Tecumseh and the Prophet: The Shawnee Brothers Who Defied a Nation

The Earth Is Weeping: The Epic Story of the Indian Wars for the American West

Shenandoah 1862: Stonewall Jackson's Valley Campaign

The Army and the Indian,
vol. 5 of *Eyewitnesses to the Indian Wars, 1865–1890*

The Long War for the Northern Plains,
vol. 4 of *Eyewitnesses to the Indian Wars, 1865–1890*

Conquering the Southern Plains,
vol. 3 of *Eyewitnesses to the Indian Wars, 1865–1890*

The Wars for the Pacific Northwest,
vol. 2 of *Eyewitnesses to the Indian Wars, 1865–1890*

The Struggle for Apacheria,
vol. 1 of *Eyewitnesses to the Indian Wars, 1865–1890*

The New Annals of the Civil War (editor, with Robert I. Girardi)

Battles and Leaders of the Civil War, vol. 6 (editor)

Battles and Leaders of the Civil War, vol. 5 (editor)

General John Pope: A Life for the Nation

The Military Memoirs of General John Pope (editor, with Robert I. Girardi)

The Darkest Days of the War: The Battles of Iuka and Corinth

The Shipwreck of Their Hopes: The Battles for Chattanooga

This Terrible Sound: The Battle of Chickamauga

No Better Place to Die: The Battle of Stones River

A Brutal Reckoning

A Brutal Reckoning

ANDREW JACKSON, THE CREEK INDIANS,
AND THE EPIC WAR
FOR THE AMERICAN SOUTH

Peter Cozzens

ALFRED A. KNOPF · NEW YORK · 2023

THIS IS A BORZOI BOOK
PUBLISHED BY ALFRED A. KNOPF

www.aaknopf.com

Knopf, Borzoi Books, and the colophon
are registered trademarks of Penguin Random House LLC.

Library of Congress Cataloging-in-Publication Data
Names: Cozzens, Peter, [date] author.
Title: A brutal reckoning : Andrew Jackson, the Creek Indians, and the epic
war for the American South / Peter Cozzens.
Description: First edition. | New York : Alfred A. Knopf, 2023. |
Includes bibliographical references and index.
Identifiers: LCCN 2022020367 (print) | LCCN 2022020368 (ebook) |
ISBN 9780525659457 (hardcover) | ISBN 9780525659464 (ebook)
Subjects: LCSH: Jackson, Andrew, 1767–1845—Military leadership. |
Creek War, 1813–1814. | Creek War, 1813–1814—Campaigns. |
Creek Indians—Southern States—History—19th century. |
Creek Indians—Southern States—History. | Indians, Treatment of—Southern
States. | United States—Territorial expansion.
Classification: LCC E83.813 .C69 2023 (print) | LCC E83.813 (ebook) |
DDC 973.5/238—dc23/eng/20220614
LC record available at https://lccn.loc.gov/2022020367
LC ebook record available at https://lccn.loc.gov/2022020368

Jacket images: (landscape) Alabama Department of Archives and History;
Creek Indian sash (detail) ca. 1830/Artokoloro/Alamy
Jacket design by Jenny Carrow

Manufactured in the United States of America
First Edition

For Antonia

The Indians fought with so great spirit that they many times drove our people back out of the town. The struggle lasted so long that many Christians, weary and very thirsty, went to drink at a pond nearby, tinged with the blood of the killed, and returned to the combat . . . breaking in upon the Indians and beating them down. [The Indians] fled out of the place, the cavalry and infantry driving them back through the gates, . . . when many, dashing headlong into the flaming houses, were smothered, and, heaped one upon another, burned to death.

      —GENTLEMAN OF ELVAS, *Battle of Mabila,* 1540[1]

The vision recurs; the eastern sun has a second rise; history repeats her tale unconsciously and goes off into a mystic rhyme; ages are prototypes of other ages, and the winding course of time brings us round to the same spot again.

      —*The Christian Remembrancer*[2]

When we got near the town . . . I saw some warriors run into a house, until I counted forty-six of them. . . . We now shot them like dogs; and then set the house on fire, and burned it up with the forty-six warriors in it. I recollect seeing a boy who was shot down near the house. His arm and thigh was broken, and he was so near the burning house that the grease was stewing out of him. In this situation he was still trying to crawl along; but not a murmur escaped him, though he was only about twelve years old.

      —DAVID CROCKETT, *Battle of Tallushatchee,* 1813[3]

CONTENTS

PART **THREE**

PART **FOUR**

PART **FIVE**

MAPS

MAP I   THE CREEK CONFEDERACY, 1790–1813

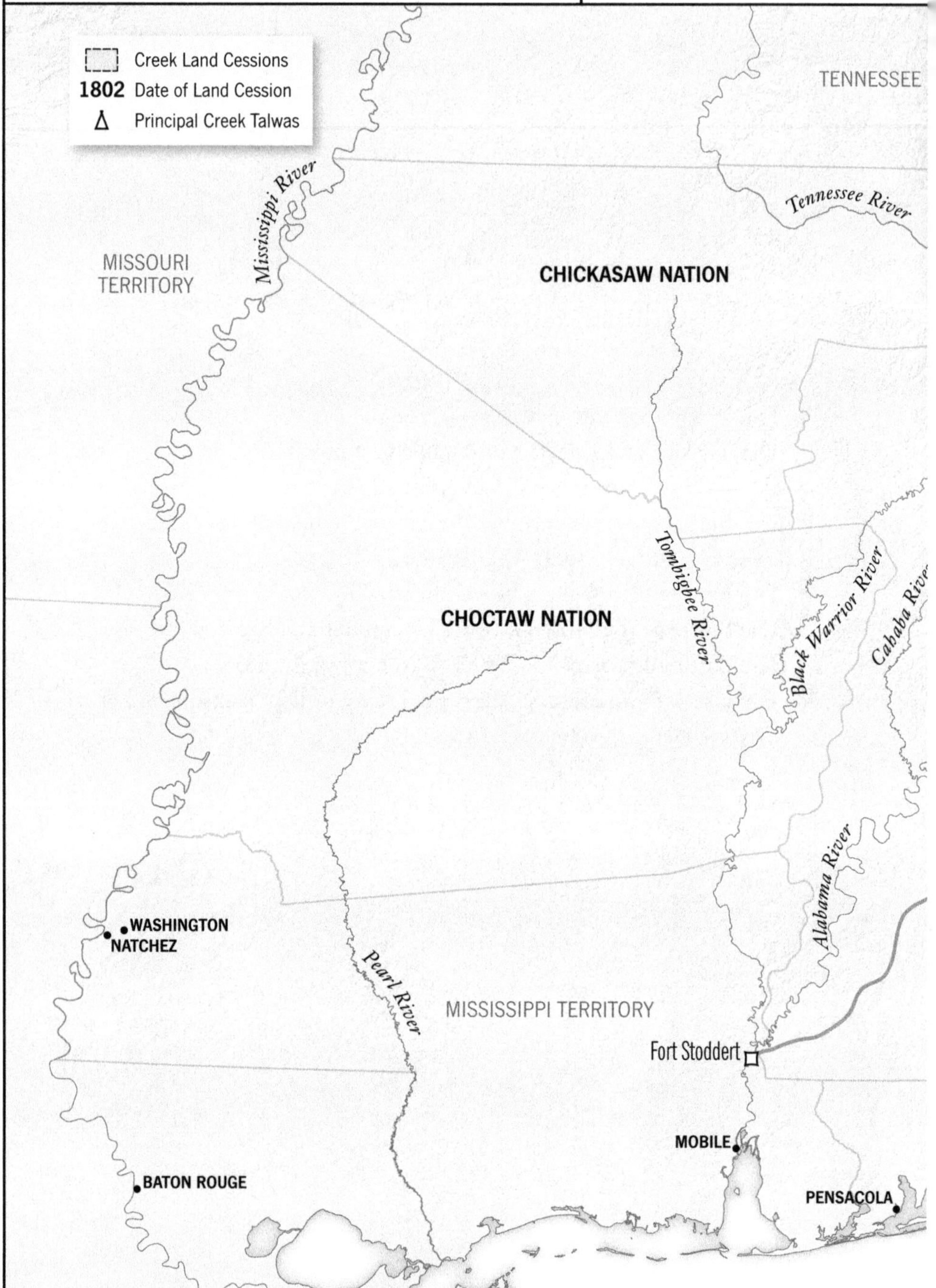

Creek Land Cessions
1802 Date of Land Cession
Δ Principal Creek Talwas

TENNESSEE

Mississippi River

Tennessee River

MISSOURI
TERRITORY

CHICKASAW NATION

Tombigbee River

Black Warrior River

Cahaba River

CHOCTAW NATION

•WASHINGTON
•NATCHEZ

Pearl River

Alabama River

MISSISSIPPI TERRITORY

Fort Stoddert ▢

MOBILE•

•BATON ROUGE

PENSACOLA•

•NEW ORLEANS

LOUISIANA

N
W ✦ E
S

0   30
Scale of Miles

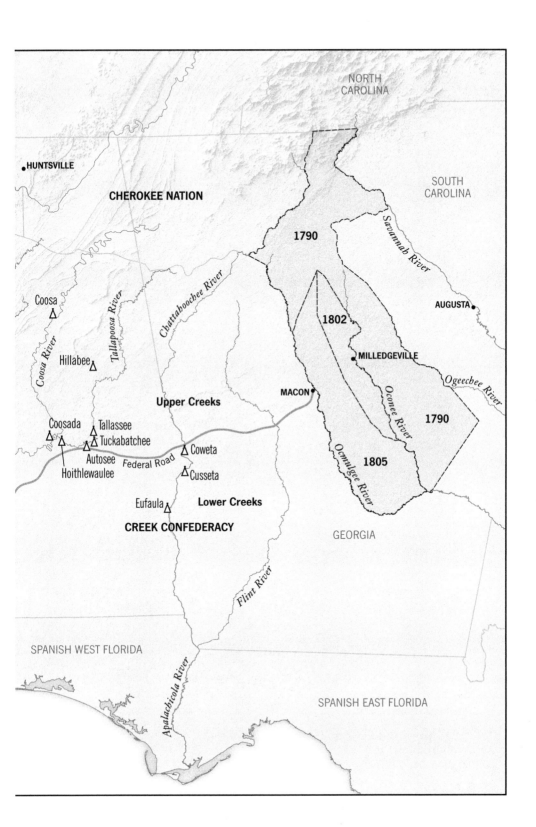

A NOTE TO READERS

The spelling and pronunciation of Creek (Muscogee) Indian place- and personal names during the eighteenth and nineteenth centuries, as recorded by white, métis (mixed-blood), and literate Creek chroniclers, varied considerably. Of course the preferences of the Creek people should be considered definitive, but absent a written language either they were unable to convey to nonindigenous (American, Spanish, and British) contacts the precise spellings of people and places, or the latter were unable to understand the Muscogee words well enough to record them with any degree of consistency. Because this is a work of history, I have tried to use the spellings most commonly employed contemporaneously, particularly by literate Creeks and métis.

When writing of the era, I also faced the question of whether to refer to the Native protagonists as Muscogees, the name by which the confederated peoples referred to themselves, or Creeks, the name bestowed on them by Anglos in their early contacts with the Muscogees, and which the Spanish also adopted. I elected to use the appellation Creek, which not only was the name given to the war that is central to this story but also was the term often employed by literate métis and Muscogees in their talks or writings.

As the Creek War opens, the reader may find the multitude of anglicized names among the Indians daunting, particularly because many of the Red Sticks, as the Creeks who fought the Americans were known, had non-Native names. I recommend the reader consult the appendix, which provides a list of the principal Creek, métis, and Red Stick leaders, to help navigate the sea of names.

Today the great majority of the descendants of the historic Creek confederacy are members of the Muscogee (Creek) Nation, a self-governed tribe located in eastern Oklahoma. With more than eighty-six thousand members, it is the fourth-largest tribe in the United States. The descendants of those few Muscogees fortunate enough to escape removal from their homeland are known today as the Poarch Creek Indians. They reside in Escambia County on the only federally recognized Creek land remaining in Alabama, about 120 miles northeast of Mobile. Despite the best efforts of the U.S. government to eradicate the Creek (Muscogee) presence from east of the Mississippi during the nineteenth century, the Poarch Creeks endure, a self-governing people dedicated to preserving their tribal culture and community.[1] I sincerely hope *A Brutal Reckoning* accurately honors the history of all Muscogees.

When non-Native authors chronicle the history of America's Native population, the question inevitably arises as to which appellation—Indian, Native American, or American Indian—is most appropriate. In this I relied on not only the historical context to guide me but also usage among indigenous peoples today. To quote from the website of the National Museum of the American Indian, "All of these terms are acceptable. The consensus, however, is that whenever possible, Native people prefer to be called by their specific tribal name. In the United States, Native American has been widely used but is falling out of favor with . . . many Native people."[2] For these reasons, as well as to obtain a better sense of historical immediacy, I most frequently use the term "Indian."

PROLOGUE

Andrew Jackson lay on a couch in an elegant room at the stylish Nashville Inn. The bed was a wreck. The cadaverous Tennessean had soaked two mattresses with his blood and stained the carpet beneath the bedstead scarlet. The place stank of dried blood, diarrhea, and the slippery-elm poultice that doctors had slathered on Jackson's shattered left shoulder and mangled left arm. Had the attending physician prevailed, there would have been no wounds to plaster. He had urged an amputation, to which the young doctor's nearly delirious patient objected. "No, I'll keep my arm," mumbled Jackson. Such was Jackson's fearsome reputation that no one presumed to dispute him. Neither did the doctor dare remove the lead ball embedded in his arm.

The fiery forty-six-year-old Tennessee militia general had no one but himself to blame for the grievous wounds that had prostrated him for three weeks and showed scant signs of improving. Cracking a horse whip and brandishing a pistol, on September 4, 1813, Jackson had provoked a pointless but violent confrontation with his former friend and militia subordinate Colonel Thomas Hart Benton on the steps of a Nashville hotel a scant hundred yards from where he now lay. Benton had just returned from Washington, D.C., where he had gone to obtain the War Department's promise to reimburse Jackson for a crippling debt the general had incurred on behalf of his Tennesseans after they were mustered into U.S. service early in the War of 1812 and then almost immediately cast aside, unpaid, ill-used, and far from home.

While Thomas Hart Benton was away, Jackson acted as second to the opponent of Benton's younger brother Jesse in a seriocomic, nonlethal duel that earned Jesse a bullet in the buttocks. Learning of the affair, a mortified Thomas Hart Benton publicly impugned Jackson's honor, a character trait the general held dearer than life itself. For that, his former subordinate must pay. "Now, you damned rascal, I am going to punish you. Defend yourself," Jackson had declared when they met. Instead, a slug and two balls from Jesse Benton's pistol punished Jackson.

While Jackson lay helpless just twelve miles from his plantation, the Hermitage, where his wife, Rachel, and their young adopted son awaited his return, events more momentous than the wounding of the West Tennessee militia's controversial commanding general gripped the citizens of Nashville. The War of 1812 was going badly for the United States. British forces menaced the Eastern Seaboard and had repelled American attempts to seize Canada. Closer to home, four days after Jackson's senseless fracas, a rider from the Mississippi Territory galloped into town bearing news of a ruthless Creek massacre of the inhabitants of a frontier stockade called Fort Mims in present-day southwestern Alabama. Horrified whites feared the slaughter portended a massive uprising of the powerful Creek confederacy, perhaps abetted by the British. Would the Tennessee frontier next fall prey to Indian depredations? The governor and Nashville luminaries met to consider their response and what if any role their incapacitated military leader might play. What could Jackson himself, feverish, gaunt, and growing thinner, unable to stand without support, wish for at such a moment? He could wish for war, with himself in the forefront.[1]

A Brutal Reckoning represents the concluding volume in a trilogy that I hope will offer readers a gripping and balanced account of the dispossession of American Indian lands by a relentlessly westering United States in the eighteenth and nineteenth centuries. It also provides a stunning lesson in how the unwavering will of one man—in this case Andrew Jackson—could set the course of a crucial era of American history and almost single-handedly win what was arguably the most consequential Indian war in U.S. history.

The principal events of *A Brutal Reckoning* largely occur concurrently with those of *Tecumseh and the Prophet: The Shawnee Brothers Who Defied a Nation*, the locus shifting from Indian warfare in the present-day Midwest to the horrific combat and colossal betrayals that largely eradicated the Indian presence in the Deep South. Only after the U.S.

government cleared the country east of the Mississippi River of its Native population was the way open for the conquest of the West, which is the subject of *The Earth Is Weeping: The Epic Story of the Indian Wars for the American West.*

A Brutal Reckoning relates a vital chapter in American history, largely forgotten but of immense consequence for the future of the United States. No other Indian conflict in our nation's history so changed the complexion of American society as did the Creek War, which lies at the heart of this book. A dispute that began as a Creek civil war became a ruthless struggle against American expansion, erupting in the midst of the War of 1812. Not only was the Creek War the most pitiless clash between American Indians and whites in U.S. history, but the defeat of the Red Sticks—as those opposed to American encroachment were known because of the red war clubs they carried—also cost the entire Creek people as well as the neighboring Chickasaw, Choctaw, and Cherokee nations their homelands. The collapse of Red Stick resistance in 1814 led inexorably to the Indian Trail of Tears two decades later, which opened Alabama, much of Mississippi, and portions of Georgia, North Carolina, and Tennessee to white settlement. That in turn gave rise to the Cotton Kingdom, without which there would have been no casus belli for the American Civil War.

The Creek War also thrust Andrew Jackson into national prominence. He began the conflict a general in the Tennessee militia whose political star seemed on the wane. Jackson's victory over the Red Sticks at the Battle of Horseshoe Bend, the climactic action of the Creek War, won him a major general's commission in the Regular army and command of the vast military district that embraced New Orleans. Without the Creek War, Jackson would never have had the opportunity to beat the British at the Battle of New Orleans and become the most celebrated general to emerge from the War of 1812. But did Jackson really deserve the accolades and the promotion that came after Horseshoe Bend? Prior to that battle his combat performance against the Red Sticks had been mixed at best. He had suffered more than one battlefield setback and had lost many of his troops to mutiny. As for Horseshoe Bend, it was not Jackson but rather his Cherokee and friendly Creek scouts acting on their own initiative—the very men he would later expel on the Trail of Tears—who won the battle for him.

Jackson commanded but one of seven columns that invaded the

Creek nation during the war. To his credit, he alone possessed the will to see the conflict through. While commanders from Georgia, the Mississippi Territory, and eastern Tennessee abbreviated their campaigns because of chronic supply shortages, enlistment problems, Red Stick resilience, and the relative indifference of a U.S. government locked in war with Great Britain, Jackson persevered. Enfeebled by a festering gunshot wound and severe chronic diarrhea, and plagued by inconstant superiors, Jackson demonstrated fortitude and personal courage rarely witnessed in American military annals. He brooked no dissent, treating his own sometimes recalcitrant troops with a harshness that astonished the militiamen and volunteers. *A Brutal Reckoning* examines Jackson's unbridled ambition, outsized sense of honor and duty, and periodic cruelty in the context of his times. His command shortcomings and successes are explored, presenting what I hope is a fair and nuanced reevaluation of Jackson the general. Such is the chronology of events, and the need to understand Creek Indian society and the factors that precipitated the Creek War, that Jackson does not stomp onto the stage until part 3 of the narrative. From the moment he plunges into the conflict, however, Jackson dominates the narrative just as he did the conduct of the Creek War. For this inevitable delay in introducing the key nemesis, first of the Red Sticks and subsequently of all southeastern Indian tribes, I beg the reader's indulgence.

The Creek confederacy represented the largest Native presence of the South. So long as the Creeks possessed their vast country, white settlement could expand no farther into what became the American South than central Georgia. It is critical to our appreciation of the challenges that Jackson confronted, then, and also a matter of fairness to the Creek people, that their early history and way of life be given its due. Jackson's successful prosecution of the Creek War cannot be adequately judged without an understanding of what came before. Neither can the richness, diversity, and perseverance of the people he conquered be appreciated without a full rendering of the events predating the conflict. This is the purpose of part 1 of our story.

The Creek War began as a civil war within the Creek community and gave rise to the Red Stick militants who precipitated conflict with the United States. It was the most devastating internecine struggle that any Native people suffered as a consequence of contact with white Americans. It was a bitter struggle pitting brother against brother, violently dividing families to an even greater extent than the American Civil War. It is a tragedy little known today, but one that merits a full rendition not only in its own right but also if one is to grasp the temper of the times and the milieu in which Jackson operated. The rise of the Red Sticks, the Creek Civil War, and its transformation into a fateful clash with the young American republic after the Red Sticks perpetrated the most horrific massacre of American and mixed-race settlers in U.S. history is the subject of part 2.

With *A Brutal Reckoning,* the Creek confederacy is restored to its rightful place among the great American Indian peoples, and Andrew Jackson joins the ranks of iconic historical figures who come in for a fresh and not always flattering reinterpretation in my trilogy recounting the grand struggle for the Indian domain of North America.

Our story necessarily begins well before U.S. encroachment on American Indian soil. It opens with the destruction of the Creeks' ancestors by Spanish conquistadors in the mid-sixteenth century and the European pathogens that accompanied them. Andrew Jackson's hardhanded brand of war, and his victory at Horseshoe Bend, had as their vicious precursor the ruthless seventeenth-century trek through southeastern North America of the Spanish conquistador Hernando de Soto. Although more than two and a half centuries separated the men, the parallels between de Soto and Jackson and the paths of destruction they carved emerge as uncannily similar. Both men conducted their respective campaigns with fierce single-mindedness. They pushed themselves to the limits of human endurance and expected their men to indulge their zealotry no matter how unrealistic their objectives might seem. De Soto and Jackson trod much of the same ground. At the Battle of Mabila in 1540, the Spaniard dealt Creek forebears the harshest defeat ever suffered by Native peoples north of Mexico at the hands of European invaders. Approximately 1,000 warriors perished in the flames and fury. Jackson broke the back of the Red Sticks at the Battle of Horseshoe Bend in 1814, fought a scant hundred miles or so east of the presumptive site of de Soto's triumph. At least 850 Red Stick warriors died defending their families and way of life against Jackson's army, a Native death count never exceeded in the two centuries of conflict between American Indians and the expanding American republic. De Soto initiated the decline of the grand American Indian culture that predated the Creeks and their southeastern contemporaries, the Cherokees, Choctaws, and Chickasaws. In shattering Red Stick resistance at Horseshoe Bend, Jackson not only brought an abrupt end to the Creek War but also set in motion the train of events that would lead to the brutal expulsion of all but a handful of Native peoples from the American South.

Andrew Jackson and his fellow expansionists reckoned the cost relatively small. In appropriating the Indian lands of the Southeast, however, the young republic had inadvertently sown the seeds of the American Civil War. Not only did the conquest of the Creek country reinvigorate a faltering slave-based cotton economy by injecting it with highly fertile soil on which to prosper under white plantation owners (the few score human chattels of dispossessed wealthy Creeks and métis had produced comparatively little in times past), but by 1860 one of the two highest concentrations of cotton production in the antebellum South was on former Creek land. Brutality in the Deep South did not end with the Creek War and Trail of Tears. It was simply replaced by the horrors of what white Southerners euphemistically called the "peculiar institution."

· PART ONE ·

CHAPTER ONE

From the Ashes of the Entrada

HERNANDO DE SOTO craved gold, glory, and gore in quantities that made even his fellow conquistadors quake. When only twenty, he quit the impoverished confines of western Spain to find his fortune in the New World. In the succeeding sixteen years, the hawk-nosed young Spaniard enjoyed dizzying success slaughtering and pillaging indigenous peoples, first in Central America and later in Peru. De Soto returned to Spain wealthy and celebrated. He won the favor of King Ferdinand and Queen Isabella, who appointed him governor of Cuba, with the expectation he would also colonize and plunder *La Florida,* as the Spanish then called North America.

Before de Soto could rightfully claim La Florida, he had to raise an army and conquer the strange country from its Native inhabitants. A less ambitious man might have been content to retire with his wealth as master of a settled island domain. But not de Soto. Vague rumors of vast gold deposits resting in the shadow of a dazzling mountain of diamond somewhere in modern South Carolina propelled de Soto onward.

De Soto had no difficulty finding Spanish adventurers to join him. In May 1539 he sailed from Havana for the west coast of what is today Florida, in seven ships with an army of six hundred men and a contingent of a hundred wives, female camp followers, black slaves, craftsmen, and priests. Crammed aboard the rocking galleons, caravels, and brigantines were 220 cavalry horses calculated to overawe the foot-bound natives; several packs of fierce hounds to track down and mangle those who fled; an ample supply of handcuffs, chains, and neck collars with which to enslave the natives; and a huge herd of hogs to supplement provisions pilfered from them.[1]

Well-disciplined but also ruggedly individualistic, de Soto's conquistadors were a colorful lot, uniformed as befitted their tastes and means. Their basic outfit consisted of a long-sleeved shirt; a short, close-fitting padded jacket (doublet); and pants, breeches, or hose. The cavalry found boots and leather gloves essential, but infantrymen made do with simple sandals. Few could afford full body armor; most wore quilted cotton or leather jackets strong enough to withstand arrows fired from short bows. Affluent conquistadors also sported sleeveless chain-mail vests. Nearly all wore helmets.[2]

De Soto made landfall near present-day Tampa Bay. European diseases—principally smallpox—preceded him. Twelve years earlier, the first Spaniards to explore La Florida had landed nearby and then passed along the Gulf Coast. In their wake the intruders and their pathogens left agony and desolation. With little remaining to despoil, de Soto plodded north toward the fabled land of riches.

Moving inland, the conquistadors met greater American Indian resistance, a natural consequence of de Soto's brutality. He burned villages that refused him slave laborers and female chattels and tossed natives who displeased him to his man-mauling hounds. In South Carolina, de Soto found neither gold nor the expected mountain of diamond, but he did meet a lovely young Indian queen who beguiled the Spaniard for a season.

Beauty, however, proved no substitute for riches, and in early 1540 de Soto marched into modern North Carolina. There he met large palisaded villages, from which he demanded food, supply porters, and women. With every mile the avaricious Spaniards traversed, their relations with the inhabitants deteriorated.[3]

No mere savages, the natives of what was to become the American South possessed the richest culture of any indigenous peoples north of Mexico. Owing their immediate allegiance to culturally similar but politically diverse and sometimes warring chiefdoms, the inhabitants belonged to the Mississippian tradition, so named because the culture—if not the people themselves—apparently originated on the banks of the Mississippi River between AD 700 and 900. These residents of what is today Alabama and Georgia spoke predominantly the Muscogean family of languages.[4] The most salient characteristic of the Mississippian tradition was flat-topped, pyramidal mounds that served as foundations for temples, mortuaries, the homes of chiefs, and other important public edifices. The villages erected around the mounds were formidable, surrounded by deep, water-filled ditches and wooden palisades with defensive towers placed at regular intervals. Larger villages sometimes had interior walls for a second line of defense.[5]

Native weapons gave thoughtful conquistadors pause. Strung with deer sinew, Indian bows were long, elastic, and exceptionally strong. The arrows, fashioned from young cane hardened in flames, had dagger-sharp flint heads. In close combat, warriors wielded short war clubs.[6]

As they entered what would become the Lower Creek country (central and western Georgia), the conquistadors met with markedly improved clay dwellings, similar to, and probably more hygienic than, the abodes of poor rural Spaniards. Native men and women wore shawls "after the manner of the Gypsies," fashioned from tree bark or grass treated to the consistency of flax. The Indians made moccasins for both sexes and loin coverings (breechclouts) for men from deerskin dressed to "such perfection" that it equaled the finest European broadcloth.[7]

De Soto, however, had come in search of wealth and glory, not to admire the Native culture. In July 1540, his expedition entered the territory of Coosa, the paramount chiefdom of the region, centered on the upper Coosa River in what is today northwest Georgia. Borne on a litter to great fanfare and accompanied by several hundred painted and plumed warriors, at the gates of its northernmost town the principal chief of Coosa greeted de Soto and his men as guests. Ancestors of the Upper Creeks, the people of Coosa were brutal slaveholders, their Native chattel laboring with severed Achilles tendons to prevent their escape. The Spaniards saw vast cultivated fields but no evidence of gold or other mineral riches. Impatient to press on, de Soto repaid the pliant Coosa chief's hospitality by putting him and several of his headmen in iron collars and chains and forcing them to serve as porters.[8]

De Soto continued south along the Coosa River into present-day Alabama. At each village, he demanded more porters and women and pillaged the few communities that dared to defy him. All went deceptively well for de Soto.

In early October, he bade a ravaged Coosa farewell and entered the central Alabama domain of Chief Tascalusa, an esteemed Native leader. At the town of Atahachi the Spaniards met him, seated regally on cushions atop a mound in the plaza, a lavish feather cape extending to his feet. Towering a foot above the tallest conquistador, Tascalusa impressed a Portuguese officer as "full of dignity; tall of person, muscular, lean, and symmetrical, the suzerain of many territories, and of numerous people, being equally feared by his vassals and the neighboring nations."[9]

De Soto and Tascalusa paid not the slightest deference to each other. As de Soto climbed the ceremonial mound to confront Tascalusa, the chief sat fixed and unimpressed. De Soto surrounded him with lance-wielding cavalrymen, placed him under arrest, and demanded four hundred male porters and one hundred women. Tascalusa took his detention in stride. He gave de Soto the porters—fine Atahachi warriors all—but told the Spaniard he would have to wait until they reached the town of Mabila, the Atahachi capital, located somewhere between the lower Alabama and the Tombigbee Rivers, before de Soto could have the women. Tascalusa tantalized de Soto with a promise of the loveliest females of Mabila. Perhaps de Soto saw in the haughty chief a kindred spirit because he acceded to Tascalusa's condition, and the entourage headed west along the bank of the Alabama River toward Mabila.[10]

De Soto expected an easy march across a compliant country. Tascalusa, however, was scarcely the passive prisoner he seemed. Unknown to de Soto, he dispatched a messenger to Mabila summoning all the warriors of his chiefdom to assemble there. De Soto's scouts cautioned their commander that the people ahead "were evilly disposed." Perhaps the expedition had best camp in the open outside the gates of Mabila rather than alongside the house that Tascalusa offered de Soto? Recklessly certain of his own invincibility, de Soto dismissed their warnings. Accompanied by a small escort of cavalry, he spurred ahead to Mabila with Tascalusa while the remainder of his command followed at a leisurely pace.

When de Soto neared the town's fifteen-foot-high beam-and-mud-daub outer walls on the cool and clear morning of October 18, 1540, the local cacique and four hundred cheering Indians festooned with ceremonial feathers and body paint sallied forth, ostensibly to welcome him. Once inside the town of eighty large houses, de Soto and his attendants settled in to enjoy an exotic and stimulating welcome in the town plaza. Fermented drinks circulated freely, and scantily clad, "marvelously beautiful women" danced for the Spaniards. While the bare-breasted dancers swirled and dipped before the mesmerized conquistadors, Tascalusa slipped away into a nearby house. Refusing de Soto's order to return to the plaza, he instead issued the Spaniards an ultimatum. They must leave immediately or suffer the consequences. Drawing his sword in response, a Spanish officer cleaved off the arm of an Indian headman. In an instant, three thousand warriors poured into the streets shouting war cries and brandishing clubs and bows and arrows. Somehow de Soto and most of his escort slashed their way out of town just as the first soldiers of the Spanish main body appeared on the open plain outside Mabila. Still in the saddle and hacking wildly with his sword, de Soto bristled with nearly two dozen arrows, none of which had penetrated his quilted armor.

The Spaniards faltered and fell back. Tascalusa's warriors helped the Atahachi porters break their chains and join the fray with weapons seized from de Soto's baggage train. The unequal battle raged into the afternoon. Spanish cavalry arrived to help balance the odds. When the infantry came up, de Soto signaled a counterattack with the blast of a harquebus. The first rush failed, but de Soto continued to throw his men against the town walls. They hacked at the plaster and cane palisades, creating a breach large enough for a few men to dart inside and set the nearest houses ablaze. The cane-and-thatch roofs ignited in a flash, and a wall of fire rolled across the town. Doomed defenders perished in the flames engulfing Mabila or at the tips of Spanish cavalry lances on the corpse-strewn plain.[11]

The wives of warriors grabbed weapons and fought "with no less skill and ferocity than their husbands," but Mabila, and with it the Atahachi culture, expired in the flames and frenzy. As twilight settled

over the carnage, dazed and wounded conquistadors glanced at the
smoldering ramparts. A lone warrior stood upon them. Despairing of
escape, he yanked off his bowstring, tossed it over the branch of a
nearby tree, wrapped it around his neck, and hanged himself.[12]

No one knows how many Indians perished in the Battle of Mabila. To
disguise de Soto's folly, Spanish chroniclers inflated the Native body
count and understated their own losses. Indian dead likely numbered
a thousand, including Tascalusa, his headmen, and the entire priestly
class. Centuries of collective civic and cultural knowledge also perished in the conflagration that foreshadowed the demise of the Mississippian tradition.

Approximately fifty conquistadors were killed or mortally wounded
at Mabila, and nearly half of the Spaniards were wounded. The expedition also lost most of its baggage and half of its horses, both devastating blows. His comrades, said one conquistador, "began to think that it
was impossible to dominate such bellicose people or to subjugate men
who were so free."

Bloodied and disillusioned, de Soto's men grew mutinous. De Soto
pushed on, however. He crossed the Mississippi and staggered aimlessly about with his dwindling band until May 1542, when he fell ill
from fever and died. A little over a year later, the remnants of the
entrada boarded rescue ships on the Gulf Coast and sailed from the
scenes of their quixotic misadventures.[13]

The Spaniards might have departed, but they left behind smallpox, a pathogen far more lethal than the carnage they had inflicted
with their swords and lances. A scourge for which the Indians had no
defenses, nor likely any explanation except divine displeasure, smallpox circulated in droplets or dust particles, infecting nearly everyone. High fevers, vomiting, and painful rashes or blisters tormented
the bewildered natives. On those fortunate enough to live, the scabs
healed after a week or ten days, leaving behind disfiguring pockmarks.
The disease also blinded many who survived. No one knows how
many Indians inhabited the South at the time of de Soto's rapacious
odyssey—some have estimated the number at nearly two million—
but in three decades following the entrada, upward of 90 percent died
from smallpox and other European viruses.[14]

The mighty chiefdom of Coosa teetered, and that of Atahachi crumbled. The people scattered simply to survive in a land bereft of unifying leadership or the once elevated culture of the Mississippian tradition. When Spaniards next visited what is today southern Alabama in 1560, Mabila lay in ruins. The few Indians who lingered amid the debris practiced a primitive agriculture, and the former chiefdom proved so barren that the Spaniards had to press on to avoid starvation. Six years later, a final Spanish expedition toppled what remained of Coosa with viruses. Afterward the Spaniards contented themselves with colonies along the Florida coast, and the curtain of recorded history closed over the region. The Indians separated, then coalesced in new and smaller groupings, scratched out small plots, and toiled at subsistence farming. Saplings and underbrush invaded the spacious clearings once tended by Atahachi and Coosa farmers. Gradually, the great forests of the South reclaimed the land.[15]

In 1670 the historical record resumed in the South when the English settled Charles Towne on the Carolina coast. From their coastal enclave, British traders edged their way inland to turn a profit at the Indians' expense. Three years later, French explorers penetrated the Mississippi valley, looking both to counter British influence and to expand their own commerce with the Indians. Spain, meanwhile, clung to the Florida settlements as buffers between its rich Caribbean holdings and the growing British presence on the Atlantic coast of North America.

The European interlopers danced about the periphery of four southeastern American Indian peoples who emerged from the remnants of the great Mississippian tradition chiefdoms. These were the Choctaws, Chickasaws, Cherokees, and Creeks. While vibrant and relatively sophisticated, theirs were simpler societies than those of their ancestors. Given the toll that European pathogens had taken, it is remarkable that cohesive cultures of any sort reemerged.[16]

Not only did they reemerge—precisely how, the natives themselves did not know—but within a century the four new Indian societies of the Deep South also prospered. Each had a well-defined domain that it zealously defended against periodic incursions by Indian neighbors. Scattered about the rolling hill country of what is today northwestern

Alabama and northern Mississippi were the Chickasaws, a tough, war-like, but comparatively small tribe of perhaps six thousand members.

To their immediate south lived the Choctaws, who numbered at least twenty thousand. The Choctaws claimed most of the Mississippi piedmont and coastal plain, as well as a sliver of western Alabama. The Chickasaw and Choctaw country lay west of the Tombigbee River, and both tribes belonged to the Muscogean language family.

The Cherokees, an Iroquoian-speaking people, controlled the Appalachian highland and piedmont areas encompassing modern southwestern North Carolina, southeastern Tennessee, and bits of western South Carolina, northern Georgia, and northeastern Alabama. They counted approximately twenty thousand members.

Ironically, the dominant Indian polity in the region was not a tribe at all, but rather a loose conglomeration of small tribes of diverse backgrounds most commonly known as the Creek, or Muscogee, confederacy. The name Muscogee (or Muskogee) comes from the Algonquian word *muskeg*, which signifies swamp or land that is prone to flooding and might have been bestowed on these Indians by their Shawnee allies. Early English settlers from the Province of Carolina called the first Muscogees with whom they came into contact Creeks because the natives resided on the upper Ocmulgee River and Ochese Creek, near modern Macon, Georgia. As Carolinians became more familiar with western members of the confederacy, they extended the appellation Creek to all of them. Having no name for their affiliated towns, the Indians took to referring to themselves as Creeks when dealing with whites.

Their realm, however, was neither the mere cluster of creeks the English name implied nor the morass the Algonquian moniker of Muscogee suggested. Numbering more than twenty thousand, and with a growing population, the Creeks claimed a vast region. When the first British colonists landed in North America, the Creek domain stretched west from coastal Georgia's Savannah River to the Tombigbee River of eastern Mississippi and south from the Tennessee River to northern Florida—an area comprising half of the present-day Deep South lying east of the Mississippi River. The Creek country rested squarely between Spanish Florida, Great Britain's Atlantic Seaboard colonies, and the southward-stretching tendrils of French Canada. All three empires would come to court the Creeks. So long as the three great European powers needed them, the Creeks prospered. The natives' fate, however, was no longer wholly their own.

The twin hearts of the Creek confederacy, if indeed the loosely affiliated towns of the late seventeenth century could be called a confederacy, were the fertile river bottoms where the rapid Coosa and Tallapoosa Rivers join to form the broad and meandering Alabama River and the central Chattahoochee River valley of today's western Georgia.

According to Creek tradition, their core towns, sometimes known as the "foundation towns," were Muscogean-speaking communities. Scholars differ as to what groupings constituted the original towns, but all agree that the Abeikas (Abihkas) and Cowetas played prominent roles. In addition to a common language and likely descent from the great Mississippian chiefdoms of Coosa and Atahachi, the affiliated towns shared a willingness to welcome non-Muscogean Indians into their fold so long as they paid ceremonial deference to the core towns and incorporated key Creek traditions. The latter condition was not particularly onerous, because southeastern tribes had much in common culturally.

The first and most potent tribe to avail themselves of Muscogee openhandedness were the Alabamas, whom the Choctaws had pushed eastward from the Tombigbee River to the western reaches of the Alabama River. Other prominent accretions included the Natchez, originally from southwestern Mississippi, several bands of the Shawnees from the Ohio valley, and the Uchees from the Savannah River country, whose languages were incomprehensible to their Muscogee allies.[17]

As the seventeenth century closed, the dominant Indian power in the Deep South, then, was a loose assemblage of largely inward-looking towns with about as much sense of common purpose as the querulous Italian city-states of Renaissance Europe had possessed. In the coming decades, it would require a threatening convergence of European powers on the edges of the Creek country to bring about a semblance of unity.

CHAPTER TWO

A Rope of Sand

THE CREEKS cherished the freedoms that accompanied their lack of a strong central authority. They also prized the security that came from belonging to one of fifty matrilineal clans—that is to say, groups of close-knit families scattered throughout the confederacy whose members believed they shared a remote female ancestor. Clans were exogamous—one must marry an outsider—and clan law reigned supreme in Creek society. Its complex set of social rules and etiquette regulated behavior and promoted a sense of fraternity with other Creek communities. Through clan membership, observed a literate Creek métis (mixed blood), the Creeks "are so united that there is no part of the [Creek] nation detached from the other, but are all linked, harmonized, and consolidated as one large, connected family, [and] there is no part of the nation but a man can find his clansmen or their connection." Wander where he may in the vast Creek country, a Creek truly was never far from home.[1]

The Creeks dated the clan system to the very origin of life on earth, and they spoke of its numinous beginnings with awe. One tale told of the emergence of the Creeks from a great fog that, as it dissipated, divided the people into clans. All Creek stories of the clan system agreed on the preeminence of the Wind Clan, particularly as peacemakers. In the coming era of European contact and conflict, the

Wind Clan would prove both a wedge for and a barrier against white encroachment.

Although the Creeks claimed a huge country, they congregated along rivers or their tributaries and reserved most of the land for seasonal hunting. Creek towns, which generally ranged between fifty and five hundred inhabitants, formed the basic political units and contained members of multiple clans. Called *talwas*, the towns enjoyed great autonomy. So tenaciously did talwas cling to their prerogatives that Theodore Roosevelt, in his monumental *The Winning of the West*, likened the Creek confederacy to a "rope of sand." In view of a talwa's near-absolute independence, it is equally accurate to translate the word as "tribe."

Beneath the talwas were the *talofas*, or villages. Lacking the public squares and ceremonial grounds unique to talwas, talofas were dependent on and often offshoots of the nearest talwa. Talofas proliferated when good farming land around the talwas grew scarce or simply because the highly individualistic Creeks wanted to put some distance between themselves and their mother community. A Creek talwa comprised both the town itself and its satellite talofas, scattered through the forest or along streams and connected by a network of trails.[2]

The Creeks believed life was an eternal struggle between peace and war, a dualism reflected in the division of talwas. There were the *Hathagalgi*, or white talwas, so styled because white was the color of peace and purity, and the *Tcilokogalgi*, or red talwas, red being the color of war. White talwas hosted peace councils and were sanctuaries for fugitives from Creek justice. Red talwas took the initiative in declaring war and planning military expeditions. Creeks proudly painted their public buildings, ceremonial articles, and even their bodies white or red according to their talwa's affiliation. Residents of similarly colored talwas considered themselves "people of one fire" and felt a bitter rivalry, bordering on hostility, toward talwas of the other color (division). So strong was the ill feeling between white and red talwas, at least in the formative years of the confederacy, that friendships, marriages, and even casual encounters rarely crossed the color line.[3]

As the confederacy matured and the European colonial presence on its periphery grew, many of the traditional distinctions between red and white talwas blurred. The mutual aversion of their inhabitants persisted, however. It found an outlet in the Creeks' favorite activity, the inter-town ball game, or *holliicosi*, which was the Indian forerunner of modern lacrosse. Far more than mere sport, holliicosi functioned as a rowdy and often bone-cracking surrogate for war that not only channeled the bellicose passions of young men but also could make or break family fortunes and alter the allegiance of talwas. Preparations for a match were exacting, and the stakes were high; three or four consecutive losses to the same talwa compelled the defeated talwa to change divisions. Fortunately for talwas with mediocre teams, inter-town games occurred only once annually.[4]

In contrast to the yearly holliicosi brawls, daily talwa life was harmonious, the ruling hand light. In peace, the civil leader, known as the *micco*, administered public affairs with the advice and consent of the talwa council. The Creeks strove for consensus. Public ridicule generally sufficed to maintain order.

An exceptional micco might exert sway beyond his own talwa. Few incentives, however, existed for the accrual of influence. Unlike their overbearing ancestral chiefs, a Creek micco must till his own fields, hunt his own game, and share his personal surplus with his people. Miccos also managed the public granary, to which all Creek families of the talwa contributed a share of their crops. In times of want, the micco distributed the communal produce according to need.

Although few ascended to the office of micco without a distinguished war record, in times of conflict talwa affairs passed to the *tustunnugee thlucco*, or great warrior, and his war council. Once peace was restored, the tustunnugee thlucco returned the reins of government to civil authorities. So long as he enjoyed the loyalty of the talwa's warriors, however, a tustunnugee thlucco's role in Creek politics remained considerable.[5]

Situated on large, crystal clear creeks or rivers, talwas were agreeable places in which to live. Numbering about sixty by the end of the eighteenth century, they had several features in common. Custom and considerations of utility dictated their layout. In the center of a talwa, on the highest available ground, stood the public square, where, in warm weather, councils and other public affairs were conducted. Four inward-facing wattle-and-daub structures painted white or red according to the talwa's divisional affiliation delineated the square. Open in front, each building consisted of three rooms with terraced rows of benches on which men sat segregated by clan. Immediately outside the square rested the bark-roofed winter council house, known as the *chokofa*. Also adjacent to the public square lay a two-hundred-yard-long rectangular ball field known as the chunky yard. Its name derived from the chunky game, in which contestants hurled poles at swiftly rolling stone disks. The chunky yard also served a macabre function. At either end of the yard stood twelve-foot-high wooden posts decorated with the scalps of slain enemies. The Creeks sometimes tortured prisoners to death, and it was to these "blood poles" that they secured the condemned.[6]

Radiating from the public grounds were residential yards that comprised households grouped by clan. A prosperous household might own four buildings laid out in an inward-facing square, with an open-air pavilion that served as the family's summer abode on one side; an enclosed cooking area perpendicular to it; a storage shed across from the cooking area in which Creek men kept their saddles (for horses descended from Spanish mustangs, bought from British traders, or stolen from white settlers), deerskins, weapons, and personal gear, and in which the family also stored corn and other produce. A rectangular wattle-and-daub, bark-roofed winter lodging house completed the square. Compared with northern Indians, for whom a single wigwam typically served all of a family's needs, and most white frontiersmen, who made do with one-room cabins, the Creeks enjoyed commodious quarters.[7]

The Creeks and their neighboring tribes differed from the northern Indian peoples in another, more profound respect: the status of women. In the patrilineal cultures of the North, women derived their property and place in society from their husbands. In the matrilineal southeastern tribes, however, women owned the homes, family property, and probably the agricultural plots, giving them far greater security and economic independence than northern women. Divorce was permissible but hardly desirable for Creek men after the birth of children because a divorced man not only was expelled from his wife's talwa but also had to maintain her and their offspring until she remarried. Creek fathers possessed another disadvantage in domestic circles. In Creek society a boy respected his maternal uncle more than his father and looked to his uncle for comfort and for guidance as he grew to young manhood.

This is not to say that Creek women had it easy. In the cosmic pecking order, men came first. Gender roles not only were clearly defined but also stood in both real and mystical opposition to each other. Women reared children; cultivated, preserved, and prepared food; dressed deerskins; and hauled firewood. Men tilled and prepared the fields, but their principal duties were hunting and war making. Fearing contamination from female "power," they obliged menstruating women, or those about to give birth, to sequester themselves in huts on the village periphery.[8]

Young women aspired to a good marriage and faithful service to their lineage. Ambitious young men found fulfillment in warfare. Preparations for its rigors began in boyhood, and advancement in male society and the wooing of a desirable mate depended on one's prowess as a warrior. Until he took a scalp, a young man lived in a kind of disgrace, obliged to serve warriors as a menial. Creek custom compelled no one to go to war, which was normally confined to sporadic, small war parties in search of a few scalps and prisoners. The entire Creek confederacy never took concerted action against a common enemy; warfare involved individual talwas, or a group of allied talwas, conducting raids on traditional foes like the Choctaws and Cherokees, against whom it was nearly always legitimate to wage war. Because opportunities to take scalps—valued as demonstrable proof of a kill—or prisoners were at a premium, aspiring Creek warriors sometimes surreptitiously murdered their own people on the margins of raids to obtain hair. The scalps of enemy women and children were always fair game, and while Creek warriors never raped women, which they feared would diminish their war powers, killing noncombatants was acceptable practice in all southeastern tribes.[9]

Creek warriors had no wish to die for their people; rather, they aspired to return home with scalps and glory, and nothing brought greater glory than a live male prisoner. Captive women and children were enslaved by clans that had lost members in battle. In bondage they did the same work as their owners. Most eventually were adopted into their owners' clan. Male captives, however, were dragged directly to the blood poles on the chunky ground. The entire talwa turned out to witness their torture and slow, hideous death by fire. Not only did Creek women mete out torture, but they alone had the right to spare a man's life, a prerogative seldom exercised.[10]

Before a talwa went to war, the tustunnugee thlucco raised his war club in a solemn public ceremony. Painted red, the Creek war club, also known as a red stick (*atássa*), was "shaped like a small gun about two feet long," said a Creek métis. "At the curve near where the lock would be is a three-square piece of iron or steel with a sharp edge driven in, to leave a projection of about two inches." If more than one talwa was to participate in a foray, the tustunnugee thlucco would send a red war club and bundle of sticks, also painted red, to each participating community. One stick in the bundle was broken each day until, on the final day, the various expeditions converged at a designated spot. Thus, the red sticks served to synchronize actions, and time was reckoned in terms of "broken days."

A war club, or red stick, was both a symbol and an essential weapon in a Creek warrior's arsenal, which by the early eighteenth century also included a musket, a tomahawk, bows and arrows, and a scalping knife. When the appointed day to depart on a raid arrived, participants gathered in the public square in breechcloth and moccasins, their bodies boldly painted. The tustunnugee thlucco emitted a sacred war whoop, and then everyone sang, danced, and fired their muskets. After ingesting a concoction of consecrated herbs, the warriors marched single file from the talwa, their thoughts fixed on killing. Once war was declared, a Creek warrior explained, "you speak to the enemy only by beating him on the head. There is no communication with him, either direct or indirect, for any reason whatsoever. Anyone who disregards this is considered a traitor and is treated accordingly." The end of hostilities, on the other hand, was absolute, at least theoretically.[11]

Much of supposed Creek bellicosity represented pure rodomontade. Open, sustained warfare between the southeastern tribes was infrequent, and even small raids were strictly a seasonal endeavor. English colonists said the Indians sought blood when the snakes were out; in other words, they waged war in the late spring, the summer, and the early fall. Late autumn, winter, and early spring they devoted to hunting. Actual loss of life was minimal; no talwa could afford heavy casualties. Although they enjoyed the ritualistic color and clamor preceding combat, few Creeks were enamored of war. Some Creek men found the whole notion of war making so repellent that they became transvestites and did women's work.[12]

Nearly all Creeks considered rituals essential not only to the smooth functioning of society but also to the averting of calamities. Central to Creek belief was the notion of separation: that things belonging to radically opposed categories had to be kept apart, either intermittently or always. Thus, women must be separated from men during menses, during childbirth, and before war making; birds and four-footed animals, as well as fire and water, must always be kept apart. The Creeks also strove to keep clean, spiritually and physically.

Men purified themselves with a highly caffeinated beverage made from roasted leaves and holly twigs called *assee,* meaning "white drink," because white symbolized purity, happiness, and social harmony. Creeks considered the beverage a gift from God, the "Master of Breath." Europeans called the strong brew the black drink because of its color. Creek men gathered in their public square weekly, or in some talwas daily, to drink from gourds a quantity equivalent in its caffeine content to two dozen cups of coffee, which they periodically disgorged. Most Europeans agreed that the black drink—which was served to male visitors along with tobacco before any council—had a pleasant taste similar to black tea. After drinking and vomiting, the men dispersed—purified from sin, brimming over with benevolence, or, in time of war, fortified for battle with a terrific caffeine high.[13]

The central Creek ritual was the annual Green Corn Ceremony, also known as the busk or the *poskitá* (literally, "to fast or purify"). Celebrated in August at the ripening of the new corn, and lasting from four to eight days, the busk represented a reaffirmation—or restoration, when necessary—of harmony between the clans of a talwa, and between a talwa and the Master of Breath. The Creeks forgave all transgressions short of murder, and life began anew.[14]

The métis George Stiggins, a chronicler of his mother's people and a participant in the Creek War, asserted unfairly that the Creeks acknowledged their creator only during the busk. In truth, most Creeks believed the Master of Breath ever present, together with otherworldly spirits benign and dreadful. And how had the Creeks come into being? A prominent eighteenth-century micco said that the first Creeks emerged from the "mouth of the ground" and hastened toward the setting sun because their appearance had angered the earth, which threatened to eat their children. The enraged earth was a huge, circular flat island resting precariously on the surface of great waters, suspended from the vault of the sky by four invisible cords attached at each of the cardinal directions. During their sojourn over its surface, the fabled Creeks discovered a thundering hill, atop which a magical stick sang and shivered. They subdued the stick and thenceforth carried replicas of it—the atássas, or red sticks—with them in war.[15]

Most Creeks believed in an afterlife but differed as to both where the soul went after death and what rewards or punishments awaited it. Some thought that the souls of the good spent eternity in an Upper World of "pleasure uninterrupted" above the sky vault; those of evil-doers wallowed in an Under World beneath the earth and waters. Others spoke of a "distant, known region, where game is plenty, where corn grows all the year round, and the springs of pure water are never dried up," juxtaposed with a "distant swamp, which is full of galling briars," devoid of women and game, in which the condemned (apparently only men) existed perpetually half-starved.[16]

Creeks assumed that evil stalked the earth. They considered tragedy that struck those who violated societal norms to be well-merited divine retribution. When bad things happened to good men, however, or when evil men prospered, there could be only one cause—witchcraft. Its practitioners appeared as fellow Creeks, but their inherent evil placed them outside the human realm. Instances of actual witch burnings were few, but the fear and loathing they evoked ran deep. Not all who touched the supernatural did so with wicked intent, however. Creeks accepted the reality of beneficent visions, dreams, and divinely induced trances—a belief on which Red Stick prophets would later capitalize.[17]

Although Creek notions of virtue and morality—particularly sexual mores—frequently offended European sensibilities, most white visitors praised Creek warmth and hospitality. The eighteenth-century French captain Jean-Bernard Bossu was such a man, and he found himself smothered with Creek kindness. When he arrived in a talwa, the micco and other leading men shook his hand vigorously and led him to the public square. There they offered him tobacco and the black drink and, on learning he was single, a lovely young woman to share his bed.

The girl was not necessarily a harlot. Creeks encouraged premarital sexual relations except between members of the same clan. Unmarried Creek women were free to use their bodies as they saw fit. When a single warrior from another talwa visited, he habitually hired a girl for a night or two.[18]

Louis Milfort, a Frenchman who lived among the Creeks in the late eighteenth century, benefited both from the promiscuity of single Creek women and from their curiosity about the sexual attributes of Caucasian males. Milfort claimed to have resisted the charms of Creek women for two years until, one evening at a festival, a particularly lovely girl flirted with him. Succumbing to her charms, Milfort snuck off with the girl to her mother's house and then climbed a rickety ladder to the girl's garret. No sooner had Milfort made the ascent than four other women appeared in the dark, seized him, yanked off his trousers, and playfully demanded he make love to all of them because they had "never yet seen a capon-warrior," meaning a Frenchman's penis. Milfort rose to the occasion. "I had to prove to these women that a French warrior is well worth a Creek warrior. I came out of the combat with honor, and my adventure was soon generally known."[19]

Had any of his paramours been married, Milfort would have been fortunate to have escaped the encounter unscathed. Creeks considered a marriage conditional until a couple celebrated a busk together, and they permitted polygamy. Unlike some tribes, which permitted extramarital affairs, they condemned adultery. The aggrieved spouse, with the help of his or her clan, punished the adulterous couple harshly, lashing their bodies and often cropping their ears. Afterward, the Creeks considered the disfigured transgressors man and wife, whether they liked it or not.[20]

Milfort undoubtedly enjoyed his nocturnal ambush. Young Creek women tended to be petite and beautiful, their languid, dark-eyed sensuality accentuated by their custom of going topless in warm weather. Creek women wore their jet-black hair plaited and then turned up and fastened on the crown of their head with a silver broach. From the wreathed topknot of hair, there flowed "an incredible quantity of silk ribbands of various colors, which stream down on every side almost to the ground." Only prostitutes used face or body paint. Creek women grew "thick and strong" as they aged, but many remained "very handsome" nonetheless. Once married, they were "discreet, modest, loving, faithful, and affectionate to their husbands," observed the early American naturalist William Bartram; husbands, in turn, were "courteous and polite to the women."[21]

In the winter, Creek women dressed in knee-length skirts of deerskin or coarse woolen cloth called stroud, matchcoats, and cloth leggings. Both sexes wore deerskin moccasins (the men sometimes went barefoot in the summer) and delighted in ear, nose, and chest ornaments; leg and arm bands; finger rings; necklaces; gorgets; and colorful headbands.[22]

Creek women were the shortest Indian females in the South; few exceeded five feet in height. Creek men, on the other hand, were quite tall. Many stood above six feet, and few were under five feet, eight inches. Their complexion was darker than that of neighboring Native peoples.

The men lavished greater attention on their appearance than did the women. They lacerated their ears, weighing down the lobes with lead until they became so elastic as to "spring and bound" with the least motion, then decorated the distended lobes with white heron feathers. Around their heads, Creek men tied broad bands adorned with stones, beads, wampum, and feathers. They tattooed their bodies with the figures of animals, serpents, stars, crescents, and the sun; miccos sometimes sported more elaborate tattoos. Unlike the women, Creek men habitually painted themselves, often with elaborate designs. When William Bartram encountered the Creeks in the mid-eighteenth century, most of the men wore ruffled linen shirts, breechclouts, and leggings, to which they added a scarlet- or blue-stroud mantle in winter.[23]

A healthy and varied diet contributed to the Creeks' fine appearance. Creek staples included corn and venison, often served in stews and supplemented with a wide variety of nutritious and delicious foodstuffs. The Creeks raised three types of corn—one for making hominy, one for flour, and a third as roasting ears. Creek women pounded and boiled the hominy into a rich gruel flavored with venison stock and left standing in large pots for family members to eat when they wished. In addition to corn, the women cultivated beans, squashes, pumpkins, potatoes, watermelons, and muskmelons by means of swidden (slash-

and-burn) agriculture in communal fields located in river bottoms or on active floodplains. The Creeks also made good use of wild fruits and vegetables. Walnuts, chestnuts, persimmons, mulberries, raspberries, plums, grapes, and greenbrier roots all found their way into the Creek diet, either fresh, fried in fritters, or preserved. Although venison constituted 90 percent of the meat the Creeks consumed, they also hunted bear, wild turkey, beaver, and bison, and speared fish with sharpened reeds. Bear meat was a breakfast favorite, and bear fat was a relished seasoning.[24]

Truly, the Creeks lived in a land of abundance—an eighty-four-thousand-square-mile mosaic of great beauty and inviting climate occupying the heart of the modern American South. The Creeks, however, defined their country and its limits not in terms of political boundaries but rather by its natural features: the piedmont, the coastal plain, the fall line, and the dominant rivers.

The piedmont, the hilly plateau separating the Appalachian Mountains from the coastal plain, was heavily forested with longleaf pine on the uplands and hardwoods like oak, sassafras, sycamore, and hickory in the valleys. Underbrush was thin. Contrary to popular belief, the region was not virgin woodland; over the centuries the Indian inhabitants had repeatedly burned off large portions of the forest to create grazing lands that stimulated growth of the deer population.

In the Creek country, the piedmont yielded abruptly to the coastal plain in a five-hundred-foot plunge of waterfalls and rapids where the Chattahoochee, Coosa, and Tallapoosa Rivers tumbled from the plateau. Rocks and shoals abounded, and the waters ran swift. The fall line hosted the best freshwater fishing in the South.

Vast forests of pine, interspersed with hickory, magnolia, and cypress, grew on the coastal plain, where rivers meandered sluggishly. Swamps, canebrakes, laurel hells, bogs, briar patches, and beaver ponds freckled the landscape. The farther south one proceeded, the poorer the land grew. Just south of the fall line, however, there ran a thirty-mile-wide and three-hundred-mile-long stretch of remarkably fertile plain, the famous Black Belt of the antebellum South, along which were located most of the Creek talwas.

Six major river systems coursed through the Creek country. Most ran generally north to south. The Savannah River marked the Creeks' eastern boundary. Next came the Ogeechee, Oconee, and Ocmulgee Rivers, all of which had their origin in the piedmont of what is today central Georgia. The Flint and Chattahoochee head in northern Georgia and run roughly parallel before joining to form the Apalachicola River and emptying into the Gulf of Mexico. The Coosa and Tallapoosa Rivers drain northeast Alabama and combine to form the languid Alabama River of pure water and excellent fishing. The westernmost rivers, the Black Warrior and the Tombigbee, formed the boundary between Creek and Chickasaw and Creek and Choctaw hunting grounds, respectively.[25]

In 1791, the American Indian agent Caleb Swan reveled in the natural delights of the Creek domain and the possibilities for exploiting them. "The climate of this inland country is remarkably healthy; the wet and dry seasons are regular and periodical. The constant breezes render the heat of summer very temperate, and toward autumn they are delightfully perfumed by the ripening aromatic shrubbery, which abounds throughout the country. The winters are soft and mild, and the summers sweet and wholesome." In short, the country "must become a most delectable part of the United States...and one day or other be the seat of manufactures and commerce." There was just one drawback as Swan saw it. "At present, it is but a rude wilderness, exhibiting many natural beauties, which are only rendered unpleasant by being in possession of the jealous natives."

Swan's ruminations were yet a century away. The threats that similar sentiments posed to the Creek way of life would come much sooner.[26]

CHAPTER THREE

Between Three Fires

CREEK WARRIORS worried. In the early 1540s, Hernando de Soto's conquistadors had thundered through the country of their Mississippian tradition ancestors with matchlock harquebuses that dealt death with smoke, lead balls, and a roar, weapons the likes of which the natives had never encountered. Just over a century later, Creek fighting men found themselves losing ground—and people—to Westo Indian warriors armed with sleek flintlock muskets, a vast improvement over the unwieldy old Spanish weapons.

A small but fearsome tribe, the Westos dealt in Indian slaves, trading captives to colonial Virginia planters in exchange for arms, ammunition, hatchets, blankets, wool and cotton clothing, metal tools, and glass beads—wondrous goods previously unknown to the southeastern Indians. That struck the Creeks as good business. First, however, they had to vanquish the irksome Westos, and for that they needed arms of their own. In 1680, Creeks of the powerful Cusseta talwa on the Chattahoochee River and the Uchee Indians of the Savannah River struck a Faustian bargain with the merchants of Charles Towne, the coastal port of the young English province of Carolina: they would extirpate the Westos in exchange for arms and ammunition and the same marvelous array of trade goods that had enticed their enemies and that soon replaced traditional tools, clothing, and adornments in Creek society. The Cussetas and Uchees made short work of the Westos, after which the Cussetas turned on the Uchees, killing scores and enslaving the remainder. In keeping with time-honored tradition, the Cussetas eventually welcomed the Uchee and Westo remnants into the Creek confederacy. The Creeks' first foray into the world of European colonial politics had gone well for them.[1]

To acquire an ongoing supply of guns and goods from the Carolinians, however, the Creeks needed something to offer them besides a temporary alliance of convenience. And so they sold other Indians into bondage. Creek slave traders found a ready market for their human wares. The emerging plantation economies of Virginia and Carolina needed Indian slave labor, and labor-starved colonies as far north as New England welcomed "Carolina Indians." Carolina officials also were eager to eliminate the potential threat posed by the Apalachee Indians of northern Florida, who were loyal to Spain, then at war with Great Britain.

The Creeks plunged deeper into the maelstrom of European imperial affairs. They swept the Gulf Coast from the lower Mississippi to Spanish Florida, gathering captives from what remained of the region's small tribes. Between 1670 and 1715 the Creeks funneled at least twenty thousand Indian captives to Carolina, becoming in the process the best-armed and most feared Indians in the South—although not, as will be seen, the finest fighters.

They might not have fully grasped the ramifications of their sudden dependence on British colonial arms and goods, but Creek men reveled in their newfound prosperity. Creek women were less enthralled with the new source of wealth. As slave catching took their men farther from home and for longer stretches than traditional hunting, male duties such as clearing the fields for farming and rearing boys fell to them.[2]

In addition to the influx of novel weapons and goods, the Creek-Carolina connection initiated two other fundamental alterations to Creek society. After they cleared Florida of most of its Native inhabitants, scores of restless Creeks migrated to the region. In doing so, they followed the usual Creek custom of incorporating survivors of the shattered Florida tribes, and later escaped black slaves. Thus were formed the Seminoles, a Muscogee word meaning "wild," or "people who camp at a distance." Gradually the Creeks came to regard their restive relatives as a distinct but allied people.[3]

. . .

It was then also that a fissure emerged in Creek society, wrought by contact with the colonial British. The Creeks split into two divisions that became known as the Upper and Lower Creeks. It is uncertain precisely how or when the separation occurred. Probably the Charles Towne traders named the two geographic clusters of talwas. The trade road from the Carolina coast forked in what is today central Georgia. The left, or lower path, led to the Chattahoochee River talwas. The right path branched off to the Tallapoosa and Coosa River talwas, as well as the more distant Alabama talwas on the Alabama River. Although most of the talwas on the latter three rivers lay directly west of the Chattahoochee communities, they were farther "up the road" from them. The principal Upper Creek talwas were those of the Abeika, Tallapoosa, and Alabama peoples. The Cowetas dominated the Lower Creek division. By the early eighteenth century, both the English and the Creeks themselves used the Upper and Lower designations. It was in the context of the Upper and Lower divisions that the term "Creek confederacy" came to have real meaning.

Because of their relative proximity to the Province of Carolina, the Lower Creeks felt the English presence first. Most of the Creek slavers, as well as the future Seminoles, hailed from talwas on the Chattahoochee and Flint Rivers. The Upper Creeks, by contrast, did not even receive their first visits from Carolina traders until the 1690s. Although they obtained arms and ammunition from the colonists, mostly in exchange for deerskins, their relative isolation largely spared them from abuse by increasingly avaricious whites.[4]

The Lower Creeks, on the other hand, became entwined in the shifting tide of colonial relations with local Indians. Conflict came courtesy of the unfortunate Yamasee Indians of Carolina. Heavily in debt and constantly hounded by their Charles Towne creditors, in April 1715 the Yamasees killed their agent and several traders. The revolt rapidly spread through the Indian nations of the South. The Lower Creeks sided with the Yamasees. Razing most of the plantation district, confederated warriors came within a few miles of Charles Towne. The fighting raged for nearly two years before the Carolinians, with the help of the Cherokees—who slaughtered a Lower Creek delegation to the tribe, an incident that caused bad blood between the two peoples for decades to come—prevailed.[5]

The Creeks and the Carolinians mended ties after the Yamasee War. The English enacted trade reforms that pleased the Indians. A rise in the availability of African slaves killed the commerce in Indian captives, but the Creeks adjusted. They tracked down runaway black slaves, for which the British Crown paid them handsomely—four blankets or two rifles for each slave returned alive, and one blanket in exchange for the severed head of a dead fugitive. The Creeks had no qualms about doing what they thought consistent with both profit and the natural order, which they believed relegated blacks to perpetual slavery.[6]

Dealing in runaways could not long sustain the Creek demand for the guns and ammunition now vital for hunting and for their defense; the metal tools that eased their labor; and the calico, woolen stroud, and duffel they had come to prefer for clothing. A change in European tastes, however, afforded them a way not merely to maintain a steady trade but also to accrue wealth beyond their wildest imaginings. Gloves, clothing, and shoes made from deerskin leather had become popular in Europe. Availing themselves of the seemingly inexhaustible herds of white-tailed deer that inhabited their country, the Creeks became commercial hunters for English leather manufacturers. Trade relations bound the Creeks to British America as firmly, to employ a Creek metaphor, as a vine winds its tendrils around a tree.[7]

The Creeks had no intention of subordinating themselves to the English colonies, however. They realized that three white fires burned beyond the borders of their country—a three-cornered imperial struggle for empire between Great Britain, Spain, and France—and that to fall into any one fire would consume them. Consequently, after the Yamasee War the Lower Creeks cultivated Spanish Florida, while the Alabamas, on behalf of the Upper Creeks, courted French Louisiana. French officials happily accepted an Alabama offer to occupy a post in their country, which the Indians would construct at their own expense. The French christened the well-built structure Fort Toulouse. It lay on the Alabama River near modern Montgomery, within a day's ride of the principal Upper Creek talwas.[8]

British colonial officials and traders deprecated the Creek policy that played the imperial powers off one another for the Indians' benefit. What they scornfully called "low politics," however, the Creeks considered a sound policy of neutrality, and they pursued it as sedulously as commercial considerations permitted. Astute Creek miccos developed a sufficient appreciation of the global conflicts that roiled Spain, France, and Great Britain to use the antagonisms they created to their own advantage.[9]

Not that the British were above low politics. To counter the French and Spanish threat and protect the Carolinas from Creek raids should the Indians have a change of heart (the Province of Carolina had divided into the colonies of North and South Carolina), the Crown granted the petition of the philanthropist James Oglethorpe to interpose a colony composed of the scrapings of debtors' prisons between South Carolina and Spanish Florida. In 1733, Oglethorpe and the first shipload of liberated debtors landed on the west bank of the Savannah River to inaugurate the Georgia colony. An astute diplomat, Oglethorpe won the friendship of the Lower Creeks, who relinquished to the British their lands between the Savannah and the Altamaha Rivers and also agreed to permit English traders to settle anywhere in the Creek country they wished. Within a few short years, the town of Augusta, Georgia, sprang up to compete with Charleston (formerly Charles Towne) for the Creek deerskin trade. Soon nearly every Creek talwa had its resident English or Scots-Irish trader, usually living with a Creek wife who helped him manage the retail end of the lucrative commerce.

The Creeks welcomed the growing English presence. Despite their suave diplomacy, free gun-repair services, and fine brandy, the French proved unable to compete commercially with the British. Neither was the relatively feeble Spanish Florida able to supply Creek wants reliably. The greater variety, better quality, and lower prices of British trade goods, combined with easy credit terms, won the grudging loyalty of Creek consumers. It was a happy time for the Creeks. Peace and prosperity saw the Creek population rise while other Indian peoples declined. Unaware that Oglethorpe's royal grant contemplated the eventual absorption of all their territory, the Creeks supposed they had secured friendly neighbors and a convenient market for their deerskins. They counted their amicable trade alliance with Georgia as "one of the most glorious events in the annals of their nation." In reality, they had taken the first step toward forfeiting their destiny to a grasping and inconstant people.[10]

· · ·

That their seemingly privileged position was in fact dangerously precarious became suddenly and painfully apparent to the Creeks in 1763, when Great Britain defeated France to end the Seven Years' War. Seismic shifts on the North American imperial map laid bare the bankruptcy of the Creek neutrality policy. Great Britain obtained Spanish Florida and divided the province into East and West Florida. Spain in turn took French Louisiana, but its presence there was weak. France withdrew from the continent altogether. No longer the objects of imperial competition, the Creek confederacy was reduced to dealing with only the British.

At first, it appeared as if the Creeks might actually benefit from British hegemony. With the royal treasury depleted by war, the British government wanted peace with the southeastern Indians. In the Proclamation of 1763, it forbade settlement beyond the Appalachians and asserted royal authority over Indian affairs. Meant to placate the natives, the proclamation proved a mixed blessing for the Creeks. Creek power and the propinquity of Spanish Florida had constrained Georgia's growth before 1763. With the Spanish threat removed, the colony expanded markedly. Within a year, the white and slave population of Georgia alone nearly equaled that of the Creek confederacy— the latter numbering between eighteen thousand and twenty thousand persons, of whom at least thirty-six hundred were warriors. To accommodate an orderly growth of Georgia, over the next decade the Crown negotiated five land cessions with the Creeks that shrank the confederacy's boundary westward to the Ogeechee River.[11]

The loss of land was trifling in its impact on the Creeks when compared with an unintended consequence of royal control of Indian affairs. Prior to 1763, colonial authorities had exercised a tight rein over Indian traders. Typically, they permitted no more than one trader to establish himself in any of the forty talwas that then made up the Creek confederacy. In for the long haul, a trader typically formed a close bond with the local micco, to whom he extended favorable rates and frequently gave presents. To cement the friendship, the micco would arrange a marriage to a niece or other female relative, and together the trader and his Creek wife would raise a mixed-blood (métis) family. The trader enjoyed the protection of the wife's clan, which became his customer base. His wife gained in prestige and often took control of her husband's trade stock. Villagers welcomed these mixed unions as visible proof of a trade alliance. Everyone benefited.[12]

The Proclamation of 1763 ruptured the tidy status quo. Confronted with a treasury depleted by war, British authorities unwisely permitted anyone able to post a small bond to obtain a "general" license to trade anywhere, rather than in a specific talwa. A wave of colonial reprobates swept over the Creek country. The new breed of peddlers found it more profitable to deal in alcohol that "bewitched" Creek men than in the trade goods the Creeks truly needed. Within a decade, the sickly-sweet aroma of West Indies tafia (a drink similar to rum) permeated all but the most remote talwas.

In a country awash in alcohol, life became cheap, and tempers grew short. While Creek men often bartered all or part of their seasonal haul of deerskins for drink, Creek women prostituted themselves for needed trade goods, and sometimes also for tafia. It was not merely single females exercising their cultural prerogative to use their bodies as they wished; increasingly, married women risked beatings and mutilation to have sex with Georgia traders, a most "monstrous set of rogues for a major part of whom the gallows groans." Creek marriages crumbled, overwhelming the mechanism of clan justice and creating bedlam in the talwas. The old breed of traders held their wives and métis children close and looked on in disgust.[13]

The Creeks had few means of combating a trade system that had turned against them. Occasionally a party of sober Creeks would ambush tafia peddlers on lonely trails, crushing their kegs but sparing their lives. Far too many Creeks, however, were addicted to tafia to truly wish to halt its flow. At the same time, the Creeks had become absolutely dependent on white trade goods. "The white people," lamented a sympathetic colonist, "have dazzled their senses with foreign superfluities." By the latter half of the eighteenth century, a good musket was worth $50 in the Creek country, "to be paid in skins or horses." A gun was hardly a superfluity, but a sample of nonlethal items in the inventory of a Pensacola trading house reveals the extent to which other items of European manufacture had insinuated themselves into every aspect of Creek life: fishhooks and lines; tin table spoons and forks; needles, thread, and silk; door and window hinges; iron corn and coffee mills; frying pans and coffeepots; gauze for mosquito nets; animal traps; ruffled shirts, gloves, hats, and silk handkerchiefs; and imported Chinese vermillion (an improved source of war paint) were among the scores of goods available at the right price in deerskins.[14]

To quench their thirst for tafia without sacrificing their own martial and their family's domestic needs, as well as to put meat on the table, Creek men hunted relentlessly. From what traditionally had been a three-month fall/winter endeavor, deer hunting came to occupy six months or more of a man's time and energy. Desperate hunters killed younger deer. Herds thinned to dangerous levels. Hunters had to travel farther afield to find game, and the Creeks and their Cherokee neighbors became increasingly unable to make their payments on British goods. Despite delivering an average of half a million pounds of deerskins annually to colonial creditors, they nevertheless descended deeper into debt. By 1773, the Creek debt totaled 670,000 pounds of deerskins.[15]

An influx of cattle also endangered the deer population. The Creeks had welcomed horses, which they called *echolucco,* meaning "big deer" in Muscogee. Most Creek men owned between two and a dozen horses, but they drew the line at cattle. Introduced to talwas by resident traders, cattle herds came to represent a new and prolific kind of private property, which accelerated a cultural shift from traditional communalism toward the materialism that European trade goods had begun. As the métis offspring of traders grew to adulthood, they too acquired cattle, as did some so-called progressive Creeks, particularly in the Lower Creek talwas. The majority "traditionalist" Creeks objected to cattle both as a cultural menace and because of the destruction that the herds inflicted on communal cornfields and the canebrakes and grasses that were prime deer-grazing grounds. They railed against the whites who fostered the new economy and wished the instigators would return from whence they had come.[16]

The whites, however, were going nowhere. Nor did the Creeks have the will to expel them, particularly after the Creeks became ensnarled in a desultory but costly war of their own making with their traditional foes the Choctaws in 1764, with whom they had long feuded over hunting land along the Alabama and Tombigbee Rivers. The tustunnugee thlucco of an Upper Creek talwa precipitated the conflict by killing a prominent Choctaw war leader and torturing several war-riors to satiate the bloodlust of his restive young men lest they instead fall out with the English, "as he knows that they must be at war with somebody." It was a bloody reminder of the inherent tension between young and old, and war and peace, which the Creeks strove to main-tain rather than ease. The Choctaws, former allies of the French who, after the British victory over their imperial friends, kept the British at arm's length from the relative safety of their southeastern Mississippi domain, wanted conflict with no one. They were hardly a people to suffer aggression unanswered, however.

The war with the Choctaws did not go well for the Creeks. Choctaw warriors were good fighters, adept at avoiding ambushes and disci-plined in battle. They also outnumbered the Creeks by at least twelve hundred men. As the conflict dragged on, some war-weary Lower Creeks drifted south to swell the ranks of their Seminole cousins in Florida. Not until October 1776, and then only with British mediation, did opposing leaders bury their war clubs "very deep in the earth."

The Creeks had merely traded one conflict for another. Three months earlier, the American colonies had declared their independence. Great Britain expected the Creeks to help it defeat the refractory colonists, with whom the Choctaws sided. The Creeks, however, reverted to their old neutrality policy, the bankruptcy of which soon became clear. Most of the deerskin merchants were British Loyalists, also known as Tories, and when they fled South Carolina and Georgia—some to Creek talwas, others to return to Great Britain—the deerskin trade tumbled. Meanwhile, the population of Georgia doubled during the Revolutionary War to sixty thousand, more than half of whom were slaves. Unruly squatters and their human chattel availed themselves of the power vacuum in the South to spill across the colony's Ogeechee River boundary into the eastern reaches of the Creek country, eager to exploit the rich riverine soil. Simultaneously, the young generation of Creek métis sought new sources of wealth. Together with vengeful Tory traders and Creek warriors whose livelihood was imperiled by the declining deerskin market, they periodically plundered backcoun-try plantations of slaves and horses.[17]

The Creeks made few attempts to help the British directly, and their most ambitious effort ended ignominiously when a Choctaw war party slaughtered fifty members of a Creek force attempting to free British and Tory friends besieged by the Choctaws and their Spanish allies. The Creeks simply could not best the Choctaws. Neither did they seem able any longer to navigate the turbulent waters of the white man's wars and politics.[18]

The Creeks emerged from the American Revolution a divided and imperiled people. To traditional inter-talwa tensions and clan jealousies, the Revolutionary War added a new and deeper layer of friction in Creek society: pro-American and pro-British factions. After the British defeat, upward of four hundred Tories formerly associated with the deerskin trade retreated with their slaves and cattle to their Creek wives' pro-British talwas, contributing their offspring to the already considerable métis population that came of age during the conflict. More than one observer was struck by the "strange medley of people... Caucasians, Indians, Africans, and several new breeds manufactured by judicious crossing" that came to characterize the Creek confederacy. The sudden profusion of adult métis Creek leaders with anglicized names also occasioned confusion. Although their Creek wives owned the property, the Tories' slave-based agriculture, métis sons, and crop-trampling herds of cattle irritated traditionalists.[19]

Creek society stood at a crossroads, with no one apparently capable of selecting a viable path for the confederacy. An unlikely leader was about to emerge, however. He would lead the Creeks—some willingly, others grudgingly—into a perilous game of power politics with a new white government and reconfigured European presence in the South. In the process, this dynamic and controversial character would deepen fissures within the Creek body politic.

His name was Alexander McGillivray. Born in 1750, he was the son of the Scottish merchant Lachlan McGillivray and his métis wife. Alexander spent his first six years in his mother's Upper Creek talwa of Little Tallassee, where maternal uncles raised him. The fair-skinned and frail Alexander enjoyed the prerogatives that accompanied membership in his mother's influential Wind Clan—that is, until Lachlan

McGillivray asserted himself as no Creek father would have dared: he took Alexander from his maternal clan to live on his Augusta plantation and then sent him to school in Charleston. Alexander thrived in colonial society; after all, he was three-quarters white, literate, and well spoken. The outbreak of the Revolution found him working in Savannah for slave importers. Lachlan departed for Scotland, and Alexander returned to his mother's people with a British commission as royal commissary (agent) to the Upper Creeks.

Alexander McGillivray never felt at home in Creek society. No warrior, he preferred books to bloodshed. Neither did he hunt. McGillivray had three things in his favor, however: his refined fluency in English, which enabled him to hold his own with white officials; a gift for intrigue and power politics; and the privileged position his Wind Clan kinsmen occupied throughout the Creek confederacy.[20]

McGillivray's chief rivals were Hopoithle Micco (the Tame King) of Tallassee and Eneah Micco (the Fat King) of Cusseta, formidable miccos who rejected the métis and "progressive" Creek slave-and-cattle culture but collaborated with American traders.[21]

Hopoithle Micco and Eneah Micco hoped to broker peace with the new state of Georgia, but it would not be easy. Five years of Creek raids had turned Georgians into inveterate Indian haters. Georgians also felt entitled to as much Creek land as they wanted because in the Treaty of Paris, which officially terminated the Revolutionary War, the British acknowledged U.S. domain over Indian country east of the Mississippi River and also quit the Floridas. Creeks were thunderstruck, but none more so than McGillivray, who railed against his perfidious former allies, declaring, "As we were not parties, so we are determined to pay no attention to the manner in which the British negotiators had drawn out the lines."[22]

Protests about British treachery gained McGillivray nothing. The geopolitical landscape surrounding the Creek country had changed profoundly. To the north, the Cherokees were locked in a bitter battle to preserve their nation against encroaching Americans. To the east, land-hungry Georgians prepared to sally forth into the Creek country. To the south, a comparatively weak Spain reclaimed the Floridas. To the west, the Chickasaws and Choctaws, for the moment at least, stood neutral.

As most Creeks scrambled to meet the new reality, McGillivray embraced the old strategy of playing competing non-Indian powers (which now effectively numbered just the United States and Spain) against one another. In the 1784 Treaty of Pensacola, he persuaded Spanish colonial officials to recognize Creek sovereignty and name him its commissary to his people, with authority to regulate trade as he saw fit. With his enhanced wealth, McGillivray built a winter plantation in Spanish West Florida. His growing legion of supporters did not begrudge McGillivray his gains. Careful not to openly undermine the authority of the miccos, he posed in public as an adviser and spokesman, which earned the thirtysomething métis the unique title of Great Beloved Man.[23]

Hopoithle Micco and Eneah Micco saw nothing great or beloved in the young upstart. They and their followers, most of whom were Lower Creeks, bore a deep-seated animus toward Spain and despised McGillivray as a self-aggrandizing Spanish lackey. To demonstrate their commitment to peace, Hopoithle Micco and Eneah Micco ceded five million acres between the Ogeechee and the Oconee Rivers to the Georgians. Most talwas denounced the Georgia land deal, and McGillivray, with five thousand warriors firmly in his camp, notified the state legislature that the hapless miccos had "no authority to cede lands."

Georgia quaked. Its militia was no match for a united Creek opposition, and no help could be expected from the weak national government that lacked even a standing army. In October 1786, Georgia's Indian commissioners requested a council with the Creek leadership. Only Hopoithle Micco and Eneah Micco showed up.[24] McGillivray, meanwhile, negotiated an alliance with the Chickamaugas, the only band of Cherokees yet resisting American intrusion. While several Upper Creek war parties helped the Chickamaugas try to sweep settlers from the Southwest Territory, as Tennessee was then known, between 1787 and 1790, Lower Creek war leaders loyal to McGillivray staged nearly five hundred raids on Georgia frontier farmsteads. Their goals were more modest than those of the Chickamauga–Upper Creek coalition. The Creeks accepted Georgia as an immutable reality. With a population of nearly fifty-three thousand whites and twenty-nine thousand slaves, Georgia stood in no danger of being overrun, although state officials often portrayed the Creek threat in apocalyptic terms. What the Creeks wanted was to clear the Oconee

River valley of unlawful settlements. Initially they contented them-selves with stealing property and burning sheds and barns, hoping that alone would drive squatters from the disputed tract. Georgians, on the other hand, retaliated with indiscriminate slaughter. McGil-livray rightly accused frontiersmen of "warring with an exterminat-ing spirit," flaying Creek women alive, cutting infants out of mothers' wombs, and stuffing the mouths of dead men with their severed penises.[25]

The violence spiraled. Vengeful Creek raiders took their share of disarticulated eyes, ears, and limbs as war trophies. With the deerskin trade in deep decline, however, they preferred to hold white women and children for ransom rather than kill or mutilate them. Creek cap-tors turned a healthy profit from kidnapping. A prepubescent girl fetched at least $10, and married women commanded up to $150. One lovesick Lower Creek métis headman paid a war party $700 (repre-senting nearly $22,000 in 2022 currency) for a pretty Georgia girl, whom he eventually wed.[26]

Although the trade was lucrative, potential buyers for white captives were limited to family members of the victims, state officials, and the occasional fellow Creek. A far broader range of potential customers existed for able-bodied blacks, inducing Creek warriors to return to their earlier role as slave traders. Creek warriors led bound blacks over the well-beaten trail to the booming slave market in Pensacola, Span-ish West Florida. There many former chattels of Georgians were sold into slavery in the West Indies. Other Creeks disposed of their black captives within the confederacy, the buyers generally being miccos, wealthy métis, or Indian countrymen, as resident white traders had become known. Some captors kept the slaves themselves, employing the black men as farmers, herders, carpenters, sawyers, and domestic servants. Creek women resented sharing their field work with men, even if the blacks were, as the Creeks conceived them, a lesser form of humanity. Infrequently, black captives were adopted into Creek clans and became warriors.[27]

In the American Constitution, McGillivray discerned a new peril both to Creek sovereignty and to his own interests. Its ratification, he deduced, would usher in a far more muscular federal government.

Sensing that the United States, rather than Spain or Great Britain, was destined to be the dominant power on the North American continent, McGillivray conspired to outflank Georgia and gain both U.S. protection for the Creeks and a guaranteed trade that he would control. It would be a tough feat to pull off; Georgia had ratified the Constitution partly on assurances that the federal government would validate the shady treaties it had made with Hopoithle Micco and Eneah Micco and also help repel Creek border incursions.[28]

McGillivray's initial foray into diplomacy with the federal government failed. In a September 1789 council on the Oconee River, U.S. commissioners demanded the Creeks recognize Georgia's claim to the disputed land without offering any compensation in return. "By God," McGillivray thundered before quitting the talks, "I would not have such a treaty crammed down my throat!"

His commissioners might bluster, but President George Washington had no desire for war with the Creeks over what he knew to be a dubious Georgia claim. With the tribes north of the Ohio River already hostile, and the newly raised Regular army small and poorly trained, the president could ill afford a two-front conflict. And so, in the spring of 1790, he dispatched a confidential envoy to invite McGillivray and a delegation of Creek miccos to the nation's capital, New York City, to sign a peace treaty "as strong as the hills and lasting as the rivers." The Creek National Council—a loose association of talwa representatives convened annually or on special occasions to consider matters of interest to the entire confederacy—accepted the proposition, and on June 10, 1790, McGillivray and a cavalcade of twenty-five miccos set out from Cusseta for the great unknown capital of the Americans.

It is hard to conceive of the amazement that McGillivray, who had never been farther north than Charleston, and the miccos must have felt as they came to comprehend the enormous population and bustling energy of the Atlantic Seaboard. The journey also appealed to their vanity. Once beyond the sullen, suspicious state of Georgia, the journey took on a triumphal aspect. Dignitaries from Richmond to Philadelphia honored the travelers. In New York City, the largest crowd since George Washington's inauguration the year before greeted McGillivray and the miccos, who were shuttled from one public celebration to another. McGillivray struck New Yorkers as a man "of an open, candid, generous mind, with a good judgment, and very tenacious memory." President Washington and Secretary of War Henry Knox, who would conduct the treaty negotiations, were privy to a less flattering appraisal of McGillivray. The métis could be bought, an Indian commissioner reported, his "importance and pecuniary emolument [being] the objects which will altogether influence his conduct."

Self-interest also motivated the miccos. On the margins of formal treaty negotiations, President Washington and Secretary of War Knox concluded a secret pact with the Creeks that granted McGillivray the rank of brigadier general in the U.S. Army and an annual pension of $1,200. Six miccos, Hopoithle Micco among them, received a handsome medal and a $100 annual stipend. The private pact also permitted the Creeks to import $60,000 a year in goods duty-free from the United States in case of an American conflict with Spain.

McGillivray and the miccos accepted the Great Father's bribes, but they also stood firmly enough for their people's interests that the public treaty, signed on August 7, 1790, granted the Creeks considerable concessions. It prohibited states from negotiating for Creek land, effectively disarming Georgia. The Treaty of New York also guaranteed to the Creek confederacy "all their lands within the limits of the United States" and permitted the Creeks to deal as they pleased with any non-Indian who "shall attempt to settle on any of the Creek lands." In exchange for an unspecified quantity of goods and a perpetual annual annuity of $1,500 payable to the confederacy, the Creek leaders yielded two-thirds of the territory that Georgia claimed under the spurious treaties of the 1780s—land that overhunting had rendered useless to the Creeks. The southern border of the cession was fixed at the Apalachee River, a short and winding Oconee tributary where game still abounded.[29]

The Treaty of New York had little impact on the Upper Creeks, and so they largely accepted it. But the Lower Creeks, whose depleted hunting lands McGillivray ceded, protested the agreement vigorously. Pocketing his bribe, the opportunistic Hopoithle Micco returned to the ranks of McGillivray's enemies. Exploiting Lower Creek unrest, William Bowles, a delusional former British army officer and adventurer, tried to supplant McGillivray with generous gifts of gunpowder to disaffected Creeks and promises of future goods at cut-rate prices. McGillivray expelled Bowles from the Lower Creek country, but the effort exhausted him. Retiring to his plantation near Pensacola, McGillivray died of a perforated ulcer and pneumonia on February 17, 1793. With him died his revolutionary dream of a unified Creek nation able to defend its land against the inevitable onrush of settlers. He alone among the Creeks had recognized that the U.S. government, however sincere its intentions, lacked the strength or will to stem the westward tide of American migration.[30]

Alexander McGillivray died as he had lived, a conflicted soul torn between two cultures. His passing left a yawning power vacuum that none was able to fill. Factionalism and local loyalties reasserted themselves. Efau Hadjo, the Upper Creek micco of the Wind Clan known to whites as the "Mad Dog," became National Council spokesman, but he lacked the prudence of his late kinsman McGillivray.

Considerable power passed to wealthy and privileged métis and Indian countrymen such as Charles Weatherford, a Scotsman married to McGillivray's half sister, and Alexander Cornells (Oche Hadjo), the literate son of a Creek woman and English father. They endorsed Efau Hadjo as spokesman, but his and their goals ultimately diverged. The Indian countrymen and métis wanted a strong Creek "national" authority capable of securing their cotton fields and slaves and preserving order. Efau Hadjo, however, was at heart a traditionalist who, in common with the miccos, was averse to war with Georgia.

Young Creek warriors bridled at their elders' passivity. They depended on warfare and horse stealing to secure honors, respect, and wives. Unlike Weatherford and Cornells, who owed their livelihood to ranching and farming, the typical Creek male survived by the hunt, or by selling horses to Pensacola traders, and thus had a keen interest in keeping out white settlers. Poor Georgians of limited prospects, boundless hatred of Indians, and undisguised scorn for government treaties were naturally drawn to the frontier. Ignoring Creek calls to vacate the land, these ruffians tightened their grasp on the Oconee valley by grazing ever larger herds of cattle in the unceded tract between the Oconee and the Apalachee Rivers. Meanwhile, Indian victories north of the Ohio River emboldened Creek militants. In late 1791, a Shawnee delegation passed through the Creek country, boasting of how a broad coalition of Ohio valley tribes had annihilated the American army on the Wabash River and cleared their country of trespassers; were the Creeks old women that they could not do the same?

Another crimson cycle of border strife appeared inevitable.[31]

CHAPTER FOUR

The Sweets of Civilization

T HE CREEK NATIONAL COUNCIL spokesman Efau Hadjo had a plan to prevent war with the Georgia squatters. He would shed Chickasaw blood instead. A warrior who prevailed over another Indian gained greater war honors than one who killed a white man, and long-standing bad blood between the Chickasaws and the Creeks provided sufficient motive to distract Creek firebrands from resuming raids on the Georgia settlements. Besting the Chickasaws should prove an easy proposition because the Creek warrior population outnumbered that of the Chickasaws by at least seven to one.

The numerical disparity counted for less than it should have, however. Simply stated, the Chickasaws were far better fighters than the Creeks, a quality that a French captain attributed to their utter fearlessness. They also had been the first southeastern Indians to acquire muskets, and their skill with them was evident. Although nearly a thousand Creek warriors answered his call in the summer of 1793, Efau Hadjo took every possible precaution when entering the Chickasaw homeland. Such was the Creeks' stealth that the Chickasaws were unaware of their presence until shooting erupted at a Chickasaw fort. Only seven warriors garrisoned the place, but overeager Creeks raised their war whoops and opened fire several hundred yards short of the walls. As the report of muskets rolled through the timber, nearby

Chickasaw warriors mounted their horses and galloped for the fort. Five of them missed the trail, stumbled into the Creek ranks, and were instantly killed. The ten surviving Chickasaws joined the small garrison. Through loopholes in the palisaded walls they kept up a steady fire on the massed enemy. Reluctant to assault even a lightly defended stockade, the Creeks, most of whom were on foot, fled. The seventeen Chickasaws and a few armed slaves galloped after the horde, gunning down nearly a hundred Creeks. A chastened Efau Hadjo acceded to a permanent peace with the Chickasaws.[1]

Efau Hadjo's clash with the Chickasaws proved more than a humiliating and bloody sideshow. As had the Creek-instigated war with the Choctaws two decades earlier, their conflict with the Chickasaws fed Native mistrust of the Creeks. For all his diplomatic suavity, Alexander McGillivray had failed to ensure a lasting peace with the United States or to unite the Creek people. Should relations with the young republic deteriorate, and ongoing Georgian incursions onto Creek soil suggested they would, the Creeks would be hard-pressed to count on support from fellow southeastern Indians.

After the Chickasaw fiasco, Efau Hadjo and his followers confronted the Georgian trespassers, who were on Creek soil to stay unless compelled to leave. Efau Hadjo recognized that the white threat demanded greater restraint than he had shown when he provoked the Chickasaws, and Creek raiders generally refrained from crossing the Treaty of New York boundaries. Georgians, on the other hand, ranged well beyond the border. More often than not they were the aggressors in the desultory warfare that smoldered from 1793 to 1795.

White provocations were considerable. In the spring of 1794, an armed rabble built stockades on the west bank of the Oconee River border and declared themselves an independent nation. Georgia militiamen, meanwhile, defied the governor and struck deep into the Creek confederacy. Their ranks included the strapping twenty-one-year-old native Virginian Samuel Dale, who would rise to legendary status in Alabama history and become known as the Daniel Boone of that state. In 1794, however, he was simply a struggling young frontiersman. His parents had died two years earlier, leaving Dale responsible for raising eight younger siblings on their hardscrabble Georgia tobacco farm. Honest, openhanded, and kind to a fault, Dale also had a hair-trigger temper and a growing reputation as a frontier brawler.

Although no Indian hater, he itched for action. "Putting a steady old man in my place on the farm, I volunteered for the service," recalled Dale, who conceded his unit's rough appearance. "Our accoutrements were a coonskin cap, bearskin vest, short hunting-shirt and trousers of homespun stuff, buckskin leggings, a blanket tied behind our saddles, a wallet for parched corn, coal flour, or other chance provisions, a long rifle, and hunting knife."

Swinging north around the Lower Creek talwas, Dale and his companions swam their horses across the wide Chattahoochee, then penetrated the pine barrens until they reached the Upper Creek talwa of Okfuskee, home to three hundred warriors, few if any of whom had raided the Georgia settlements. Their innocence mattered little to the Georgians, who attacked at dawn. Startled warriors spilled from their dwellings. Dale's company murdered thirteen and seized ten others, torched a few homes, and then galloped off. Scouting ahead of the company on the return march, Dale and another militiaman chanced upon two warriors asleep in a makeshift shelter. Dale killed one, but the other Creek darted into a canebrake. Dale picked his way through the tall and tough vegetation until a single musket shot felled his companion. Throwing himself behind the Georgian's corpse, Dale waited until the Indian emerged in a low crouch and "glided through the cane like a serpent," evidently thinking to kill Dale and then escape. "I cocked my rifle, and the instant I got sight of his head I pulled the trigger, but misfired," Dale recollected. "Before I could re-prime, he was upon me, with his knife at my throat, and his left hand twisted in my hair. At that instant one of our troop fired, and, leaping to my feet, I plunged my knife into the Indian's bosom. But he was already dead, shot through the heart, and, without a spasm or a groan, he fell heavily into my arms." With a flourish of frontier chivalry, the Georgians wrapped the "brave fellow's" blanket around him, broke his musket, laid it across his body, and departed. Dale never said what happened to the ten captured Creeks.[2]

By late 1795 the federal government had had enough of the irksome Georgians. Secretary of War Timothy Pickering ordered two hundred Regular troops to the Georgia frontier with orders to keep the peace, even if it meant shooting Georgians. Meanwhile, President Washington directed the Indian superintendent for the southeastern tribes to assemble the Creeks for a peace council.[3]

Washington knew better than to trust the timorous superintendent, who rarely ventured from his Savannah office, to conduct the proceedings. Instead, he appointed three veteran statesmen to negotiate with the Creeks. They included Senator Benjamin Hawkins, who would ultimately wield greater authority over the Creeks than Alexander McGillivray had ever attempted, not to strengthen Creek independence, but to attempt to break it by means of a beneficent paternalism—in short, to save Creek lives at the cost of the Creek way of life.

George Washington thought Benjamin Hawkins an "ingenious gentleman" and ideal member of the peace delegation on which the president placed such high hopes. In a U.S. Senate already strained by sectional suspicions—northern states distrusted the motives of Southerners toward the Indians; southern states resented northern interference in matters over which they remained reluctant to concede federal authority—the North Carolinian's good humor, patience, and rectitude made him widely popular and trusted. Largely forgotten today, Hawkins stood tall in his time. Born in 1754 to a self-made and industrious tobacco planter, he attended the College of New Jersey at Princeton, where he developed a lifelong passion for language studies. In the autumn of 1777, Hawkins quit his studies to join General George Washington's staff with the rank of colonel, serving principally as interpreter for the many French officers in the Continental army. Chronic stomach ulcers and fevers eventually compelled Hawkins to return to North Carolina, where he was elected first to the state legislature and later to the Continental Congress under the Articles of Confederation. Assigned to the committee on Indian affairs during his first term, Hawkins displayed a deep sympathy for the Indians and a fascination with their languages.[4]

As head of the American delegation, Hawkins did not disappoint. On June 29, 1796, he, his fellow commissioners, and Creek leaders signed a pact of "peace and friendship" known as the Treaty of Colerain, in which all parties bound themselves to the terms of the earlier Treaty of New York. The Creeks consented to the building of military posts in their country—a huge concession to which they yielded in the hope that Regular army garrisons would protect them from the relentless Georgians. In consideration of the "friendly disposition of the Creek nation," the Treaty of Colerain awarded the Indians $6,000 in goods and the services of two blacksmiths, one to be employed in the Upper Creek talwas, the other among the Lower Creeks. The treaty concluded, the Americans and Creeks parted amicably.[5]

President Washington knew that treaties alone, no matter how honestly negotiated, offered only a brief respite from the intermittent violence on the southern frontier. Not only the Creeks but also the Cherokees and Chickasaws dwelled in a precarious peace with their American neighbors. On taking office, Washington had advocated a policy of fair, government-regulated trade with the Indians, supplemented by a program to promote their "civilization"—in other words, to convert them into American-style small farmers. Congress eventually authorized the president to establish and regulate nonprofit trading houses known as Indian factories in the Indian country. In the hands of a competent agent, so the thinking went, Indian factories would provide a potent tool for reshaping Native cultures.

For the program to stand a chance, however, Washington needed to find a competent Indian agent. Fortuitously for the president, Benjamin Hawkins was available. He had opted against another Senate bid and, while a commissioner to the Creeks, had developed a burning desire to better their lot through farming and simple industry on smaller tracts than their hunting economy required. The Georgians and Tennesseans would get the land they coveted; the Indians would prosper in their new lives and eventually become assimilated. Gender roles would be upended: men must necessarily abandon the chase in favor of ranching and planting, and women abandon agriculture for the presumably more congenial work of "household manufactures." It was, Hawkins reckoned, their only hope for survival. What the Creeks might wish was irrelevant; they had no notion of the unabating pressure to expand the new United States westward. Hawkins would be their savior, or so he thought.

On August 29, 1796, President Washington presented the Cherokee nation with "the first general or principal Agent for all four southeastern nations of Indians, Colonel Benjamin Hawkins, a man already known and respected by you. I have chosen him for this office because he is esteemed for a 'good man,' has a knowledge of Indian customs, and a particular love and friendship for all the southeastern tribes." As well as for Indian women, Washington might have added had he known that Hawkins had become smitten with them. In a letter to a lady friend explaining why he had accepted a seemingly dead-end post far from the comforts of civilization, Hawkins had confessed his "*love* for the red woman and determination to better if practicable their situation." None were more alluring or appeared to Hawkins to be more amenable to "civilizing" programs than the women of the Creek confederacy.

The men, however, were another matter. They "are bred in habits proudly indolent and insolent, and they will reluctantly and with great difficulty be humbled to the level of rational life," he wrote shortly after settling into a small log cabin in Cusseta, his temporary quarters until the planned Indian agency was built on the east bank of the Flint River. Apart from his infatuation with Creek women, it was logical that Hawkins should settle among the Creeks. The Cherokees had largely been subdued militarily, their lands reduced to make room for western North Carolina and Tennessee settlers. The Chickasaws and Choctaws retained their countries, which were then well removed from westering whites. The Creeks presented the greatest potential source of friction with the government. Inducing them to abandon the hunt in favor of farming also would open western Georgia and perhaps even portions of modern Alabama to settlement by poor white farmers and wealthy landowners who ached to escape the confines, increasingly limited opportunities, and depleted soil of the Atlantic Seaboard. Consequently, Hawkins concentrated his efforts on the Creeks. His foray into their society began inauspiciously, however. No sooner had he arrived in Cusseta than a severe attack of gout laid him up for a week. Although "sometimes not able to turn in my blankets," the bedridden Hawkins was "constantly crowded with visitors and obliged to attend to the headmen and warriors of twelve towns." Through an interpreter of uncertain ability, he explained to them his "civilizing" program. The Creek men were baffled. Give up hunting? Violate divinely ordained gender roles and labor like women in the fields? "They told me they did not understand the plan," wrote Hawkins. "They could not work, they did not want ploughs, it did not comport with the ways of the red people, who were determined to persevere in the ways of their ancestors."[6]

Neither persistent poor health nor what he regarded as the obtuseness of Creek men would deter Hawkins from pursuing his civilizing mission; after all, it was to ensure their survival that he had come among the Creeks.

The battle for the Creek soul had begun.

Soon after recovering from his illness, Benjamin Hawkins undertook a long and hard tour of all but the most distant Creek talwas, which were home to the Alabama and Koasati peoples, who were closely allied by intermarriage and common interests. Hawkins never really grasped their reality, and his lack of understanding of affairs in the confederacy's western reaches would have baleful consequences in the coming years. His itinerary was nonetheless impressive. Hawkins visited eight important Upper Creek talwas and also spent considerable time in the principal Lower Creek talwa of Coweta and among the Uchees. Everywhere he went, he recorded progress made in ranching and farming, the political predilections of the people, the number and mood of the warriors, and the impressions of the leading Creek métis and the Indian countrymen (white men with Creek wives), with whom he spent much time. Not a religious man himself, Hawkins appeared uninterested in Creek spirituality, nor did he display any appreciation of the clan system. Nevertheless, his tour gave him a far better understanding of the Creeks than any government official had previously possessed. Hawkins, however, filtered his conclusions through an ethnocentric lens. He believed that the Creeks must have a strong national government capable of enforcing laws, which he himself would craft, if they were to "fulfill their engagements with us." He began to speak of the Creek "nation," a concept utterly foreign to the Creeks, for whom sacrosanct clan and talwa affiliation prevailed. How to hold the Creeks accountable as a people and manage them efficiently was Hawkins's challenge. He must marginalize the hundreds of autonomous clan leaders and mold a small class of political leaders whom he could cajole, bribe, or bludgeon into accepting his civilization policy.

To achieve his purpose, Hawkins would remake the Creek National Council into a muscular governing body answerable to him. He created legislative districts with appointed delegates, whom he encouraged to form an executive committee with which he might work. Hawkins also designated Tuckabatchee as the Upper Creek "capital"—a concept foreign to the Creeks—and Coweta as that of the Lower Creeks. The National Council would meet annually, alternating between Tuckabatchee and Coweta. That these talwas were home to Hawkins's subagents meant that council business would be conducted under the watchful eye of an American official. Annual sessions would begin with a "State of the Nation" address by Hawkins, in which he would communicate matters pertaining to his civilization policy to the leading men of the Creek nation. The National Council was to elect a speaker, or "head chief," to preside over its deliberations, "deliver the voice of the nation," and presumably work hand in glove with Hawkins.

Having set the structure of Creek governance—at least theoretically—Hawkins told the first gathering of the reimagined National Council at Tuckabatchee in May 1798 what he expected. The Creeks wanted to discuss ongoing white infringement on their land, particularly by the hogs and cattle that were denuding Lower Creek hunting grounds of the vegetation upon which the deer population depended. Hawkins, however, had other priorities. To exact domestic justice, he demanded the Creeks enact laws that would eviscerate clan authority, replacing clan enforcers with "law menders" answerable only to the National Council. Moreover, Hawkins insisted the Creeks permit him alone to deal with external threats and also to punish white trespassers. Any Creeks who interfered were liable to be shot. The National Council acquiesced.[7]

To succeed, Hawkins needed willing confederates among the Creeks. These he had. Being nearer to the Indian agency and to the faithless Georgians, few Lower Creeks challenged Hawkins; on the contrary, they welcomed his protection.

Hawkins had four prominent allies in the Upper Creek talwas, three of whom hailed from Tuckabatchee. The first was Alexander Cornells. Hawkins and Cornells had formed a fast friendship during the Colerain treaty council. Hawkins admired the charming and handsome métis, who could pass for a white man, and put Cornells on the government payroll as subagent to the Upper Creeks. Efau Hadjo also threw in his lot with Hawkins and became the first speaker of the reimagined National Council. His friend Hopoie Micco, a slaveholder and cattle rancher who ruled a lesser Upper Creek talwa, emerged as perhaps the most zealous Upper Creek proponent of Hawkins's program. The crusading Indian agent's fourth ally, whom Hawkins never entirely trusted, was the opportunistic and guileful Big Warrior, also of Tuckabatchee. A giant of a man, he suffered from partial albinism. Many Americans thought Big Warrior insincere in his professions of friendship, but no one ever offered any proof against him. Born about 1760, Big Warrior was just coming into his own when Hawkins arrived. He would develop into a Creek political presence as prominent as his name suggested.[8]

Benjamin Hawkins's civilization policy rent the fabric of Creek society. It aggravated old tensions, inflamed more recent differences, and created new schisms. Having lost much of their hunting land to Georgian despoliation and to their own overhunting for a deerskin trade now in sharp decline, the Lower Creeks increasingly embraced aspects of Hawkins's agricultural program. A growing European market in southern cotton also induced some Lower Creek men and Creek métis in both parts of the confederacy to take up cotton cultivation in addition to cattle and hog ranching. Notwithstanding the friendship Hawkins enjoyed with the Tuckabatchee headmen and with miccos intent on gaining a seat on the National Council, the majority of Upper Creeks tried to distance themselves from Hawkins's schemes. The deepening rift between the two divisions was reflected in their preferences respecting government presents and annuities: the Upper Creeks took theirs in guns and ammunition; the Lower Creeks preferred hoes, axes, plows, and spinning wheels.[9]

Hawkins enjoyed mixed success with Creek women, many of whom took to the spinning wheel cheerfully. They refused, however, to sacrifice their societal prerogatives, which ranching—a purely masculine endeavor—threatened to erode. As livestock multiplied, ranchers moved their families from the talwa households that women controlled to new settlements where men ignored matrilineal norms. Perhaps the growing tensions between Creek men and women escaped Hawkins's notice because he reported proudly, "The raising of stock is more relished by the Creeks than any other part of the plan devised for their civilization."

There was no missing the upsurge in genuine prostitution, however. It was the one economic realm in which Creek men could not compete. Without realizing he was largely the cause, Hawkins complained in 1802 of the growing number of women who "think of no support but prostituting their granddaughters or daughters. On this they confidently rely for clothes and food and spoke of it as a cheap and easy way of acquiring both."

The very landscape was changing. Fenced-in cotton fields and pastures belonging to acculturated Creeks and mestizos, who also installed locks on their cabin doors, began to squeeze out communal cornfields. The Creek customs of charity and mutual support withered, especially in the Lower talwas—changes that gratified Hawkins. The Creeks had "tasted the sweets of civilization and began to know the value of property and the necessity of defending it." Unimaginable a generation earlier, by the first decade of the nineteenth century, the Creeks were splitting into haves and have-nots.[10]

If President Thomas Jefferson had his way, all American Indians east of the Mississippi River would have markedly less of one commodity—land. George Washington and his one-term successor, John Adams, had refrained from demanding major land cessions. Jefferson, however, assumed office in 1801 keen to acquire every inch of Indian country between the Appalachians and the Mississippi River he could without provoking war. Two considerations drove his avarice. First, he needed land to facilitate the expanding Jeffersonian "Empire of Liberty." Only by moving westward, Jefferson believed, could Americans maintain the republican society of independent yeoman farmers that he idealized and not descend into the black swirl of urban misery that blighted much of the Old World and propelled the rise of autocrats. Second, at least until the 1803 Louisiana Purchase rendered the point moot, Jefferson wanted to seed the region west of the Creek confederacy with American settlements to counter Napoleonic France, the potentially belligerent successor to the vast Spanish claims beyond the Mississippi.

Jefferson had no doubt that his vision, which coincided with the wishes of a majority of Americans, would prevail. First, however, he believed he must have more land. The Atlantic Seaboard groaned beneath the weight of a burgeoning citizenry. In Georgia alone, the population doubled during the last decade of the eighteenth century. By 1800, there were 101,066 whites and 59,699 slaves residing between coastal Georgia and the Oconee River. In April 1802, the Jefferson administration concluded a compact with Georgia that recognized both federal and state expansionist dreams. Georgia waived all claim to the eighty-six million acres then well beyond its reach—the Creek, Choctaw, and Chickasaw homelands that lay between the state's present-day border with Alabama and the Mississippi River. The vast cession became known as the Mississippi Territory. In exchange for the paper transfer, Georgia received $1.25 million and a promise that the United States would as "early as the same can be peaceably effected" extinguish for Georgia's use Indian title to all lands within the state—in other words, nearly half of the Creek confederacy.[11]

For the time being, Jefferson trod lightly with the Creeks. In a May 1802 council at Fort Wilkinson, a federal outpost on the Oconee River, Creek delegates ceded the contentious Altamaha River tract and part of the land lying between the Oconee and the Ocmulgee. In return the Creeks received a perpetual annuity of $3,000 ($80,000 in 2022 dollars); annual salaries (bribes) of $1,000 apiece for treaty signatories; goods valued at $10,000, which were distributed to the council chiefs to dole out as they desired; and another $10,000 to satisfy Creek debts at the U.S. Indian factory.

Although he probably pocketed a bribe, the unseemly proceedings nevertheless sat poorly with Efau Hadjo, who aired a new grievance. A third white frontier had emerged, consisting of settlers who came via the Gulf of Mexico to clear land, cultivate fields, and build homes on the lower Tombigbee and Alabama Rivers in a portion of the new Mississippi Territory that also was Creek country. Efau Hadjo warned that their presence portended trouble: white settlements hemmed the Creeks in from the east, north (the state of Tennessee), and now the southwest, and the Choctaws lay on their western border. The meekness with which the Creeks had endured encroachments since the 1796 Treaty of Colerain caused the federal commissioners—Hawkins among them—to ignore Efau Hadjo's plea. Shortly thereafter, Efau Hadjo stepped down as speaker of the National Council. The pliant Hopoie Micco replaced him.[12]

The Creeks enjoyed a three-year hiatus from further American land grabs. That is not to say that President Jefferson had ceased to advocate his Empire of Liberty or contemplate its implications for the Indians. In February 1803, Jefferson wrote privately to the two principal Indian superintendents, William Henry Harrison and Benjamin Hawkins. They were subordinates of the secretary of war, but Jefferson wanted them to know his own thinking, candid and unfiltered. The tribes north of the Ohio River, for which Harrison bore responsibility, were small and comparatively weak. Toward those that resisted "civilizing," Jefferson directed Harrison to take a hard line. "Should any tribe be foolhardy enough to take up the hatchet at any time, the seizing the whole country of that tribe, and driving them across the Mississippi, as the only condition of peace, would be an example to others, and a furtherance of our final consolidation." Harrison had his instructions, and he worked diligently to dispossess the Indians of their country.[13]

The greater size and strength of the southeastern Indian nations required considerable caution and forbearance on the government's part. In a private letter to Hawkins dated February 18, 1803, Jefferson gave the agent his instructions. Hawkins welcomed them; his views accorded entirely with those of the president. What the Creeks might wish he deemed irrelevant; enlightened white men such as he and the president must think for them. And Jefferson's judgment in the matter of the Indians' future was fixed:

> I consider the business of hunting as already become insufficient to furnish clothing and subsistence to the Indians. The promotion of agriculture, therefore, and household manufacture, are essential to their preservation, and I am disposed to aid and encourage it liberally. This will enable them to live on much smaller portions of land, and, indeed, will render their vast forests useless but for the range of cattle; for which purpose, also, as they become better farmers, they will be found useless, and even disadvantageous. While they are learning to do better on less land our increasing numbers will call for more land, and thus a coincidence of interests will be produced between those who have land to spare, and want other necessities, and those who have such necessities to spare, and want lands. This commerce, then, will be for the good of both, and those who are friend to

both ought to encourage it.... In truth, the ultimate point of rest and happiness for them is to let our settlements and theirs meet and blend together, to intermix, and become one people.... I feel it consistent with pure morality to lead them towards it.

Although Jefferson's intentions were commendable in the context of his time, they reflected ignorance of southeastern Indian culture. That the Creeks and their ancestors had been practicing agriculture for centuries, that deeply ingrained gender roles mitigated against men taking up farming, and that the Creeks might actually prefer their way of life were of no concern to Jefferson when measured against the needs of the growing American republic.

The inevitability of American expansion became apparent on April 30, 1803, when the United States purchased from Napoleon Bonaparte the territory of Louisiana, 828,000 square miles of land nominally held by France but in fact populated overwhelmingly by American Indians. Although the Native denizens of the West could be expected to fight for their land, Jefferson thought it ample enough to one day accommodate the southeastern tribes.

The president shared his views on the subject with the thirty-six-year-old former senator Andrew Jackson, then a judge on the Tennessee Supreme Court. Jackson had registered his "disgust" with the Indian policy of Jefferson's political rival and presidential predecessor, John Adams, by resigning his Senate seat in 1798 after a brief stint in Washington. While president of the Senate, Jefferson had derided Jackson as an ambitious hothead. Now he saw in him a potential advocate of his expansionist plans. "The acquisition of Louisiana is of immense importance to our future tranquility, inasmuch as it removes the intrigues of foreign nations to a distance from which they can no longer produce disturbances between the Indians and us," Jefferson wrote to Jackson on September 19, 1803. "It will also open an asylum for these unhappy people in a country which may suit their habits of life better than that they now occupy, which perhaps they will be willing to exchange with us, and to our posterity, it opens a noble prospect of ... an extant of country under a free and moderate government as [the world] has never seen."

Little could President Jefferson have imagined that his brief missive would form the blueprint for war, dispossession, and the bloody and

agonizing American Indian Trail of Tears westward orchestrated by
the Tennessee magistrate to whom he wrote of a glowing future for
white Americans.[14]

To Benjamin Hawkins, Jefferson conceded that transforming the
Native peoples would take time. Two matters, however, could not
long be postponed. In the first instance, the president cautioned
Hawkins that influential Georgians suspected the agent had "thrown
cold water on [the Indians'] willingness to part with lands" that
Georgia insisted it needed. Unable to "resist so strong a pressure,"
Jefferson "beseeched" Hawkins to persuade the Creeks to surrender their residual tract between the Oconee and the Ocmulgee Rivers. Hawkins negotiated the sale, only to have the Senate reject the
transaction on the grounds that Hawkins had offered too much for
the land.

The federal government also required a second concession from
the Creeks. Having recently acquired New Orleans in the Louisiana
Purchase, the Jefferson administration wanted to fashion a horse path
wide enough to accommodate postal riders and travelers from Washington, D.C., to New Orleans, or at least to Mobile, which was then
part of Spanish West Florida. The only practical route lay across the
Creek country. Metaphorically speaking, the Creeks must acquiesce
to the insertion of a narrow vein that would pump the white man's
blood through their heartland.[15]

Just seventy years had passed since the Creeks made a gift of land
to James Oglethorpe and his colonists. The gesture, which the Creeks
offered from pure self-interest, backfired horribly. It had enabled the
creation of the state of Georgia that now threatened to engulf much
of their country. Neither an alliance with Great Britain during the
American Revolution, a subsequent season of raids against trespassing
settlers, nor two treaties with the fledgling United States had guaranteed the integrity of their boundaries. An expansionist in the White
House and like-minded men such as Andrew Jackson in the state gov-
ernments of Tennessee and Georgia eyed the Creek country greedily.
They lacked only the pretext and the military strength to scoop up
Creek soil. The Creeks would talk again to the Great Father, unaware
that time was not on their side.

．　．　．

William McIntosh had an eye for opportunity. Born in Coweta around 1778 to a Scottish Tory captain and a Creek mother of the Wind Clan, McIntosh (Tustunnugee Hutke) was among the most promising—from a white American perspective—of the new generation of métis. He owned many slaves and cattle, and his clan affiliation and generous nature won him influential Creek supporters. Through his father, who settled in Savannah after the Revolutionary War and married a prominent local lady, McIntosh also had well-connected white kinsmen willing to accept him into Georgia society. His appearance certainly put those uncomfortable around Indians at ease. Tall, well built, of strong intellect and gentle manners, McIntosh looked every bit the handsome Scottish gentleman. Black hair, which he wore in the white man's style, with sideburns extending to his rugged jawline, and dark, piercing eyes were all that betrayed his Indian blood. McIntosh's manner of dress, though a bit eccentric—he sported an enormous ostrich plume in his headdress—also had more in common with Georgia gentlemen than Creek warriors. Although illiterate, McIntosh spoke fluent English. A confidant of Benjamin Hawkins's, by 1805 the twenty-seven-year-old McIntosh was well on his way to dominating the assimilationist Coweta Creeks.[16]

The Creeks appointed McIntosh to a six-man delegation chosen to negotiate the horse-path treaty with President Jefferson in Washington in the autumn of 1805, which greatly enhanced his standing. When Hopoie Micco took ill before the delegation departed, its members selected McIntosh, rather than his fellow métis delegate Alexander Cornells, as spokesman.

Benjamin Hawkins and the Creek delegation reached the capital in late October. They excited only mild interest. A British traveler considered the Creeks scarcely worth a second glance because "the Creeks are nearly civilized, and from the dress of the greater number, there was no distinguishing them from the American citizens—some indeed were a little darker than the inhabitants of the Southern states." A British diplomat thought them colorful, but he also saw nothing of the savage in their demeanor or dress. "When I went to visit them, they all rose from the ground where they had been seated in conversation, gave me their hands and touched their hats; they had the appearance of coachmen, each being dressed in a blue coat, with a red collar and gold lace around the hat."[17]

The business of treaty making began on November 2. To the delight of the young métis spokesman, President Jefferson greeted the group as "Friend McIntosh and Chiefs of the Creek Nation." He thanked the Great Spirit for seeing them safely to Washington, then turned to reasons for their presence. First the land cession: Hawkins had erred; there was no precedent for so high a price, nor was the government prepared to pay more than a "reasonable" amount for the Oconee-Ockmulgee tract. As for the postal path, Jefferson offered inducements that must have stirred McIntosh's acquisitive soul. Enterprising Creeks who settled near the trail would profit from ferries, toll bridges, stagecoach stops, and taverns, all of which they would control, with the rates they charged subject to Hawkins's approval. Jefferson told the Creeks that the Louisiana Purchase rendered the road imperative. The Napoleonic Wars would presumably end one day, and the United States must be prepared to defend what it had purchased against Great Britain, with whom relations were strained. A postal path would provide a first step by connecting New Orleans, the crown jewel of the Louisiana Purchase, with the United States. Contrary to Spanish propaganda, Jefferson assured the Creek delegates, the Americans would never relinquish nor be driven from Louisiana. The Creeks were hemmed in, plain and simple.

The following day, McIntosh replied on behalf of the delegation. A rough-hewn eloquence and hard logic pervaded his speech. He denied that the price agreed upon for the Ocmulgee-Oconee tract was too high; on the contrary, his Creek forefathers had parted with land too cheaply. But no more. "We find since we have grown up, they partly gave their land away; we now find they gave too much of it away." Obviously referring to himself and Alexander Cornells, he continued, "When it is almost too late, we have young half-breed men now grown up among us that have learning, that have been taught the value of land." Jefferson capitulated; the government would honor the price Hawkins had offered. Despite the potential for profit the postal path offered him, McIntosh argued against it on the grounds that recalcitrant Upper Creeks would likely cause trouble.

Negotiations continued another eleven days. In the end, the Creeks got a fair price for the Oconee-Ocmulgee tract, Jefferson got his postal path, and McIntosh profited nicely. The First Treaty of Washington, signed on November 14, 1805, mandated that the Creek signatories "will have boats kept at the several rivers for the conveyance of men and horses, and houses of entertainment established at suitable places on said path for the accommodation of travelers." In what stank of a corrupt bargain, each Creek treaty signatory was promised $500 from the coming year's Creek annuity. Work on the four-foot-wide postal path—which was to run from Athens, Georgia, to Fort Stoddert, a federal stockade on the west bank of the Mobile River, just below the confluence of the Tombigbee and Alabama Rivers near present-day Mount Vernon, Alabama—would not begin until 1806, but McIntosh immediately laid plans for a ferry across the Chattahoochee River. Although not a delegate, Big Warrior staked claims to ferries and toll bridges in the Upper Creek country. So too did Hopoie Micco. Several other wealthy miccos entered the stagecoach and inn businesses.

As McIntosh had predicted, cries of protest arose among rank-and-file Upper Creeks, as well as those leaders denied a share of the profits. None were angrier than the Alabamas and the Koasatis. The postal path would cut their country in half, and settlements at its southwestern terminus would bite into their hunting grounds. Two furious Koasati warriors remonstrated with war clubs, murdering Hopoie Micco in the winter of 1805–1806.[18]

Hopoie Micco became the first Creek leader to have his blood splashed on the tattered fabric of the Creek confederacy. He would not be the last.

CHAPTER FIVE

The Hungry Years

MORAVIAN MISSIONARIES were a persevering lot. Members of a small but intensely evangelical German sect, the Moravians enjoyed success among Indians vastly disproportionate to their numbers because they dedicated themselves unselfishly to their work and respected Indians for the people that they were rather than considering them merely souls to be saved. So it was that two members of the North Carolina congregation came to the Creek country in the summer of 1804 to start a mission among the Upper Creeks. Benjamin Hawkins suggested they visit Tuckabatchee first. There, he said, the people were "kindly disposed toward strangers and white people."

Their sojourn began and ended at Tuckabatchee. "An extensive survey was out of the question because of the scarcity and excessive price of food," explained the Moravians. In fact, "food could rarely be bought at any price because of famine conditions throughout the Creek country. All we were able to obtain was what little Colonel Hawkins could give us out of his depleted stock."[1]

The Moravian missionaries had witnessed the initial stages of an eight-year stretch of misery that the Creeks called the "Hungry Years." It began with widespread crop failures in 1803. The depleted deer population yielded little during the winter hunt, and by the spring of 1804 prospects were dire, particularly in the Upper Creek

talwas that had resisted ranching. In earlier times, the public grana-
ries might have alleviated food shortages. Wealthy Creek and métis
converts to Hawkins's civilization policy, however, had ceased contributing their excess crops, preferring instead to sell them on the open
market. While prosperous ranchers "lived on their beef and milk," the
poor grumbled and grubbed for berries and roots.

The famine ground on. In July 1807, Hawkins reported "a greater
scarcity of corn than was ever known in this country.... Some have
actually starved." The yearly Creek annuity could have saved lives,
but rich miccos and their acculturated supporters hoarded the money.
They scorned their traditionalist countrymen as meriting what befell
them. The hungry, however, did not suffer meekly. From their wealthy
neighbors, they stole corn, cattle, cloth, powder, and guns—anything to
keep alive. Hawkins too suffered theft. The Creek Agency was robbed
numerous times, including once by a gang of old Creek women who
made off with eighty heads of cabbage.

Returning escaped slaves to their white masters became a popular
and profitable way to avoid starvation. The state of Georgia paid a
$12.50 reward ($250.00 in 2022 currency) for each captured runaway, a
considerable sum in the Creek country. With the population of Georgia growing to a quarter million by 1810, of whom roughly half were
black slaves, there was no shortage of escapees lurking in the swamps
and forests. When actual runaways were lacking, some Creeks surrendered blacks who had been living among them as adopted tribesmen.

In 1808, the Creek harvest again came up short. A "progressive"
micco boasted selfishly to Hawkins, "I am the first chief who ploughed
and adopted the plan of civilization and am clothed and fed by it."
The elder chief Hopoithle Micco, whose opposition to Hawkins's programs exasperated the superintendent, addressed a letter to President
Jefferson lamenting his people's poverty. "Our goods are so very dear
that we cannot clothe ourselves. Such as have stocks of cattle and
hogs can clothe themselves, but others must and do go naked." Well-
dressed progressive Creeks shrugged and tended to their cattle.

Nature showed no mercy either. In 1810 a severe spring hurricane
delayed the planting season. A long drought claimed most of the
crops, and a yellow-fever epidemic ravaged the confederacy. The year
1811 offered no respite. Hawkins's own scientifically cultivated crops
withered under the summer sun. A Moravian missionary at the Creek

Agency found "the ground so hard from the steady heat of the sun that everything within range of its rays is burned." Traveling down the Chattahoochee, he saw scarcely "a house where several [Creeks] were not ill with fever and some were in bed." Miccos and beloved men wandered the forest drunk. Offering the appalled Moravian missionary a plate of vermin-ridden and moldy meal—all she and her children had—the wife of one inebriate snarled that her husband and his cohorts were "swine and lay about the woods like pigs."

Hawkins saw opportunity in Creek misfortune. With the approval of the pliant National Council, he drew orders on the annuity to reward Creeks who hewed to his civilization plan. Despite losing his own model crops, Hawkins remained confident that hunger would compel recalcitrant Creeks to adopt his programs. Week after week, the hot sun blighted the Creek cornfields. Upper and Lower Creek leaders quarreled over annuity shares. Factions grew harder than the thirsty soil.[2]

And then the night sky spoke, whether to warn of impending desolation or to offer hope for their deliverance, the suffering Creeks could not say.

The Great Comet of 1811 first became visible in the Creek country in August. With each passing day, it grew clearer and rose higher and brighter until it conquered the heavens with a coma 50 percent larger than the sun and a tail stretching 100 million miles. Invariably frightened by comets of any dimension, the Creeks likened them to snakes chasing the moon. Some believed that comets portended war. One as immense as this might even herald the apocalypse. On September 19, 1811, the celebrated Shawnee war leader Tecumseh rode into Tuckabatchee beneath the preternatural light of the Great Comet. Perhaps he could interpret its meaning.

Tecumseh, however, was scarcely a disinterested observer. He had traveled from his village six hundred miles to the north in present-day Indiana, intent on winning Creek adherents to his northern Indian confederation. For Tecumseh, the comet was a welcome traveling companion and harbinger of great change, which he would effect. His parents had named him for a shooting star that swept across the night sky at the moment of his birth; Tecumseh derives from the Shawnee word *nila-ni-tkamáthka,* meaning "I cross the path or way" of a living being. Because Tecumseh was born into the tribe's Panther Clan, the animal whose path he crossed was a panther—no ordinary panther, but rather a miraculous creature of transcendental existence that lived in the water but periodically burst across the skies as a comet. The panther, celestial or commonplace, was a formidable creature both in the Ohio valley and in the Creek country.[3]

The forty-three-year-old Tecumseh was a strong, handsome man; Indians and whites alike found his aspect arresting. He stood five feet eleven and had a larger frame than most Shawnee males. "Too heavy-built to be swift on foot," said a federal government official who knew him well, the muscular Tecumseh was "altogether formed for strength and to endure great hardships." He also had quick reflexes and excellent hand-eye coordination. His complexion was a matter of debate. Some whites thought him darker than the norm; others imagined his complexion lighter than that of most Indians. Most whites admired his high, broad forehead, slightly hawkish nose, and exceptionally fine, large white teeth. When at ease, Tecumseh was "very gay and playful" with his fellow warriors and possessed a warm and winning smile. What most struck whites about his facial features were his deep-set hazel eyes, which added a brooding intensity to his expression.[4]

Tecumseh was no stranger to the Creeks. His father had lived much of his life in a Shawnee talwa among the Upper Creeks and had taken a Creek woman as his first wife. Tecumseh had Creek kin, and as a young man he had fought with the Chickamaugas and their Upper Creek allies against American settlers in the Southwest Territory (Tennessee). Restless young Creek warriors frequently paid extended visits to Tecumseh's Indiana village. They returned home with gripping tales of the alliance of northern tribes that the Shawnee war chief and his younger brother, the Prophet Tenskwatawa, had assembled to oppose further white encroachment on Indian land in the Great Lakes region. Tecumseh hoped to convert the four southeastern peoples— the Choctaws, Chickasaws, Cherokees, and Creeks—to their cause. The Choctaws and Chickasaws rebuffed the renowned Shawnee, and he had yet to visit the Cherokees. Tecumseh held high hopes, however, that the Creeks would join him. If Tecumseh succeeded in recruiting only the disaffected Upper talwas, his sojourn would have been worth the effort.

Tecumseh did not travel alone. In addition to the Great Comet, a splendidly bedecked and ecumenical entourage accompanied him. There were seven Shawnees, including Tecumseh; six Kickapoos; six Winnebagos; and two Creeks. Apart from Tecumseh, the key member of the party was the forty-year-old Creek warrior Seekaboo, who had long resided with the Shawnees. An accomplished warrior, brilliant orator, and agile interpreter dedicated to propagating the Shawnee brothers' creed, Seekaboo spoke fluent English, Shawnee, Choctaw, Muscogee, and the trade jargon of the southeastern tribes, Mobilian. Nothing, however, physically distinguished Seekaboo from the others. Tecumseh erased all outward tribal distinctions among the men, insisting they dress alike to convey their core message: We are all one Indian people with a common destiny.

And so they had ridden as one. The Creeks appreciated fine costuming, and Tecumseh indulged their tastes. He and his men wore buckskin hunting shirts, leggings gartered beneath the knees, breechclouts, and multicolored beaded moccasins. They shaved their heads until just three flowing braids remained. These they garnished with hawk feathers. Around their heads they wrapped red flannel bands. On each arm they wore silver bands—one above and one below the elbow, and a third on the wrist. Around their necks hung silver gorgets, and heavy silver rings dangled from their ears. Semicircular streaks of war paint ran from eye to cheekbone. Their temples bore a small red dot, their chests a large red circle.

They carried new .60-caliber British Indian-trade flintlock muskets, tomahawks, and scalping knives. Tecumseh's attire varied from the others in only one respect; instead of wearing hawk feathers in his braids, he crowned his head with two crane feathers: one the bird's natural white color, symbolizing peace, and the other painted red, connoting both council and conflict. As befitted the somber purpose of their expedition, Tecumseh and his men rode black ponies.[5]

Tecumseh and his retinue were the most highly anticipated of several outside delegations scattered among the five thousand Creeks and métis who crowded the public square of Tuckabatchee. A motley collection of white traders, free blacks and slaves, Spaniards, and spies of varying loyalties mingled on the margins. Copious quantities of pungent black drink steeped in large kettles. Tobacco smoke blanketed the public square. Seen through rifts in the smoke, the setting was spectacular. Situated on a broad flat, Tuckabatchee stretched for nearly three miles along the west bank of the Tallapoosa River. Hogs rooted on the talwa perimeter. Cattle and horse herds belonging primarily to métis grazed in vast pasturelands beyond bright fields of waving mature corn. A mile and a half above Tuckabatchee roared a tall waterfall, spilling its flow over shoals that divided the river into two swift-flowing channels as it passed the talwa.[6]

The occasion for the boisterous gathering was the annual National Council, which Benjamin Hawkins had called two days before Tecumseh arrived. Ostensibly, Hawkins sought formal, public Creek acquiescence to expand the four-foot-wide postal path through the confederacy into a sixteen-foot-wide road capable of accommodating soldiers and heavy wagons in the event of war with Great Britain, which appeared increasingly probable. Should war break out, New Orleans would be a probable British objective. Because the British could be expected to court dissident Creeks, the contemplated road would also enable American troops to strike readily at any talwas that might consider switching sides, a point Hawkins kept to himself.

Great Britain and the United States nearly went to war in June 1807, when the British warship HMS *Leopard* fired on the frigate USS *Chesapeake* off the Virginia coast. Still at war with Napoleon Bonaparte in Europe, Britain had sent a squadron to blockade French ships in Chesapeake Bay that were attempting to buy American supplies. Several Royal Navy seamen jumped ship, and local American authorities granted them sanctuary. One of the deserters joined the crew of the *Chesapeake,* which provoked the captain of the *Leopard* to blast away at the *Chesapeake* until the outgunned American frigate struck its colors and surrendered not only a British-born deserter but also three Royal Navy deserters of American birth. The confrontation outraged the American public. War fever gripped the land. Rather than risk a conflict for which the United States was unprepared, President Jefferson imposed an embargo on British goods, a response that satisfied few and brought economic hardship to much of the nation.

On the American frontier, the *Leopard-Chesapeake* affair raised the specter of a British-instigated Indian uprising should the United States and Great Britain go to war. That fear was particularly acute in the

Northwest (today's Midwest), where the Shawnee brothers' doctrine of Indian political unity and cultural renewal flourished and British Canada loomed as an unfriendly neighbor likely to aid the disaffected Indians. Thoughtful Southerners also worried; they knew that the Royal Navy had a long reach. "In case of a war with Great Britain we expect to have warm work here," fretted George Gaines, the authorized government trader (Indian factor) to the Choctaws. "Should she land many troops in West Florida, we shall not be disappointed, for the Creeks, a most powerful nation of Indians, often express a partiality for the British government, and one third of the Choctaws would be glad to have an opportunity of being troublesome to us."[7]

At the time of the Tuckabatchee council, American relations with Great Britain remained severely strained. As its conflict with Napoleon ground on, Great Britain forced more American sailors into the thinly stretched Royal Navy. Besides holding this and other maritime grievances, President James Madison, who succeeded Jefferson in 1809, believed not only that Britain's presumed support of Tecumseh and Tenskwatawa's restive northern Indians impeded American expansion but also that Canada threatened national growth. A small but vocal group of recently seated congressmen espoused the violent annexation of the British possession and the outright extirpation of the Shawnee brothers and their northern allies, as well as any southeastern Indians who might make common cause with them.

Upper Creek intransigence gripped the Tuckabatchee National Council, and with good cause. The postal route had proved a continuing source of friction. Hawkins had done his best to mitigate Indian annoyance. He ignored an order from the postmaster general that only white men be employed as postal riders, a measure that would surely have inflamed even the most progressive Creeks. Americans who tried to evade ferry charges proved another irritant. Again Hawkins intervened on behalf of the Creeks, reminding potential travelers—who must have special passports to use the path—that the Creeks owned and operated the ferries. All profits belonged to the Creeks, and the only white men exempt from ferriage fees were those on public business.

The Creek National Council also refused to permit American-owned horse-changing stands on the route and reminded the government of other restrictions on white travel that the Treaty of Washington imposed. Displaying admirable restraint, Creek miccos told Hawkins that "they were greatly embarrassed at the repeated misunderstanding of the treaty stipulation relative to a post path through their land by every man who came from the government and had anything to do with the path or transportation of the mail." The most recent federal official "had come on with his wagon and commenced building bridges contrary to what they understood their treaty stipulation with the president to be. It is not," they emphasized, "to be a road but a path with logs over the creeks."

As if American misuse of the postal path were not a sufficient irritant, a thriving market in black-market liquor, weapons, ammunition, and other goods peddled by unlicensed American traders with the connivance of profiteering Creeks developed on the principal waterways of the confederacy. Complicit miccos might wink at the smuggling along the Coosa, the Tallapoosa, and the Alabama, but there was near-unanimous opposition to violations of the Ocmulgee River boundary between Georgia and the Creek confederacy.

To Hawkins's immense relief, Creek tactics toward interlopers had evolved to reflect a changed reality. Georgia was now a heavily populated state with a sizable militia. It could also draw on federal support in the event of armed strife. So the Creeks resorted to a hard-edged door-to-door diplomacy to which neither Hawkins nor Georgia officials could object. Apparently at Hopoithle Micco's behest, the National Council dispatched representatives to visit every Georgian settlement lying over the boundary line and "demand rent for the fields cultivated, twenty-five cents a head for cattle, and fifty cents a head for horses ranging on their lands, and the discontinuance of such unwarrantable conduct for the future." The squatters paid up.[8]

By his own admission, Hopoithle Micco was "a very old man," but not so feeble as to miss the long-term danger that the Americans posed. On September 1, 1811, from a trading house in West Florida, he dictated a letter to his "friend and ally" the king of England, lamenting that "it is now a long time since their old friends [the British] had left them, and he longs to see them again." The Americans were "on the very doorsteps" of the Spanish towns of Pensacola, St. Augustine, and Mobile. Hopoithle Micco feared their loss would doom the Creeks. Could not the British do something to rescue the Creeks from their current "deplorable state"?[9]

While old Hopoithle Micco appealed—in vain, it turned out—to the British, young Creek warriors—patriots or dissidents, depending on one's perspective—resisted American migrants with death threats, beatings, and what whites considered extortion. Margaret Eades, then a young girl bound for Louisiana, recalled one such incident. Sloshing through a muddy stretch of the postal path, her caravan halted under a drenching rain at a stream, over which the Creeks had laid a few slender poles. A party of warriors standing guard demanded a steep toll that Eades's party refused. Rather than pay, the white men set their slaves to work downstream cutting trees to fashion their own bridge. The furious Creeks would likely have killed them, Margaret Eades averred, had not her uncle, a onetime Creek captive who spoke Muscogee, intervened. Drawing an old Revolutionary War sword from one of the wagons, he berated the warriors as "fools who could never whip the whites." Should they try, "their nation would be destroyed." After hearing him out, the Creeks "raised their blankets around their shoulders and moved off, doggedly shaking their heads."[10]

More irritants arose. As if intent on inciting the exasperated Creeks to war, in 1810 the state of Tennessee and the federal government attempted to open free river navigation between Tennessee and Mobile by way of the Coosa and Alabama Rivers—straight through Upper Creek country. A united National Council rejected the gambit. Hawkins sided with the Creeks, but Secretary of War William Eustis overruled him. He directed the Choctaw factor Edmund P. Gaines to survey a water route from Fort St. Stephens (seventy miles north of Mobile) to the Tennessee River. Creek warriors intercepted Gaines and escorted him home. The secretary of war nonetheless persisted. Without giving notice to the Creeks, he directed Lieutenant John R. Luckett to survey the postal path east from Fort Stoddert (thirty miles north of Mobile) to determine the feasibility of expanding it into a military road. With reckless abandon, Luckett carved mile markers in Roman numerals into thick trees, reaching the ninety-ninth milepost before three hundred warriors detained him. They brought him and his small detachment, disarmed but unhurt, before an Upper Creek council. Admonishing Luckett that "the measuring and marking of their country" must cease, the council returned the lieutenant and his men to Fort Stoddert.[11]

The Upper Creeks had had enough. Hopoithle Micco scolded

Hawkins: "You ask for a path, and I say no." Alluding to Gaines's and Luckett's abortive surveys, as well as to several illicit branch trails already in use by American travelers, he insisted, "The officers must not be going through our lands to hunt paths. I spoke last summer to you and to the president about paths through our country. I told you no, it would bring trouble. My chiefs and warriors will never say yes—I hope it will never be mentioned again."[12]

At the September 1811 Tuckabatchee National Council, with Tecumseh watching for an opportunity to sway the Creeks in his favor, Hawkins resurrected the government demand for a broader road. A heated but bogus debate ensued, bogus because Hopoithle Micco and his allies in council were unaware that Hawkins had co-opted the Lower Creeks and enough Upper Creek miccos to render any objections to the proposed Federal Road meaningless. Moreover, under the supervision of Brigadier General Wade Hampton, commander of the Orleans Territory, work had already begun at both ends of the postal path. Several weeks before the Tuckabatchee council convened, Eustis told Hampton to commence felling trees, reinforcing bridges, creating trails through swamps with logs laid side by side transversely, and widening the existing trail. Negotiations be damned; Hampton was to clear a way for soldiers and heavy artillery to reach New Orleans before war with Great Britain erupted no matter the cost. The Creeks were mere impediments, their likely objections of no concern to the Madison administration.[13]

Tecumseh knew that he had no legitimate business before the Creek National Council. Such was his fame that council members nevertheless wanted to hear what he had to say. Asked twice to address the council, he demurred because "the sun had gone too far." Finally, on the third day of the proceedings, in a bit of theatrics that Tecumseh undoubtedly orchestrated, his warriors interrupted the council with whoops and yells, brandishing a sacred war pipe. They urged Creek warriors to smoke from it and join their cause. The miccos angrily intervened, unanimously rejecting the pipe and its symbolism.

Order restored, Tecumseh addressed the National Council. His brother Tenskwatawa, the Shawnee Prophet, had sent him to impart to the Creeks his doctrine of Indian renewal and of spiritual cleansing, avowed Tecumseh. Smoothly dissembling, he assured Hawkins and the chiefs that he rejected war with the United States; the Great Comet apparently did not portend strife. Rather, the Indians should "unite in peace and friendship among themselves and cultivate the same with their white neighbors." More than that Tecumseh would not say publicly until Hawkins departed.

Each night in the public square, Tecumseh and his men captivated the Creeks with the "Dance of the Lakes," which Tecumseh said the Master of Life had imparted to Tenskwatawa.

The dancers jerked, twitched, grimaced, and fell into trances but gave no further hint of their true purpose. Hawkins was not impressed. Weary of menacing dances and endless Creek bickering, the superintendent announced that he had come not to seek approval of a widened road but to inform the Creeks that work had commenced. Opponents seethed but at length ratified an agreement suitable to Hawkins. On September 29, the agent headed for home, confident the Creeks would accept the inevitable.[14]

The Upper Creeks had no idea how to respond. Perhaps Tecumseh would provide an answer. Even after Hawkins left, however, Tecumseh took care to keep his message from hostile ears. No white men and few métis were admitted to the brightly painted, thatched-roof town rotunda where he at last delivered his speech. Claiming to be a mere vessel of the divine, Tecumseh declared that the Master of Life, through his brother Tenskwatawa, had dictated what he was about to say. Tecumseh might have cloaked himself in verbal celestial trappings, but in truth he had reshaped Tenskwatawa's original revivalist creed into his own intertribal political and military doctrine aimed at thwarting American encroachment on Indian lands.

"Brothers, there are two paths," Tecumseh began. "One is light and clean. The other is covered with clouds. If you take the dark path you may lose your lands. Perhaps the United States may wish to exchange lands with you. We advise you to keep your lands. The lands we now have are not [as] good as we had formerly. Brothers, the Indians often suffer by taking bad talks; do not listen to bad talks." Tecumseh refrained from advocating outright hostilities with the United States. Rather, he groped for a Creek commitment to the Shawnee brothers' alliance, with war a last resort to defend remaining Indian lands east of the Mississippi—and then only with British aid. Seekaboo finished interpreting, and Tecumseh awaited the Creek response. He had cause to be hopeful. The Upper Creek leaders Big Warrior and Captain Isaacs, the turbulent, forty-three-year-old head warrior of Coosada, had greeted him warmly, sharing tobacco with Tecumseh as a token of esteem when he arrived at Tuckabatchee. Captain Isaacs had also traveled secretly to Spanish Mobile that summer and bought fifty pounds of gunpowder. Only Captain Isaacs knew how he meant to use it. A "cunning and artful scamp," Isaacs tended to tack with the prevailing wind.

The wind blew cold on Tecumseh's cause. Here in council, Big Warrior and Captain Isaacs kept silent. The council member William Weatherford spoke first. He addressed Tecumseh brusquely. Weatherford's demeanor and dress were calculated to impress; his personal magnetism and distinguished lineage assured him a rapt audience. Born near Coosada, three miles below the junction of the Coosa and Tallapoosa Rivers, William Weatherford was the great-grandson of a French captain and Sehoy, the beautiful matron of the Wind Clan. His grandfather was Lachlan McGillivray, his grandmother, Sehoy II. Alexander McGillivray was his uncle. His parents were the wealthy Scottish trader Charles Weatherford and Sehoy III, which cemented his ties to the Wind Clan. Weatherford, however, was far more than simply the beneficiary of a distinguished lineage. The thirty-year-old Koasati métis was a brilliant orator in a culture that placed a premium on rhetoric. He spoke fluent English and French and passable Spanish but refused to learn to read and write. Weatherford took pride in his illiteracy and considered himself Creek, with a profound regard for Creek spirituality. He had no quarrel with whites; in fact, he dressed like a prosperous if eccentric white plantation owner. Tall, muscular, and slender, standing six feet tall and weighing about 165 pounds, Weatherford preferred to wear a fine black broadcloth jacket, a black vest, black breeches, elegant boots, a black hat encircled by a beaded band, and a broad, heavily beaded waistband—all of which accentuated his auburn hair, mild black eyes, and light complexion.

Weatherford loved horses. His father had built a trading post on a high bluff overlooking the Alabama River and laid out a fine racetrack nearby. Both father and son devoted themselves to breeding and training fine horses, and the crowds that attended the Weatherford races contributed greatly to the family's considerable wealth. A generous host, William Weatherford opened his plantation doors to dissipated young Alabama and Koasati warriors, over whom Weatherford, a sober man, exerted boundless influence.

Here at Tuckabatchee, Weatherford minced no words with Tecumseh. He rejected the Shawnee's "bad talk" and suggested he leave the Creek nation posthaste. The Americans were too strong for the Indians, and the notion of meaningful British help was laughable, argued Weatherford, because a quarter century earlier, when the Americans were far weaker, they had defeated the British. In the event of war, he concluded, neutrality remained the best policy. A visiting Cherokee chief also rejected Tecumseh's overture, and the Lower Creeks unanimously denounced him.

Big Warrior offered Tecumseh no help. The Shawnee's message confused him, or so he later told Benjamin Hawkins. As sentiment turned against Tecumseh, Big Warrior suggested in private council that Tecumseh be executed on the Tuckabatchee chunky field. Weatherford condemned Big Warrior as a coward, and the notion appalled even the most progressive Lower Creek chiefs: Tecumseh had come to them from the Shawnees, a friendly tribe, and done nothing to warrant punishment. Go he must, but in peace, as he had come.

Tecumseh had been dealt a hard blow. Neither his eloquence nor the refulgent Great Comet sufficed for Tecumseh to prevail. Although nothing remotely resembling an alliance emerged, Tecumseh did persuade some thirty warriors, including Big Warrior's eldest son and at least one war leader, to accompany him to the Shawnee brothers' village to meet the Prophet Tenskwatawa himself. They and several dozen other Upper Creeks had succumbed to the seductive appeal of Native spiritualism. To instruct potential converts to Tenskwatawa's particular creed, Tecumseh prevailed upon Seekaboo, his Creek protégé and traveling companion, to remain behind.[15]

In persuading Seekaboo to proselytize among disaffected Upper Creeks, Tecumseh had made a decision that was to have shattering consequences for the entire Creek confederacy and radically alter the course of history in the American South.

· PART TWO ·

A WORD TO THE READER: Keeping track of who's who in the impending Creek War can be daunting, a bit like reading a Russian novel. Most of the principal Creek leaders were métis (persons of mixed parentage) who had Scots-Irish fathers and went by their anglicized names or their American-bestowed monikers when dealing with non-natives. This may be jarring to readers unaccustomed to historical American Indian figures whose names appear more similar to those of encroaching white settlers than of Native Americans. Compounding the difficulty readers may face is the absence of a single Red Stick or pro-American Creek or métis personality who dominates the story. Both Red Stick and traditional Creek leadership was diffuse, and power decentralized, so that even the most noteworthy personages appear only sporadically.

To ease the way, I list the principal personages in an appendix at the close of the book. I encourage the reader to consult it as frequently as necessary.

Always bear in mind also that the Red Sticks are a faction of the larger Creek people. Although a distinct entity, the Red Sticks were either full-blooded Creeks or Creek métis.

CHAPTER SIX

Rise of the Red Sticks

T HE INDIAN FACTOR George Gaines was glad to be home. His encounter with quarrelsome Creeks who had taken exception to his government-contracted river survey a year earlier had frightened him. Potential conflict between the United States and Great Britain loomed large. Gaines understood that a war between the two powers would likely pit the southeastern tribes against one another in bloody border clashes. Gaines could take some solace in knowing that his trading house at Fort St. Stephens, an ungarrisoned stockade on the upper Tombigbee River, sat snug in the friendly Choctaw nation. Despite his fears, Gaines still counted Creeks among his customers. One of the most reliable was a "cunning" chief named Oceochemotla who ruled over a breakaway settlement at the falls of the Black Warrior River. Oceochemotla and his men patronized Gaines's store in the spring and the fall. They were amiable enough, trading both with the Choctaws and with Gaines, and always paid their debts promptly.

Consequently, Gaines felt no cause for concern when in late autumn 1811 Oceochemotla and thirty or forty warriors banked their canoes laden with peltries and furs alongside his factory. Oceochemotla had never been friendlier. "The old chief was exceedingly desirous to make me believe he was very much attached to me," Gaines recollected. He also wanted to avail himself of an offer Gaines had made to increase his credit limit. Previously content with $100, Oceochemotla now insisted on a credit line of an "old hundred" ($1,000). Gaines balked, however. "I answered that the times had changed—the British government had a misunderstanding with the president which might end in a war, and it would be unwise in me to permit him to contract so large a debt, and very imprudent to do so." After some fruitless haggling, both agreed to sleep on it and "tell each other [about] our dreams in the morning." Oceochemotla and his men drew off, but the chief's interpreter, a local named Tandy Walker who had lived among the Creeks as a blacksmith, tarried. Beckoning Gaines into a dark thicket, Walker warned him that Oceochemotla's band, together with other Creeks settled farther up the Black Warrior River, intended to join Tecumseh and the British when war came; they wanted to secure all the goods they could before the invincible British expelled Gaines, as they surely must.

The next morning Oceochemotla returned hopefully. What had Gaines dreamed? "I dreamed there was war," the factor averred. "The English came over in their ships and engaged some of the northern tribes of Indians to help them fight, but they were soon whipped by the president's warriors, and the English were driven back over the 'Big Water.'" And what had Oceochemotla dreamed? "That my good friend sold me all the goods I wanted." Gaines apologized; his own dream must guide him. He gave Oceochemotla the usual $100 in credit. The chief made his purchases and then paddled away. Gaines never saw him again.[1]

Oceochemotla had fallen under Tecumseh's sway. Seekaboo, meanwhile, labored to win a wide allegiance of Upper Creeks to Tenskwatawa's moral teachings and to Tecumseh's political and military coalition. He instructed his listeners—Creek and métis alienated from their wealthy, recreant elder miccos—in Tenskwatawa's intricate doctrine of spiritual renewal. Seekaboo found the nativist soil fertile in the Upper Creek country. The Federal Road had been the last straw for angry young warriors, and aspiring mystics exploited their fury. The absence of Christian inroads among the Creeks also lightened Seekaboo's work. Bible-quoting missionaries were commonplace in the North. From Indians opposed to the Shawnee brothers' program, they received a good hearing. Mere words, however, were insufficient in the South. Benjamin Hawkins had advised Moravians intent on proselytizing in the Creek country in 1804 that the Creeks, suspicious of Christianity, welcomed white craftsmen but distrusted those who "came only as teachers or as missionaries." The progressive métis Alexander Cornells told another prospective missionary not to waste his time on the Creeks. Although they had no Bible, Cornells insisted that the Creeks knew God "without a book; they dream much of God; therefore they know it."[2]

With their own religious tradition to draw on, Seekaboo's Creek acolytes had no more intention of mimicking Tenskwatawa's doctrine than they had of accepting Christian dogma. Instead, they integrated those elements of Tenskwatawa's teachings that most closely aligned with their own spiritual upbringing to fashion a mixed faith.

One tenet of Tenskwatawa's creed particularly pleased the traditionalist Creeks who had rejected Hawkins's civilization plan, as well as the poor whom it had left behind. Tenskwatawa promised that the "Master of Life had taken pity on his red children and wished to save them from destruction" provided they return to communal living. Indians who accumulated "wealth and ornaments" would "crumble into dust," but those who shared their possessions with fellow believers would die happy. "When they arrived in the land of the dead, [they] would find their wigwam furnished with everything they had on earth."

The Master of Life (or as the Creeks knew him, the Master of Breath) insisted that the Indians shun the Americans. He had revealed their true aspect to Tenskwatawa. They were the by-products of the foam and scum that rolled onto the coast of the Great Salt Lake (the Atlantic Ocean), usurpers of Indian land whom the Master of Life despised.

A band of Alabamas from Coosada who made the long trek to the Shawnee brothers' village of Prophetstown in present-day eastern Indiana to confer with Tenskwatawa returned with an aggressive injunction. The Shawnee Prophet had told them that the Master of Life "in his wrath would assist the Indians in the recovery of their lands and country, which he had made on purpose for their special use." War with the American interlopers was inevitable. Not all whites were evil, however. Indians were to treat the English and Spaniards as "their fathers or friends, and to give them their hand, but they were not to know Americans on any account, but to keep them at a distance."

Tenskwatawa's advocacy of friendship with the English and Spaniards accorded not only with his and Tecumseh's plans but also with the interests of Great Britain and Spain. In 1811, the two European powers were allied in the struggle against Napoleon Bonaparte, who had occupied Spain and placed his brother Joseph on the throne in Madrid. Spanish guerrillas joined the fight against the French, a bloodbath that would eventually cost nearly 400,000 Spanish lives before ending in 1814. In the meantime, the legitimate Spanish government clung to a few rebellious provinces, too weak and distracted to concern itself much with affairs in North America. Spain hoped to retain its Florida possessions, but in the event of a British and American breach it could contribute little materially.

In addition to his good feelings for the British and Spaniards, Tenskwatawa preached strict dietary practices. Indians were to eat no foods that whites cooked or that were foreign to their culture. They were to shun salted foods and must relinquish their cattle and hogs and eschew beef and pork as unclean. It was permissible, however, to keep horses. The Master of Life had given the Indians "the deer, the bear, and all wild animals, and the fish that swim in the water." These species, together with corn, beans, and other Native crops, must suffice for Indian needs.

Impoverished Creek disciples who owned few if any cattle or hogs appreciated Tenskwatawa's strictures against keeping domestic stock, and all Creeks could understand his prohibition against consuming "salt victuals," which were forbidden during the busk (poskitá) and also during initiation ceremonies, salt being considered a pollutant.

The Shawnee Prophet also addressed the loss of deer during the Hungry Years. The Master of Life had shown him that deer, now so scarce east of the Mississippi River, were merely "half a tree's length" underground and would reappear in abundance if the Indians followed Tenskwatawa's teachings. Not only that: if the Indians obeyed, then the Master of Life also would cause a cataclysmic upheaval and bury the Americans beneath the earth forever.

Tenskwatawa emphasized another obstacle to the creation of an Indian Eden, an impediment consistent with Creek belief. While the Americans were children of the *Motshee Manitou,* or Evil Spirit, they were not its most active or insidious agents on earth. That distinction belonged to Indian witches, who labored ceaselessly to thwart the Master of Life's will and to spread chaos among the Indians. Those who declined to repent must die.[3]

The earliest and most fervent Creek apostles of Seekaboo styled themselves prophets. To widen the appeal of the new doctrine and legitimize their own roles as seers, they weaved Creek faith and practice into Tenskwatawa's teachings. The Creek prophets also borrowed liberally from the busk. Rites of purification such as fasting, the destruction of old things in order to make way for collective renewal, the significance accorded sacred numbers, the performance of esoteric chants, and the prominence given men in rituals all became central to their dogma. As visible symbols of their station, the Creek prophets carried five-foot-long staffs with cow's tails tied to the end and occasionally blackened their faces and draped their bodies in feather mantles, as had mystics of the Mississippian tradition.

The Creek prophets also adopted many of the trappings and ways of the traditional Creek *kithlas,* or "knowers," a select group of holy men who claimed to commune with the Master of Breath, practiced clairvoyance and sleight of hand, entered into self-induced trances, and shook in the presence of heretics. From these practices, the kithlas claimed to obtain supernatural powers—as would the new generation of Creek prophets. Whether such histrionics would win them adherents remained to be seen.[4]

Josiah Francis was a torn and tormented man. The forty-year-old métis son of an American silversmith and an Alabama woman, he had tried all his adult life to exist in both Creek and American society. The strapping six-footer learned English and Spanish, took up silversmithing, and also worked as a trader in his native talwa of Autauga for John Forbes and Company, a British firm that enjoyed a near monopoly in private trade and commerce in the Floridas and the Creek country. Francis's fellow métis and a rival for the Creek soul, George Stiggins, dismissed him as a "man of no talent, very still and reserved in his manners in the ordinary scenes of life... of no turn to command respect or esteem." In one sense Stiggins was right; by 1812, Francis was in debt nearly $1,000 to Forbes and Company. On the other hand, he excelled in his parallel profession of medicine man. He officiated at the annual Autauga busk and other sacred ceremonies. As his debt grew, so too did his lamentations over the erosion of traditional Creek values. Francis denounced the evils of Hawkins's civilization plan but appreciated the value of good relations with the Spaniards and British.

Seekaboo took early notice of Josiah Francis. Considering him the ideal candidate for head prophet of the Alabamas, in 1812 Seekaboo performed the rites needed to effect his transformation. He locked Francis in a cabin and then chanted and danced around the place for ten days. On the eleventh day, Francis emerged, cloaked with prophetic powers and the ability to communicate with the Master of Breath but temporarily blind, or so he said. Mystified townsmen led him about for several days until Francis declared his vision restored, whereupon he enlisted prospective prophets.[5]

Creek men who became followers of Francis and his fellow prophets needed a means by which to identify themselves and their adherents. Because they were warriors, it was only natural that these revivalists of sacred Creek values—for that is how they saw themselves—would adopt the signal item of traditional Creek weaponry as emblematic of their cause: the atássa, the red war club, or as it and its bearer would become known to Americans, the Red Stick.

Seven decades later, an aged métis explained to an amateur American historian the labor and care that went into making the atássa and the manner of its use. Recalled the old man,

> The winter huckleberry and the white oak runner were the forest growth exclusively used in making the red stick, as the wood of both is exceedingly hard and tough. The warrior would select a bush having a single, large, bending root. He cut his stick about three feet long, leaving about seven inches to the root, or club end. After stripping off the bark, he began about two inches from the end of the root, and beveled down two sides of the bend to a sharp edge, about five inches long, so that this beveled part bore some resemblance to the curving blade of a hatchet. After this, the stick was thoroughly seasoned over a fire.... The stick was then painted red, with the exception of the club end, which part the warrior expected to dye red in the blood of an enemy. The paint generally used was made of a soft, red stone.... The

stick received several coats of the paint. After the last coat had become dry, a hole was then bored through the handle, about five inches from the end, and a strong loop of buckskin or deer's sinew was fastened therein.

Warriors wielded the red stick with one hand, their wrist inserted in the sinew loop to prevent their losing hold of the weapon. In battle, warriors tried to strike their victims on the head with the sharp edge of the red stick. A single stroke often sufficed to inflict death.[6]

Seekaboo and his protégé Josiah Francis, known among believers as Hillis Hadjo, or "Crazy-Brave Medicine," recruited prophets readily from the ranks of Upper Creek medicine men, but enlisting rank-and-file followers proved difficult. Francis marshaled a litany of tricks to attract adherents. When touching a nonbeliever, he would jerk and tremble. He claimed that a spirit had taught him how to fly and to live underwater. To prove the latter claim, Francis would enter a stream and then vanish beneath the water for days at a time. He likely swam underwater while breathing through a straw. When he reached a point beyond view, Francis would emerge and hide in the woods before swimming back to the spot where he had entered the water. Eventually these stunts drew recruits, but not enough. Two months after Tecumseh left, Francis superintended the first Dance of the Lakes in the Creek country. His gathering proved a bust. Only forty warriors attended, far too few to have any real impact on Upper Creek politics. It would take more than clever stunts or fantastic claims to win over enough Creeks to further Tecumseh, Tenskwatawa, Seekaboo, and Josiah Francis's dream of a pan-Indian front against American encroachment.[7]

Although Francis and Seekaboo's Creek and métis followers remained few, they at least had a collective name for themselves: they were the Red Sticks.

It was 2:20 a.m. on Monday, December 16, 1811, by the white man's reckoning. A sound like massed cannon fire, or the blast of huge stores of gunpowder, rent the stillness of a Louisiana Territory night. An instant later the earth's surface trembled, rolled, and burst open. Horizontal undulations resembling huge ocean waves traveled for miles, growing higher until they fractured, spurting sand, coal, and hot water as high as treetops. Flashes of light danced across the land. A dark, sulfurous vapor arose. Trees bent earthward, their boughs interlocking. Gaping fissures, landslides, and floodwaters reshaped the landscape. At the village of New Madrid, the epicenter of the earthquake, cabins collapsed, and the cemetery slid into the churning Mississippi River. Residents staggered, vomiting and disoriented, about the dirt streets, awaiting the final judgment.

Fewer than a dozen whites died in the cataclysmic five-minute-long shock, and the earth swallowed up seven Indians. One who escaped death told of being sucked into the ground to a depth of two tall trees before upward-roaring water disgorged him. The warrior waded or swam four miles before reaching dry land. His explanation of the horrifying occurrence: the Shawnee Prophet had summoned the earthquake to wipe away the white man.

The first shock of the New Madrid earthquake, together with the strongest of the nearly three thousand aftershocks lasting two months, was felt across the entire nation. Young Margaret Eades was journeying on the Federal Road with her family and fellow immigrants to Louisiana when the initial tremor shook the earth. Horses broke loose, wagon chains swayed and jingled, trees tilted and intertwined, and "every face was pale with fear and horror." Frightened Creeks came to their camp with an explanation of the fearsome phenomenon: Tecumseh, they said, had "stamped his foot for war."[8]

There were undoubtedly Creeks who saw in the New Madrid earthquake a portent of coming strife. Most, however, were more concerned with the mundane business of getting along under Benjamin Hawkins's civilization plan, reconciling themselves to the deepening tensions between Upper and Lower Creeks and the continued presence of Georgia squatters west of the Ocmulgee, and adjusting to the ever-growing number of white travelers on the Federal Road, which the army had completed in just a few short months. By early April 1812, nearly a hundred immigrants to the Mississippi Territory passed the Creek Agency weekly. Many Creeks must have felt as if a white noose were tightening around their collective necks.

Neither the earthquake nor its aftershocks slowed the flow of emigrants or the reckless disregard of the Ocmulgee boundary that Georgians exhibited. It was more than some young Creek warriors could bear. Often fueled by frontier liquor, they lashed out individually or in small parties, usually for plunder.[9]

Most travelers negotiated the Federal Road safely, but in the spring of 1812 two elderly white men, Thomas Meredith and Arthur Lott, were killed on the trail. Neither slaying was premeditated, nor was the hand of the nascent Red Stick movement or its prophets evident in either. Benjamin Hawkins, however, demanded swift retribution from the National Council. The Lower Creek métis William McIntosh stepped forward to lead the "law menders" in tracking down the fugitives.

McIntosh was a good tracker, but his contempt for Creek tradition overruled his better judgment. Navigating forest, canebrakes, and swamps, he pursued Lott's killer to Tallassee, a white talwa. At Tallassee, one of the wanted men claimed sanctuary and the protection of its ruling figure, Hopoithle Micco. Thinking himself safe, he faced McIntosh's posse openly in the public square, whereupon McIntosh shot him dead. Infuriated at McIntosh's transgression, Hopoithle Micco and his followers swung to the side of the prophets and the fledgling Red Sticks.[10]

The violence continued. A frontier raid far more inflammatory than the shootings of Meredith and Lott, with women and children as the principal victims, threatened to bring the weight of an infuriated State of Tennessee to bear on the Upper Creeks. The outrage occurred at the isolated homestead of the settler Jesse Manley near the mouth of Duck River, about seventy miles west of Nashville. Upper Creeks considered the region their legitimate hunting grounds. Sporadic Creek attacks on settlers continued from the 1790s until 1808. A four-year hiatus ensued, but expectation of war with Great Britain, and a fear that Creeks and their presumptive British instigators would rekindle frontier depredations, had most Duck River frontiersmen on their guard.[11]

Not so Jesse Manley and his fellow settler John Crawley. In May 1812, they left their families and ventured down the nearby Tennessee River to buy corn. Before departing, Crawley took his wife, Martha, and four children to the Manley cabin, where Mrs. Manley was recovering from the birth of her third child. Crawley and Jesse Manley asked a male boarder named Hays to watch over their families in their absence.

No sooner had the two men left than a party of between five and eleven rancorous Upper Creeks chanced upon the Manley homestead. They were returning to the Black Warrior River country after a dispiriting sojourn at Prophetstown. They had fought in the Battle of Tippecanoe the previous November, a struggle precipitated when the Indiana Territory governor, William Henry Harrison, availed himself of Tecumseh's absence to attack the Shawnee brothers' village. Harrison prevailed, and Tenskwatawa and his followers temporarily scattered. As was the Indian custom, the defeated warriors vowed to wreak vengeance on frontier settlements.[12]

At the Manley place, war whoops rent the gentle May morning. Outside, warriors bludgeoned to death and scalped two of the Crawley children. They also killed the boarder Hays. Bursting through the cabin door, they bashed Mrs. Manley's infant against a wall, slew her older children, and then scalped and shot Mrs. Manley twice at close range, the powder burning out one of her eyes. Leaving her for dead, they hauled a terrified Martha Crawley across the Tennessee River, but not before she hid her other two children in a cellar.

Two or three days after the raid, John Crawley and Jesse Manley returned to the plundered, corpse-strewn cabin. Breathing fitfully, Mrs. Manley lay on her blood-soaked bed. She lingered several days before dying.[13]

Martha Crawley's ordeal, on the other hand, had just begun. The war party dragged her through deep forests and over obscure Indian paths to the edge of their Black Warrior River talwa, where a sympathetic Creek woman warned Crawley that her captors intended to kill her; already they had dug her grave. Crawley acted fast. Picking up a tin cup under the pretense of going to a spring for water, at nightfall she darted into a dense spinney of oak and pine and crept into a hollow log. There she hid until morning. For three days she wandered, cold and hungry, before staggering into Tuscaloosa in the hope of a better reception. She was taken to a house where several Indians had gathered. Again she feared the outcome, and again a Creek woman helped her flee. She stumbled through the woods until sunset the next day, when a warrior caught up with her and ordered her back to Tuscaloosa at gunpoint. For Martha Crawley, there appeared no escaping death.[14]

Help came from afar. The Choctaw Indian factor George Gaines was at home one evening when his Creek métis neighbor Tandy Walker paid him a call. A Creek friend from Tuscaloosa had told Walker of the battered Crawley's presence there. When the two men hesitated, Gaines's wife interceded: Walker must try to purchase her freedom. The kindhearted Walker consented.

Two weeks later, he and Martha Crawley appeared on Gaines's doorstep. "She was in bad health, her mind a good deal impaired by suffering; her limbs and feet were still in a wounded condition caused by the brush, briars, etc. she was forced to walk through after she was captured by the Indians," recalled Gaines. His wife "took charge of her, ordered a tepid bath, and furnished her with comfortable clothing. After a week's tender nursing, her mind appeared to be restored." Not long thereafter, Martha Crawley was reunited with her husband and the two children she had hidden in the Manley cellar. Her recovery, though not recorded, surely must have been long and hard.[15]

In Tennessee, the Manley-Crawley raid evoked past horrors and seemingly presaged new atrocities. That pioneers had committed similar acts of barbarity against Indian women and children in years past never entered white calculations. The specter of Indian depredations on a scale unseen for decades stalked lonely homesteads and roused towns already tense with the expectation of war with Great Britain. For six months, President James Madison had delayed the day of reckoning while Speaker of the House Henry Clay and his fellow "War Hawks" in Congress strummed a bellicose refrain. Reluctantly, President Madison submitted a war message to Congress on June 1, 1812, enumerating the hostile acts that Britain had committed against the "independent and neutral" United States. All had occurred on the high seas, in British or European ports, or along the American coastline except one, which Madison blamed on the Shawnee brothers and their supposed British abettors. "In reviewing the conduct of Great Britain toward the United States our attention is necessarily drawn to the warfare just renewed by the savages on one of our extensive frontiers, a warfare which is known to spare neither age nor sex and to be distinguished by features peculiarly shocking to humanity," said Madison of the Battle of Tippecanoe and the subsequent Indian revenge raids. He offered nary a nod at American lust for Indian land as a cause of hostilities; Native unrest could be accounted for only by British "interpositions." On June 18, Congress returned a declaration of war against Great Britain.[16]

Although the Madison administration had taken no steps to prepare for war beyond a halting and badly managed mobilization, it could not neglect the vulnerable border with Canada, where the British forces were concentrated, or their Indian allies then massing in northern Indiana and Ohio. All available Regular troops, together with northern volunteers and militia, marshaled for invasions of Canada. The Madison administration fixed its gaze northward. For the foreseeable future, the southern states and territories would have to resist any Indian uprisings below the Ohio River themselves.

Most Tennesseans feared that the Creeks would take up arms against the United States on behalf of Great Britain. John Sevier, one of the state's founders and a distinguished Revolutionary War–era Indian fighter and former governor, believed all the southeastern tribes dangerous. "There is not the least confidence to be placed in savages. I would not trust neither Chickasaws, nor Cherokees too far. They have been much attached to the British, and no doubt there is yet some of the old friendship remaining," the elder Sevier advised his son. "As for the Creeks, they are sure to join the British, whatever they may other ways pretend, as they are as great a set of villains as ever lived."

Andrew Jackson shared Sevier's sentiments. The politicking forty-five-year-old had leveraged his popularity to obtain a commission as major general of the West Tennessee militia. In the Crawley-Manley raid he saw a golden opportunity to employ his militiamen, learn for himself what military leadership skills he possessed, and eliminate the Indian scourge from the entire Southeast. "My heart bleeds on the receipt of the news of the horrid cruelty and murders committed by a party of Creeks on our innocent wives and little babes," he wrote to Tennessee's governor, Willie Blount (the younger half brother of the former governor William Blount), on June 4. "They must be punished, and our frontier protected, and as I have no doubt but they are urged on by British agents and tools, the sooner they can be attacked, the less will be their resistance, and the fewer will be the nations or tribes that we will have to war with. It is therefore necessary for the protection of the frontier that we march into the Creek nation, demand the perpetrators at the point of the bayonet, [and] if refused, that we make reprisals and lay their towns in ashes." Jackson had placed himself on a rhetorical collision course with the Creeks; the Manley-Crawley raid, he hoped, would provide the necessary catalyst for a physical confrontation.[17]

Both a passion to purge the country of the presumed Native lackeys of the British he so despised and the chance to fulfill the former president Jefferson's expansionist dream motivated Jackson. Governor Blount, on the other hand, owed his distrust of the Creeks largely to greed. An Indian-hating land-grabber—the Cherokees called him the "Dirt King"—Blount cast as keen an acquisitive eye on the Creek country as did the most avaricious Georgian. More cautious than Jackson, Blount initially declined to sanction the full-scale invasion of the Creek country that his militia general advised. He instead ordered out two punitive expeditions to find Martha Crawley and punish those responsible for the slaughter on the Manley homestead. More than five hundred Tennessee militiamen volunteered, but they had little to show for their effort. The first expedition turned back at the Tennessee River for want of supplies; the second riddled an innocent Creek hunter in the back with musket balls before giving up the search.[18]

Blount was far from satisfied. He offered Secretary of War William Eustis a lurid and false account of the vicious treatment Martha Crawley purportedly continued to undergo at the hands of the Creeks (at the time Blount wrote, Crawley was recovering at the Gaineses' home). "It is said that those Creeks take that poor woman from town to town, in their nation, naked, and exultingly dance around her as their captive." Belatedly adopting Jackson's brutal counsel, the governor insisted that the only remedy lay in an outright invasion of "the Creek nation . . . as the best way of keeping peace." Blount declined to suggest where the careworn secretary might find soldiers sufficient for such an endeavor while mobilizing to fight Great Britain (Jackson thought his untried militiamen sufficient; Blount did not). Blount also intimated that Benjamin Hawkins shielded the guilty Creeks and accused him of "neglect" for not having captured and returned them to Tennessee to suffer Volunteer State justice.[19]

Although preoccupied with stalled invasions of Canada and likely British reprisals against northern border states, Eustis knew the truth. Hawkins, who learned of the Manley-Crawley raid less than two weeks after it occurred, had written to Eustis on May 25, a full month before Blount's first hectoring letter, that "the chiefs will meet in one week, and we shall see what can be done." Because clans could be expected to shield their own from the law menders, Hawkins advised Eustis that "likely...a show of force will be necessary within the agency" and hoped that the district military commander would have the necessary troops.

As the agent had hoped, and Blount and Jackson likely regretted, cooler heads prevailed among the Creeks. The Upper Creek leader Big Warrior assured Hawkins that law menders would "overtake that gang as quickly as possible and punish them, take the woman [Martha Crawley] and deliver her up to the white people, and collect all stolen horses which have been brought in our land by these villains." With Big Warrior's promise, a chance at cheap glory eluded Jackson.[20]

William McIntosh again assumed command of the law menders. They tracked the "gang" deep into the rugged and remote western reaches of the Creek country. The law menders killed one laggard, but the rest of the fugitives either melted into sympathetic Chickasaw towns along the Tombigbee or rejoined Tecumseh's people, with whom most had been living for several years. Despite that setback for National Council–decreed justice, as the year 1812 drew to a close, tensions appeared to calm in the Creek confederacy. Travel along the Federal Road resumed unimpeded. The work of McIntosh's posse had had a salutary effect, at least for the time being. The miccos and war leaders of the Lower Creeks remained unequivocally on the side of the United States—not necessarily out of affection for Americans, but because they were hemmed in and the British had proven fickle friends in the past. "The chiefs...say... that if the British should make an offer of arms, they will endeavor to restrain their young men from accepting of them," Hawkins continued, "or if they should accept them, from using them against their friends the United States—that they depended for safety, not on arms and ammunition, but on the friendship of the president; that they are surrounded and have no back country to fly to, and if they had, they would not change their present situation for any prospects founded on uncertainty."

General Wade Hampton, the military district commander who had supervised construction of the Federal Road, seconded Hawkins's assessment. In the autumn he journeyed the length of the road without incident, lodging at Creek- and métis-owned inns and drinking at their taverns. Granted, the Red Sticks and their prophets did not frequent the taverns, keeping largely to their talwas or stealthily recruiting converts. They nevertheless remained a minority among the Upper Creeks, few of whom, though restive, were ready to risk war with the United States.[21]

The quiet in the Creek country did nothing to soften the din of the Tennessee Assembly, where loud demands for Indian extirpation were the order of the day. On September 15, the benighted legislators—intent on appearing as patriotic as their forefathers, who had wrestled with Indian war parties for what now was quiet countryside—demanded the governor call up ten thousand militiamen for border duty to avert "horrid scenes of savage barbarity." For good measure, the state legislature also directed Governor Blount to tell Benjamin Hawkins to either extradite the vanished Creek fugitives to Tennessee within twenty days or watch its volunteers "exterminate the Creek nation." War with Great Britain was not enough; Tennesseans—with Jackson in the forefront—were intent on slaughtering any Indians who might remotely pose a threat to their state and then appropriating land emptied of its rightful inhabitants.[22]

The Upper Creek war leader Little Warrior had no fear of saberrattling Tennesseans—or of any other Americans. He had lived most of his adult life with the northern Shawnees, and, as an apostle of Tenskwatawa, Little Warrior fought with Tecumseh's confederated tribes and the British as they compiled one victory after another during the opening months of the War of 1812. Tecumseh and his British allies captured the American bastion of Detroit and the entire Army of the Northwest, the principal U.S. force in the region. Simultaneously, another Indian force massacred the garrison of Fort Dearborn, on the site of Chicago. Prospects darkened for the pan-Indian confederacy in the late autumn, however, when Tecumseh fell ill, a roving patrol of Kentucky volunteers razed Prophetstown, and a reconstituted army under William Henry Harrison prepared to retake Detroit from the British and Indians and then invade Canada.

Somehow in the bitter, blighted winter of 1812–1813, the Shawnee brothers managed to feed the smattering of warriors who assembled in their makeshift camp on the Wabash River in the expectation of renewing the war against the Americans in the spring of 1813.

Most of Tecumseh's Indian allies, including Little Warrior and his coterie of nine Creeks, remained with the British. On the frigid morning of January 22, they together scored a victory that must have sent the spirits of the convalescent Tecumseh soaring. General Harrison had hoped to gather four thousand men and cross the ice-covered Detroit River to attack the British in present-day Ontario. But Major General James Winchester, a willful and bungling subordinate, advanced to the small settlement of Frenchtown in southern Michigan Territory without informing Harrison. Seizing the opportunity to deal a blow to Winchester's exposed command, the British and Indians attacked. With the Americans more interested in gathering firewood than keeping watch, and their senior leaders lodged comfortably in the rear, the allies made short work of Winchester's command. In the most decisive victory either side had achieved to date, on January 12, 1813, the British and Indians killed 290 Americans, mostly Kentucky volunteers, and captured six hundred others. Two days later the triumph was tarnished, however, when drunken Indians—Little Warrior's party likely among them—massacred sixty prisoners. The Battle of Frenchtown nevertheless ended Harrison's planned invasion and returned the momentum of the War of 1812 in the Northwest to the British and Indians.[23]

Exhilarated by the gore at Frenchtown, Little Warrior and his warriors repaired to the Shawnee brothers' camp to learn their plans and the role they expected the Creeks to play. Tecumseh enjoined Little Warrior to return to the Creek confederacy with a message: Come spring, Tecumseh would rejoin the British. Together, they would crush Harrison's army, after which he would travel south to help lead the Creeks against the Americans. Tenskwatawa also told his southern disciple to enjoin the Creeks to "take up the hatchet against" the United States. The Shawnee brothers assured Little Warrior that the Creeks would receive ample arms and ammunition from the British.

A Shawnee delegation would follow Little Warrior in a month or two with further instructions. In the meantime, Tecumseh told Little Warrior he "must spill the blood of white people on their return," presumably to present wavering Creeks with a fait accompli.[24]

Little Warrior obliged. On February 9, 1813, his party debouched on the north bank of the Ohio River, seven miles from its mouth near present-day Mound City, Illinois. Crossing the ice-littered Ohio was their first concern. Tracing the frozen riverbank, they found both the means to navigate the Ohio and a target to satisfy Tecumseh's call for the white man's blood. Three small boats lay invitingly beside two cabins. In the doorway of one cabin stood a settler named Clark. Dismounting, the Indians ambled up the bank. Clark knew one of the Creeks, who spoke English, and, shaking the Indian's hand, offered the warriors a meal. Resting their muskets against the outer wall, the warriors filed indoors. While they crowded around the table, Clark told his wife to cook them a meal. A neighbor who had dropped by earlier sat down with the Creeks.

The Indians devoured the food, then rose. Two warriors blocked the doorway. Two others stood behind the Clarks' neighbor. "You be stout man," said one in halting English. "You be strong man. Can you run fast?" With that, the Creek beside him drew his tomahawk from his belt and struck at the man's head. He dodged. The blade skimmed his forehead, slicing off flesh from his eyebrow and exposing the bone. Bleeding profusely, the wounded neighbor plunged to the door, knocked over one of the Creeks, and sprinted through the snow toward a partially frozen creek. Four Creeks followed. The Clarks' neighbor leaped onto the ice, but it broke beneath his weight. Struggling waist deep through the chill water and pushing aside ice blocks, he attained the far bank. The Creeks gave up the chase and turned back. Lingering for a moment, the shivering man watched the warriors gun down Clark at the cabin door; his wife already lay dead inside, her skull split open from a hard tomahawk blow. The Creeks also shot dead the owner of the adjacent cabin in his doorway and then converted his cabin into a charnel house. A lesser war leader named the Tuskegee Warrior grabbed the dead man's pregnant wife. Stripping her naked, he sliced open her belly, yanked out the fetus, and drove it onto a chimney peg. Scooping out the dying woman's entrails, he scattered them about the cabin for the hogs to later feast upon. The

Tuskegee Warrior's followers killed one child, then absconded with the remaining two. Whether they murdered or kidnapped them, no one ever learned.

After plundering both cabins, the Creeks piled into the three boats, paddled across the broad Ohio River, and then resumed their homeward journey, content to await the consequences of their brutal audacity.[25]

CHAPTER SEVEN

Civil War

THE STUNNING British and Indian victory at Frenchtown that fed Little Warrior's bloodlust also removed American pressure on Upper Canada, at least temporarily. The Michigan Territory remained in the hands of Tecumseh and his British allies, and northern Ohio appeared vulnerable to their combined force. During the early months of the War of 1812, the British also had repulsed American attacks on Lower Canada. Although the British Canadas stood defiant while American generals and politicians wallowed in recrimination and doubt, British prospects nevertheless were far from bright. With the war against Napoleon Bonaparte still raging in Europe, Great Britain had few resources with which to bolster its North American possession. Examining the outlook for 1813, British leaders sought a way to divert American troops from the Canadian border and also put pressure on the United States to come to terms. Their solution: impose a naval blockade centering on Chesapeake Bay and land troops on the Maryland shores. As land clashes began in the spring of 1813 a mere seventy miles northeast of the nation's capital, the Madison administration lost most of what little interest it had in affairs on the volatile southeastern frontier.

. . .

Hard times continued in the Creek country. Complaints against the United States mounted, and Creek tempers grew shorter. The Creek annual annuity for 1812—payable before the end of the year—was overdue. A perplexed and anxious Benjamin Hawkins repeatedly queried Secretary of War John Armstrong about the cause of the delay but got no reply. Flagging American fortunes in the war with Great Britain likely preoccupied the marginally competent Armstrong, and the Treasury might have lacked the disposable funds required to meet its treaty obligations. Nevertheless, the Creek miccos needed the money owed them to settle bills at the Indian factory, pay their warriors, and provide for their elderly.[1]

The Hungry Years had ended, but good crops did not improve the lot of the average Creek. Instead, Hawkins's civilization plan had rent the social fabric of Lower Creek talwas and impoverished the dissolute, who were legion. In a moment of candor, Hawkins confessed to his assistant, the Upper Creek métis micco Alexander Cornells, that "the love of rum has almost destroyed Cusseta and Uchee; whole families live by stealing from me. They even kill my cattle to get the skins to buy whiskey." Enough Creeks and métis prospered, however, to permit Hawkins to cling to the illusion that his program was succeeding. Rather than question the underlying assumptions of the civilization plan, he blamed the increase in inebriates and thieves on miccos who "will not do their duty."[2]

Federal provocations mounted. Not only did the government withhold the Creek annuity, but Secretary Armstrong also ordered Hawkins to persuade the Upper Creeks to open the Coosa River to Tennesseans, a mandate intended to exploit a sudden shift in the strategic balance in the Southeast. In April 1813, Major General James Wilkinson, the commander of the military district embracing Louisiana and the Mississippi Territory, captured Mobile from the feeble Spanish garrison, barring one potential port to the British should they strike at the Gulf Coast. The Mobile District became part of the Mississippi Territory, and the prospect of a new market thrilled Tennesseans.

Hawkins attempted to present Big Warrior and William McIntosh with a fait accompli. "As we are now in possession of Mobile, you will soon see people from Tennessee coming down [the] Coosa with their produce to market; when you see that, you will see you are friends,"

Hawkins disingenuously assured the Creeks. "No one has a right," he added menacingly, "to prevent...people from going to Mobile and New Orleans through any of the waters of the United States."[3]

Navigation of the distant Coosa was of no concern to the compliant McIntosh, but it meant a second white artery through the heart of the Upper Creek homeland. Both Big Warrior and Alexander Cornells refused Hawkins. "I have stated this to you," thundered Big Warrior, "the [Creek] nation was obliged to give up the public road, and they knew that would bring trouble on them.... If they have to give up the waters of the Coosa, it will hurt the feelings of the Creeks; it will not do. You thought you would mention this waters [*sic*] to them, to bring trouble on them, and destruction at once; you mean to destroy us, on these waters, in trying to make use of it, when we don't allow it."[4]

The vise tightened on Hawkins. He was at a loss how to proceed, as his equivocating answer to Secretary Armstrong revealed: "Navigation of the Coosa...is alarming in a high degree to the Creeks, as they are fearful the whiskey trade down that river will bring ruin to their nation. But it must be got over some way, as, very soon, Tennessee must be gratified on this point."[5]

In fairness to Hawkins, he was in no state to cope with stress. Since at least October 1812, he had been bedridden with rheumatism, fever, and a persistent cough. In January of that year, the fifty-seven-year-old Hawkins had nearly died of what he described as pleurisy.[6] With his health precarious, in the matter of neither the delinquent annuity nor navigation of the Coosa River had he been able to address the Creek leadership personally.

Then came a crisis more profound than any that had confronted Hawkins during his sixteen years as Indian superintendent. From the Chickasaw Indian agent in late March 1813, Hawkins learned that Creek adherents of the Shawnee Prophet (Little Warrior's war party) had murdered seven white families near the mouth of the Ohio River, the corpses "most cruelly mangled, showing all the savage barbarity that could be invented." After boasting of their deed to some Chickasaws, the perpetrators had continued on to the Creek country carrying the scalps and bearing talks from Tenskwatawa. Although his informant exaggerated the body count, Hawkins knew he must punish the murderers or else risk war. These were no random slayings by "thoughtless, wild young men," Hawkins reminded Big Warrior and his fellow Upper Creek leaders, but deliberate, premeditated atrocities. Promising that William McIntosh and his Lower Creek law menders would help if necessary, Hawkins insisted the Upper Creeks send out their own enforcers on behalf of the National Council to apprehend Little Warrior and his coterie and bring them to the agency. "The guilty must suffer for their crimes," he warned, "or your nation will be involved in their guilt." Unable to travel, Hawkins dispatched an assistant to Tuckabatchee to keep the pressure on the National Council. McIntosh and his men thundered up the Federal Road for the Upper Creek "capital" as well.[7]

No sooner had Hawkins sent the Upper Creek chiefs his ultimatum than a rider from Tuckabatchee presented him with an urgent message: two white travelers had just been shot on the Federal Road, one of whom died; the National Council would convene at Tuckabatchee at once to consider its options.[8]

As tensions rose, loyalties blurred. Big Warrior, always one to place his own interests first, flirted with Josiah Francis and the Red Sticks, likely to gauge their strength and the prospects of British intervention in the Southeast.[9] Neither he nor the other principal Upper Creek miccos and war leaders wanted an open rupture with the United States, at least not yet. After deliberating twelve days, the National Council authorized William McIntosh and his Lower Creek law menders and an Upper Creek party under Tustunnugee Hopoie to track down Little Warrior and his adherents.

In the gray morning twilight of April 18, 1813, William McIntosh, Tustunnugee Hopoie, and their men entered a white talwa—in which Creek law prohibited violence—and quietly surrounded a wattle-and-daub house that offered sanctuary to at least some of the guilty Red Sticks. McIntosh waved a few warriors forward to force the door. Hearing them approach, its occupants fastened the latch, gave a war whoop, performed a hasty war dance, and then opened fire from the windows. A musket ball broke an arm of McIntosh's nephew; another shattered a hand of Alexander Cornell's son. Little Warrior's lieutenant, the subchief Tuskegee Warrior, taunted the attackers, boasting that he had "killed and eaten white people... and cut open the white woman near the mouth of the Ohio." His defiant display ceased when the defenders ran out of ammunition, whereupon McIntosh's men torched the house. The Tuskegee Warrior perished in the blaze. Crawling to the doorway, two wounded Red Sticks begged for mercy. The law menders dragged them twenty yards from the house and then tomahawked them to death. Two other Red Sticks ran toward the nearby Coosa River. One was shot dead; his companion swam to the far bank and escaped badly wounded.

Little Warrior was nowhere to be found. Talwa informants told the law menders that the fugitive war leader had passed the night on the opposite bank of the Coosa. Perhaps to test his fidelity, McIntosh and Tustunnugee Hopoie chose Captain Isaacs to lead a search party.

Since rebuffing Tecumseh's overtures at the November 1811 Tuckabatchee council, Captain Isaacs had done well for himself. The magical aspects of the Shawnee Prophet's faith had evidently intrigued him, or perhaps he simply saw in them a technique for winning over the credulous. Already a respected war leader, Captain Isaacs soon became an accomplished conjurer. He spoke passionately of the "wonderful things he could do and the miraculous things he had done," and people believed him. Like Josiah Francis, he dove into the water and vanished for days. On the river bottom, Captain Isaacs claimed to have communed with "an enormous and friendly" serpent who revealed to him the future—which did not include making war on the whites or on progressive Creeks. By the spring of 1813, Captain Isaacs was the most esteemed prophet in the Creek country and an existential threat to Josiah Francis.[10]

In executing the National Council's mandate, Captain Isaacs earned the undying enmity of the Red Sticks. He and his party of law menders trapped Little Warrior in a swamp, where the renegade resisted with a pistol, musket, and then bow and arrows before expiring in a hail of musket balls.[11]

At Hoithlewaulee, also a white talwa, Captain Isaacs slew two of Little Warrior's remaining accomplices. A third lingered mortally wounded for nearly a day and before dying issued a word of warning. "He told the townspeople that the nation would be ruined for killing him and not taking the Prophet's talk."

That left only the Federal Road assailants, who it turned out were simple thieves, not Red Sticks. Returning to their talwa, one of the two got drunk and, displaying a fine saddle, bragged, "The master of this saddle I have left on the road dead, and I have a heap of money." In this instance, clan justice prevailed. The uncles of both suspects helped kill them.

The fugitive Creeks were now all dead. What that portended for the Red Stick cause was uncertain.[12]

As the spring of 1813 drew to a close, Benjamin Hawkins thought he had the Creeks well in hand. "From the present disposition of the Creeks there is nothing to be apprehended from them," he assured Georgia's governor, David Mitchell, on May 31. "The chiefs are as well convinced as I am that their existence as a nation depends on the observance of their treaty stipulations with the United States." A week later, Hawkins expressed similar sentiments to Secretary of War Armstrong. "If I find any symptoms of hostility among [the Creeks], I shall apprise you of it without delay." Exasperated with disruptive whites, he added, "If my fellow citizens on the frontiers will withdraw their intrusions on Indian rights and be honest, they have but little to apprehend. If they will but only lend their confidence to the officers of the government and cooperate with them for the public peace and happiness, we should go on very well and ease the timid mind of a frightful load."[13] For these missives, Hawkins would later be accused of blindness to conditions in the Creek country, if not treasonous intent.[14]

Six weeks before Hawkins wrote to Mitchell, the *Georgia Journal* had offered the governor a more penetrating appraisal of matters in the Creek confederacy. The unnamed correspondent foresaw—and welcomed—bloodshed. War, he averred, could only benefit rapacious frontiersmen:

The Creeks are divided into two parties, and it is yet uncertain which will prevail. Most of those who own property (and some of them have large plantations and many negroes) are anxious for peace, as they have everything to lose and can gain nothing by war. The more indigent Indians, and particularly the young warriors, are eager to display their prowess in war and to acquire property by plunder. It is supposed by some that civil war will break out among them and save us the trouble of chastising their insolence and violence. The commencement of war with us will be the signal for their destruction. Our frontier is thickly settled with a brave and hardy population, who wait only for the word to strike a blow, which if it does not exterminate, will drive them forever from the territory they now occupy.[15]

In death, Little Warrior and his adherents achieved martyrdom. Among both militant Red Sticks and wavering Upper Creeks, the chiefs who ordered their deaths became the objects of opprobrium because they had not consulted the clans of the condemned as Creek law required, which rendered the subsequent executions illegitimate. Far from being ritualized affairs designed to impress common Creeks with the power and justice of the National Council, the death sentences had been conducted as sneak attacks on sanctuary talwas. The very lack of ritual, consultation with the clans of the guilty, or respect for the sanctity of white talwas revealed the council's weakness. The council could assassinate, but it could not assert authority in the time-honored Creek manner. The struggle for the Creek soul accelerated.

While the National Council floundered, Josiah Francis and the Red Sticks furtively consolidated their growing strength. They assembled in forests or on the margins of talwas. Clandestine Red Stick runners urged undecided Creeks to kill those among them who had rejected the old ways, had done the white man's bloody bidding, had accumulated vast wealth at the expense of their fellow Creeks, or had acceded to Hawkins's civilization plan.

It was a gruesome edict, but one the Red Sticks held essential to restore the true civilization that the traditional Creek order represented—a return to purity guided by their prophets, who in turn drew upon the divinely bestowed wisdom of the Shawnee Prophet. Much of Red Stick doctrine remains obscure, but it is clear that they abided by their prophets' admonition against using trade goods—guns and ammunition excepted. Casting aside white man's clothing, Red Stick warriors vowed to fight naked or dressed only in a loincloth and red-colored boots or moccasins. They abandoned the elaborate silver and brass ornaments and glass beads popular with most Creeks and shaved their heads. They left just a narrow roll of hair brushed straight back from the forehead, on which they placed an equally slender headdress. Their prophets taught them to reject all forms of wealth, retaining a particular antipathy for livestock, which trammeled communal hunting grounds and cornfields. The Shawnee Prophet preached that right living would bring back the deer; how better to restore grazing ground than to cleanse the land of cattle? In the event of war, slaughtering cattle also would have the practical benefit of depriving Creek enemies of a primary food source.

The tails of slaughtered cattle became amulets. In battle, they would serve the same function as human scalps, encouraging comrades and frightening foes. The prophets instructed warriors to tie the appendages to their arms, while they themselves bore red-dyed cow's tails as symbols of their office.

Little Warrior's death generated an influx of scantily clad, cattle-hating recruits to the Red Stick ranks. Most were Upper Creeks, but a considerable contingent from the Lower talwas of Coweta and Cusseta, together with perhaps forty disaffected Uchees, also joined up. New prophets emerged. They included the repugnant but gifted Alabama métis Paddy Walsh. The son of a "murdering, despicable swamp Tory" who had fled from South Carolina to the Creek country after the Revolutionary War, Paddy Walsh lost his father while a child. Standing just five feet two, with a hairline that ran low on his forehead and a wide mouth that "made him look almost inhumanly ugly," Walsh had a sharp mind. A gifted linguist and accomplished orator, he spoke Muscogee, Alabama, Chickasaw, and Choctaw fluently and typically carried his point in council. The métis George Stiggins also considered Paddy Walsh, for better or worse, "the greatest prophetic warrior that the Creeks ever had."

Seekaboo, meanwhile, shuttled from talwa to talwa, surreptitiously initiating other prophets. The thirty-two-year-old métis Peter McQueen, the head warrior of Tallassee and a commercial farmer and slaveholder whose Scots-Irish father had been the first trader to settle among the Creeks, became a Red Stick political and war leader. A wealthy member of the Wind Clan, he was a nephew of Alexander McGillivray's. Whites who knew him called McQueen "shrewd, sanguinary, and deceitful," which probably meant he got the better of them. Adding a welcome dose of prestige, old Hopoithle Micco also joined the Red Sticks. The cause reinvigorated him, and he boasted widely "of his bows, his arrows, and his magical powers."[16]

As the movement grew, the Red Sticks sought new forest lairs, well removed from talwas of doubtful fidelity, where they could perform the Dance of the Lakes and other purifying rituals freely and which could serve as defensive strongpoints in the event of attack. That summer, they laid out three Red Stick bastions strategically located in the Upper Creek country.

Between visitations "from the Lord," Josiah Francis likely commanded the new Alabama Red Stick bastion, Eccanachaca, located on the western flank of the Creek confederacy. Although more properly translated as "beloved or sacred ground," the spot became known to Americans as the Holy Ground. Admirably cradled amid a heavy growth of mixed forest a quarter mile below the south bank of the Alabama River and thirty miles west of present-day Montgomery, Alabama, the two hundred households of the Holy Ground benefited from rich soil and abundant deer, wild turkey, and waterfowl. Eighty more families lived in a satellite village on a nearby stream. All told, Josiah Francis counted between two hundred and three hundred warriors loyal to his fledgling cause. He sanctified the council house. Around the perimeter of the Holy Ground he drew a mystic protective circle, which he said the Master of Breath would prevent Creek nonbelievers or white men from entering.[17]

Sixty-five miles east of the Holy Ground, in marshy land between Hoithlewaulee and Autosee, just north of the Federal Road, and about twenty-five miles east of modern Montgomery, a second Red Stick stronghold—the name of which is not known—took shape. Having overthrown their miccos in favor of the prophets, the people of Hoithlewaulee and Autosee welcomed the hundreds of Red Sticks and their dependents from lesser talwas along the Coosa and Tallapoosa who gravitated to the site.

Tohopeka, the third Red Stick rallying point, rested in a horseshoe-shaped bend of the Tallapoosa River sixty-six miles northeast of modern Montgomery that the Creeks called *Choloco Litabixee* (Horse's Flat Foot). An enormous encampment, Tohopeka was to be occupied as the need arose by warriors from six nearby Abeika talwas under the leadership of the métis chief Menawa. Work began at once to erect an elaborate log barricade across the exposed neck of the bend.[18]

The Red Sticks were fortifying themselves for war while Benjamin Hawkins spoke hopefully of a Creek future under the government's civilization policy.

At Tuckabatchee, Big Warrior and the "old chiefs" who had ordained the killing of Little Warrior also "forted up." They erected a palisade around the talwa's public square in expectation of a Red Stick assault. A frenzied urgency drove their efforts; they knew they were marked men. The federal military district commander, Major General James Wilkinson, also understood their plight. Leaving Fort Stoddert with his family and a twenty-man army escort en route to a new assignment in the North, Wilkinson found the Federal Road and adjoining Creek communities deserted. The few people he met babbled "wild reports" of impending strife, "consternation and terror in every countenance." A friendly Creek intercepted him with an appeal from a terrified Big Warrior for an interview. "He . . . lives in fear of his life, as his antagonists are daily making converts and increasing in strength, with the avowed intention to destroy him and all who have been concerned in the execution" of Little Warrior and his men, Wilkinson wrote to a friend on June 25. After assassinating the offending chiefs, the Red Sticks "expect to intimidate the rest of the nation to join them, and then it is their intention to make war on the whites. This seems to be the general impression, but no one can tell or even guess where a blow will be struck." Wilkinson ignored Big Warrior's plea and hurried out of the Creek country as fast as his carriage would carry him.[19]

Big Warrior fretted prematurely. He was not Josiah Francis and Paddy Walsh's first target. That distinction went to the prophet turned executioner Captain Isaacs, who must be "cast down from the pinnacle of his fame" before the Red Sticks could gain "ascendancy over the multitude." First, Josiah Francis and Paddy Walsh intended to discredit Captain Isaacs; then they would kill him. They proclaimed that the Master of Breath had revealed that Captain Isaacs's supposedly benevolent serpent familiar was in fact a diabolical spirit who instructed him in witchcraft. His talwa (Tuskegee) proscribed him; his portion was to be death by fire. Reverential followers warned Captain Isaacs of his impending fate. Gathering the store of gunpowder and lead that he had cached, Captain Isaacs and his retinue rode out of

Tuskegee for the friendlier confines of Tuckabatchee. Furious at having been foiled, the Red Sticks plundered and burned Captain Isaacs's
farm and killed two of his warriors who had lingered in the neighborhood. From Tuskegee, Francis and Walsh proclaimed their intention
to march on Tuckabatchee and execute Big Warrior, Alexander Cornells, and all the other collaborationist chiefs.[20]

The Red Sticks nearly caught Big Warrior and Alexander Cornells
unawares. Big Warrior and two other chiefs had assembled at Cornells's house in Tuckabatchee preparatory to a meeting with Superintendent Hawkins at the Creek Agency, scheduled for June 16. "Idle
young people" advised them of what Cornells dismissed as "some
fooleries" in other talwas, but they "had heard of nothing hostile from
any quarter." A credible report that Peter McQueen and Hopoithle
Micco had "given an ear" to the Red Stick fanatics startled them, and
they asked the talwa's war leader to query the men, both of whom
denied any affiliation with the Red Sticks. When similar reports from
other quarters seemingly confirmed the allegations, the hastily gathered Upper Creek representatives to the National Council dispatched
a second runner to McQueen and Hopoithle Micco with a message
meant to conciliate but that could only inflame the Red Sticks. "You
are but a few Alabama people," began the misinformed chiefs. "You
say that the Great Spirit visits you frequently; that he comes in the
sun and speaks to you; that the sun comes down just above your heads.
Now, we want to see and hear what you say you have seen and heard.
Let us have the same proof you have had, and we will believe what we
see and hear." Misjudging the source of Red Stick rage, the Tuckabatchee chiefs concluded, "You have nothing to fear; the people who
committed murder [Little Warrior and his men] have suffered for
their crimes, and there is an end to it."

As if the misguided message itself were not bad enough, the chiefs
chose as its bearer a man who had helped kill Little Warrior. The
prophets condemned and executed him, then used his scalp as a
recruiting device. Their brief return message to Tuckabatchee stated
their bleak purpose: they were coming to kill Big Warrior, Cornells,
Hawkins, and "the old chiefs who had taken his talks"; after "this war
among themselves, they would be ready for the white people." Lest

there be any doubt of their invincibility, the prophets warned that they possessed the power to "destroy by an earthquake, render the ground soft and miry, and [cause] thunder."[21]

Big Warrior and the Tuckabatchee headmen scrambled to save themselves, their African American slaves—Big Warrior owned at least eighty—and their people. They appealed to the seven nearest Upper Creek talwas for reinforcements, but all refused to oppose the prophets. With a small escort, Alexander Cornells rode under cover of darkness to the Lower Creek talwas for help; if Hawkins permitted it, he would also call on the governor of Georgia. Cornells stopped first at Coweta. The talwa's sympathetic war leader hastened to Tucka-batchee with fifty warriors, leaving word for others to join him when they returned from the hunt. Cornells had markedly less success at Cusseta, where he discovered the micco and headmen cowering in the forest, preferring to make excuses for the prophets rather than confront them. On June 22, a disgusted Cornells left to confer with Hawkins.

At the Creek Agency chaos reigned. Most of the white and métis women and children residents of the sprawling Flint River concern had fled to Georgia, and many white residents of Lower Creek talwas had abandoned their homes in favor of the agency. A now wide-awake Benjamin Hawkins reassured two Moravian missionaries that the agency was secure; "nevertheless," wrote one, "we are able to see from the numerous precautions he is taking that he anticipates trouble."[22]

Hawkins had limited options. The storeroom contained just eleven extra muskets and a little powder to augment the weapons of the corporal's guard of Regulars posted at the agency. His namesake military post, Fort Hawkins, forty miles east on the Ocmulgee River, was also undermanned. Perhaps Hawkins took some comfort knowing that Red Stick plotting also had caught others unprepared. "The chiefs are much surprised that the plan of the prophets should have been so long kept a secret from them," related Alexander Cornells. "They looked on it as a sort of madness and amusement for idle people. But, during this period, it was secretly gaining strength and converts, and where least expected, burst forth in acts of murder, confident of its strength."[23]

Hawkins's first concern was not for the Creeks. With uncharacteristic cynicism, perhaps born of anger at what he undoubtedly regarded as a betrayal by the people for whom he had labored so long, he suggested to Governor Mitchell that if the conflict proved purely a civil war, the best course might be to ignore the strife until a clear winner emerged. The Red Sticks, however, had also vowed to make war on the whites, and that was clearly intolerable. No sooner had Cornells delivered his report than Hawkins persuaded an intrepid interpreter and four equally courageous Lower Creek headmen to venture into the Red Stick camp at Tallassee with a message from him asking why they hated the whites—as if Hawkins were oblivious to a generation of border provocations and encroachment by Georgians—and warning them of American military might.[24]

Hopoithle Micco ridiculed the superintendent. The Red Sticks had no intention of "throwing aside the war sticks." They would fight until they had put to death those culpable for Little Warrior's murder, and Hopoithle Micco cast the blame broadly. First, the Red Sticks would reduce Tuckabatchee to ashes, after which they would march to Coweta and destroy it as well. From there, the Red Sticks would slaughter every Georgia settler west of the Ogeechee River. There they would pause, rest, and then continue their campaign of death and plunder to the Atlantic coast. Tecumseh and the British, meanwhile, would slay all Americans north of the Red Sticks' line of march. Hopoithle Micco proclaimed his men well armed with bows, arrows, and war clubs. With these and "the magic powers he possessed," concluded Hopoithle Micco, "aided by the British and Shawnees, who were now coming from the Northwest and were now more than halfway to him, he was able to crush the Americans and would do it." As the old chief ranted, a subordinate prophet muttered angrily to Hawkins's runner that the prophets of Alabama had begun prematurely. They were to have waited until Tecumseh arrived.[25]

Hopoithle Micco was either delusional or egregiously misinformed. Tecumseh was not coming—neither then nor ever. He had assembled the largest Indian fighting force ever seen on the North American continent, nearly six thousand warriors. While Hopoithle Micco crowed of the Shawnee's impending arrival, however, Tecumseh was eight hundred miles away, preparing with his British allies to make one final attempt to wrest control of the Northwest from William Henry Harrison by attacking his forts in northern Ohio. Tecumseh's Indian confederacy was tenuous, and the British mustered fewer than a thousand men. Together they faced steep odds. Affairs in the Creek country, to the extent they were even aware of them, had no place in the calculations of Tecumseh or the British commander.[26]

Big Warrior knew nothing of the Red Sticks' strategic isolation. Aware only that he faced mortal danger, the normally voluble Creek cowered in his makeshift fort on the Tuckabatchee council grounds, hoping that reinforcements and gunpowder, of which his 190 warriors had precious little, would arrive before the Red Sticks attacked.

They did. While the Red Sticks lingered near Autosee dancing and making magic, Captain Isaacs rode into Tuckabatchee with 200 warriors and, strapped on packhorses, his precious barrels of gunpowder. Next came 231 warriors from Coweta and Cusseta, the war leader of the latter talwa having upbraided his micco and headmen for their "pusillanimous conduct" when Alexander Cornells met them. Several warriors from Kialijee, a talwa up the Tuscaloosa that the Red Sticks had razed when its council rejected the prophets' call to arms, also straggled into Big Warrior's fort. Although still afraid, Big Warrior had a respectable 600 fighting men crammed in his fort together with several hundred noncombatants. A shortage of food and water appeared their greatest enemy.

On July 2, the first Red Sticks, a war party of Autosee men, filtered into the outskirts of Tuckabatchee. Brandishing firebrands and war clubs, they set fire to the barked roofs of several houses. That caused Big Warrior to send out women to gather what corn they could—something he should have done much sooner. Six warriors guarded them. As the women snapped ears of corn from stalks in the communal field, the Tuckabatchee warriors collided with the Autosees, who had just slaughtered a hog. The Tuckabatchees fired first, and three Autosee men fell dead—the first Red Stick casualties of the Creek Civil War. The rest ran off, and the Tuckabatchee warriors and the women returned to the fort.

It was an inauspicious beginning to the grand Red Stick march of destruction. Hopoithle Micco, Paddy Walsh, and the prophets were furious. Invoking the tradition of the extended busk, they agreed that their warriors should lay siege to Tuckabatchee for seven days. On the eighth day, they would storm the fort and make short work of its heretical defenders. Big Warrior estimated the enemy at twenty-five

Andrew Jackson, nemesis
of the Creek people.

Hernando de Soto, the Spanish
conquistador who cut a bloody swath
through what was to become the
Creek country.

Hernando de Soto Burns Mabila by Herb Roe. De Soto's brand of warfare against the Native peoples of the Mississippian tradition bore an uncanny similarity to that later waged by Andrew Jackson against the Creeks.

Italwas by Dori DeCamillas. An evocative rendition of a typical Creek talwa. The chunky field may be seen in the left middle ground, the public square in the center, and the winter council house in the right middle ground.

James Oglethorpe, founder of the Georgia colony. An astute diplomat, he won the trust of the Lower Creeks.

A partial family group on the Georgia frontier, typical of the whites who squatted on Creek land in the late eighteenth century.

Benjamin Hawkins, Indian agent. His paternalistic
"civilization" program undermined traditional
Creek society, creating the fissures that would
precipitate the Creek Civil War.

Josiah Francis, Red Stick métis prophet. Francis
painted this self-portrait while in London after the
Creek War.

Jim Boy, Red Stick prophet and war leader.
He was known to shake violently in the presence of
nonbelievers.

Big Warrior.

Big Warrior, an opportunistic Upper Creek leader particularly reviled by the Red Sticks. He owed his survival to Benjamin Hawkins and the Georgia militia.

Hopoithle Micco. Once a leading accommodationist, he later became a fervent and delusional Red Stick leader, believing he could clear the entire southern United States of white men.

William McIntosh, Lower Creek métis. Perhaps the wealthiest man in the Creek confederacy, McIntosh fought with the Americans in the Creek War and later facilitated dubious U.S. government land grabs for his own personal gain.

Pushmataha, one of the three principal chiefs of the Choctaw nation. He stood squarely with the Americans of the Mississippi Territory against the Red Sticks.

A mid-twentieth-century photograph of the Burnt Corn Creek battlefield.

A typically dramatic and stylized nineteenth-century depiction of the Fort Mims massacre. (There were, for instance, no cannons frowning from the fort's lone blockhouse.)

John Floyd, the capable commander of Georgia forces at the Battles of Autosee and Calabee Creek.

ABOVE Rachel Jackson, who frequently implored her beloved husband to return home during the course of the Creek War. RIGHT Andrew Jackson as a major general in the Regular army, exhibiting no trace of the shoulder wound that caused him unimaginable suffering during the Creek War.

John Coffee, the talented and fiercely loyal lieutenant to Andrew Jackson.

John Cocke, major general of the East Tennessee militia, who Jackson wrongly accused of sabotaging his operations.

Thomas Pinckney, the capable departmental commander who appreciated Jackson's gifts and tolerated his shortcomings.

hundred, but he likely exaggerated. The Red Sticks in the aggregate could not have exceeded five thousand warriors, a significant number of whom were then at the Holy Ground with Francis or completing defenses under Chief Menawa's command at Tohopeka.

The days spent at Tuckabatchee passed poorly for the prophets. The Red Sticks managed to kill or drive off all the cattle and horses except the few secured in the fort. In the desultory skirmishing and one abortive assault that followed, however, they lost thirteen men, including a prophet shot through the head while uttering magical incantations within range of the Tuckabatchee riflemen. The defenders lost only one man wounded. Perhaps guessing the prophets' plan, on the seventh evening the Lower Creek leaders persuaded Big Warrior to retreat to Coweta. While he and his followers crossed the Tallapoosa River unimpeded, Red Stick warriors set Tuckabatchee ablaze. Hopoithle Micco had won a hollow victory.[27]

The Red Sticks now looked to their rear. They consolidated control over the Upper Creek country, often brutally. Warriors slaughtered cattle and hogs with no regard for their own long-term food needs, and plundered, beat, or killed proponents of Hawkins's civilization policy. At Okfuskee, Red Sticks murdered the progressive micco and four headmen, stripped naked a métis woman who taught weaving to the women of the talwa, then broke her looms and shredded her cloth supply. An eighteen-year-old Alabama prophet named Letecau returned to his native talwa of Aubecooche with eight disciples, ostensibly to demonstrate the Dance of the Lakes to the doubting micco and headmen. Curious townspeople followed the prophet to the bank of the upper Coosa River to watch the sacred performance. Letecau and his youthful adherents danced frantically. Suddenly they gave a war whoop and clubbed three headmen to death. Aubecooche onlookers dove into the river. Swimming to the far bank, they took a circuitous path back to the talwa, assembled their warriors, and hastened to the scene of the slaughter, where the triumphant Red Sticks continued to dance. Exhibiting more courage than good sense, a headman entered their circle. They felled him with war clubs, then shot him full of arrows. The Aubecooche warriors retaliated, killing Letecau and his coterie and taking the youthful prophet's scalp. Fearing retaliation, the entire population of Aubecooche took refuge in a friendly Cherokee town, as did the residents of three neighboring talwas.

. . .

As July 1813 drew to a close, the Red Sticks, with twenty-nine of the thirty-four Upper Creek talwas in their camp, repeated their promise to abolish heresy. "The declaration of the Prophets," Big Warrior told Benjamin Hawkins, "is to destroy everything received from the Americans [and] all the chiefs and their adherents who are friendly to the customs and ways of the white people; to put to death every man who will not join them; and, by those means, to unite the nation in aid of the British and Indians of the Lakes against their white neighbors, as soon as their friends the British will be ready for them."[28]

Mighty words, but the Red Sticks failed to make good on Hopoithle Micco's pledge to march against Coweta or to attack white border settlements, much less sweep their way to the seaboard. Although the battle for Tuckabatchee cost the Red Sticks few lives, it exhausted most of their powder and lead. Withdrawing to their camp near Autosee, the prophets and war leaders contemplated their next move. On the matter of negotiations, the Red Sticks were of one mind. They refused to receive "any talks from Colonel Hawkins or the white people."[29]

Benjamin Hawkins retaliated as best he was able. His rheumatism having abated, he organized a limited Lower Creek counteroffensive to keep the Red Sticks occupied until the Georgia militia—which was eager to enter the fray on behalf of the friendly Creeks—was mustered, armed, and provisioned.

Several dozen Lower Creek warriors defected to the Red Sticks. Every leader of consequence stood by Hawkins, however. The unpredictable Uchees had 18 who turned traitor, but 175 Uchee war leaders and warriors reported to the agency ready to punish both the Red Sticks and their own faithless tribesmen. Washing his hands of Big Warrior, who "dreads the conflict and is much under the influence of fear," Hawkins looked instead to William McIntosh, who did not disappoint. With 375 Lower Creek mounted warriors, he thundered across high and open pine barrens toward the Tallassee home of Hopoithle Micco and Peter McQueen, swam the swift-running Tallapoosa River, and galloped into the abandoned talwa, the populace having hastily fled to the Red Stick enclave outside Autosee. Kettles, pots, deerskins, and cowhides lay strewn about. In Peter McQueen's personal storeroom, McIntosh's raiders discovered salt stacked nearly to the ceiling and a considerable supply of the forbidden substance in most other family compounds. Carrying all the plunder they were able, McIntosh's raiders set fire to the talwa and its cornfields before returning to Coweta.

McIntosh's success emboldened the Lower Creeks. In August, small war parties combed the country west of Coweta. They killed an occasional Red Stick warrior, captured a twelve-year-old member of Peter McQueen's family and four of McQueen's slaves, retrieved stray cattle and horses, and despoiled deserted dwellings.[30]

Although Hawkins had balanced the score for Tuckabatchee, he nonetheless felt frustrated. Lower Creek leaders were generally as timid as Big Warrior. "Our chiefs are so much under the influence of fear, I no longer rely on their reports, but with great limitation," he complained. Georgians also proved an irritant. Lawless frontiersmen intent on killing Indians preyed on friendly Lower Creeks. Peaceable settlers clamored for protection and accused Hawkins of ignoring them when blame lay with the War Department. Overwhelmed with mismanaging the war against Great Britain, Secretary of War John Armstrong had ignored every letter from Hawkins since the outbreak of the Creek Civil War. By mid-September, Hawkins had had enough. "As I hear nothing from you relative to the communications [that] I have made to you on Indian affairs, I have judged it advisable to have an understanding with myself on my situation here," carped Hawkins. After deducting agency expense he had paid for himself, Hawkins had earned less than $3,000 in more than a decade as superintendent. Perhaps it was time the president found a replacement. "He owes it to his high standing and to me to send him on; in doing so, he will do me no injury, or excite the least resentment. This department," concluded Hawkins, "has always been strewed with thorns." Let someone else endure their stabs.[31]

CHAPTER EIGHT

Stark Mad

P ETER MCQUEEN knew that the Red Sticks lacked the powder and lead needed for protracted combat. They also had no means of repairing their numerous defective muskets. Old Hopoithle Micco might fantasize of becoming a Creek incarnation of Hernando de Soto; McQueen would focus on the realities of waging with inferior arms and minimal powder and ball what Red Stick orthodoxy would necessarily make a two-front war.

Provoking a war on two fronts is seldom a good strategy, particularly when the aggressor will likely be outnumbered. It borders on the irrational when there exists the potential for a third front—in the Red Sticks' case, the state of Tennessee with its land-grabbing governor, Willie Blount, and combat-hungry militia general Andrew Jackson. This, however, is precisely the prospect that confronted the Red Sticks when they raised their war clubs in July 1813. Their prophets assured them that the British and Tecumseh's northern Indians would tip the balance in their favor.[1]

The Red Stick second front comprised eighty thousand acres of soggy cypress and tupelo-gum forests, meandering bayous, and stagnant marshes resting between the Mobile and the Tensaw Rivers. The rank region abruptly terminated twenty-five miles north of Mobile at what was known as the "Cutoff," a channel of the Alabama River that flowed west into the lower Tombigbee River several miles above the true confluence of the two watercourses.

To comprehend the violence that was about to erupt, a look backward is in order. Beginning in 1765, the Creeks and Choctaws permitted British colonists to settle on high, dry ground on the west banks of the Mobile and Tombigbee Rivers between Mobile and the Cutoff. By mutual agreement, land north and east of the Cutoff belonged to the Creeks, an understanding that endured after British control of the Floridas passed to Spain, which in turn ceded the country to the United States in 1795. The American government flouted the accord and built a stockade named Fort Stoddert on a bluff of the Mobile River, ostensibly to defend Americans legally settled on the west bank of the Tombigbee. By 1800, however, 500 American settlers and their 250 slaves squatted on the east banks of both the Tombigbee and the Alabama Rivers.[2]

Upper Creek leaders bristled. Alexander McGillivray complained that "droves of Americans upon the Tombigbee...not content with the British limits which now compose the Spanish, have spread and extended themselves over a great space of Choctaw and our hunting grounds." He barely prevented the Alabamas and Koasatis from banding together with the Choctaws to expel them. McGillivray averted violence, but the intrusions intensified. "The people of Tombigbee have put their cattle in the fork on the Alabama hunting grounds, and they have gone a great way on our lands," declared the National Council spokesman Efau Hadjo in 1802. "I want them to be put back; the Indians begin to complain and will soon do mischief." Confronted with government inaction, his successor, Hopoie Micco, threatened, "It is not stock only we complain of; we find that houses are built on our lands, and fields are cleared and cultivated.... If they do not move off, we shall consider these things as our property and act accordingly."[3]

The Jefferson administration sent the surveyor of public lands to Fort Stoddert to investigate. He discovered that some two hundred families had "effected their cultivation upon ground where the native right remains unextinguished." Dispossessing them would be hard. Indigo, cotton, corn, rice, and tobacco all flourished on their unlawful Tensaw farms. Cattle grazed in the pine barrens. With its easy access to the Gulf of Mexico, "nothing can prevent this country from taking

MAP 2   THE TENSAW AND LOWER TOMBIGBEE COUNTRY, 1813

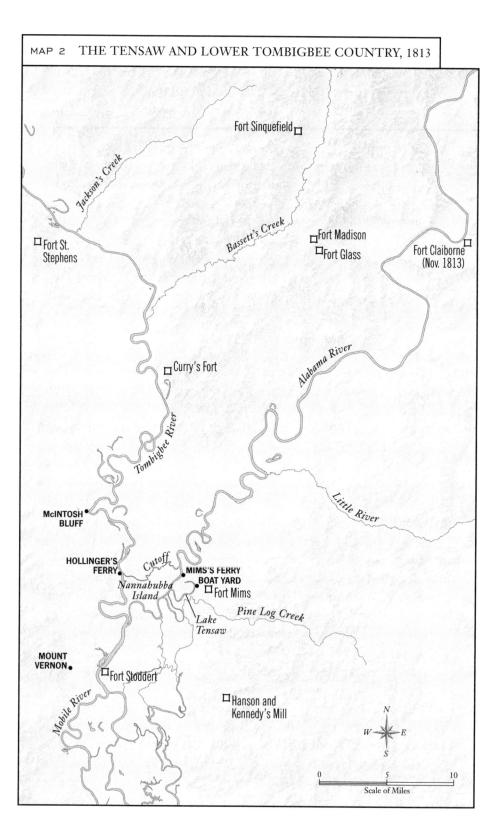

a decided lead in the commerce of the West [Indies]. Nature seems in this region to have been lavish of its bounties."

The American trespassers, however, disgusted the surveyor. They were "with few exceptions illiterate, wild and savage, of depraved morals unworthy of public confidence or private esteem; litigious, disunited, and knowing each other, universally distrusted of each other." Hostile to the laws of any government, the squatters were "almost universally fugitives from justice, and many of them felons of the first order."

The Federal Road opened the door to a slightly better class of Americans, mostly travelers bound for the booming Natchez District of the Mississippi Territory, far removed from the Creek country. Enough of the newcomers, however, settled in the Tensaw by 1810 to raise its population to 733 whites and 517 blacks. Two years later, the number climbed to nearly 2,000. What the road had wrought incensed the Alabamas and the Koasatis. As they saw it, a cancer had emerged on the western margin of the Creek country that endangered their very way of life. Traditionalists—that is to say, the have-nots of Hawkins's civilization policy—became increasingly desperate to extract it.[4]

More than just a sanctuary for undesirable Americans, the Tensaw District posed an internal threat to Creek sovereignty because many of its inhabitants were Creek or métis emigrants from Alabama and Koasati talwas who eschewed traditional ways. Although unmentioned in the government surveyor's report, they represented the wealthiest, most reputable, and influential residents of the Tensaw—slaveholders, ranchers, cotton planters, and entrepreneurs who embraced the American-style market economy. Although they maintained their mothers' clan affiliations, these Tensaw transplants resisted efforts by their native talwas to assert authority over them.

Alexander McGillivray had been the first notable Creek to settle in the Tensaw. He built a plantation on Little River, a tributary of the Alabama River in the upper reaches of the region, and encouraged members of his mother's Wind Clan to join him there. Several métis who would play prominent roles in the Creek War availed themselves of McGillivray's offer. They included his nephews David Tate and William Weatherford and his clan allies Sam Moniac and Richard

Dixon Bailey. When McGillivray died, the European-educated Tate became headman of the Little River Creeks. Many American residents of the upper Tensaw took Creek wives, strengthening communal ties with their métis neighbors.

McGillivray's kin flourished. The American-educated "Dixon" Bailey, who quit his talwa for the Tensaw because his fellow Creeks habitually butchered his hogs and cattle "whenever they trespass on fields under cultivation," piloted a ferry across the delta for travelers crossing to the Mississippi Territory. Sam Moniac ran a stage station from his home on the Federal Road. Both men also had thriving plantations on the Little River. The Weatherford family operated a lucrative horse-racing track that drew sportsmen and gamblers from as far away as Natchez.

As the Tensaw prospered, Benjamin Hawkins and Governor David Holmes of the Mississippi Territory vied to assert control over the district. Creek leaders construed the machinations of Hawkins and Holmes as a threat to their sovereignty. They also disapproved of the warm welcome Tensaw métis accorded American settlers. Smoldering resentment turned red hot during the Hungry Years, the prolonged blight to which the thriving economy of the wealthy Tensaw Creeks proved immune.

The miccos of other Upper Creek talwas gradually joined their Alabama and Koasati colleagues in trying to discipline the Tensaw métis. In 1809, the ubiquitous Captain Isaacs entered the Little River country with a dozen warriors to collect taxes on cattle and flatboats. Some paid the tax in the spirit of traditional Creek charity. But not Dixon Bailey. The beefy, dark-complexioned métis and his aged Creek mother came to blows with the warriors before Captain Isaacs backed off. Neither man forgot the incident. Both vowed revenge and awaited an opportune catalyst. By the summer of 1813, the ascendant Red Sticks—particularly their Alabama and Koasati prophets—ached to reassert talwa authority over the Little River heretics or, failing that, to excise the Tensaw cancer not merely from their body politic but also from the face of the earth.[5]

The degree to which the Red Stick leadership coordinated their actions in July 1813 is a matter of conjecture. Chief Menawa and the

Abeikas appear to have been busy building their fortified camp at Tohopeka while Hopoithle Micco attacked Tuckabatchee with his contingent of Red Sticks. Peter McQueen, either by mutual agreement with the old war chief or on his own initiative, removed himself to Josiah Francis's Holy Ground preparatory to leading a large party to Pensacola to demand from the Spaniards the arms and ammunition that all Red Stick factions needed. Although perhaps not aware of the cause—the ongoing Peninsular War that ravaged Spain—the Red Sticks recognized that Spanish authority over West Florida was tenuous. Concluding the time ripe for a muscular approach to the Spanish governor, McQueen hoped to enlist the principal Red Stick prophet in his endeavor.

A bit of the luster had rubbed off the supposed magic of Francis. Two months earlier, he had written a letter in Spanish (a language of which he knew not a word) to the governor at Pensacola, purportedly an entreaty gentler than that which McQueen now intended. When Red Stick skeptics suggested that the letter "looked more like a paper full of crooked marks than writing," Francis protested that the Master of Breath had given him the gift of Spanish literacy. Fearful of divine retribution should that be true, sixty warriors reluctantly carried the missive to Pensacola. The governor, Mateo González Manrique, demanded to know why they had handed him a sheet chock-full of chicken scratches. Stammering their innocence, the duped envoys begged González Manrique's pardon. After a hearty laugh, the governor told them he had half a mind to return a similarly unintelligible letter to Francis informing him he had neither arms nor ammunition to give him. González Manrique forbore embarrassing Francis further, but the Red Sticks returned to the Holy Ground empty-handed.[6]

Brutal and belligerent, Peter McQueen intended to overawe González Manrique with Red Stick might and to punish any Creek apostates he might meet along the way. In mid-July, McQueen set out from the Holy Ground with twenty-four Red Stick headmen, three hundred warriors, and a packhorse train to carry home the ammunition and supplies they expected the Spanish governor to lavish on them. Josiah Francis nominally led the Alabama contingent. Jim Boy (Tustunnugee Emathla) led the Koasatis. Tall and strikingly handsome, Jim Boy was a muscular mulatto of dubious parentage. The putative son of a Koasati micco, he seems to have in fact been the adopted child of the chief's favorite slave, also a large-framed mulatto. In any event, Jim Boy reveled in the role of prophet. He periodically fell into trances, convulsed violently, grinned wildly, and boasted of his ability to deflect the white man's bullets or to sink an attacking enemy in muck and mire of his own creation.[7]

The illiterate McQueen also carried a packet of great importance, or so he thought. Removed from Little Warrior's corpse by the martyr's nephew, the Red Sticks believed it contained a letter from a British general in Canada to the governor of West Florida, requiring him to furnish the Red Sticks with guns and ammunition. Perhaps the letter was sealed, or else no literate Red Stick read it, because the document in question was merely a letter of introduction. McQueen and his followers believed otherwise, however, and they bragged of it to every American and Tensaw métis they met on the road to Pensacola. Because the beleaguered Madison administration feared a British offensive on the Gulf Coast, government officials credited the rumored letter as proof that the British were instigating the Creeks to make war on the United States, a preposterous notion. The British had considered neither a campaign in the Southeast nor involving themselves with the Red Sticks. The British were on the defensive in Canada and just beginning operations in the Chesapeake Bay that threatened Baltimore and Washington, D.C., and no British commander in North America had the authority to open yet another front. The Americans, however, knew little of royal military policy, and fables flourish when facts are few.[8]

The early Tensaw métis settler Sam Moniac hoped to keep clear of the Red Sticks, whose depredations threatened both his life and his wealth. That he habitually wore a large medal that George Washington had given him during the Treaty of New York proceedings undoubtedly infuriated the Red Sticks. In the spring of 1813, he quit his home on the Federal Road in favor of his more distant Little River plantation. While he visited Pensacola to sell steers, his sister and brother joined the Red Sticks. Probably at Peter McQueen's behest, they absconded with most of his Little River stock and thirty-five of his slaves.

Concern over his abandoned property got the better of him, and Moniac slipped back to his Federal Road residence at the very moment Jim Boy and his Koasatis camped on his grounds en route to Pensacola as part of McQueen's expedition. What followed mystified Moniac. "Jim Boy shook hands with me and immediately began to tremble and jerk in every part of his frame, and the very calves of [his] legs were convulsed until he entirely lost his breath." Jim Boy explained that the salt Moniac consumed caused the convulsions; the Master of Breath had instilled in the prophets a repugnance of salt so that they might better identify Creek apostates. Moniac dissembled smoothly. "Jim Boy asked me what I meant to do," he recalled. "I said that I should sell my property and buy ammunition and join them." Evidently mollified, Jim Boy expounded on Red Stick plans. Moniac, who was deposed on the matter in August, might have embellished Jim Boy's threat as payback against the Red Sticks for destroying much of his property. "He told me," swore Moniac, "that they were going down to Pensacola to get ammunition," after which they would make a general attack against all Americans in the Mississippi Territory, Tennessee, and Georgia; that "the war was to be against the whites and not among the Indians themselves; that all they intended to do in that way was to kill those who had taken the talk of the whites, [such as] the Big Warrior, Captain Isaacs, and William McIntosh." Oddly, Moniac said nothing of Red Stick animosity toward his fellow Tensaw métis.[9]

Moniac might have exaggerated the scope of most Red Sticks' destructive ambitions, but their rage was real enough. On the dark-wooded Federal Road, a mail carrier—probably a Creek métis—suddenly found himself surrounded by outriders from Peter McQueen's procession. They seized his mailbag. Then, as he rode away, the Red Sticks fired a volley at him, killing his horse. The mail carrier escaped on foot through the forest.

In Burnt Corn Springs, a hamlet at the intersection of the Federal Road and the Great Pensacola Trading Path (better known as the Wolf Trail), McQueen's Red Sticks inflicted more pain before turning south on the final leg of their journey to the West Florida capital. They targeted the trading house and plantation of its most prominent resident, the métis James Cornells, first cousin of the assistant Indian agent Alexander Cornells. The newlywed Cornells was absent, but the Red Sticks burned his corncribs, plundered his house, beat a friend of his nearly to death, and seized his white bride, Betsy Coulter. Carrying her with them to ransom in Pensacola, McQueen's sunbaked cavalcade pounded down the dusty trading path through dry pine barrens with high hopes.[10]

Pensacola was a sprawling town laid out in the Spanish fashion. It rested beside a bay of the same name. Five main streets, punctuated by thirty squares, ran parallel to the water. Brick or stucco homes, replete with ironwork verandas and interior courtyards, afforded the town a languid charm. Two large swamps flanked Pensacola on the east and west. A six-gun redoubt built of wood and sand guarded the northern approach to the town. The governor's palace stood in the main square, called the Plaza de Armas, between Pensacola Bay and the three-story frame barracks that quartered the capital's garrison, which numbered no more than four hundred men. Three blockhouses guarded the Plaza de Armas. Ten brass cannons and a few dismounted brass howitzers lay scattered beneath a fourth blockhouse, which served as the magazine.

On the afternoon of July 20, McQueen and his Red Sticks rode past the outer redoubt and fanned out around the Plaza de Armas. They expected much, unaware that Pensacola was a castle in the sand, erected on the crumbling edge of a receding Spanish empire. Its Florida holdings had never been Spain's most valuable possessions, but rather were intended as a bulwark to prevent American filibusterers from endangering Cuba and Central America. With Mobile already lost, the captain general of Cuba, Juan Ruiz de Apodaca, whose jurisdiction included the Floridas, knew that Pensacola could not long be held with the forces available to him; he wished only that Governor Mateo González Manrique make a good showing if attacked. Considering that his troops were few and underfed, González Manrique doubted he could accomplish anything without an Indian alliance. The difficulty was, he had little to offer the Indians. As early as January 1813, he had complained to Ruiz de Apodaca that a shortage of supplies from Cuba had reduced the garrisons to a ration of watery stew and bread.[11]

Peter McQueen met González Manrique in a public conference that evening. Shaking the governor's hand warmly, the métis proclaimed, according to González Manrique, "that the object of his mission was to inform me that the continued aggressions of the Americans to take over their land had put the Creeks in the position of declaring war, that as allies of the Creeks and of their brothers the English, he hoped [I] would take an active part in the war, and moreover would provide them the arms and ammunition they needed, as well as victuals and various other articles they lacked." González Manrique temporized. He had neither the means to make war on the United States nor the authority to arm the Red Sticks, but he would give them powder, ball, and food, and would refer their request for weapons to the captain general in Havana. As for the British letter from Canada, the governor told them it was merely a letter of introduction. González Manrique thought Peter McQueen left his office "apparently satisfied."

The next morning, July 21, McQueen reappeared with five compatriots, including Jim Boy and Josiah Francis, for a closed conference, to which González Manrique acceded. Once inside the governor's private office, McQueen accused González Manrique of the "vilest treachery." The governor "had given his hand but not his heart." González Manrique had duped the Red Sticks; he "was a friend and not an enemy of the Americans, as they had foolishly imagined." The governor remonstrated with McQueen; he was indeed their friend but must obtain the captain general's permission to dispense guns and swords—permission he had no doubt would be granted. In the meantime, he would give them his surplus powder, lead, and supplies. Outwardly mollified, the Red Sticks left.

They next paid a call on John Innerarity, the Pensacola agent of John Forbes and Company. The lanky, thirty-year-old, stern-faced Scotsman owned the grandest residence in town. A two-story, gable-roofed structure fronting Pensacola Bay, it boasted floor-to-ceiling windows to admit the pleasant bay breezes and a large veranda running the length of the house on the landward side. The company storehouse, which the Red Sticks had heard was filled to the rafters with gunpowder and balls, stood temptingly nearby.

Early on the morning of July 22, Innerarity awoke to find his estate overrun with Red Sticks, including a convulsive Jim Boy, who "trembled and grinned horribly." While McQueen harangued the Scotsman for supplies, Innerarity dissembled. "I told them I had none but this would not satisfy them, [so] I took them up the loft of the brick store and showed them the empty barrels." Exasperated, McQueen and the Red Sticks rode off to the Plaza de Armas. Unknown to them, Innerarity had moved his huge stock of powder and lead to the Spanish post of Fort Barrancas, six miles distant. The Red Sticks had missed the chance to obtain enough munitions to fight a long war.[12]

At 11:00 a.m., the time set for the Red Sticks to receive their "gifts," McQueen and his interpreter burst into the office of González Manrique, who was then chatting with the parish priest. The governor must augment the gifts, or the Red Sticks would not accept them, pronounced McQueen. González Manrique shrugged. "I told them that was fine, that I had nothing more to give them and that if they didn't want it to leave it." Swearing the Red Sticks would kill any Spaniard they encountered outside Pensacola, McQueen stormed out of the palace. Moments later, a cacophony of war whoops burst forth on the Plaza de Armas. Red Sticks hurled insults at the scattering townspeople. Hearing that two Americans were in town, warriors went from house to house, breaking down doors in search of them. The Americans—one of whom was the Tensaw métis David Tate, the other William Pierce, owner of a Tensaw cotton mill—darted into the army barracks, where they were afforded protection. Before his presence became known, Tate conversed with his fellow Tensaw métis James Cornells's captive wife, Betsy Coulter, who had been sold to a Frenchwoman. Coulter warned him that her captors had vowed to kill all the whites and métis in the Tensaw once they procured enough powder and ball.[13]

González Manrique hastened to contain the chaos. Rolling cannons into the Plaza de Armas, the garrison and militia formed ranks and challenged the mounted Red Sticks. Confronted by artillery, the warriors wilted. McQueen sheathed his saber and begged the governor's forgiveness. Blaming the disturbance on "hotheaded young warriors," he agreed to accept whatever goods the Spaniards offered them. McQueen also apologized to Innerarity for the violence of his rhetoric. In view of the depleted stores in Pensacola, the Red Sticks did rather well. The gifts that they slung onto their packhorses included 2,100 pounds of musket balls, 2,000 flints, 1,050 pounds of powder, 400 powder horns, 100 razor blades, 300 pairs of scissors, 32 barrels of flour, 25 bags of corn off the cob, 200 pounds of coffee, 400 pounds of sugar, and—surprisingly acceptable to the Red Sticks—4 bags of salt.[14]

On July 24, Jim Boy and the Koasatis left Pensacola. Before departing McQueen, Francis, and their retinues tarried to regale the trepidatious residents with the Dance of the Lakes.

Although glad to be rid of the Red Sticks, González Manrique feared for what the future might hold. "Under the best of circumstances war would not be in the interest of Spanish Florida, but under present conditions it presents a new affliction that could reduce the province to pecuniary," he wrote to Captain General Ruiz de Apodaca. "[War] will close off the source of fresh meat for the garrison and townspeople, which they have been buying from residents of the Tensaw and other American neighbors and will cause public credit to suffer." So desperate did the situation appear that the governor applied to Innerarity for a private loan to buy meat.

Innerarity also dreaded war. His brother ran the Forbes and Company store in Mobile, which might well become a Red Stick target. Much of what McQueen said was "balderdash," Innerarity wrote to his brother. Nevertheless, "the league seems to be very formidable, and I fear will daily gain much additional strength. They have all gone stark mad, and the fermentation will communicate like wildfire. They will spill much innocent blood with the ammunition which the governor involuntarily gave them."[15]

Word of the Red Stick visit to Pensacola traveled fast. David Tate and William Pierce, who came so near to losing their lives to rampaging Red Sticks on the Plaza de Armas, had been in Pensacola as spies for Colonel Joseph Carson, the commanding officer at Fort Stoddert. Their report, together with the testimony of Sam Moniac, James Cornells, and other Americans and métis who encountered McQueen, sparked a frenzy of flight and fort building by frightened Tensaw residents, which the discordant response of local military authorities only intensified.

Harry Toulmin, the district magistrate, sounded the alarm on July 31. A proponent of Benjamin Hawkins's civilization policy, the forty-seven-year-old immigrant son of a dissident English Unitarian preacher had accurately downplayed the concerns of skittish settlers the year before, calling fears of war with the Creeks "greatly exaggerated." Toulmin also had fustigated the district militia commander Colonel James Caller for attempting to provoke hostilities.

Caller epitomized the worst element of the Tensaw white community. A swaggering, corrupt, land-swindling Indian hater, wealthy in land and slaves, he had come to the Tensaw in 1798 and immediately sought to dominate local politics for personal gain. Not surprisingly, Caller and Toulmin became bitter enemies. In 1810, the territorial governor thwarted Caller's attempt to organize a filibustering foray against Spanish Mobile and Pensacola. In the summer of 1812, Caller dispatched a party of "rangers" to murder Indians. After firing on a peaceable Creek hunting party and beating some inoffensive Choctaws senseless, the miscreants dispersed. They had come dangerously close, rued Toulmin, to pushing the Creeks into the arms of the Spaniards.[16]

By the end of July 1813, however, even Judge Toulmin had to admit that the Tensaw urgently needed Colonel Caller's services. Refugees crowded Fort Stoddert. Civilians from the upper Tensaw congregated at Fort St. Stephens, a solid stockade built by the French a century earlier on a bluff above the west bank of the Tombigbee, nearly seventy miles north of Mobile. Nine-tenths of the American and métis farms in the Tensaw were abandoned, their occupants hiding in the swamps or "forting up" in more than a dozen makeshift blockhouses and stockades near the Cutoff. East of the Tensaw forts, silence prevailed. "All intercourse between this country and Georgia has ceased. The carrying of the mail is completely suspended," Toulmin advised territorial authorities. "The general commotion through the Creek nation is a matter of notoriety. Their plantations are neglected and uncultivated, and the houses of all who reside near the road are abandoned. The state of things seems a prelude to war."[17]

Brigadier General Ferdinand L. Claiborne, the commander of the Mississippi Territory Volunteers, concurred. At the first word of unrest, he hurried his brigade from Baton Rouge to Fort Stoddert. When he reached the Mobile River stockade on July 30, Claiborne found the population of the Tensaw "in a state of utmost confusion and alarm. They were flying from all quarters to the west side of the Tombigbee, leaving behind them rich and highly cultivated farms, with immense crops and stocks of cattle an easy prey to the hostile Indians."

Claiborne did not panic easily. A forty-year-old former Regular army officer, he had fought at the Battle of Fallen Timbers in 1794 against the confederated tribes of the Old Northwest. In 1805, Claiborne resigned his commission, moved south, and settled in Natchez. Popular and honest, he prospered in business and soon became speaker of the territorial legislature and commander of the militia. American unpreparedness at the outbreak of the War of 1812 placed a premium on men with military experience, and in March 1813 the secretary of war appointed Claiborne brigadier general of the Mississippi Territory Volunteers, directly subordinate to the commander of the Seventh Military District. Unlike Judge Toulmin, Claiborne disliked Hawkins's program; he had long favored a hardhanded policy toward the Creeks. Nevertheless, Claiborne and Toulmin worked well together.[18]

Troop shortages and a difficult superior officer constituted Claiborne's immediate problems. Expirations of enlistments reduced his "brigade" from 600 infantry and 150 cavalry to a mere 341 poorly armed infantrymen. Governor Holmes activated eight militia companies, but it would take time for them to traverse the innumerable swamps, ramshackle bridges, and rudimentary roads between the Natchez District and the Tensaw frontier. With the paltry force then at hand, Brigadier General Thomas Flournoy, successor to the command of the Seventh Military District after Wilkinson's departure, expected Claiborne not only to protect the frontier from the Red Sticks but also to help defend Mobile against a British or Spanish attack, a threat that existed largely in Flournoy's imagination. Not that Flournoy possessed much of an imagination. Querulous and incompetent, the thirty-eight-year-old former Georgia attorney had been handed a brigadier general's commission in the U.S. Army by a bungling War Department despite no prior military experience. Although he and Claiborne were both brigadier generals, Flournoy commanded the district. His Regular commission also trumped Claiborne's volunteer rank. Flournoy would prove nearly as great an impediment to Claiborne's effective exercise of field command as the Red Sticks.[19]

The infamous packet from Canada that Little Warrior had allegedly been carrying when killed also concerned Claiborne. He questioned neither the Red Stick representation of its contents nor word that the Spaniards had liberally furnished them with arms and ammunition.[20]

At least Claiborne would have to fight only dissident Creeks. The Choctaws, who could have tipped the balance decisively in the Red Sticks' favor, wanted nothing to do with them. While Peter McQueen undertook his turbulent trip to Pensacola, other Red Stick emissaries traveled to the Choctaw nation, urging them to forget their old rivalry and together make war on the whites. For two days, the Red Sticks vainly sought to breach the Creek tradition "to never shed the blood of white men in war." Even the frenetic Dance of the Lakes, which so inspired the Red Sticks, lured to their banner only thirty or forty of what the Choctaw chief Moshulitubbee—who had played host to Tecumseh two years earlier—dismissed as "restless and misguided" young Choctaw warriors. It was a body blow to Red Stick prospects in a conflict that had yet to begin in earnest.[21]

A week elapsed between the time Judge Toulmin first became aware of Peter McQueen's mission to Pensacola and the welcome arrival of General Claiborne's depleted Mississippi Territory Volunteers at Fort Stoddert on July 30. The intervening days had been interminable. Tensaw whites and métis shared in the "confusion and distress." Ethnic differences vanished in the face of the common danger. Together they erected stockades and huddled in tents within the pine walls, enduring long nights fraught with fear of sudden war whoops resounding in the forests, or of red war clubs shattering the skulls of the sleeping.[22]

Tensions ran especially high at Fort Madison, a settlers' stockade raised on a ridge of scrub pine six miles west of the Alabama River and some eighty miles northeast of Mobile. Cluttered and claustrophobic, it was typical of the improvised Tensaw forts. Métis and white frontiersmen together had dug a trench three feet deep, into which they drove pine logs fifteen feet high to form a perimeter. The men cut portholes eight feet apart and eight feet from the ground and built tall benches from which to fire. They erected crude blockhouses at the northeast and southwest corners. At all four inside corners, the men raised high scaffolds covered with earth. Every night, they lit pitch-pine fires that cast a quivering glow over the surrounding forest. Pickets walked nervous beats close to the walls. Inside the one-acre compound, at least three hundred civilians cowered in tents or crude wooden shelters, deplored the rudimentary sanitation, and prayed for dawn.

Two hundred and twenty-five yards to the south, the similar but slightly smaller Fort Glass went up. It sheltered another two hundred frightened frontiersmen until occupied by a welcome detachment of soldiers. Shortly thereafter, all five hundred area residents crammed into Fort Madison. A neighboring gristmill, cotton gin, and numerous prosperous plantations made Forts Madison and Glass important bastions. Fortunately for the defenders, their numbers included the clear-headed and tough Sam Dale, who had been on the verge of returning to Georgia when the citizens begged him to assume command of Fort Glass. "Well," he replied after considering the offer. "My life is no more valuable than anybody else's, so I will stay with you." After the troops occupied Fort Glass, Dale became de facto co-commander of Fort Madison. With his decision to remain, Dale had taken his first step toward becoming an Alabama legend.[23]

The Creek War, the cataclysmic conflict between the Red Sticks and the United States that would reshape the American South, commenced north of Fort Madison on July 25, 1813, with a minor chance encounter. A party of armed civilians hunting stray cattle caught three Red Stick warriors unawares and disarmed them. Two of the whites, James Smith and Mark Hayes, guarded the Red Sticks while the others searched for the cattle. Carelessly stacking their weapons against a tree, the settlers trudged into the timber, leaving Smith and Hayes alone with the Indians. The captives cast hard glances at the muskets and whispered to one another in Muscogee. Suddenly they sprang toward the tree. Hayes shot one dead. Smith seized a light shotgun and a warrior simultaneously. Holding the shotgun waist-high with his free hand, he fired its load into the back of the third warrior. Then, dropping the shotgun, he drew his knife and stabbed through the heart the man in his grasp. The work of two or three seconds, Hayes and Smith's exploits were hailed by their comrades as a "remarkable achievement." Three dead Red Sticks meant little in the larger scheme of things, however. The pitch-pine fires still burned at the four corners of Fort Madison during the long, hot Tensaw nights, and pickets scanned the forest for Indians.[24]

They came up the trail from the south one bright and sunny late-July morning. Making no effort to conceal themselves, two hundred unarmed warriors and seven chiefs approached slowly in triple file, dressed in hunting shirts, blue loincloths, fringed leggings, and buckskin moccasins. Rings of red paint encircled their eyes. Beads and silver ornaments swung rhythmically on their chests. Six war leaders distinguished by headdresses of hawk plumes and eagle feathers and heavily beaded waistbands composed the first rank. Forty feet in front of the war leaders strode a broad-shouldered, full-chested figure five feet, ten inches tall. His mouth was large, his lips thick, and his cheekbones prominent. Not handsome by any means, he possessed, said a white onlooker, an "inexplicable attribute which belongs only to the truly great, that which forces the ejaculation, 'Who is that?' from all observant strangers." His dress alone would call attention to the forty-three-year-old Indian. He wore a complete blue military uniform with epaulets, a ruffled shirt, a blush sash around his waist, high black boots, and a black fur hat, to the right side of which was fastened a large, circular, silver ornament. Slightly behind him walked his interpreter and his manservant, both uniformly dressed in striped hunting shirts, blue loincloths, and black hats.

A crowd of expectant spectators thronged the front gate of Fort Madison. As the uniformed Indian drew closer, he recognized the militia captain Henry Rivière, an old friend. "My brother!" exclaimed Pushmataha. "Yes, indeed, my brother!" replied Rivière as the two men clasped hands. Turning toward his warriors, Pushmataha waved a hand. With military precision, they formed a crescent three lines deep facing the fort—the shortest men in the front rank, the tallest in the rear. He then commanded, "Sit down," and the warriors seated themselves cross-legged. After conversing for half an hour with Captain Rivière, Pushmataha stepped into the crescent of seated warriors and spoke. They had waited patiently because Pushmataha was the most revered of the three principal chiefs of the Choctaw nation. He had risen through the ranks by virtue of his prowess in battle against the hated Osages, who prowled the Choctaws' western border. In common with his countrymen, he took pride in never having shed white blood.

Pushmataha's eloquence, a quality that the Choctaws esteemed, was on full display now. He reminded his warriors that he had led them across the Tombigbee to reassure the Americans that the Choctaws wished to help them. "The white people were now on the eve of war with the Muscogees [Creeks]. From time immemorial the Choctaws and the Muscogees had been enemies, and they could never travel together on the same warpath," declaimed Pushmataha to his men.

Turning to the crowd, Pushmataha assured them that "if at any time they wished their services in the impending war, that every Choctaw warrior standing before them would rejoice to march to battle with them against the Muscogees." After the interpreter finished, the whites and Creek métis milled about Pushmataha with words of thanks. Addressing his crescent of warriors, Pushmataha announced, "Come, I am going," and began to walk back down the trail. The warriors followed single file. Watching them depart, the denizens of Forts Madison and Glass breathed easier knowing they had Indian allies in their darkest hour.[25]

CHAPTER NINE

Terror in the Tensaw

THE PROSPECT of killing Creeks thrilled Colonel James Caller.
Two years earlier, civil authorities had squelched his half-baked
scheme to slay Spaniards in Mobile. No one now, however,
objected to his expedition into the Creek country. Caller's political
rival Judge Toulmin even permitted his son to join the colonel and his
125 raw militiamen, and the army captain in command at Fort Stoddert
volunteered to serve under Caller. General Claiborne also endorsed
Caller's plan to intercept the Red Sticks returning from Pensacola and
seize the ammunition they carried before it could be employed against
the Tensaw settlements.[1]

Despite his dubious reputation, Caller's calculations were sound.
Before quitting Pensacola, Peter McQueen had spoken openly of his
plan to rendezvous with seven hundred fellow Red Sticks a hundred
miles east of Fort St. Stephens, distribute the Spanish ammunition,
and then strike the Tensaw. The Red Sticks traveled leisurely up the
Wolf Trail in at least two well-separated parties, with Jim Boy commanding the lead group and its powder-and-ball-laden packhorses.[2]

Caller's ragtag command cantered out of Fort St. Stephens on the
morning of July 25, 1813, looking more like frontier sportsmen than
fighters. No two men dressed alike. Caller's martial trappings included
a calico hunting shirt, civilian trousers, a tall, cylindrical military cap

called a shako, and riding boots. His men carried whatever weapons they owned, from squirrel rifles to shotguns. At Fort Glass, a small company under Sam Dale fell in with them. The next morning Caller's men crossed the broad Alabama River in canoes, their horses swimming alongside. Swinging south, they met Dixon Bailey and thirty métis and progressive Creek volunteers. Caller's augmented force of two hundred passed the night of July 26 at the junction of the Federal Road and the Wolf Trail near the pillaged home of James Cornells.[3]

Tuesday, July 27, 1813, dawned clear and hot. Caller started down the Wolf Trail. Abruptly his scouts returned at a gallop. They had spotted a "large body" of unsuspecting Red Sticks encamped no more than two or three miles down the trail. The Indians, reported the scouts, were cooking their breakfasts or relaxing beside a gushing spring on the far side of a steep ridge. Packhorses grazed unguarded. About six hundred yards south of the springs, obscured by a swampy, snarled canebrake, ran Burnt Corn Creek. Pine barrens composed the intervening ground.

At 11:00 a.m., Colonel Caller held an informal council of war. "Where shall we fight them?" Caller asked his officers. Opinions varied. Some wanted to prepare a dismounted ambush and await the Indians' approach. Others urged a rush over the ridge into the Indian camp. Offering a prudent alternative, Sam Dale volunteered to go ahead alone and "ascertain the force of the Indians and the proper position to fight them." His comrades rebuked him. "We can whip the damned redskins anywhere, and whip them to hell," crowed one officer. "[I] can go as near hell as any of you," Dale snarled. "You are on the road there and may go ahead and be damned."[4]

Forming his six companies into three columns, Caller ordered a charge. He might have intended the men to dismount on the near side of the ridge and attack down the far slope on foot. Most, however, "were still in the saddle and discharged their pieces before they dismounted, which was extremely injudicious," recalled a lieutenant. Their ragged volley struck only two people: a Creek woman cooking breakfast and a slave who fell while fleeing the Red Sticks, who retreated into the swamps bordering Burnt Corn Creek.

Colonel Caller had surprised Jim Boy and his eighty Koasati warriors. Just sixteen had muskets. The others carried only war clubs and scalping knives. Jim Boy later said that if Caller had pressed his

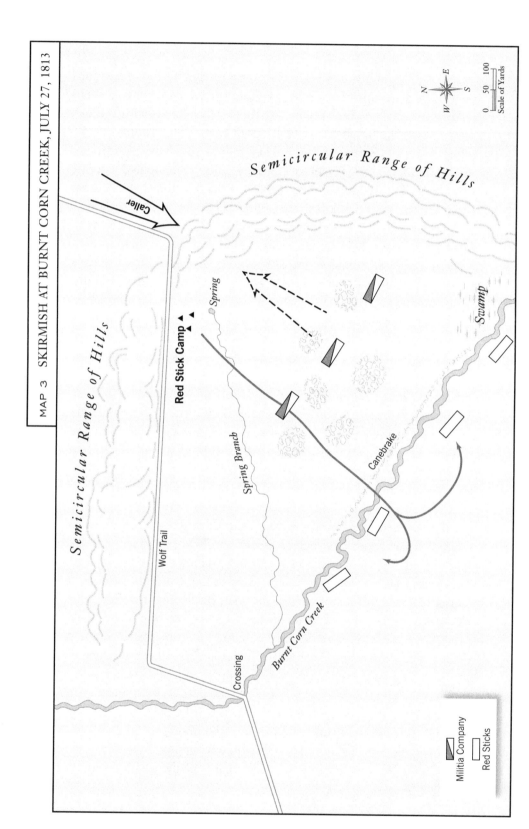

MAP 3   SKIRMISH AT BURNT CORN CREEK, JULY 27, 1813

Semicircular Range of Hills

Semicircular Range of Hills

Caller

Spring

Red Stick Camp

Wolf Trail

Spring Branch

Canebrake

Swamp

Burnt Corn Creek

Crossing

N
E
W
S

0   50   100
Scale of Yards

Militia Company

Red Sticks

advantage, the Koasatis would have lost heart and gone home. Caller's attack, however, unraveled quickly. Few of his men took the elementary precaution of securing their horses. At least twenty animals, Caller's mount included, galloped straight into the hands of the Red Sticks. Captains Bailey, Dale, and Benjamin Smoot pressed the assault with their companies, but most of the militiamen lingered in the rear, plundering the Indian camp and rummaging the Creek packhorses.

Hidden in the canebrake, the lightly armed Red Sticks hurriedly painted for battle while those with muskets kept up a sporadic fire that halted the three attacking companies in the pine barrens. For perhaps forty-five minutes the two sides traded fire. The militiamen got the worst of it. Two privates fell dead. A dozen men were wounded, including Sam Dale. "While reloading my piece, I received a ball in my left side, which ranged round the ribs and lodged against my backbone," he recalled. "I vomited a good deal of blood and felt easier, and one of my men reloaded my rifle for me." As Dale struggled to stand, Dixon Bailey begged Colonel Caller for permission to rush the Red Sticks. Caller, however, insisted on consolidating his command at the base of the ridge.

He failed. "Someone unfortunately, in a loud voice, sounded the word '*retreat*,' a word that can never be uttered among raw and undisciplined troops in the presence of an enemy without fatal consequences," recollected Dale. "A general panic ensued, and the militia—who had fought bravely and would have charged into the swamp had they been ordered so to do—hearing the fatal word, fled from the field."[5]

Raising a war whoop, the Red Sticks emerged from the canebrake on foot, but the mounted militiamen retreated faster than the Indians could pursue. Most went home, some with booty-laden Indian packhorses in train. About seventy militiamen regrouped long enough to cross the Alabama River together before they too scattered. No one had seen Colonel Caller, and few probably much cared what had befallen him. As it turned out, Caller had lost both his horse and his way. He wandered in the woods for fifteen days before a search party found him, starving and half-mad.[6]

Despite losing two warriors killed and five wounded, together with much of the powder and lead from Pensacola, Jim Boy and the Koasatis were elated. The easy victory at Burnt Corn Creek, wrote the métis George Stiggins, "gave them an exalted opinion of their own valor and prowess and a most contemptible opinion of the Americans who, they were confident, were touched by a cowardly spirit by the will of the Master of Breath, so that they would have less trouble in destroying them."[7]

Dixon Bailey kept his métis company intact after Burnt Corn Creek. He also exacted a bit of revenge for the defeat. Riding north into the Upper Creek heartland, Bailey ransacked the homesteads of several Red Stick leaders, including Peter McQueen, before returning to Fort Mims, a Tensaw settlers' stockade in which he had sheltered his family. The inhabitants greeted him as a hero. Bailey must have known, however, that Red Stick retribution would overtake him wherever he went.[8]

Despair gripped the Tensaw. "I think as soon as these Indians find themselves [ready], they will endeavor to revenge themselves on our frontier," the commanding officer at Fort St. Stephens advised General Claiborne. Judge Toulmin agreed, warning Governor Holmes that "the Indians no doubt regard us as old women, and the next conflict will be bloody."[9]

William Weatherford, the prominent Tensaw métis nephew of the late Alexander McGillivray who had rebuked Tecumseh at the Tuckabatchee council two years earlier, tried to keep clear of the Red Sticks. He hoped "their frenzied delusion ... would blow off like a tornado in a short time [and] that they would become more calm, sociable, and less devilish toward each other," recalled Stiggins. Early that summer, Weatherford and his brother-in-law Sam Moniac took a cattle-trading trip to the Mississippi Territory, after which Weatherford traveled to Pensacola. Returning to his talwa just before the fray at Burnt Corn Creek, he found his children gone; to compel his allegiance, the Red Sticks had absconded with them and all his movable property to the Autosee-Hoithlewaulee enclave. For the sake of his hostage family, Weatherford pretended to espouse the Red Stick cause. He hoped to lead his family to the Tensaw, but Burnt Corn Creek decided his fate. After the affair, his Tensaw friends assumed he had turned traitor. Reluctantly, Weatherford cast his lot with the Red Sticks.[10]

Josiah Francis, Peter McQueen, Paddy Walsh, Seekaboo, and Jim Boy welcomed Weatherford warily to their war council at Hoithlewaulee. Despite his rhetoric about razing the Tensaw settlements, McQueen had returned from Pensacola intending to use the newly procured powder and ball to attack Upper Creek collaborators and the Cowetas. The clans of those killed or wounded at Burnt Corn Creek, however, demanded retribution against the Tensaw militia—particularly against Dixon Bailey and his métis volunteers. Because they were known to have rejoined their families at Fort Mims, the stockade became the avengers' objective. Before formally agreeing, the council asked Weatherford, who knew many of the defenders intimately, if an attack on Fort Mims could succeed. Aware that their minds were already made up, Weatherford endorsed their designs.

Weatherford's unexpected agreement won him both the council's "unbounded confidence" and the command of the war party. Josiah Francis declined to accompany the expedition. He likely resented the role accorded Weatherford and also feared the attack would fail. In Francis's stead, the council elected the prophet Paddy Walsh to serve as the war party's spiritual leader.

Runners carried bundles containing twenty red-colored twigs to each of the thirteen participating talwas. One twig was to be broken each day; on the final "broken day" the constituent forces were to converge at a designated rendezvous. To conceal their movements, warriors from three talwas would demonstrate against Coweta. Well pleased with themselves, the Red Stick leaders at Hoithlewaulee snapped the first twig and awaited the day of reckoning with the Tensaw traitors and their American accomplices.[11]

Sixty-six-year-old Samuel Mims had accomplished much in life. One of the first white settlers in the Tensaw, he married well, and Mims and his wife, Hannah, now owned one of the largest plantations in the region, located on fine, fertile ground seventy-five yards east of the sinuous Tensaw Lake. In 1813, the elderly couple lived comfortably with Samuel's older brother David in a large two-story frame house that included a shingled roof and two verandas, as well as an adjacent kitchen and smokehouse. Close by were a blacksmith shop, loom house, hewed-timber springhouse, and two corn houses. Slave quarters stood well removed from the household, so too did the family's three stables.[12]

As rumors of a pending Red Stick incursion grew, the Mimses offered their property for a stockade to shelter white and métis neighbors and their slaves. After Burnt Corn Creek made Red Stick reprisals a near certainty, the flow of refugees to Fort Mims increased. By early August there were at least three hundred civilians and twenty militiamen crowded into tents, lean-tos, board shelters, and crude cabins within the one-and-a-quarter-acre stockade. A third of the inhabitants were white, a third métis, and a third black slaves. Fifty or more small children and dozens of dogs roamed the compound. No proper latrines existed, only outhouses over shallow holes. Mosquitoes and flies thrived in the dirty confines. Occupants regularly slipped beyond the gates of the "filth pen" to the cooling waters of Tensaw Lake or the Alabama River.

Although filthy, Fort Mims at least appeared formidable. If adequately manned, it would easily withstand attack because Indians had an almost preternatural dread of assaulting stockades. The fort's eleven-hundred-foot perimeter consisted of upright, split-pine posts, with leftover posts planted around the loom house. Gun portholes—loopholes in frontier parlance—were spaced at three- to four-foot intervals in the wall about three feet off the ground. A single unfinished blockhouse rose from the southwestern corner of the compound.[13]

From his headquarters at Mount Vernon, a cantonment fourteen miles southwest of Fort Mims on high ground above the low-lying, insalubrious Fort Stoddert, General Claiborne hastened to bolster Tensaw defenses. He received no help from his superior, General Thomas Flournoy. The feckless district commander, who had taken ill, remained fixated on the security of Mobile. In his fevered imaginings, the Creek uprising was a Spanish ploy to draw troops away from Mobile so that the Spaniards might retake it. Flournoy not only refused to detach for frontier duty a single Regular army soldier but also prohibited Claiborne from furnishing ammunition to anyone not mustered into service by the territorial governor. Neither could Claiborne issue a single musket without first obtaining Flournoy's consent. Not unreasonably, Claiborne had suggested a preemptive strike against the westernmost Red Stick talwas. Judge Toulmin endorsed the move. Flournoy, however, not only rejected the suggestion but also withheld reinforcements to prevent Claiborne from taking the offensive.[14]

Although he had few troops to spare, Claiborne did what he could to strengthen the settlers' stockades east of the Tombigbee. He detached the capable colonel Joseph Carson with 200 men to protect civilians north of the Cutoff and Major Daniel Beasley with 170 Mississippi volunteers and 30 militiamen to defend the Tensaw settlements.[15]

Claiborne had placed the fate of the Tensaw settlers in the hands of a melancholy wastrel. A thirty-year-old native North Carolinian, Daniel Beasley had come to the Natchez District with a law degree and high hopes for a bright future on the frontier. They were shattered abruptly one morning in 1811 or 1812 when he killed a man in a duel. Overwhelmed with remorse, Beasley sank into a profound depression. His favorite pastimes—drinking, whoring, and gambling—lost their allure. To friends, he confided his earnest desire to "engage in a lawful warfare in hopes that he might be killed in the service of his country and thereby terminate the misery of his earthly existence."

Perhaps Beasley's dashing appearance and eight-year stint as a county sheriff impressed Claiborne. Standing five feet ten, with dark eyes and hair, Beasley presented what a Tensaw militiaman conceded to be a "very fine-looking and determined countenance." In any event, when summoned to active duty at the outbreak of the War of 1812, Claiborne left the management of his plantation to Beasley. After one of his best officers resigned in February 1813, Claiborne offered Beasley a major's commission in the First Mississippi Territory Volunteers. Rejuvenated by the prospect of a heroic demise, Beasley accepted.[16]

On August 1, Beasley and his men tramped through Fort Mims's east gate. The major liked what he saw. "I have viewed the country around and have determined to continue at this place," he advised Claiborne. "We have had no hostile Indians about as yet, but it is believed by the inhabitants here that they will come." Apparently, Beasley did not share their apprehension. After permitting the twenty local militiamen to elect their own captain—they unanimously selected Dixon Bailey—Beasley and the garrison settled into a decidedly nonmilitary regime of card playing, gambling, and drinking.[17]

Claiborne might have felt something amiss because he visited the post less than a week after his protégé assumed command. The men had likely stashed the playing cards and liquor before his visit, but Claiborne found enough awry to trouble him. He admonished Beasley to finish the blockhouse, build at least two more, muster all able-bodied and willing adult-male civilians into the volunteer service, send out regular patrols, and above all not to underestimate the Red Sticks.[18]

Claiborne's words fell on deaf ears. Beasley extended the east wall and front gate fifty feet to accommodate the tents of the Mississippi Territory Volunteers, but he neither built additional blockhouses nor hurried completion of the existing one. As the days passed with no sign of Red Sticks, discipline eroded. The garrison left the front gate ajar day and night. Silt and sand filled the groove it dug in the earth. The strength of several men would be needed to shut the gate, should anyone deem that fundamental precaution prudent. Inhabitants came and went as they pleased, soldiers slept off hangovers in the stables outside the gates, housewives did laundry or bathed discreetly in Tensaw Lake, and couples fornicated in the canebrakes or on a tupelo-shaded island.

Major Beasley gambled away his days and drank well into the nights. "We are perfectly tranquil here and are progressing in our works as well as can be expected considering the want of tools," he assured Claiborne. By late August, detachments to other vulnerable stockades reduced Major Beasley's strength to a hundred territorial volunteers and forty-five militiamen. Late-arriving refugees raised the number of civilians packed into Fort Mims to nearly four hundred. Escaping the fetid interior of the fort was of greater concern to its denizens than the chance of a Red Stick assault. General Claiborne also grew complacent. Assuming Beasley had followed his instructions, he proclaimed Fort Mims "capable of repelling the six nations of Indians," a reference to the fierce Iroquois confederacy of bygone days.

Beasley said nothing to dispel the general's faith in the fort or in him, asking only for two dozen extra muskets to arm citizen volunteers. Beasley's indifference also infected his officers. On August 24, Lieutenant Spruce M. Osborne, the post surgeon, asked Claiborne for a transfer closer to the probable scene of action. Believing Fort Mims safe, the twenty-eight-year-old University of North Carolina graduate had only one fear: that after the conflict ended, he would be asked, "Where were you on such a day when the enemy were routed?" Six days later, Osborne would have his answer.[19]

. . .

In thirteen talwas across the Upper Creek country, the final red twigs snapped. Warriors assembled in the public squares, gyrated, shrieked, and twirled their war clubs to the discordant drumbeat of the Dance of the Lakes, and then were gone. On August 24, the day Lieutenant Osborne penned his request for a transfer, 750 Red Sticks rendezvoused fifty miles northeast of Fort Mims and held a great war dance. The next morning, with William Weatherford, Paddy Walsh, and Jim Boy in the lead, they rode or walked single file past abandoned Tensaw plantations, along a rough, forested trail that led directly to Fort Mims. Their step was unhurried; their fears of assaulting a stockade assuaged by the numinous assurances of their prophets. This was the season of the "Big Ripening Moon," the traditional time of the busk and of spiritual renewal—a propitious moment to purge the Tensaw with blood.[20]

William Weatherford was lost in a private hell. Having joined the Red Sticks under duress, he had little desire to shed blood, be it Creek, white, or métis. During a pause in the march to Fort Mims, Weatherford chanced to be in a cornfield with Dixon Moniac, the brother of Sam Moniac, and a few Red Stick warriors when a scouting party of whites led by Dixon Moniac's father approached. As the elder Moniac came into range, his son raised his musket to shoot him. Slapping it aside, Weatherford whispered sharply, "If your father is to be killed, let someone else do it." He ordered everyone to hold their fire, and the riders passed safely.

In attacking Fort Mims, Weatherford risked losing a woman dear to him. Twice a widower, Weatherford had fallen in love with Lucy Cornells, the famously beautiful métis daughter of James Cornells. After Peter McQueen's vandals burned their house, Cornells and his daughter had taken refuge in the fort. Now an irresistible force propelled Weatherford toward tragedy.

Weatherford tried to give Fort Mims's defenders a chance to prepare themselves. If they appeared alert, he might persuade the warriors to forgo an assault, notwithstanding their prophets' guarantees of victory. He not only did everything possible to slow the march but also permitted several captured slaves to escape in the hope they would warn the garrison.[21]

Warnings both genuine and spurious came apace to the frontier stockades, but not from the slaves on whom Weatherford relied. On August 21, a Choctaw warrior with a sterling reputation among white residents stumbled into Easley's Fort, an outpost eighty-five miles north of Mount Vernon on the border with the Choctaw nation. Visibly agitated, he swore that four hundred Red Sticks from the Black Warrior River talwas had appropriated a small Choctaw village nearby, intending to descend on Easley's Fort in four or five days. Should the whites doubt his word, the Choctaw told them that they "were at liberty to tie him and keep him, and if at the expiration of six days" no Red Sticks appeared, "he would agree to have his throat cut." A mail rider from the Chickasaw Agency brought corroborating evidence to General Claiborne and Judge Toulmin at Mount Vernon. Chief Pushmataha had told the man that a large Red Stick war party had assembled on the Black Warrior with a handful of Choctaw turncoats and were engaged in the Dance of the Lakes, after which they would seize Easley's Fort and then move against Colonel Carson's command at the confluence of the Tombigbee and Alabama Rivers. While scores of families poured into Mount Vernon from the northern settlements "much alarmed," General Claiborne set out with eighty men for Easley's, the "most exposed" fort in the district. Before Claiborne departed, a reliable resident of the Tensaw reported that upward of eight hundred warriors were en route to attack Fort Mims. Claiborne passed the intelligence on to Beasley. With Claiborne distracted by what proved a phantom menace, Beasley was on his own.[22]

And what of the guilt-ridden, hard-drinking major, who Claiborne thought would "give a good account" of himself? As William Weatherford hoped, Beasley did not lack for warnings of the Red Stick approach. The first came on August 14 when one of Sam Moniac's young slaves, out searching for a horse in a swamp beside the Alabama River, swore he saw Indians. Beasley dismissed the incident. A string of seemingly false alarms dulled Beasley's sense of impending danger as effectively as the liquor he guzzled. "Day after day, [scouts] that would be sent out would come in hastily and give information of approaching hordes of Indians," recalled a civilian occupant of Fort Mims. "Major Beasley would send off command after command in search of them. They would as often return with great disappointment and report to the major no Indians, nor signs. These [frequent] disappointments brought the major and his command into a state of false security. All got to believe that no Indians would approach."

At 5:00 p.m. on August 29, two young slaves sprinted through the open east gate, swearing they had counted twenty-four warriors lurking two miles distant. Beasley dispatched the twenty-nine-year-old captain Hatton C. Middleton and twenty men, with the slaves to guide them to the spot. At sundown, Middleton returned; he had seen no Indians or sign of Indians. Beasley exploded. Summoning the slaves' owners, John Randon and Josiah Fletcher, he demanded they whip the lying miscreants to end the rumormongering. The métis Randon acquiesced, but Fletcher, a longtime white Tensaw resident, refused. Enraged at the rebuff, Beasley ordered Fletcher and his family expelled from the fort. Mutual friends intervened. Beasley agreed to countermand his order, and Fletcher consented to the boy's punishment. At 11:00 a.m. the next day, he was to be tied to a post and publicly lashed one hundred times.

Night fell. Mosquitoes whirred and flies buzzed unseen in the dark, rank compound. Officers and men drank and caroused. Dogs yelped and snarled. Women and children settled in for another fitful night's sleep amid the noise and filth. The dim light of a new moon offered a murky outline of the open east gate. It stood invitingly ajar.[23]

The youthful slaves had spoken truthfully. Indians lay just beyond Fort Mims, far more than the two dozen that the boys had counted. On the afternoon of August 29, the entire Red Stick war party stopped six miles east of the fort to refresh themselves. As the warriors rested, two men from Captain Middleton's detachment rode into view on a trail three hundred yards distant. More interested in gossiping than scouting, they were unaware of the crouching throng that watched them. The warriors debated; some wanted to shoot them, but the majority, Weatherford included, argued that a negative report from the scouts would better serve their purposes.

After the two slothful scouts turned back, the Indians pressed forward to within three-quarters of a mile of Fort Mims. Halting for the night in tall timber, the warriors stripped to their breechcloths and painted themselves for the impending battle. After dark, Weatherford and two reliable warriors reconnoitered the fort. No sentries challenged them. They peeped through the loopholes but saw only a few glimmering campfires. The open east gate, however, convinced Weatherford that he had been right to spare the scouts.

Returning to the Red Stick bivouac, Weatherford assembled the principal war leaders to discuss the plan of attack. With Lucy Cornells's welfare likely on his mind, he counseled his subordinates to kill no women or children; they had come, he said, "to fight warriors and not squaws." War leaders growled their disapproval. Doubts about Weatherford's loyalty resurfaced. Dissenting war leaders accused him of having a "forked tongue and white breast," more interested in sparing not only Lucy but also his own relatives, of whom several had sought sanctuary in the fort. Was he truly a warrior? they wondered. After all, he neither painted himself nor stripped for battle in the Creek fashion; he would go into the fight dressed like a white man in a hunting shirt and trousers.

The prophet Paddy Walsh interrupted. He suggested the warriors rush the walls of Fort Mims, holding their fire until they possessed the loopholes. Walsh would magically render five warriors invulnerable to white men's weapons, after which the bulletproof Red Sticks would enter the fort and perform a war dance. Their safe return would be the omen for a general rush into the compound. Walsh promised the battle would claim at most three Red Stick lives. He also pledged to run around the fort three times at the onset of the assault in order to deaden the defenders' bullets. Not daring to question the powers of a prophet, Weatherford consented.[24]

Private Nehemiah Page of the First Mississippi Territory Volunteers awoke in his tent on Monday, August 30, 1813, with a hangover. First light washed the eastern slopes of the sky above the forest. The sparse stars melted away like snowflakes on stone. Army drummers beat reveille into Page's throbbing skull. The heat, humidity, and claustrophobic confines of Fort Mims compounded his pain. Everywhere he looked there were people—four hundred men, women, and children packed inside the one-and-a-quarter-acre stockade. Private Page had gotten drunk the night before to celebrate the completion of the fort's only blockhouse. It was not much of an achievement, because regulations, common sense, and Claiborne's orders called for one blockhouse at each corner of a fort, but it provided as good an excuse as any for the twenty-eight-year-old militiaman and his comrades to drink.

Page negotiated the teeming settlers, slaves, and scampering dogs on his way to roll call, then fell into a straggling line of 146 volunteers and local militiamen. Slapping at swarming mosquitoes, he declared himself present. Afterward Page staggered outside the open eastern gate and dropped down to sleep in one of Sam Mims's stables. Neither his companions nor his superior officers objected. There were no drills scheduled and no patrolling or regular sentry duties. Several of the militiamen still lacked muskets.

Other occupants of the fort slipped out that morning after Private Page. A group of women, some bearing infants, gathered on the bank of Tensaw Lake to bathe and do laundry. An adolescent métis couple swam past them, intent on making love on a shaded island. Zachariah McGirth, a forty-three-year-old former Tory who had married Alexander McGillivray's widow, left her and their six children in the fort and with two slaves took a boat to their farm three miles upriver to collect pumpkins and corn. John Randon's slave, carrying the painful welts raised by the flogging of the day before, exited the gate to tend to his master's cattle grazing a mile east of the fort. Instead of cattle, he nearly stumbled into a thicket replete with crouching Red Stick warriors. One whipping had been enough. Rather than return to Fort Mims and again face the lash for reporting what he had seen, the boy ran off.

As the sun climbed higher, the heat and humidity rose apace, inducing a languor that few in the fort were inclined to shake off. Certainly, Major Beasley did nothing to animate the garrison. Unlike Private Page, who merely nursed a morning hangover, Beasley was drunk. With a bottle by his side, he composed a rambling letter to General Claiborne complaining of the unreliability of the militia but bragging that he had "improved the fort and have it much stronger than when you were here." As for the rumored Red Sticks, the soldiers were "anxious to see them."

The morning dragged on. At 11:00 a.m., Beasley directed drums beat to summon the fort's tenants to witness the punishment of Fletcher's slave. Soldiers and families gathered about the whipping post. Someone struck up a fiddle. The unfortunate young slave embraced the post and awaited the lash strokes. Drummers lifted their drumsticks.

Pounding horse hooves interrupted the flogging. Drawing rein at the fort's east gate, James Cornells shouted to Major Beasley that he had just seen a dozen warriors in the woods, evidence enough that the long-expected attack on Fort Mims was at hand. Unknown to William Weatherford, his beloved Lucy Cornells and her father had taken refuge at Pierce's Mill, a small stockade nearby. James Cornells habitually left Pierce's Mill early each morning to check on his Alabama River ferry.

The fuddled Beasley waved Cornells off; he must have "only seen a gang of red cattle." To which the incredulous métis replied, "That gang of red cattle would give him a hell of a kick before night." Fuming, Beasley stammered an order for his immediate arrest. Cornells galloped away in disgust, the drums beat, and the lash cracked on the boy's bare back.

In a ravine east of Fort Mims, 730 Creek warriors rose in unison from a tangle of cypress and tupelo-gum trees and surged toward the fort. The rhythmic tramping awoke Private Page. Peering through a gap in the stable's hewn logs, he glimpsed a sobering sight—hundreds of men, painted black, red, or a mix of red and black, each stripped to his loincloth, from the back of which dangled a severed cow's tail. Some warriors carried muskets, others bows and arrows, but all brandished the distinctive curved red war clubs of the Red Sticks. Their moccasin-muffled footfalls growing firmer, they dashed past Page to cover the final hundred yards to the open east gate. Intently watching a card game, the lone sentry had his back to the attackers. The instant the last Indian passed the stable, Page sprang out toward the Alabama River. He never looked back.[25]

Thirty yards separated the sprinting warriors from the east gate before a startled sentry discharged his musket and darted into the tent-filled ground occupied by the Mississippi Territory Volunteers. Recumbent or seated, the unsuspecting volunteers struggled to their feet. Most of their muskets were unloaded; many were stacked carelessly about the yard. Sword in hand, a suddenly lucid Major Beasley shoved his way toward the gate. He threw his entire weight against it, but the gate would not budge. A Red Stick war club ended his effort, and he slumped to the ground, having achieved the heroic demise he desired.

A burly slave took his place and clubbed several Red Sticks with the butt end of a musket before others bludgeoned him to death. The Indians made short work of the territorial volunteers. Captain Middleton collapsed mortally wounded. Shot twice, Spruce M. Osborne was carried to a cabin by two volunteers. He asked the men to take him back outdoors so that he might watch the battle until he died. The remaining volunteers darted into cabins or sheltered themselves in the smokehouse, corn houses, or loom house.

In their wake came Paddy Walsh's five chosen men, who paused to perform the Dance of the Lakes. One of their number, a Shawnee, was feathered "from top to toe." Paddy Walsh had assured them that they were bulletproof, that musket balls would split in two when striking them. Walsh's magic had not touched Dixon Bailey's musket, however, and the métis captain put a bullet in the gyrating, feathered Shawnee. Three other dancers also dropped, shot or slashed to death by swords, before the last of them scampered back through the gate. After the war whoops of the dancers subsided, David Mims inexplicably wandered out of his brother's house to survey the scene. A musket ball struck him in the jugular vein. Crying, "Oh God, I am a dead man," the old settler flopped and twisted, the blood spurting "like the sticking of a hog."

Outside the fort, Paddy Walsh began his ceremonial run around the perimeter. His magic again failed, and he fell with a bullet wound. Undeterred, Walsh called on the nearest warriors to toss aside their muskets and bows and arrows and rush into the fort with only scalping knives and war clubs. None paid him any heed.[26]

A fatal flaw in the fort's defenses became evident to the Red Sticks: the walls had far more loopholes than defenders. Encircling the stockade, warriors fired through those not in use. William Weatherford, meanwhile, told warriors to shove fence rails against the protruding barrels of the defenders' muskets, which would stop up the loopholes they used.

With Beasley and Middleton dead, the only organized resistance inside Fort Mims came from Dixon Bailey's small company, which held a short stretch of the north wall. Bailey had had the foresight to place extra loaded muskets beside the loopholes assigned his men, and they poured a withering fire on Red Sticks in that sector.

For two hours the fighting raged. On the west side of Fort Mims,

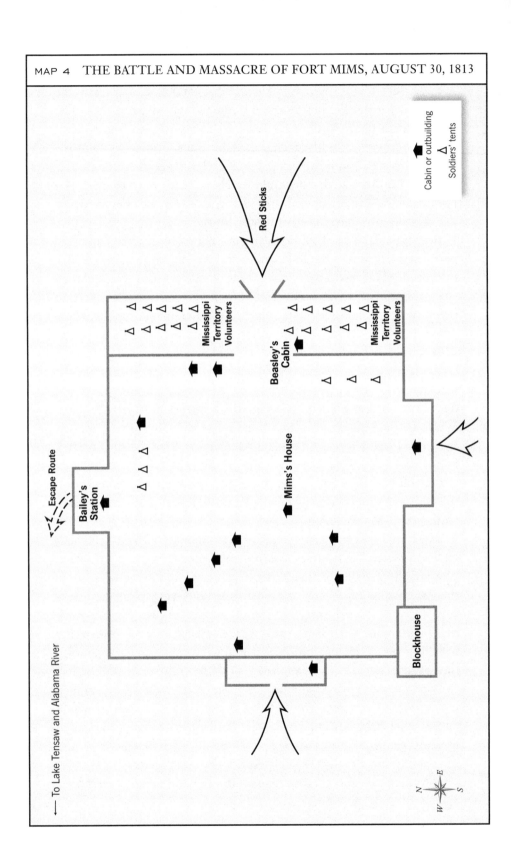

MAP 4   THE BATTLE AND MASSACRE OF FORT MIMS, AUGUST 30, 1813

Cabin or outbuilding

△
Soldiers' tents

Red Sticks

Mississippi Territory Volunteers

Beasley's Cabin

Mississippi Territory Volunteers

Mims's House

Escape Route

Bailey's Station

Blockhouse

To Lake Tensaw and Alabama River

N
E
W
S

warriors labored to cut a hole in the inner gate (Beasley, in yet another lapse, had left the outer gate agape). Other warriors scaled the blockhouse, which Beasley had neglected to man, and traded fire with militiamen who drove them off after an hour. Weatherford ran into the compound with a small contingent of Red Sticks shouting, "Dixon Bailey, today one or both of us must die."

War whoops, musket fire, the screams of frightened women and children, and the yelping of dogs blended in a terrifying cacophony. Gun smoke hung low and thick in the humid air. Although the Red Sticks owned most of the outer wall, too few warriors followed Weatherford into the fort to decide the struggle. At 3:00 p.m., the Red Sticks withdrew several hundred yards to tally their losses and decide their next move.[27]

Weatherford saw a chance to end the slaughter. He argued against renewing the assault because the defenders had been adequately humbled; the Red Sticks need not carry the place and suffer additional losses. Inwardly, he shrank from the indiscriminate massacre of women and children that would likely cap a complete Red Stick victory. Unable to dissuade the war leaders, who vowed to kill him should he persist in his disputatious ways, Weatherford mounted his horse and rode to his half brother David Tate's planation, twelve miles distant.[28]

The battle resumed with greater fury. Warriors cut a jagged hole in the split-pine posts along the southern wall. They shot flaming arrows through the gap toward the Mimses' kitchen and smokehouse. Both caught fire. A wind sprang up. Blowing embers set the Mimses' house ablaze. "Then it was," recalled the civilian surgeon Dr. Thomas G. Holmes, "that horror and dismay was to be seen in every face in the fort."

Beside a covered well near the blockhouse, eight unarmed Spanish deserters from Pensacola huddled in prayer. Nearly starved, they had taken refuge in Fort Mims the night before and were fed on orders from Dixon Bailey. Now the Red Sticks methodically clubbed them to death where they knelt.

Gasping and choking, the defenders of the Mimses' house, together with women and children who had sought shelter on the second floor, spilled into the open. Some dashed to a cabin on the north wall that Bailey defended. With boundless bloodlust, Red Sticks cut down others in their tracks. "The way that many of the unfortunate women were mangled and cut to pieces is shocking to humanity, for many of the women who were pregnant had their unborn infants cut from the womb and lay by their bleeding mothers," Dr. Holmes remembered. All the women, he continued, "were stripped of every article of clothing; not satisfied with this," the Red Sticks "scalped every solitary one, [taking] the skin of the whole head so as to make many scalps."

With the end near, Holmes loosened several weak posts in the wall behind the cabin Dixon Bailey defended. Dixon, his brothers James and Daniel Bailey, and the few other militiamen yet alive held off the Red Sticks until the refugees from the Mimses' house blocked their line of fire. Twenty-three-year-old Nancy Bailey, wife of James Bailey, acquitted herself admirably, reloading muskets and shotguns. Not so Private Samuel Mathews, who lay on the ground shivering with fear, the sweat "running from him as freely as though he had been deluged with water from a river." Nancy Bailey enjoined him to stand up and fight like a man. When he refused, she repeatedly pricked him with a bayonet; "all to no purpose," lamented Dr. Holmes, "for he lay like an ox."[29]

Cinders from the Mimses' house soon set Dixon Bailey's bastion ablaze. Smoke engulfed the defenders and clustered civilians. With further fighting useless, flight became the best hope for survival. Down went the posts that Holmes had loosened. The doctor passed through the gap with a slave woman named Hester. Pausing to look back, Hester glimpsed her master staggering about with both hands gripping his shattered jaw. Then a bullet ripped through Hester's arm. Dr. Holmes hurried her along until they became separated. Despite her wound, Hester swam both the Alabama and the Tombigbee Rivers to safety.

Bleeding profusely, Dixon Bailey also slipped through the breach just behind Holmes. Moments later, nearly 150 Red Sticks dashed around the northwest corner of the fort and started after the survivors, who ran toward the thickets and swamps adjoining Tensaw Lake. Bailey unloaded both barrels of his shotgun into the nearest pursuers. That was the last Dr. Holmes saw of him. Bailey's decomposing body was later found in a swamp, hunched against a cypress stump.

Daniel and James Bailey lay dead beside the burning cabin. Red

Sticks asked the métis Nancy Bailey to which family she belonged. Pointing to her husband's corpse, she declared herself the spouse of "that great man you have murdered there." The Red Sticks knocked her down, sliced open her belly, and scattered her entrails. Starting a bonfire, warriors tossed both the dead and the wounded into the flames.

There were occasional acts of kindness amid the carnage. When the Mimses' house went up in flames, the teenage métis Susan Hatterway, whose white husband lay dead, took a four-year-old métis girl in one hand and a black slave girl in the other and said to them, "Let's go out and be killed together." To Hatterway's amazement, no one molested them. On the contrary, one bloodstained, begrimed, and war-paint-covered warrior beckoned anxiously to her. She somehow recognized him as a family acquaintance. Claiming them as his prisoners, the compassionate Red Stick eventually took the three to Pensacola, where he turned them over to mutual friends.

Before bolting through the breach, Josiah Fletcher asked one of his slaves to look after his wife, unaware she was already dead. As Fletcher rushed out, several warriors shouted to one another to kill him. One of them, recognizing Fletcher as a longtime friend, kept the knowledge to himself but told his companions that he wanted the honor of killing the white man. They agreed, and off ran the warrior after Fletcher. In a thicket beyond sight of the fort, he overtook his friend. Apologizing for having frightened him, he told Fletcher to hide until dark and then run for all he was worth.

Left in the fort without her husband, Levitia "Vicey" McGirth awaited her end along with her four daughters. Vicey's young son lay dead, and all around her warriors busied themselves slaughtering women and children. When it came Vicey's turn, the blood-splattered warrior before her suddenly lowered his tomahawk. His scowl softened into an expression of "pity and gratitude." Gathering up her children, he claimed them and Vicey as his slaves and guided the family out of the fort. In anticipation of the Red Stick return march to Josiah Francis's Holy Ground sanctuary, he acquired horses for them. The thoughtful warrior was named Sanota. Several years earlier, he had appeared at the McGirth home, starving, homeless, and friendless. The McGirths raised him as an adopted son. He lived with the family until the seductive call of the Red Sticks lured him away.[30]

By 5:00 p.m. the Battle of Fort Mims—and the subsequent Red Stick massacre of noncombatants—was over. No one can say with certainty how many perished that day. The death toll among the fort's occupants was likely between 250 and 300, of whom half were white, a quarter métis, and a quarter black. The Red Sticks spared at least half of the slaves, to be placed in Creek bondage, sold, or adopted. Red Stick dead probably numbered at least 100, with estimates ranging from the prophet Josiah Francis's claim of just 30 to the métis George Stiggins's count of 202. Regardless of the precise total, the Red Sticks had been badly hurt, none more so than Paddy Walsh. Not only had he endured three bullet wounds, but his impotent magic also outraged the Red Sticks. That night, clan members whisked him away in a canoe. With Weatherford gone and Walsh at least temporarily discredited, the Red Stick war party quit the smoldering ruins of Fort Mims, made camp in the surrounding forest, and started for home at sunrise the next day. They plundered neighborhood plantations but made no attempt to attack the two hundred inhabitants of Pierce's Mill.[31]

When the rumble of rifle fire from Fort Mims first rolled through the forests to his plantation, Zachariah McGirth and his two slaves stowed their provisions and rowed back down Tensaw Lake. Running their boat into a canebrake beyond the stockade, they hid until the firing ceased. Billowing smoke coiled above the timber; the crackle of consuming flames replaced the shrieks, war whoops, and musketry. At twilight, McGirth approached the ruins. Dogs scampered about in stunned silence. Bodies lay heaped in piles, some still bleeding, others smoked with fire, all scalped and mutilated. In a vain hunt for Vicey and the children, McGirth and his slaves examined corpse after corpse. At nightfall McGirth rowed for Fort Stoddert with one burning desire: to avenge himself on the Red Sticks.

Dr. Holmes lay concealed in a thicket until certain the last Indian had gone to sleep, then set off through the pines. After walking a mile, he stumbled on the entire Red Stick camp. Halting within ten feet of the nearest slumbering warrior, he edged away, only to stagger again among sleeping Indians. Finally able to keep a straight line, Holmes walked several miles and then hid in a swamp, where he remained for four days without a morsel of food before a passing militia patrol carried the famished physician to Fort Stoddert.[32]

On the bluff above Fort Stoddert, the gunfire from Fort Mims had been plainly audible. Watching smoke rise on the horizon, Judge Toulmin held Major Beasley's buoyant morning letter in his hand. A week later, armed with the lurid tales of survivors, he wrote General Claiborne the obvious conclusion: "The massacre at Mims will long, I trust, prove a useful lesson to the people of this country. It will teach them in language of awful solemnity that courage without caution is of little avail."[33]

In sitting out the Fort Mims expedition, the prophet Josiah Francis had exercised an overabundance of caution. When he learned not only that it had succeeded but that his fellow prophet Paddy Walsh also had been wounded and consequently lost face, Francis scrambled to reassert himself as the leading Red Stick seer. He and the war leader Dog Warrior were roaming the Tensaw east of Fort Madison with their own war party of a hundred followers when Fort Mims fell. Concluding that Fort Madison was too strongly defended to attack (the garrison had already learned of the Fort Mims catastrophe from a breathless survivor), Francis and Dog Warrior swung north to examine the prospects for storming Fort Sinquefield, a half-acre stockade with a two-story blockhouse situated on wooded tableland. During their ten-mile march, the Red Sticks came upon an unexpected sight. Although aware of the danger, the families of Ransom Kimbell and Abner James had quit the stifling confines of Fort Sinquefield for the cooler and roomier Kimbell cabin a few miles from the post. Late at night on August 31, recalled a member of the household, "the dogs ran out furiously and barked violently, while the sounds of running human feet were so distinctly and alarmingly heard that Mrs. James, with admirable presence of mind, blew out the candle." Inexplicably, the families tarried at the Kimbell place.

At 3:00 p.m. on September 1, they paid for their negligence. Ransom Kimbell and Abner James were standing outside when the war party stormed the cabin. Leaving their families to perish, they made for Fort Sinquefield. It was over in a matter of minutes. Bursting into the cabin with war clubs in hand, Red Stick warriors crushed skulls and scalped the occupants, then vanished. Fourteen mangled bodies bore mute testimony to the butchery. A cool rain fell that night. The drops revived a badly wounded daughter of Abner James. Finding her one-year-old son still alive, she hobbled off toward Fort Sinquefield. A burial party discovered them the next morning, shivering in a hollow log.[34]

Sixty people occupied the rectangular palisade near Samuel Sinquefield's log cabin. Imprudence was apparently a Tensaw trait. Despite the risk of attack, the morning of September 2 found nearly everyone outside the stockade. An oxcart loaded with the Kimbell and James dead had creaked up the trail at dawn. The men hastily interred the corpses but lingered for a graveside service. Escorted by two or three guards, nearly two dozen women washed clothes at a spring on low ground 275 yards southwest of the main gate. The guards had stopped halfway downhill, seated themselves on a log, and drowsed.

As the mourners dispersed, someone called the grieving Ransom Kimbell's attention to an odd rustling in the forest, saying, "Look yonder, what a fine gang of turkeys." Josiah Francis had chosen excellent camouflage. The approaching gaggle were Creek warriors stooped low; their heads encircled with upright turkey feathers and cow's tails dangling from their shoulders. Unable to catch the burial detail, they whirled toward the women at the spring. A quick-thinking mounted volunteer gathered the fort's dog pack and with the sixty snarling canines charged the astonished warriors. The dogs grappled with the Red Sticks long enough for all the women to enter the stockade but one—who, pregnant and exhausted, fainted just short of the gate. An exultant warrior sank a tomahawk into her skull, ripped off her scalp, and slashed open her belly.

Thwarted in their initial sally, Francis's warriors sought cover behind the Sinquefield cabin and large pine trees seventy-five yards from the fort. When the first shot from the fort sputtered harmlessly, the Red Sticks shouted, "They are almost out of powder." A métis defender replied in Muscogee, "Come on and we will show you whether we are almost out of powder." From the upper story of the blockhouse a crack marksman boasted after killing a warrior, "That makes five redskins I have turned over today." Peering through the loophole for a new target, he toppled backward, blood spurting from a fatal neck wound. For two hours the firing continued until Francis and Dog Warrior withdrew, less nine warriors dead. They had killed only two enemy: the unfortunate pregnant woman and the proud marksman.[35]

The Red Sticks had had enough. Neither Josiah Francis nor Paddy

Walsh had been able to protect them. With seventeen of the twenty settler stockades standing unmolested, they withdrew. Lacking a coherent plan, the Red Sticks broke up into small foraging and raiding parties, more concerned with gathering foodstuffs than sustaining the war.

In truth, the Red Sticks had little with which to fight. "Our muskets now are totally rusty," Josiah Francis wrote to Governor Mateo González Manrique shortly after Fort Mims. "We are poor and in need of everything. The locks of our muskets are aging; we need new ones; also blankets to cover our nearly naked bodies; powder, balls, and knives. We hope that you will supply our necessities before the winter cold because we are resolved to defeat our enemies whenever the occasion presents itself." In exchange for Spanish largesse, Francis offered to retake Mobile for the Spaniards.

González Manrique wanted no part of Francis or his proffered help. Not only did the beleaguered governor have nothing to give the Red Sticks, but he also had only enough rations to feed the Pensacola garrison for another month. The civilian population was in equally dire straits. "I have fully instructed that this miserable town give no assistance to anyone," he wrote to the captain general in Havana in early October. "Perhaps because of my poor explanation you don't understand the truly critical and extreme situation in which I find myself." Rather than incur Francis's wrath by refusing him outright, González Manrique temporized, telling the prophet that he had not yet received an answer from Havana to Peter McQueen's original request.[36]

Other Red Sticks came begging. In early September, Alexander McGillivray's nephew the métis Alexander Durant, whose father had died defending Fort Mims, and Thomas Perryman pleaded with González Manrique for weapons and ammunition, presumably for both the hostile band of Lower Creeks and Hopoithle Micco's Upper Creek Red Sticks. Durant and Perryman possessed greater decorum than had Peter McQueen. Although they too brought a large war party to Pensacola, the two clearly saw that the Spaniards "can neither help themselves nor us." Visiting a British warship in Pensacola harbor, Durant and Perryman appealed to their "father" the king of England. An answer from London would be a long time forthcoming. For the foreseeable future, the Red Sticks were on their own.[37]

General Claiborne knew nothing of the Red Sticks' problems. Swept up in the prevailing panic after Fort Mims, he braced himself for the next massacre and searched for a scapegoat. Claiborne lacked the counsel of Judge Toulmin, who with most Mount Vernon residents and refugees had fled to Mobile. Others hastened west, but matters appeared little better in that direction. Panic gripped the Natchez District, and thousands of residents descended on the territorial capital of Washington amid rumors that Red Stick war parties had come within a day's ride. Beside Mount Vernon and Fort Stoddert, in the Tensaw region only Forts St. Stephens, Madison, and Glass were defended, the latter two because a recuperated Sam Dale and the garrisons disobeyed Claiborne's order to abandon the posts, around which nearly a thousand terrified settlers had gathered.[38]

Claiborne was as stampeded as the most credulous civilian. With only three hundred troops under his direct command, Claiborne saw little hope for resisting the three thousand Red Stick warriors he supposed lay ready to batter the Tensaw defenses. Without reinforcements, he advised Governor Holmes on September 4, "the whole country promises to be destroyed." Judge Toulmin also despaired. "I daily look for accounts of fresh attacks and further massacres, and I know no part of the country that will be safe," he wrote to Holmes. "Without immediate and effectual succor from Georgia and Tennessee, the whole country on the waters of the Mobile will be laid waste and abandoned."[39]

Apart from their proximity to the theater of war, Georgia and Tennessee loomed large strategically because General Flournoy continued to refuse Claiborne reinforcements. Fearful of the impotent Spaniards, he held his two Regular regiments at Mobile, expecting a reincarnated Hernando de Soto to try to raze the place. Judge Toulmin left a meeting with Flournoy dumbstruck. "I am truly alarmed and astonished as to the delusion which prevails with regard to this Indian war," he wrote to Claiborne a week after Fort Mims. "General Flournoy says to me, 'The Creeks are for war, but it is impossible that they commence it until their civil war is finished.'"

Who could have possibly put such an absurd notion in the general's head? Only Benjamin Hawkins could inspire such a belief, reasoned

Toulmin, to which only an imbecile of Flournoy's stamp could cling after Fort Mims offered "positive evidence" of Red Stick intentions. In a long and doleful letter to President James Madison, Toulmin accused both Flournoy and Hawkins of gross incompetence. Claiborne, however, was not at liberty to traduce his superior officer; consequently, he directed all his ire at Hawkins. To Flournoy, Claiborne simply observed, "Colonel Hawkins's communications for some time past have unfortunately had a tendency to lessen our apprehensions and to beget a belief of our almost perfect security." But to Toulmin, he thundered, "The wealth of the Indies would not compensate me or make me easy under a blunder such as Colonel Hawkins has imposed on our government and its officers."

Claiborne had his scapegoat. Now he must prepare for a second Red Stick offensive that even the normally well-informed Chief Pushmataha thought probable. Regaining something of his composure, on September 12 Claiborne assured Toulmin, "We are prepared for them, come where they may."[40]

The Red Stick menace notwithstanding, decency demanded the interment of the rotting corpses at Fort Mims. Reluctant to add to the death toll in a country he thought swarming with Red Sticks, Claiborne waited a week before sending a squad under the capable Captain Joseph P. Kennedy to "examine the fatal field" and then return posthaste. "Our little band marched in gloomy solitude to the fort," reported Kennedy. The sickly stench of death hung heavy in the timber. At the soldiers' approach, flocks of buzzards took to the air, and dogs slinked away from the partially consumed carcasses of the dead.

The place was an abattoir. Only the blockhouse, a few scorched pickets, and the east gate had escaped the flames. Hundreds of red cow-tail banners and discarded war clubs lay scattered about. Human bones littered the ashes of the Mims house. At the gate "lay Indians, Negros, men, women, and children in one promiscuous ruin." The decomposing remains of Major Beasley, presumably identified by his uniform, were crumpled behind the gate. Inside the stockade, Kennedy counted the bodies of forty-five men, women, and children in a single heap, stripped of their clothing and scalped. Red Stick warriors had shoved fence poles up women's vaginas or impaled their bodies on stakes. The decaying corpse of a young white woman thought to have been pregnant with twins lay with its stomach slashed and a putrid fetus on either side. Weakened by retching, Kennedy and his men wobbled back to their boat.

On September 22, Claiborne ordered Kennedy out again, this time with nearly three hundred men to bury the dead and, in case they were attacked, to "fight to the last extremity." Only the buzzards and dogs were on hand to greet the burial detail, however. Digging a long trench, the men consigned to the earth the remains of 247 dead whom they concluded from bits of clothing or their butchered state to be whites, blacks, or friendly métis. Those corpses thought to be Red Sticks they heaved in a pile and covered with rails and brush.

Zachariah McGirth accompanied the burial detail. Collecting the bodies of a woman and six children he assumed to be those of his family, he placed them gently in the trench. Afterward he volunteered for the most dangerous duty imaginable—service as a government courier between Claiborne's headquarters and distant Fort Hawkins, Georgia. Shaving his head and painting himself like a Red Stick warrior, he set out on the first of many long, lonely rides along the dark and dismal Federal Road, unaware that his wife and children were alive as the captives of a kindhearted Red Stick warrior.[41]

· PART THREE ·

CHAPTER TEN

The Emergence of Old Hickory

ZACHARIAH MCGIRTH was hardly alone in wanting to avenge the calamity at Fort Mims. Judge Harry Toulmin did his best to ensure that the entire nation shared the horror and outrage that gripped the people of the Tensaw. A week after the fort's destruction, he penned a long and graphic letter to a North Carolina editor that dwelled on the slaughter of white women and children. Reprinted throughout the United States in October 1813, it had the desired effect. Fort Mims became a national rallying cry for vengeance against the Red Sticks. Total war was to be the price they paid, retaliation as complete and unsparing as that meted out at Mabila two centuries earlier by Hernando de Soto.[1]

There was just one catch. The U.S. government had neither the troops nor the inclination to respond to an Indian conflict on the southern frontier promptly or adequately. The war with Great Britain, now in its second year, had evolved into an exhausting slugfest along the Canadian border in which neither side had gained a clear advantage, and to which both nations dedicated most of their available manpower. A British naval squadron prowled Chesapeake Bay and terrorized towns on the eastern shores of Maryland and Virginia but failed in its goal of diverting American forces from Canada. In the autumn of 1813, the Madison administration pinned its hopes on twin offensives, one under William Henry Harrison to retake Detroit and neutralize the British and Indian threat from Upper Canada (Ontario), the other to capture Montreal via the St. Lawrence River. As for General Flournoy, even widely credited rumors that eight thousand Red Sticks, armed at Pensacola, intended to attack Georgia and Tennessee failed to distract him from his fixation on New Orleans and the phantom Spanish threat. Only one force—the twenty-five hundred western Tennessee volunteers commanded by the fiery, forty-six-year-old militia major general Andrew Jackson—stood ready and eager to punish the perpetrators of the Fort Mims massacre. Indeed, Jackson and his political ally the Tennessee governor Willie Blount had requested War Department permission to stage a preemptive strike—in concert with the Georgia militia if possible—against the Red Sticks a full month before Fort Mims. Beset with worries over the northern campaigns and Chesapeake Bay, the secretary of war waved off Jackson, Blount, and the governor of Georgia with a vague admonition to do whatever they thought appropriate.[2]

Fighting came naturally to Andrew Jackson. His entire life had been a struggle punctuated by interludes of domestic tranquility in the company of his wife, Rachel, whom he deeply loved. Jackson was born into adversity in the South Carolina piedmont on March 15, 1767. His Scots-Irish father, for whom he was named, worked himself to death on his hardscrabble farm during his wife Elizabeth's pregnancy. The widowed Elizabeth Jackson moved with Andrew and his older brothers, Hugh and Robert, into the crowded home of her sister, where she assumed the role of housekeeper and nanny to her eight nieces and nephews. The Revolutionary War interrupted what for Andrew was a brawling, defiant boyhood born of a lack of parental supervision. At age thirteen, Andrew, as well as his brothers, was thrown into the ugly partisan warfare between Patriots and Tories that raged through the South. As "men hunted each other like beasts of prey, and the savages were outdone in cruelties to the living and indignities to the dead," Andrew Jackson witnessed unimaginable horrors. Captured in a raid that reduced his aunt's home to ashes, he suffered a blow from an English officer's sword that creased his skill and left in him an abiding hatred of all things British. He contracted smallpox in a British prison camp and would have died had his mother not secured his release.

No sooner had he recovered than his mother succumbed to cholera contracted while administering to other prisoners. Both of his brothers also died in a war that scarred Jackson for life.[3]

At age fifteen, the orphaned Andrew Jackson threw himself into the postwar turmoil of a tentative new nation. Fortified with enormous reserves of energy, self-reliance, and self-esteem, and possessed of a burning passion to succeed, an almost preternatural power of persuasion, and unimpeachable integrity, the adolescent Jackson clawed his way upward. He read law, obtained his license to practice in North Carolina, and in 1788 migrated west to become at age twenty the public prosecutor for the Mero District of North Carolina, as Middle Tennessee was then known. Jackson settled in Nashville, then a rough-and-tumble frontier town of a few hundred people lodged in houses, cabins, tents, and nondescript shelters on the bank of the Cumberland River. The Indian menace remained real. Upper Creek and Chickamauga war parties stalked the countryside. Six months after arriving, Jackson volunteered for an expedition to punish "savages" who had attacked the outskirts of Nashville. Although a mere private, he earned his comrades' praise as "bold, dashing, [and] fearless." It was the first of several such outings he would undertake during six years of intermittent clashes with Indian raiders.[4]

Jackson clearly had charisma, and part of his appeal derived from his appearance. Erect and thin—he stood six feet tall and seldom weighed more than 145 pounds—Jackson exuded rawboned toughness and strength. A shock of sandy hair offset blazing blue eyes of disarming intensity. They transfixed a female acquaintance. Jackson "was by no means good-looking," she recalled. "But his eyes were handsome. They were large, a kind of steel-blue, and when he talked to you, he always looked straight into your own eyes ... as much as to say, 'I have nothing to be ashamed of, and I hope you haven't.' This and the gentle manner he had made you forget the plainness of his features."[5]

Certainly, Rachel Donelson Robards, the daughter of a Nashville founder, saw beyond Jackson's plain features. A raven-haired, dark-eyed vivacious beauty, she won Jackson's heart handily, and the pair eloped to Spanish Natchez in 1791. Both were twenty-four years old. There was just one difficulty: unknown to either of them, Rachel was still married to her abusive husband, who had abandoned but not yet divorced her. For nearly three years Andrew and Rachel unwittingly cohabitated in Nashville as adulterers, and she also a bigamist until Rachel's wastrel husband finally divorced her.

No one in Tennessee society thought any less of Rachel. Thomas Hart Benton, who would later square off against Andrew Jackson in a raucous gunfight, swore that a "more exemplary woman in all the relations of life, wife, friend, neighbor, mistress of slaves, never lived, and never presented a more quiet, cheerful, and admirable management of her household. She had not education, but she had a heart, and a good one, and that was always leading her to do kind things in the kindest manner." Rachel might have borne feelings of guilt because she became an exceedingly pious evangelical. That did not prevent her and Jackson from enjoying themselves, however. Avid dancers, they made a curious pair, she "short and stout," he tall and rail thin. They longed to have children but were unable to conceive. Rachel suffered great distress during Andrew's absences, which, as his judicial and then political career matured, grew increasingly frequent. He too deplored their time apart. "I have this moment received your letter," read a typical missive to Rachel. "What sincere regret it gives me on the one hand to view your distress of mind, and what real pleasure it would afford me on the other to return to your arms, dispel those doubts that hover around you, and retire to some peaceful grove to spend our days in solitude and domestic quiet."[6]

Circumstance and ambition, however, fated Jackson to a life far from solitary or quiet. Shortly after arriving at Nashville, he won the patronage of William Blount, an insatiable land speculator who served first as governor of the Southwest Territory (as Tennessee was known from 1790 to 1796) and then as senator from the young state of Tennessee. While ascending the ladder of Tennessee politics, Jackson also speculated in land—amassing, losing, and then regaining a fortune. In 1791, Blount appointed him attorney general for the Mero District (Middle Tennessee). In 1796, Jackson became Tennessee's first member of the U.S. House of Representatives, and a year later entered the Senate. Young and brash, Jackson failed miserably in that august chamber. The president of the Senate, Thomas Jefferson, had little love for him. "His passions are terrible," Jefferson later wrote. "He could never speak on account of the rashness of his feelings. I have seen him attempt it repeatedly, and as often choke with rage. His passions are, no doubt, cooler now; he has been much tried since I knew him, but he is a dangerous man."[7]

Jackson resigned his seat after less than a year and withdrew to the more hospitable environs of Tennessee politics. In 1798 he won election to the state supreme court. He served until 1804, when he resigned to devote himself to his new plantation, the Hermitage, and to his duties as a major general in the Tennessee militia, a position to which he had been elected two years earlier.

On the frontier, the militia provided the principal defense against Indian incursions. Militia service also gave men a unique sense of belonging and fraternal companionship that not even the church could equal. The Uniform Militia Act of 1792 required all able-bodied men between the ages of eighteen and forty-five to enroll in the state militia and furnish their own arms and equipment. The act also permitted states to organize and train their militia as they saw fit. In time of war, Congress could federalize militiamen as volunteers with inducements of cash bonuses or land grants, as it would do during the War of 1812.

Some men treated militia duties as a lark or a chance to molest peaceable Indians. Not Jackson. After reprimanding a local militia commander for an "unwarrantable murder committed on an Indian in your country," he demanded the colonel break up a party his major had organized to hunt down Indian camps beyond the state border. "The militia are considered to be the bulwark of our national peace, prosperity, and happiness, and for an officer thus to violate the law and hazard the peace of our country is such an example to those of a lower grade that it must meet with . . . his immediate arrest and court martial."[8]

In his personal life, Jackson sometimes fell short of his rigid standards of discipline, once with fatal consequences that would pain him for life. A slight misunderstanding over the "merest wordplay" arising from his passion for horseracing brought him into conflict with Charles Dickinson, a well-connected young dandy who insulted both Jackson and his prize racehorse. Jackson challenged Dickinson to a duel. Dueling had lost favor in Nashville, so on May 30, 1806, Jackson and Dickinson repaired to Kentucky to settle their grievances. The duelists drew lots, and Dickinson won the privilege of shooting first. Raising his pistol, he fired. The ball slammed into Jackson's chest. A puff of dust rose from his coat vest. Jackson raised his left arm, covered his throbbing wound, clenched his teeth, and stood still.

"Great God," cried Dickinson. "Have I missed him?" Ordered back to his mark, Dickinson awaited Jackson's return shot. Slowly and deliberately, Jackson raised his pistol, took aim, and squeezed the trigger. The hammer halted at half cock. Jackson coolly drew back the hammer and fired again. The bullet struck Dickinson just below the ribs, and he bled to death on the spot. Only then did Jackson open his coat to reveal his own blood-soaked shirt. Dickinson's bullet had lodged so near Jackson's heart that the slug could not be removed. The wound healed improperly, and for many years to come, it would cause Jackson intense pain. Much to Jackson's surprise, the encounter also saddled him with a reputation as a violent and vengeful man. Nashville society shunned him.

Jackson nearly lost far more than the esteem of fellow Tennesseans. In 1805, the former vice president Aaron Burr, himself a pariah for having killed Alexander Hamilton in a duel, visited Jackson at the Hermitage with a bold scheme that thrilled his host. Like most Tennesseans, Jackson longed to rid the southeastern frontier of the Spanish presence, which would guarantee uninterrupted free passage of Tennessee goods down the Mississippi. When Burr revealed his intention to raise a force to eject the Spaniards, Jackson eagerly offered his support as a militia commander. Only later did Jackson learn Burr's true objective, which was not only to expel the Spaniards but also to wrest New Orleans from American control and create an empire of his own. Jackson scrambled to extricate himself from his role as an unwitting accomplice to treason. Burr's plans came to naught, and Jackson weathered the storm of Burr's subsequent trial. Both President Jefferson and his successor, James Madison, however, harbored doubts about Jackson's loyalty to the United States. Madison's misgivings were partly personal; Jackson had supported his political opponent James Monroe in the 1808 presidential election. Bruised but not beaten, Jackson withdrew to the Hermitage, tended to his planting and fluctuating prosperity, and looked hopefully to future glory as the nation slid toward war with Great Britain.[9]

. . .

Jackson came a step closer to realizing his desire to repay Great Britain for having orphaned him during the Revolutionary War when in February 1812 Congress called for fifty thousand volunteers for federal service to be raised from state militias. "Citizens!" he proclaimed from the Hermitage. "Your government has at last yielded to the impulse of the nation. Your impatience is no longer restrained. The hour of national vengeance is at hand. The eternal enemies of American prosperity are again to be taught to respect your arms!"[10]

Then came a new enemy. While Jackson anticipated a formal declaration of war, the Crawley-Manley massacre on the Duck River in May 1812 widened his wrath to include the Creek marauders, who, he reckoned, were tools of nefarious British agents. Assuring Governor Willie Blount (the half brother of William Blount) that he could muster twenty-five hundred willing militiamen at a moment's notice, Jackson pestered him repeatedly in June and July for permission to exact retribution. When Blount vacillated, Jackson presented him with an ultimatum that would have done Hernando de Soto proud. "I shall wait no longer than July 20 or 25," declared Jackson. "With such arms and supplies as I can obtain, I shall penetrate the Creek towns until the captive with her captors are delivered up and think myself justified in laying waste their villages, burning their houses, killing their warriors, and leading into captivity their wives and children until I do obtain a surrender of the captive and the captors."[11]

Word of Martha Crawley's release reached Nashville just days before Jackson intended to march against the Creeks. Although deprived of an immediate casus belli, Jackson retained his goal of conquering the Creek confederacy; he merely delayed the day of reckoning and—now that war with Great Britain had been declared—broadened his objective to include the seizure of West Florida. To his "patriotic volunteers," Jackson proclaimed,

> The War has now begun. Your Brothers in arms from the Northern States are passing into the country of your enemies [Canada]; and (I know your impatience) you burn with anxiety to learn in what theatre your arms will find employment. Then turn your eyes to the South! Behold in the province of West Florida, a territory whose rivers and harbors are indispensable to the prosperity of the Western, and still more so, to the eastern Division

of our state. Behold there likewise the asylum from which an insidious hand incites to rapine and bloodshed, and who will renew their outrages the moment an English force shall appear in the Bay of Pensacola. It is here that an employment adapted to your situation awaits your courage and your zeal; and while extending in this quarter the boundaries of our Republic to the Gulf of Mexico, you will experience a peculiar satisfaction in having conferred a signal benefit on that section of the Union to which you yourselves immediately belong.[12]

Jackson had divined British designs on the Gulf Coast. His Majesty's government looked longingly to the day when victory over Napoleon would permit Great Britain to widen the scope of the war against the United States. But while President Madison and the War Department trembled at the potential for a two-front war, Jackson reveled in the prospect that an American victory—which he took as a given—offered to open vast new lands to southern speculators and settlers. That meant dispossessing not only the Spaniards and Creeks but also all the southeastern tribes. He rhapsodized publicly on the golden future their discomfiture would offer his fellow Tennesseans. "Imagination looks forward to the moment when all the southern Indians shall be pushed across the Mississippi, when the delightful countries now occupied by them shall be covered with a numerous and industrious population; and when a city, the emporium of a vast commerce, shall be seen to flourish on the spot where some huts, inhabited by lawless savages, now mark the junction of the Alabama and Tombigbee rivers." A trail of Indian tears westward; a road to white abundance southward. The forty-five-year-old Tennessee militia general had articulated his life's ambition; he lacked only the authority to achieve it.[13]

For four fretful months, Jackson awaited orders to move anywhere action beckoned. In the autumn of 1812, Tecumseh blunted an American offensive into western Ontario, after which he cooperated with British troops to capture the invading army and with it the critical American outpost of Fort Detroit. All Ohio lay exposed to Indian depredations. Jackson accordingly shifted his gaze northward. "The unpleasant news of General [William] Hull's surrender to the British and their savage allies, received this day, may make aid in that quarter desirable," he wrote to Governor Blount on September 8. "It will give me pleasure, with your approbation, to march to the relief of that quarter without delay." Blount had no say in the matter, however; Jackson must await War Department instructions.[14]

At the end of October, they came. The Ohio front had stabilized. Jackson was to descend the Cumberland and Mississippi Rivers to reinforce Major General James Wilkinson at New Orleans against an expected British southern offensive. Jackson dutifully appointed December 10 the date for his militiamen to rendezvous at Nashville and muster into U.S. service as volunteers for a one-year term that was to expire on December 10, 1813—a date that would burn itself into the consciousness of his men. The volunteers must supply their own uniforms of brown or blue homespun coats, hunting shirts, pantaloons, and dark socks.[15]

When assembly day dawned bitterly cold, nature tendered Jackson his first command challenge. Snow lay deep on the ground, and the Cumberland River froze for only the second time in living memory. To Jackson's amazement, two thousand volunteers nevertheless filed into town. For want of shelter, they bivouacked in the snow, burning in one night the one thousand cords of wood Jackson had expected would suffice until they embarked. A sheltering tavern beckoned him, but Jackson instead passed the night tramping among his shivering soldiers, dragging drunken men within reach of campfires, and shaking slumbering, half-frozen sentries awake. At daybreak Jackson at last retired to the tavern to warm himself. Seeing him, a civilian who had spent a comfortable night in a warm bed remarked that it was a "shame" that men had to sleep outdoors while the officers enjoyed the best accommodations in town. "You damned infernal scoundrel, sowing disaffection among the troops! Why, the quartermaster and I have been up all night, making the men comfortable. Let me hear no more such talk," Jackson growled, glancing at the hearth, "or I'm damned if I don't run that red-hot andiron down your throat." The critic decamped.[16]

Bureaucratic ineptitude handed Jackson a second leadership challenge. He saw the flotilla carrying his fourteen hundred infantrymen (six hundred cavalrymen traveled overland) safely downriver to Natchez, Mississippi Territory, the scene of his illegal marriage to Rachel and now U.S. soil. There he received a dispatch that left him thunderstruck. Far from urging him forward to glory, General Wilkinson told Jackson to remain at Natchez because there were neither sufficient provisions nor quarters ready for his men at New Orleans; neither had the British appeared anywhere along the Gulf Coast. Jackson assented but chafed at inactivity. Perhaps his splendid volunteers, "the best young men" of western Tennessee, could be better employed in the North. "Shall the safety of the lower country admit, and the government so order, I would with pleasure march to the lines of Canada, and there offer my feeble aid to the army of our country and endeavor to wipe off the stain on our military character occasioned by the recent disasters," he wrote to Wilkinson. Two weeks passed with no answer. And then in mid-March came an order from the new secretary of war, John Armstrong, that wrung from Jackson both wonder and wrath. Dated five weeks earlier, it read,

War Department, February 6, 1813

Sir: The cause of embodying and marching to New Orleans the corps under your command having ceased to exist, you will, on the receipt of this letter, consider it dismissed from public service and take measures to have delivered over to Major General Wilkinson all the articles of public property which may have been put into its possession.

    You will accept for yourself and the corps the thanks of the President of the United States.

                                                    J. Armstrong

Thrusting the order at his friend, former aide, and now regimental commander Colonel Thomas Hart Benton, Jackson fumed, "Dismissed? Dismissed where? *Here?* Five hundred miles by land from home? Dismissed without pay, without means of transport, without provision for the sick?" Benton agreed that Jackson should disobey the order but cautioned the general against sending too "severe" a reply. Jackson, however, was not to be dissuaded. "If it was intended by this order that we should be dismissed [five] hundred miles from home, deprived of arms, tents, and supplies for the sick, of our arms and supplies for the well, it appears that these brave men, who certainly deserve a better fate and return from their government was intended by this order to be sacrificed ... to pass through the savage land where our women and children and defenseless citizens are daily murdered," he wrote with understandable hyperbole. Jackson intended to march to Nashville, where he expected the men to be paid, and then—and only then—dismiss them. Still in a rage, Jackson also penned an accusatory letter to President Madison, asking how in good conscience he could abandon the patriotic Tennesseans and "even strip our sick of every covering and surrender them to pestilence and famine." Requisitioning wagons, teams, provisions, and medicine on his own credit, Jackson led his volunteers up the old Natchez Trace.[17]

Jackson acquitted himself magnificently on the tortuous march home. Giving his three horses to sick soldiers, he trudged alongside his men day after day. His rapid and tireless pace on the narrow, wooded path won for him a lifelong sobriquet. First a Tennessean remarked that the general was "tough." Another soldier observed that he was "tough as hickory." The troops began calling him "Hickory." As their admiration mounted, they added the affectionate prefix "Old." Jackson liked the nickname. He also appreciated the warm reception accorded him on his return to Nashville in late April. "Long will their General live in the memory of the volunteers of West Tennessee for his benevolent, humane, and fatherly treatment to his soldiers," avowed *The Nashville Whig*. "If gratitude and love can reward him, General Jackson has them." Old Hickory also had a huge debt because the War Department refused to reimburse him the expenses incurred in bringing his men home. Thomas Hart Benton hurried to Washington, D.C., to try to right the injustice.[18]

One last military task remained to Jackson—that of releasing his volunteers from service, a seemingly routine exercise that would nearly prove his undoing. Before they disbanded, the enlisted men received from Old Hickory the following signed certificate:

I certify that ___ enrolled himself as a volunteer under the acts of Congress of February sixth and July sixth, 1812, and has served as such under my command, on a tour to the Natchez country, from the tenth [of] December, eighteen hundred and twelve, until the twentieth April, eighteen hundred and thirteen, and is hereby discharged.

ANDREW JACKSON, Maj. Gen.

Contemplating their discharge, two soldiers asked Jackson if it freed them from further service between then and December 10, 1813, the end of the one year for which they had enlisted. They "need not debate on that," Old Hickory assured them; the act under which they had volunteered was repealed and the discharge was "final."[19]

Jackson returned to Rachel's waiting arms at the Hermitage the "most beloved and esteemed of private citizens in western Tennessee." He had seen much hard marching but no fighting in a war that still raged. That he would serve again, if called, there could be no doubt. How his discharged volunteers might respond to a second summons, however, was anyone's guess.[20]

Andrew Jackson passed a gratifying spring at the Hermitage. He welcomed the public adulation, basked in the affection of his wife, and radiated the joy that came with fatherhood. He and Rachel had longed for children but had been unable to conceive. In 1809 her sister-in-law had had twins. Being of delicate health and already saddled with several children, she gave one of the twins to the Jacksons to raise as their own. They named the boy Andrew Jr.

His militiamen knew Old Hickory as tough, but he treated the toddler with a profound paternal tenderness unfathomable to those familiar only with his volatile public persona. Calling on the Jacksons one evening, Thomas Hart Benton found Andrew Jackson seated in a chair, a lamb and his namesake child on his lap. Handing the animal to a servant, Jackson stammered that Andrew Jr., weeping because the lamb was alone outside, had begged him to bring it indoors. The gesture moved Benton. "The ferocious man does not do that," he averred. "Though Jackson had his passions and his violence, they were for men and enemies—those who stood up against him—and not for women and children, or the weak and helpless; for all of whom his feelings were those of protection and support."[21]

Unless they were slaves. By 1813, a row of rickety huts on the Hermitage was home to at least twenty, on whom Jackson meted out punishment with whip and chains. When Rachel complained to him that her maid Betty had "put on some airs and been guilty of a great deal of impudence," Old Hickory publicly flogged her. Should she again misbehave—Betty apparently had washed the clothes of white neighbors without "the express permission of her mistress"—Jackson would give her fifty lashes, a brutal penalty that might well prove fatal. To runaway slaves, Jackson showed no mercy. Recovering four of his own, he felt "compelled to place two of them in irons for safekeeping until an opportunity offers to sell or exchange them."

Although they were slaveholders with large acreage, the Jacksons lived modestly, as dictated by their fluctuating finances, which might collapse should Colonel Benton fail to persuade the War Department to pay Old Hickory's Natchez-expedition debt. Their home was a square two-story, single-chimney, three-room log cabin—one room on the ground floor and two upstairs. A second and smaller cabin stood twenty feet from the main house. A covered walkway connected the two structures. Such was the Hermitage in 1813.[22]

Jackson's domestic tranquility ended abruptly. In June, William Carroll, a talented young militia captain who had impressed Jackson on the Natchez campaign but alienated other junior officers by his arrogance and "dandyism," asked his former commander to serve as his second in a duel with Jesse Benton, the hot-tempered brother of the very man in whose hands Jackson's fortunes then rested. A startled Jackson tried to decline because his age and station rendered acceptance "extremely injudicious." Carroll persisted, however, and after a futile attempt to persuade Benton to drop his challenge, Jackson assented. The June 14 duel was as ludicrous as the grounds for it were trivial. Both participants took bullets, Carroll in the thumb and Benton a grazing shot across the buttocks.

Thomas Hart Benton returned from Washington to find his younger brother the butt of jokes for the mortifying spot in which he had been hit. Thomas Hart Benton blamed Jackson for the affair, his outrage the greater because he had persuaded the War Department to assume Jackson's military debts. When Jackson learned that the elder Benton had publicly disparaged him as a dishonorable rogue, he "swore by the Eternal" that he would horsewhip him the first chance he got. All Nashville braced for a clash that most thought absurd.

The showdown occurred on the morning of September 4, 1813, five days after Fort Mims fell. Had the antagonists known that a courier was then pounding the road to Nashville with news of the massacre, they would likely have forgotten their petty grievances. As it was, Jackson went out of his way to provoke a needless confrontation. Learning that the Bentons were staying at the City Hotel in Nashville, he rode into town with his nephew Stockley Hays and his friend and fellow planter John Coffee on the pretext of picking up mail. The three took rooms at the nearby Nashville Inn. Sauntering along the sidewalk from the post office to their lodging, they approached the City Hotel, where Thomas Hart Benton lingered in the doorway, staring daggers at them. Jesse Benton hid inside. Both carried pistols.

"Do you see that fellow?" whispered Coffee.

"Oh yes," replied Jackson, "I have my eye on him."

As they came abreast of Thomas Hart Benton, Jackson whirled to face him, brandishing a whip. "Now, you damned rascal, I am going to punish you. Defend yourself."

Benton reached in his breast pocket. Jackson drew a pistol and backed him into the hallway. Emerging from the barroom, Jesse Benton raised his pistol, loaded with three balls, and fired. One ball shattered Jackson's left shoulder, severing the artery; another pierced Old Hickory's left upper arm and buried itself near the bone; the third barely missed him. Pitching forward, Jackson fell hard on the floor, blood spurting from his shoulder and oozing down his arm. Coffee and Hays joined the fray. Pistols were fired and daggers wielded, but when bystanders finally pulled the belligerents apart, only Jackson had been hurt badly. Carried to a room in the Nashville Inn, Jackson soaked two mattresses in blood before doctors stanched the bleeding. A young physician recommended amputation. "I'll keep my arm," countered Old Hickory. No one dared contradict him. Neither did the doctors attempt to extract the ball. They slapped a poultice of slippery elm on the wounds. For the next three weeks, Jackson lay prostrated from loss of blood. Hounded by Jackson adherents, the Bentons left town.[23]

Less than a week after Jackson's wounding, an express rider from the Mississippi Territory galloped into the Tennessee capital with news of the Fort Mims massacre. On September 18, senior Tennessee militia officers and Nashville civilian notables gathered in committee to fashion a response. No one doubted the propriety of war with the Red Sticks. "I hope to God," said a Tennessee senator, echoing the sentiments of his constituents, "that as the rascals have begun, we shall now have it in our power to pay them for the old and new." Tennesseans need look only to their own recent past, when Indian attacks were frequent and the state was neglected by the federal government, to empathize with the traumatized citizenry of the Tensaw. Because the War Department, far more concerned with fighting the British on the Chesapeake Bay than punishing hostile Indians on the nation's periphery, showed no inclination to move quickly against the Red Sticks, Tennesseans would fill the void. The local luminaries resolved to succor the threatened settlers, suggesting that a regiment of volunteer cavalry be marched into the hostile Creek country to "give immediate check to their ravages, exterminate their nation and abettors, and save thousands of the unoffending women and children on our frontier." Infantry regiments would follow as soon as they could be mustered, organized, and provisioned.[24]

It was a tall order for a single mounted regiment. Jackson, however, had absolute confidence in the ability of its commander, his close friend and confidant the forty-one-year-old colonel John Coffee, to blaze a trail to ultimate victory. "General Coffee is a consummate commander," Jackson would write. "He was born so. But he is so modest that he doesn't know it." Coffee looked soldierly too. "Never did I see so fine a figure," a contemporary wrote. "He is upwards of six feet in height, and proportionally made. His face is round and full and features handsome. His hair and eyes black, and a soft serenity diffuses his countenance. He is as mild as the dew drop, but deep in his soul you see very plain [a] deliberate, firm, cool and manly courage. He must be a host when he is roused."[25]

Its business concluded, the Nashville committee appointed Colonels Coffee and William Martin, who had served in the Natchez expedition, and Major General John Cocke, commander of the East Tennessee militia division, to present its proposals to Governor Blount and the convalescent Old Hickory, recumbent in his room at the Nashville Inn. At Jackson's side sat young John Reid, owner of a saltpeter concession in the Chickasaw nation. Already a devoted protégé of Jackson's, Reid had agreed to act as his aide-de-camp despite having an expectant wife at home. He doubted, however, that Old Hickory would be able to take the field anytime soon. "I left the general [the] day before yesterday, who appeared to be in good spirits, calculating on a speedy recovery and resolved at all hazards to go against the Creeks," Reid wrote to his mother on September 19. "But

I am apprehensive that his situation is much more dangerous than he supposed it to be." Jackson, his arm in a sling, suffered from excruciating pain that periodically clouded his thinking. He assured his visitors, however, that he would assume command "as soon as the freemen of Tennessee can be collected to march against the foe."

Although pleased that Old Hickory would overcome his "present temporary indisposition" and take the field, Colonel Martin wondered how he intended to recall the veterans of the Natchez expedition in view of his having discharged them. Jackson brushed Martin's concern aside. The secretary of war, Old Hickory said, had subsequently informed him that he lacked the authority to discharge volunteers; consequently, they were still on active service and would be until December 10, 1813. On Jackson's word and Governor Blount's assurance that the men would be paid for the entire year, Martin and his officers dispersed to assemble their veterans. Newly raised militia, which would constitute half of Jackson's infantry, were subject to just three months' service under the Militia Act. Jackson asked General Cocke, whose later date of rank subordinated him to Old Hickory, to arrange provisions for both Cocke's East Tennesseans and Jackson's westerners while in the field. Cocke passed the request to the contractor at Knoxville, who warned that he could only deliver supplies if the Tennessee River rose higher. His focus narrowed by the pain of his only partially healed fracture, Jackson neglected to fully consider the implications of enlistment terms or the vagaries of supply. In the months to come, both would torment Old Hickory as acutely as his mangled shoulder.[26]

The martial enthusiasm of the moment, however, overrode all other concerns. Governor Blount authorized the raising of five thousand volunteers (to include veterans of the Natchez expedition), evenly divided between Jackson's West Tennessee Division and Cocke's East Tennessee Division. The Tennessee legislature resolved to pay for the war with state funds if the federal government faltered in its obligations. In "an act to repel the invasion of the State of Tennessee by the Creek Indians, and to afford relief to the citizens of the Mississippi Territory," the legislature cast the impending contest as a matter of self-defense, a not entirely disingenuous posture given the many seemingly credible reports received in Nashville of Red Stick activity near the state's southern border. A local militia commander, for instance, reported that the larger part of the population of Huntsville, then a young but thriving town just north of the Tennessee River, was "flying to Tennessee for protection [from] the merciless savages."

Old Hickory ardently exploited the rumors, half-truths, and frontier fears to spur recruitment. A florid general order on September 28 proclaimed, albeit prematurely, his complete recovery:

> Brave Tennesseans! Your frontier is threatened with invasion by the savage foe! Already do they advance towards your frontier, with their scalping knives unsheathed, to butcher your wives, your children, and your helpless babes. Time is not to be lost. We must hasten to the frontier, or we will find it drenched in the blood of our fellow citizens.
>
> I am commanded by Gov. Blount to call into the field at the shortest delay possible two thousand men of my division.... The present crisis will try the patriotism of my division. Your country relies on it. Your general has the utmost confidence that the full number will appear at the day and place, well equipped and ready to meet the foe.
>
> The health of your general is restored. He will command in person.[27]

Governor Blount and Old Hickory were clear on the unprecedented opportunity that the present crisis presented. Victory over the Red Sticks would be but the prelude to dispossessing all Creeks of their lands, dislodging the Spanish from West Florida, and preventing the pernicious hand of Great Britain from grasping the Gulf Coast. "These objects once effected," rhapsodized Blount, "each southern and western inhabitant will cultivate his own garden of Eden, and will, through the natural channels placed by a wise and just Creator, ... export his own produce, and import such comforts as he may think desirable, by the shortest routes of communication with the ocean." Tennessee's "defensive" invasion of the Creek country was to be a war of conquest.[28]

Polly Crockett begged her husband, David, not to go to war. They had only just settled on their latest homestead—the peripatetic twenty-seven-year-old Tennessean frequently uprooted his family—and had two young boys to raise. David wrestled with his emotions. (The future American icon—the "king of the wild frontier"—never cared for the nickname "Davy.") Although a proficient bear hunter, he doubted his fitness for combat. "There had been no war among us for so long, that but few who were not too old to bear arms knew anything about the business," he recalled. "I, for one, had often thought about war and had often heard it described, and I did verily believe that I couldn't fight in that way at all." Then too there was Polly's plea to consider. "She said she was a stranger in the parts where we lived and that she and our little children would be left in a lonesome and unhappy situation if I went away." A sense of a larger loyalty won out, however. "It was mighty hard to go against such arguments as these," David Crockett ruminated, "but my countrymen had been murdered, and I knew that the next thing would be that the Indians would be scalping the women and children all about there if we didn't put a stop to it." Besides, the term of service was only three months, and the $65.99 in prospective pay hardly paltry. On September 24, he enlisted as a private in the Second Regiment of Mounted Riflemen of General Coffee's cavalry brigade.[29]

The twenty-year-old Richard K. Call had no qualms about enlisting. The well-heeled nephew of a Kentucky senator, he was studying in a private academy near another uncle's Tennessee plantation when Jackson issued his appeal for volunteers. Whether martial ardor or merely a wish to escape "present restraints" moved him, Call could not say. His enthusiasm proved contagious, however, and he persuaded nearly every student of military age to enlist with him. The kindly academy president entreated Call to reconsider. He "spoke of the importance of the present time to myself and my companions for scholastic improvement, if rejected now never regained." Although "in part deaf to his entreaties," he did talk most of his schoolmates into returning to their classes.

Call started for Nashville proud of his soldierly mien. He was, he later recalled, "a slender, beardless, grenadier-looking fellow, habited in a hunting shirt of some dark hue, relieved by a fringe of bright yellow, a leather belt around my waist, in which I carried a tomahawk and long hunting knife." Call also carried a journal in which to record his adventures.

Call's first glimpse of greatness came unexpectedly. Loitering with a gaggle of fellow volunteers at the junction of two dirt roads, one of which led to the Hermitage, Call spotted a carriage bouncing toward him, a rider some distance in the rear. As the carriage drew alongside, the driver asked that one of the volunteers speak to the ladies. Call stepped forward with alacrity, falling into a pleasant conversation with Rachel Jackson and her two nieces. While Mrs. Jackson inquired "with the kindness of manner so peculiarly her own" about Call's life and ambitions, General Jackson overtook the carriage. Rachel introduced the young volunteer to her husband. The torment unmistakable, Old Hickory bent down to shake Call's hand. "He was still suffering pain and looking pale and emasculated," remembered Call. "His graceful manly form, usually erect, was now bent with pain, while he still carried his arm in a sling. The expression of his countenance was grave and thoughtful, and his cheek pale. Yet there was something in the liniments of his face, a slumbering fire in his pale blue eyes that made me recognize the presence of a great man." Little could Call imagine then that he was destined to forge a long and loyal friendship with the commanding general or to become a future territorial governor of Florida.[30]

Jackson went to work with as much vigor as his wounds permitted. On September 25, he directed his two infantry brigades to rendezvous at Fayetteville, a village ninety miles south of Nashville, no later than October 4. On September 27, he directed Colonel Coffee to hurry to Huntsville with what men he had to allay the town's fears. Governor Blount and Jackson next asked John McKee, the widely esteemed former agent to the Choctaws, to take the pulse of the Choctaw nation and ensure their neutrality, if not active support. To Governor Holmes of the Mississippi Territory, Jackson lamented his debility. "The late fracture in my left arm will render me for a while less active than formerly," but "still I march, and before we return if the general government will only [keep] hands off, we will give peace."

Old Hickory overestimated his stamina. His thinking clouded frequently. On September 29, for instance, he repeated orders to Coffee for "fear my letter was not intelligible, hurried on all sides with start-ing my runners, to endeavor out of the mass of contradictory rumors and information through so many contradictory channels, to acquire some correct information—added to the pain of my arm—all com-bined to confuse my ideas."

By October 4, Coffee had collected nearly thirteen hundred mounted men at Huntsville. The infantry assembled at Fayetteville as ordered. Jackson, however, could not keep the pace he had set for himself. When the time came to start for Fayetteville, he needed help merely to mount his horse. His left arm hung in a sling. He could not wear the left sleeve of his coat; neither could he bear the weight of an epaulet. Bolts of pain so severe they caused him to lose conscious-ness sporadically shot through his shoulder. "It could not have been a pleasant thought," reflected an early biographer, "that he had squan-dered in a paltry, puerile, private contest, the strength he needed for the defense of his country."[31]

Before Old Hickory could hope to vanquish the Red Sticks, he must first master his own agony.

CHAPTER ELEVEN

Invasion of the Tennesseans

I N SEEKING to take the war to the Red Sticks on their home soil, Andrew Jackson confronted a strategic challenge as acute as his pain. His difficulty arose from the inability of a harried and unevenly led War Department to pay sufficient attention to the implications of the Red Stick outbreak. As mentioned earlier, the Madison administration declined to commit Regular troops to the contest and failed to coordinate the actions of the Mississippi Territory, Georgia, and Tennessee to combat it. Neither did the War Department immediately appoint an overall commander. Even if it had, the great distances involved between invading columns, the difficult and inadequately mapped terrain of the Creek country, and lack of reliable communications would all work against concerted action. With General Flournoy keeping a tight rein on Claiborne in the Mississippi Territory and the Georgia militia unprepared, it would be up to the convalescent but aggressive Jackson to invade the Red Stick domain first, and over the most difficult approach. There would, in essence, be at least three separate incursions with which the Red Sticks would have to contend, but at least they would not come simultaneously. Two would likely follow a predictable course. Troops from the Mississippi Territory and Georgia could march most of the way to the nearest Red Stick talwas or strongholds by way of the Federal Road. Jackson, on the other hand,

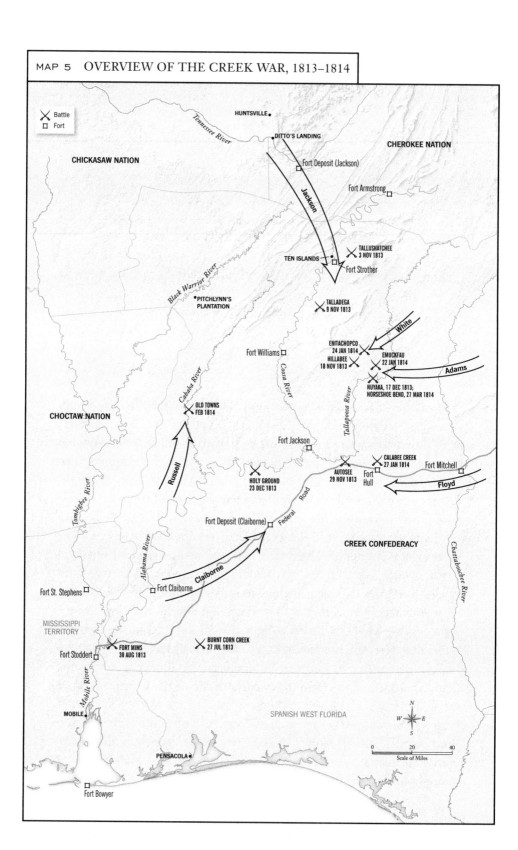

MAP 5 OVERVIEW OF THE CREEK WAR, 1813–1814

Battle
Fort

HUNTSVILLE

DITTO'S LANDING

CHEROKEE NATION

CHICKASAW NATION

Tennessee River

Fort Deposit (Jackson)

Fort Armstrong

Jackson

TALLUSHATCHEE
3 NOV 1813

TEN ISLANDS

Fort Strother

Black Warrior River

PITCHLYNN'S
PLANTATION

TALLADEGA
9 NOV 1813

White

ENITACHOPCO
24 JAN 1814
HILLABEE
18 NOV 1813

EMUCKFAU
22 JAN 1814

Fort Williams

Cahaba River

Coosa River

Adams

NUYAKA, 17 DEC 1813;
HORSESHOE BEND, 27 MAR 1814

CHOCTAW NATION

OLD TOWNS
FEB 1814

Tallapoosa River

Russell

Fort Jackson

CALABEE CREEK
27 JAN 1814
Fort Mitchell

AUTOSEE
29 NOV 1813

Fort
Hull

HOLY GROUND
23 DEC 1813

Floyd

Tombigbee River

Federal Road

Fort Deposit (Claiborne)

CREEK CONFEDERACY

Chattahoochee River

Claiborne

Alabama River

Fort St. Stephens

Fort Claiborne

MISSISSIPPI
TERRITORY

BURNT CORN CREEK
27 JUL 1813

Fort Stoddert

FORT MIMS
30 AUG 1813

SPANISH WEST FLORIDA

N
W   E
S

Mobile River

MOBILE

0   20   40
Scale of Miles

PENSACOLA

Fort Bowyer

would have to negotiate mountains, streams, and dense forest with only the occasional Indian path to ease the way.

Andrew Jackson's route of march into the upper reaches of the Creek confederacy would also pass through the western edge of the Cherokee nation. It was of incalculable advantage to Old Hickory, and of equal peril to Red Stick prospects, that the Cherokees opted to ally themselves with the Tennesseans.

The Cherokee decision would have come as no surprise to Tecumseh, who during his autumn 1811 peregrinations had found the Cherokee country a world turned upside down. Two decades earlier, he had fought with Cherokee militants (the Chickamaugas) against American encroachment. Cherokee politics and culture, however, had undergone a dramatic upheaval that doomed his mission. Slavery proved to be the most significant driver of cultural change. Among slaveholding Cherokees, Indian agents found the "desire for individual property very prevalent." A curious irony of their long years of war with white interlopers made the Chickamaugas the leading slaveholders in the Cherokee nation; they had amassed large numbers of slaves during their many raids on American settlements. Far from a majority of Chickamaugas owned slaves, but those who did constituted the political elite. They, together with Cherokee leaders who benefited from government bribes and control of annuity payments to tribesmen, consolidated authority over their people.

Opposition emerged to the land cessions and to the government chiefs, as it had north of the Ohio River, but Cherokee militants faced unique geographic constraints. The Indiana Territory was sparsely settled, and Tenskwatawa and Tecumseh always had the option, if necessary, of retiring northwest to regroup in the upper Great Lakes region, then largely free of whites. The 12,400 members of the Cherokee nation, however, were wedged between the populous states of Tennessee and Georgia. They had no place to go except far, far to the west, and permanently. Beginning in 1808, the government tried to persuade the Cherokees to do just that—to "remove" themselves west of the Mississippi River. The ill-conceived initiative had two consequences, both of which facilitated Cherokee unity. Some 1,000 of the most militant tribe members voluntarily emigrated, while the heretofore accommodationist Cherokee national leadership opposed forced removal. The government backed down, and the Cherokee chiefs' strong stand on behalf of tribal rights enabled them to defuse opposition to their rule. Rather than risk their tenuous hold on their homeland by siding with the Red Sticks, in September 1813 the Cherokee National Council officially placed its warriors at the president's disposal. As their energetic agent Return J. Meigs observed, "There appears an enthusiasm to turn out which I did not think proper to repress."

On October 7, Meigs mustered a Cherokee regiment into federal service for three months. At Andrew Jackson's insistence, the Cherokees received the same pay as white soldiers. Colonel Gideon Morgan, a thirty-nine-year-old Indian countryman married to a Cherokee, commanded the regiment. He was the only white officer. To distinguish themselves from the Red Sticks, the Cherokees wore white plumes in their hair. At least three hundred warriors answered the initial call, with more expected to enlist. For the moment, however, the Cherokees would be spectators. Fearful of leaving their nation exposed to Red Stick retaliation should Jackson falter, they first had to be assured that Old Hickory had the wherewithal to win.[1]

Private David Crockett was about to face his first test as a wartime leader. Colonel Coffee had kept Crockett and his seven hundred fellow mounted volunteers busy in camp near Huntsville drilling, caring for their mounts, and jerking beef, the latter a prosaic but crucial task because the civilian contractors whom Jackson and Coffee depended on had stumbled. "Flour is not to be had, and old corn is scarce," Coffee told Old Hickory, who had yet to advance with the infantry. "It might be well for you to stimulate them...for the movements of an army entirely depend on the exertions of the contractors."

While fretting over food, Coffee also ordered Major John H. Gibson to take "trustworthy" volunteers and scout across the Tennessee River for Red Sticks. Gibson selected Crockett because he was "good with the rifle" and also gave him the privilege of choosing a scouting companion. Crockett picked his young friend George Russell. When Gibson grumbled that Russell "hadn't beard enough; he wanted men, not boys," Crockett had a ready retort: "I didn't think that courage ought to be measured by the beard, for fear a goat would have the preference over a man." The major yielded. On October 3, he forded the broad and swift Tennessee River at Ditto's Landing with Crockett, Russell, and ten other mounted riflemen.

Plunging southeastward into the pine-barren wilderness on an Indian trail, Major Gibson made seven uneventful miles that day. The next morning, he divided the party in twain. Bearing no grudge over Crockett's earlier insolence, Gibson placed him in charge of a five-man detachment to reconnoiter a separate trail and rejoin the major at dusk fifteen miles farther on. Crockett reached the rendezvous on time, but the night passed with no sign of Gibson. The next morning, Crockett made his first command decision. He would scout on, with or without the major. After a twenty-mile ride his party paused at the cabin of a white man named Radcliff, living there with his Creek wife and their métis sons on the edge of the Creek country. The couple fed Crockett's detachment, but they were edgy. Radcliff had reluctantly entertained ten painted Red Stick warriors only an hour earlier; should they return, he told Crockett, "they would kill us and his family with us."

Dinner over, Crockett's men saddled up, all but two or three who, frightened by Radcliff's tale, suggested turning back. Determined to continue, Crockett used their dread against them. "I knew some of them would go with me, and that the rest were afraid to go back by themselves, and so we pushed on."

Crockett's mounted riflemen resumed their nocturnal odyssey, their destination a camp of friendly Creeks eight miles distant. A full moon in the clear night sky eerily illuminated the deep pine forest. Hooves pounded toward them from around a bend in the trail. Pulling rein, Crockett's men met two well-armed blacks mounted on Indian ponies. Former slaves, they had escaped their Red Stick captors and were trying to return to their white owner. The men were brothers, and both spoke Muscogee. Crockett sent one to Ditto's Landing, and the other accompanied him to the Creek camp.

Crockett found the friendly Creeks—forty men, women, and children huddled in the forest. They proved welcoming but skittish hosts. While Crockett and Russell amused themselves in bow-and-arrow target shooting by pine light with Creek boys, the former slave conferred with the warriors. They were worried, he told Crockett, that the Red Sticks would punish them for entertaining Tennesseans. Crockett allayed their fear with humor: "I directed him to tell them that I would watch, and if one would come that night, I would carry the skin of his head home to make a moccasin." His promise of vigilance notwithstanding, Crockett dozed. Abruptly a scream awakened him. Within minutes, the Creeks vanished. The former slave briefed Crockett on the source of the alarm. On approaching, a Creek runner from Talladega, the friendly talwa of the renowned micco Chinnabee, had emitted a shriek of warning. A large Red Stick war party, he announced, had been crossing the Coosa River all day at a place called *Oti Palin,* or Ten Islands, a chain of wooded islets stretching several miles along the Coosa some seventy-five miles south of Huntsville. Crockett hastened back to Colonel Coffee with the news. "We fed our horses, got a morsel to eat ourselves, and cut out" at dawn.

Crockett reached camp before noon, his hard riding for naught because Coffee rejected the report of a mere private. "I was so mad that I was burning inside like a tar kiln," fumed Crockett, "and I wonder that the smoke hadn't been pouring out of me."

The next morning, October 6, the errant Major Gibson reported in. He too had encountered runners from Talladega, whose warnings both corroborated and expanded on Crockett's intelligence. The Red Sticks, they said, had consolidated their forces at the Hickory Ground, a talwa about 170 miles south of Ditto's Landing. They intended to detach between eight hundred and a thousand warriors to attack the Georgia frontier, while the remainder, perhaps three thousand, advanced to "meet Jackson high up on the Coosa ... to save him the trouble of going all the way." A perplexed Coffee urged Jackson to hurry forward with the infantry. "I am at a loss," he confessed, "to know what position I had better take ... for the protection of the inhabitants here."[2]

Although Crockett was rightfully frustrated, he and Russell had acquitted themselves well on their first military foray, cementing a friendship that would endure until a pitiless March morning twenty-three years later in San Antonio de Béxar, Texas, at a crumbling ex-Spanish mission called the Alamo.

The friendly Creek informants either misread Red Stick intentions or deliberately misrepresented them in order to speed American retaliation. Their reports also implied greater Red Stick unity of purpose and of forces than existed. The want of documentary evidence makes Red Stick activity in the weeks following Fort Mims impossible to trace with any kind of precision. It is clear, however, that further offensives against the Americans were not a priority. Rather, Red Stick leaders—their men low on ammunition and lacking British or significant Spanish support—looked to defend their country from counterattacks and settle scores with Creeks who continued to defy them. They also had to contend with the food shortages that their wanton slaughter of livestock had created.

The Red Sticks were also more dispersed than Major Gibson's informants assumed. William Weatherford lingered in the Tensaw with enough warriors to keep General Claiborne off balance. The floundering Hopoithle Micco lurked within a day's march of Coweta, which the Red Sticks would need to destroy before ever contemplating a spoiling attack on the Georgia border. The nearest Red Sticks, whose crossing of the Coosa at Ten Islands so concerned Colonel Coffee, numbered fewer than two thousand warriors and were not after the Tennesseans. Peter McQueen, who had emerged as a principal Red Stick leader, had sent them to capture the talwa of Talladega, kill Chinnabee, and compel his men to help them defend the Red Stick northern border against Jackson. In short, the Red Stick strategy was to consolidate their hold on the Creek country; brace for attacks from the Mississippi Territory, Georgia, and Tennessee; and hope for British or Spanish aid.

They would get no help from Tecumseh. On October 5, 1813, he fell at the Battle of the Thames in Upper Canada (modern Ontario), an American victory that shattered the northern Indian confederation, which dwindled from nearly six thousand warriors to fewer than four hundred. Under the unsteady hand of a bewildered Tenskwatawa, the stalwarts melted into the Canadian wilderness to eke out a precarious existence on decidedly meager British largesse.[3]

Spurned by their fellow southeastern Indians and deprived of northern allies, the Red Sticks were on their own.

Andrew Jackson rode in agony. The Benton fight had shattered more than his shoulder. It ruined his health and aggravated his natural irritability. He had left his sickbed too soon, and severe diarrhea plagued him. When the spasms came and his bowels weakened, Jackson's staff would bend a half-severed sapling for the general to hunch over, arms drooping, until the symptoms subsided. The only medicine he took was weak gin and water. He grew gaunt, and his face took on a yellowish cast. Old Hickory struggled to control his temper. Pain permeated his every decision.[4]

Such was the commanding general's state when on October 11 he received Coffee's dispatch imploring him to hurry forward in expectation of a Red Stick onslaught. Disguising his debility well, Old Hickory animated the infantrymen "with his voice and his looks [until] their ardor became irresistible." Alternating between a fast walk and a jog, they covered the remaining thirty-two miles to Huntsville before nightfall.[5]

When it became apparent that the Red Sticks did not intend to attack, Jackson fashioned his plan to thrust deep into their country. As his admiring aide John Reid explained it, "We expect to be joined by an equal number soon from East Tennessee and then penetrate as far as the confluence of the Coosa and Tallapoosa, where a junction will be formed with us by the forces from Georgia. I say this is expected, though not by me. Unless we should meet with a very powerful resistance from the Creeks, I do not think the forces from either quarter will ever be able to overtake us."

Neither, it appeared, would provisions. Nashville and East Tennessee civilian contractors offered a litany of excuses for their inability to meet the army's needs. A despairing Jackson appealed widely for help. In a circular letter to General Flournoy, Governors Blount of Tennessee and Mitchell of Georgia, and the Choctaw agent John McKee, Old Hickory confessed, "There is an enemy whom I dread much more than I do the hostile Creeks... I mean the meager monster 'Famine.' Willingly I would endure the worst of all Earthly evils than see my army starving in the enemy's country." While supplies trickled in from Tennessee, Jackson consolidated his forces at a new stockade in the Cherokee nation named Fort Deposit.[6]

Jackson neglected no potential food source. To keep his men from starving and deprive the Red Sticks of sustenance, he would wage total war and, if possible, live off the country. In a measure intended both to gather food and to clear his right flank, Jackson ordered Colonel Coffee to eliminate hostile talwas along the Black Warrior River.

The burly Virginian set out on October 14 with his regiment of eight hundred mounted men, among them David Crockett. Two days later, on the east bank of the broad and placid Black Warrior, they entered an empty Creek village. The corn stood unharvested, but apart from a hundred bushels that the Tennesseans picked from the stalks, they found no food. Pushing on another eight miles, Coffee came upon a talwa on the site of present-day Tuscaloosa. It too was deserted. After plundering the corncribs and stripping the stalks, the Tennesseans burned fifty buildings and the council house. Loath to press farther upriver without a guide—for all Coffee knew, he might be riding into an ambush—and with no food left except parched Indian corn, after eight days the colonel returned to Fort Deposit.[7]

Old Hickory would not be there to greet Coffee. On October 22, Cherokee couriers brought Jackson news that prompted him to march posthaste against the Red Sticks. The Cherokee chief Path Killer had entertained two Red Stick emissaries at Turkey Town, the principal Cherokee settlement on the upper Coosa. Advising him that Red Sticks had indeed forded the Coosa at Ten Islands and intended to attack Chinnabee at Talladega, his Red Stick visitors suggested the Cherokee leader "be cautious how [he] acted." Badly outnumbered, Path Killer took the only sensible course open to him. "A peaceable policy has been pursued with them," he informed Jackson, "as my situation required me to do so."[8]

Jackson, however, felt more than a match for the Red Sticks, whose numbers he had revised downward to a thousand. Moreover, he had pledged to protect Chinnabee. "Do not grow dispirited, but if you should be attacked, hold out obstinately for a few days, when I will come to your relief," Jackson wrote to the old micco three days earlier. "If one hair of your head is hurt, or of any who are friendly to the white, or of your family, I will sacrifice a hundred lives to pay for it."

Trusting Coffee to catch up with him, on October 24 Jackson left Fort Deposit to keep his promise. Although his men had only six days' rations, Old Hickory clung to his plan to penetrate deep into the Red Stick heartland and, he assured Chinnabee, "teach all the bad spirits in your nation a lesson they have long stood in need of," even if he had to "live upon acorns." His aide John Reid predicted a less savory diet. "We shall be compelled, I expect, to eat our horses."

Before striking out for the Ten Islands, Jackson issued a proclamation articulating the tactics he would employ, his expectations of his troops, and the hazards that lay ahead:

> It is an enemy barbarous in the extreme that we have now to face. Their reliance will be upon the damage they are capable of doing you whilst you are asleep.... Our sentinels must never sleep, nor our soldiers be unprepared. Our soldiers must lie with their arms in their hands, and the moment an alarm is sounded they must move to their respective positions without noise and without confusion. They will thereby be enabled to hear the orders of their officers and to obey them with promptitude.
>
> Great reliance will also be placed by the enemy in the consternation they shall be able to spread through our own ranks by the horrid yells with which they commence their battle; but brave men will laugh at the subterfuge by which they hoped to alarm them. It is not by howling and screams that death is inflicted, and you will hail their howling approach by a substantial salute with the bayonet. What Indian ever stood the charge of a bayonet? The order for the charge of the bayonet will be the signal for victory!

Jackson also reorganized his army, separating the volunteers and militia into distinct brigades. The First and Second Regiments of Tennessee Infantry Volunteers formed the First Brigade, Brigadier General William Hall commanding. The First and Second militia regiments made up the Second Brigade under Brigadier General Isaac Roberts. Colonel Coffee caught up with the army at the end of October to find himself promoted to brigadier general in command of a mounted brigade twelve hundred men strong, which represented nearly half of Jackson's disposable force of twenty-five hundred troops.[9]

Jackson's command was an irregularly uniformed lot. Most soldiers wore cotton or coarse linen trousers, long-tailed civilian shirts, and "hunting shirts," which were thigh-length single- or double-layered jackets with shoulder capes attached to provide additional warmth. Some men donned animal-skin caps, but most preferred floppy civilian felt hats of varied design. The rank and file wore sturdy, high-topped farmer's work shoes; most officers sported fine boots. Canvas or leather leggings provided additional protection against brush and briars. Regulations called for uniforms to be dyed blue for infantry and black for riflemen, which faded rapidly to a dirty gray. Officers dressed in elaborate civilian-style coats with a single epaulet and braid. Cavalrymen boasted expensive high-topped riding boots.[10]

Jackson used his mounted arm aggressively. On October 26, the day after he crossed stunningly beautiful mountains, vibrant in their autumnal leafage, and entered the Creek country, Jackson dispatched two hundred horsemen under Lieutenant Colonel Robert Dyer to ransack the Creek settlement of Littafuchee, twenty miles west of their route of march. Cherokee scouts guided Dyer's detachment. Whether Jackson truly feared Littafuchee harbored Red Sticks or simply wanted to add to his meager food stores is unknown. The headman Bob Cataula certainly wanted no trouble with anyone. Having resisted the recruiting efforts of bullying Red Sticks, Cataula and his thirty-two followers—mostly women and children—settled in the game-scarce pine barrens to distance themselves from the impending war and tend their ninety head of cattle and hundred acres of corn. They lived in tranquil isolation until the chill morning of October 27, when Dyer's boisterous Tennesseans rousted them from their cabins. The blameless Creeks offered no resistance, believing, Cataula later said, "that they would be safer with the whites than with their own people."

Dyer treated them shabbily. The cattle ran off before he could commandeer them, but the colonel emptied the Creeks' corncribs, pillaged their homes, burned the place to the ground, then herded the inhabitants to the army camp. The whole affair appalled John Reid. When Dyer returned with his captives, Reid rose from his cot to commit his disgust to writing. "It is now about 3:30 a.m. and they have just arrived, bringing with them about [thirty] prisoners, men, women, and children," he wrote to his wife. "I have never been more affected in my life than I was by the cries of some of the children when they arrived at our fire. They had been traveling the whole night through an incessant rain and were exceedingly naked, cold, and hungry." His fellow officers ridiculed Reid's "supplications for mercy" toward the prisoners. "I am afraid I was not born for a warrior," he confessed. "I cannot bear to see any severity exercised even toward the men who are brought in and are wholly within our power. I was astonished to find such an immense majority against me upon this subject." Reid had signed on with a hard lot of men—how hard, he would soon discover.

That they took delight in tormenting Indians who were not even enemies did not bode well for the forthcoming campaign. Perhaps Jackson
felt a pang of remorse because he sent the captives on to the Nashville
jail for "safekeeping." The ladies of the town clothed and saw to the
comfort of the displaced Creeks, and the gentle Bob Cataula became
something of a local favorite.[11]

After disposing of his first prisoners, such as they were, Jackson
pressed on along a narrow Indian trail down the west bank of the
broad Coosa River. As they neared the Ten Islands on November 2, his
men beheld a breathtaking spectacle, the "wild and picturesque" falls
of the Coosa. "The Falls," marveled the young volunteer Richard Call,
"with its rushing waters, breaking in foam over the rocks, covered with
waterfowl rising and shrieking as they flew, and mingling their wild
notes with the loud murmuring water gave a grandeur to the scene."
Just below the thundering drop, Jackson's engineers marked the foundation of Fort Strother, which Old Hickory intended to make the base
for his proposed invasion of the Upper Creek heartland.[12]

    While perspiring infantrymen hauled and hewed timber for the
planned stockade, William Carroll's horse soldiers forded the Coosa
upstream on a mission to eradicate another Creek community. Their
target was no defenseless talofa like Littafuchee, but rather the Red
Stick talwa of Tallushatchee, which stood eight miles east of the Ten
Islands—dangerously close to Jackson's left flank. Why the approximately two hundred resident warriors of Tallushatchee and their
eighty family members did not withdraw on Jackson's approach and
consolidate forces with the Red Sticks targeting Talladega is something
of a mystery; they knew the Tennesseans had crossed the Creek border in strength. Perhaps their prophets had promised to render them
invincible. In any event, Tallushatchee rested silent and unsuspecting.

Dawn on November 3, 1813, broke clear and chill over the clearing
that cradled the clapboard cabins of Tallushatchee. As the darkness
melted, General Coffee and nine hundred troopers glided undetected
through the pine barrens. Two of Chinnabee's warriors guided them.
Eager for scalps and plunder, seventeen Cherokee scouts also accompanied the Tennesseans.

Three miles short of Tallushatchee, Coffee divided his command into two parallel columns—the left element composed of the cavalry, the right of the mounted riflemen. The cavalry was to deploy in an arc on one side of the talwa, the mounted riflemen on the other.

The Tennesseans resumed the march. At sunrise, they began to close the noose around Tallushatchee. Suddenly the "drums of the enemy began to beat," recalled Coffee, "mingled with their savage yells, preparing for action." Armed with muskets, bows and arrows, and quivers that each contained fifty arrows, the warriors spilled from their cabins. The war leader took his place in the center of a hollow square. He was ready to turn his attention to whichever side of the formation most needed him, confident that at least his scalp would emerge from the struggle in friendly hands because Creek warriors pledged to die rather than permit an enemy to carry off a dead war leader's scalp. If the war leader were badly wounded, the warrior nearest him would finish him off, remove his scalp, and retreat with a cry for the warriors to break ranks, rally around a ranking warrior, and resume the fight. Such in theory were Creek tactics. Executing them among the cabins, noncombatants, and as yet unseen ring of Tennesseans surrounding Tallushatchee would prove difficult at best.[13]

Colonel Coffee opened the fray. As the Red Sticks formed for battle, he hurled a company of mounted rangers toward them. The rangers galloped to within musket range, fired some scattered shots, and then lured the Red Sticks to pursue. The warriors yelled and ran after the rangers "like so many red devils," said David Crockett, who watched the opening scene from his place among the mounted riflemen. Catching sight of Crockett and his comrades, the massed Red Sticks veered toward them, unaware of the long line of cavalrymen in the timber on the opposite side of Tallushatchee. "We then gave them a fire," Crockett recalled, "and they returned it, and then ran back into their town." Coffee ordered the encircling files to advance dismounted. Pandemonium ensued. "The Indians soon saw they were our property," continued Crockett. Women and children darted from the cabins to surrender. Crockett saw seven women clutch at the hunting shirt of a stunned soldier. He also counted forty-six warriors who ran inside a single cabin for a last-ditch defense. As Crockett's company approached the place, a woman sat in the doorway prepared to resist. "She placed her feet against the bow she had in her hand, and then took the arrow, and, raising her feet, she drew with all her might and let it fly at us, and she killed a lieutenant," marveled Crockett, who had never before seen a man killed with bow and arrow. His enraged companions fired at least twenty musket balls into the woman. Her death elated the Tennesseans, and they showed the Red Sticks in the cabin no mercy. "We now shot them like dogs," Crockett confessed. Bullets easily penetrated the thin clapboard walls, shredding those inside with splinters, balls, and buckshot. To complete the carnage, Crockett's detachment set the cabin ablaze, burning the wounded inside to death. The gore made an indelible impression on Crockett. "I recollect seeing a boy who was shot down near the house. His arm and thigh was broken, and he was so near the burning house that the grease was stewing out of him. In this situation he was still trying to crawl along; but not a murmur escaped him, though he was only about twelve years old."[14]

The cold-blooded, systematic slaughter spread across the battlefield. General Coffee not only made no effort to halt it but also excused the brutality as a consequence of the purported ferocity of Red Stick resistance. Their resistance might or might not have been ferocious, but it certainly was ineffective. Outnumbered four to one and with no time to reload their muskets after their first shots, the warriors relied on bows and arrows, which in the blinding smoke they likely fired wildly. Coffee lost just five men killed and forty wounded, most of them slightly. Tallushatchee, on the other hand, was a smoldering ruin thick with the stench of death. Scarcely a warrior survived. Coffee initially counted 135 corpses on the field, a figure revised upward to 186 dead after the flames subsided. He took eighty women and children prisoners, leaving twenty wounded noncombatants behind when he abandoned the place that night.[15]

Old Hickory and John Coffee thrilled at the outcome of the lopsided Battle of Tallushatchee. "We have retaliated for the destruction of Fort Mims," Jackson boasted to Governor Blount. So pleased was Jackson at the brutality that he issued an order forbidding his men to give quarter to Red Stick warriors in future engagements—assuming the Red Sticks dared to stand and fight again. Dismissing Tallushatchee as "a small skirmish," Coffee assured his wife that the Red Sticks "will [never] meet us—they have no kind of chance—our men will drive them wherever they find them."[16]

Not everyone in the army shared Jackson and Coffee's conquistador-like exuberance. On the morning of November 4, a militia infantry battalion combed the wreckage of Tallushatchee. John Reid accompanied the unit and felt sorry he had. "I rode over the field of battle when all was still," he wrote to his wife. "It is impossible to conceive so horrid a spectacle. I long to see you and the children."[17]

Richard Call was a member of the battalion. The carnage sickened him. "I saw it in its worst aspect, when the horror of danger had passed, when I could excite no feeling of passion in my breast, to control my sympathy and sorrow for human suffering. Humanity might well have wept over the gory scene before us." Call did. "We found as many as eight or ten dead bodies in a single cabin, sometimes the dead mother clasped the dead child to her breast, and to add another appalling horror to the bloody catalog, some of the cabins had taken fire, and half-consumed human bodies were seen amidst the smoking ruins. In other instances, dogs had torn and feasted on the mangled bodies of their masters. Heartsick, I turned from the revolting scenes."[18]

Cherokee warriors from nearby Turkey Town did more than gawk or shed tears; they eased the anguish of survivors. After the white soldiers departed, they gathered twenty women and children who would otherwise have died, carried them home, dressed their wounds, and fed them—basic tenets of civilized warfare that evidently had not occurred to Coffee or Jackson.[19]

Hunger had hardened most of the Tennesseans as surely as did their hatred of the enemy. Reduced to half rations, soldiers grumbled over the lack of bread and scarcity of beef. General Coffee retrieved no provisions from Tallushatchee, preferring instead to set the corncribs and cornfields ablaze. A ravenous David Crockett and several of his companions took matters into their own hands. Combing the battlefield, they discovered a potato cellar under the wreckage of the very cabin that Crockett had watched claim the lives of forty-six warriors. They hauled out a large cache of unappetizing tubers. "Hunger compelled us to eat them," Crockett remembered, "though I had a little rather not, if I could have helped it, for the oil of the Indians we had burned up on the day before had run down on them, and [the potatoes] looked like they had been stewed with fat meat."[20]

Most men are capable of acts of compassion, at least on occasion. So too was Andrew Jackson. Before dispatching the Tallushatchee captives to Huntsville, he visited them in camp. A neglected and malnourished infant caught his eye. Concerned the baby might perish,

Jackson asked the Creek women to suckle him. "No," they snarled. "All his relations are dead. Kill him too." Images of his own tortured youth passed through his mind, and he had the infant Lyncoya brought to his tent. There, among his few remaining provisions, Jackson found some brown sugar. Mingled with water, it kept Lyncoya alive until the newborn could be sent to Huntsville, where he was nursed at Jackson's expense, and then taken to the Hermitage. "When I reflect that he as to his relations is so much like myself, I feel an unusual sympathy for him," Jackson wrote to Rachel by way of explaining the new addition to their family. "Charity and Christianity say he ought to be taken care of, and I send him to my little Andrew, and I hope [you] will adopt him as one of our family." Rachel consented, and Lyncoya became the Jacksons' second adopted son.[21]

While their commander administered brown sugar to the infant Lyncoya, his troops scrounged for whatever morsel of food they could find. Rations were all but gone. Contemplating the gaunt horses corralled beyond his tent, John Reid again had a nauseating premonition of consuming his mount. He attached no blame to Old Hickory. On the contrary, his esteem for Jackson, to whose unrelenting pain and disabling bouts of diarrhea Reid bore witness, only grew. "Never was a general sent out so poorly provided for by the government as General Jackson," Reid wrote to his father on November 6. "Were he anything less than he is, the whole expedition would speedily come to nothing. But he seems to derive additional animation from the difficulties he has to encounter. He is determined to push the enemy to the gates of Pensacola and to destroy that place if it furnishes them assistance. He will remain here for a week for the purpose of obtaining supplies to enable him to push on to his object."

Or so Reid and Jackson hoped. The very next evening, however, runners from Chinnabee brought word that a thousand Red Stick warriors drawn from nine talwas (perhaps co-commanded by an infamous Hillabee Creek métis known as Billy Scott and perhaps also by the head warrior of the talwa of Wewocau) had besieged Chinnabee's people. The 154 friendly Creeks crowded into a hilltop stockade belonging to a métis trader named Lashley that overlooked Talladega, some forty miles south of Fort Strother. They were low on food, water, and ammunition.

Jackson hesitated not a moment. "We shall set out in three hours to their relief," Reid scribbled hastily to his wife. "God knows when or where we shall make our next meal." Leaving the sick and wounded, the baggage, and a token guard at the as yet unfinished Fort Strother, Jackson started for Talladega at midnight with twelve hundred infantry and eight hundred cavalry and mounted riflemen.[22]

Old Hickory exuded as much confidence as his emaciated face and frame could project. Not only did he outnumber the Red Sticks, but he also expected reinforcements and provisions from East Tennessee. Brigadier General James White, commanding a brigade in John Cocke's division, had left his base at Turkey Town, assuring Jackson he would join him at the Ten Islands on the afternoon of November 7. The addition of White's brigade and the wagonloads of supplies that would presumably accompany him clinched matters for Jackson. "Not withstanding all privations and difficulties," Old Hickory wrote, he would "[break] down the Creek force and make them fully sensible that they have been indebted for their safety to our forbearance alone." Pensacola beckoned; Talladega was to be only the first encounter of an inexorable march through the heart of the Creek country. Although disappointed that White had not yet shown up, Jackson set out to bring a swift end to the war.[23]

Fortunate was the man in Jackson's army who had even a single day's ration. Neither the horrors of Tallushatchee nor hunger, however, prevented Richard Call from appreciating the splendor—and hazards—of the march beneath a moon that "shown brilliantly." For thirty miles, the trail stretched "rocky and uneven." Foaming water swept over the shoals where the army was to cross the Coosa. "Arriving here," remembered Call appreciatively, "each horseman took up a footman behind him, and sometime before day the whole army had passed over, and we resumed our march." Before them unfolded a series of high, thickly forested hills swathed in autumnal red and orange, alternating with deep, dark valleys. Wolves and all manner of game roamed the land, which was prime Creek hunting country. On the horizon rose Cheaha Mountain (the highest point in modern Alabama), named for a legendary chief. The sweet smell of pine and abundant creeks and cool springs made the trek as pleasant as hunger—or in Jackson's case, loose bowels and a throbbing shoulder—permitted.

MAP 6   THE BATTLE OF TALLADEGA, NOVEMBER 9, 1813

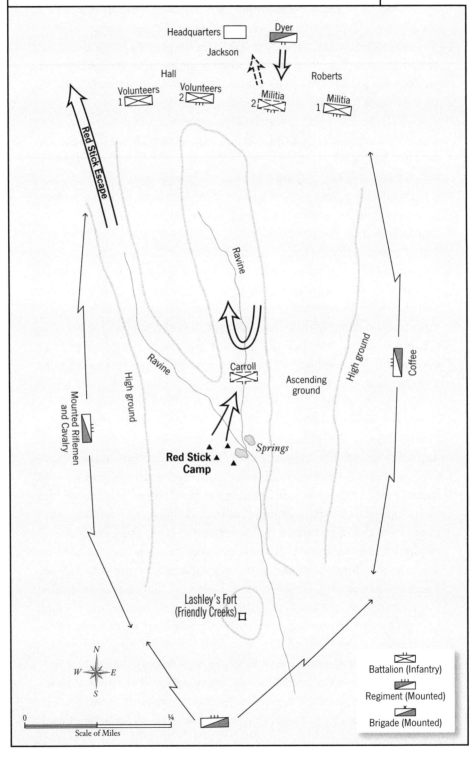

Headquarters

Dyer

Jackson

Hall

Roberts

Volunteers 1

Volunteers 2

Militia 2

Militia 1

Red Stick Escape

Ravine

Ravine

High ground

High ground

Coffee

Carroll

Ascending ground

Mounted Riflemen and Cavalry

Springs

Red Stick Camp

Lashley's Fort
(Friendly Creeks)

N
W   E
S

0   ¼
Scale of Miles

Battalion (Infantry)

Regiment (Mounted)

Brigade (Mounted)

November 7 and 8 passed uneventfully, with no sign of General White or his supply train. Optimistic nevertheless, Jackson made camp at midnight beside a sparkling creek six miles northwest of Talladega. Old Hickory dispatched scouts to reconnoiter the Red Stick position and, after his aide John Reid relieved him of his overcoat, which his limp left arm prevented him from removing himself, settled in for a few hours' sleep. To Jackson's surprise, Chinnabee appeared before his campfire. The old micco had left his people at Lashley's fort to meet White's column. As astonishing as was the micco's presence, it paled beside the dispatch he bore from General White. Rather than marching to protect Fort Strother, White had—on the "positive orders" of General Cocke—reversed course to rendezvous with his immediate superior, who was then erecting his own storage depot (Fort Armstrong) deep in the Cherokee country 240 miles northeast of the Ten Islands. A shocked Jackson read the worst into the missive. Unaware that Cocke too was chronically short of rations, or that—far from bringing with him bounteous foodstuffs—White commanded a near-mutinous brigade on the verge of starvation, Jackson wrongly suspected treachery born of East and West Tennessee rivalry at its worst. "I have no doubt," he wrote to Rachel, "but this order by General Cocke to General White was intended to cripple me and defeat my intended operations."[24]

Although deprived, as he saw it, of a chance to end the Creek War, Old Hickory nevertheless resolved to deal the Red Sticks at Talladega a fatal blow. At 3:00 a.m. on November 9, his scouts returned with a heartening report. The Red Sticks had not encircled Chinnabee's people. Rather, they were congregated around two springs in a shrub-choked valley a quarter mile short of Lashley's hilltop fort, content to let hunger, thirst, their prophets' incantations, and periodic exhortations win over the heretics. The scouts told Jackson he might approach the long valley from the north through open pine forests with little fear of detection.

At sunrise the army halted on the northern rim of the valley. A half mile distant, the Red Sticks lay encamped and apparently still asleep, with no sentinels posted—a chronic Creek tactical vulnerability. Jackson quietly arranged his troops in battle order. He told Coffee to deploy his mounted men on the high ground to the east and west of the valley, with flanks touching behind Lashley's fort. To

David Crockett's delight, Chinnabee's adherents streamed from the stockade, waving and crying, "How-dy-do, brother, how-dy-do?" The infantry, meanwhile, formed in column where it stood, Colonel Roberts's militia brigade on the left and Colonel Hall's volunteers on the right. Colonel Dyer, the despoiler of Littafuchee, retained 250 cavalrymen as a reserve. With the valley effectively encircled, Jackson began the battle with an old Indian tactic designed to draw the Red Sticks toward the infantry on the high ground. He sent Colonel William Carroll, to whom he indirectly owed his shattered shoulder, into the valley with three companies to roust the Red Sticks from their camp. From his place in the infantry line, Richard Call watched Carroll's party vanish down the slope. "Then came moments longer than hours, each filled with bounding hope and thrilling expectations, yet no sound is heard," recollected Call. "At length a volley fired by the gallant band bring us the foe, and there is heard a yell from that deep valley glen, as if legions of demons had broken loose upon the earth."

Carroll's men had waded through tall grass and shrubs to within eighty yards of the Red Stick camp before exchanging fire with the Red Sticks, who had likely been awakened by the thundering hooves on the ridges above them and the ballyhoo from Lashley's fort. The Tennesseans withdrew as planned, and the Red Sticks swarmed after them. Their prophet buoyed the warriors with assurances that the white soldiers' musket balls would "crush into dust and fall harmlessly at their feet."

Painted scarlet and stripped to their breechclouts, the pursuing warriors inspired precisely the sort of dread that General Jackson had hoped to prevent in his pre-campaign proclamation to the army. "The Creeks are far from wanting in bravery," John Reid acknowledged. "Indeed, from all I have seen I am of the opinion they possess a greater share of it than our men. I am sure no white men would have undertaken an attack as they did. And they are men too of far the most gigantic stature I have ever seen." Several overawed militia companies broke and ran. Jackson, who sat mounted eighty yards away, plugged the gap with Dyer's reserve.

On came the Red Sticks. Recalling his father's reluctance to shoot during his first battle in the Revolutionary War, the volunteer private Andrew Jackson Edmondson wondered if he would prove any more capable of killing a man. "Never will I forget my feelings when I raised my gun to fire. I had heard my father say [of] his first effort he could not get his gun to his shoulder for trembling—I drew mine up, and I thought took pretty fair aim." Edmondson squeezed the trigger simultaneously with his entire brigade. Smoke rolled down the ridge, and the Red Sticks reeled in confusion. "Neither their strength nor their valor can avail them without discipline," observed John Reid. "Fifty of their warriors might perhaps best fifty of ours, but they certainly know not how to make a proper disposition against large numbers of men." (They had never had to do so, Reid might have added.)

Repelled on one front, the Red Sticks rallied and charged Coffee's line. "They came rushing forward like a cloud of Egyptian locusts and screaming like all the young devils had been turned loose, with the old devil of all at their head," David Crockett wrote. "The warriors came yelling on, meeting us, and continued until they were within shot of us, when we fired and killed a considerable number of them." Crockett described the ensuing slaughter: "They broke like a gang of steers and ran across to our other line, where they were again fired on; and so we kept them running from one line to the other, constantly under a heavy fire."

After throwing themselves in vain at Jackson's lines for at least an hour, several hundred warriors slipped through a gap between Hall's brigade and Coffee's cavalry and made for the distant mountains. Richard Call's battalion pursued. The Red Sticks "were defeated, routed, and they fled, but it was not the flight of cowardly retreat; they fell fighting," averred the Tennessean as the cavalry rapidly outpaced him and his fellow infantrymen. After three miles Coffee's troopers halted the chase. Coffee and Jackson thought the damage done sufficient. "Wherever they ran, they left behind them traces of blood," gloated Old Hickory, "and it is believed that very few will return to their villages in as sound a condition as they left them."[25]

The battle ended before 9:00 a.m. Jackson lingered long enough to count 299 Indian dead. Perhaps another 200 Red Sticks died during the retreat. Jackson's tactic of deliberate fire delivered in close order— only the climactic bayonet charge was lacking—paid off. Old Hickory suffered just fifteen killed and eighty-five wounded, including one regimental commander shot in the shoulder and another through the bowels. He had inflicted a shattering but by no means war-ending defeat on the Red Sticks; they were too numerous and too decentral-

A BRUTAL RECKONING

ized to buckle under the twin blows of Tallushatchee and Talladega. Old Hickory understood that, but concern for his sick and wounded and hunger—his men, most of whom had been on half rations or less for at least two weeks, had no food left, and Coffee's horses had not eaten corn in two weeks—compelled him to withdraw.[26]

The army had "borne without murmuring" deprivation in the face of the enemy, but they expected a bountiful recompense at Fort Strother. Instead, reported a stunned Richard Call, "on our return to the Ten Islands, hungry, weary, and exhausted with hard fighting and marching, to find little or nothing to eat, when we fully expected to find abundance, murmurs of discontent were heard at every campfire, spreading like contagion until the whole camp became infected." A mortified Jackson discovered the stores at Fort Strother—to which he had contributed his own private rations for the sick—all but exhausted. His fury with the bungling civilian contractors responsible for the shortages was boundless, a sentiment his deputy quartermaster angrily echoed. "Provisions are in the greatest abundance at Fort Deposit. Why in the name of God have not the contractors packed them on horses to the army, if wagons and teams could not be procured?"

Jackson's army considered the laurels of victory a bitter substitute for beef and biscuits. Like ravening wolves, soldiers circled Old Hickory's headquarters with petitions to disband. Meeting on November 14 with his field officers, Jackson struck a compromise: a corporal's guard would hold down Fort Strother while he led the army to Fort Deposit, confident that "when their appetites are satiated and their sense of duty revived," they would "return cheerfully to the standard of their country" with him.[27]

Amid the grumbling, Jackson received one welcome indication that his victory had not been barren. The warriors of Hillabee, a substantial Upper Creek talwa situated on an eponymous tributary of the Tallapoosa River sixty miles southeast of Fort Strother, had defected from the Red Sticks after the battle and wanted to open peace talks. Addressing Old Hickory through the trusted white husband of a Hillabee woman, the humbled Hillabees offered to lay down their arms, pledge loyalty to the United States, and accept whatever other terms Jackson might dictate.

Old Hickory hastened to exploit the crack in the Red Stick ranks. He would welcome the Hillabees on the condition that they restore any prisoners or property taken from whites or friendly Creeks, surrender those among them who had instigated the war or killed white citizens, share with his army what extra food they might have, and contribute warriors to battle the remaining Red Sticks.[28]

The Hillabees would likely have accepted Jackson's terms, and the wedge among the Red Sticks, once opened, would undoubtedly have widened. A miscue by General Cocke, however, killed any hope of ending hostilities.

When General Cocke issued the recall order to White on November 7 that so infuriated Old Hickory, he knew both of Coffee's victory at Tallushatchee and of Jackson's chronic supply shortages. Supply deficiencies were hardly Jackson's fault, nor unique to his command. The entire war effort was a logistical nightmare for which the blame in large measure rested with Congress. To cut costs, in 1802 Congress abolished the quartermaster and commissary departments in favor of civilian agents whose interest lay principally in balancing their books and lining their pockets. Troops were fed by private contractors so intent on turning a profit that they often delivered poor provisions or chiseled on the authorized quantity.

General Cocke had called a council of war to consider the question of succoring Jackson. Acceding to its "unanimous wish," Cocke wrote to White, "If we follow General Jackson's army, we must suffer for supplies, nor can we expect to gain a victory. Let us, then, take a direction in which we can expect to share some of the dangers and glories of the field." With Jackson fighting his way down the Coosa, the obvious—and nearest—objective for the East Tennesseans were the Red Stick talwas along the Tallapoosa River, particularly Hillabee and its outlying talofas. Unaware of the Hillabee peace overtures, on November 11 Cocke ordered White to take a mixed command consisting of cavalry, mounted infantry, and Colonel Gideon Morgan's Cherokee regiment and destroy the Hillabee sanctuaries. White's force suffered no less from want of provisions than had Jackson's. It carried just three days' rations for a two-hundred-mile expedition likely to last at least ten days.[29]

Navigating a rough and rocky country, White's raiders first fell upon the deserted talwa of Little Okfuskee, which they torched. Next, they set flame to Auchenaulgau, an abandoned Red Stick talwa of ninety-three dwellings, before turning up the gravelly bank of Hillabee Creek toward their principal target. On the evening of November 17, White halted amid a dense growth of pine, oak, and hickory six miles short of the Hillabee talwa. A thick bank of clouds obscured the thin sliver of moon. Dismounting, the riflemen and Morgan's Cherokees crept through the forest to encircle the unsuspecting Hillabees. At daybreak on November 18, they fell upon a people patiently awaiting Jackson's response to their surrender offer. The Cherokees were at the forefront of a slaughter that claimed the lives of 64 unresisting warriors and yielded 256 prisoners, most of them women, children, and the elderly. "We lost not a drop of blood," White reported before steering his captive-laden column homeward amid drenching rains, well pleased with his part in avenging Fort Mims. When told of the encounter, which derailed the armistice with the Hillabees, Old Hickory expressed no anger. Congratulating General Cocke on White's massacre, he observed, "This, added to the affairs at Tallushatchee and Talladega, will I think oblige the enemy to respect our arms."

On the contrary, the surviving Hillabee warriors, enraged at what they construed as duplicity on Jackson's part, fought from that day forward with a fury and doggedness born of hatred and despair.[30]

As the twin Tennessee offensives sputtered to an inconclusive end, the Red Sticks braced for the next incursion. The aspirations of Jim Boy, Peter McQueen, and other exuberant Red Stick leaders to sweep the Creek borders clean of Americans—declared before the Fort Mims massacre had enraged the nation—now clashed with the hard realities of Spanish and British vacillation and the numerical superiority of a divided, distracted, but still potent United States. In the wake of Jackson's victories at Tallushatchee and Talladega, the Red Sticks abandoned any notion of conquest. Instead, said George Stiggins, they became "more cautious and [thought] how they might evade total annihilation." The razing of Tallushatchee and Littafuchee in particular demonstrated the indefensibility of individual talwas; thus it was that General White found Little Okfuskee and Auchenaulgau deserted. The Hillabees, thinking themselves safe while negotiating peace, had paid a high price for trusting the Americans.

The Red Sticks realized they must consolidate in their three enclaves. In early December, at least a thousand warriors and their families from the remaining fourteen Red Stick talwas along the Tallapoosa River gathered in the enclave near Autosee (twenty-five miles east of modern Montgomery, Alabama). A nearby war camp became home to Peter McQueen's Tallassees. Fifty miles to the north, the able chief Menawa and the Abeikas strengthened their defenses at Tohopeka, and fifty miles west of Autosee, Josiah Francis and most of the Alabamas and Koasatis hunkered down at the Holy Ground while William Weatherford staged small spoiling attacks in the Tensaw.

Hillabee prisoners swore that their comrades were "not yet beaten." War leaders threatened future assaults against the Lower Creeks and assured British contacts that they mustered twelve thousand warriors. The Red Sticks' dissembling, however, could not disguise their poverty. Corn rotted on the stalks in the fields of abandoned talwas. Red Stick warriors combed the forests for what wild game remained. Women scoured the woods for fruits, nuts, and roots, and the war leaders "loudly supplicate[d] British arms and ammunition."

Perhaps, in spite of their prophets' assurances to the contrary, the Master of Breath had turned his back on the Red Sticks. "If, as they contemplated, this was so," recorded George Stiggins, the Red Sticks "were determined to meet the foe despite all hazards and take death if so ordained, for a man could die but once."[31]

CHAPTER TWELVE

The Red Sticks Resilient

G OVERNOR DAVID MITCHELL of Georgia was at wit's end. Just days after the Red Sticks besieged Tuckabatchee on July 2, 1813, and well before Jackson was ready to march, he enlisted twenty-five hundred Georgians for federal service. Mitchell's personal promptitude, however, availed him little. The indifference of the Madison administration toward the Red Sticks and their potential for weakening the American hold on the Gulf Coast continued. Equipment shortages also intervened to retard preparations. Not until the end of August were the Georgia volunteers able to gather at Fort Hawkins on the Ocmulgee River. Once assembled, they expected to advance promptly to relieve Tuckabatchee and secure the Georgia frontier. Instead, weeks passed with nothing but short rations and sickness to show for the volunteers' promptness. "This little army has been badly provisioned with victuals since it encamped," grumbled the forty-two-year-old private James Tait in September. "Much and just complaint has arisen; I hope we shall be taken more care of in ... the future."

Governor Mitchell agreed, but he could get nothing from the federal government beyond bad advice and empty pledges. Preoccupied with Canada and the Chesapeake Bay, the War Department had neither the resources nor the inclination to combat Indian strife on the southeastern frontier with Regular troops. The feckless secretary of war, John Armstrong, suggested that the Tennessee and Georgia volunteers assemble somewhere in the Cherokee nation and jointly strike the Red Sticks. An incredulous Mitchell responded that Armstrong's strategy would "leave the frontier entirely exposed to the incursions of hostile savages." With that the Madison administration bowed out. "As the expedition against the hostile Creeks is very interesting to Georgia," Secretary of State James Monroe wrote to Mitchell by way of explanation, "will be carried on principally within the limits of that state, and the president has high confidence in your ability to command it with advantage to the United States, he desires that you would take charge of it." Monroe's flippant missive would have sat poorly with Willie Blount and Andrew Jackson, had they been aware of it. Not that either was averse to cooperating to the extent possible with the Georgians, but their own state's interests demanded an immediate assault from Tennessee.

To compound Governor Mitchell's difficulties, neither Madison nor Armstrong offered him the means with which to prosecute a campaign. The governor needed arms, ammunition, tents, camp equipage, blankets, shoes, forage for horses, and medical supplies in quantities far beyond the capacity of the U.S. Army quartermaster at Savannah to provide. The military district commander, Major General Thomas Pinckney, writing from Charleston, could offer only moral support. As for Mitchell's material needs, Pinckney "feared we shall be embarrassed to procure them." Moreover, the U.S. Army contractor in Georgia refused to transport supplies beyond the state line.

Mitchell also knew little of Tennessee's intentions. Not until early October did Willie Blount communicate with his Georgia counterpart, and then only to convey the strength of Jackson and Cocke's commands and a promise to "from time to time advise you of their march, positions, movements, and intended attacks."[1]

Amid the disarray, Mitchell could rely on one constant in his favor: the capable and concerned commander of the Georgia brigade, Brigadier General John Floyd, a native South Carolinian born in 1769 to fanatically patriotic parents. During the Revolutionary War, his father taunted Loyalists by wearing a gorget engraved "Liberty or Death." After the conflict the Floyd family moved to the Georgia coast. As a young man, Floyd prospered first as a boatbuilder and then as one of the state's principal land- and slaveholders. Watching the general conduct a review of the regiment to which he belonged, Private James Tait was impressed. "[Floyd] was dressed in a blue frock coat, with very splendid epaulets and rich gold lace. He is a man of stature, about the middle size, of a dark complexion and formed for strength, appearing to possess the capacity, so necessary for a commander, of enduring much fatigue." General Floyd also struck Benjamin Hawkins as a "brave, active, intelligent officer." Scraping together state funds from diverse accounts and wheedling a moderate amount of federal money, Governor Mitchell fitted out Floyd's brigade sufficiently for the general to advance from Fort Hawkins to the Creek Agency in early October.[2]

Later that month, President Madison finally awoke to the Creek threat and the need to coordinate the efforts of Tennessee, Georgia, and the Mississippi Territory to suppress the outbreak before the British exploited it to seize the Gulf Coast. When Governor Mitchell unexpectedly resigned, Madison appointed Major General Thomas Pinckney, commander of the Sixth Military District headquartered in Charleston, to "take direction" of all operations against the Red Sticks.

Pinckney would prove a superb choice for a difficult mission. A distinguished soldier, statesman, and politician, the vigorous and intellectual sixty-three-year-old South Carolinian enjoyed wide popularity. His father had obtained for him the best possible European education. During a sixteen-year residence abroad, Pinckney earned a degree from Christ College, Oxford, and studied military science in France. Pinckney also developed a lifelong love for classical Greek, which he read fluently. He returned to America in 1774. While in England, Pinckney's patriotic ardor won him the epithet of "Little Rebel." At the outbreak of war in 1775 he became a captain in the First South Carolina Regiment. Later promoted to major, he served as aide-de-camp to General Horatio Gates. At the Battle of Camden, a musket ball shattered his leg and he was captured, ending his active service.

After the war Pinckney became a staunch Federalist and served a term as governor of South Carolina. A favorite of President George Washington's, Pinckney accepted appointment first as U.S. minister to Great Britain in 1792 and then as envoy extraordinary to Spain in 1794. In the latter capacity, he negotiated the Treaty of San Lorenzo, which granted Americans the right to use the port of New Orleans and established a clear boundary between the United States and

Spanish Florida—both key steps toward future American expansion in the Southeast. Returning to the United States, Pinckney became the Federalist candidate for vice president in the 1796 election. Alexander Hamilton backed Pinckney enthusiastically. "This gentleman," declaimed Hamilton, "has been all his life distinguished in the South for the mildness and amiableness of his manners, the rectitude and purity of his morals, and the soundness and correctness of his understanding, accompanied by a habitual discretion and self-command which has often occasioned a parallel to be drawn between him and the venerated Washington."

Despite Hamilton's endorsement, Pinckney finished behind the Democratic-Republican Thomas Jefferson in the balloting, and the awkward ticket of the Federalist John Adams and Jefferson took office. After two terms in Congress—during which he came to know and like his fellow representative Andrew Jackson—Pinckney retired to his plantation with "little taste" left for public life. At the outbreak of the War of 1812, he reluctantly accepted command of the Southern Division (Sixth Military District).[3]

Until the Creek outbreak, Pinckney's overriding concern had been to fortify Southern harbors against attack by the mighty British fleet. The War Department gave him no hint of what instructions, if any, it had provided to Governor Mitchell, nor did it address the inevitable command conflict that would arise because Pinckney's mandate to manage the Creek conflict placed at his disposal Regular troops belonging to the inept and spiteful Seventh Military District commander, Thomas Flournoy. Pinckney also knew nothing of Jackson's activities. Their mutual respect, however, mitigated against willful misunderstandings. On November 16, unaware that Jackson had already retired to Fort Strother, Pinckney sent him a "general outline" of how he thought the Creek campaign had best be conducted. "Until I shall have received more correct intelligence," allowed Pinckney, "it would be improper to issue instructions a compliance wherewith might be rendered inexpedient by circumstances of which I am ignorant." The South Carolinian proposed that four forces— Jackson's division, Cocke's division, Floyd's brigade, and a command composed of Claiborne's Mississippians and the Third U.S. Infantry, the latter wrested from General Flournoy—converge at the junction of the Coosa and Tallapoosa Rivers (fifteen miles northeast of today's

Montgomery, Alabama). There a well-garrisoned supply depot was to be constructed to permit uninterrupted operations throughout the Creek country until the Red Sticks were subdued. Each command was expected to build and garrison forts along its respective route of march to preoccupy the Red Sticks and prevent them from uniting.

Pinckney knew better than to set any timetables, or to expect the four armies to move in concert over such a vast expanse. Communications were uncertain at best; dispatches between Pinckney at Charleston and Flournoy's New Orleans headquarters, for instance, had to travel through Tennessee and down the Mississippi or along the old Natchez Trace.[4]

Andrew Jackson welcomed Pinckney's plan. "I am happy to find from your letter of instructions that my ideas correspond so well with yours as to the proper mode of prosecuting the war," he wrote to his new commander on December 3. "It is certainly correct that a mere temporary incursion into the enemy's country will not produce those beneficial and lasting effects . . . which our government expects." Apologizing for having had to withdraw after Talladega, Old Hickory swore to push to the confluence of the Tallapoosa and Coosa "with as little delay as possible." Whether that be a matter of weeks or months, Jackson did not venture to say.[5]

That the Red Sticks might develop plans of their own seems not to have occurred to Pinckney or Jackson. The notion, however, haunted Big Warrior and the other friendly chiefs holed up at Coweta. "I have begged of you all this long summer to come and help us and no assistance from you yet," Big Warrior wrote to Benjamin Hawkins in early October 1813. "I am so frightened that I have no more talk." The Red Sticks also noticed the inertness of the Georgia volunteers. No sooner did Jackson turn back to Fort Strother than Hopoithle Micco and Peter McQueen combined forces to try to starve Coweta into submission.

Big Warrior grew desperate. With the endorsement of William McIntosh and Alexander Cornells, on November 18 he appealed to Hawkins and Floyd to act before the Red Sticks, who outnumbered the friendly warriors two to one, might compel him to capitulate. "They are killing everything and burning all of the houses. We can't turn out to fight them on account of our women and children, and we cannot leave our entrenchments for fear of them getting possession." Big Warrior could not comprehend the Georgians' delay. "You have had full time to come. The hostile party are in the open pine woods. If you was [*sic*] here, it is a good place to fight them. If they make off, you will have trouble to find them."[6]

Floyd had his men on the march to Coweta the same day. He had finally procured enough weapons and ammunition, but his brigade suffered from other supply shortages—"the contractors and quartermaster department...have been a dead weight," he grumbled to his wife—and from colds, fevers, diarrhea, and other camp maladies.

The Red Sticks had no wish to fight Floyd. Before the Georgia brigade crossed the Chattahoochee River, they fell back sixty-six miles to their stronghold. Floyd paused to build a supply depot, which he named Fort Mitchell, on the Federal Road adjacent to Coweta. That gratified Big Warrior. Neither he nor Floyd, however, believed either the friendly Lower Creek talwas or the Georgia frontier would truly be secure until the Red Sticks gathered alongside Autosee were crushed.[7]

Autosee itself was a singular place. The boyhood home of Dixon Bailey, it was far older than most talwas. Four hundred years earlier the site had been home to Mississippian-tradition Mound Builders. After the Spanish destroyed the town during the entrada, Creeks primarily of the Serpent Clan settled on the spot. The talwa flourished, growing to at least two hundred household compounds. When the American naturalist William Bartram visited Autosee in December 1787, he met more "venerable chiefs and warriors" than he had in any other talwa. The winter council house, or chokofa, a wattle-and-daub conical structure, also was much larger than those he had seen elsewhere. Bartram admired the artistry of the public square. Vibrant paintings "extremely picturesque or caricature" covered the walls of the principal structure. The columns supporting the piazza of the summer council house were "ingeniously formed in the likeness of vast speckled serpents." A forty-foot-tall pine pillar that rose just beyond the public square particularly intrigued Bartram. Round and tapering to a point from a base three feet in circumference, the pillar was as much a mystery to the Autosees as it was to Bartram. Their ancestors had discovered the pillar, and it still towered above the talwa when Red

Stick prophets consecrated their adjacent enclave as a sacred refuge second only to Josiah Francis's Holy Ground.[8]

At first blush, Autosee and its environs appeared ill-suited for defense. The talwa backed onto the Tallapoosa River, making it vulnerable to an attack from the south. The nature of the near bank, however, compensated somewhat. It dropped abruptly six feet, creating a natural firing step before falling another thirty feet to the water. A thick curtain of reeds and brush lined both the upper and the lower ledges. Beneath the tangle, four feet from the water's edge, a band of slick clay followed the twisting course of the river. As further protection against attack, the five hundred Autosee warriors had dug caves for their families and carved well-concealed bunkers in the lower ledge.

The Red Sticks also had clear fields of fire for several hundred yards south of Autosee before the open plain yielded to the prevailing pine barrens and hardwood forests that stood between the talwa and the Federal Road. Just west of Autosee, within a large looping bend of the Tallapoosa, the inhabitants had burned away the native canebrakes to plant corn. The bare cornstalks had withered in the November cold, removing any vestige of concealment. From the talwa to the mouth of Calabee Creek, a mile to the east, the ground was also cleared.

Of far greater moment to Red Stick prospects at Autosee than terrain considerations were the presence of fifteen hundred additional warriors and their families, drawn to the consecrated sanctuary. Within a loop of the Tallapoosa five hundred yards west of Autosee, Red Sticks from eight nearby talwas and talofas had erected two hundred cabins. East of Autosee, Peter McQueen camped with his Tallassee followers. Five miles downriver at Hoithlewaulee, the gnomish prophet Paddy Walsh waited with a strong contingent of Alabama warriors. By common consent Coosa Micco, who was both the civil and the military leader of Autosee, assumed command of the combined Red Stick forces. To guard against surprise, Coosa Micco posted scouts along the Federal Road. The Creek leaders had seemingly done everything possible to prevent a second Talladega.

General Floyd started for Autosee on November 25 in biting cold. He had assembled a strong but hardly overwhelming force. His Georgia brigade consisted of 650 infantry and riflemen, 200 horsemen, and a 100-man artillery company hauling several old brass British cannons, captured relics of the Revolutionary War. Even antiquated cannons terrified Indians, however, and the Red Sticks had yet to encounter artillery of any sort. Five hundred friendly Creeks—Cowetas under William McIntosh and Tuckabatchees commanded by the gifted young war leader Mad Dog's Son—accompanied the expedition. Floyd's men carried five days' rations; the general hoped to deliver a swift and decisive blow against Autosee and then return to Fort Mitchell before food ran out. General Pinckney's plan for a protracted campaign in the Red Stick heartland—at least insofar as the Georgia column was concerned—would have to wait.

After a brief bivouac, at 1:00 a.m. on November 29, Floyd's Georgians and the friendly Creeks left the Federal Road and plunged into the frosty pine barrens and dismal forests to negotiate the final eight miles to Autosee. At daybreak they paused just short of the open field fronting the talwa. "The scene was truly interesting," Floyd wrote to his wife. "The morning was calm, clear, and intensely cold; the fields appeared covered with snow from the excessive frost." The general felt confident. Unaware that the adjacent sanctuary, or stronghold, existed, he intended to surround Autosee by placing his right wing at the mouth of Calabee Creek and the left wing on the bank of the Tallapoosa west of the talwa. McIntosh and Mad Dog's Son, meanwhile, were to ford the Tallapoosa just downriver and deploy on the far bank behind Autosee to cut off the Red Stick escape route. All seemed well in hand until the sun rose and distant objects grew visible. In the loop of the Tallapoosa where he had intended to anchor his left wing, Floyd descried the Red Stick sacred sanctuary. Equally disconcerting, several hundred warriors were gathering in front of both it and Autosee in two separate squares, punctuating their war cries with taunts for the Georgians to come on.

While Floyd contemplated the changed circumstances, Private Tait, shivering in his brown fringed hunting shirt, cape, and trousers, wondered at the Red Sticks' near nakedness. "There were but few of them who were not in a state of [partial] nudity. Whether from necessity or choice, I cannot pretend to say. Why from the former, for where are their dressed deerskins? Why from the latter, for it was very cold?"[9]

The Red Sticks intended to fight stripped and painted not for want of time to dress or for lack of winter wear but because such was their practice. Coosa Micco had spent the night conferring with his close friend and confidant Tewasubbukle, a prominent Alabama prophet, about the upcoming battle. They were still in "deep and private conversation" when a warrior who had camped deep in the forest in anticipation of an early-morning turkey hunt sprinted into Autosee to warn of the soldiers' approach. Coosa Micco acted fast. He ordered noncombatants to swim the Tallapoosa and disperse. Those too infirm or elderly to cross the icy water crouched in caves dug into the riverbank. Gathering hastily, the Red Stick war leaders accepted Tewasubbukle's proposition that the prophet command the contingent at the sanctuary town and that Coosa Micco lead the forces gathered at Autosee, including Peter McQueen's Tallassees and old Hopoithle Micco's contingent. Scarcely had the warriors assembled in their respective formations, which stood five hundred yards apart, than a scout told Coosa Micco that the soldiers were maneuvering in the hoarfrost-tinted timber beyond the open plain. Mounting his horse, Coosa Micco galloped about, cautioning his men to be brave and not waste their precious ammunition "in fear."[10]

General Floyd, meanwhile, altered his tactics to confront the unexpected second Red Stick formation. Three infantry companies and one rifle company wheeled to the left and started en echelon toward the prophet Tewasubbukle. Two troops of light dragoons carrying pistols and sabers trotted behind them. The remainder of the brigade under General Floyd swept out of the woods to confront Coosa Micco.

The thunderous onset of battle stunned Floyd. He struggled to convey its horror to his wife, writing, "The sereneness of the morning, the yells of the savages, the firing of our artillery, and the incessant prattling of the musketry and rifles; the dead laying promiscuously over the field, and the rolling pillars of smoke issued by the devouring flames preying on the savages' dwellings, in addition to the columns produced by the repeated discharge of our artillery and the light sheets produced by the repeated discharge of small arms were in various figures fantastically floating in the air."[11]

A musket ball caught Floyd in the kneecap. The Georgian reeled but stayed in the saddle. On the far side of the plain, a round of grapeshot blew Hopoithle Micco off his horse, gravely wounding him. Despite repeated cannonading that "shattered their miserable huts to pieces," the Autosees and their allies held their ground. Then dragoons charged the sacred enclave. They killed Tewasubbukle and dispersed part of his force. Coosa Micco galloped from Autosee to rally them, but the dragoons had inflicted irreparable damage. The major commanding spurred his horse into the scrum, sabering several Red Sticks and scattering the rest. "Mercy was asked by some of the poor devils," recalled Private Tait, "but none shown." The slaughter astonished Tait. "They retired behind the bank of the river and as they were shot rolled into the stream.... Some were killed in swimming across."[12]

Coosa Micco's attempt to rally the fallen Tewasubbukle's warriors nearly cost him his life. He returned to his own men with two musket balls in his body and a saber slash across the cheek. His horse staggered beneath him, shot through the neck and body. Faint from loss of blood, Coosa Micco dismounted and waved his men back toward the steep riverbank. A few paused to fire at the approaching Georgians through chink holes in the houses until grapeshot riddled the structures. Fires spread swiftly. "Everything was consumed in the town," wrote the wounded but lucid Floyd. "Dogs, cats, and some of the savage tenants fell victim to the devouring flames."[13]

The tumult drove some to recklessness. The brigade quartermaster William Tennille spurred his horse after the withdrawing Red Sticks until a volley brought his mount down on top of him. Freeing himself from the dead animal, Tennille found he was alone between the lines. A musket ball broke his right arm; another ripped through his thigh. A group of Red Sticks rushed forward to scalp him but halted when he leveled his pistol at them. The weapon misfired, and the warriors edged closer. Drawing his saber with his left hand, Tennille held his assailants at bay until a detachment of dragoons rescued him. The quartermaster's histrionics won him wide respect but cost him his arm.[14]

The Autosee and Tallassee warriors fell back to the twin bluffs above the Tallapoosa. After a brief but bloody clash in the bordering reed brakes and thickets, Floyd called off the attack. As he later explained, his men could not see the Indians on the riverbank without peering over the upper bluff and exposing themselves to close-range fire. The general also saw little point in prolonging the contest because the friendly Creeks had been unable to ford the Tallapoosa and surround Autosee; the water, they claimed, was too high and too cold (but not, apparently, too cold for the women and children of the Red Stick warriors to cross). Floyd redeployed his Creek allies on his right flank, where "they fought with an intrepidity worthy of any troops." Three other factors persuaded Floyd to retire. First, assuming he could pry loose those women and children who had sheltered themselves in the caves beside the river, Floyd had no way of transporting them to Fort Mitchell. Second, his men had exhausted their rations. Finally, he expected Red Stick reinforcements from nearby Hoithlewaulee to appear momentarily.

At 9:00 a.m., with Coosa Micco's warriors driven from the plain and Autosee in flames, the Georgians reassembled for the return march to Fort Mitchell. Not so the friendly Creeks. They stayed to despoil the Red Stick dead and the few unburned buildings. Letting their guard down, they were caught unprepared when the Hoithlewaulee Red Sticks suddenly attacked them, briefly closing their line of retreat. In the melee, the Tuckabatchees lost their leader, the "shrewd, well-disposed, and enterprising" Mad Dog's Son, whose death Floyd "regretted very much." With that limited measure of Red Stick revenge, the Battle of Autosee ended. For reasons known only to himself, Paddy Walsh and his Alabamas never entered the fray.[15]

Red Stick losses were far heavier than those of the Georgians. Floyd estimated he killed at least two hundred of the two thousand warriors engaged, although some of his soldiers thought enemy dead were only half that number. The Red Sticks, for their part, acknowledged eighty killed and one hundred wounded. Floyd reported losing eleven soldiers killed and fifty-four wounded. The friendly Creeks paid dearly for lingering to loot, losing seventeen killed and thirty-one wounded.[16]

Both General Pinckney and Benjamin Hawkins counted Autosee a defeat for the Georgians because Floyd had been unable to establish a permanent post in the Red Stick country. Their criticism was unfair. Pinckney had not communicated his expectations to Floyd, who intended a sharp search-and-destroy expedition and accordingly planned his retreat in advance. Floyd was rightly pleased with the outcome of Autosee. He had razed not only Autosee, a principal Red Stick talwa, but also one of three supposedly impenetrable Red Stick sacred refuges, more than doing his part to avenge Fort Mims. The battle might have been a tactical draw, but it damaged Red Stick morale, largely by demonstrating that at least one of their sanctuaries was not necessarily the divinely shielded stronghold that the prophets represented it as being.

Whether Josiah Francis's vaunted Holy Ground or Chief Menawa's log barricade at Tohopeka would prove better able to repel American invaders remained to be seen.[17]

General Floyd's brigade and his Creek allies were gone. The Mississippians had yet to move against the Holy Ground, and Jackson's Tennesseans showed no inclination to stage a second incursion against the northern reaches of the Red Stick dominion, for the defenders of which Tohopeka was the rallying point.

The Red Sticks on the Tallapoosa River, however, had not seen the last of Georgian invaders. Against his better judgment, General Pinckney had yielded to the demand of the new Georgia governor, Peter Early, that a reconnaissance in force be staged against the upper Tallapoosa Red Sticks who—in the governor's mind at least—posed a threat to exposed Georgia settlements on the Ocmulgee River. Command of the expedition went to Brigadier General David Adams, who recruited 530 mounted riflemen on short notice. Pinckney understood that such a small force could only plunder, burn, and perhaps get into serious trouble; it could not take and hold territory, which the general considered crucial to defeating the Red Sticks.[18]

With Governor Early's good wishes, on December 15 Adams's ragtag outfit forded the broad Chattahoochee River beneath a cold stinging rain. Conferring with his officers and Creek guides on the west bank that afternoon, Adams decided to stage a surprise attack on the nearest target, the Red Stick talofa of Nuyaka, thirty miles due west. Into the wet and gloomy wilderness plunged the Georgians, confident that they would enjoy the element of surprise against the three hundred warriors believed to be haunting the upper Tallapoosa River.[19]

They were sorely mistaken. A few hundred yards below Nuyaka, the Abeika chief Menawa and twelve hundred warriors were concentrated at Tohopeka, the third of the three sacred Red Stick strongholds. Two miles downstream lay Emuckfau, a sizable talofa. Another eighteen miles downstream was Okfuskee, a large talwa that claimed both Emuckfau and Nuyaka as satellite villages. In short, the area toward which Adams rode swarmed with Red Sticks.

The Georgians' objective had an ironic name. Laid out in 1777, the talofa was renamed Nuyaka—the Muscogee pronunciation of "New York"—thirteen years later to celebrate Alexander McGillivray's peace treaty with President Washington. Nuyaka consisted of eighty-five dwellings on a level terrace at the western base of a long chain of rolling, rocky hills clad in hickory and pine.[20]

The Georgians had scarcely begun their march when they stumbled on a small forest settlement of eleven crude huts known as Mad Warrior's village. It stood empty. The residents had fled toward Nuyaka moments earlier. Adams burned the dwellings and pressed on, the smoke curling above the treetops a clear clue to any nearby Red Sticks that something was amiss. Three miles short of Nuyaka, Adams halted and bivouacked for the night. Under the impression he could still surprise the Red Sticks, he prohibited his wet and trembling soldiers from lighting campfires.

At dawn on December 17, Adams assembled the grousing mounted riflemen in three columns to attack Nuyaka. Emerging from the rock-strewn forest above the talofa, an embarrassed Adams found the place abandoned. While his men looted and then torched Nuyaka, Adams contemplated his next move. Disobeying orders, a few soldiers wandered off. A musket cracked, and a Georgian dropped with a shattered shoulder. War whoops and taunts rose from the far bank. That decided it. Mumbling something about short rations and rising waters, Adams promptly retreated.[21]

The Red Sticks were content to let the outnumbered Georgians leave. They could rebuild Nuyaka handily if they chose. Moreover, with most of their warriors on foot, the Red Stick war leaders likely saw no point in chasing mounted men, particularly when there were matters more pressing: specifically, to finish constructing defenses around Tohopeka so formidable that no sane white soldier would dare approach the place and also to muster the forces necessary to repel the inevitable advance of the Mississippians. While Chief Menawa busied the refugees from Nuyaka as well as his own Abeika warriors with completing the strongest and most complex fortifications American Indians had ever raised in case Jackson should return, the prophet Josiah Francis and a reluctant William Weatherford assembled their Alabama and Koasati followers at the Holy Ground to dispute any incursion from the Mississippi Territory. Meanwhile, the third major

Red Stick concentration, the Creeks of Autosee and neighboring lower Tallapoosa communities, recuperated from their recent clash with Floyd's Georgians.

The Red Sticks had been bloodied but hardly beaten.

So long as the dawdling Brigadier General Thomas Flournoy commanded the Seventh Military District, matters moved slowly in army circles in the Mississippi Territory. The Choctaw chief Pushmataha, however, proved both a man of his word and decisive. In late July 1813, he had assured apprehensive white and métis residents of the Tensaw that if war came, he would "rejoice to march to battle with them" against the Red Sticks. After Fort Mims he quickly made good on his pledge. Accompanied by George Gaines, the Indian factor at St. Stephens, he traveled to Mobile to offer his services to General Flournoy, who could no longer pretend the Red Sticks posed no threat.

Nevertheless, the meeting was a bust. Pushmataha spoke eloquently of his reasons for wanting to fight: to protect the American settlements; to avenge the deaths of friends at Fort Mims; and most important, to restrain his warriors, a few of whom had joined the Red Sticks. If "not engaged soon by the general," Pushmataha feared, they all would desert to the hostiles. To Gaines's chagrin, Flournoy "rudely rejected" the great chief's appeal. Returning to St. Stephens, a baffled Pushmataha remarked to Gaines that "the great warrior [Flournoy] was in his opinion of very small caliber." Stumbling to assuage the chief's wounded dignity, Gaines told Pushmataha that a "much greater warrior," Andrew Jackson, was coming to "set matters right."

While Gaines and Pushmataha related their misadventure to the angry and disbelieving populace of St. Stephens, a perspiring messenger from Mobile on a lathered and panting horse pulled rein before them: Flournoy had reconsidered; he would accept the Choctaws into the federal service at full pay. "A shout of exultation rose up from the crowd," recalled a relieved Gaines, "and all was joy, and among the number, Pushmataha felt exceedingly rejoiced."[22]

Brigadier General Ferdinand Claiborne, commander of the Mississippi Territory Volunteers, did not. His troubles with Flournoy predated Fort Mims and continued after the massacre. Tensaw settlers remained huddled at Fort St. Stephens, Fort Stoddert, and lesser stockades while their crops withered, cattle strayed about the countryside, or roving Red Stick foraging parties from Josiah Francis's Holy Ground rustled them. Claiborne's search-and-destroy missions netted nothing. Leaping into ravines, melting into swamps, gliding across rivers and streams in hidden canoes, the Red Sticks were always a step ahead of their pursuers. Claiborne guessed that no more than a hundred Red Sticks roamed the Tensaw, but they sufficed to paralyze the district.

William Weatherford might have led some of the raiders; his movements in the autumn of 1813 are obscure. He likely spent most of his time shuttling between the Holy Ground and his nearby plantation. That he had a hand in Red Stick activity in the Tensaw after Fort Mims, however, can be counted certain.

Claiborne again proposed to take the war to Red Stick talwas as Andrew Jackson was about to do, but Flournoy refused his request. He permitted his frustrated subordinate only to build a fort at a perpendicular precipice known as Weatherford's Bluff on the lower Alabama River to interdict the Red Stick foraging parties and to stock supplies for General Jackson, whom Flournoy expected momentarily to barrel through the Creek country. Otherwise, "to cover the [Tensaw] frontier and defend the inhabitants while gathering their crops" and search for secreted Creek canoes should be Claiborne's principal objectives.[23]

As chance would have it, a simple canoe clash changed the course of events in the Tensaw. The doughty Captain Sam Dale, recovered from the wound he sustained at Burnt Corn Creek, initiated the contest. His and several other militia detachments had been beating the bush for Red Stick foragers without success. In early November, Dale obtained the permission of Colonel Joseph Carson (Claiborne's principal subordinate) to take forty-five militiamen and scour the Alabama River between the charred remains of Fort Mims and Weatherford's Bluff for signs of Indians. After Dale set off from Fort Madison, Colonel Carson ordered Captain William Jones's company of Mississippi Territory Volunteers, thirty or forty strong, to reinforce him.[24]

The frosty morning of November 12 found the searchers on both banks of the Alabama. Captain Dale and twelve of his men were cooking a breakfast of sweet potatoes and beef in a small field on the east bank opposite Randon's Landing, the site of the abandoned plantation of the métis John Randon, who with his wife and three daughters had perished at Fort Mims. Captain Jones's company and the remainder of Dale's contingent were breaking bivouac on the west bank, 150 feet distant. The river ran deep but placid; canoes shuttled the men from shore to shore.

Dale was on his guard. A dozen recently extinguished cooking fires smoldered near his campsite, and several scaffolds for drying meat rose beside them. A large Indian foraging party likely prowled the forest beyond, but no Red Sticks were to be seen until 10:30 a.m., when Dale and his men espied a thirty-foot-long and four-foot-deep canoe cut from a single immense cypress tree—the sort of conveyance the Creeks used to transport corn by water—round the river bend above them. Eleven Red Stick warriors manned the boat. Nineteen-year-old Jeremiah Austill watched their approach awestruck. "All [were] painted and naked except their flaps and a panther skin round the head of the chief extending down his back in a robe," recalled the sinewy, six-foot-two-inch-tall youth, who like his companions wore homespun linen trousers and a hunting shirt. "They were sitting down with their guns erect before them."

Dale and his small party unleashed a volley at the warriors, hitting no one. Two Red Sticks leaped from the canoe and swam for shore. Reloading his musket, James Smith, a stout, strongly built twenty-five-year-old, fired again. One swimmer rolled over in the water dead. The Red Stick canoe veered toward the center of the river. Dale yelled at his men on the far bank to pile into their largest canoe and challenge the Indians. Eight men obeyed. They paddled toward the Red Sticks until one militiamen lost his nerve. "Live Indians, by God! Back water, boys! Back water!" he screeched, and the canoe withdrew.

An infuriated Dale decided to attack the Red Stick canoe with the only boat he had—a square-bottom dugout capable of carrying just four men. Dale, Smith, and Austill piled in, the latter taking post at the prow. A free black man known as Caesar reluctantly paddled. The small boat weaved and bobbed toward the Red Stick canoe. At twenty yards' range, the three men stood up gingerly and discharged their weapons. Dale's and Austill's muskets misfired. Stumbling as he squeezed the trigger, Smith saw his shot splash harmlessly in the river. Most of the Red Sticks held their fire and waited for the foolish white men to come alongside. An impatient Indian hurled his tomahawk at Dale, the blade grazing the captain's thigh; another fired but missed.

As the two canoes touched, a Red Stick barked at Dale, "Now for it, Big Sam!" A moment later the panther-skin-robed warrior brought his clubbed musket down on Austill, who dodged but caught a hard blow on the hand before Dale and Smith slayed his assailant, the captain's musket stock splintering when it cracked open the Indian's skull.

The three white men fought with focused ferocity. "Not one word was spoken on either side that I heard after the first blow," recalled Austill, who took a blow from a war club that opened a deep gash in his head. Caesar handed Captain Dale his own musket and bayonet and steadied the boat while Dale and Smith leaped into the Indian canoe and bayoneted warriors. Within minutes, every Red Stick lay dead. Austill stepped into the Indian canoe. Two inches of blood soaked his shoes. Together Austill and Dale cast the Indian corpses into the river.

Austill later learned that there had been three hundred Red Sticks in the woods on the east bank watching the contest. After seeing the three white men slaughter nine of their fellow warriors, they fled. William Weatherford might have led the raiding party; in any event, it vanished from the Tensaw.[25]

The Canoe Fight burnished Sam Dale's reputation as the Mississippi Territory's premier Indian fighter, heartened Tensaw residents, and might have prevented a second wave of Red Stick raids. It also coincided with Generals Pinckney and Claiborne's first steps toward an offensive against the Red Sticks, a shift in strategy facilitated by the unceremonious departure of the annoying General Flournoy. On November 6, Flournoy received War Department orders to detach the Third U.S. Infantry Regiment for duty against the Red Sticks. Deprived of half his force, Flournoy quit Mobile with his remaining Regulars—and the garrison at Pierce's Mill, which Governor Holmes had deemed critical to protecting the Tensaw—and returned to New Orleans to defend the Gulf Coast against the flickering phantom of British invasion. Before leaving, he tried again to rein in Claiborne. "You had better never fight a battle than run the risk of defeat," counseled Flournoy. Not content with giving advice, he crippled Claiborne's mounted arm by dismissing from the federal service a contingent of Natchez dragoons that had proven of great worth in shielding the Tensaw settlements. Like Claiborne, its commander, Major Thomas Hinds, had offended Flournoy by urging an offensive against the Red Sticks.[26]

Freed from Flournoy's interference, Claiborne sent him a politely worded farewell jab—"I must acknowledge [that] it was intended that you should act on the seaboard, not participate in the Creek War; the taking of the 3rd Regiment from you is evidence of that"—and then advanced his Mississippi Territory Volunteers to Weatherford's Bluff. Claiborne celebrated both its natural grandeur and its strategic significance. "I am on the east bank of the Alabama River, thirty-five miles above Mims," he wrote to Governor Holmes on November 21. "The bluff is very high with a limestone point, commanding an extensive prospect. From this position we cut the Indians off from the water and from growing crops. We also render their communications with Pensacola more hazardous." To that end, Claiborne detailed Pushmataha—gratified finally to be campaigning alongside the Americans—with fifty-one warriors and a detachment of Mississippi volunteers to assume a blocking position on the Wolf Trail.[27]

General Claiborne also marveled at the unclaimed wealth around Weatherford's Bluff. Large cattle herds wandered loose. At least fifteen thousand barrels of corn and an "abundant" crop of pumpkins stood ripe for the taking. "Most of these crops," reported Claiborne sadly, "were cultivated by friendly half-breeds, the greater part of whom fell at Mims."

The vagaries of communication over a vast and hostile country continued to hamper American operations. At the very moment Andrew Jackson's famished army retired to Fort Strother, Claiborne set about amassing provisions for Old Hickory, whom he expected to rendezvous with at Weatherford's Bluff. Claiborne also began construction on a two-hundred-square-foot stockade anchored on stout blockhouses and shielded by an artillery lunette that commanded the Alabama River. His officers insisted the general christen the stockade, which was completed in ten days, Fort Claiborne.[28]

On November 28, Lieutenant Colonel Gilbert Russell, an ambitious Regular army officer, marched into Fort Claiborne with the Third Regiment. His last orders from General Flournoy had been to "cooperate" with Claiborne. Neither Russell nor Claiborne needed prodding from General Pinckney; both ached to invade the Red Stick country. When word of Jackson's plight reached them in early December, Claiborne and Russell were ready to march with their combined force of a thousand men. Their objective was the prophet Josiah Francis's blessed refuge the Holy Ground. So long as Red Stick war and foraging parties came and went from there with impunity, the Tensaw would enjoy no peace.[29]

Josiah Francis took great pride in Eccanachaca, the "sacred or beloved ground" that his American opponents labeled the Holy Ground. He had built the town of two hundred homes on a parcel of elevated land that Francis claimed the Master of Breath had chosen and consecrated solely for the Red Sticks. Most of the residents were Alabamas, and they erected a new tribal council grounds on the site. The late Tecumseh's emissary Seekaboo, who had been instrumental in inciting the civil war among the Creeks, also resided there.

The Holy Ground rested on the south bank of the Alabama River, approximately twenty-five miles east of present-day Selma, Alabama, on lovely, fertile soil, surrounded by marshy woodland prodigious in its variety of trees. Two dozen types of oaks grew in the vicinity. Hickory, cypress, sycamore, and longleaf pine enclosed the village and lined the earthen riverbank, which in places rose to a height of twenty feet.

The Holy Ground covered fifty acres. No trails approached the place; the Red Sticks accessed the town by canoe. A brook running from an ample spring on the eastern margin of Eccanachaca supplied residents with abundant clear, cool water. Two deep ravines, each about two hundred yards long, joined and emptied into the Alabama River just beyond the southwestern edge of the Holy Ground. Josiah Francis ordered a line of stakes driven into the earth from the brook, around the village to the mouth of the twin ravines. He also laid out a long, two-foot-high, consecrated pile of finely split pine and cypress logs across the neck of land. Finally, Francis described an invisible "wizard circle" around the Holy Ground, beyond which the Master of Breath would permit no apostate to tread. Should the unseen circle prove deficient, the softwood rampart would spontaneously combust, subjecting intruders to a fiery death. Verily, pronounced Francis, the boundary of the Holy Ground would prove the "grave of white men."[30]

. . .

General Claiborne's troops objected to an expedition against the Holy Ground for reasons more mundane than the dubious prospect of divinely wrought immolation. On December 8, Claiborne's aide handed him a respectfully worded entreaty from the company-grade officers of Colonel Carson's regiment of Mississippi Territory Volunteers begging him to scrap the movement: "Considering that winter and the wet season have set in, the untrodden wilderness to be traversed; the impossibility of transporting supplies for want of roads; that most of our men are without winter clothing, shoes, or blankets; that a large majority of those ordered to march will be entitled to their discharge before the expedition can be accomplished, we trust that the enterprise may be reconsidered and abandoned." There was no hint of mutiny. The petitioners would "cheerfully obey your orders and carry out your plans."[31]

Sam Dale scoffed at the petition. He dismissed most of the signatories as young dandies from the Natchez District too "accustomed to the comforts, [and] many of them to the luxuries of life" to withstand hard campaigning. General Claiborne, however, considered the matter sympathetically. "Their objections were stated with the dignity, feeling, and respect which these officers had always manifested," he reported. His mind, however, was made up: on December 13, the expedition would depart Fort Claiborne on the 120-mile march, initially along the Federal Road and then through trackless forest and swamp to the Holy Ground. "As soon as the order to march was issued, each man repaired promptly to his post," averred the appreciative general.[32]

Claiborne's column was a heterogeneous lot, consisting of Colonel Russell's 550 regulation blue-and-white-clad Regulars; Colonel Carson's homespun-clothed Mississippi Territory Volunteers; mounted riflemen; a small militia battalion, of which Sam Dale's company formed a part; and Pushmataha's Choctaw battalion, augmented to 150 warriors, for a total strength of 950 officers and men. Claiborne was keen to settle scores: friendly Creeks told him that the Holy Ground hosted not only the prophet Josiah Francis but also that "inimical . . . half-breed chief" William Weatherford, whom vengeful Mississippians yearned to kill for his supposed complicity in the Fort Mims massacre.[33]

Weatherford had not intended to settle at the Holy Ground. After

Fort Mims he seems to have shuttled between the sacred place, his plantation, and a second home on the Federal Road, while perhaps occasionally directing raiding parties in the Tensaw. Not until mid-December, when he learned of Claiborne's preparations to invade, did Weatherford and his friend and Scots-Irish métis neighbor Malcolm McPherson relocate to the Holy Ground. So too did the métis John Moniac, whose brother Sam Moniac, friend to and brother-in-law of Weatherford, had resisted appeals to join the Red Sticks.[34]

General Claiborne's column slogged northeast along the Federal Road toward Francis's blessed refuge. Sam Moniac acted as chief guide. A hard, chill rain fell intermittently, churning the trail to a pasty ooze and slowing Claiborne's pace to ten miles a day. Atop a soggy pine barren beside the Federal Road, overlooking a dark and dismal watercourse called Big Swamp Creek, Claiborne left his mud-streaked wagons and baggage and his sick, together with a hundred-man work party to construct a small stockade that—perhaps taking a cue from Andrew Jackson—he named Fort Deposit. The next morning, December 23, 1813, in subfreezing cold, his troops left the road and swung due north on a slippery trek "through woods without a track to guide them." Relieved of encumbrances, the men made better time. They closed to within two or three miles of the Holy Ground before Claiborne halted at 11:00 a.m. to prepare for the attack.

Employing tactics similar to those of Generals Jackson and Floyd, he divided his force into three columns intended to encircle the Red Stick enclave. Colonel Carson and his eighty territorial volunteers deployed to the right. The militia and Pushmataha's Choctaws deployed to the left. Colonel Russell's Third Infantry formed the center. To Major Henry Cassels, Claiborne accorded the difficult task of inserting the small battalion of poorly disciplined, untested mounted riflemen into the half-mile gap between the south bank of the Alabama and the northern edge of the Holy Ground to seal off the river as an escape route.[35]

Claiborne's preparations did not go unnoticed. William Weatherford, Malcolm McPherson, and several other Red Sticks had ventured into the woods south of the Holy Ground that raw and overcast morning to reconnoiter. Pulling rein within range of Russell's infantry, they exchanged a few shots and then galloped back to the Holy Ground to prepare for battle. Not that they had much beyond the prophet

MAP 7   THE BATTLE OF THE HOLY GROUND, DECEMBER 23, 1813

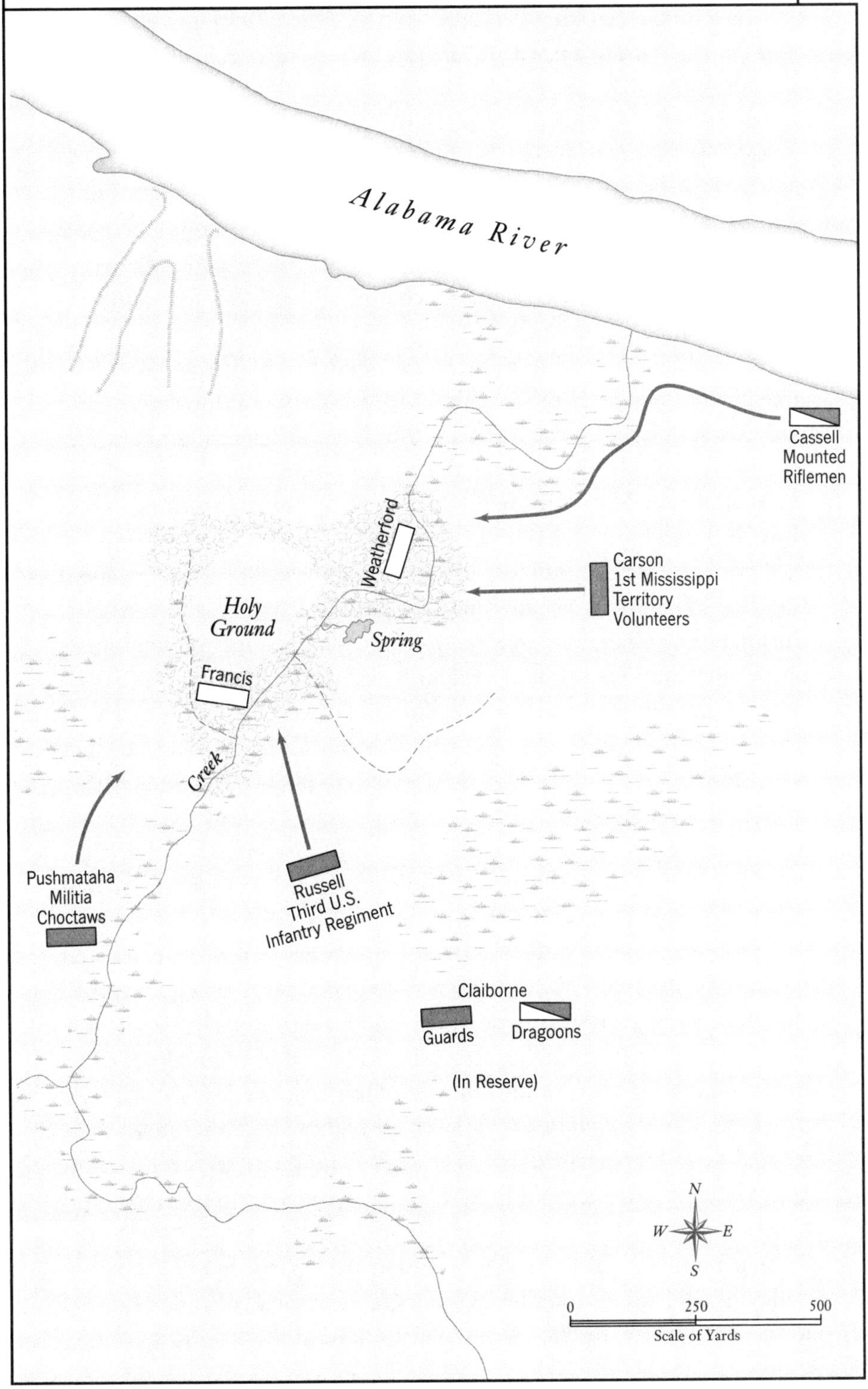

Alabama River

Cassell
Mounted
Riflemen

Weatherford

Holy
Ground

Carson
1st Mississippi
Territory
Volunteers

Spring

Francis

Creek

Russell
Third U.S.
Infantry Regiment

Pushmataha
Militia
Choctaws

Claiborne

Guards   Dragoons

(In Reserve)

N
W   E
S

0   250   500

Scale of Yards

Francis's magic circle and sacred ring of fallen timber with which to resist the Americans. Most of the warriors of Eccanachaca either were engaged at Autosee or had gone north to fight Jackson. Clutching their red war clubs, the two hundred warriors present waited and watched hopefully for the Master of Breath to strike down the approaching Americans. Possessing less faith in divine intervention, William Weatherford ordered the women, children, and elderly out of the Holy Ground and urged the thirty black men who resided in the town—either escaped slaves or chattel of the Red Sticks—to help check the impending attack.[36]

General Claiborne's plan unraveled before a shot was fired. The pine barrens between his front line and the Holy Ground shimmered with a coat of ice atop six to twenty-four inches of standing water. The troops plunged ahead, breaking the ice and wading slowly forward for three hundred chilly yards before debouching onto dry ground—wet, shivering, and badly separated.

Before closing on the Holy Ground, Claiborne and Russell halted the Third Infantry to enable the left and right columns to catch up. Pushmataha's Choctaws and the militia re-formed for the final push, but Major Cassels's mounted riflemen and Colonel Carson's Mississippi volunteers had vanished in the thick forest. A consequence of what Colonel Russell decried as his "stupidity and cowardice," but what was in fact an impenetrable swamp barring his way, Major Cassels failed to seal off the riverbank escape route. Colonel Carson, on the other hand, was overly eager to begin the contest. Rather than flank the Holy Ground from the east as ordered, Carson instructed his Creek guide to lead him to the southeastern edge of the sanctuary.

Carson's command numbered only eighty waterlogged and untested volunteers. To Francis's frightened followers, however, who watched the Mississippians pass effortlessly through the prophet's magic circle and then step easily over the sacred ring of logs, they seemed superhuman. Francis and most of his followers summarily fled. A subordinate prophet and his stauncher set of perhaps eighty adherents stood their ground near Weatherford, who lay with some thirty to forty Koasati and Alabama followers and black men behind long logs directly in Carson's path.

At a hundred yards' range, Weatherford's party opened a sharp volley of rifle and musket fire. Dispersing, Carson's volunteers edged forward from tree to tree. As they neared Weatherford's line of logs, they espied a small knot of warriors standing in the timber unleash an "incessant shower" of arrows at them. Their holy man exhorted the warriors to hold fast. His aspect struck the whites as gallantly ludicrous. "A prophet was seen in the midst," a Mississippian recalled, "frantically running to and fro, waving a cow tail dyed red in each hand and giving vent to the most unearthly yells."

The Red Sticks' aim was execrable. They hit no Mississippians. Neither did they unnerve Carson. He motioned several men around Weatherford's left. Squatting behind trees, they delivered an enfilading volley that killed or wounded several Red Sticks. The logs began to leak Indian men rearward. The black defenders, however, fought tenaciously.

After thirty minutes of fighting, the battle turned decisively in Carson's favor. Resting his musket against a tree and taking deliberate aim, a private named Gatlin shot the gyrating prophet, stretching him "lifeless on the ground" with a ball in his chest. The Red Stick bowmen fled.

Emerging from the timber behind Carson, the timorous Major Cassels entered into the fray with his mounted riflemen, and Weatherford's remaining defenders broke and ran. As their men scattered, Weatherford and Malcolm McPherson quit the logs, mounted their horses, and galloped away. Carson's troops ached to give chase. "Boys," Carson shouted. "You seem keen, go ahead and drive them."[37]

A brief but deadly pursuit ensued. Several Red Sticks toppled to the ground, shot in the back. The survivors congregated on a low bluff overlooking the Alabama. Some swam its icy but placid waters; others splashed through the swamp that Major Cassels had been unable to penetrate, their "yells of disappointment and rage" audible to Carson's men. A warrior silhouetted on the bluff grimly entertained the Mississippians with his defiance until, recalled one soldier, "mortally wounded and tossing in his death agony, he rolled headlong down the steep bank to the earth below."

Carson's men had little compassion for the Red Sticks. In the Holy Ground public square they found a tall pine post adorned with the putrefying scalps of Fort Mims victims, and in Weatherford's cabin they grabbed a letter from the governor of Spanish West Florida, González Manrique, congratulating the Red Sticks on the massacre. Unlike Jackson's Tennesseans, however, the Mississippians committed no atrocities. Not so the Choctaws, who reached the battlefield with General Claiborne and Russell's Third Infantry just as the firing petered out. A stray bullet caused momentary merriment among Pushmataha's warriors. Piercing a cane stalk, it struck Hoentubbee, a Choctaw chief who two years earlier had shown Tecumseh uncommon hospitality, square in the chest. Supposing himself mortally wounded, Hoentubbee cried, *"Sallishke"* ("I am dead"). When his warriors saw that the ball had left only a welt, they laughed heartily at their embarrassed leader.

Claiborne rewarded Pushmataha's fidelity. He permitted the Choctaws the privilege of ransacking the town and mutilating the enemy dead. Grateful Choctaw warriors scalped the fallen Red Sticks but scorned the hair of dead blacks as "trophies unfit for warriors." Fastening both Red Stick and black men's bodies with grapevines to their horses' tails, they galloped about the grounds, dragging the dead behind them until torn to shreds. The Choctaws also came away with two hundred abandoned horses. After the Choctaws sated their taste for plunder and gore, Claiborne set the Holy Ground ablaze. As the flames licked the planks of one cabin, the door swung open, and a runaway slave stepped out. Scarcely had he cleared the threshold when a dozen or more musket shots ripped him apart. Up in smoke with the two hundred cabins of the Holy Ground went more than fifteen hundred barrels of parched corn. With no wagons to haul it, Claiborne had his troops stuff their pockets with as much corn as they could carry before burning the rest.

Claiborne claimed to have slain thirty enemy at a cost of just one man killed and five wounded; other accounts place the number of Americans wounded at twenty. A black survivor later testified that Red Stick fatalities amounted to just seven Indians and eight blacks killed.[38]

William Weatherford survived in fine style. He and Malcolm McPherson were the last Red Sticks to quit the Holy Ground, and Weatherford's audacious escape (McPherson's identical act slipped into the historical dustbin) became a staple of later Alabama lore, just as did Sam Dale's exploits in the Canoe Fight. Tarrying on the edge of the Holy Ground until mounted infantrymen nearly encircled them, Weatherford and McPherson galloped down a long hollow toward the riverbank, only to pull up short at the edge of a ten- or twelve-foot bluff overlooking the water.

A leap was their only alternative. Turning his horse, Weatherford rode back up the ravine thirty yards to get the distance needed to accelerate for the jump. Aiming the animal toward the bluff, Weatherford drove his spurs into its flanks. Horse and rider dashed up the bluff, vanished over the top, and plunged into the river. They sank for a moment, resurfaced, and then the horse swam for the opposite shore. Bullets splashed the water like hail.

On the far bank, just out of range, Weatherford dismounted. Removing the saddle and blanket, he inspected his prized animal for wounds. A bullet had sliced off a lock of mane; otherwise the horse was untouched. Calmly wringing water from the blanket, Weatherford saddled the animal, mounted, gestured obscenely at the exasperated riflemen, then rode away. McPherson emerged from the river a few moments after. Together they spread word of the devastation wrought to the second of the three sacred Red Stick strongholds.[39]

The death and destruction dragged on. As Claiborne's camp stirred at dawn on Christmas Eve, a few scattered shots greeted them from the opposite shore of the Alabama. Spotting an Indian canoe on the far bank, Colonel Russell offered $50 to anyone who would swim over and retrieve it to ferry men across to dislodge the hidden Red Sticks. A soldier accomplished the feat unscathed. When he returned, Jeremiah Austill—apparently eager for another canoe fight—paddled an equally enthusiastic Pushmataha and six Choctaw warriors across the Alabama. No shots greeted them, and they concealed themselves on the bank until Austill returned with six soldiers. Together they tracked their Red Stick tormentors to their camp in a canebrake. Silently, Pushmataha motioned his warriors and the soldiers into position behind logs or trees. When all were in place, the chief yelled in Choctaw, "Shoot, shoot, kill all, kill," the meaning of which the soldiers readily comprehended. The surprised Red Sticks offered no resistance. The Choctaws claimed to have slain and scalped eighteen, clearly an exaggerated count, but both Pushmataha's warriors and the soldiers did return to camp with armloads of booty.[40]

While Pushmataha and Austill entertained themselves on the far bank, Major Cassels's mounted riflemen pounded up the near shore of the Alabama to torch a talofa the Red Sticks had constructed eight miles east of the Holy Ground near Weatherford's plantation. En route they stumbled upon three Shawnee compatriots of the Red Sticks. Retreating into a stand of reed, the Shawnees refused all entreaties to surrender. For two hours they kept the mounted riflemen at bay. After Cassels slayed them, he continued on to his objective. Before nightfall he plundered and burned the sixty dwellings of the deserted talofa. Claiborne advanced the rest of his army to Weatherford's plantation, and everyone passed a miserable night beneath a cold drenching rain.[41]

While his troops nibbled on parched corn, Claiborne spent Christmas Day 1813 weighing his options. He was exhausted, but Colonel Russell wanted to press on another forty miles to Hoithlewaulee. Its destruction would eliminate yet another significant Red Stick talwa. Colonel Carson and his officers, however, had no stomach for Russell's scheme. Meeting privately with Claiborne, they persuaded the general to end the campaign. He later enumerated the reasons for turning back: the troops lacked decent clothing and shoes, the volunteers and militia had not been paid for several months, and provisions were scant, mostly just parched corn and rancid flour.[42]

On January 1, 1814, General Claiborne's army ceased to exist. The Mississippi Territory Volunteers marched from Fort Claiborne to Mount Vernon to receive their pay and discharge papers. Laden with plunder and scalps, Pushmataha and his Choctaw warriors returned triumphantly to their villages. Claiborne resigned his commission and headed home with the hearty thanks of the citizens of the Tensaw. His expedition had terminated whatever vestige of danger had lingered there. At St. Stephens, a grand parade was held in his honor. "On every countenance the gleam of joy appeared to beam," recalled a townsman. "The name of Claiborne, his gallant officers and men, resounded from one end of the town to the other, and the night was passed with a general rejoicing such as was never before experienced at St. Stephens." With profound relief, civilians abandoned the squalid frontier forts and returned to their farms. They left behind the graves of those, mostly children, who had succumbed to disease and malnourishment while confined in the close and insalubrious stockades.[43]

General Claiborne had given much to save the Tensaw. Although just forty-two when he quit the army, the quarrels with Flournoy, the stress induced by unreliable contractors, and the rigors of campaigning had broken his health and wrecked his finances. Political foes pilloried him for failing to prevent the Fort Mims massacre and for not exploiting his victory at the Holy Ground. Bankrupt and exhausted, Claiborne died at his Natchez plantation in March 1815.

The irascible and ambitious Colonel Russell, in command at Fort Claiborne with his Third Infantry and the local militia, encouraged much of the criticism of Claiborne's conduct of the Holy Ground expedition that the general's political opponents unjustly leveled against him. No sooner had Claiborne left his eponymous fort than Russell gave General Pinckney his self-serving take on the campaign. "The project failed," he bluntly asserted, "and after killing a few Indians, burning a few towns and committing some capital blunders, we contented ourselves with what we had done and marched back." Pinckney, however, need not worry; Russell assured him that as an enterprising Regular army officer he would come up with a plan to bring the Red Sticks permanently to heel.[44]

As 1813 ended, Red Stick prospects appeared mixed. The numinous ring around the Holy Ground had proven evanescent, its earthly defenses inadequate. Two American stockades (Fort Strother and Fort Hull, the latter constructed by General Floyd on the Federal Road) polluted Red Stick soil. The Red Sticks had repelled four invading columns, but at considerable loss. The more sober-minded among them might have wondered whether they had provoked a war they could not win, that Fort Mims had perhaps been fueled by mad passions with no regard for future consequences. Most, however, retained faith in their prophets' assurances that Spanish arms and ammunition would begin to flow like water; the British would come in their great ships; the redcoat soldiers would disembark and together with their Red Stick friends humble Creek nonbelievers, sweep the Creek borders clean of Americans, and render the Red Stick domain inviolable.

General Pinckney likewise faced uncertain prospects. With the Mississippi Territory Volunteers disbanded and the Tennessee and Georgia contingents recuperating, Pinckney had only Russell's Third Infantry immediately available. The possibility of reinforcements was doubtful at best. The year 1814 opened with the United States facing uncertain prospects in the mid-Atlantic states and struggling to salvage some sort of success on the Canadian frontier. Both tasks would grow increasingly difficult after the defeat of Napoleon Bonaparte and his exile to the island of Elba in April. While the United States continued to commit most of its newly raised Regular army regiments to the Canadian theater, Great Britain was able greatly to augment its naval forces in the Chesapeake Bay and along the Atlantic Coast and to reinforce its ground commands in both Canada and eastern Maryland. Annapolis, Baltimore, and the District of Columbia all suddenly became vulnerable to British attack. Pinckney could expect little from a War Department that might have to decamp on short notice.

Despite the chilling implications for the American South of a Red Stick victory—particularly if facilitated by British assistance—the Creek War stood as a stalemate of marginal concern to the beleaguered Madison administration.

CHAPTER THIRTEEN

All We Lack Is Powder and Lead

JOSIAH FRANCIS and his acolytes needed a scapegoat to allay their people's murmured hints of apostasy. Why had the Holy Ground fallen, contrary to the great prophet's predictions, charms, and incantations? Had Francis's invisible barrier and cordon of consecrated logs been charlatanism? While Francis squirmed, a loyal lesser prophet stepped forward with an explanation for the fiasco: there had been a traitor at the Holy Ground who, by means of contrary charms, had doomed the sacred defenses.

The traitor must be identified, and treason punished. Two days after the Holy Ground imbroglio, at the temporary camp of the town's dispossessed, the accuser directed that a huge bonfire be built, and all the surviving prophets and warriors summoned to form a circle around it. They were to dance a prescribed number of times around the blaze. The man upon whom the most particles of soot fell would necessarily be the guilty party, black—as in the blackness of soot—being emblematic of evil. The prophet's instructions were carried out, and the filthy unfortunate put to death. The faithful rejoiced, doubters recanted—and Francis fled. Naturally timid, he declined to risk either his prestige or his life on further prophesying. Instead, he and a handful of adherents sought refuge in Pensacola under the pretext of appealing to the British to support a cause that to them now appeared doubtful.[1]

·   ·   ·

In January 1814, William Weatherford and Peter McQueen also journeyed to Pensacola. Weatherford also apparently questioned Red
Stick prospects after the Holy Ground. Between 500 and 750 fighting
men out of an initial warrior strength of approximately 4,000 were
dead, and an untold number had been wounded. More ominous than
the destruction of the Holy Ground, Autosee, Talladega, and several
other talwas and talofas—dwellings and council grounds could always
be rebuilt—was the loss of the foodstuffs and supplies they had contained. Winter came, and with it hunger and privation. The profligate
slaughter of livestock that the prophets had ordained now threatened
homeless followers with starvation.

There were hopeful prospects also, however. To reiterate, the
Americans had made no lasting inroads in the Red Stick country. At
Hoithlewaulee, the Red Sticks could muster two thousand warriors
from the untouched lower Tallapoosa and Coosa River talwas at short
notice, while Chief Menawa counted perhaps twelve hundred men
at Tohopeka on the upper Tallapoosa, likewise undisturbed. The
morale of most warriors remained high. Even before he learned of
Claiborne's withdrawal, the Red Stick métis John Durant wrote to
his brother Sandy, "We have had two powerful armies [Jackson's and
Floyd's] in our country but they have had to run back faster than they
came. The Creeks have been counted cowards; they turned out to be
brave soldiers. All we lack is powder and lead."[2]

In Pensacola, Weatherford, McQueen, and their large entourage
of warriors wheedled a few horse loads of ammunition for the Red
Sticks at Hoithlewaulee, but there was no food to be had. In retaliation for Spanish aid to the Red Sticks, limited though it was, General
Flournoy sealed off New Orleans and Mobile. "The national ware-
houses in West Florida are empty," Governor González Manrique
wrote, alerting his superior in Havana. "The people only have flour,
and there is a complete lack of all types of stew and salted meat."
Fresh food too was almost depleted. The governor urged Havana to
consider the "critical state of the province" and immediately ship provisions to Pensacola. The Red Sticks no longer were merely a nuisance
to González Manrique; their antics jeopardized the very survival of
Spanish West Florida.[3]

. . .

In sole command of the Mississippi Territory frontier after Claiborne resigned, Lieutenant Colonel Gilbert Russell ached to achieve the decisive victory over the Red Sticks that had eluded the general. While Weatherford and McQueen were in Pensacola soliciting powder and lead, the striving Russell petitioned General Pinckney for permission to stage a waterborne offensive along the Alabama River against Hoithlewaulee and points east. If he were able to assemble nine hundred men and enough boats to carry ninety days' supplies, Russell felt certain he could break the back of Red Stick resistance. Pinckney appreciated Russell's aggressive spirit but doubted him capable of assembling more than the six hundred Regular troops then at Fort Claiborne; the Mississippi Territory Volunteers had mustered out, and the local militia consisted of fewer than a hundred men. Pinckney counted on the armies of Andrew Jackson and John Floyd, once they recovered, to put an end to the Creek War in 1814. He instructed Russell to build or secure the necessary boats, load them with provisions, and then advance cautiously to the confluence of the Coosa and Tallapoosa Rivers in support of Jackson and Floyd. Altering his ambition to accommodate his orders, Russell assembled his flotilla.

Then the peevish General Flournoy intervened—for ill, as was his wont. Dozens of boats suitable for navigating the Alabama River floated idle and decaying in the harbors of New Orleans and Mobile. They were the property of the Seventh Military District, however, and Flournoy would not release them to Russell. Neither would he grant Russell the tools or quartermaster supplies necessary to build his own boats. Because the Third Regiment had been stripped from his command, Flournoy felt no obligation to cooperate with Russell. As far as he was concerned, Pinckney could send Russell what he needed overland across Red Stick country.[4]

Stymied in his larger plans, Russell sought action closer to home. Small, far-ranging Red Stick foraging parties periodically prowled the Tombigbee and Tensaw Districts. They represented an annoyance rather than a real threat or opportunity for serious combat. At the end of January 1814, however, Russell received word that four or five hundred enemy warriors were congregated at a place known as the Old Towns on the lush and lovely Cahaba River, eighty miles north of

Fort Claiborne (and forty miles northwest of present-day Selma, Alabama). Marshaling the five hundred members of the Third Regiment fit for duty, Russell set out from Fort Claiborne toward the presumed Red Stick assemblage. With Russell traveled two militia companies under Sam Dale, one of which was led by Jeremiah Austill's father.

Because the troops were to travel a trail too primitive for wagons, Colonel Russell ordered Captain James Dinkins to take two barges outfitted with cannons and laden with provisions up the Alabama and Cahaba Rivers to rejoin the regiment just below the Old Towns before the soldiers' six-day rations ran out.[5]

Nothing went as planned. The "wretched guide" who led Russell's column became hopelessly lost. Ten days elapsed before the famished soldiers reached the rendezvous, only to find no sign of Dinkins's barges. Pressing on, Russell entered the Old Towns ready to give battle, but instead encountered only fifteen or twenty deserted Creek cabins scattered about a bluff overlooking the Cahaba.

Sam Dale sympathized with his commander's predicament. "Colonel Russell was in a tight place and roundly damned his luck. He could find no Indians and had lost his barges." Russell knew better than to press his luck. Lieutenant Joseph M. Wilcox, an eager young West Point graduate, accepted the colonel's proposal that he take an Indian canoe and with three volunteers paddle downriver in search of Dinkins. Wilcox was to tell the wayward captain to return to Fort Claiborne. While Russell and Wilcox conferred, hungry troops set fire to the cabins to flush out their resident rodents. "I saw a soldier offer two dollars for a rat," said Dale. "The offer was rejected; the owner demanded ten dollars." Scrounging hickory nuts and acorns and slaughtering Russell and Dale's horses for meat, the ravenous soldiers idled at the Old Towns for four days on the off chance Dinkins might appear, then stumbled back to Fort Claiborne. The return march consumed six days and the men's strength with it. Exposure to the elements and exhaustion so inflamed the bullet wound Sam Dale had received at Burnt Corn Creek that he quit the army to recuperate.

Dinkins and his barges awaited Russell at Fort Claiborne. The captain had missed the mouth of the Cahaba River and continued up the Alabama before realizing his error. Instead of trying to correct his course, Dinkins returned to Fort Claiborne, bearing the precious provisions and the cold corpse of Lieutenant Wilcox.

David Crockett. The famed frontiersman saw action as a Tennessee mounted rifleman in Jackson's first campaign against the Red Sticks.

Richard Call. The future governor of the Florida Territory served Jackson faithfully throughout the Creek War as an enlisted man and junior officer. Call's account of his wartime service ranks among the best.

Tennessee Volunteers by Keith Rocco. An excellent depiction of the typical Tennessee Volunteers that turned out for service under Jackson.

Battle of Tallushatchee. General Coffee's attack on the Red Stick talwas featured gut-wrenching brutality committed by numerous mounted riflemen.

Battle of Talladega. A stirring and stylized depiction of the Red Stick defeat from an early Jackson biography.

Jackson faces down a brigade of hungry and discontented volunteers in a nineteenth-century rendition. Richard Call said his apparently "supernatural appearance . . . awed and petrified" the rebellious Tennesseans.

The Holy Ground Battlefield, likely the spot where William Weatherford and his mount leaped into the Alabama River.

Menawa, the most capable Red Stick war leader and Andrew Jackson's principal opponent.

The Battle of Enitachopco, a near brush with annihilation for Andrew Jackson.

Cherokee warriors cross the Tallapoosa River in rear of Tohopeka.

Cherokee warriors infiltrate Tohopeka. Their audacious crossing of the Tallapoosa River and assault on the Red Stick village turned the tide of battle at Horseshoe Bend.

The Thirty-Ninth U.S. Infantry charges the Red Stick breastworks at Horseshoe Bend.

The Red Sticks defend their barricade at Horseshoe Bend.

Sam Houston in later life. His exploits at Horseshoe Bend won him Andrew Jackson's admiration.

Andrew Jackson rides over the Horseshoe Bend battlefield after the day's carnage.

The surrender of William Weatherford, one of the most storied moments of the Creek War.

Opothle Yoholo, an eloquent spokesman and genuine defender of Creek interests. He vigorously opposed the government removal program.

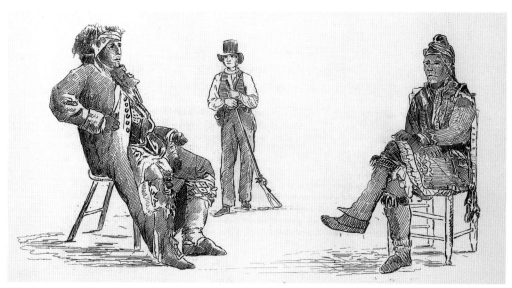

Chiefs of the Creek nation in 1829, with one of the ubiquitous Georgia squatters on Creek land.

The lone survivor of Wilcox's party told Russell a tragic tale. Ten miles downriver from the Old Towns, the lieutenant and his inexperienced paddlers had upset their canoe. They lost a musket overboard and soaked all their ammunition except a handful of cartridges that they had carried in their pockets. Undeterred, the men righted the boat and resumed their trip, expecting at any moment to encounter either Dinkins's barges or the Alabama River. Traveling through the night and deep into the following afternoon, they instead chanced upon a Red Stick encampment, likely warriors under Paddy Walsh who had abandoned the Old Towns ahead of Colonel Russell. Paddling furiously, Wilcox's party eluded 150 howling and jeering pursuers and swung east into the Alabama River. For two days Wilcox's party struggled upriver, pausing for only thirty minutes in a canebrake to rest and finish the last of their food. On the third afternoon, the famished men spotted two Red Stick canoes on the horizon. Grounding their canoe and ducking into a canebrake on the north bank of the Alabama, Wilcox and his two soldiers—one militiaman had deserted during their rest stop the day before—hoped to hide until nightfall before resuming their journey.

They never got the chance. At dusk, the Red Sticks attacked, intent on capturing them. A brief struggle ensued. With clubbed muskets, the trio killed two warriors and drove off the others, who carried with them Wilcox's canoe. After staggering aimlessly through swamps until dawn, Wilcox abandoned the search for Dinkins. He and the two men began fashioning a cane raft with which to cross to the south bank; from there, they would walk to the Federal Road and then head home.

A canoe bearing eight Red Sticks interrupted their labors. The Indians poured a volley at the soldiers. One man fell with a bullet through the knee, and the other fled, leaving Lieutenant Wilcox to his fate. Ten minutes later, Dinkins's barges hove into view. The Red Sticks paddled off, and the squeamish surviving soldier led the detachment to the ambush site. There lay Wilcox and the other man weltering in gore, their skulls cleaved with tomahawks. Both lingered a few minutes before dying—the only army casualties of Russell's expedition.[6]

Colonel Russell's fiasco marked the end of army operations staged from the Mississippi Territory. Neither would the Choctaws contribute much more to the war effort. Apart from Pushmataha's ardent contingent, the Choctaws proved half-hearted allies. Most, at least, resisted repeated Red Stick entreaties to switch sides. Governor Blount of Tennessee and Andrew Jackson had been the first American officials to recognize the need to obtain if not the active cooperation, then at least the neutrality of the northeastern Choctaws, over whom Pushmataha exercised no influence. In late September 1813, the former Choctaw agent John McKee, who retained the confidence of both that tribe and the neighboring Chickasaws, traveled from Nashville at Old Hickory's behest to confer with both peoples. Should conditions appear favorable, McKee was to lead them against a presumably fortified Red Stick village on the Black Warrior River and clear Jackson's right flank.

Establishing himself at the lower Black Warrior River plantation of John Pitchlynn, the capable U.S. interpreter for the Choctaws, McKee spent three months wrangling with the northeastern Choctaws, whose cunning leader, Chief Moshulitubbee, stalled until certain the Americans could prevail before committing to fight for them. He made repeated demands of McKee for powder, lead, and supplies. The harried emissary shuttled between Mobile and Pitchlynn's place with the requested munitions, which never seemed to suffice. In mid-December, McKee lost patience and threatened to tell General Jackson that Moshulitubbee was an enemy.

Moshulitubbee and his Choctaws took notice. Aware that Jackson had thrashed the Red Sticks at Tallushatchee and Talladega, they wanted no trouble with Old Hickory. Word of Claiborne's destruction of the Holy Ground removed any doubts they had about siding with the Americans. They even pledged to fight those of their warriors who had joined the Red Sticks on the Black Warrior River. The Chickasaws, who had made innumerable excuses for their inaction, also promised Jackson that they not only would put to death any Red Sticks who entered their nation but also would contribute two hundred warriors to the Choctaw expedition, which John McKee was to command. On January 12, 1814, a satisfied McKee set out with Moshulitubbee and four hundred Choctaw warriors to scour the Black Warrior River. Eight days later they entered the Red Stick village, its occupants having absconded. McKee burned the place and then turned back. The tardy Chickasaws joined him on the return march, content to have proven their fidelity to the Americans without the need to shed blood.[7]

With McKee's brief raid—consequential only for compelling the previously noncommittal Choctaws and Chickasaws to take sides in the war—the curtain closed on combat in the western part of the Red Stick country. A decisive blow against the Red Sticks would have to come from the north or east—and soon. American prospects, however, were mixed. As will be seen, Andrew Jackson's army had unraveled from a variety of causes, including chronic food shortages, debate over enlistment expirations, and the need to provide for families back home. What remained of his command huddled in camp at the northern margins of the Red Stick country. Similar problems threatened to upend General Floyd's Georgia brigade.

General Pinckney, consequently, was eager to spill Red Stick blood before Georgia enlistments expired on February 25. Unsubstantiated rumors that British ships had landed arms and ammunition for the Creeks, and perhaps even troops in Spanish West Florida, fed Pinckney's anxiety. General Floyd, who had recuperated from his Autosee wound, also wanted to fight again. A grateful Pinckney approved a second Georgia expedition, but supply deficiencies—the perennial bugaboo of American commanders in the Creek War—delayed Floyd's departure from Fort Mitchell until mid-January 1814.

At least Floyd knew where to find the enemy. Chief Menawa's large but untested Abeika contingent of twelve hundred warriors, drawn from six talwas, was gathered at Tohopeka awaiting Old Hickory's return. Another four hundred warriors lingered at Okfuskee in case Colonel Russell should reappear, and fifteen hundred more had congregated at the confluence of the Tallapoosa and Coosa Rivers between Hoithlewaulee and the charred remains of Autosee, ready to repel a second strike from either the Mississippi Territory or Georgia. It was against this third aggregation that Floyd finally marched west on January 17 with a force of eleven hundred militia and five hundred friendly Lower Creek and Uchee warriors. Three days later Floyd paused at Fort Hull, twenty-four miles east of Hoithlewaulee, to prepare his men for battle.[8]

Then the skies opened. For the next four days a cold hard rain pummeled the troops and friendly Creeks and reduced the Federal Road to muck. On January 25, Floyd resumed the march. He made just three miles on the spongy trail. The day after was no better. Weary of repeatedly wrestling his heavily laden wagons out of axle-deep mud, Floyd halted after two miles. Waving the wagons back to Fort

Hull, he redistributed the ammunition, entrenching tools, and six days' provisions on light carriages and packhorses and then filed his soggy command into the woods in search of a suitable campsite. A mile north of the Federal Road and seven miles south of present-day Tuskegee, Alabama, he found a spot to his liking—a slight rise on the south bank of Calabee Creek, overlooking a broad swamp of the same name. Forming a rough square two lines deep, the soldiers rested on their arms. Floyd placed his precious artillery, just two small, wooden-wheeled cannons mounted "navy-style" on wooden carriages, in the center of camp.

The gray light of a cloudy winter's afternoon filtered through the forest. Ample time remained before dark to fortify "Camp Defiance," as Floyd christened the bivouac, but he issued no such orders. Here and there, soldiers stacked logs in front of their positions. Most men, however, contented themselves with a hot meal and the prospect of a fitful night's rest on the cold and damp earth. Before drifting off to sleep, Private James Tait glimpsed the friendly Creeks blacken their faces over burned stumps and logs. "This is their way," he mused, "in order to exhibit to their enemies as ugly an appearance as possible."[9]

Floyd's army had not marched unnoticed. Red Stick scouts posted on the Federal Road apprised the prophet Paddy Walsh of Floyd's approach well before the Georgian's expedition became bogged down at Fort Hull. The scouts also spotted the dreaded cannons. With a resilience common to Red Stick prophets, Walsh had overcome the feebleness of his medicine at Fort Mims, recovered his following, and recuperated from his bullet wounds. Here was a fresh opportunity not only to prove the value of his incantations but perhaps also to claim the role of principal war leader.

Sending swift runners to neighboring encampments, Walsh called for a rendezvous and a council of war at Hoithlewaulee. William Weatherford and his friend and confidant William "Bit Nose Billy" McGillivray, the métis son of a Scots trader who had assumed the sur-name of the great Creek diplomat, answered the prophet's summons. So too did Jim Boy. With them they brought the ammunition recently obtained in Pensacola. Peter McQueen was absent, having elected to remain in the Spanish West Florida capital temporarily to manage

Creek interests there. The métis chronicler George Stiggins placed the number of warriors who responded to Paddy Walsh's call at 1,274.

The four Red Stick leaders bickered over a plan of attack. At a contentious council on the evening of January 26, Walsh urged a "close and severe" assault on Floyd's camp while the soldiers slept. If the Red Sticks penetrated the enemy square before daylight, they would continue the fight; if not, they would retreat. Jim Boy endorsed Walsh's proposal. Weatherford and McGillivray, on the other hand, thought it preposterous to encounter the enemy thinking, "I am to be defeated in the end." A "man could not fight hard with a limit on himself to run off at a certain time," they argued. For their part, "they would fight as long as they could see any chance; they wanted no limitations on their battle."

Weatherford offered an alternative. Conceding the wisdom of a night assault, he suggested Paddy Walsh lead three hundred warriors stealthily toward one side of the Georgians' square until discovered, after which they should batter their way through the line with tomahawks and war clubs, rush to the center of the camp, kill the officers in the tents in which they slept, and then fight their way out. The instant Walsh's warriors raised their war whoop, the remaining Red Sticks would attack the other three sides of the encampment. An attack at close quarters against groggy, leaderless troops would shatter Floyd's army and send both the survivors and their Creek stooges flying for the frontier.

It was a sound plan, and likely would have succeeded in mauling if not annihilating the Georgians. Walsh and Jim Boy, however, accused Weatherford of wishing to see them killed in a suicidal charge that he and McGillivray lacked the courage to lead. Furious at having their courage challenged, Weatherford and McGillivray offered to lead the storming party or die in the attempt. To break the impasse, Walsh called for three hundred volunteers. Aware that the prophets opposed Weatherford, only a handful came forward. Weatherford swore and stormed about, threatening to go home rather than see lives wasted in Paddy Walsh's fainthearted "half-fight." With McGillivray reluctant to leave, however, Weatherford yielded. He would do his best to squeeze victory from Walsh's defeatist scheme.[10]

· · ·

While their leaders squabbled, the Red Stick warriors trembled expectantly beside tiny campfires in the cold muck of Calabee Swamp, a mile west of Floyd's command. Stripped to their breechclouts and painted red, they ached to deal the detested Georgians and the Lower Creek and Uchee apostates a mortal blow. Less than two hours of darkness remained when the contentious Red Stick commanders' conference broke up. A heavy white frost had formed. Walsh, Jim Boy, Weatherford, and McGillivray dispersed to advise the junior war leaders of the final plan and its timid subscript of quick victory or daybreak retreat. The Red Sticks were to edge forward noiselessly in their soft moccasins, crawling as they neared the American picket line. Rising, they would emit a war whoop and charge the front and flanks of the camp. It was imperative that they capture the cannons; Weatherford and McGillivray would direct the effort against the guns, while Paddy Walsh and Jim Boy presumably led a flanking party each.

Wrapped in a blanket, the twenty-two-year-old private Allen Brooks drowsed beside a crackling campfire when the high-pitched Indian war cry pierced the black stillness. Stupefied, Brooks stumbled about looking for his shoes. Musket balls whizzed past. Turning in the direction of a dull thud, he glimpsed a cousin collapse, blood spurting from a fatal shot to the forehead. Gradually, Brooks's company formed a ragged line several hundred feet behind their campfire. Other units also fell back, compressing the already tight square that comprised Camp Defiance.

The bivouac's bold name failed to inspire. Troops panicked as the dimly visible Red Sticks rushed toward them out of a roaring dark rendered deeper by the sulfurous cloud of gun smoke that quickly blanketed the ground. Officers also succumbed to the terror. One frightened lieutenant scampered to a hay bed and burrowed inside. Captain Samuel Butts, a close friend of Floyd's who had managed supplies and provisions for the Autosee campaign, set a better example. Shot through the body, he propped himself against a tree and then called for his brace of pistols in order to "dispatch two of the enemy should they appear near enough." The friendly Creeks were worse than useless. At the first fire they abandoned the line and huddled in the center of camp.[11]

Fortunately for the defenders, General Floyd maintained his composure. Stepping from his tent at the first fire, he struck a match, squinted at his pocket watch, and made a mental note of the time. It was 5:20 a.m., just forty minutes until daybreak. Mounting his milk-white horse, Floyd galloped to the front. A bullet slammed into his aide-de-camp's mount, and the man tumbled hard to the ground. Three balls struck the regimental commander, Colonel Daniel Newman, leaving his troops momentarily leaderless.

Beyond the front line, two sentinels lay dead. The men of one picket post fired a volley into the gloom and then swung clubbed muskets at the shadowy Red Sticks. Repudiating the cowardice of the Lower Creeks, the twenty-nine-year-old métis Timpoochee Barnard, son of a longtime Scots trader and Uchee mother, sallied forth with his Uchee warriors to rescue the isolated detachment. For his audacious act, the red-turbaned Barnard won the esteem of a thankful General Floyd.

With the sentinels either dead or integrated in the firing line, attention turned to Floyd's two cannons, commanded by Captain Jeff Thomas. The contracting ranks left them dangerously exposed, and Red Stick warriors fired with deadly accuracy at the gun crews whenever cannon flashes illuminated them. They shot four of seven crewmen on one cannon, and for a time it appeared that they would overrun both guns. Then a cannon flash revealed to Captain Thomas that his gunners had overshot their mark; the Red Sticks were crawling—not running—up the slope on which the guns stood. Thomas barked an order to lower the muzzles. Using their muskets as levers, several nearby infantrymen lifted the carriages. Cannon blasts swept the front with canister shot. The small iron balls ripped apart the forward-most warriors and caused the rest to recoil. Taking heart, General Floyd yelled, "Hold your ground, boys, it will soon be daylight, and then we will give them hell." To which William Weatherford retorted above the din, "Yes, damn you, and we will give you hell before daylight comes!"[12]

Brave words, but the battle had turned against the Red Sticks. Uncertain shafts of light from the rising sun knifed through the gun smoke. Red Stick ammunition ran out. "Give me some bullets, give me some lead," a Georgian who understood Muscogee heard the warriors call to one another. No longer shielded by darkness, Weatherford's Red Sticks receded into the swamp. Paddy Walsh fell gravely wounded. So too did Jim Boy. The leaderless attackers on both flanks withdrew, their line of retreat etched in blood.

Floyd counterattacked. He wheeled his flank regiments into line and drew his rear ranks forward. A troop of dragoons galloped ahead, slaying with sabers fifteen slow-running Red Sticks. After a mile, Floyd called a halt. Trudging back to camp, Private Allen Brooks heard a low moan emanating from a small canebrake. He approached the spot cautiously. There lay a wounded Red Stick, his leg broken and mangled. Grieved at his cousin's death, Brooks put a bullet through the man's brain. Resuming his trek, Brooks stepped over a large, hollowed-out pine log, unaware that a warrior crouched inside it. Back at camp, Brooks waited for his comrades to rejoin him. As they neared the pine log, the hidden Red Stick abandoned his refuge and bolted past. "In the twinkling of an eye," said an astonished Brooks, "scores of rifles were fired upon him, and he fell, riddled with bullets."[13]

Private Brooks's cold-blooded killing of the disabled warrior marked one of the few atrocities to occur during the forty-five-minute battle and subsequent pursuit. For the most part, the Georgians treated wounded Red Sticks kindly. Perhaps to compensate, in their minds at least, for their cowardice during the battle, their Lower Creek allies fell upon the Red Stick dead with unbridled savagery, however. "The friendly Indians exercised great barbarity upon the bodies of our enemy's slain. They ripped them open, cut their heads to pieces, took out the heart of one, which was borne along in savage triumph by the perpetrators," attested the horrified Private James Tait. "Strange to tell, [they] cut off the private parts of others. One dead Indian was hoisted upon a dead horse, and as he would tumble off, the savage spectators would cry out, 'Whiskey too much.' What bestial conduct."[14]

Paddy Walsh survived. Relatives carried him to a canoe and paddled the wounded métis down the Alabama River to an isolated canebrake where he could recuperate unmolested either by prowling whites or by Red Sticks angry that his medicine and battle plan both had failed. After his wounds healed, Walsh fled to the western edge of the Creek country, content to let the conflict run its course.[15]

With Paddy Walsh out of the war and Jim Boy incapacitated, it fell to William Weatherford and the lesser prophets to reorganize the lower Tallapoosa and Coosa Red Sticks after their repulse. Not only had they failed to deal the Georgians a mortal blow, which the Red Sticks would likely have done had Weatherford's tactics been adopted at Calabee Creek, but fifty warriors also had been killed and an uncertain number wounded in the brief but bitter clash. Floyd had lost seventeen men killed, most in the opening moments of battle and in the struggle for the cannons.

More threatening to Red Stick chances in the lower Tallapoosa and Coosa region than their casualties was the diminishing stock of food. There had been no time since hostilities had begun in which to harvest corn and little opportunity to hunt. Unable to work the land, the women grubbed for berries and acorns, while the men likely regretted their wholesale slaughter of hogs and cattle during the heady early days of the war. Returning with a Red Stick scalp taken near Tuckabatchee shortly after the Battle of Calabee Creek, Timpoochee Barnard's Uchee scouts told General Floyd that the Red Stick "women and children are running off nearly perished and would desert if they could." Apart from keeping their families together, after Calabee Creek the men showed little interest in anything. "The defeat silenced the old and new war dance and whoop of many of the most conspicuous warriors," related George Stiggins, "[and] the lower-town [Red Stick] chiefs appeared to be paralyzed and inattentive to national affairs."[16]

Few warriors were more despondent than the remnant of a small party of young Choctaws from Moshulitubbee's town who had thrown in with the Red Sticks at the start of the war. Most died at Calabee Creek. Hopeful of forgiveness, the survivors headed home. Theirs was a harsh welcome. Despite his early sympathy for the Red Stick cause, Chief Moshulitubbee ordered their immediate arrest and execution. Fratricidal strife had overspilled the Creek frontier.[17]

The demoralized lower Tallapoosa and Coosa Red Sticks at least would not have to contend again with Floyd. His army lay in shambles. Expecting supply wagons that never materialized, Floyd held his ragged, poorly clad militiamen at Camp Defiance for five days after Calabee Creek. Many lacked shoes and blankets, which the friendly Creeks had appropriated during the Georgians' counterattack. Excepting Barnard's Uchees, Floyd was happy to see them go. "The aid of friendly Indians, I had never any reliance on," he wrote to Pinckney. "They cannot be persuaded to venture an inch beyond the army and have been in every influence in which they have acted a disadvantage to us." The needs of the wounded caused Floyd to put the able-bodied on half rations. Weakened by hunger and exposure, several score fell ill with measles, and a number died. Mutinous murmurings wafted their way to headquarters. A sympathetic Floyd yielded. On February 1 his army shuffled back down the Federal Road, first to Fort Hull, which he garrisoned with a detachment of recently arrived Regulars under Colonel Homer Milton and 140 militiamen who volunteered to remain behind, and then on to the Georgia state capital of Milledgeville to muster out.

Other fresh troops were also on the way. General Pinckney had assembled two new volunteer regiments, one from North Carolina and the other from South Carolina. When they reached Fort Hull, presumably no later than mid-February, Colonel Milton was to assume overall command and cooperate with General Jackson in his next thrust toward the Red Stick heartland at the junction of the Coosa and Tallapoosa Rivers, whenever it came.

Both the citizens of Milledgeville and his own officers and men applauded Floyd's leadership. They blamed commissary agents and contractors for the Georgia brigade's inability to contribute more. All regretted that "reasons beyond [Floyd's] control should have prevented the termination of the Creek War by the troops of our own state."[18]

General Floyd quit the service with a clear conscience. To Andrew Jackson, he explained why he had aborted his expedition after Calabee Creek:

> The uncertainty of receiving supplies so dispirited the men who now lost all hopes of being able to penetrate further into the enemy's country without the risk of starvation at the end. Besides this the men had been called into service in summer attire, which is now worn out, and the men nearly naked. The expiration of their term of service, and the season for agricultural pursuits fast approaching, many of the men are poor and their families dependent on their labor for support, began to reflect on their situation and their interests and happiness. Disaffection soon began to discover itself, and I possessed not means but by orders and threats,

which would have availed nothing, in checking a sentiment that but too generally pervaded the ranks and required considerable address to overcome. A resort to force without means would have broken up the army. I therefore without effecting to know existing malcontents, ordered the army to fall back.

In justice to the militia under my command, I can assert that they are brave, and have entered the service with great zeal, have yielded to subordination, and acquired discipline as long as they entertained a hope of rendering service, but they have been shamefully supplied.[19]

If Floyd expected sympathy for his plight from Old Hickory, he was looking to the wrong man. Jackson probably cast Floyd's missive aside scornfully. He had overcome greater obstacles at immense personal cost. If necessary, Jackson would prosecute the war to a finish himself.

· PART FOUR ·

CHAPTER FOURTEEN

Tennesseans to the Rear

RUMINATING ON the relationship between full rations and victory, Napoleon Bonaparte observed, "There is no subordination with empty stomachs."[1] In the waning weeks of 1813, Andrew Jackson was to experience the hard truth that lay behind Napoleon's dictum. While Claiborne and Floyd fought their final contests against the Red Sticks independently of each other, Jackson wrestled with inadequate supplies, insubordination, and his own pain-racked constitution at camps far from the scenes of battle.

True to the promise he had made to his officers, on November 14 Jackson withdrew from Fort Strother toward Fort Deposit to meet supplies supposedly on the way. Haggard and hungry though they were, few soldiers really wanted to find food at Fort Deposit, so eager were they to go home. The aide-de-camp John Reid feared the army would collapse. "You have no conception of the ungovernable state of the men," he wrote. To Jackson's immense relief, and to his troops' dismay, after marching just a dozen miles, they met a drove of 150 cattle. Slaughtering, cooking, and consuming them was the work of a minute. Filled with "beef and valor," the soldiers felt capable of coping even with the wrath of Old Hickory, or so they thought. When Jackson issued the order to return to Fort Strother, one defiant company instead set out for home. Others prepared to follow them. Beneath a cold rain, General Coffee and a small party of cavalrymen watched the renegades approach, uncertain how to respond.

Suddenly General Jackson, Major Reid, and a "few faithful friends" drew up beside Coffee. Forming the mounted men astride the trail, Jackson told them to fire on the would-be deserters should they persist. "By the immaculate God!" thundered Jackson. "I'll blow the damned villains to eternity if they advance another step!" There was no need for bloodshed; one look at Old Hickory sufficed to send the refractory company scuttling back to its encampment.

Jackson's troubles were far from over, however. Ignoring the entreaties of its senior officers, nearly the entire brigade of volunteers also decided to desert. One thousand determined men lined up on the soggy Tennessee-bound trail. Galloping to the scene, Jackson grabbed a musket from a soldier and rode to the head of the column. A startled lieutenant, Richard Call, remembered his appearance. "General Jackson suddenly and unexpectedly, as if he had dropped from the skies, approached in my rear, unseen by me until he passed me. His countenance was like a thundercloud charged with tempest."

Old Hickory halted. Major Reid and General Coffee drew rein beside him. Emaciated and racked with pain from his festering shoulder wound, his left arm in a sling, Jackson leaned the musket on his horse's neck, vowing to shoot the first man who tried to pass him. "He gave vent to his furious indignation and wrath," continued Lieutenant Call. "He told them that he had not there the power to punish them, or to prevent their disgrace, but if they went, then we would follow them to their houses and have every man put to death who dared to abandon the campaign until honorably discharged." Abruptly changing tack, Jackson blamed the officers, saying that if they had done their duty, the men would have emulated their example.

The mutineers stood beneath the drumming rain in sullen silence, "awed and petrified," said Call, "by what seemed his supernatural appearance." Old Hickory softened. He appealed to their patriotism lightheartedly. "Come on, my brave fellows. I have now abundant supplies. Follow me but a few weeks longer, and we will end this savage war. We will drive the Red Sticks and their friends the British into the sea at Pensacola, and then you shall have the long-corked claret and a dance with the pretty girls." Gradually, a few soldiers and junior officers—Lieutenant Call among them—left the column and joined

Jackson, training their muskets and pistols on the disaffected men. The rebellious troops dispersed. Order was restored.[2]

With each passing day, however, prospects for holding together the army dimmed. Supplies fell woefully short of Jackson's promise. Cold and dampness permeated the camp. "The army is becoming exceedingly unhealthy," Major Reid wrote dejectedly to his wife on December 3, "and several of the wounded, and more of the sick, have lately died."

Jackson shared in his soldiers' suffering. "From my late exposure to the inclemency of the weather," he confided to General Pinckney, "the wound of my arm, and the want of rest, my health is a little impaired." The pain he could endure. What Old Hickory could not abide, however, was seditious rumbling. Word reached headquarters that General Hall's brigade of volunteers, which had enlisted on December 10, 1812, for one year's service, intended to demand its discharge on December 10, 1813. At first, Jackson dismissed the news as the camp gossip of idle soldiers, confident that another battle with the Red Sticks would restore their patriotism.

Prospects for staging another expedition appeared promising. Although flour and meal were in perilously short stock, the contractors had provided ample pork and beef. General Cocke's fifteen hundred East Tennesseans were expected to reach Fort Strother on December 12. Jackson also counted on the imminent return of General Coffee's mounted brigade, which he had permitted to rest, refit, and forage north of the Tennessee River. Jackson also knew of Floyd's partial victory at Autosee. As soon as Coffee and Cocke arrived, he would march southward and deal the Red Sticks a "final blow."[3]

Hunched in his marquee (a spacious, conical-topped canvas tent), coat draped over his wounded shoulder, scribbling or dictating to Major Reid the necessary orders for his contemplated offensive, Old Hickory struggled to accept the possibility that his beloved West Tennessee volunteers lacked his fervor for victory over the Red Sticks. Unburdening himself to a prominent Tennessee clergyman, Jackson wrote on December 3, "I left Tennessee with the bravest army, I believed, that any general ever commanded. I have seen them in battle, and my opinion of their bravery is not changed. But their fortitude— upon this too I relied, has been too severely tested. You know not the privations we have suffered, nor do I like to describe them. Perhaps I was wrong in believing that nothing but death could conquer the spirits of brave men." Nevertheless, the war must continue. "New volunteers must be raised to complete a campaign which has been so auspiciously begun by the old ones," insisted Jackson. "You have said, if I needed your assistance, it would be cheerfully afforded. I do need it, in a high degree...in summoning volunteers to the defense of their country." Jackson looked to his young protégé Major William Carroll to spur the recruitment of volunteers, and he sent him to Nashville together with the reliable Brigadier General Isaac Roberts, who also needed new men to fill the depleted ranks of his militia brigade, which disease and battle losses had reduced to half strength.[4]

Of those officers yet in camp Jackson could trust only Major Reid implicitly. Not only were Carroll and Roberts gone, but Old Hickory's close friend and confidant John Coffee lay in bed in Huntsville seriously ill. Perhaps his near isolation, incessant pain, and chronic diarrhea induced Jackson to indulge breaches of the chain of command. On December 4, the regimental commander Colonel William Martin circumvented his immediate superior, General Hall, and wrote Old Hickory that he would lose the entire brigade of volunteers on December 10. "On that day they will claim their discharge as a matter of right," averred Martin. The men were sorry, but most were poor farmers who must return home to tend to family business or they would be ruined. "They feel a pride of having fought under [Jackson's] Command" and "have received him as an affectionate father." They hoped to part on cordial terms.

A disconsolate Jackson responded that he had applied to Governor Blount for permission to discharge the men and to authorize new volunteers to "complete a campaign which has been so happily begun and thus far fortunately prosecuted." In the meantime, the volunteers must remain beyond their term of service. He would construe any attempt to leave as mutiny and desertion, which "*shall* be put down, so long as I retain the power of quelling them, and when *deprived* of this power, I shall, to the last extremity, be still found in the discharge of my duty."[5]

Martin persisted in advocating the volunteers' legal right to depart, leading Jackson to conclude that what he really faced was a conspiracy of brigade officers to undermine him. He simply could not conceive that his men did not share his single-minded obsession to win the war, that they might have concerns more pressing than crushing the Red Sticks. On the evening of December 9, Fort Strother nearly blew itself apart. What triggered the showdown between Old Hickory and the volunteers is uncertain. Jackson maintained that General Hall came to his tent sputtering that his men were in "a state of mutiny and making preparations to move forcibly off." In fact, most were asleep or chatting by their campfires. All wanted to go home, but none contemplated desertion. No matter. Jackson dashed off the following order: "The commanding general being informed that an actual mutiny exists in the camp, all officers and soldiers of the First Brigade will, without delay, parade on the west side of the fort and await further orders."[6]

Lieutenant Call stood in General Hall's large tent with the other brigade officers "for what purpose I knew not." Hall was about to speak when someone announced that Major Reid was galloping through the brigade camp. In an instant the officers dispersed, each to his respective unit. No sooner had Call returned to his campfire than word came for the brigade to form outside the west gate of Fort Strother. "It was then about 8:00 p.m., dark as night can be and cold, calm and silent as death, while the atmosphere was charged with a dense mist." The volunteers formed mutely. Above them on a long ridge the militia brigade appeared. Atop a small hill a hundred yards distant stood two six-pounders, their frowning tubes intermittently made visible by the flickering linstocks in the gunners' hands. "Here we stood in breathless silence and expectation for several moments," remembered Call.

At length General Jackson rode out of the fort. Pausing at the center of the brigade line, he barked, "The General expects obedience from every soldier. Shoulder arms!" The men stood frozen. "Shoulder arms!" he again shouted. "As if by irresistible impulse," Call said, "every soldier obeyed with an energetic simultaneous slap of the hand on the musket, which made it ring like music along the line." Jackson breathed hard. "This was the grating moment in my life," he later told Rachel. "I felt the pangs of an affectionate parent, compelled from duty, to chastise his child to prevent him from destruction and disgrace, and it being his duty he shrunk not from it—even when he knew death might ensue."

Old Hickory dismounted at one end of the line. Sublimating his solicitude for the soldiers' suffering, he harangued and then dismissed each company in turn with a pledge to blow the volunteers to shreds should they persist in their designs to desert. The men were dumb-struck. "The general charged us with being in a state of mutiny, which was the first intimation I had of any such a disposition," averred a private. "There was dissatisfaction, but nothing like the appearance of mutiny." The precise language of Jackson's threat seared itself into the memory of Lieutenant Call. "Now, gentlemen, where is the man who dare tell me he will go home tomorrow, for by the eternal God who made me, he shall not," Old Hickory growled. "If you do go home, you shall pass over the body of your general. If you are prepared for the conflict, speak! I am ready. You see my artillery on the hill." Remount-ing after the last company broke ranks, Jackson, blanched by nervous exhaustion, melted into the night.[7]

December 10 dawned cloudy, gray, and as "gloomy as the hearts and minds" of the volunteers. Jackson's outburst only kindled the mutinous spark he had sought to extinguish. Glancing about, Lieu-tenant Call observed officers and men alike "with glowering discon-tent settled on their cheerless, sullen obedience to the discipline of camp." The young subaltern wanted out of Hall's brigade. Hoping to resign his commission in favor of serving as a private in Jackson's personal guard, Call visited the general in his marquee. "I found him alone, sitting at the entrance, with the elbow of the right arm resting on his knee, and his head reclining on his hand in deep thought." To Call's chagrin, Old Hickory rejected the lieutenant's offer brusquely. Silently, Call strode off, "feeling a pride in having done my duty." He had walked scarcely a dozen yards before Jackson called him back. Apologizing for his rudeness, Jackson explained, "No, Lieutenant, I cannot permit you to leave your company; as young as you are, you may be of great service; your example cannot fail to produce a good effect." Old Hickory ruminated a moment. Suddenly he exclaimed, "By the eternal God, if I had 500 such men, I would put an end to the mutiny before the sun sets."[8]

The mutiny had existed only in Jackson's mind; the volunteers remained in camp. It was clear, however, that he could expect noth-ing further from them in the way of active campaigning. Accordingly, he instructed General Hall to march his men to Nashville and do with them as Governor Blount saw fit. Before promulgating the direc-tive, Old Hickory appealed one last time to the volunteers to recon-sider. At Jackson's order, Hall's brigade assembled for dress parade on

December 13. Into the hollow square rode Major Reid. With a "clear manly voice," he read a lengthy, "eloquent and powerful appeal to their feelings of pride and patriotism." Only two men were moved by it to remain: a Captain Williamson and Lieutenant Call. That afternoon, the volunteers who had followed Jackson to Natchez in 1812 and shattered the Red Sticks at Talladega turned their backs on him and headed home.[9]

Although the infidelity of the West Tennessee volunteers "pierced his heart," Jackson's spirits lifted with the arrival at Fort Strother of General Cocke and 1,450 East Tennesseans on December 12. He ordered a three-gun salute fired in their honor and paraded Hall's soon-to-disband brigade to greet the East Tennesseans. "They are fine material," he informed General Coffee, adding giddily, "I must move on the enemy. It would be treating [Cocke's] troops, who I know are brave, impolitely not to give them a fandango."

Jackson's warm feelings went unreciprocated. Unknown to him, General Cocke had had to resort to threats and cajolery to persuade his men to march the fifty miles from their camp at Fort Armstrong to Fort Strother. Few wanted to fight the Red Sticks any longer. Most common soldiers, be they from East or West Tennessee, were tired of a war that meant hunger, hard marching, and further neglect of farm and family—all to kill Indians who no longer seemed to pose any threat to the folks at home, if they ever really did. The East Tennesseans' mood soured further when they mingled with Hall's departing volunteers, who struck the East Tennessee captain Jacob Hartsell as a hard-looking lot. "There was more confusion than I ever saw in my life at one place. There could hardly be anything done for the cursing and swearing amongst the men."

When Jackson learned that the enlistments of the East Tennessee volunteers were to expire in two weeks, he turned bitter. Old Hickory and General Cocke kept to their respective marquees at opposite ends of the campgrounds. Three days after Cocke's arrival, Jackson told him to return to Fort Armstrong to gather provisions, disband his volunteers, and recruit fifteen hundred new troops for six months of service. Cocke's eight-hundred-man militia regiment, meanwhile, remained at Fort Strother, consuming precious rations and grumbling.

A false rumor spread through their camp that Jackson intended to hold them for six months, which nearly precipitated a real mutiny. "Some swore that before they would stay three months, they would kill General Jackson," Captain Hartsell recalled. "Some swore that they would desert. Some said that they would lose all their wagons before they would stay any longer."[10]

General Roberts's brigade of West Tennessee militia also unraveled. Desertions had reduced it to no more than six hundred men. Imitating Hall's volunteers, they insisted that Jackson honor the expiration of their three-month enlistment on January 4, 1814.

With Hall's volunteers gone and both the East and the West Tennessee militia unreliable, Old Hickory looked to John Coffee to salvage the cavalry because he felt he must take the offensive. Creek scouts had advised him of Floyd's withdrawal after Autosee and of the Red Sticks' regrouping on the Coosa River a scant sixty miles to the south. "Something effectual and decisive must be done immediately," Jackson wrote to Coffee. "The enemy, building their hopes upon our late unhappy distractions, are assembling below us. Delay, while it diminishes our strength will increase theirs. Hasten to form a junction with me and bring along every particle of breadstuff that can be procured."[11]

Coffee was unable to oblige his old friend. Not only was he still bedridden, but his men too had caught the discharge bug, which Coffee feared would metamorphize into outright desertion once they met Hall's infantry. As it was, most of the troopers who had rendezvoused in Huntsville after refitting now refused to recross the Tennessee River. All claimed the right to a discharge on December 24. As Hall's malcontents filed into Huntsville, Coffee despaired. "I am really ashamed to say anything about the men of my brigade doing anything ever again," he professed to Jackson on December 20. "They have been so distracted for some time past, and they are now lying encamped with that unholy body of infantry that deserted you." A week later, only the partly recuperated Coffee and two dozen officers of his once proud brigade remained. The tiny band retained a disproportionate number of enslaved attendants, and they were afterward known as the "Black Corps."[12]

David Crockett was among those who left. He went home with the vast majority of Coffee's mounted brigade, happy that his soldiering days were behind him. "The weather began to get very cold, and our clothes were nearly worn out." On December 29, 1813, Crockett obtained his discharge and pocketed $65.99 for his service, plus a comparatively liberal allowance for travel expenses and the use of his horse.[13]

Contemplating the collapse of Hall's and Coffee's brigades, Old Hickory wondered if the Red Stick prophets had hexed his army. "The sedition and mutiny have been such throughout the whole body of volunteers, both cavalry and infantry, that it is impossible for me to say whether I shall have any force," he mused to Rachel. "The physic of the Indian prophets must have seriously worked upon them to occasion these men, once so brave, once so patriotic, to conduct so strangely and so disgracefully to themselves and country."[14]

Perhaps the prophets had poisoned the mind of Governor Blount as well. On December 22, Blount rejected Jackson's appeal that he raise new volunteers on the doubtful grounds that it was strictly a federal matter. Instead, Blount suggested that Old Hickory abandon Forts Strother and Deposit and withdraw to the Tennessee frontier. An incredulous Jackson railed at the governor's timidity. The Madison administration had called on Tennessee for five thousand volunteers. On the assumption the state would maintain that number in the field, the War Department had based its strategy, such as it was. "God forbid," snarled Old Hickory, that he become an instrument in disappointing the national government and exposing Indian allies to Creek revenge. Scarcely containing his anger, Jackson adjured Blount to display a bit of backbone:

There are times when we must disregard punctilious etiquette and think only of serving our country. What is really our present situation? The enemy we have been sent to subdue may be said, if we stop at this, to be only exasperated.

Is it sound policy to abandon a conquest thus far made and deliver up to havoc, or add to the number of our enemies, those friendly Creeks and Cherokees who, relying on our protection, have espoused our cause and aided us with their arms? Is it good policy to turn loose upon our defenseless frontiers 5,000 exasperated savages to dip their hands once more in the blood of our citizens?

You have only to act with the energy and decision the crisis demands, and all will be well. Send me a force engaged for six months, and I will answer for the result; but withhold it, and all is lost—the reputation of the state, and yours and mine along with it.[15]

Not content with a single slap at the governor, shortly after midnight on December 29, Jackson dictated to his depleted aide-de-camp Major Reid a second scolding of Blount. Frequently repeating himself in a rambling and bilious epistle, Old Hickory mocked Tennessee's chief executive with the same merciless intensity that drove his own emaciated body and overburdened mind. "Are you my dear friend sitting with your arms folded recommending me to retrograde to please the whims of the populace," challenged Jackson. "Let me tell you it imperiously lies upon both you and me to do our duty regardless of the consequences or the opinions of these fireside patriots, those fawning sycophants or cowardly poltroons who after all their boasted ardor would rush home and let thousands fall victim to my retrograde—let us take a view of the real state of things and see how you and myself would appear in the painting. Arouse from your lethargy," Old Hickory howled. "Call out the full quota authorized and despise the fawning smiles or snarling frowns of miscreants. The campaign must rapidly progress, or you are forever damned!"[16]

Jackson's fanatic devotion to crushing the Red Sticks—an obsession perhaps derived largely from his personal loathing of the British, whom he feared might combine with the Red Sticks to conquer the entire Deep South—also burned fiercely in a letter to Rachel. So too did a manly resignation to fate. "I am here," he wrote from his marquee beneath a cold gray rain, "and by the orders of General Pinckney compelled to remain." Pinckney had expected him to rendezvous with Floyd's Georgians, but with the militia about to depart, Old Hickory could do no more than try to hold Fort Strother with Lieutenant Robert Armstrong's artillery company, his personal guard, and the scout company—the only men willing to serve beyond their enlistments. "But fear not, my better self," he assured Rachel, "the guardian angels will protect us and support us under every trial, danger, and difficulty so long as we are engaged in a righteous cause." Jackson ardently hoped that General Coffee would recover soon, because without him "I lose my best prop."[17]

While Coffee convalesced, Old Hickory clashed with his other remaining high-ranking subordinate, Brigadier General Isaac Roberts, just returned from his recruiting drive in Tennessee with 190 new militiamen. On his return, Roberts had passed the angry officers and men of Hall and Coffee's brigade. Uncertain what reception to expect from the mercurial Jackson, Roberts ordered the newcomers to bivouac three miles short of Fort Strother while he conferred with the commanding general.

Neither Jackson nor Roberts could expect any guidance regarding terms of enlistment from the indecisive Governor Blount. Neither could they look to the Madison administration for much in the way of precedent or policy. After fighting broke out, American efforts to mobilize an effective fighting force to defeat the British had consisted largely of stopgap half measures dictated by a Congress divided over the wisdom of the war itself and administered by a poorly organized and chronically understaffed War Department that struggled even to function in peacetime. "In the deplorably wretched condition of the War Department, it was impossible either to begin the war or to conduct it," lamented a congressional War Hawk.

At the outset of the war, the incentives offered to volunteers were paltry, and only six volunteer regiments were raised during the entire war to augment the elusive goal of ten Regular regiments. Congress increased pay and bounties in 1813. Despite the best efforts of southern members, however, Congress neglected to arm the militia, establish uniform terms of service, or clarify its relation to the Regular establishment until 1814. The War Department wanted to draft the militia into the Regular army, a move for which Congress had no stomach, and the Regular army never reached its authorized level of fifty-seven thousand men. In a word, chaos prevailed from the top down.[18]

Captain Jacob Hartsell witnessed the fraught reunion of Roberts and Jackson, held in plain view of the soldiery. Roberts asked Jackson if he would accept the recruits for three months; Old Hickory replied that not less than six months would suffice. Rather than yield the point, Roberts swore he would encourage them to go home, which he did. As for his brigade, Roberts insisted Jackson discharge the men on January 4, 1814, in accordance with the terms of their enlistment. Some of them, Roberts urged, were "very poor men and had no other way of making a living but to farm." "That matters nothing," Jackson retorted. "When men [are] at war, they must stay till they had done their country's service," period of enlistment be damned. Cursing viciously, the two generals drew their swords. Officers hastened to separate them. Jackson and Roberts withdrew to their tents and scrawled bitter notes to each other.[19]

New Year's 1814 at Fort Strother passed in somber silence. In his marquee, Jackson brooded over the injustices done him. "I have exerted every nerve to progress with the campaign," he wrote to Coffee. "As soon as I get over one difficulty another presents itself or is raised by the expressions of the governor [and] the mutiny of the troops, all occasioned by the underhanded designs of officers who wish to raise their popularity on my downfall." There could be no compromise. Either an officer shared Jackson's zeal for the war, or he was a scheming traitor.[20]

Jackson's next clash with fractious Tennesseans came on January 4, the date Roberts's brigade claimed for its discharge. The evening before, Old Hickory had issued a general order forbidding any man to leave post without his permission. He might as well have written it on the wind. Dawn came, and not a sentinel nor the officer of the guard, a Lieutenant Kearley, was to be found at his post. Dozens of tents had vanished, their owners already on the road home. An enraged Jackson directed Kearley's immediate arrest. Told the lieutenant refused to surrender his sword on the grounds he was a "freeman and not subject to the orders of General Jackson," Old Hickory assembled his staff and personal guard, thirty men in all, and with them stalked across camp to confront him. As the general approached, a group of armed militiamen formed a line behind Kearley, as if to prevent his arrest.

Lieutenant Richard Call looked on in dread. What transpired Call later termed "the most exciting and painful spectacle" he ever witnessed. Halting before Kearley, Old Hickory leveled a pistol at the lieutenant's breast. The militiamen and Jackson's guard raised their muskets at one another. Major Reid gingerly slipped Kearley's sword from its scabbard. Jackson declined to receive it. "No, sir," he snapped. "He must deliver it himself, or I will put him to death." Kearley complied. Muskets were lowered, and bloodshed averted. Learning that

Kearley's superior officers in the brigade had put him up to the act of defiance, Jackson freed the lieutenant after a brief imprisonment. "Lieutenant Kearley," Old Hickory said, "you are the only brave man in your corps, and as I respect courage even when erring, I shall liberate you. You may go home with honor, while the rest shall retire in disgrace." Roberts's brigade did not wait for the lieutenant, but left at once, a surly gaggle eager to vilify Jackson to the folks at home. Only two officers and twenty-nine men of the brigade stood by Old Hickory, among them Lieutenant Call, whom Jackson at last permitted to serve as a private in his personal guard.[21]

Ten days after Jackson's showdown with Lieutenant Kearley, the East Tennessee militia returned to Fort Armstrong to be discharged. Little more than an armed mob, they wreaked havoc on the Cherokees, shooting cattle, hogs, and horses and bullying the populace for the sheer pleasure of it, outrages that an infuriated Jackson reminded General Cocke were "contrary to the rules of war, the laws of nations and civil society, and well calculated to sour the minds of the whole [Cherokee] nation against the United States." Not only had Jackson lost most of his army, but the lawless East Tennesseans also were jeopardizing his invaluable alliance with the Cherokees.[22]

As darkness descended on Fort Strother, a dim ray of light shone on the horizon. Derided as a nettlesome dandy by Tennessee officers envious of Jackson's partiality to him, Major William Carroll was at least partially rewarding Old Hickory's faith in him. Almost singlehandedly, he recruited eight hundred mounted volunteers in West Tennessee and ordered them to rendezvous in Huntsville in late December. Jackson had asked Carroll to secure a six-month enlistment, but the new men were enrolled for only sixty days' service, the consequence of a bureaucratic error. Old Hickory's first inclination was to discharge the men. Then a false rumor reached Jackson that the British were landing troops at Pensacola to reinforce the Red Sticks. Placing no credence in the story, General Pinckney suggested Jackson simply hold his ground until the Thirty-Ninth U.S. Infantry, a new regiment then recruiting in East Tennessee, joined him in two or three months. Jackson, however, not only believed the rumor but also intended to act against the Red Sticks before the phantom British command reinforced them. As he told the seemingly lethargic Governor Blount, "The moment of extremity is not a moment for hesitation or wavering." Directing Carroll to bring his mounted contingent on to Fort Strother no later than January 10, 1814—in time to bid the East Tennessee militia farewell—he planned to "cross the Coosa River and recommence operations" the day after they arrived.

It was a long shot, and Jackson knew it. "I shall meet the enemy about sixty miles below here. God knows what the result will be, but I hope it will add no additional disgrace to Tennessee," he told Blount. "My force is feeble, but I trust pretty well purified by the late purgation. Has Tennessee really come to a dead stand?"[23]

CHAPTER FIFTEEN

Jackson Courts Disaster

TENNESSEE HAD not come to a dead stand, as Jackson supposed. Old Hickory had not been left to fight the Red Sticks with only a battalion of untested sixty-day volunteers and a handful of loyal veterans. No one in higher office intended to abandon Jackson, if only he would wait. On January 3, 1814, the chastened Governor Willie Blount ordered a levy of twenty-five hundred troops from the West Tennessee militia and a thousand men from East Tennessee for three months' service against the Creeks. General Pinckney also directed the Thirty-Ninth U.S. Infantry Regiment, then completing recruitment in Knoxville under the command of Colonel John Williams, the former attorney general of Tennessee, to report to Jackson as soon as possible. Despite the ominous British presence in the Chesapeake Bay and on the Canadian–New York border, which might well portend twin offensives, the War Department at last had awakened to the need to dispatch at least one Regular regiment to help Jackson.

Jackson would welcome the Regulars. As for the militiamen, however, neither their projected number nor their period of enlistment was what Jackson had requested. But they were all that the political climate in Tennessee would bear. With the War of 1812 entering its third year in apparent stalemate and the Red Stick threat receded from the Tennessee frontier, enthusiasm for military duty waned. General

Pinckney thought the new Regulars and militia would prove sufficient to deal the Red Sticks a final defeat. "The largest computation that I have heard of the hostile Creek warriors made by any competent judge is 4,000," Pinckney counseled Jackson. Allowing for at least 750 casualties to date, and their irregular supply of guns, powder, and lead, the Red Sticks should be no match for a similar number of well-armed and tolerably trained troops. Consequently, Pinckney concluded, "I would recommend that you should not embarrass yourself with the sixty-day mounted men."[1]

Old Hickory, however, was obdurate. He had what he considered compelling cause to risk an immediate advance with Carroll's mounted militia. To keep soldiers so "full of ardor to meet the enemy" idle until their discharge would both discourage future enlistments and constitute a waste of state funds. Jackson also thought a quick strike necessary to protect the lightly defended Fort Armstrong, where considerable stores were stockpiled, from what the post commander feared was an imminent Red Stick attack. Finally, Jackson further saw his limited offensive as an essential diversion to prevent the Red Sticks on the Upper Tallapoosa (Menawa's Abeikas) from falling on General Floyd's rear when he staged his second advance from Georgia in January 1814, a concern that General Pinckney did not share.[2]

To what extent Jackson's stated reasons for leading Carroll's raw troops into battle reflected true military necessity (as he saw it) or were simply a pretext to cover his innate combativeness only Old Hickory himself knew. His faithful but discerning aide-de-camp John Reid saw nothing to condemn in either the man or his methods, however. "The world is greatly mistaken if it supposes that the general is too rash and precipitate as a commander," Reid told his brother. "He is indeed a man of enterprise—full of ardor—and of the most rapid movements, but although he never felt personal fear, he is, I believe, the most cautious manager of an army that ever was appointed to conduct one. The reason is he would dread a defeat as the worst of all earthly calamities, and ten thousand times worse than death." Carroll's sixty-day men applauded Jackson's aggressiveness. "Old Hickory is the boy for the reds and a day of settlement is at hand," wrote a militiaman on learning of the pending expedition.[3]

.   .   .

The métis Chief Menawa had no dread of Tennesseans. On the contrary, the Abeika war leader owed his reputation for fearlessness to laurels won at their expense. In the days before Tennessee statehood, Menawa had routinely despoiled the Cumberland River valley of horses. His exploits earned him the early moniker of Hothlepoya, or "the Crazy War Hunter." Frontiersmen and Creek warriors alike respected his audacity and ingenuity, and the former also appreciated his reluctance to shed blood unless cornered. Menawa's exploits brought him vast wealth. By the time he abandoned his predatory ways, Menawa owned a store, more than a thousand head of cattle and as many hogs, and several hundred horses, which made him an unlikely but genuine convert to the Red Stick dogma. He also carried on a brisk trade in furs and pelts with the Spaniards in Pensacola.

Notwithstanding his wealth, Tennesseans also granted Menawa a genuine liberality. The story was told that Menawa, returning from a particularly fruitful excursion, met a tired white pedestrian trudging a forest trail with no companion but a hound, his horse having run off. To ease the man's burden, Menawa bestowed on him a fine mount worth $200. In exchange, he asked only for the hound so that he would have a trophy to display in place of the forfeited horse. "The acquisitive propensity of so heroic a person," an admiring American official observed, "is not excited by the value of the thing stolen, but by the glory of the capture."

Well aware of their leader's reputation, Menawa's twelve hundred warriors exuded confidence. They trusted not only in Menawa but also in the strength of the elaborate breastworks they had built to defend the refuge for themselves and some twenty-five family members at the village of Tohopeka in the horseshoe-shaped bend on the Tallapoosa (located seventy miles southwest of modern Montgomery, Alabama). Should the Tennesseans prove foolish enough to approach, the Abeikas expected an easy triumph.[4]

Jackson set out from Fort Strother on January 15, 1814. In addition to his untried militiamen, he had Lieutenant Robert Armstrong's small artillery company (of which Richard Call was now a member) dragging its one six-pounder cannon, a 48-man infantry company stitched together from faithful volunteers, two scout companies of 60 men each, and General Coffee's "Black Corps," for a total force of 930 officers and men with which to tackle Menawa's large and eager Red Stick assemblage. "All were sensible to the hazard of the enterprise, but all felt equal confidence in the skill, prudence, and daring intrepidity of their gallant leader," averred Call.

Splashing across the icy Coosa River, Jackson's column directed its march toward Okfuskee, thirty miles to the southeast. At Talladega, Jackson welcomed into his ranks 65 Cherokees and 235 friendly Creeks. Of the former, the Cherokee agent told Jackson proudly, "They now behave well; they are proud to bear arms and to act in the field with their white brothers. There can be no doubt of their fidelity," he added, "but they must be entirely guided by our councils." To distinguish themselves from the Red Sticks, Jackson's Indian allies stuck white plumes in their head wrappings, giving them from a distance the appearance of a flock of egrets.[5]

For two days after passing Talladega, the army and its Native auxiliaries ambled through an "open and beautiful" country. On January 21, they entered the hills bordering the Tallapoosa River. Near the abandoned talofa of Enitachopco, Jackson's scouts stumbled upon their Red Stick counterparts, who hurried off without a fight. As sunset settled over the land, Jackson encountered a web of fresh trails, all merging into a large, "much beaten and lately traveled" road trending toward Tohopeka, rather than in the direction of Okfuskee as Jackson had expected. At nightfall, Creek guides reported the large and boisterous Red Stick village of Tohopeka, just three miles distant, its occupants engaged in a frenetic war dance. The guides said nothing to Jackson of the formidable log barricade, which perhaps they could not see in the failing light. Presented with indisputable evidence that the enemy had "concentrated to give us battle," Jackson bivouacked on the "best site the country would admit," a commanding eminence near the narrow, shallow, and occasionally swirling waters of Emuckfau Creek two miles north of Tohopeka.

Jackson chose his ground well. A level pine barren extended half a mile to the front, flanks, and rear before descending into a deep valley of dense cane and a narrow stream. He also deployed his men carefully. The militia lay down in a hollow square beside small campfires. In case of a night attack, they were to form ranks fifteen paces behind the campfires so as to illuminate attacking Red Sticks. Within the square the artillery company and Indian allies camped beside the army's baggage and tethered horses. Jackson doubled his sentinels, who stood two hundred yards beyond the campfires. "Being prepared at all points," reported Jackson, "nothing remained to be done but to await their approach if they meditated an attack, or to be in readiness if they did not to pursue and attack them at daylight."[6]

Menawa had no intention of passively awaiting an assault. With the audacity that had made him a matchless horse thief, he led his warriors beyond the Tohopeka barricade before daybreak on January 22. He was a conspicuous figure. Mounted on a fine horse, Menawa wore a bearskin headdress adorned with the horns of a large bull. Counting on the element of surprise, superior numbers, and the confusion a predawn attack would cause, he expected to disperse the Tennesseans as handily as he had stolen their horses in bygone years. Menawa, however, was unaware of Old Hickory's practice of waking his army early. At 4:00 a.m., the soldiers arose, dressed, and stood vigilant. Two hours passed quietly. With morning twilight teasing at the horizon, Jackson permitted the men to prepare their breakfasts.

No sooner had the militiamen crouched about their cooking fires, remembered Richard Call, than "the crack of a rifle, succeeded by a shrill war whoop, called everyone to arms." The Red Sticks had crept so close before being discovered that they struck the main line almost simultaneously with the fleeing sentinels. Shrieking the watchword, "Stick to it," the stampeded sentinels shoved their way through the militia ranks and "ran for their lives." As ordered, the soldiers formed behind their campfires with muskets leveled. Their wait was brief. "The enemy, yelling like demons, rushed on with great impetuosity," Call wrote. "They came within range of the light, and some of them so near that when they fell under the steady aim of our cool brave men, they fell in our fires."

Menawa threw the bulk of his forces against Jackson's left flank and left rear. The militia held, but their ranks thinned. Jackson ordered a forty-man company, his only reserve, to the threatened sector. They did not lack for officers. Colonel Carroll accompanied them, as did General Coffee and his Black Corps. The fight raged for thirty minutes until, deprived of the cloak of darkness, the Red Sticks abandoned the field.

Jackson and Coffee conferred briefly. Coffee agreed to lead four hundred militiamen and most of the friendly Indians after the retreating Red Sticks, but first they had to hunt down their horses in the gun-smoke-shrouded camp. The delay permitted the Red Sticks to withdraw to Tohopeka. One look at the log barricade persuaded Coffee to end the pursuit; without artillery support, he calculated the Red Stick defenses impenetrable.

At 11:30 a.m., Coffee's mounted militiamen and their dejected Indian allies, who had few scalps to show for their troubles, returned to camp. Tethering their horses, the soldiers returned to their places in line. A reckless few wandered into the valley behind camp in search of dead Red Sticks, unaware that plenty of live enemy lurked nearby because Chief Menawa had followed Coffee back to Emuckfau for a second try at Jackson's lines. At noon he attacked. First a Red Stick contingent emerged from the valley behind Jackson's camp and fired on the trophy hunters. General Coffee, his brother-in-law Major Alexander Donelson, the officers of the Black Corps, and perhaps fifty of Jackson's veterans ran out to meet the assailants. Jackson was about to send 150 Indians to reinforce Coffee when a large Red Stick force approached through the pine barren to his front.

Menawa had struck Jackson's rear as a feint to draw men from the front line, but the diversion itself nearly broke Jackson's ranks. General Coffee fell, shot in the right side. An instant later a bullet bore through Major Donelson's brain. Only the timely appearance of the métis Colonel Richard Brown and his Cherokee warriors prevented greater carnage among the Tennesseans. Richard Call recorded the Cherokee daring: "Mounted on a fleet horse of the hardy Indian breed, [Brown] dashed alone towards the cane brake, turned suddenly at a right angle and passed rapidly near and parallel with the hidden foe, drawing their fire as he went, and whenever the curling smoke arose from the thicket, a mounted Cherokee with uplifted tomahawk dashed in, and with fatal blow dispatched the defenseless warrior before he could reload his rifle." It would not be the last time that the Cherokees turned an action decisively in Old Hickory's favor.

With his diversionary contingent slaughtered and Jackson's front line holding, Menawa broke off his second assault. Sorting out their mounts, the militiamen galloped after the vanishing Red Sticks, only to find them again tucked safely behind their breastworks at Tohopeka. When the soldiers withdrew, Menawa sent several dozen scouts to harass the Tennesseans' camp.[7]

The short winter's afternoon deepened. Shadowy Red Sticks weaved from tree to tree just beyond the line of sentinels. Burial details furtively dug graves for the five Tennessee dead, burning brush over the site to obliterate traces of the freshly turned earth and so prevent Indian warriors in search of scalps from disinterring the corpses later. Other men made litters to carry their twenty-three wounded comrades cross-country as comfortably as the bitter cold and the rugged terrain would permit. They fashioned poles from long, stout branches, two per litter. These they secured with leather or rope at a width sufficient to drape over the back and cinch to the belly of the lead and trail horses. Between the animals, the blanket-draped poles swayed uncertainly with their mangled human cargo. Three men were assigned to each litter: one to steer the lead horse, one the rear animal, and the third to prevent the wounded passenger from rolling off.

Most of the militiamen passed the waning hours of January 22 hauling logs into place to create rough field fortifications; everyone from Old Hickory to the lowest private expected a night attack. Sentinels were doubled. Few men slept. Through fleecy clouds a feeble light fell upon the pine barrens. Snapping branches or rustling bushes generated ragged volleys from the frightened guards, who invariably stumbled into camp trailed by phantom warriors. No sooner was order restored than the entire process repeated itself. Richard Call dozed off toward daybreak, only to be startled awake by a man who scurried aimlessly about the bivouac shrieking, "Indians in the encampment, Indians in the encampment," until he ran smack against a tree. Recovering from the shock, he sheepishly confessed that he had dreamed of warriors overrunning the camp and then sounded the alarm while sleepwalking. It was the first good laugh the men had enjoyed in days.

No attack came that night. Menawa evidently calculated that sleeplessness and stress were more effective in depleting the soldiers than another lunge at their camp.[8]

Although Old Hickory inflicted far greater casualties than he sustained at Emuckfau—he claimed to have slain fifty Red Sticks, nearly all during Coffee's pursuit and the afternoon counterattack—he could hardly count the battle a victory. Indeed, Jackson seems to have recognized how close he had come to disaster. Of Menawa's dual assaults, he confessed to Rachel that "in these affairs my wounded were so increased and my horses starving, my men in some degree began to be panic struck. I could not advance and burn the town but determined to . . . commence my march for [Fort Strother] on the morning of the twenty-third." Adopting a supercilious tone with General Pinckney, he claimed that the Battle of Emuckfau had demonstrated how to defeat the Red Sticks. "The cowardly dogs cannot stand a charge," he asserted. "It is by this way alone the Indians can be killed; to stand and fight they outhide and outshoot us. It is by the charge I destroy from eight to ten of them for one they kill of my men."[9]

That might have been a fine lesson for the future, but Jackson's sole concern as January 23 dawned was to safely withdraw his weary command to Fort Strother. At 10:00 a.m. the troops rode out of camp in three columns, with the wounded and baggage in the center followed by the artillery company and its single small cannon. Flanking parties and an advance and rear guard kept watch for Red Sticks. At one point a deep cane-laced defile bisected the trail. Fearing an ambush, Jackson negotiated its slopes cautiously. After covering twelve miles that day, the army bivouacked a quarter mile short of another ominous ravine, through which meandered the twenty-to-thirty-foot-wide Enita-chopco Creek. "Another night of successive alarms ensued, while to add to our discomfiture rain fell heavily, which without tents made it exceedingly difficult to keep our arms and powder dry," said Richard Call. "As the night before, the sentinels frequently fired and ran within the fortifications, but no attack was made."[10]

Jackson's scouts had spotted Red Sticks on the flanks and in the rear of the army during the day's march, darting from tree to tree, just out of range. After the night passed quietly, Jackson prepared for the next potential threat—an ambush when the army negotiated the steep banks and reed fringes of Enitachopco Creek on January 24. Rather than follow the main trail, he ordered a fatigue party to cut a new path across open woodland to an alternate ford six hundred yards downstream.[11]

With little brush to clear, the workmen had the new trail ready rapidly, and shortly before sunrise Jackson got his command under way. He formed a strong rear guard of three columns with orders to face about and envelop the enemy in the event they attacked. Most of his command and their Creek allies forded Enitachopco Creek at the improvised ford unmolested, the only obstacle a thin scrum of reed growing along the water's edge. Next came the wounded, swinging painfully on litters between horses. They too ascended the far bank without incident while the militiamen who made up the rear guard waited their turn.

A musket shot and a war whoop announced the advent of the Red Stick assault. Jackson had divined Menawa's intentions. Before dawn, the Red Stick chief had arrayed between five hundred and eight hundred warriors in ambush at the trail ford; realizing he had been duped, Menawa hurried cross-country to intercept the Tennesseans before they splashed across the creek.

Jackson welcomed the challenge. "I felt rejoiced," he wrote to Rachel. "The ground was of my own choosing, and I knew that if the men would stand and fight, I would destroy nine out of every ten of the enemy." But the militiamen, untutored in open combat, panicked. Colonel Nicholas Perkins, commanding the right column of the rear guard, tried to arrange his men in a dismounted battle line facing rearward toward the oncoming Red Sticks. Only a few obeyed. Neither his thundering oaths nor his drawn sword prevented the rest from galloping across the ford. Perkins mounted and followed his frightened men to a hillock on the far bank. Although well removed from danger, they again refused his order to dismount and form ranks.

Lieutenant Colonel John Stump's left column mimicked the craven example of Perkins's troopers, stampeding "like bullocks" straight across the creek into the midst of the litter bearers and trailing elements of the main body.

Colonel Carroll, in command of the center column, fared better; he rallied twenty-five to thirty-five men to resist the onrushing Red Sticks. Carroll's party would likely have been annihilated had Colonel Brown and his Cherokees not come crashing down on the Red Sticks' flank—a crucial contribution that Jackson neglected to acknowledge in his battle report.[12]

At the ford, Old Hickory swore and fumed while the mob washed past him. "My salutations were harsh, my orders peremptory," he told Rachel. When no one listened, he tried to draw his sword. It stuck in the scabbard, however, and "in the attempt I had like to have broken my left arm, or I should have halted the fugitives."[13]

Private Call needed neither oaths nor saber strokes to show him where his duty lay. He had just forded the creek when the commotion caused by the collapsing rear guard commenced. Glancing about, he spotted Old Hickory staring in wonderment at the wall of approaching fugitives. "I ran up and found General Jackson at the ford, who without speaking pointed at the opposite side." Splashing back over the stream, Call dodged the oncoming mass and made for Lieutenant Armstrong's artillery company.

Armstrong clearly needed help. The lieutenant and his two dozen men were dragging their six-pounder up a slope to rake the Red Sticks. While several strained at the gun, Call and the remaining men ascended the hill and delivered a musket volley into the nearest warriors, momentarily halting them. No sooner had the artillerymen wheeled the cannon into place than they discovered that they had forgotten to bring up the rammer and priming iron. With no time to spare, they improvised. One man used his musket as a rammer; another employed his musket's ramrod as a priming iron. A blast of canister blanketed the slope with smoke. As the gunners loaded a second round, Lieutenant Armstrong fell mortally wounded; his last words were "Save the cannon." Three more artillerymen dropped in rapid succession.

Old Hickory praised the artillery lavishly in his report, but his commendation was pure balderdash. With no reputation at stake, Richard Call wrote honestly of the affair. The fire of the single cannon, he confessed, produced no more impact on the Red Sticks than pebbles tossed in a surging wave. "The artillery was used with little effect, although fired repeatedly, as the Indians fought from tree to tree and could only be touched by the well-aimed rifle or musket. The Indians were in front and on both sides of us and near at hand. And our men were falling so fast that we could not have stood it much longer."[14]

In justice to the artillery, however, its mere presence—together with that of the Cherokees—slowed the Red Stick attack long enough for General Coffee, who had risen from his litter, Colonel Carroll, and several company-grade officers to muster enough troops for a mounted counterattack. The Red Sticks gave way, and Coffee and Carroll chased them nearly to Tohopeka.

Jackson's army had barely escaped annihilation. Major Reid swore that he counted nearly two hundred dead Red Sticks on the Enitachopco Creek battlefield. His claim rings false; Indian losses were likely fewer than a hundred. Jackson clearly prevaricated concerning his own casualties, admitting to only five killed. General Coffee, in a letter home, said the army suffered thirteen dead and forty-seven wounded.[15]

Regardless of how many Red Sticks he might have slain, Old Hickory had no intention of tarrying on the battlefield. He neither interred his dead nor fashioned litters for the wounded. Corpses were heaved onto horses, their riders holding the dead in place. Wounded unable to sit upright in the saddle were similarly slung onto horses. Just minutes after the militiamen returned from their aborted pursuit, the army moved out.

The troops bivouacked at sunset on the "beautifully level" earth of a dense forest. Spirits were low. "It was a gloomy night," remembered Private Call, "made so by the sad task of burying the dead, which work we did by torches, the flickering and uncertain light of which added to the funeral gloom of the scene." Jackson passed the time sitting on a stump beside a campfire outside his tent, his horse saddled and bridled beside him. As the first orange streaks of dawn fingered the eastern sky, the men broke camp and resumed their march. Descending the rugged hills of the Tallapoosa country onto the plains of Talladega, Call said, "we all breathed more freely from a sense of safety." The next day, January 26, 1814, the army reached Fort Strother, ending their eleven-day expedition through the northern reaches of the Red Stick realm.[16]

Menawa's warriors were in good spirits. They boasted around their Tohopeka campfires of having driven Jackson back across the Coosa. Lest that become the universal opinion, Jackson hurriedly assured General Pinckney that the campaign—although it neither created a permanent presence in the Red Stick country nor inflicted crippling casualties—had been worth the risk. Old Hickory offered five benefits of his brush with disaster, three of which were dubious. Jackson contended that he had made a "most fortunate diversion" in favor of Floyd's second offensive. In fact, Menawa's Abeika Red Sticks had not aided the Tuckabatchee bands when Floyd attacked Autosee, nor was there any reason to believe they would have done so at Calabee Creek. Old Hickory also suggested that he had forestalled a strike against the supply depot at Fort Armstrong, but the Red Sticks never contemplated any such action. Jackson swore that he had dealt Red

Stick morale a hard blow, when his abrupt retreats after Emuckfau and Enitachopco actually reinvigorated them. Jackson's contention that he had "beneficially employed" the sixty-day volunteers had merit only because they had escaped disaster at Enitachopco. There could be no disputing his claim, however, that he had explored and cut a road through "the enemy's country to the point where their forces will probably be concentrated."[17]

Jackson's slanted report had the desired effect because at that juncture in the War of 1812 Americans were eager for uplifting news, whether able to confirm its veracity or not. Although he had counseled against it, General Pinckney applauded Old Hickory's expedition and the "intelligent bravery and good conduct" he and his troops had displayed. "I take the liberty," he wrote to the secretary of war, "of drawing your attention to the communications of General Jackson. Without the personal firmness, popularity, and exertions of that officer, the Indian war, on the part of Tennessee, would have been abandoned at least for a time." Pinckney recommended Jackson be promoted to brigadier general in the Regular army whenever a vacancy occurred.[18]

Plenty of Tennessee veterans would have preferred to see Old Hickory cashiered. "Some of the old volunteers are venting their spleen against you," Jackson's friend John Overton advised him from Nashville. Former enlisted men grumbled to their neighbors about Jackson's arbitrary conduct, harsh discipline, and questionable ability. Some whispered falsely that he had been drunk on duty. Colonel Edward Bradley of the disbanded First Tennessee Volunteers published tracts in state newspapers critical of Jackson, which won Bradley and his disaffected subordinates a sympathetic audience among the "lower elements" of Tennessee society. Jackson need not worry, however. He must view "the whining of Bradley, etc., as the wind that passes by," counseled Overton, "neither exciting antipathy, nor observation, except regret for their weakness and want of patriotism."[19]

Jackson did fret, however. His shoulder still pained him acutely, persistent diarrhea plagued him, and his always precarious constitution teetered on the brink of collapse. He would, however, persevere. "The snarling curs may grin, lie, and falsely swear, but they will die with their own bite," Jackson assured General Coffee, who was on leave recuperating from his Emuckfau wound. To Rachel, Jackson wrote at the end of January, "My station is arduous and my duty severe. I will perform it. As to the vile slanderous vipers, I despise them as the crawling worm that rolls through the slime untouched, unnoticed by any."[20]

Rachel was fed up with her husband's sense of duty, which she considered misplaced. Lonely, frazzled, and fearful for his safety, she simply wanted him to come home. Jackson had written to her truthfully of the Emuckfau fiasco, sugarcoating nothing (in contrast to his robust and cheerful missive to General Pinckney). Her husband's brush with disaster and her nephew Alexander Donelson's death in the battle sent her into a tailspin. "My Dearest Life," she appealed to her husband from the Hermitage in her faulty, error-ridden, but heartfelt prose,

> I received your letter by express. Never shall I forgit it. I have not Slept one night sin[c]e.... I Cryed aloud and praised my God for your safety. How thankful I was. Oh, my unfortunate nephew. He is gone. How I Deplore his Loss, his untimely End.
>
> My Dear, pray Let me conjur you by every Tie of Love to Let me see you.... I have borne it untill now; it has thrown me into feavours. I am very unwell. How long oh Lord will I remain so unhappy, no rest, no ease. I cannot sleepe. All can come home but you. I never wanted to see you so much in my life. I must see you. Pray, my Darling, never make me so unhappy for aney country. You have been gone a Long time six months. In all that time what has been your trails, dangers, and Diffyculties. Oh Lorde of heaven until we meete. Let it not be Long from your Dearest friend and faithfull wife until death.[21]

Rachel's supplication saddened Jackson. He remained as wedded to his notion of duty, however, as his sobriquet Old Hickory suggested. To Rachel, he responded with a firmness grounded in their shared sense of providential design. "My love, I am grieved to think of the pain my absence occasions," he began.

> But when you reflect that I am in the field and cannot retire without disgrace, I am in hopes that your good sense will yield

to it a little while with resolution and firmness, and my love as
it reflects my safety, when you reflect that I am protected by
the same overruling Providence when in the heart of the Creek
nation as I am at home, his protecting hand can shield me as well
from danger here as there. . . .

I have therefore to request that you will retain your usual
firmness—and should it be the will of Divine Providence to
smile upon my honest exertions, I have a pleasing hope of seeing
you before long. [If] I get my supplies shortly, I will soon put an
end to the Creek War. As soon as this is done and I can honorably retire, I shall return to your arms on the wings of love and
affection to spend with you the remainder of my days in peaceful
domestic retirement.[22]

Much work remained to be done before Jackson could return to the
Hermitage. He knew he had been lucky with the sixty-day volunteers.
"The disorder that prevailed amongst officers and men in our late
excursion," he wrote to an ally confidentially, "was a striking example,
and a sufficient warning never to enter the country of our enemy with
troops not reduced to some kind of obedience and order."[23] Consequently, he must build a new army, one both free from enlistment
disputes and responsive to his brand of discipline, which the betrayals
of the "mutineers" were to render harsher. He must also secure a reliable flow of supplies to permit an unremitting and decisive campaign
in the Creek country.

Jackson operated on multiple administrative fronts simultaneously.
Four days after returning to Fort Strother, he released the sixty-day
volunteers with a month remaining on their enlistment. It was a sound
decision in terms of army logistics; they would only consume precious
provisions while contributing nothing productive. It was also a good
move politically. As Richard Call observed, Old Hickory dismissed
the sixty-day men "flushed with victory," which ensured they would
counter the baleful influence of the disgruntled former volunteers
then traducing Jackson back in Tennessee. Jackson singled out Call for
special praise, presenting him with a personal letter of appreciation
for his loyalty and gallant service at Enitachopco Creek. Thus began
the lifelong collaboration that would culminate in Call's appointment by the future president Jackson to the territorial governorship
of Florida.[24]

Even as Old Hickory boosted young Call, he settled scores with those he believed had wronged or failed him. On February 3, he arrested four captains of Brigadier General Isaac Roberts's West Tennessee volunteer brigade on charges of "sedition, mutiny, desertion, and disobedience of orders." He also urged Governor Blount to deny General Roberts's resignation until he too stood trial. A court-martial found the four captains guilty but gave them light sentences because it concluded that Roberts bore responsibility for their conduct. On February 19, the general was arrested, tried, convicted of mutiny, and cashiered.

Holding Colonel Nicholas Perkins accountable for the collapse of the rear guard at Enitachopco Creek, Jackson also hauled him before a court-martial. Although Jackson wanted him shot, the tribunal acquitted him on charges of disobedience of orders and cowardice and restored him to command of his mounted regiment, which had already mustered out.

Jackson also eliminated the threat, more imagined than real, posed by Major General John Cocke, whom he unjustly assumed had sabotaged his November 1813 campaign against the Red Sticks. Brigadier General George Doherty, a sixty-five-year-old Revolutionary War veteran and an intriguing East Tennessee political rival who commanded a newly recruited militia brigade in Cocke's division, told Old Hickory that Cocke was instigating mutiny among the six-month volunteers and slandering Jackson's good name in the bargain. An enraged Jackson demanded Governor Blount arrest and court-martial Cocke. Various delays occurred, and a year passed before Cocke was tried and ultimately acquitted.[25]

James Parton, a sympathetic but fair-minded early Jackson biographer, attributed Jackson's petulant and unjust vengeance against the "grossly misrepresented" General Cocke to a temperamental defect that led Old Hickory to "imbibe prejudices readily and hold them tenaciously." His precarious health certainly contributed to his rancor. Returning to Fort Strother on March 10 from a two-month furlough, Major John Reid found the general "nearly worn out with sickness." That Jackson intended to ruin Cocke is evident. During the Cocke affair, Major Joseph Anthony, another of Jackson's aides-de-camp, resigned because disgruntled former volunteers had slandered him, and he felt compelled to return to Tennessee to correct the record. Jackson deeply regretted both the "foul aspersions that envy and cal-

umny had raised against" Anthony and the need to accept his resignation. "If we did not live in the age of falsehoods and slander this would
have astonished me very much," he wrote to the major, unaware that
he was a willing consumer of smears when it came to General Cocke.
Anthony, however, must go back home to redeem his honor because,
continued Jackson with emphasis, "*the life of a man is not worth possessing
when his reputation is gone.*"[26]

While he smashed former subordinates and perceived rivals, Old
Hickory also at long last assembled an army worthy of the name. Help
came to him from an unexpected quarter. Since the start of the Creek
War, Andrew Jackson had had nothing but trouble with East Tennesseans, be they inept contractors, sullen militiamen, or imagined adver-
saries such as General Cocke. It was an East Tennessean, however,
who orchestrated the reinforcements Jackson would need to launch a
sustained campaign against the Red Sticks.

Hugh L. White, a distinguished Knoxville politician, attorney, and
member of the Tennessee Court of Errors and Appeals, had taken a
deep interest in the welfare of the state's soldiers. He made no distinction between those of the rival eastern and western districts. Hearing that Jackson's men were subsisting on "roots and acorns," in late
November 1813 he left his comfortable seat on the bench and journeyed
to Fort Strother. Grateful for his visit, Jackson beseeched the judge
to use his influence to speed the arrival of the Thirty-Ninth Infantry
Regiment. White agreed to what he imagined would be a simple task
because the regimental commander, Colonel John Williams, was his
brother-in-law.

Returning to Knoxville, a chagrined White learned that the War
Department, in response to another of the interminable rumors of
an impending British invasion of the Gulf Coast, had reassigned the
regiment to duty in New Orleans. White urged Williams to insist that
the War Department rescind the orders. Jackson's "condition is very
deplorable," the judge told his brother-in-law. "His men have all abandoned him except his lifeguard." Unless Williams came to his aid, "the
country would be overrun by savages, the inhabitants become victims of every species of cruelty, and the reputation of their state forever blasted." The two men talked through the night before Williams

yielded. To shield Williams from official recriminations for bucking the War Department, General Pinckney also ordered him to march to Fort Strother rather than New Orleans.

Jackson had high hopes for the Regulars. They "will give weight to my orders, enable me to keep down mutiny, and introduce subordination into the ranks, all important to success and a speedy termination of the Creek War," he assured Pinckney in mid-February 1814. For nearly six months, Jackson had endured a suppurating shoulder wound, a useless arm, chronic diarrhea, and, as he saw it, mutinous subordinates. Alleviating his own agony was beyond Jackson's means, but with a solid core of Regulars on whom he could rely, final victory at last appeared within reach.[27]

CHAPTER SIXTEEN

A Slow, Laborious Slaughter

L ATE WINTER RAINS beat a steady tattoo on the fabric of Old Hickory's marquee. Inside, Jackson lay prostrated by a severe cold. He passed the gray days dictating letters to his aides, grumbling to the medical staff who poulticed his throbbing shoulder, and stumbling outdoors to relieve his loose bowels in the waterlogged latrines of Fort Strother. Despite his misery, Jackson maintained a rosy manner that bordered on the obsequious in correspondence with his commanding officer, General Pinckney. "I feel much indebted to you for your instructions, and view of my future operations," he gushed in a March 4 missive. "They are judicious, well calculated to ensure safety and success, and shall be kept in view. Be assured, General, it will always afford me pleasure to receive any instructions from you; your wisdom and experience would under any circumstances give them great weight."[1]

Private John Woods also felt miserable. Standing guard on a cold, dreary late February morning without a blanket or breakfast to warm him played hard on the seventeen-year-old West Tennessee volunteer. Below the legal age, he was under no obligation to render military service. Nevertheless, he had left the farm of his "respectable" family in early January 1814 to volunteer, enlisting in the same company in which his elder brother served. It was Woods's misfortune to belong to the rabble that General Roberts had recruited in December 1813 and that had decamped when Jackson refused to grant the men a discharge. Although his comrades accepted Jackson's subsequent proffer of a parole and returned to Fort Strother (Woods had joined the unit after their pardon), the men remained in bad odor with the commanding general.

Hungry and shivering, Woods obtained the permission of the officer of the guard to return briefly to his squad tent to get his blanket and a quick breakfast. While he ate, the officer of the day happened by. Taking umbrage at the trash littering the ground outside the tent, he demanded the occupants immediately police the area. All obliged except Woods, who kept eating. The officer cursed Woods and ordered him to join his companions. Between forkfuls of food the youngster snarled that he was on guard duty, with permission to leave his post briefly. The officer peremptorily ordered him back to his post. Woods refused. Words passed between them. When the officer directed a soldier to arrest his tentmate, Woods primed his musket and swore he would shoot the first man who tried to seize him.

A standoff ensued. It lasted long enough for someone to alert Jackson that a mutineer had leveled his musket at the officer of the day. "Which is the damned rascal?" barked Old Hickory as he emerged from his marquee. "Shoot him! Shoot him! Blow ten balls through the damned villain's body."

By the time Jackson reached the squad tent, Woods's comrades had persuaded him to surrender his musket and himself. Jackson ordered him placed in irons and whisked off to the camp of the recently arrived Thirty-Ninth U.S. Infantry, to be held in close confinement pending a court-martial.[2]

No one, least of all Woods himself, expected the youngster to suffer serious consequences for his rash act. A long record of leniency belied Jackson's bluster that morning about shooting the "damned rascal." Since assuming command in October 1813, Old Hickory had put no one to death, much less approved a harsh sentence for breaches of discipline. He had remitted two death sentences, both of which had been rendered for aggravated offenses. In that respect he was typical of militia officers, who were loath to impose draconian Regular army punishment on their state brethren. On October 24, Jackson reduced a corporal in rank for using disrespectful language to his captain. Four days later, five cavalry privates found guilty of desertion were transferred to the infantry, compelled to forfeit their horses, and forced to wear their hunting shirts wrong side out for two weeks with the word "Deserter" emblazoned on the back; Jackson remitted the sentence of two of the men because "they were of tender years." Nine soldiers who pleaded guilty to desertion on December 4 were sentenced to have one side of their faces painted black and their coats inverted with the label "Deserter" painted on them, and were compelled to ride a wooden horse fifteen minutes a day for three days. Jackson commuted the death sentences of a lieutenant and an ensign convicted of desertion to "dismissal from the service with infamy."[3]

The mass desertions of December and January had hardened Old Hickory, however. "A fellow has mutinied," he said of Private Woods's transgression, "and I expect he will have to be shot."

On a bleak and soggy March 12, in open forest between two tents, the court-martial convened. Woods sat upright on a log, sullen and defiant in the belief that though he might be condemned to death, the sentence would never be carried out. Pacing the grounds out of Woods's hearing, Jackson snarled to the officers sitting in judgment, "Be cautious and mind what you are about; for by the eternal God, the next man that is condemned, I won't pardon, and this is a hearty, hale young fellow."

The court-martial rendered its verdict. Woods was to be shot in two days by a detail of a sergeant and twelve riflemen from the Thirty-Ninth Infantry. On March 14, the army drew up in a square to witness the execution. It was an enormous assemblage because Jackson at last had his desired reinforcements. In addition to the six hundred Regulars in their smart blue coats, white pantaloons, and tall black hats, a brigade of East Tennessee militia and a reconstituted cavalry brigade under John Coffee witnessed the terrible proceedings: more than three thousand officers and men watching one young man pay the ultimate penalty for disobedience. Woods sat in the center of the square on a stool, his eyes tied with a handkerchief. He endured the adjutant's reading of a perversely prolix and inexcusably inaccurate general order that Jackson had written to a youth on the edge of eternity. "While under the immediate command of General Roberts, you were one of those who in violation of your engagement, of all the principles of honor, and of the order of your commanding general, rose in mutiny and deserted," proclaimed the adjutant. "You were arrested and brought back, and notwithstanding the little claim you had to mercy, your General . . . thought proper to grant you a pardon." Woods must have flinched in terror. Not only was the charge false—he had enlisted after the desertion—but it rendered a last-minute reprieve unlikely. Nevertheless, observed a soldier whose brother stood before the condemned Woods as a member of the firing squad, neither he, his brother, "nor a single man in the army, least of all the criminal, expected he would be shot till the word 'Fire,' and [twelve] bullets pierced him at once."

The execution stunned the army; no other militia general then serving the United States would have sanctioned the execution except Jackson. How he came to believe Woods had been a deserter is not known, but the impact on the army proved salutary. "That night not a word was heard in camp," recollected a soldier. "[We] were all as silent as death. What an effect! General Jackson had no more plague with mutinies."[4]

At the very moment twelve musket balls slammed into the young John Woods's chest, Andrew Jackson sat in his marquee, composing a letter to General Pinckney laying out his design for a final offensive against the Red Sticks. Old Hickory had no compunction about shooting Woods; he regretted only that Doherty's East Tennessee militia brigade was not on hand to see the execution.

Jackson promised Pinckney that he would root out the "numerous and troublesome" Red Sticks at Tohopeka under Chief Menawa. Beforehand, he would construct a supply depot fifty miles down the Coosa River from Fort Strother and a similar distance west of Tohopeka. High water from the incessant spring rains made the site readily accessible by flatboat. The Regulars would take charge of the boats, provisions, and magazine stores. They also would build and if necessary defend the depot, which was to be named Fort Williams in honor of the regimental commander. Should no threat materialize to Fort Williams, the Thirty-Ninth would march overland to rendezvous with the rest of the army on the Emuckfau Creek battlefield.

Jackson had amassed a formidable volunteer force, of which the Thirty-Ninth U.S. Infantry was the core. The conspiratorial, sixty-five-year-old brigadier general George Doherty led the East Tennessee militia brigade. Brigadier General Thomas Johnson, a forty-seven-year-old surveyor and state politician, commanded the West Tennessee militia brigade. Each brigade consisted of two regiments and numbered approximately thirteen hundred men. John Coffee led a nine-hundred-man reconstituted cavalry brigade that comprised two regiments of mounted riflemen and an additional five hundred eager Cherokee volunteers under Colonel Gideon Morgan and a hundred Lower Creeks under William McIntosh. A two-gun artillery battery and a scout company rounded out Jackson's army.[5]

Old Hickory benefited not only from superior numbers—deducting his January losses, Menawa now mustered approximately a thousand warriors (the number fluctuated depending on the inclinations of individual Red Sticks)—but also from reliable intelligence, the latter courtesy of the Kialijees, a band of neutral Upper Creeks whose talwa lay in the heart of Red Stick country. Abandoning their homes in February for the safety of Talladega, they briefed Jackson on the component talwas of Menawa's largely Abeika force and confirmed its resolve to "hold [Tohopeka] to the last." Tohopeka "will be the hot bed of the war party until destroyed," concluded Jackson.

Assuming he prevailed over Menawa, Jackson intended to resupply at Fort Williams and then push southward toward the juncture of the Coosa and Tallapoosa Rivers to crush Autosee and Hoithlewaulee warriors believed to have reassembled at the Hickory Ground. In that enterprise, General Pinckney assured Jackson he would be assisted by the three hundred Regulars of the Third U.S. Infantry under Colonel Homer Milton, then holding Fort Hull, together with a brigade of North and South Carolinians, should the latter reach the front in time. Nothing would remain thereafter but to mop up Weatherford's Alabamas and Koasatis.[6]

Rachel's prayers would accompany Jackson in what he had assured her would be his final fights before retiring to the Hermitage for good. Her heart bled for him. With Calvinist fortitude, perhaps pretended, she wrote to Jackson on the eve of his departure from Fort Strother, "The Daingers and trials, perels, and DiffyCulties dayly awaits you but I see you have set your foot on a rock that never Can be shaken. Oh, how often I have thanked the supreme Governor that rules and Directs the just and virtuous. You say his overruleing Power is more Conspicuous in the field of battle then in our peacfull dwelings. Shurely that is Correct. It's Christian. I Can almost say thou arte a Cristian. I hope you are goodness, and virtue points oute all your ways."

Private John Woods had been in his lonely forest grave but a week when Rachel penned those words.[7]

Old Hickory moved methodically. On March 16, the militia and their Indian allies left Fort Strother for the putative site of the planned supply depot, fifty-nine miles downriver. Colonel Williams and the Regulars, meanwhile, wrestled their provision-laden flatboats through low water and dodged shoals. Six days elapsed before marching men and battered boats reunited and work began on Fort Williams. A palpable thrill of impending and decisive victory animated the army. "We shall with as little delay as possible move to [Tohopeka]," wrote John Reid. "Having destroyed, as I hope in God we shall, a pretty powerful and daring confederacy which is there collected, we shall return to our deposit, procure fresh supplies, and march to the Hickory Ground, where I hope the Creek War will be terminated."[8]

While his aide-de-camp forecast triumph, Jackson feared ruin. Colonel Williams had been able to transport rations sufficient for only ten days, a quantity Jackson calculated would be consumed on the "excursion" to Tohopeka. Without a stockpile sufficient for forty days in the field (some 200,000 rations of bacon and bread), he would find himself exactly where he had been during the dark days of November 1813 when "discontent and mutiny" thwarted his plans.[9]

Old Hickory objected to provisioning his Cherokee and Creek contingent, which he regarded as a nuisance rather than an asset. Despite the Cherokees' sterling performance at Enitachopco Creek, the chance that they or his Creek auxiliaries might contribute materially to the impending battle seems never to have occurred to Jackson.[10]

For three days axes sang, trees tumbled, and logs were hewn. While fatigue parties fashioned Fort Williams, large detachments roamed the Coosa River valley below the stockade site in search of Red Sticks. They ran off a few stragglers, encountered a web of fresh trails leading toward Tohopeka, and applied the torch to three Red Stick talofas and one talwa. Only a Cherokee war party drew blood, killing four Red Stick warriors and taking five prisoners.[11]

.   .   .

The candles burned late into the night of March 23 at headquarters. Jackson dictated a long general order to John Reid, to be read to the troops before daybreak on March 24. Alternately cajoling and coercive, sprinkled with liberal doses of both hyperbole and sound military logic, Jackson's proclamation to his "Fellow Soldiers" presented them with the prospect of "manifesting your zeal to your country and avenging the cruelties committed upon our defenseless fellow citizens by the infuriated Creeks." The only Red Stick atrocities committed on Tennessee soil had been the raid on the Manley homestead and abduction of Martha Crawley in May 1812, events that were never far from Jackson's mind. Nonetheless, he continued, "our borders must no longer be disturbed by the war-hoop of the ruthless savage or the cries of the suffering victims." Evidently harking back to Fort Mims, he exclaimed, "That torch which they lighted up on our frontier has blazed and must blaze again in the heart of their nation. They shall see by its blaze, the gleaming of that sword which their cruelties and treacheries has compelled us to unsheathe." Having worked himself and presumably his soldiers to a fever pitch, Jackson enjoined them nevertheless to be merciful. On the chance anyone had forgotten John Woods's execution, he hammered home the need for "discipline and strict subordination." Victory would be achieved by the charge. "In that moment you will see your enemy flying in every direction before you," Old Hickory assured the men. "Your general pledges his reputation upon this, and he is willing to add the further pledge of his life." Jackson expected nothing less from the army. As judge, jury, and executioner, he warned, "Any officer or soldier who flies before the enemy without being compelled to do so by superior force and actual necessity shall suffer death."[12]

With Old Hickory's words soaking their souls, in the predawn twilight of March 25, his troops drew twenty-four rounds of ammunition and an eight-day supply of rations consisting of bacon, jerked beef, and "bread stuff." At 5:00 a.m. the army melted into the dark and trackless wilderness leading to Tohopeka, fifty-two miles to the east. Deducting 450 men to garrison Fort Williams and a strong guard at Fort Strother, Jackson took the field with 3,200 soldiers and allied warriors, giving him a solid three-to-one superiority in numbers over the Red Sticks.[13]

With their barricade before them and the Tallapoosa River behind them, Chief Menawa's warriors waited confidently. Women and the elderly tended to their daily tasks, children played, and dogs darted among the log cabins tucked in the horseshoe-shaped bend of the Tallapoosa. Its waters were high and ran fast from recent rains. Canoes fringed the near bank. In the unlikely event soldiers breasted the barricade, the canoes would provide a rapid means of escape for Creek noncombatants. Few warriors, however, intended to abandon the place no matter what the outcome. They had assembled from six Abeika communities—most prominently Okfuskee, Hillabee, and Nuyaka—to fight or die defending the Red Stick doctrine. That bold spirit characterizes Creeks to this day. "It is part of our ethos as a people that we see those Red Stick warriors taking a last stand," explains a prominent tribal citizen. "That piece of information is handed down: we take the last stand. We call ourselves *Este Maskoke Ispocogees:* 'the last people.' We take 'last stands' and pull together. The people pull together in these moments of extreme danger. And that is what they were doing at Horseshoe Bend—pulling together."[14]

Not that the Abeika Red Sticks saw a literal last stand in the offing. They had had seven months to prepare their defenses, time they put to excellent use, creating the most imposing Indian-built fortifications the American army would ever confront. A 350-yard-long wall of thick pine logs, stacked five or six high and held in place with upright pine posts and props, zigzagged across the neck of the hundred-acre peninsula. In places the breastworks rose to a height of eight feet; nowhere were they less than five feet high. Sharpened stakes protruded diagonally upward from ground level toward potential attackers. Clay chinking filled gaps between the logs. Two rows of firing ports were cut in the logs at regular intervals, permitting defenders to shoot standing or kneeling while protected from return fire. There might also have been a lower rear wall composed of an earthen embankment held in place with smaller logs and upright posts. A log-floored ditch or walkway might have run between the two walls, assuming the rear wall existed. Archaeologists who have examined the site, of which nothing remains aboveground, differ on the question of a ditch and rear wall, which seems an unlikely precaution for the Red Sticks to have taken because none harbored the slightest concern of an attack from the rear. They considered the bend in the Tallapoosa, which their prophets had blessed, a barrier as inviolate as their man-made barricade.[15]

Then there was the enemy himself. Nothing in the armed horde with which the Abeikas had wrestled at Emuckfau and Enitachopco suggested that white soldiers possessed the wherewithal required to storm breastworks. The Red Sticks could not know that their nemesis Jackson had assembled a real army, well disciplined and determined to fight, impelled onward by the added motivation of Old Hickory's threat to shoot anyone who shirked their duty. To ensure that the soldiers would be easy targets for their own fire, the Red Sticks cleared portions of the ground to their front not already denuded in building the breastworks.

Unthinkable though the breaching of their barricade was, the Red Sticks nevertheless fashioned fallback positions behind the breastworks, where the ground inclined gently to a tangled, thickly forested rise that tapered off at the village. Scattered across the fifty or sixty acres of rough, high ground, these secondary defenses resembled shallow foxholes shielded by stacked logs.

The Abeikas also took comfort from the divine hand that lay gently over Tohopeka. Their tribal prophets, whose incantations grew louder as Jackson's Tennesseans drew nearer, assured them that the village and its defenses rested on consecrated land impassable to white men. A visiting William Weatherford had heard such protestations before. Unwilling to endure another Holy Ground fiasco, on March 26 he and his pregnant wife packed their belongings and left Tohopeka.[16]

Weatherford timed his departure impeccably. Six miles northwest of Tohopeka, Jackson's army bivouacked near the Emuckfau battlefield. Conferring with his confidant General Coffee, who had glimpsed the ominous potential of the Indian barricade during his abortive pursuits of the Red Sticks at the Battle of Emuckfau, Jackson devised a simple but ingenious plan—theoretically at least—to obliterate the Abeika warriors and their refuge. At daybreak, Coffee would ride down the Tallapoosa with his mounted brigade, consisting of two regiments of seven hundred Tennessee militiamen, Colonel Gideon Morgan's five hundred Cherokees, and William McIntosh's hundred Lower Creeks. They were to ford the river three miles southwest of Tohopeka, come up on the Abeikas from behind, and throw a cordon around the far bank of the horseshoe-shaped bend to prevent escape. Coffee also was to keep a weather eye west toward Okfuskee, where he and Jackson mistakenly believed a second Red Stick force had gathered. Old Hickory, meanwhile, would march directly against Tohopeka with the infantry and the artillery company, batter gaps in the breastworks with his two cannons, and then launch a grand bayonet charge against the weakened Abeika defenses. The Red Stick peninsular refuge would become an inescapable death trap.[17]

Or so Jackson thought until he saw the barricade stretched before him. "It is impossible to conceive a situation more eligible for defense than the one they had chosen, and the skill which they manifested in their breastwork was really astonishing," he later told General Pinckney. "It extended across the point in such a direction that a force approaching would be exposed to a double fire, while they lay entirely safe."

John Reid also wondered at the Abeikas' handiwork. "You can scarcely imagine a situation stronger by nature or rendered more secure by art. It was impossible from the zigzag form of the wall . . . to take it with any advantage without cannon, even if you had possession of one of its extremities."[18]

Jackson waved his two cannons—a hefty six-pounder mounted on a sturdy wooden carriage and a delicate, short-barreled three-pounder—forward to an open knoll a mere eighty yards from the nearest stretch of the breastworks to begin the task of splintering the Red Stick defenses. While the gun crews dragged their pieces up the slope, Jackson's infantry filed into lines of battle within easy musket range of the enemy. Old Hickory's headquarters guard, which doubled as a scout company, spread out in the rolling field below and to the left of the artillery. Anchoring its left flank on the wooded fringe of the Tallapoosa, Colonel Williams's six hundred blue-coated Regulars, bayonets shimmering, deployed in close order opposite the barricade. Whenever Jackson saw fit to order a charge, they would bear the brunt of the battle. To their right and in rear of the artillery knoll, the Second East Tennessee Militia, casually outfitted in felt top hats and long fringed coats, came into line. The First East Tennessee Militia, a portion of its front facing the south bank of the Tallapoosa, out of sight of the barricade, completed the main line of battle. Each regiment counted approximately three hundred men fit for duty. The West Tennessee militia brigade, six hundred strong, constituted the

MAP 8 THE BATTLE OF HORSESHOE BEND, MARCH 27, 1814

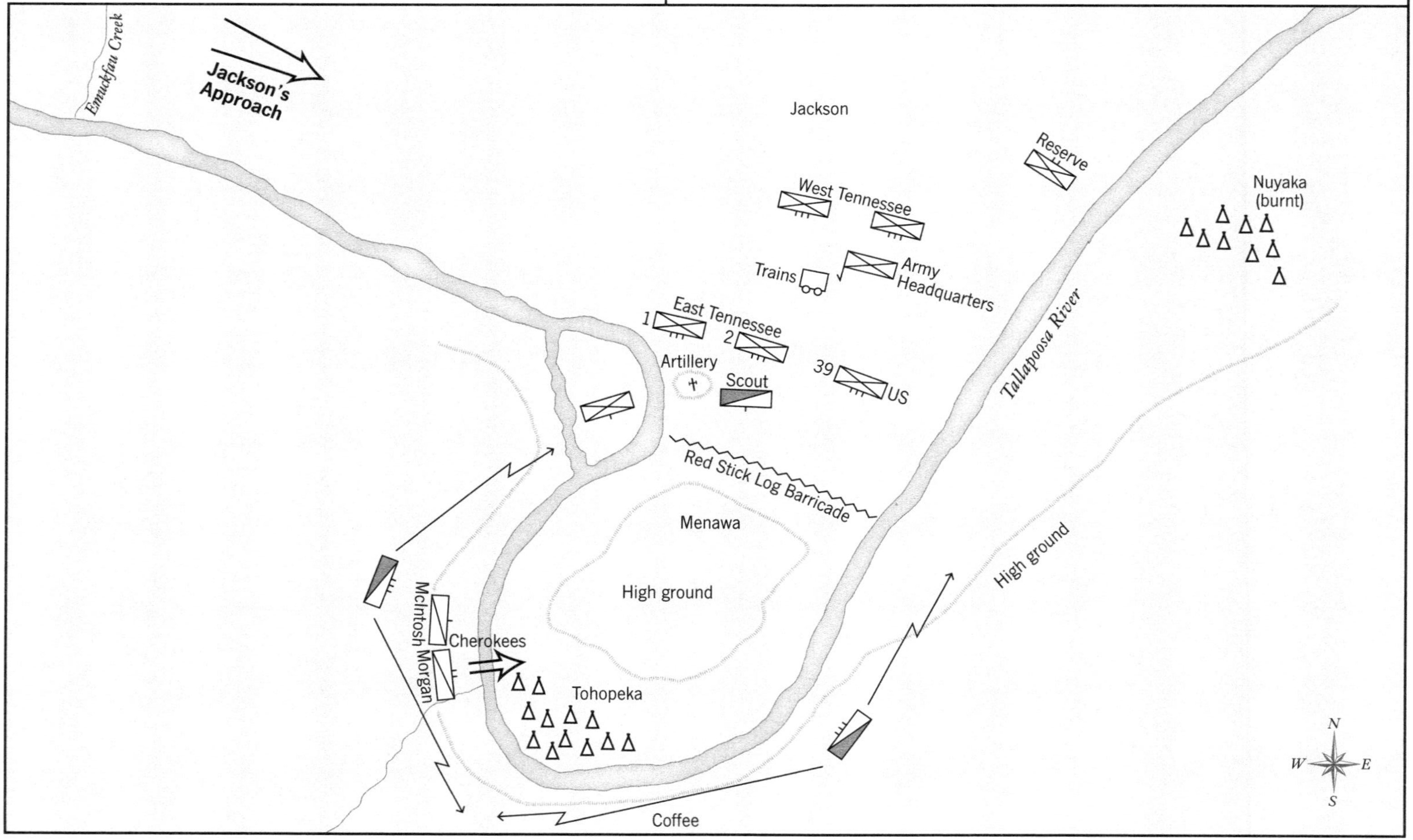

reserve line. Between the two lines Jackson marshaled his wagons and planted his headquarters flag. A small rear guard, whose apparent duty was to resist any Red Sticks who might find their way to the battlefield from the north, rounded out Jackson's formations. All told, he mustered just under two thousand fidgety infantrymen.

Behind their barricade, a thousand fiercely festooned warriors howled and mocked their opponents. In language colorful and obscene, English-speaking Red Sticks taunted the soldiers to attack. Most were painted for battle. The colors black and red predominated. Some warriors stripped to their breechcloths; others sported linen shirts. Nearly all wore leather leggings. Those lacking muskets clutched bows and arrows. The warriors also tucked war clubs and tomahawks in their belts for use in the unlikely event any soldiers lived long enough to scale the barricade.

The cannoneers trained their pieces on the center of the barricade. At 10:30 a.m. the guns boomed their smoky greeting. Their light-caliber balls bounced off the massive pine logs. Subsequent shots had no greater effect. Jackson seethed. "Such was the strength of the wall that it never shook." A few of the small three-pound balls embedded themselves in the clay chinking between logs, but the two-gun barrage on the barricade "had no effect to demolish it or to drive the enemy from behind it," confessed Colonel William Carroll.

Old Hickory later crowed that his riflemen felled any Red Sticks foolish enough to show their heads during the feeble cannonade. The warriors, however, clearly had the upper hand. Eleven artillerymen crumpled around their cannons. Firing safely through loopholes, Red Sticks also wounded several Regulars. On the forward slope of the high ground behind the barricade, in plain sight, three Abeika prophets waved cow-tail banners, chanted, and danced, delighted that the Master of Breath blew the force from the Tennesseans' cannonballs before they struck.[19]

An hour passed, and then another. Old Hickory appeared out of ideas. Unwilling to risk a charge, he simply continued the cannonade. As their losses mounted, the Regulars grew restless, perhaps none more than the twenty-one-year-old Ensign Samuel Houston, the future first president of the Republic of Texas. Certainly, no one in his regiment understood Indians better than did Houston. A nonconformist by nature, at age fifteen Houston abandoned the Kingston general store in which he clerked to live with the Cherokees, whose country abutted his family's East Tennessee farm. The Cherokees took to the strapping white adolescent. The chief of the band adopted him, naming Houston "the Raven" after the bird the Cherokees believed symbolized good luck and wanderlust. Houston had not bucked the family traces entirely, however. He regularly visited his widowed mother and siblings, wheedling money from her with which to purchase a generous quantity of gifts for his adopted Cherokee kin.

In 1811, Houston returned to frontier society, fluent in Cherokee but intent on filling the gaps in his white education. He studied under a tutor and opened a school for local children. Debt, however, soon drove him to resume clerking. Houston loathed the work no less than he had three years earlier. When the opportunity to enlist in the Thirty-Ninth presented itself, he grabbed it. A friend recalled the moment when Houston "took the silver dollar." Following the custom of the day, a recruiting detail paraded up the dirt thoroughfare of Kingston with fife and drum. Silver dollars glinted on the drumhead as tokens of enlistment. Houston stepped forward, snatched a coin, and "was then forthwith marched to the barracks, uniformed, and appointed the same day as a sergeant." Shortly after Houston left Kingston, admiring friends secured for him an ensign's commission.

Ensign Houston cut a fine figure in uniform. Powerfully built, at six feet, two inches tall, he towered over most of the men of his platoon. His deep, commanding voice and eyes, as brilliant a shade of blue and as transfixing as those of Old Hickory, enhanced Houston's natural gift for leadership.

Staring intently at the gun-smoke-draped barricade, the young ensign awaited his first test of combat.[20]

General Coffee had had no trouble getting his men into position undetected by the Red Sticks before the artillery barrage began. His U-shaped line rested on a wooded bluff a quarter mile from the Tallapoosa. Unknown to the warriors who manned the barricade a mile to the north, or to the noncombatants who clung to their cabins during the cannonade, escape was now impossible.

The stalemate at the barricade annoyed the Cherokees as much as it did Sam Houston and the Regulars. Unlike the soldiers, however, they had no intention of standing still. Watching the Abeika women and children dart about their village, safeguarded by only a handful of fighting men, the Cherokee second corporal Charles Reese devised a scheme to break the impasse. To his tall and burly nephew, aptly named Tucfo, meaning the Whale, he proposed, "Why not let us go down that ravine, swim across, and get some of those canoes so as to get General Coffee's command across and attack the Creeks from behind?" The thirty-seven-year-old liked the notion. He and Reese started toward the riverbank. A third warrior fell in with them, and together they swam the swollen, 120-foot-wide Tallapoosa. The plan nearly went off without a hitch. "Upon reaching the opposite shore I received a gunshot wound from the enemy," recollected Tucfo. Easing the big man into a canoe, Corporal Reese and his other companion paddled it and another boat back to the far shore, where their comrades had gathered to lay down a covering fire for them. "By this exploit, our warriors were enabled to cross the river and obtain other canoes by which they succeeded in carrying over a force strong enough to attack the enemy in the rear," affirmed Tucfo.[21]

The daring of Corporal Reese, Tucfo, and the third Cherokee proved contagious. Other Cherokee warriors piled into the two canoes and paddled to the far side of the river. Some engaged the Red Sticks in the village while others brought more canoes to fellow Cherokees eager to cross over. The veteran captain William Russell and his scout company descended the bluffs to await their turn also.

When his Cherokees began their spontaneous surge across the Tallapoosa, Colonel Gideon Morgan galloped off to alert Major Lemuel P. Montgomery, commanding the left wing of the Thirty-Ninth Infantry, to the unfolding assault on the Red Stick rear. Returning to the Cherokee regiment, Morgan counted nearly two hundred of his warriors already across the river. Captain Russell and some of his men were also over, as were William McIntosh and several dozen Lower Creeks. This mixed force had carried Tohopeka and were battling the Red Sticks for control of the near slope of the wooded high ground between the village and the barricade. Abeika noncombatants huddled in their cabins or bolted up the ridge, covered by Red Stick warriors. Marshaling thirty more Cherokees, Morgan plunged across the Tallapoosa and joined the fray himself. After an hour of skirmishing from tree to tree, Morgan took a musket ball to the right temple, "which had like to have terminated my existence." The nearest Cherokees watched him "dance like a partridge" and then collapse. Moments before losing consciousness, Morgan "heard the heavenly intelligence that the 39th had charged the breastworks."[22]

The twenty-eight-year-old Major Lemuel P. Montgomery bore more than a passing resemblance to his friend and mentor Andrew Jackson at a similar age. Born of Scots-Irish immigrant parents, Montgomery attended an academy in North Carolina, read for the bar, and then set up practice in Nashville. Tall and slender, he possessed a countenance "indicative of observation and thought." He had neither Jackson's roughness nor his quick temper, however, being admired for his wit, liberality, and modesty. Altogether he appeared a man destined for great things.[23]

Montgomery had delivered Gideon Morgan's message promptly to Colonel Williams, who in turn urged Jackson to storm the barricade to relieve pressure on Morgan's warriors. Jackson demurred, however. General Doherty also implored the commanding general to attack, but Old Hickory, perhaps fearing a slaughter, again declined to give the order to charge.

It was noon. Like Jackson, Menawa faced a tactical dilemma. His warriors were holding their own against the Cherokees but needed help to retake the village and rescue the women, the children, and the elderly trapped behind Cherokee lines. Reluctantly, Menawa detached warriors from the barricade to meet the threat to his rear. Others, concerned for the safety of their families, broke away of their own accord.

Jackson finally realized he had no alternative but to charge. The cannons had fired seventy rounds to little effect, and eleven gunners lay wounded on the knoll. Cherokee audacity had attenuated Menawa's front line. Further delay would gain Old Hickory nothing. At 12:30 p.m., Jackson gave the necessary orders, and the fourteen-year-old drummer boy of the Thirty-Ninth Infantry beat the long roll. Officers barked out final commands, the men straightened their ranks, and then the blue-coated regiment surged forward. A West Tennessee militia company and a scout detachment squeezed into the front line to the left of the Regulars. Several companies of East Tennessee militiamen fell in on the right. The artillery knoll and south bank of the Tallapoosa prevented most of Doherty's brigade from joining in the initial rush, but enough soldiers surged forward to thrill Major John Reid. "Never were men more impatient for a charge than those by whom it was now to be made. The least deliberation must have convinced everyone that many must fall in the perilous undertaking, but no one deliberated. It was a moment of feeling and not of reflection."[24]

Agony and death awaited them at the barricade. Wherever they were able, soldiers thrust muskets through loopholes emptied when Red Sticks withdrew their weapons to reload them. Warriors, in turn, regained the apertures when the soldiers reloaded. Occasionally, soldiers and warriors wrestled their weapons through the same loophole. "In many instances," averred Major Reid, "the balls of the enemy were found welded to the muzzles of our guns." Rushing the breastworks on foot with his men, Major Montgomery fired his pistol through a vacant loophole, killing an Indian. A return shot through the same opening wounded Montgomery. Hoisting himself to the top of the barricade, he turned, waved his hat, and urged his men to scale the works. A musket ball crashed into Montgomery's skull, cutting short a promising life.[25]

Private James Love crossed the barricade first. As he leaped to the ground on the Red Stick side, a hurled tomahawk caught him in the chest and split apart his ribs. Love survived but bore a huge scar for life. His fellow enlisted man Jesse Webb fared little better. Scaling the barricade, he was riddled with musket balls. The first struck him in the right arm. A second ball bore into his left groin. A third pierced the right side of his chest. A Red Stick war club separated his breastbone, prostrating him "at the same moment an Indian mounted me to take a trophy from my head," Webb remembered, "but fortunately [he] was prevented [by] a fellow soldier bayoneting him."[26]

The fight was bitter but brief. Cheering Regulars rapidly punched gaps in the sagging Red Stick ranks. On the extreme right of the regimental line, Ensign Sam Houston climbed the barricade with his platoon. He slashed at Red Sticks with his sword until a barbed arrow buried itself in his right groin. Hobbling about exhorting his men, Houston kept on his feet until the warriors retreated to a log-roofed redoubt beside the riverbank. Then, bleeding and helpless, he sank to the ground. Houston begged a fellow officer to extract the arrow. The man tried, but the arrow refused to budge. He tugged at it again with the same result. Furious and perhaps delirious with pain, Houston raised his sword and threatened to cleave the officer's skull if he failed a third time. The man yanked hard, and the arrow came out, together with a mass of tissue and a torrent of blood. Struggling rearward, Houston delivered himself to the regimental surgeon, who stanched the flow of blood.[27]

No one attended to Menawa. He lay unconscious amid a heap of slain warriors. Six musket balls had perforated his body. When he recovered, the chief found himself weltering in blood, his hands clutched firmly about his musket. The battle had swept past, but straggling shots and rippling volleys told him that the killing was far from over. Rising slowly to a seated posture, Menawa saw a soldier pass nearby. With deliberate aim, the man fired. A ball plowed through Menawa's mouth from cheek to cheek, carrying away several teeth. He slumped back amid the dead.

The Abeika prophets were beyond worldly ministrations. John Reid took particular delight in witnessing a grapeshot slice off the jaw of one, whom he mistook for Menawa, calling it a "very appropriate punishment for his impostures." With Menawa presumably dead, and the principal prophets undoubtedly dead, the leaderless Red Sticks retreated to the high ground, forming pockets of resistance behind their fallback positions. That they were doomed was evident to one warrior, who said his brother warriors dropped around him "like the fall of leaves."[28]

After the collapse of the barricade, the Battle of Horseshoe Bend degenerated into a five-hour slaughter that ended only with nightfall. Despite Jackson's general orders before the battle calling for restraint, atrocities and needless deaths abounded. Separated from his parents, a small Abeika boy ran about the village bewildered until a soldier crushed the child's skull with the butt of his musket. An officer upbraided the man for his barbarity. "Oh, it is all the same," replied the murderer. "He will make an Indian someday."

The old died with the young. A wizened man whom one member of Russell's scout company guessed to be at least ninety sat on the ground in the village, busily pounding corn in a mortar, apparently oblivious to the carnage and the crackling of burning cabins. Most of the scouts ignored the harmless and perhaps dementia-plagued character. One man, however, deliberately killed him in cold blood. He did so, he told his disgusted companions, "so that he might tell his people at home that he had killed an Indian." A mortally wounded Abeika woman with a crushed left arm exacted a measure of revenge. When a squad entered her cabin in search of concealed warriors, she raised herself up, fastened an arrow to a bowstring, and sprang the bow with her knee, instantly killing the squad leader. She died in a hail of bullets.[29]

When it became apparent the battle was lost to them, few Red Stick warriors bothered to fight on. Notwithstanding their pledge to make a last stand at Tohopeka, most were reluctant to die needlessly. Unaware that Coffee's riflemen lined the timbered far bank, nearly three hundred warriors leaped into the Tallapoosa, hoping to swim to safety. Some shoved logs into the water, to which they clutched while crossing.

Those who took to the river never had a chance. Rifle shots exploded the skulls of swimmers like overripened melons. Those clinging to logs "would drop like turtles into the water," a rifleman recalled. Several corpses came to rest against the riverbank; others vanished beneath the water. Many more likely floated downriver. No more than thirty warriors escaped the battlefield, most of whom waited until nightfall to swim the river. By then, concluded one of Coffee's troops, "the Tallapoosa might be truly called a river of blood, for the water was so stained that at 10 p.m. it was very perceptibly muddy, so much so that it could not be used."[30]

Warriors who chose to honor their pledge to make a last stand on the peninsula fought and died until just two apparent clusters remained: the Red Sticks who had taken refuge in the log-roofed redoubt in the ravine near where Sam Houston had been wounded, and a second cohort that clung to the riverbank beneath an overhanging bluff.

General Jackson tried to halt the carnage. Dismounting and sheltering himself behind a large oak tree, he told a Muscogee-speaking scout to call on those in the redoubt to surrender. They replied with musket shots. A ball glanced off the tree near Old Hickory's head and struck the scout in the shoulder. That ended Jackson's peace overture. Artillery could not be brought to bear on the declivity, so Old Hickory called for volunteers to storm the place. Sam Houston, who lay near enough to hear the summons, labored to his feet, grabbed a musket, and called on his men to follow him. Staggering down the rocky ravine as twilight settled over the forest, Houston came within fifteen feet of the redoubt before two musket balls struck him simultaneously, one in the right arm, the other in the shoulder. With ebbing strength, Houston ordered his men to charge, only to discover instead that he was alone. Despite his mangled groin and shattered right arm and shoulder, Houston staggered back up the ravine before collapsing. After dark, soldiers burned the redoubt, immolating its occupants.[31]

The Red Sticks clustered beneath the overhang above the riverbank also expired gruesomely. Coffee's men on the far bank alerted approaching Regulars to their presence. Several Regulars injudiciously crept to the edge of the bluff and looked over; they paid for their foolishness with musket balls through the head. More prudent soldiers dug a ditch the length of the overhang, into which they drove a row of long, sharpened pine stakes. They kicked the stakes, and the ledge toppled onto the Red Sticks, burying them alive.[32]

Night fell. The occasional musket shots, which signified Red Stick survivors rooted out and dispatched, at last ceased. The grisly work of counting corpses and slaughtering holdouts would resume at daybreak. Soldiers and Indian allies lay down amid the dead. The lurid glow of burning cabins lit the forest.

Surgeons tended to the wounded. Sam Houston received only cursory care. A doctor bandaged his groin and extracted the bullet from his right arm. He was about to probe for the second musket ball when another surgeon suggested he desist. Houston, he said, had lost too much blood to survive the night, better not to torture him gratuitously. Laying Houston aside on the ground, the surgeons ministered instead to men whose odds of recovering they judged better. Houston, however, refused to die. Shivering with cold, tormented by thirst, and racked with spirit-shattering pain, he passed the night alone and ignored. When daybreak confounded the surgeon's prediction, Houston was placed on a litter and carried swinging and jolting between two horses sixty excruciating miles to Fort Williams, where he might expire in relative comfort. Instead, Houston survived to chart the course of the future Republic of Texas.[33]

Menawa awoke. Grief gripped his soul. The corpses that surrounded him and the unearthly light of the burning Tohopeka confirmed his people's fate. Menawa's cause was ruined, his blood-soaked body seemingly wrecked. In common with Sam Houston, however, Menawa had a strong will to live. He crawled to the river, slid down the bank, found a canoe, and shook it loose from its mooring. Reclining in the boat, Menawa let the current decide his destiny. He drifted downriver until the canoe ran aground in a swamp in which some Abeika women and children had been secreted by their husbands before the battle. Easing their mangled and insensible chief from the canoe, the women poulticed his wounds.[34]

While Menawa clung to life, at daybreak on March 28, Jackson ordered a count made of the Red Stick dead. The detail assigned the task hit upon a grim but effective way to prevent double counting: they sliced off the tip of the nose of each corpse they tallied. Not only were the soldiers desecrating the dead, but they also were unwittingly marking the Red Stick dead as criminals because Creek law punished thieves by slitting their noses.

While the count went on, battlefield ghouls amused themselves by fashioning bridle reins from the skin of dead warriors. Frontiersmen had perfected the practice in which some of Coffee's troopers now indulged. Beginning at the calf, a souvenir hunter would make two parallel incisions with a knife about three inches apart, running the incisions up the leg and along the side of the victim's back to the shoulder blade, then across to the opposite shoulder, and from there down the other side of the back to the other calf. Removing the strip between the incisions yielded a U-shaped fleshy contrivance that, when dried, became part of the mounted rifleman's tack.

The Cherokees, meanwhile, abducted Abeika women and children as war prizes. They kept some as slaves; others they sold to the soldiers, who euphemistically referred to young abductees as "pets" rather than "property," usually purchased for their own children's amusement. The going price for a boy was $20. Unlike the recipients of trafficked children, Lieutenant Benjamin Wright of the Thirty-Ninth Infantry acquired an infant humanely. He had slain a warrior during the battle and stripped off his silver gorget and other ornaments as souvenirs. Perhaps scrounging for more trinkets, he peered into a clump of bushes near the river. Instead of baubles, he found an abandoned baby. Wright named the infant Moses and raised him as a son.[35]

Two young warriors also received a new lease on life. Captured that morning concealed in underbrush, they were brought to Jackson, who, after questioning them about Red Stick casualties, saw to it that they were well cared for. Sent to Nashville, the men became apprenticed to tradesmen, and both eventually became skilled mechanics. Sixteen other Red Sticks were less fortunate. Detected that morning beneath an overhang along the riverbank, the men were all killed, the tips of their noses added to the gory count.[36]

The nose collectors reaped a large harvest. They deposited at headquarters 577 nasal tips. General Coffee calculated that his mounted riflemen had slain nearly 300 Red Sticks in the river, for a total of at least 850 warriors killed, marking the Battle of Horseshoe Bend as the largest loss of warrior lives in a single clash on the North American continent since 1540, when Hernando de Soto had slaughtered the defenders of Mabila a scant hundred miles or so west of the site of Old Hickory's bloody triumph. Neither would the chilling death count ever be exceeded during the long course of the Indian Wars, either in a single engagement or in a prolonged struggle such as the Great Sioux War.

The cost to the army was trifling by comparison: just 26 soldiers were killed and 107 wounded at Horseshoe Bend. The Cherokees suffered disproportionately high casualties, losing 18 of their best warriors killed and 36 wounded. John Coffee had little to say about the Cherokees or friendly Creeks (who lost 5 killed and 11 wounded) or their contribution to victory in either his report or his personal correspondence. Jackson, for his part, merely acknowledged their "great gallantry" without suggesting they played any appreciable role in the outcome.

Others were more forthcoming and rightly credited the Cherokees with having turned the tide of battle. "Gentlemen of rank and character who were present at the decisive battle at the Horseshoe have told me that the daring, intrepid, and preserving bravery of the Cherokee warriors probably saved the lives of 1,000 white men," the Cherokee Indian agent Return J. Meigs reported. "It has made among them widows and orphans, and they deserve well of the United States." Colonel Williams recognized the debt he owed the Cherokees. "Had it not been for the enterprise of the Cherokees in crossing the river," he acknowledged, "nearly [my] whole regiment would have been cut to pieces."[37]

.   .   .

At a dark and brooding council beside a boulder-strewn, turbulent creek twenty miles from the ruins of Tohopeka, Menawa learned the extent of the catastrophe that had befallen his Abeikas. The reports of talwa and talofa leaders shocked him. Not more than twenty warriors from Okfuskee had escaped the slaughter, none from Tuckabatchee, and only three from Nuyaka. Jackson had also burned and pillaged Okfuskee. Not a vestige of Menawa's vast material wealth remained. He was as poor as the most abject member of his band. For three days he and the other council principals grieved and contemplated their future. They neither ate, drank, nor permitted their wounds to be dressed. At the close of the third day, Menawa recalled, "it was determined that the Indians should return to their respective homes, submit to the victors, and each man make his own peace as best he might." The bloody Abeika defeat at Horseshoe Bend and the subsequent dispersal of the survivors slashed Red Stick fighting strength by more than a third.[38]

Returning to Fort Williams to rest and refit his army, Jackson was guardedly optimistic that Horseshoe Bend would hasten the war's end. Writing to Rachel of the battle, he concluded hopefully, "What effect this will produce upon those infatuated and deluded people I cannot say. It is probable that they may now sue for peace. Should they not, if I can be supplied with provisions, I will give them, with the permission of Heaven, the final stroke at the Hickory Ground." How soon that might be, no one could venture to say. Food was short, and the horses were so worn down that General Coffee feared they would all die. Nevertheless, Old Hickory assured Rachel, "All is now content—no murmuring to be heard." Jackson not only had won a staggering battlefield victory, albeit in large measure because of Cherokee boldness, but also had finally conquered his own army.[39]

CHAPTER SEVENTEEN

An Elusive Peace

THE TENSAW PLANTER Zachariah McGirth owed an immeasurable debt of gratitude to the Red Stick warrior who had saved his wife and children's lives at Fort Mims seven months earlier and whose corpse lay putrefying on the Horseshoe Bend killing grounds. Only hours before the Red Sticks staged the attack that started the Creek War, McGirth had left Fort Mims on an errand. Supposing his family had perished in the slaughter, the grieving McGirth courted death as a government courier over the Federal Road. His suicidal impulse went unrewarded, however. Discharged in early 1814, McGirth wandered the streets of Mobile, alone and bereft. A few weeks after Horseshoe Bend, a friend approached him with unexpected news: there were people down at the wharf who urgently wished to see him.

At the dock bystanders directed him to a canoe in which a woman and six children huddled, naked but for the blankets they clutched about them. Asked twice if he knew them, McGirth replied that he did not. Throwing off her blanket, the woman revealed her face and nude figure. It was his wife, Vicey, and his six children, whom he imagined he had buried after Fort Mims. To her stunned husband, Vicey related her harrowing tale. She told him of the Creek warrior Sanota, whom they had raised as a foster son, and the protection he had afforded them until a sense of duty took him from the Hickory

Ground to Tohopeka. Perhaps aware that he was on a one-way trip to eternity, Sanota told Vicey she must fend for herself from then on. When word of his death reached her, Vicey fled the prevailing pandemonium at the Hickory Ground with her children. After toiling through a hundred miles of forests and swamps, their clothing shredded beyond use, the family reached their Tensaw home, only to find the country deserted. Vicey pieced together a rude hut and grubbed for potatoes to keep her children alive. A patrol of Tensaw volunteers chanced upon her in a potato patch, naked and nearly starved to death. Aware that her husband was in Mobile, they paddled the family downriver to the remarkable reunion on the wharf.[1]

Vicey McGirth had been fortunate. Notwithstanding the catastrophe at Horseshoe Bend, the Alabama and Koasati Red Sticks, together with those from the Coosa and lower Tallapoosa River talwas, had little incentive to surrender captives. Despite heavy losses, they had repelled invading columns from both Georgia and the Mississippi Territory. Their leaders shunned further combat after Calabee Creek but hardly felt conquered. Nor, it seems, did any except the Abeikas, who had all but ceased to exist as a people. Including their losses at Horseshoe Bend, the total Red Stick death toll to date likely topped two thousand, or just over half of the able-bodied male Red Stick population.

Although few contemplated surrender, the Red Sticks had no wish to tangle with Old Hickory again. In addition to their heavy casualties, the Red Sticks had lost any semblance of unity. Surviving prophets continued to enjoy a measure of influence, but principal loyalties reverted to talwas and clans. William Weatherford and his predominantly Alabama and Koasati followers took refuge on a spit of land in the Alabama River east of the Holy Ground known as Moniac's Island. Peter McQueen's Tallassees and Josiah Francis's Alabama adherents camped a dozen miles below Hoithlewaulee along Catoma Creek, just south of present-day Montgomery. Several hundred Red Sticks and their families decamped for Pensacola. The inhabitants of the six talwas that lay cradled near the union of the Coosa and Tallapoosa Rivers congregated for mutual support at Hoithlewaulee.[2]

It was against Hoithlewaulee that Jackson intended to move next. He expected an easy conquest and lacked only the supplies necessary to realize it. "The victory [Horseshoe Bend] is so complete and decisive that I calculate on a very feeble resistance in the future, and all that I want to finish the campaign and give a lasting peace to our southern frontier in a few days is a sufficient supply of provisions, for which I must in part look to you," he told his assistant quartermaster on April 1. While awaiting supplies, Jackson roused his troops for the final push. "Our enemy are not sufficiently humbled since they do not sue for peace. Buried in ignorance and seduced by their prophets, they have the weakness to believe they shall still be able to maintain a stand against our arms," sneered Old Hickory. "We must undeceive them. They must be made to atone for their obstinacy and ... [be] driven from their last refuge."[3]

On April 7, Jackson left Fort Williams with three thousand men carrying eight days' rations to administer the death blow. It would require a fifty-mile trek over a rugged, trackless land bisected by countless creeks to reach Hoithlewaulee. Jackson hoped to attack the Red Sticks on April 11, but nature intervened on their behalf. "The march was a continued fall of rain," related John Coffee, the worst conditions a Tennessee army had yet endured. A cold, relentless downpour pummeled the slippery hillsides. Streams overflowed their banks. When Jackson's drenched command stumbled into Hoithlewaulee on April 14, they found the talwa deserted. The enemy had vanished across the Tallapoosa. Most withdrew to the Escambia River on the Alabama-Florida frontier or sought Spanish protection in Pensacola. Others slipped across the Coosa River to the western margin of the Creek country, among them the invalid Menawa. An enraged Old Hickory reduced Hoithlewaulee and three neighboring talwas to ashes.[4]

Brooding got the better of Jackson, and he blamed the Red Stick escape on Colonel Homer Milton, the Regular army officer in command at Fort Hull. In early April, Milton's small Regular detachment had been reinforced by the advance guard of the Carolina Brigade, a mixed force of North and South Carolina volunteers then confronting high waters, measle outbreaks, insufficient wagons, and food shortages on its march through western Georgia. Benjamin Hawkins, apparently feeling his presence necessary at the denouement, had come from the Creek Agency to Milton's camp. Together, they superintended the building of Fort Decatur, the penultimate link in the chain of forts that General Pinckney had envisioned stretching from the Georgia frontier to the fork of the Tallapoosa and Coosa Rivers. The stockade arose just eight miles east of Hoithlewaulee. The Red Sticks did not interfere with Milton's construction work, and the colonel reciprocated by permitting them to escape.

Before leaving Fort Williams, Jackson had hoped only that Milton might "make a diversion" on his behalf. Now he all but accused Milton of upending his plans, not only by failing to give battle to the Red Sticks, but also by denying him badly needed provisions. General Pinckney was partly at fault; he had assured Jackson that Milton would at some indeterminate time attack Hoithlewaulee. Pinckney took Jackson's displeasure in stride, suggesting that such contretemps were common to "military life." To "prevent any future misunderstandings of this sort," however, he would take charge of operations in the field. The courtly South Carolinian was then only a two-day ride from Jackson's headquarters.[5]

Old Hickory had left behind the smoldering ruins of Hoithlewaulee and sidled a few miles downstream to Tuskegee, a vacant talwa of thirty or forty Creek abodes nestled on a forty-six-foot-tall bluff at the fork of the Coosa and Tallapoosa Rivers. Scarcely visible beneath the underbrush were brick and mortar traces of the old French Fort Toulouse. Below the bluff, the two mighty rivers of the Upper Creek country approached within a quarter mile of each other before curving outward to create a three-thousand-acre peninsula of forest and canebrake. Tuskegee marked the ideal site for the final and most imposing link in Pinckney's chain of Creek country forts.[6]

Old Hickory's tirade about the dilatory Milton might have struck General Pinckney as petty, perhaps even silly in view of Jackson's prodigious accomplishments, which he looked forward to acknowledging when he met the Tennessean: the single-minded, indefatigable Jackson had brought the Creek War effectively to a close.

Contemplating the tranquility of the Tuskegee countryside, Brigadier General John Coffee anticipated a general peace. "We reached this place so long sought for yesterday. The Indians have all fled; they are running in all directions. Numbers are coming in and begging forgiveness. Some are running towards Pensacola, while others are hiding in the swamps. Our fighting is over, the [Creek] nation is conquered, and all we have to do is to establish a sufficient number of posts to retain control of this country," he wrote to his wife hopefully on April 18. "Now I think I can see the way clear when I shall be able to return home and remain in quiet with you and enjoy the blessings of private and social life the remainder of my life."[7]

William Weatherford had little hope of future happiness. In early talks with surrendering Red Sticks, Old Hickory had demanded that they seize Weatherford so that "he might be dealt with as he deserved" before Jackson would accept their protestations of friendship. Weatherford knew this. To spare his comrades the humiliation of turning him in, Weatherford decided to submit to the mercurial Jackson, come what may. On April 17, he departed Moniac's Island with fifteen slaves taken at Fort Mims and a small escort of warriors to watch over them. Leaving his human cargo and attendants outside army lines, Weatherford approached the nearest sentinel and asked where he might find the headquarters tent. His presence excited no alarm. Soldiers had become accustomed to seeing both surrendering Red Sticks and friendly Creeks come and go. There was nothing threatening in Weatherford's demeanor. He carried no weapon and wore only tattered moccasins and buckskin breeches. The black-haired, bare-chested rider also had white skin and spoke fluent English; perhaps he was not even an Indian. The obliging sentinel pointed the way to Jackson's marquee.

Dismounting at a respectful distance, Weatherford strode calmly toward the tent. Benjamin Hawkins happened to be sitting outside. Instantly recognizing the visitor, he exclaimed, "By the great Alexander, here is Weatherford." Jackson, who had been inside dictating letters to Major Reid, at once strode outside, sword in hand. Walking firmly forward, Weatherford asked, "Is this General Jackson?"

"Yes," Jackson replied.

"I am Bill Weatherford."

"How dare you show yourself at my tent after having murdered the women and children at Fort Mims!" Jackson sputtered. "I had directed that you should be brought to me confined; had you appeared in this way, I should have known how to treat you."

"I am in your power—do with me as you please," answered Weatherford, who calmly but emphatically denied responsibility for the slaughter of civilians at Fort Mims; he had counseled hard against pressing the attack to its horrific conclusion and ridden off before the massacre occurred. Jackson softened. Extending his hand, he said, "I am glad to see you, Mr. Weatherford."

"General Jackson, I have come in to surrender," said Weatherford as he shook Jackson's hand.

"I am glad to hear it," Jackson replied.

"Our warriors are killed and scattered, our ammunition is out, our women and children are naked and starving," continued Weatherford. "If we had warriors and something to eat, we would fight on."

"You are a brave man," said Jackson, "and I glory in your spunk." With that, he led Weatherford through the canvas door of his marquee.[8]

Weatherford's piercing black eyes and gentlemanly comportment transfixed John Reid. "Weatherford was the greatest of the barbarian world," he told a friend. "He possessed all the manliness of sentiment—all the heroism of soul.... [If you] could see his looks and gestures—the modesty and yet the firmness that were in them."

Jackson and Weatherford conversed well into the evening, sharing a jug of rum to lubricate the proceedings. As the liquor flowed, Jackson's regard for Weatherford soared. "General Jackson, as if by intuition, seemed to know that Weatherford was no savage and much more than an ordinary man by nature and treated him very kindly indeed," recalled Major Reid. Another acquaintance of both Jackson and Weatherford attested, "I have heard General Jackson say that if he was capable of forming anything like a correct judgment of a man on a short acquaintance, that he pronounced Weatherford to be as high-toned and fearless as any man he had met with."

Before parting, the two men settled on terms: Jackson would issue rations to Weatherford's starving followers, and Weatherford would help Old Hickory track down and induce Red Stick holdouts to surrender. As for the fifteen slaves Weatherford brought with him, Jackson also accepted them—officially on behalf of the government, but actually to work, for a time at least, in the fields of the Hermitage when he went home.[9]

A return to the Hermitage and a reunion with Rachel were indeed drawing near. Red Sticks streamed into Jackson's camp, the forts in the Upper Creek country, and Hawkins's Creek Agency to surrender unconditionally and beg for food. They turned over slave, white, and métis captives taken at Fort Mims and elsewhere in the Tensaw. Famished Red Sticks were also eager to escape the wrath of roving pro-American Creek vigilantes looking to settle scores.

The army treated capitulating warriors and their families kindly. To prevent their starving, a genuine concern given that most Red Stick communities and crops had been destroyed, in the coming weeks government stores would issue rations to approximately eighty-two hundred refugees.[10]

The destinies of Red Stick leaders varied. Jim Boy went home to await his fate. The desire to fight having long since left him, Hopoithle Micco submitted to confinement the day before Weatherford rode into Jackson's camp. In an admirable display of forgiveness, Benjamin Hawkins tried to intercede on his behalf. Withal, Hawkins remained fond of the old man who had dedicated much of his life to subverting the agent's civilization policy. Hopoithle Micco's guards, however, roughed him up so badly that he died before Hawkins could effect his release.[11]

Paddy Walsh likewise met a hard end. Still intent on inflicting pain on Americans and apostate métis, the surly bantam stalked the edges of the Tensaw country for nearly a year before his own people betrayed him to Mississippi territorial authorities. He was imprisoned at Fort Claiborne to stand trial for having killed two settlers in retaliation for the murder of his aunt by Tensaw vigilantes. Somehow Walsh escaped, only to be seized and returned to his captors by former Red Sticks fearful of army retribution. Brought before a drumhead court-martial, he was convicted of murder and hanged. No evidence had been presented against him, and the interpreter had given false answers to the court.[12]

Peter McQueen was captured shortly after Horseshoe Bend but escaped army clutches and made his way to West Florida. Josiah Francis also "absconded," as Jackson put it. Not only did Francis elude capture, but he also managed to set himself up with several women in a handsome suite of apartments in Pensacola, while three hundred of his male followers camped under the guns of the Spanish redoubt.

With Tecumseh dead, and both the northern Indian alliance and the Red Stick movement in shambles, the prophet Seekaboo decided to lose himself among the Seminoles of Florida. He was never heard from again.[13]

While the Red Stick refugees who conceded defeat enjoyed reasonable treatment by the government, and those who gathered along the Escambia River contemplated fighting on, perhaps with help from their Seminole cousins, another group of former fighters rode a one-way trail to oblivion. They were Choctaw renegades, a remnant of a few score turbulent young warriors who, spurning the tribal proscription against shedding white blood, had joined the Red Sticks at the outbreak of hostilities. Most perished in the Battle of Calabee Creek. A few had thrown themselves on the mercy of the Choctaw chief Moshulitubbee, only to be arrested and executed. Regretting their misplaced allegiance, the remaining survivors petitioned for the right to come home. Pushmataha took it upon himself to reply on behalf of the Choctaw leadership. They were free to return, he said, so long as they followed a path that Pushmataha prescribed and advised him regularly of their progress.

The way led between two high hills near the present city of Demopolis, Alabama. As the humbled turncoats neared the spot, Pushmataha deployed warriors on both sides of the defile. When the last traitor entered the killing zone, Pushmataha's men opened a withering fire. The renegades were slain to a man.[14]

There was a festive air in Tuskegee as April 1814 drew to a close. The former Upper Creek talwa overflowed with soldiers. Shortly after William Weatherford left to help track down wayward Red Sticks in the Cahaba River region, Major General Joseph Graham, clad in a secondhand dress uniform that the North Carolina governor had sold him, rode resplendently, if a little thread-worn, into Jackson's camp at the head of his brigade of North and South Carolina militiamen. Colonel Milton accompanied him with his Regular companies, which merged with Colonel Williams's battle-hardened Thirty-Ninth U.S. Infantry to form a single brigade. Two additional artillery companies and a troop of dragoons rounded out the largest army force yet assembled in the Creek country.

Relations between Jackson and Milton were likely frosty, but General Graham was a man after Jackson's heart. A slender, long-faced Scots-Irishman from the North Carolina backcountry of "mannerly bearing" and an enthusiastic scholar, Graham had grappled with Tories

and Banastre Tarleton's dreaded British cavalry in the same neighborhood as had Jackson during the Revolutionary War. Eight years older
than Old Hickory, Graham suffered nine wounds in a single battle
and rose in rank from private to major before age twenty-one. After
the American Revolution, he dedicated himself to developing an iron
furnace, which proved highly profitable, and to education, serving as
an early trustee of the fledgling University of North Carolina in Chapel Hill.[15]

When General Pinckney arrived to assume command on April 20,
the celebrating began in earnest. Pinckney hosted as lavish a banquet
in Jackson's honor as army rations permitted. Outside Pinckney's
ample marquee, Carolina militiamen and Regulars entertained the
Tennessee rank and file with "soldierly hospitality" and toasted their
gallantry in "many a flowing mug of regulation whiskey." The fes-
tivities spilled over into the next day. When the bacchanalia ended,
General Pinckney announced at 3:00 p.m. on April 21 that Jackson and
his men were free to leave. Two hours later, Old Hickory and his
tipsy Tennesseans were on the trail homeward. After they left, Graham's militiamen began the work of transforming Tuskegee into Fort
Jackson. The prospective post was intended to be a sturdy, five-angled
fortification that would anchor Pinckney's network of Creek country
forts and pay tribute to the Tennessee militia general who had made
it possible.[16]

As much as he appreciated the adulation, Jackson departed the Creek
country deeply troubled. The War of 1812 was going poorly for the
United States. By the spring of 1814 the comparative positions of Great
Britain and the United States had shifted markedly. When the war
began, Great Britain had been locked in a brutal struggle with Napoleon Bonaparte. The Crown had considered the American conflict a
minor irritant rather than a threat serious enough to warrant diverting
scarce military resources. The collapse of France in the spring of 1814
opened new opportunities for Great Britain. The strategic myopia of
the congressional War Hawks, principally Kentuckians and Tennesseans, who had precipitated the War of 1812, then became apparent.
Congress had denied the Madison administration the funds needed
to build a fleet, and now the mighty British navy, relieved from war

with France, blockaded American ports and roamed the Atlantic coast at will. American trade stagnated, a collapse of American finances appeared imminent, and New England wanted out of the war. In addition to stepping up its efforts on the Atlantic coast, Great Britain began to plan a second major invasion of the United States from Canada so as to transform a heretofore annoying defensive war into a crushing victory over its former colonies.

In light of declining American fortunes against Great Britain, the Madison administration had little stomach for prolonging the conflict with the Red Sticks. The harried president and his War Department wanted to terminate the war on terms that punished Creek malefactors without being so harsh as to provoke further trouble. Evidently expecting Jackson to emerge victorious, ten days before the Battle of Horseshoe Bend, Secretary of War John Armstrong advised General Pinckney of the terms under which a Red Stick capitulation would be accepted. Pinckney was to conduct treaty negotiations "in a form altogether military," assisted by Benjamin Hawkins to the extent he judged appropriate.

The intended surrender terms were lenient indeed. "As soon as [the Red Sticks] shall express a desire to put an end to the war," Pinckney was to propose that they cede land enough to indemnify the United States for the cost of the war, cease all contact with the Spaniards, deliver up the "prophets and other instigators of the war," and permit the government to open roads through their country and construct military posts and trading houses "as may be deemed necessary and proper."[17]

Jackson bristled when Pinckney apprised him of Secretary Armstrong's instructions. The government, Old Hickory argued, should decline to negotiate and simply dictate the harshest possible terms. "The commissioners appointed to make a treaty with the Creeks [should] have little to do but assign them their proper limits," he advised Armstrong before departing the Creek country. "Those of the friendly party who have associated with me will be easily satisfied, and the remainder of the hostile party, pleased that their lives were spared them, will thankfully accept as a bounteous donation any district which may be allowed them for their future settlement." Jackson considered a narrow strip running from the Georgia line past Horseshoe Bend to the Coosa River and north to the Cherokee frontier more than enough land for the friendly Creeks, with perhaps a sliver of land below the Federal Road allocated to Big Warrior's people. In sum, Jackson advocated the outright appropriation of two-thirds of Creek lands.[18]

Tennesseans united behind Old Hickory in objecting not only to the lenient terms the Madison administration offered but also to the absence of Tennessee representation on the treaty commission. There was a general feeling that Pinckney, although an "amiable man of talents," would let the Red Sticks off too easy, and that Hawkins, in view of his previous sympathy for the Creeks, was "unworthy of any national trust." Tennessean suspicions appeared borne out when Pinckney amended Armstrong's instructions to indemnify friendly Creek losses during the war and to remunerate chiefs who had distinguished themselves as American allies. These were wise and just alterations, but they rankled Tennesseans who thought only of their own sacrifices and the decisive role the state had played in winning the war.[19]

For a brief season, complaints of federal pliancy took second place in Tennessee to adulation of Andrew Jackson. Old grudges were cast aside. Disgruntled former subordinates fell silent. East Tennesseans suppressed their jealousy of their West Tennessee rivals. "Already, General, it is the common theme of conversation that you must be our next governor," an old friend assured Old Hickory. Prominent former critics "speak of you in terms even of affection. There is not a word said in this country but is not in terms of respect, if not of admiration." Rachel, who as usual suffered from sundry ailments, gloried in her husband's triumphs while longing for his return. "Once more you have been Led from The field of battle in safety and one of the most Daingerous interprises of any History Ever recorded. Murciful God how he has Smileed on us and Crownd your patriotic Zeale with unequaled successes with Glory and Honor for yourself and country."[20]

Nashville hailed Jackson as a conquering hero. On May 14, local luminaries accompanied Old Hickory to the outskirts of town, where a cheering crowd conducted the frontier Caesar to the courthouse. With Old Hickory rode little Lyncoya Jackson, decked out "more like a puppet than anything else." Rachel and their adopted son Andrew, dressed in a "nicely made" suit, stood beside the dignitaries. Behind

Jackson trudged the Tensaw slaves that William Weatherford had surrendered to him.

Speeches, dinners, and banquets in Jackson's honor lasted a week. Governor Blount presented Jackson with an honorary sword on behalf of Governor Holmes and the people of the Mississippi Territory in recognition of his "preeminent services to his country, the happy effects [of which] have been so immediately felt by the citizens of this territory."[21]

Jackson had no doubt but that he had won a strategically decisive victory that would contribute to both the humbling of Great Britain and further national expansion. Addressing a rowdy and receptive gathering at Nashville's Bell Tavern on May 16, he proclaimed,

The success which attended our exertions has indeed been very great. We have laid the foundation of a lasting peace to those frontiers which had been so long and so often infested by the savages. We have conquered. We have added a country to ours, which, by connecting the settlements of Georgia with those of the Mississippi Territory, and both of them with our own, will become a secure barrier against foreign invasion, or the operation of foreign influence over our red neighbors in the South, and we have furnished the means not only of defraying the expense of the war against the Creeks, but of that which is carrying on against their ally Great Britain.[22]

It was a stirring speech, but events in the Creek country would prove Jackson's assurances premature.

CHAPTER EIGHTEEN

Betrayal at Fort Jackson

WILLIAM WEATHERFORD was a man of his word. In late May he induced seventy former Red Stick warriors to accompany him and a three-hundred-man expedition under the North Carolina colonel J. A. Pearson on a sweep of the central Alabama River valley southeast of the Cahaba River. Their objective was to persuade Alabama and Koasati holdouts to surrender to General Graham at Fort Jackson. Pearson and Weatherford combed the region for fifteen days. Without a single loss of life, they brought in nearly 330 Indians, of whom 94 were warriors. Not that Weatherford was averse to shedding blood to subdue recalcitrant bands. Several weeks later, he joined Colonel Joseph Carson's Mississippi Territory dragoons in a cross-border raid of a Red Stick settlement near Pensacola. Angry British officials claimed the invaders "killed all the Indians they could lay hands on" and "took what women and children could be found."

Carson's expedition seemingly confirmed General Graham's conviction that the remaining Red Sticks "will fight only in self-defense when they do not expect quarter." So sanguine was Graham that little remained to be done but accept the surrender of dispirited and starving former Red Sticks, and then feed them, that he began disassembling his brigade well before its mid-July discharge date. Culling scores of enfeebled militiamen, many of whom should never have been recruited to begin with, he sent a steady stream of subpar soldiers in jolting wagons back over the bumpy Federal Road to the Georgia settlements. Company first sergeants scratched from the muster rolls those suffering from any of a litany of complaints: general debility, consumption, dropsy, deafness, inflammation of the liver, weakness of the system, asthma, sore legs, accidental bayonet wounds, blindness, general emaciation of the system, and nervous weakness.[1]

William Weatherford tried to go home, and the effort nearly cost him his life. Old Hickory might have absolved him of blame for the atrocities at Fort Mims, but Mississippi Territory residents had not. Recoiling from death threats, he took refuge inside Fort Claiborne. The post commander, Colonel Gilbert Russell, not only accommodated him but also assigned to Weatherford a guard party of presumably reliable men. They included James Cornells, who bore a bitter hatred of Weatherford. Just a year earlier, Weatherford had been deeply in love with Cornells's daughter Lucy, but war had nipped the budding romance. McQueen's Red Sticks burned the Cornellses' home and took James Cornells's wife captive, ransoming her in Pensacola before the Battle of Burnt Corn Creek. Under the mistaken assumption that Weatherford had participated in the kidnapping, Cornells vowed to kill him should the opportunity arise. Learning of Cornells's intentions, Weatherford objected to him as a guard. When that failed, Weatherford confronted Cornells. Would he slay him in prison? "No," replied Cornells. "I will take no advantage of you while you are here and I am guarding you. But when this time is over, I intend to kill you." Weatherford seemed satisfied. "Well, if you will take no advantage of me on this occasion, I will trust myself to you." Cornells, meanwhile, learned that Weatherford had played no role in the abduction of his wife or the burning of his property. The men became fast friends.[2]

It was clear there could be no reconciliation between the U.S. government and the Red Sticks who had fled to West Florida. In late April, Lower Creek chiefs cautioned Benjamin Hawkins not to expect Peter McQueen, Josiah Francis, or their seventeen hundred followers to surrender. "They were proud, haughty, brave, and mad by fanaticism" and would mistake any government overture as a sign of weakness. Although the most culpable, they had endured the least. Better, the Lower Creeks advised, to give them a taste of what Jackson had administered to the Abeikas at Horseshoe Bend.

An American visitor to Pensacola asked a Red Stick warrior, whose family clearly suffered from hunger and want, why he did not seek American protection, knowing that if he did so he would receive ample provisions. "No," the man snarled, "he was waiting for the English. They would be here in about a month with a great many men, arms and provisions, and he intended to go to war again." In the meantime, he and his compatriots would steal cattle from Tensaw settlements—a food source their prophets had forbidden during the heady days of the Red Stick uprising—or wheedle rations from the Spaniards. The inquisitive American dismissed the warrior as delusional.[3]

On May 10, 1814, four days before Andrew Jackson reached Nashville, two British frigates dropped anchor in the brilliant blue waters of Apalachicola Bay, two hundred miles southeast of Pensacola. Rowing ashore, a landing party of British Royal Marines disembarked on the white-sand beach and penetrated inland, combing the hardwood forests and cypress and tupelo swamps for Indians ready to rally to the British cause. Ten days later, on board the HMS *Orpheus,* Captain Hugh Pigot conferred with ten Red Stick chiefs about cooperating to reconquer Creek lands and expel the Americans from Baton Rouge, Mobile, and ultimately New Orleans. While the conferees made grand plans and reaffirmed their historic bonds of affection, reinvigorated warriors helped themselves to the two thousand new English muskets and a supply of powder and ball deposited for them on the beach. A Royal Marine captain also disembarked to train the Red Sticks and their Seminole cousins in Western ways of war.[4]

As we have seen, Captain Pigot's presence was the consequence of a radical change in British military strategy occasioned by the defeat of Napoleon Bonaparte. Victory over the French freed up troops and ships for the invasion of the Gulf Coast that Americans had long feared. The British objective was to capture New Orleans and gain control of the lower Mississippi River, which would compel the United States to abandon its attempts to seize Canada and divert resources to reopen the vital southern commercial and military artery.

Captain Pigot assured his superior officer, Vice Admiral Sir Alexander Cochrane, the newly installed commander of the North American station, that the task would be far easier to accomplish than His Majesty's government assumed. The minor Red Stick chiefs whom Pigot entertained beguiled him with a bogus narrative of their war against the United States. Not only did they apparently neglect to mention the Horseshoe Bend imbroglio, but they also told Pigot that the Red Sticks were strong, unified, and expected aid from the Choctaws, Chickasaws, Cherokees, Seminoles, and Georgia slaves eager to rise up against their masters. Of Red Stick fidelity to the king, the conniving chiefs left no doubt. They were "his dutiful children in this part of the world" and needed only additional arms and ammunition to fight on his behalf. With Pigot's encouragement, the chiefs assured Admiral Cochrane, "We have always been in our hearts Englishmen, and never shall any nation induce us to forget the love we bear for our Father King George and the British nation. To you we look for assistance so as to [show] the Americans the horror of war, which they have inflicted on us, and would you only land a small body of troops, we are certain all the Indians now forced to serve America will join with hearts and souls the British cause and drive them completely out of all the lands of which they have robbed the different Indian nations and all they themselves possess in these parts."[5]

Pigot endorsed the chiefs' desperate gambit to retrieve victory from the jaws of defeat. Grossly overestimating Red Stick numbers and just as badly miscalculating American determination to hold Mobile and New Orleans, Pigot concluded that three thousand British troops landed at the ports would be "joined by all the Indians, with the disaffected French and Spanish, to drive the Americans entirely out of Louisiana and Florida." He estimated Red Stick and Seminole numbers at twenty-eight hundred armed and ready to fight and another thousand waiting in the swamps near Pensacola for British muskets.

It was later said that the prospect of prize money caused Pigot to support Red Stick fantasies. Whatever Pigot's motivation, a credulous Admiral Cochrane became enamored of his scheme. In early July, Cochrane ordered Brevet Major Edward Nicolls and a hundred Royal Marines, then in Havana, to carry more arms to the Red Sticks, train them in European tactics, and induce a regiment's worth of Georgia slaves to rally to the Union Jack. In the meantime, Captain Pigot commissioned George Woodbine, a white Jamaican trader well known to the Creeks, a brevet captain in the Royal Marines. He assigned him as British agent to the Red Sticks and Seminoles assembled at Apalachicola Bay. Until the British were able to send supply ships, Woodbine was to provision the Indians from the Forbes and Company store at Prospect Bluff, a few miles up the Apalachicola River. Two noncommissioned officers circulated among the warriors, teaching close-order and bayonet drill.[6]

Word of Captain Pigot's machinations traveled fast. The opportunistic Big Warrior, who attended a talk with the British, told Benjamin Hawkins what had transpired. He also assured the agent that he had rejected Pigot's proffer of arms and predicted the British would bring only "ruin and bad talk." Although tempted to switch sides, Big Warrior remained faithful to the Americans who had saved him from Red Stick vengeance early in the Creek War. Peter McQueen, on the other hand, welcomed the British warships as enablers of a Red Stick reconquest of the Creek country. He had been on the verge of surrendering at Fort Claiborne when Red Stick runners told him of Pigot's largesse. Immediately he reversed course for Apalachicola Bay. McQueen's change of heart, together with rumored British overtures to the Choctaws and Chickasaws, greatly troubled the Choctaw factor George Gaines. "I had been preparing for a trip to Tennessee to see my friends and relations, and most of my neighbors had been as busy in devising and executing ways and means to make themselves as comfortable as they were before the war. But today we are all down in the mouth," he wrote to his brother in early June. If reports of British intrigue were true, concluded Gaines, "we shall have even a warmer summer than the last."[7]

Andrew Jackson hoped for a summer warm with the love of family. Rachel, his adopted son Andrew, little Lyncoya, and the Hermitage all needed his attention. His shoulder wound was on the mend. Jackson thought most of the floating bone fragments had been expelled from the suppurating hole in his shoulder during the rigors of the campaign, but he still endured periodic bouts of severe diarrhea. Above all things, he needed rest. As a concerned John Reid put it, "His health was still delicate and rendered retirement essential to its restoration."[8]

Jackson, however, could not divest himself from the fate of the country he had wrested from the Red Sticks. From the Hermitage in late May he fumed over what he considered unwarranted government leniency and strategic myopia. Obtaining just enough Creek land to reimburse the cost of the war was insufficient, reasoned Jackson. "The grand policy of the government ought and must be to connect the settlements of Georgia with that of the [Mississippi] Territory and Tennessee," he told Colonel John Williams, "which at once forms a bulwark against foreign invasion and prevents the introduction of foreign influence to corrupt the minds of the Indians." Only a corridor of "wealthy inhabitants, unmixed by Indians," between the Creek country and Spanish West Florida, buttressed by military might, could secure the integrity of the frontier. Moreover, the Cherokees who had contributed so mightily to Jackson's victory must yield their remaining land in Tennessee for cash or an equivalent portion of the Upper Creek country. "Our national security requires it; their security requires it. The happiness and security of the whole require this salutary arrangement." The whole, that is, except the Indians, whose happiness in Jackson's calculations counted for little.[9]

Jackson's aggressive musings were about to reshape federal Indian policy in the South. On May 22, in acknowledgment of Old Hickory's victory at Horseshoe Bend and absent other suitable candidates for high command (American officers continued to perform miserably against the British), Secretary of War Armstrong offered Jackson a brigadier general's billet in the Regular army and command of the Seventh Military District (comprising Louisiana, Tennessee, the Mississippi Territory, and the Creek country), with its two understrength Regular regiments and the soon-to-depart Carolina brigade. Should Jackson accept, President Madison wished him to "proceed without delay to Fort Jackson and consummate the arrangements committed to General Pinckney in relation to the hostile Creeks."

Jackson accepted with alacrity. Before again bidding farewell to Rachel, he received an added honor. William Henry Harrison, who defeated Tecumseh and his British allies in western Ontario the year before, had just resigned his major general's commission in disgust over federal policy. It now went to Jackson. The higher rank emblazoned on his uniform jacket, Old Hickory left Nashville on June 25. With him as aides-de-camp rode John Reid and Richard Call, the latter restored to the rank of lieutenant.[10]

Old Hickory's fifteen-day sojourn to Fort Jackson afforded him ample opportunity to contemplate the Creeks' destiny. From Fort Deposit southward he witnessed hungry, bewildered, and frightened former Red Sticks crowd supply depots to draw a measly three-quarters of a pound of flour and one-quarter pound of beef or pork daily. In common with fellow westerners like Colonel Williams, with whom he had shared his initial thoughts on the matter, Jackson considered the administration's proposed terms for dealing with the Red Sticks far too lenient. Unlike most westerners, whose objections arose largely from land hunger, as a military man Jackson's primary concern—for the moment at least—was frontier security. He believed the borders of Georgia, Tennessee, and the Mississippi Territory must be removed from the threat that Peter McQueen, Josiah Francis, and the remaining hostile Red Sticks posed, particularly because it appeared that the Spaniards and British intended to abet further conflict. He also understood the need both to help and to isolate those already surrendered. "It is enough to make humanity shudder to see the distressed situation of the Indians. Eight thousand are kept alive, being fed by the government daily," he wrote to Rachel. "And I fear, should they be supported by foreign aid, we will have half of the men we are feeding to keep from starvation to fight."[11]

On the morning of July 10, Jackson reached the eponymous post that would serve as department headquarters and play host to the treaty council. The place appalled him. Under General Graham, the garrison had lapsed into a lassitude befitting the southern summer heat and absence of a firm guiding hand. The fort was less than half finished. Small-pine pickets intended for stockade walls instead rotted in piles. No effort had been made to remove undergrowth from inside the compound or chop down timber outside it to create clear fields of fire. Jackson would need at least six months to make the place defensible. On July 15, the Carolina brigade would head home, and with Colonel Williams's Thirty-Ninth U.S. Infantry patrolling the West Florida frontier, Old Hickory would have on hand at the fort only the 541 officers and men of the Third U.S. Infantry present for duty at the decrepit post.

Withal, Old Hickory adopted a bold front. The day after arriving, he directed Benjamin Hawkins, who had returned to the Creek Agency, to advise friendly Creek war leaders and miccos to report to Fort Jackson for a treaty council on August 1. Jackson expected Hawkins to come back posthaste and notify the "chiefs of the hostile party who have submitted as also those who have any desire to submit" of the time and place of the council. Jackson would attack and reduce to "unconditional submission" those who held back. Jackson also demanded that Red Stick stragglers on the Cahaba and Black Warrior Rivers repair to Fort Jackson immediately; their "destruction," he advised Hawkins, "will attend a failure to comply with these orders."[12]

They came, those few Red Stick leaders north of the West Florida border who had escaped either death at Horseshoe Bend or murder at the hands of their disillusioned followers. Menawa did not attend, and none who did were major figures in the Red Stick movement. Friendly Creek miccos and war leaders predominated. Colorfully attired with the feathers, turbans, jewelry, and other regalia of their offices, they were in good spirits. General Pinckney had promised to compensate them for their war losses; foraging Red Stick warriors and American soldiers had slaughtered their cattle and hog stocks in about equal measure, and the former had razed several of their talwas and talofas. The conciliatory Pinckney had also pledged to remunerate friendly chiefs and warriors whose land fell within whatever territory the United States demanded the Creeks cede. That the Great Father would compel the Red Sticks to relinquish much of their country the friendly Creeks accepted as just; that they might lose more than a fraction of their own land never occurred to them. Had they been privy to Jackson's disparaging remarks about their integrity, they would have approached the council apprehensively. In point of fact, Old Hickory had little use for the Creeks who had served faithfully under him. They had "entered the ranks of an invading army," he told John Reid, to exterminate their own people. It mattered not to Jackson that the Red Sticks merited punishment; the friendly Creeks were no better than "traitors to their country and justly deserving the severest punishment." Jackson evidently saw his Creek allies in the same light as the Tories who had tormented him during the American Revolution.[13]

The Creeks normally commenced councils casually and with an elastic concept of deadlines. The proceedings at Fort Jackson were no exception. It took an impatient Jackson three days to marshal the miccos and war leaders. Meanwhile, a cavalcade of Cherokee chiefs rode into Fort Jackson with their agent Return J. Meigs to "protect their interests" in the pending settlement.

On the dreary and drizzly morning of August 5, 1814, Jackson presented the Creeks with his terms. All began well enough. Stepping outside his spacious marquee, he shook hands vigorously with the Cherokees and allied Creeks. "I am charged by your father the president of the United States to say to you chiefs and warriors that your conduct has met with his entire approbation," announced Jackson. The chiefs uttered their appreciation. Turning to former Red Sticks, Jackson continued, "I am happy to meet you once more at peace with the United States and your own nation, and to call you friends and brothers. War is a dreadful calamity; it has reduced your whole nation to misery and ruin." The Creeks concurred.

"Friends and brothers," he boomed at the broken Red Sticks, "you have followed the counsel of bad men and [made] war on a part of your own nation and the United States. This war has cost the United States a large sum. You must yield as much of your land as will pay this sum." The friendly Creeks likely smirked with satisfaction. And then Jackson stunned the entire assemblage. "But [the land] must be taken from your whole nation, in such a manner as to destroy the communication with our enemies everywhere. Your brothers the friendly Creeks will agree to it."

They decidedly did not. That evening the friendly Creeks met in private council to consider Jackson's demands. He wanted twenty-two million acres of land, more than half of the Creek domain, or roughly three-fifths of the present state of Alabama and one-fifth of Georgia. He also expected all of the Creeks to abandon the hunt in favor of farming, apprehend or shoot the "prophets and bad men" still on the run—principally, Peter McQueen and Josiah Francis—and permit the United States to construct roads through and to build forts inside their reduced territory. Particularly troublesome to once wealthy and severely self-interested Creek leaders, Jackson had said nothing of General Pinckney's pledge to compensate their personal losses. With one sharp political stroke, Jackson clearly sought to enfeeble the Creek people. There was a touch of evil genius in Old Hickory's stratagem; he would end the war by concluding a harsh peace treaty with his allies. The angry Creeks coined a sober new sobriquet for the author of the monstrous terms: from that night forward Jackson would be known to them as Sharp Knife or Pointed Arrow.[14]

MAP 9   THE CREEK CONFEDERACY AFTER THE TREATY
OF FORT JACKSON, 1814

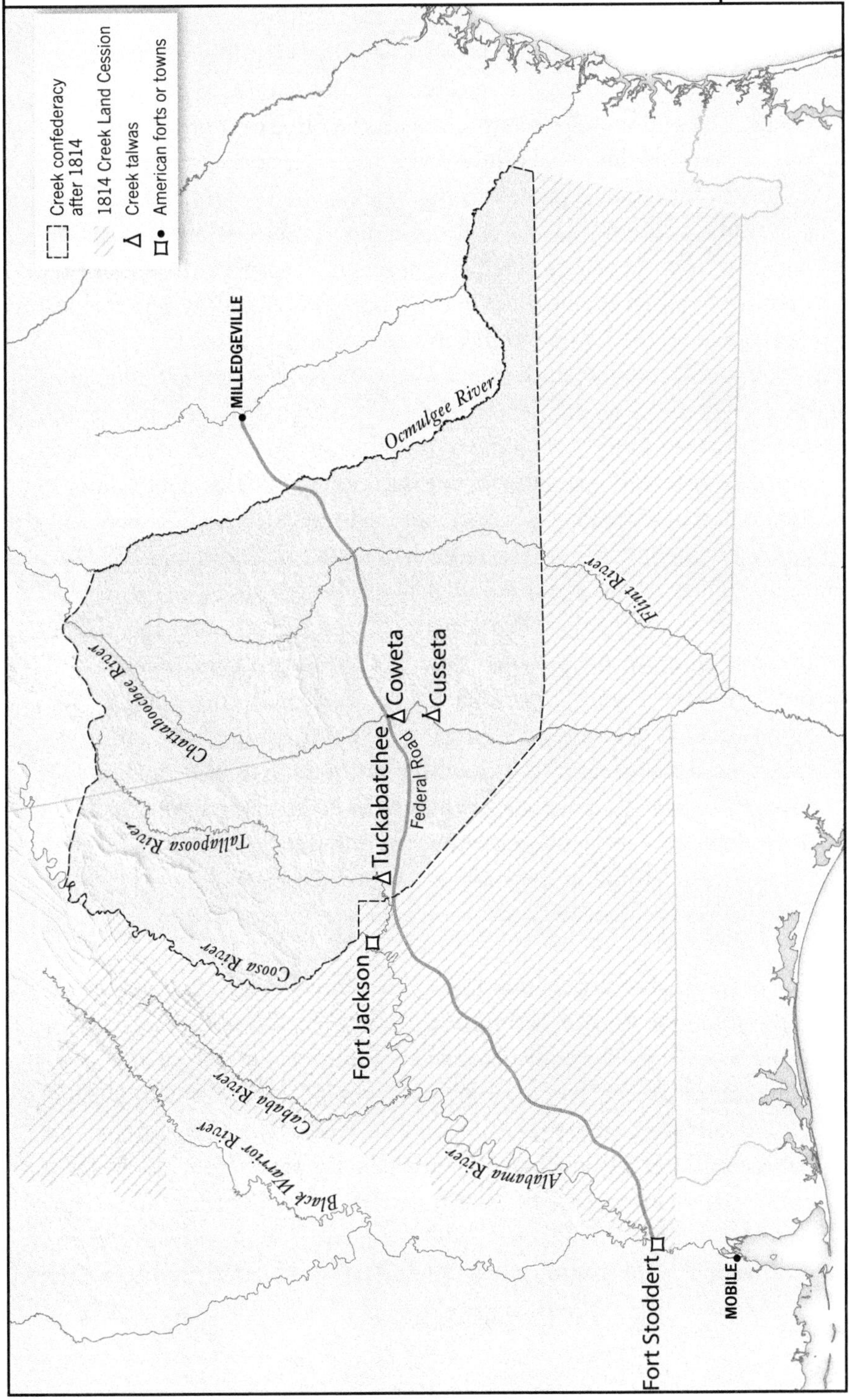

Creek confederacy
after 1814

1814 Creek Land Cession

△ Creek talwas

□● American forts or towns

MILLEDGEVILLE

Ocmulgee River

Flint River

Chattahoochee River

△Coweta
△Cusseta

△Tuckabatchee

Federal Road

Tallapoosa River

Coosa River

Fort Jackson

Cahaba River

Black Warrior River

Alabama River

Fort Stoddert

MOBILE

Rather than confront Jackson, the Creeks appealed first to Benjamin Hawkins, upon whose compassion and influence they relied. As spokesman for the pro-American Upper Creeks, it fell to Big Warrior to entreat their old friend to intercede with Sharp Knife to soften the terms. The spilling of white blood and the Creek National Council's punishment of the perpetrators "was the sole cause of war amongst us and nothing else," protested Big Warrior. Why should the faithful Creeks be made to pay for the misdeeds of the Red Sticks? Besides, with a potent Red Stick force still active in West Florida, it was premature to talk of expenses. "This way presented to us gives us alarm. I hope and beg the United States to settle on easy terms."[15]

Jackson knew he had dealt the Creeks a hard blow. "Whether they will agree to the terms, or in part fly to the Spaniards, as yet I cannot say," he wrote to Rachel on the night of August 5. He had no intention of softening his demands, however. Although Hawkins did nothing to encourage Big Warrior to believe better terms possible, his open sympathy for the Creeks only excited Jackson's contempt, and Big Warrior's appeal to the agent enraged him. He was already predisposed against the chief. When Big Warrior had first broached the subject of compensation for property losses, the general threatened to put him in chains. Ranting irrationally now, Jackson excoriated Big Warrior, whom he considered a "man of great duplicity," and his fellow friendly chiefs. He scolded them for not having either handed over Tecumseh, who Jackson said was at the time he visited the Creeks an avowed enemy of the United States (he was not, having neither called for war nor committed any hostile acts), or shot him themselves. Jackson also accused the friendly Creeks of having hoped for Tecumseh and the British to prevail over the United States.

To Big Warrior's plea that talk of land cessions be postponed until the remaining Red Sticks were defeated, Jackson responded, "We know the war is not over—and that is one reason why we will run a line between our friends and our enemies." Friendly Creeks had no grounds for complaint, snapped Old Hickory; had it not been for American intervention, they would have no land left at all. Perhaps at Hawkins's insistence, Jackson relented on the matter of individual property claims. Should they sign the treaty, Hawkins would record their requests for remuneration. "I will send them to your father the President of the United States. You will be paid honorably everything you ought to have, but we must first know our friends from our enemies," said Jackson. "Consult—and this evening let me see and know who will sign it and who will not." He would coerce no one, but those who rejected the treaty would be "given provisions to go to Pensacola," and thereafter be counted as enemies. On that cheerful note, the August 7 council terminated.[16]

Big Warrior and his compatriots again consulted with Benjamin Hawkins. He evidently encouraged them to make the best of a bad bargain: sign the treaty, as Jackson insisted that they do, so long as he agreed to submit with it their claims and General Pinckney's promise to honor them. Because the chiefs were more interested in their own losses than the greater good of their people, they yielded. On the morning of August 9, Big Warrior summoned Jackson and Hawkins to the Creeks' private council square. After Big Warrior and the Creek war leader Shelocta, who had fought with Old Hickory, eloquently but futilely appealed to Jackson not to seize the rich lands west of the Coosa, they accepted the treaty. Of the thirty-six war leaders and miccos who made their mark on the document, only one was a Red Stick, and he of little consequence.

The Creek signatories tried to appear masters of their own fate. They would honor Sharp Knife in accordance with Creek custom, and in so doing create a fictive tie of kinship with him. As Big Warrior professed to Hawkins, "The general has done much for us, and we wish to do something for him."

"You saved my life, and I am thankful for that," Big Warrior now told Jackson. "We have put our heads together and counselled on it and have come to one opinion about it, and what we should do. We, the Creek nation, give you three square miles of land, to be chosen where you like, from that we are going to give up." They made the same gift to Hawkins.

Jackson demurred. He would dispose of the gift to "clothe their poor naked women and children." The Creeks rejected his offer, more in sorrow than anger; they gave him the land so that he might live on it. Jackson extricated himself, in a manner of speaking. He promised to seek President Madison's opinion of the propriety of his accepting their gift and be bound accordingly. Hawkins never hesitated. "I have been long among you, and grown gray in your service," he said with true feeling. "I shall continue to be friendly and useful to you while

I live, and my children, born among you, will be brought up to do the same. I accept your present and esteem it the more highly as it resulted from the impulse of your own mind and not from any intimation from the general or me."

Jackson might have winced at Hawkins's implied rebuke of his heavy-handed treatment of the Creeks, to which the agent took profound exception. Hawkins considered the Madison administration's instructions to General Pinckney the only legitimate basis for dealing with the Creeks. Old Hickory had his treaty, however. It granted everything he demanded and far more than the government had requested.

In forwarding the Treaty of Fort Jackson and sundry related documents to Washington, Jackson hastened to explain to the secretary of war why he had exceeded instructions. "Considerations interesting to the United States, relative to the Spanish dominions immediately south of us, induced me to procure the cession of all the Creek lands of consequence, bounding on foreign claims of territory, in order to prevent future connections injurious to our tranquility." Jackson could have accomplished as much, and recouped the cost of the war, with a far smaller cession. His fellow westerners knew that, and they looked forward to grabbing as much of the Creek country as possible. "This acquisition of territory contains some very valuable land," salivated a Nashville editor, "and will no doubt be sold to a considerable advantage as soon as the government authorizes it."[17]

The land was valuable indeed. Old Hickory had acquired 21,086,793 acres of prime Upper and Lower Creek hunting grounds, together with much of their richest farmland—the "cream of the Creek country," as Jackson put it—which would ultimately go under the auction hammer for speculators and settlers. Although not then apparent, Jackson had set the pattern of land seizure and removal that was to doom not only the Creeks but also all the Indians of the Southeast and later of the American West.

Old Hickory had no time to savor his success. An acrimonious exchange of letters with Governor González Manrique convinced Jackson that the militarily feeble Spaniards would not—in fact could not—expel the Red Stick fugitives from West Florida. Unknown to Jackson, the nominally neutral governor had conceded control of Pensacola to a detachment of Royal Marines, the vanguard of a British invasion force then massing in the Caribbean to attack Mobile and New Orleans. At long last, the British were coming.

The threat that Peter McQueen and Josiah Francis's warriors alone posed paled beside the prospect of several thousand British veterans of the Napoleonic Wars, backed by an immense fleet, wresting control of the Gulf Coast from the United States and, together with the fugitive Red Sticks, reversing all the United States had accomplished in the Creek War.

Old Hickory moved quickly. With a promptness remarkable even for the peripatetic Jackson, he marshaled the Third U.S. Infantry and within forty-eight hours of signing the Treaty of Fort Jackson embarked for Mobile, the loss of which would jeopardize New Orleans. Tennessee militiamen drawn from Forts Deposit and Strothers would hold Fort Jackson in the absence of the Regulars; Governor Blount would hastily muster others to reinforce Jackson in the field.

Before Old Hickory left Fort Jackson, Big Warrior called his attention to the Red Sticks south of the treaty line. Big Warrior had forfeited his talwa and nearly lost his life to the Red Sticks; he had no desire to repeat the experience. Likening McQueen and Francis's followers to a ravening pack of wolves deprived of dens, Big Warrior warned they would fall on the pro-American Creeks after Jackson left. "They were not completely cowed and would be yet killing us. Let us follow them and kill them," implored Big Warrior. Jackson, however, could not be bothered with Big Warrior's predicament. "If you kill them, I will kill you," Jackson snarled. "Let them alone; the war is ended with the Indians." With that, he rode off. A baffled Big Warrior, whose shrewdness had extricated him from countless crises, was left to ponder what sort of a friend he and the peaceable Creeks had in Sharp Knife Jackson, or if they had in him a friend at all.[18]

· PART FIVE ·

CHAPTER NINETEEN

A Scalp for a Scalp

A SURREAL EUPHORIA gripped the foes of the United States in the South. The Red Sticks languishing in Spanish West Florida saw the British as their salvation—an ally capable of restoring their homelands and, more urgently, of rescuing their people from looming starvation. Together with East Florida Seminoles, they gravitated to the British agent Captain George Woodbine and to Major Edward Nicolls, who disembarked on the Gulf Coast with a hundred Royal Marines in August 1814.

Unaware how thoroughly Old Hickory had thrashed the Red Sticks, the British also expected great things from their new allies. Admiral Cochrane even predicated his impending Gulf Coast campaign on a strong Red Stick and Seminole force to augment his British troops, which the credulous Captain Pigot, who had opened relations with the Indians in May, assured him he would have. "Thank you for the weapons!" Peter McQueen and Josiah Francis wrote to Pigot in June. "Land a few British troops, and we shall help them drive the Americans out of the Gulf region." Pigot forwarded their buoyant promise to Cochrane together with continually exaggerated reports of Indian strength. In return, the Red Sticks and Seminoles received a wondrous—and bogus—assurance, perhaps written by Pigot. "The British and other powers have conquered France, and seven powers are now united against America. A little before the white frost, you will hear of smoke all around the United States, in the seaports, and the burning of powder. The war is just beginning. There will be several armies landing in different places. His Majesty King George said the seven powers would be able and were determined to conquer America, and the British would be masters of it." The Red Sticks and Seminoles "need not be deceived; the British would fulfill their promises and never leave this land again." Perhaps the missive left Josiah Francis feeling inadequate; what prophet could have divined such a deliverance?[1]

Admiral Cochrane had cause for optimism beyond Pigot's glowing dispatches. He had what he considered troops enough to assume the strategic offensive against the Americans. A British counteroffensive from Canada nearly conquered upstate New York. In August, while Old Hickory browbeat the friendly Creek chiefs at Fort Jackson, Cochrane landed an expeditionary force near Washington, D.C., that burned the capital and dispersed the Madison administration before reembarking. Cochrane reserved his highest hopes, however, for the Gulf Coast. Confident he could rapidly arm and organize at least twenty-eight hundred Red Sticks and Seminole warriors, the admiral requested far fewer British troops for his planned attacks on Mobile and New Orleans than he otherwise would have. Cochrane even expected Lower Creek talwas that had remained neutral during the Creek War to flock to his colors.[2]

Captain Woodbine knew better. In a remote clearing called Prospect Bluff, fifteen miles up the languid Apalachicola River, he erected a fort and supply depot alongside the assorted buildings of the Forbes and Company trading concern. Woodbine's fort eventually became the rallying point for Indian and black (runaway slave) opponents of the United States. Even as Admiral Cochrane spoke so expectantly of formidable Indian allies, however, Woodbine counted only the filthy, famished followers of Josiah Francis, clad in rags and scratching out a meager existence in the surrounding swamps. From the destitute Red Sticks, Woodbine might muster nine hundred warriors, but he needed muskets to arm them and food to sustain them. Despairing of both, in late July he led the Red Sticks from his isolated post to Pensacola. There a British squadron transporting Major Nicolls and his Royal Marines met them in August. Abandoning any pretext of Spanish neutrality, Governor González Manrique permitted the British to convert Pensacola into a base of operations against Mobile, in part because Jackson's bellicose correspondence had convinced him that Old Hickory intended to attack the town.[3]

The thirty-five-year-old Nicolls, a fiery Irish abolitionist with a brilliant combat record who had earned a lieutenant's commission at age fifteen, made himself de facto governor of Pensacola. He treated the Spaniards with disdain and liberated their slaves for British military service. Together Nicolls and Woodbine lifted flagging Red Stick morale and also recruited a fair number of Lower Creek warriors angered by the Fort Jackson Treaty. Rations became regular. Woodbine paid miccos and war leaders $2 and warriors $1 a day. Nicolls distributed three hundred British uniforms to fortunate warriors who, an informant told Andrew Jackson, proudly "paraded the streets" of Pensacola in their fine scarlet jackets.

From Mobile, Jackson fired off his most menacing missive to Governor González Manrique to date. "Information having been received by me that the refuge banditti from the Creek nation are now drawing rations from your government and under the drill of a British officer in Pensacola with your knowledge (if not approbation) for resuming their acts of barbarity against the citizens of our frontier, I have directed my patrols to reconnoiter the country north of the Spanish line and treat all those renegades who are caught above the line as enemies until you explicitly avow them to be under your jurisdiction and hold yourself accountable for their conduct," thundered Old Hickory. If they killed or depredated, Jackson would retaliate not "on the heads of helpless women and children . . . but on the head which countenanced and excited the barbarity"—that is to say, the governor himself. "An eye for an eye, tooth for tooth, and scalp for scalp."[4]

Finding himself figuratively under Old Hickory's scalping knife, González Manrique was surely pleased to see the British initiate their plan to clear the Americans from the Gulf Coast. On September 15, a four-ship British squadron bearing Major Nicolls, his Royal Marines, and 180 Red Sticks under Josiah Francis and Peter McQueen attacked Fort Bowyer at the mouth of Mobile Bay. The British expected to reduce the redoubt handily. After landing the Royal Marines and Red Sticks on a spit of land six miles east of Fort Bowyer, the squadron sailed contemptuously close to the fortification. The British, however, underestimated Jackson, who had bolstered the fort's defenses. Its guns crippled the British flagship and sent the squadron packing. Nicolls, meanwhile, launched a frontal assault on Fort Bowyer with the Red Sticks and the Royal Marines that withered under American musketry, rekindling the Red Sticks' dread of Old Hickory. Rather than permit the disillusioned Red Sticks to sow doubts about British might among their comrades at Pensacola, the squadron bypassed the town and unloaded Josiah Francis, Peter McQueen, and their warriors at Apalachicola Bay.[5]

It was a pointless precaution. The Red Sticks in Pensacola soon learned for themselves not only the relative weakness of the British but also the long reach of Old Hickory. Not even the American president could stop him. Jackson ignored half-hearted admonitions from Madison to respect Spanish neutrality. Exercising what he termed "the broad principle of self-preservation," in early November Jackson invaded West Florida with four thousand troops and seven hundred Choctaw Indian allies. By rooting out the Red Sticks and their redcoat abettors from Pensacola, Jackson believed he would "put an end to the Indian war in the south, as it will cut off all foreign influence." His health continued precarious; he had just recovered from a severe and prolonged fever, during which the last and largest bone fragment had seeped from his shoulder.

The ease with which Jackson took Pensacola compensated for his pain. At daybreak on November 7, Old Hickory's army advanced in two columns. The two hundred Spanish defenders abandoned their fort and fled through the streets to the British squadron anchored in the harbor. Major Nicolls, who occupied Fort Barrancas in Pensacola Bay with his Royal Marines and Red Sticks, blew up the place and rowed for the safety of ships. Having no need to hold the town, with a fine rhetorical flourish Jackson returned Pensacola to González Manrique. The "enemy having disappeared and the hostile Creeks fled to the forest, I retire from your town and leave you again at liberty to occupy your fort." "May God preserve your life many years," replied the humbled governor.[6]

The Red Stick defenders of Fort Barrancas rode the tide of defeat to Apalachicola Bay and thence upriver to Prospect Bluff, the pine- and palm-shaded sanctuary where their brother warriors and their families, perhaps eighteen hundred in all, awaited them. Major Nicolls and

Captain Woodbine transformed the backwater Babylon, where Red Sticks, Seminoles, runaway slaves, civilian traders, and British redcoats mingled on easy terms, into a daunting bastion. There were so many armed blacks that Americans called the place the Negro Fort. Nicolls, the ardent abolitionist, had become as genuinely committed to the Red Sticks and Seminoles as he was to blacks. He encouraged small cross-border raids into Georgia while awaiting the appearance of Admiral Cochrane and the grand invasion force that would capture New Orleans and, Nicolls hoped, help the Red Sticks reclaim their homeland.[7]

Admiral Cochrane still espoused the Red Stick cause. He had less need of Indian allies, however, because His Majesty's government had given him eight thousand redcoats, far more troops than he had requested. Nevertheless, when he sailed into the Gulf of Mexico on December 5, 1814, Cochrane issued a proclamation addressed "To the Great and Illustrious Chiefs of the Creek and Other Indian Nations" soliciting their "active support and cooperation" in reducing New Orleans. Cochrane's prose was lofty, his promises sublime. "The same principle of justice which led our Father to wage war of twenty years in favor of the oppressed nations of Europe animates him now in support of his Indian children. And by the efforts of his warriors, he hopes to obtain for them the restoration of those lands of which the People of Bad Spirit have basely robbed them."

Few Indians answered the admiral's call. They had witnessed how handily Andrew Jackson and his "people of bad spirit" had bested Nicolls's Royal Marines and the British Father's warships at Fort Bowyer and Pensacola. Those who did respond left Cochrane's patronizing second-in-command, Vice Admiral Edward Codrington, more amused than impressed. Invited aboard Cochrane's flagship, Josiah Francis and a small retinue of chiefs and warriors ascended the gangplank to suppressed laughter and mild revulsion. "We had the honour of these Majestic Beasts dining with us two days, and we are disgusted with a similar honour here today," snuffled Codrington. The vice admiral stood aghast: the Indians had no notion of how to properly wear the uniforms the British bestowed upon them, tying trouser legs around their waists as if the fine pantaloons were savage breechcloths.

"Some of them appeared in their own picturesque dresses at first, with the skin of a handsome plumed bird on the head and arms; the bird's beak pointing down the forehead, the wings over the ears, and the tail down the pole," Codrington wrote to his wife. "But they are now all in hats (some cork, gold-laced ones), and in jackets such as are worn by sergeants in the Guards, and they have now the appearance of dressed-up apes."[8]

Codrington's snickering was short-lived. As guests of Admiral Cochrane, on January 8, 1815, Josiah Francis, Peter McQueen, and their scarlet-attired compatriots witnessed the ferocious inevitability of Old Hickory. In thirty minutes of brutal slaughter on a plain just southeast of New Orleans, Andrew Jackson's numerically inferior army inflicted more than two thousand casualties on attacking redcoats at a cost of just sixty-two men killed, wounded, or missing. Perhaps the horrified Red Sticks muttered words of consolation to their hosts, invoking Horseshoe Bend to express their empathy. Was the reed-thin Tennessean against whom they had fought so hard perhaps a reincarnated Hernando de Soto, and Horseshoe Bend and the Battle of New Orleans merely inescapable reprises of Mabila? It certainly must have seemed so to the Red Stick and Seminole onlookers.[9]

Admiral Cochrane, however, refused to abandon the struggle for the Gulf Coast, if for no other reasons than to keep Jackson immobilized and to distract American strategists from Canada. With his army battered, the admiral again turned to the Red Sticks and Seminoles. Remarkably, given what they had seen at New Orleans, Josiah Francis and Peter McQueen pledged to cooperate. Unquestionably, the pugnacious Major Nicolls played a large part in reinvigorating them. He had strengthened the defenses at Prospect Bluff, added to the stock of arms and ammunition, and claimed to have thirty-five hundred Creeks, Seminoles, and blacks eager to fight, the more so because Cochrane's plan called for strikes against the Georgia frontier—a prospect innately appealing to the Indians, except those who were spies for Benjamin Hawkins. When the old agent heard of Nicolls's scheme, he roused himself with an energy he had never displayed during the Creek War, assembling nine hundred Lower Creek warriors and fifty army dragoons in early February 1815 to square off against the Irish major and his confederates. A bitter battle appeared in the offing in the West Florida backcountry. Suddenly, however, both sides drew off, and the pine barrens and cypress swamps fell silent.[10]

· · ·

Nicolls and Hawkins had received the startling news simultaneously: the War of 1812 was over. After months of acrimonious negotiations, the United States and Great Britain had signed a peace treaty at Ghent, Belgium, on December 24, 1814. Nearly two months elapsed before news of the accord reached the combatants on the Gulf Coast. It was a document of great moment to the Red Sticks. With a few strokes of the white man's quill, Article IX of the Treaty of Ghent reversed the outcome of the Creek War—at least in terms of the lands the Creeks had lost. It obligated the warring nations to make peace with their indigenous foes and to restore to the Indians "all possessions, rights and privileges which they may have enjoyed, or been entitled to in 1811," effectively nullifying the Treaty of Fort Jackson. The Red Sticks, it would appear, could go home, and the friendly Creeks could reclaim the lands they had ceded to Sharp Knife, portions of which were already stained with white settlers. Perhaps Old Hickory could be broken after all.

The Madison administration begrudgingly acknowledged its obligations. "In pursuance of the stipulations of the Ninth Article of the Treaty of Ghent," the secretary of war informed Jackson in June 1815, "the President is confident that you will cooperate with all means in your power to conciliate the Indians, upon the principles of our agreement with Great Britain."

Jackson disobeyed. Conciliate the Creeks? Return their land? Not a chance. The Treaty of Fort Jackson was his treaty. It would stand, both the Madison administration and His Majesty's government be damned. As for the Red Sticks, Old Hickory argued disingenuously that because they were "residents" of Spanish West Florida, Article IX did not apply to them. Having signed the Treaty of Fort Jackson, the friendly Creeks had no recourse to Article IX either. Well aware that Jackson spoke not only for himself but also for powerful western interests that increasingly dominated the Democratic-Republican Party, neither the secretary of war nor President Madison dared overrule him. And so Jackson continued to remove friendly Creeks from the ceded country unimpeded. The chiefs protested to Benjamin Hawkins but feared to challenge the savage victor of the Battles of Horseshoe Bend and New Orleans, now freed from further conflict with the British.[11]

The Red Sticks, on the other hand, were not without hope. Before quitting the Gulf of Mexico in March 1815, Admiral Cochrane left behind Edward Nicolls (recently promoted to colonel), his Royal Marines, several pieces of artillery, a large stock of arms and ammunition, and three warships to protect the Indians at Prospect Bluff "until such time as they are restored to their possessions in terms of the treaty of peace." When it became clear that the Americans intended to renege on their obligations under Article IX, Colonel Nicolls made a compact with the Indians that, if His Majesty's government ratified it, would extend formal British recognition to the Creeks in exile, effectively creating both a military alliance and a British enclave on the Gulf Coast. The Red Sticks agreed to keep the peace until London ruled on Nicolls's proposed treaty. They selected Josiah Francis, whose dismal performance as a prophet had converted him to a rational pragmatist, to represent their interests.

On June 16, 1815, two days before the Battle of Waterloo sealed Napoleon's fate forever, the three British warships then in Apalachicola Bay lifted anchor with Colonel Nicolls, the Royal Marines, Francis, his adolescent son, and three Red Stick attendants aboard and sailed for the distant land of the Great English Father. On the waves with the mixed assemblage rode the Red Sticks' last best hope.[12]

The British ship bearing Josiah Francis dropped anchor in the Thames on August 14. The courteous, English-speaking Francis strode the streets of London bedecked as he thought proper to pay due homage to his benefactors. He wore the scarlet coat of a British general, a scarlet cap, long scarlet stockings, and a pair of gentleman's black shoes and carried a long-stem pipe to smoke during his idle moments, which proved plentiful. His garish dress likely astonished some Londoners, the more so because his métis roots (his father was English) endowed him with a complexion closer to that of an Englishman than an Indian. None, however, were more astonished by Francis's presence than the British government, which had no advance notice either of Nicolls and Francis's voyage or of the presumptuous Irish colonel's treaty. The two men, in fact, might have reached London before the document.

Francis had counted on meeting the prince regent on arrival. Instead, months dragged emptily by. No one from Whitehall or the royal family cared to see the former prophet. Nicolls maintained Francis, his son, and the three other Red Sticks at his own expense. He gave them food, lodging, winter clothes, and the sundry items needed to endure a long stay in cold and damp London. How Nicolls's twenty-three-year-old wife, Eleanor, and their three young children responded to their exotic guests is not known.

Untutored in Creek-U.S. relations, the secretary of war and colonies Earl Bathurst investigated the matter extensively. He communicated with Admiral Cochrane and other knowledgeable officials to understand the context and ramifications of Nicolls's agreement. A year passed before the British government received Francis, and then it was to deliver a shattering message. Denied the long-promised audience with the prince regent, Francis, dressed for the occasion "in a most splendid suit of red and gold," heard instead from Earl Bathurst that His Majesty must repudiate Nicolls's treaty. Good relations with the United States were paramount for a war-weary Great Britain; a compact with the expatriate Red Sticks would only jeopardize the peace. Bathurst could merely suggest that the Red Sticks try to coexist with the Americans. To salve their conscience, the British lavished gifts and money on Francis in the prince regent's name and gave him a ceremonial commission as a brigadier general.

To avoid antagonizing the United States, Bathurst tried to keep the visit a secret; he assumed the best way to prevent word of it from leaking was to detain Francis as long as possible. Not until December 1816 did His Majesty's government grant Francis passage on a British vessel. Word of Francis's presence leaked nonetheless. American newspapers mocked the pomp and circumstance that greeted the "savage" when he attended a birthday ball in honor of the emperor Nicholas aboard a visiting Russian warship. "The double sound of the trumpet announced the arrival of the patriot Francis, who fought so gloriously in our cause in America," read a passage reprinted from a London daily. "He was dressed in a most splendid suit of red and gold and by his side he wore a tomahawk, mounted in gold, presented to him by the prince regent. He appeared much delighted with the appearance of the frigate."

Before departing for home—wherever home might be after his two-year hiatus from the turbulent Southeast—Francis entrusted his son to Colonel Nicolls. He wanted the boy to have the benefit of a good English education.[13]

.   .   .

In June 1817, Josiah Francis stepped ashore on the sandy, salt-grass-laced Spanish and Seminole soil of Apalachee Bay into the welcoming arms of his fellow Red Sticks. Francis, however, would rather have sailed on to Bermuda and forgotten the horrors of war. Perhaps to reassert whatever authority he might have lost during his absence, Francis lied robustly about his visit to the British Father. Announcing that he bore a "talk" that he had had with the prince regent "in person," Francis called for an immediate council of the Red Stick miccos and war leaders near present-day Tallahassee. The local agent of John Forbes and Company thought the return of the "notorious" Francis portended trouble and might even prove "the ruin of those scoundrels."

By "those scoundrels," the trader meant the fugitive Red Sticks, the Seminoles, and the runaway slaves congregated between the Apalachicola and the Suwannee Rivers in the panhandle portion of Spanish East Florida. Few if any Red Sticks or blacks resided west of the Apalachicola any longer; Andrew Jackson, who now enjoyed the lofty title of commander in chief of the Southern Division of the U.S. Army, had destroyed the Negro Fort the year before, killing most of the male runaway slaves.

Francis found his tribesmen well on the road toward amalgamation with the Seminoles. Peter McQueen had established a village of his Tallassee followers near the Suwannee River. Other Red Stick bands likewise resided alongside Seminole towns. Before attending the council that he had called, Francis took care to place his métis wife and two daughters temporarily at the old Spanish settlement of St. Marks, seven miles north of which he would construct his own village on the bank of the clean and clear Wakulla River, his nearest neighbors the languid manatees that paddled curiously past.

Within six months of his return, Francis had attracted a following of thirty-five hundred Seminoles and displaced Red Sticks. Realizing that he had stuck his hand into a tinderbox, in which the slightest spark might set off a conflagration potentially fatal to the remaining Red Sticks, Francis trod gently. While proclaiming that the prince regent had promised him powder and ball to defend the Red Sticks' new home, he cautioned against provoking the United States. Also, speaking more like the late Tecumseh than a Red Stick agitator, Francis urged Indian unity against the common American enemy. Most of the expatriate Red Sticks agreed with him; the resident Seminoles, having seen their borders violated, were less inclined to forbear the encroaching Americans.[14]

So long as Sharp Knife Jackson cast a menacing shadow across the Gulf Coast, the chances for peace were slim. President James Monroe, the successor to James Madison, also coveted Spanish Florida but was reluctant to provoke a conflict. Whether Monroe could legitimately send a force into Spanish East Florida to avenge Seminole attacks on American troops, including the slaughter of a thirty-four-man detachment traveling to Fort Scott, a new stockade just north of the international border on land the Seminoles long claimed as their own, was a matter of debate. Nevertheless, on December 26, 1817, Secretary of War John C. Calhoun ordered Old Hickory across the international boundary, vesting him "with full power to conduct the war as he may think best," in consequence of "the increasing display of hostile intentions by the Seminole Indians." Calhoun made no mention of the Red Sticks, but Jackson knew that no one in the Monroe administration would object if he exterminated them.[15]

From his Nashville headquarters, Andrew Jackson marshaled the military resources of the Department of the South, activating a thousand Tennessee militiamen to supplement his five hundred Regulars. The Lower Creek chief William McIntosh gathered eighteen hundred Creek warriors to help Old Hickory stamp out the Red Sticks and punish the Seminoles. Jackson and McIntosh reached Fort Scott on March 9, 1818, the soldiers having marched 450 hard wilderness miles in forty-six days to "chastise a savage foe who combined with a lawless band of Negro brigands, have for some time past been carrying on a cruel and unprovoked war against the citizens of the United States," declared Jackson.[16]

Old Hickory had lost none of his ruthless efficiency. Within two months he had razed every Red Stick, Seminole, and black settlement in the East Florida panhandle and sent the stunned and starving survivors reeling deep into the interior of the province, from whence they would renew their struggle against the Americans seventeen years later. William McIntosh, whom Jackson referred to as "general," inflicted the heaviest single blow of the First Seminole War on April 12, when his Creeks and a detachment of American dragoons slew thirty-six of Peter McQueen's Tallassee warriors and captured ninety-seven women and children. To forestall Spanish interference, Jackson also briefly took St. Marks and Pensacola, acts of dubious legality that caused the Monroe administration no end of diplomatic headaches.

The campaign cost the soldiers and their Creek allies little beyond broken-down horses, disintegrating shoes, and shredded uniforms. Old Hickory, on the other hand, was utterly spent. He would have liked to press on, seize St. Augustine, and then sail to Cuba to "ensure the security of our Southern frontier," but lacked the wherewithal to pursue his quixotic fancy. In declaring the First Seminole War over, Jackson also wrote to President Monroe on June 2, 1818, of his own woes. "I am at present worn down with fatigue and by a bad cough with a pain in my left side which produced a spitting of blood, has reduced me to a skeleton," he scribbled fitfully. "I must have rest."[17]

Josiah Francis would enjoy eternal rest. He had paid the ultimate price of Old Hickory's fatiguing fury. Francis had tried to escape the impending conflict. Before Jackson's army descended on St. Marks, he and a Red Stick leader named Himollemico had asked the British Indian agent whether any vessels capable of carrying off their families, followers, possessions, and cattle might soon put into the bay. The agent said that a schooner was expected presently. No sooner had they spoken with the agent than word of approaching Americans reached them. Francis and his followers decamped into the tangled and marshy woods that fringed the coast and awaited succor. One morning they descried a ship plying the waters toward St. Marks, the Union Jack waving welcomely from a topmast. Emerging from the brush, Francis and Himollemico pushed off for the ship in a canoe. As an expression of his fealty to the Crown, Francis wore his scarlet British general's uniform with a brace of pistols buckled around his waist and the gold-mounted tomahawk presented to him in London tucked into his belt. The Indians boarded the gangplank cheerfully and stepped at once into captivity; the vessel was an American warship flying the British flag to disguise its bellicose purpose from the Spanish garrison at St. Marks.

When told of their capture, Jackson ordained that Josiah Francis and his companion be taken ashore and hanged. As the noose was fitted about his neck, a scalping knife allegedly slipped from Francis's sleeve. According to the probably apocryphal account, he had hoped to slit Jackson's throat before his own execution. The American press took great pleasure in Josiah Francis's demise. He had been "outlawed by his countrymen for his perfectly savage propensities, was a murderer by trade, a favorite at court, and the ally of England," croaked a Baltimore editor.[18]

There would be no opportunity for newspapers to celebrate a similar end to Peter McQueen. After the First Seminole War, he and his surviving Tallassee adherents fled deep into Florida, where they blended with the Seminoles until the two peoples became indistinguishable. McQueen's later movements are obscure. He apparently settled for a time along the alligator-infested Peace River deep in modern Florida. Leaving behind a grandson who would obtain fame as the great Seminole chief Osceola, McQueen and his wife eventually plunged into the Everglades. They came to rest on a barren, sunbaked island on the Atlantic coast off Cape Florida near the tip of the future state. There McQueen died in 1820 or 1821. His widow returned to the Creek country to begin a new life. Of her late husband, it could at least be said that he had died far from the reach of grasping Americans.[19]

CHAPTER TWENTY

Shades of Genocide

P ETER MCQUEEN'S WIDOW became engulfed in a titanic migration that seemed destined to swallow what remained of her country. The end of the War of 1812 and Spain's cession of Florida to the United States in 1821 released an expansionist swagger and chest-pounding American nationalism contemptuous of any Indians who dared to impede the growth of the Republic. In 1817, Mississippi became a state with a population of seventy-five thousand. Nearly thirty thousand Americans, assimilated métis, and their human chattel were comfortably settled along the Tombigbee River or in the Tensaw District. Congress created the Alabama Territory from the ceded lands lying east of Mississippi. In 1818, Sam Dale led an expedition to root out or kill a band of Red Sticks who not only refused to relinquish the region but also occasionally murdered white pioneers. Subsequent sweeps by the territorial militia eliminated the few holdouts.

Settlers and speculators from Virginia, the Carolinas, Tennessee, and Georgia swept over the land Old Hickory had wrested from the Creeks at Fort Jackson. "The axes resounded from side to side, and from corner to corner," recalled an early chronicler of Alabama. "The stately and magnificent forests fell. Log cabins sprang, as if by magic, into sight. Never before or since has a country been so rapidly peopled." In December 1819, Alabama achieved statehood. Its eastern boundary rested along the Coosa River opposite the compressed Creek country.[1]

Few took greater pleasure from the swelling white and slave population of the Deep South than did Major General Andrew Jackson. National security demanded the "permanent settlement of all the lands acquired from the Creek Indians," Old Hickory advised the incoming president, James Monroe, on Inauguration Day 1817. The more land that could be wrested from the Creeks, the better. Jackson begged Monroe to dispense with negotiations. "I have long viewed treaties with the Indians as an absurdity not to be reconciled to the principles of our government," counseled the commander of the Department of the South. They might have been necessary when the nation was weak, but no longer. Jackson regarded all Indians within the territorial limits of the United States as "subject to its sovereignty," with only a "possessory right to the soil for the purpose of hunting and not the right of domain." Make small farmers of them, protect them in their rights so long as they behave, but by no means treat with them as if they enjoyed even a semblance of independence. Such was Jackson's guiding philosophy.[2]

President Monroe rejected Jackson's call to abrogate the treaty system, but both he and his secretary of war, John C. Calhoun, recognized as clearly as did Jackson that the United States no longer need fear or appease the southeastern tribes. They "are becoming daily less warlike, and more helpless and dependent on us," wrote Calhoun. "They have, in a great measure, ceased to be an object of terror and have become that of commiseration. The time seems to have arrived when our policy towards them should undergo an important change.... Our views of their interest, and not their own, ought to govern them."

Such a paternalistic policy would have been inconceivable before the Creek War.[3]

President Monroe made no secret that he intended to seize as much remaining Creek land—and that of the other southeastern tribes—as possible. It was, he told Congress in his first annual address, part of the natural order of things for the Indians to evolve or give way. "The hunter state can exist only in the vast uncultivated desert," pontificated Monroe. "It yields to the more dense and compact form and greater force of civilized population, and of right it ought to yield, for the earth was given to mankind to support the greatest number of which it is capable, and no tribe or people have a right to withhold from the wants of others more than is necessary for their own support and comfort." Those "others" were white planters and their slaves. The Monroe administration encouraged not only the Creeks but also all southeastern tribes that might object to the emigrant tide to quit their compressed homelands and remove themselves west of the Mississippi River.[4]

A broken and dispirited people, the Creeks were hard pressed to defend their interests. Red Stick refugees who had lingered on the periphery of the Creek country rather than cast their lot with the Seminoles gradually stole back to their ruined talwas, but the communities they and other Upper Creeks rebuilt never attained their former influence. Lower Creek talwas, by contrast, began to shed residents unable to survive on the game-depleted land left to them. The métis generally fared better. Most became farmers in the white man's fashion. Some of the miccos partnered with Georgia whites to erect inns and stores along the Federal Road, frequently selling goods at exorbitant prices to their own people. As the 1820s opened, most Creeks sank into poverty. A general apathy settled over the land, and Creeks increasingly turned to liquor to escape the drudgery of existence.[5]

Creek leaders offered scant remedy. Self-interested, superannuated miccos dominated the National Council. Corpulent and cautious, the aging Big Warrior continued to control the Upper Creeks who had resisted the Red Sticks. His principal counselor was Opothle Yoholo, an eloquent spokesman and genuine defender of Creek interests. Reaching beyond their island in the encroaching sea of whites, Opothle Yoholo and other aspirants to leadership made common cause with literate, sophisticated Cherokee chiefs who seemed better able than the Creeks to hold the avaricious Americans at bay. The largely ineffectual, perhaps senile Lower Creek micco Little Prince was speaker of the nation. After spending a year as Andrew Jackson's guest at the Hermitage, William Weatherford retired from Creek politics and worked to mend his relations with the whites and métis of the Tensaw. So far as neighboring Georgians were concerned, the real power among the Creeks rested with William McIntosh, who well understood that Georgians wanted to expel the Creeks from the state.

The governor, after all, had run on a platform of replacing "all the red for a white population."[6]

McIntosh's prominence in Coweta made him speaker of the Lower Creek talwas. The National Council found the suave métis useful because he could navigate both Creek and American societies. Georgians, for their part, regarded him as a reliable hero of the Creek and First Seminole Wars. At a banquet held in his honor at Augusta in late 1818, the citizenry applauded the "prepossessing and dignified" McIntosh. "His features are strongly marked, entirely devoid of the wild, vacant, unmeaning stare of the savage," wrote a newspaperman. "We have seen him in the bosom of the forest, surrounded by a band of wild and ungovernable savages. We have seen him too, in the drawing room in the civilized walks of life, receiving the mead of approbation which his services so justly merit. In each situation we found him the same, easy and unconstrained in his address and uniform in his conduct."[7]

Cupidity got the better of McIntosh, and he conspired with two particularly loathsome Georgians to add to his considerable wealth at the expense of his mother's people. The first reprobate was the former governor David Mitchell, named Indian agent when Benjamin Hawkins, broken in body and spirit, died in June 1816. A military surgeon on duty in Georgia found Mitchell's appointment abhorrent; he likened it to letting the fox into the proverbial henhouse. "The most important duty of the agent is to see that justice is done between the Indians and the government and citizens of Georgia," the doctor ventured. "But I know [Mitchell] well and cannot entertain a doubt but that in all his decisions he will lean to the side of Georgia—the state in which he is popular, and where the popular cry is exterminate the savages!" Or at least deprive them of their extensive holdings, which comprised one-third of present-day Georgia.[8]

The other nefarious Georgian in the unfolding Creek tragedy was George Troup, elected governor in 1823. Determined to rid the state of Creeks, the wildly self-righteous Troup resorted to chicanery, bluster, and threats so extreme to achieve his ends that fellow Georgians dubbed him "the mad governor." He and McIntosh were cousins.[9]

McIntosh and Mitchell, whose children wed in August 1818, targeted Creek annuities, most of which they pocketed to satisfy Creek debts incurred at their monopolistic store. They also began to carve away Creek land in Georgia. In 1818, Mitchell obtained two tracts that

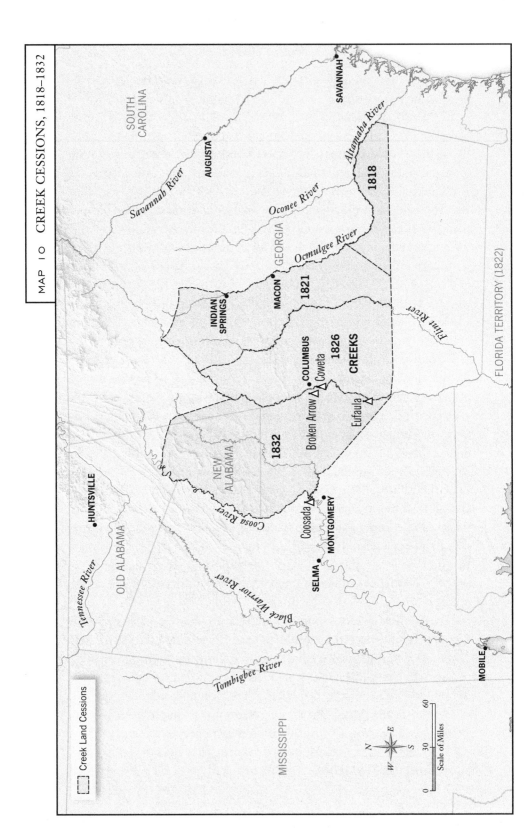

MAP 10 CREEK CESSIONS, 1818–1832

made up the northeastern extreme of the Creek country—one parcel between the Apalachee and the Chattahoochee Rivers, the other south of the Ocmulgee and the Altamaha—for which the Creeks were to receive $120,000 over a ten-year period. In December 1820, McIntosh hosted talks at his tavern located on the west bank of the Ocmulgee at Indian Springs, the mineral waters of which the Creeks held to have great curative powers. The Upper Creeks boycotted the negotiations, but McIntosh manipulated the doddering Little Prince into ceding a five-million-acre swath between the Ocmulgee and the Flint Rivers for $450,000 ($11 million in 2022 dollars), of which $250,000 would be reserved to reimburse the exaggerated depredation claims of frontier Georgians. Much of the rest would line McIntosh's pockets. Grateful commissioners rewarded McIntosh with a thousand-acre reserve surrounding his Indian Springs property and an adjacent tract encompassing his plantation, both on the west bank of the Ocmulgee. Lower Creek treaty signatories and other prominent McIntosh allies also were compensated.[10]

Outraged Upper Creeks cautioned McIntosh that he strode a fine line between wealth and death. Even the heretofore malleable Little Prince deserted him. In May 1824, Big Warrior, Little Prince, and Opothle Yoholo called a council at Tuckabatchee to draw up an unambiguous declaration of future policy. Two educated young Cherokees attended to record the proceedings (the Cherokee nation also bristled at Governor Troup's bullying). What emerged from the council was a plaintive mix of lamentation and edict. "In times of our forefathers we had a large bound of country and went through the woods after the game as if there never was to be an end to that mode of life," the attendees reflected. "Our nation was strong and never met a nation that was equal to us in warfare." That is, until the Creeks met Old Hickory. "Our crazy young men made a war with the white people and General Jackson was compelled to raise an army and come in and break them down." Now their lands were much reduced. "We have only a sufficiency to support ourselves upon, should we even resort to the greatest economy." Consequently, no Creek must speak of parting with even a single acre. Concluding with a thinly veiled threat to McIntosh, the council declared, "We are Creeks. We have a great many chiefs and headmen but, be they ever so great, they must all abide by the laws. We have guns and ropes, and if any of our people should break these laws, those guns and ropes are to be their end."

The council reconvened in October 1824 in response to a Monroe administration summons to discuss new land cessions with two federal commissioners at year's end. The chiefs reenacted the law against unauthorized land sales and appealed to the conscience of "our Christian brothers, the white people," to reject attempts to dispossess them. The council again put McIntosh and his clique on notice, declaring, "We deem it impolitic and contrary to the true interest of this nation to dispose of any more of our country. Any authority heretofore given to any individual, either written or verbal, has long since been revoked and done away with. Therefore, it is resolved by the chiefs in council that a copy of this be transmitted to some editor of a public newspaper for publication."[11]

Their words fell on deaf ears. On February 12, 1825, at his Indian Springs tavern, McIntosh, thirteen lesser chiefs, and fifty Creek men of no rank accepted a treaty that ceded to the United States all remaining Creek land in Georgia as well as the northern two-thirds of their Alabama realm. In exchange, the government granted the Creeks an equal number of acres on the distant Arkansas River, which neither McIntosh nor the other signatories had ever seen, and "$400,000 to the nation migrating," although only McIntosh and his followers intended to move. McIntosh would also receive $25,000 for his Indian Springs property and other holdings.

Few signatories had even a remote idea to what they affixed their marks, and some of the names were forged. The treaty commissioners had made liberal use of bribes, deceit, and chicanery, but McIntosh agreed to the cession only after they promised him American protection and payment to him of the first $200,000 in funds for Creek migration. As the métis prepared to sign the document, which had been written in secret and divulged to Creek delegates only moments earlier, Opothle Yoholo, who attended the gathering on behalf of an ill Big Warrior, cautioned McIntosh, "My friend, you are about to sell our country; I now warn you of your danger!"[12]

McIntosh knew the risk he ran. He hoped, however, to take his questionably obtained gains and resettle on the distant Arkansas River before his opponents on the National Council responded. Already, incensed Upper Creeks had threatened to cut the throats of McIntosh and his confederates and hang their heads "by the road for a show." To forestall grisly retribution, McIntosh appealed to Governor

Troup, who pledged to employ Georgia militia against any Creeks who harmed him or interfered with Troup's dream of an Indian-free Georgia.[13]

In late March, an acutely lucid Little Prince summoned McIntosh to appear before the National Council to answer charges. Feigning illness, McIntosh declined. Council members had no patience for McIntosh's stalling tactics. Big Warrior was dead, and the Upper Creeks dour. The council tried McIntosh for treason in absentia and sentenced him to death. It remained only for the law menders to carry out the sentence.

Having led the law menders against Creek fugitives from National Council justice prior to the Creek War, McIntosh understood both their reach and their wrath when aggressively commanded. On this occasion, the council chose well. They bestowed leadership on the battle-scarred Menawa, who despised McIntosh. To his credit, he initially declined to lead the law menders because tradition called for an impartial hand to carry out a death sentence, but the council insisted.

Accompanied by at least one hundred warriors—some witnesses to what transpired placed the number as high as four hundred—Menawa rode to McIntosh's property on the afternoon of April 29. The executioners hid themselves in the forest surrounding the tavern because Creek law called for the death sentence to be carried out at daybreak. Unknown to them, McIntosh intended to leave for an inspection of the Arkansas River tract that morning. The law menders acted first, however. Arising before dawn, they set fire to a shed beside the tavern to illuminate the grim proceedings. As the white guests and female occupants of the tavern bestirred themselves, Menawa yelled for them to come out. No harm would befall them; he intended to kill only McIntosh and any others complicit in the Indian Springs travesty who chanced to be present. McIntosh's Cherokee wife, daughter, and their white guests stumbled out. Then the warriors tossed firebrands at the place. McIntosh's son Chilly escaped through a back window, plunged into the Ocmulgee River, and swam to safety. Not so his father. The flames briefly silhouetted McIntosh and an aged Coweta micco before the open front door, and a musket volley wounded the métis and killed his accomplice. Bleeding badly, McIntosh stumbled upstairs. From a second-floor window he returned his assailants' fire until the flames drove him back downstairs. Shot several times as he staggered outside,

McIntosh fell. The law menders dragged him a short distance by his feet. McIntosh raised himself on an elbow, glared defiantly, and then died with a knife plunged into his chest. Menawa's executioners fired at least fifty bullets more into McIntosh's corpse. Justice had been served; the National Council had reasserted itself as a power with which to be reckoned.[14]

William Weatherford enjoyed a far more tranquil later life than had the conniving McIntosh. After the Creek War he farmed on the east bank of the Alabama River, a mere thirteen miles northeast of the site of Fort Mims. He and Sam Dale became close friends. To Dale, Weatherford explained why he chose to settle so close to the scene of past horrors. "He said that his old comrades, the hostiles, ate his cattle from starvation; the peace party ate them from revenge; and the squatters because he was a damned Redskin," recalled Dale. " 'So,' said he, 'I have come to live among gentlemen.' "

Weatherford grew wealthy. He accumulated at least three hundred slaves and a stable of fine horses. Realizing he had tried to prevent the massacre of noncombatants, local whites and métis not only forgave Weatherford for Fort Mims but also came to respect his "bravery, honor, and strong native sense."

Weatherford demonstrated his finer traits during a murderous fracas in 1820. A crowd had gathered for an estate sale. For reasons not recorded, two ruffians assaulted an old man named Bradberry. One smashed a pitcher over Bradberry's head; the other plunged a knife into the back of his neck. As he lay bleeding in the dirt, the two killers threatened to slay anyone who intervened. Everyone froze except the fifty-four-year-old Weatherford. "These, I suppose, are white men's laws," he bellowed. "You stand aside and see a man, an old man, killed, and not one of you will avenge his blood. If he had one drop of Indian blood mixed with that which runs upon the ground there, I would instantly kill his murderers, at the risk of my life." Bystanders begged him to act. They assured Weatherford that the white man's law would protect him. Weatherford drew a long silver-handled dirk and then stomped toward the murderers. Seizing the nearest by the throat, he held him while others tied him up. The thug's knife-wielding accomplice surrendered without a struggle. "Billy Weatherford," he said, "I am not man enough for you."

William Weatherford remained a Creek at heart, intimately in tune with nature and moved by its augurs. On February 24, 1824, while hunting with friends, he made a disturbing prophecy after a companion killed an albino deer. Profoundly distressed, Weatherford said that one of them would soon perish; the white stag was a "token" of impending death. The next day, Weatherford fell seriously ill. In his delirium he saw his deceased second wife, reputed to have been the most beautiful woman of the Alabamas, standing beside his bed, waiting to lead him to the spirit world. Weatherford died on March 24. Repairing to a remote grove of bushy oak and saplings, friends buried him beside his mother beneath a small cairn.[15]

Reasonable white men recognized that the killing of William McIntosh represented a "public execution by the laws of the nation"—a just, if harsh, punishment for illegally selling Creek land. Reasonable men, however, were at a premium in Georgia. Governor Troup called for a survey of the Indian Springs treaty lands, activated the militia to discourage disgruntled Upper Creeks from interfering further, and announced that Georgians would greet any federal attempt to abrogate the deal as grounds for secession or civil war.

The fellow Democratic-Republican James Monroe would likely have capitulated to Troup's saber rattling, but he was no longer president. The newly inaugurated president, John Quincy Adams, accorded a full and fair hearing to the competing Creek missions that descended on the capital in the autumn of 1826: a "tribal" delegation under Opothle Yoholo dispatched by the National Council to urge the Great Father to rescind the Treaty of Indian Springs, and a delegation of pro-McIntosh Lower Creeks led by Chilly McIntosh, which demanded blood revenge for his father's "murder" and immediate recognition of the accord so that they might collect the money due them and begin their move west.

Before leaving for Washington, Opothle Yoholo met with the federal army commander in Georgia, the fair-minded brigadier general Edmund Gaines. With Little Prince's mental faculties declining rapidly and Big Warrior's son of marginal ability, Opothle Yoholo had become the de facto head of the Creek nation, less the McIntosh faction. The superintendent of Indian affairs considered him a "cool, cautious, and sagacious" interlocutor, with "a tact which would have done credit to a more refined diplomatist." Opothle Yoholo also impressed Gaines. He advised Secretary of War James Barbour that the Creek speaker and his party would "readily lay down their lives upon the land in which the bones of their ancestors are deposited and die without resistance, that the world shall know that the Muscogee Nation so loved their country [that] they were willing to die rather than sell or leave it. They appeal thus to our magnanimity, and I cannot but say, I trust and hope that their appeal will not be unavailing."[16]

President Adams and Secretary Barbour heeded Gaines's advice. They tried to satisfy both Opothle Yoholo and Chilly McIntosh as best as they were able, exercising enormous forbearance during nearly two months of intermittent negotiations with the visiting Creeks. At last, on January 17, 1826, Opothle Yoholo reluctantly agreed to cede all Creek territory in Georgia east of the Chattahoochee River (the Creeks subsequently ceded an overlooked remnant) in exchange for retention of their Alabama holdings, annual annuities, and an explicit annulment of the Indian Springs Treaty. The agreement was called the Treaty of Washington.

Although he contemplated suicide over the loss of the Georgia country, Opothle Yoholo nevertheless accomplished something no Indian leader had, and which no other ever would: he had persuaded the United States to abrogate a ratified treaty. Additionally, the Creeks won back their lands in Alabama, together with federal guarantees of protection against encroachment. Adams advised the Senate that the Treaty of Washington was the best deal he could strike; Opothle Yoholo made a similar report to the Creek National Council.[17]

While most of the Lower Creeks living east of the Chattahoochee sought refuge in the five-million-acre Alabama tract, the historic seat of the Upper Creeks, the McIntosh faction began their move beyond the Mississippi River. The rupture lacked the violence of the Creek Civil War, but the physical separation was equally profound. In May 1827, a federal agent guided Chilly McIntosh and four companions on an exploratory visit to their prospective home in what is today eastern Oklahoma. There they received a hearty welcome from the roving Osages, who claimed the region, and from Cherokee emigrants. Pleased at the prospect of allies against his tribe's sworn enemies the Pawnees, an Osage chief offered his daughters to Creek leaders in marriage. After nearly a year among the Osages, Chilly McIntosh returned to Alabama to mend ties with Little Prince and prepare his people for their journey. In council, he spoke enticingly of the "fertility of the soil, abundance of grass, and the salubrity of the climate." With his Osage friends, McIntosh had participated in his first buffalo hunt and was eager to return, either as micco or in a subordinate role, it mattered not to him.

In January 1828, Chilly McIntosh and 739 Lower Creeks and métis started up the Tennessee River by steamboat for Fort Gibson, the Indian agency in today's eastern Oklahoma with which they would be affiliated. By year's end, at least 1,400 members of McIntosh's faction had emigrated. In the succeeding five years, another 1,000 moved west from Alabama, until by the end of 1833 some 3,000 Lower Creeks had uprooted themselves, of whom 2,459 survived the rigors of travel and acclimation to their new homes. Many of the early emigrants were prosperous, slaveholding métis who laid out plantations along the rich river valleys, hoping to replicate the homes they had left behind.[18]

No president was truly a friend to the Indian, and James Monroe and John Quincy Adams both had advocated voluntary emigration of the southeastern tribes. Neither of them had pressured the tribes to move, however, and Adams had bristled at Governor Troup's interference in federal Indian policy. He also had opposed Alabama's attempt to exercise legal jurisdiction over Creeks living within state boundaries, recognizing in the scheme the seeds of forced dispossession.

The erudite and introspective northerner, however, lost the election of 1828 to Andrew Jackson. Fellow Southerners keen to expand the Cotton Kingdom to the exceptionally fertile plain that constituted the heart of the Creek country in Alabama expected Old Hickory to mandate Indian removal. With this expectation, 97 percent of eligible voters (landholding white men) in Georgia and Alabama cast their ballots for Jackson.[19]

Old Hickory did not disappoint. His only personal link to the Creeks had been his adopted son Lyncoya. Jackson had high hopes for him, even contemplating sending him to the U.S. Military Academy. Illness intervened, however. At age seventeen, Lyncoya died of tuberculosis. The Creeks now were merely an irritant to Old Hickory.

In his first annual address, Jackson denied the right of the Creeks to maintain a sovereign presence in Alabama and sustained the state's right to impose its laws on them. "I informed the Indians inhabiting parts of Georgia [Cherokees] and Alabama [Creeks] that their attempt to establish an independent government would not be countenanced by the Executive of the United States and advised them to emigrate beyond the Mississippi or submit to the laws of those states." Jackson added, disingenuously, that "this emigration should be voluntary, for it would be as cruel as unjust to compel the aborigines to abandon the graves of their fathers and seek a home in a distant land." He counted on a devious and crushing application of Alabama law on the Creeks to render their forcible removal unnecessary.[20]

In calling for the "voluntary" emigration of Native peoples to lands west of the Mississippi, Jackson had articulated the issue that would define his presidency. As his second-term vice president, Martin Van Buren, recalled, "There was no measure, in the whole course of his administration, of which he was more exclusively the author than this."[21]

Congress enacted the necessary legislation. The Indian Removal Act of 1830 provided "for an exchange of lands with the Indians residing in any of the states or territories, and for their removal west of the river Mississippi" to such land as the president deemed suitable. The Choctaws, Cherokees, Chickasaws, and friendly Creeks who had facilitated Jackson's victories in the Creek War were as clearly in the government's crosshairs as were former Red Sticks. Old Hickory could pull the trigger with a clear conscience. The Removal Act, he wrote to the Choctaw métis John Pitchlynn, "was a measure I had much at heart and sought to effect because I was satisfied that the Indians could not possibly live under the laws of the states. If now they shall refuse to accept the liberal terms offered, they only must be liable for whatever evils and difficulties may arise. I feel conscious of having done my duty to my red children, and if any failure of my good intention arises, it will be attributable to their want of duty to themselves, not to me."[22]

That the Indians might see their "duty to themselves" differently than did Jackson troubled him not. The "evils and difficulties" arose for them at once. No sooner had Jackson signaled that he would not protect the Creeks from Alabama than its courts began to harass them. No less a personage than Opothle Yoholo was hauled before the Montgomery County Circuit Court on bogus charges of "trespass with force and arms" and the destruction of property. A good lawyer got him off, but most Creeks had no notion of how to navigate the white man's legal system, particularly when it was manipulated against their interests.[23]

With the courts behind them, in 1831 white interlopers from across the South swarmed into the Creek country. Many were fugitives from justice, louts who peddled illicit liquor to the dispirited Creeks or robbed them of livestock and property. The better class of trespassers erected squatter's cabins and cleared Creek forests for farming. Meanwhile, starvation and smallpox stalked the rightful inhabitants of the land. The Creek Indian agent, an honest man who pitied his charges, bought what he could for them on credit, but the Jackson administration rebuffed his appeals for help. "Let a practice obtain for them," pontificated Secretary of War and Jackson sycophant John Eaton, "that whenever hungry the government will interpose, and then resting upon that expectation, they will make no exertions for their own relief." In other words, let them move west and "prosper" or stay where they were and chew tree bark.

When the Creek National Council challenged Eaton with reports by relocated kinsmen who said the western land was fit only for a graveyard, the secretary dismissed their concerns churlishly. "The country your nation possesses west of the Mississippi River you say is not healthy. This surely is not correct; all the accounts we have here are opposed to your statement. Many of your people, as you well know, speak highly" of the western tract, Eaton continued. "Join them and the rest of you will be happy also. But at the place you are, and under the government of the laws of Alabama, you cannot be so." Otherwise, Eaton insisted they suffer in silence any misfortunes that their obstinance might occasion.

Not all federal government officials exhibited Eaton's contempt for Indian lives. Between July and December, the post surgeon at Fort Mitchell vaccinated more than seven thousand Creeks against smallpox, but many others died.[24]

When Eaton's replacement, Lewis Cass, proved no more disposed to protect them than had his predecessor (Secretary Cass, like Eaton, spoke for Old Hickory), the Creek National Council made a final desperate play to save something of their people's homeland. Opothle Yoholo and his fellow council members well understood the grav-

ity of the times. The preceding autumn they had hired one William
Moor, apparently a reputable Alabamian, to investigate the extent of
white intrusion. After "a disagreeable tour of thirty days" through
the diminished Creek country, Moor counted 185 illicit homesteads.
Calculating each family at 8 persons, he estimated that 1,480 whites
had invaded Creek lands. That was not the worst of it. Many others
had merely blazed and cut their initials on trees to demarcate the
tracts they expected to occupy when the Creeks were forced west.
"If the present Congress or the general government does not interfere on your behalf," forewarned Moor, "your country will be entirely
overrun, and all the land fit for cultivation immediately occupied by
this class of invaders." Avaricious whites were the vultures; peaceable
Creeks and their country the carrion.[25]

The Creek National Council hoped to save their land and preserve something of their sovereignty by formally surrendering both.
On March 24, 1832, a delegation of Upper and Lower Creek headmen
signed what became known as the Treaty of Cusseta. Under its terms,
the Creeks ceded all of their lands in Alabama to the United States. In
exchange, the Jackson administration pledged to expel intruders, survey the 5,200,000-acre cession, and allot 2,187,000 acres to individual
Creek heads of household in severalty. The remaining acreage would
be open to white settlement. With the treaty, the Jackson administration ceased to recognize the Creeks living in Alabama as a legitimate
Indian nation. It closed the Creek Agency at Fort Mitchell and shifted
all formal relations to the Creeks living in the Indian Territory west
of the Mississippi.

From the National Council's perspective, the treaty appeared a
clever bargain. The council intended for their people to take their
individual land allotments in blocks clustered about their old talwas.
This would maintain some semblance of traditional life and National
Council authority in local matters.

The reality proved otherwise. White cotton planters eager to shift
the center of production from the tired soil of the southern coastal
states deeper inland saw the Treaty of Cusseta, which opened three
million acres to their slave-based economy, as an opportunity too
good to be missed. Speculators, planters, and poor whites looking
to better their hardscrabble lot not only swarmed into the ceded
land, which became known as New Alabama, but also aggressively
swindled unsophisticated Creeks out of their lawful allotments.

Whiskey peddlers and corrupt traders contributed to the shady proceedings. They sold their shoddy and vile products on credit after
inducing their Creek customers to sign mortgages on their property
as security.

There were plenty of Creeks to exploit, plunder, and cheat. In 1832,
the federal government took a census of the Alabama Creeks for the
purpose of issuing land patents. For the first time, the precise number
of Creeks residing in the Old South was ascertained: 14,142, including
445 black slaves, were enrolled in the Upper talwas, and 8,552, including 457 slaves, in the Lower talwas.[26]

Conditions in what remained of the Creek country worsened.
Mob resistance abetted by local courts frustrated federal attempts
to remove white intruders. White thugs drove Creeks from their
homes, burned their houses and crops, and stole their livestock. The
common Creek did not understand deeds, contracts, and other legal
papers, making them easy prey for swindlers who lubricated devious
transactions with whiskey, bribed impoverished Creeks into selling
the property of their neighbors, or simply forged instruments of sale.
The National Council was powerless against Alabama courts, which
invariably sided with whites. A visiting New Yorker who attended the
last Green Corn Ceremony (busk) held by the Creeks in their homeland in 1835 condemned the blatant fraud perpetrated on his Indian
hosts, writing home,

> What the diplomatists could not achieve was forthwith attempted
> by speculators;... and the Indian independence straightway
> began to disappear. Certain forms were required by government
> to give Americans a claim to these Creek lands. The purchaser
> was to bring the Indian before a government agent. In the agent's
> presence, the Indian was to declare what his possessions were
> and for how much he would sell them. The money was paid in
> presence of the agent, who gave a certificate, which ... authorized
> the purchaser to demand protection from the national arms, if
> molested. All this was well enough, but it was soon discovered
> that the speculators would hire miscreants and drunken Indians
> to personate the real possessors of lands, and having paid them
> the money, would take it back as soon as the purchase was com-
> pleted, give the Indian a jug of whiskey or a small bag of silver
> for the fraud, and so become lords of the soil.

The visiting New Yorker attempted to convey the danger that surrounded law-abiding Creeks, continuing,

> On one side, white rogues—border cutthroats—contending, through corrupted red men, for the possessions of those among them who, though honest, are unwary. On another side, the cheated Indian-robber of his brethren, wheedled by some fresh white cheat... Even the judges are accused of being, covertly, sometimes as bad as any of the rest....
>
> I beheld a fine, gentle, innocent-looking girl—a widow, I believe—come up to the [federal] investigator to assert that she had never sold her land. She had been counterfeited by some knave. The investigator's court was a low barroom. He saw me eyeing him, and someone told him I was travelling to take notes.... He seemed to shrink and postponed a decision.
>
> The ill-starred red people here are entirely at the mercy of interpreters, who, if not negro slaves of their own, are half-breeds—a worse set, generally, than the worst of either slaves or knaves.[27]

Vagrant Creeks roamed the country, hopeless and dejected. Starving and destitute though they were, they nonetheless refused to leave the neighborhood of their former homes. Decent Alabamians, army officers, and federal officials implored the Jackson administration to halt the land fraud, but Secretary of War Cass dismissed the matter as beyond the reach of federal authority. The deputy federal marshal and Canoe Fight veteran Jeremiah Austill did not. Determined to protect his former foes from the most blatant white outrages, he confronted a particularly notorious criminal, Hardeman Owens, whom Austill called "the most daring man I have ever met with, and one of the most dangerous." Recently appointed commissioner of roads and revenue in one of the counties the Alabama legislature had created in the Creek cession, Owens appropriated a prosperous Creek farm for himself. Not only did he drive the owner from his home, but he also "dispossessed... a young girl of another farm of 100 acres of valuable land and broke her arm for complaining," reported Austill, "and with others (among them a dentist), robbed the Indian graves—the dentist for the teeth, and Owens for the silver ornaments and beads, which are always buried with the Indian dead, and these he afterwards sold in his shop."

With troops from Fort Mitchell, Deputy Austill tried to evict Owens from the Creek cession. Playing the part of penitent, Owens beckoned Austill to enter his home. Creek complainants warned Austill that the house was mined. While the deputy stood in the yard contemplating his next move, Owens slipped outdoors. Suddenly the house exploded. The miscreant tried to shoot his way to safety, but an army private killed him. Owens's death caused angry squatters, concerned they might be next, to band together for mutual defense. The county court issued warrants for the arrest of Austill and the commanding officer of Fort Mitchell. Gradually the fury subsided, but incidents such as this compelled Secretary Cass reluctantly to call for an investigation into Creek-land fraud in late 1835.[28]

Happily for Cass, war intervened. White rogues eager to interrupt inquiries into their despicable dealings and hasten the recognition of their bogus land titles incited roving bands of victimized Lower Creeks to stage raids across the Chattahoochee River against those whom the Creeks thought responsible for their discomfiture. They concentrated on farms and plantations in the neighborhood of Columbus, Georgia, a town that harbored land swindlers and liquor peddlers. Fair-minded Alabamians saw the conflict for what it was—yet another vicious fraud perpetrated on the Creeks. "The war with the Creeks is all a humbug," opined *The Montgomery Advertiser*. "It is a base and diabolical scheme devised by interested men to keep an ignorant race of people from maintaining their just rights and to deprive them of [their] small remaining pittance.... We do trust that these blood suckers may be ferreted out and their shameful misrepresentations exposed." Seven hundred concerned Alabama citizens forwarded a memorial to the House of Representatives demanding that Congress investigate the "fraudulent contracts" that precipitated the violence. As the governor of Alabama explained, "The frauds and forgeries practiced upon the Indians to deprive them of their lands...and the vice and intemperance introduced upon them by a class of white men, and the destitute, almost starving condition to which they were reduced by [them]... excited the [Creeks] to hostilities."[29]

Culpability played no part in the calculations of the Jackson administration, however. Canceling his own fraud investigations, Secretary

Cass ordered out the army and militia to suppress the uprising, after which all Creeks were to be "collected and sent immediately to their country west of the Mississippi, by military force if necessary." The Choctaws had proceeded the Creeks westward; now, through no fault of their own, the Creeks were to face removal.

The so-called Second Creek War was a brief but bloody burlesque. Upper Creeks joined the army in suppressing the "hostiles." At least fifty of the so-called hostile Creek men, women, and children died in one clash alone. In an ironic twist, Jim Boy, formerly one of the principal Red Sticks, teamed up with Opothle Yoholo to command the nearly two thousand Upper Creek warriors who allied themselves with the army, an act that almost precipitated a second Creek civil war. Several hundred other Upper Creeks sought refuge among the Cherokees to escape removal, only to find themselves expelled with their Cherokee protectors two years later.

The prolonged and brutal reckoning between the Creeks and Andrew Jackson was about to end. What can rightly be labeled the Creek Trail of Tears began in July 1836 when government officials herded 2,498 Lower Creeks designated as hostile onto steamboats for the journey first to Montgomery and then overland seven hundred miles to Fort Gibson for resettlement with the McIntosh faction, which grudgingly accepted them into their community. The men boarded the boats bound in irons; wailing women and children embarked destitute and clad in rags, deprived even of cooking pots. At Montgomery, "the spectacle exhibited by them was truly melancholy," recorded a newspaperman. "To see the remnant of a once mighty people fettered and chained together forced to depart from the land of their fathers into a country unknown to them is of itself sufficient to move the stoutest heart."[30]

But not the hearts of Old Hickory, Lewis Cass, or the white scoundrels who fleeced and harassed the Creeks even as they departed. A total of 14,609 Creeks left Alabama during 1836 for the western Creek nation in five groups under army auspices. The following year the army transported 5,000 more. A few Creeks hid in Alabama swamps and canebrakes awhile longer; only a handful escaped deportation.

Similar agonies accompanied each exodus. While yet on Alabama soil, reported Lieutenant John Sprague, the army attendant of one Creek group, "a large number of white men prowled about, robbing them of their horses and cattle and carrying among them liquor which caused an alarming rate of intoxication. Men who had had claims upon these distressed beings now preyed upon them without mercy. Fraudulent demands were presented and unless some friend was near, they were robbed of even clothing." Other whites entertained themselves shooting Creek dogs while the animals swam the Coosa River; an Alabamian watched "many an Indian shed tears as his dog was killed." Aged and infirm Creeks climbed off wagons and sank down in the dirt to dream of the past and die lonely deaths. Sprague lacked the means to ease Creek agony. "Persistent appeals were made to me to clothe their nakedness and to protect their lacerated feet," said Sprague, who could offer nothing beyond what the crooked Alabama civilian contractors who conducted the removal claimed the government had paid them to feed and transport the Indians they despised. Had the Creeks "been permitted to retain the fair proceeds of their lands," lamented the lieutenant, "they would have had the means of procuring additional supplies for their comfort."[31]

The trail the evicted trod was easy to trace. Nearly a quarter century later, the German sportsman Frederick Gerstaecker chanced upon a stretch of the Creek path while hunting near the Ozark Mountains of Arkansas. Mute evidence of hardship and horrors lingered along the weed-strewn trail and in the dark forests. Returning home, Gerstaecker ruminated on what he had witnessed, imagining the scenes that had left such scars and decrying the policy that yielded such tragedy, writing,

> Numerous holes cut in the fallen trees showed where the squaws had pounded their maize to make bread. More melancholy traces were visible in the bones of human beings and animals which were strewed about. Many a warrior and squaw died on the road from exhaustion, and the maladies engendered by their treatment; and their relations could do nothing more for them than fold them in their blankets and cover them with boughs and bushes to keep off the vultures which followed their route by thousands and soared over their heads, for their drivers would not give them time to dig a grave and bury their dead. The wolves, which also followed at no great distance, soon tore away so frail a covering and scattered the bones in all directions.

This is a sad instance of the abominable haggling spirit so prevalent in America. The government, to avoid trouble, had contracted with individuals for a certain sum, which was quite sufficient to have conveyed the poor Indians comfortably, but they were obliged to part with all they had for bread, selling their rifles and tomahawks, horses going for two and three dollars; and, while they died of hunger and distress, the contractors made a fortune.[32]

Gerstaecker authentically evoked for his European readers the horrors of the long Creek Trail of Tears. Creeks who endured it recounted similar tales of their travails. "The command for a removal came unexpectedly upon most of us," a survivor later told her granddaughter Mary Hill. "Wagons stopped at our homes and the men in charge commanded us to gather what few belongings could be crowded into the wagons. We were taken to a crudely built stockade and joined others of our tribe. Even here, there was the awful silence that showed the heartaches and sorrow at being taken from the homes and even separation from loved ones."

Then the journey west began. Mary Hill's grandmother continued,

Many of us fell by the wayside, too faint with hunger or too weak to keep up with the rest.... A crude bed was quickly prepared for these sick and weary people. Only a bowl of water was left within reach; thus they were left to suffer and die alone.

The little children piteously cried day after day from weariness, hunger, and illness.... These were once happy children—left without father and mother—crying could not bring consolation to these children. The sick and the births required attention, yet there was no time and no one was prepared.

Death stalked at all hours, but there was no time for proper burying or ceremonies. My grandfather died on this trip. A hastily cut piece of cottonwood contained his body. The open ends were closed up, and this was placed along a creek.... Some of the dead were placed between two logs and quickly covered by shrubs, some were shoved under the thickets, and some were not even buried but left by the wayside.

It is no wonder, then, that Gerstaecker encountered so many scattered human bones on his outing in the shadows of the Ozarks.

No provision was made for natural obstacles encountered on the march. At one point on their trek a Creek contingent was compelled to wade for six days through an enormous swamp, struggling at night to find hillocks or other high ground on which to escape the spongy bottomlands and snatch a bit of sleep. Lamentations loud and long arose from the fetid country. Compulsively opening, inspecting, and retying her pitiful bundle of belongings, a Creek woman wailed, "I have no more land, I am driven away from home, driven up the red waters. Let us all go, let us all die together, and somewhere upon the banks we will be there."

"The Indian will vanish," Creek elders had prophesied when the first Americans came among them. That time had seemingly come. "Now," the Creeks repeated to one another on the trail, "the Indian is on the road to disappearance."[33]

The Creeks did not disappear. That thousands perished during the removal or soon after is apparent from census data. A population of 21,792 Creeks was enrolled under the Cusseta Treaty of 1832. Adding the McIntosh faction, which had already emigrated, brings the total number of Creeks to well over 23,000. Not until 1859 was a careful census again taken of the Creeks. The population was found to have dropped to 13,537. Clearly, little more than half of the Creeks uprooted from Alabama lived to rebuild their society—today's Muscogee (Creek) Nation of eastern Oklahoma—in the strange land into which they were cast.

From his seat in the House of Representatives in 1841, the former president John Quincy Adams reflected on the expulsion of the Indians from the Southeast. His colleagues had asked him to accept the chairmanship of the Committee on Indian Affairs. Adams, however, could not disguise his abhorrence of an Indian policy—propelled by his political opponent Andrew Jackson's "fraudulent treaties and brutal force"—that to him was beyond hope of reform. "It is among the heinous sins of this nation, for which I believe God will one day bring them to judgment—but at His own time and by His own means," predicted Adams, who wanted no part in the "profligate corruption." And so he turned his "eyes away from this sickening mass of putrefaction and asked to be excused from serving as chairman of the committee."

Adams also blamed the states of the Deep South for their "utter prostration of faith and justice" in driving the Indians from their dwellings, and he expected divine retribution to be visited on them as well. Alabamian and Georgian beneficiaries of Creek removal would have laughed scornfully at the New Englander's mawkish musings, had they known of them.

No sooner had the Creeks been expelled than slavery cast its baleful net over the rich soil that had run through the Creek heartland. The cotton economy boomed. Outside the Cotton Belt, in pine forests once the domain of the Lower Creeks, large herds of cattle and droves of hogs thrived. The prosperity that came at the expense of the dispossessed Creeks endured scarcely two decades, however, before Adams's avenging God wrought judgment on the usurpers in a great and terrible civil war, a cataclysm from which elderly Creek survivors of the horrors of 1813–1814 might have taken a mordant satisfaction.[34]

APPENDIX

Creek and Métis Personages

Dates of birth and death are given when they are known or can be conjectured with some degree of confidence. I hope this appendix will prove useful to readers in navigating the maze of Creek, Red Stick, and métis leaders.

ALEXANDER CORNELLS (OCHE HADJO): Upper Creek métis. Government interpreter, subagent to the Upper Creeks, and a close ally of the Indian superintendent Benjamin Hawkins.

ALEXANDER McGILLIVRAY (HOBOI-HILI MICCO) (1750–1793): Upper Creek métis. The most influential Creek leader in Muscogee history. The son of a Creek mother of the powerful Wind Clan and a Scottish trader father, he was not only literate but also well educated. McGillivray parlayed his family status, education, and knowledge of trade to become a fabulously wealthy planter and slave owner, as well as the primary intermediary between the Creek confederacy and the British, Americans, and Spanish in the 1780s and early 1790s, often working to play the foreign powers off one another to his own and to the Creeks' advantage.

BIG WARRIOR (TUSTUNNUGEE THLUCCO) (CA. 1760–1825): Upper Creek. A man of imposing stature, the opportunistic and wealthy principal chief of the Upper Creeks did not like Americans, but he believed it was in both his own and his people's best interests to ally themselves with them. The Red Sticks detested him.

CAPTAIN SAM ISAACS (TOURCULLA) (BORN CA. 1764): Upper Creek

métis. The head warrior of Coosada, Captain Isaacs initially embraced the Red Stick prophetic movement, but quickly spurned it. He became a staunch foe of the Red Sticks and lost his wife to a Red Stick war party.

CHILLY MCINTOSH (1800–1875): Lower Creek métis. The son of William McIntosh, he led the first Creek contingent westward to the Indian Territory in 1828. Becoming a Baptist minister, he allied himself with the Confederacy during the American Civil War, commanding the Second Regiment of Creek Mounted Volunteers with the rank of colonel.

CHINNABEE: Upper Creek (Natchez). A staunchly pro-American micco whose talwa of Talladega was besieged by the Red Sticks.

DAVID TATE (1779–1829): Upper Creek métis. Son of the British Indian agent David Taitt and half brother of William Weatherford, he sided with the Americans during the Creek War.

HOPOIE MICCO (DIED 1805): Upper Creek political leader. A pliant spokesman of the Creek National Council and advocate of Benjamin Hawkins's "civilization" program, he was assassinated by inflamed traditionalists.

HOPOITHLE MICCO (CA. 1755–1814): Red Stick political and war leader. An early accommodationist, the prominent Upper Creek leader came to resent the cultural changes wrought by "progressive" Creeks and métis and ultimately to embrace the Red Stick cause.

JAMES CORNELLS (BORN CA. 1772): Upper Creek métis. The pro-American Cornells was a trader, planter, and the first cousin of Alexander Cornells.

JIM BOY (TUSTUNNUGEE EMATHLA) (1790–1851): Red Stick prophet and war leader. An early convert to the Red Stick cause, he survived the Creek War and later raised units of Creek volunteers to fight with the Americans in the so-called Second Creek War and in the First Seminole War.

JOSIAH FRANCIS (HILLIS HADJO) (1770–1818): Red Stick métis prophet. A principal instigator of the Creek Civil War and also among the most ardent advocates for war with the whites, he fled the Creek country after the Battle of the Holy Ground.

LITTLE PRINCE (TUSTUNNUGEE HOPOEI) (DIED 1832): Lower Creek. Pro-American head chief of the Lower Creeks.

LITTLE WARRIOR (DIED 1813): Upper Creek Red Stick war leader who resided much of his life with the Shawnees. Little Warrior's massacre of white settlers on the Ohio River and subsequent execution by Creek law menders helped precipitate the Creek Civil War and earned him the status of martyr among the Red Sticks.

MENAWA (CA. 1765–CA. 1840): Red Stick métis war leader. Arguably the most capable Red Stick military figure, he lost all his immense wealth in the Creek War and nearly forfeited his life leading the Abeika Red Sticks at Horseshoe Bend.

OPOTHLE YOHOLO (CA. 1798–1863): Upper Creek. The adroit and principled successor to Big Warrior as Upper Creek spokesman, Opothle Yoholo came to prominence in the 1820s, first as a fervent opponent of government attempts to purchase remaining Creek lands east of the Mississippi River and later as an outspoken critic of Creek removal.

PADDY WALSH (DIED 1815): Red Stick prophet and war leader. A rival of Josiah Francis for the role of head prophet of the Red Sticks.

PETER McQUEEN (CA. 1780–1820): Red Stick métis political and war leader. The head warrior of Tallassee, McQueen was a prosperous planter and slaveholder who became an early and fervent convert to the Red Stick cause.

RICHARD DIXON BAILEY (1778–1813): Upper Creek métis. A wealthy planter and commander of a métis volunteer company, he was particularly reviled by the Red Sticks.

SAM MONIAC (TOTKES HADJO) (CA. 1781–1837): Upper Creek métis. An affluent slave-owning planter and stage station owner, Moniac was the staunchly pro-American brother-in-law of William Weatherford.

SEEKABOO: A multilingual Creek mystic and avid follower of Tecumseh and Tenskwatawa who long lived with the Shawnees. He helped create the Red Stick movement.

WILLIAM McINTOSH (TUSTUNNUGEE HUTKE) (1775–1825): Lower Creek métis. Perhaps the wealthiest man in the Creek confederacy, McIntosh fought with the Americans in the Creek War and later facilitated dubious U.S. government land grabs for personal profit.

WILLIAM WEATHERFORD (1781–1824): Upper Creek Red Stick. Son of a wealthy Scottish trader and a Creek woman distinguished in the powerful Wind Clan, Weatherford was coerced into a leadership role in the Red Stick movement. Americans wrongly blamed him for the massacre of civilians at Fort Mims.

ACKNOWLEDGMENTS

I would like to express my heartfelt thanks to my friends and distinguished fellow historians S. C. Gwynne, Bob Drury, and Jim Rasenberger for their close reading of my manuscript and their invaluable suggestions for improving it. All are exceptional writers and researchers whose works I unreservedly recommend to anyone with an interest in American history.

I also wish to express my deep gratitude to the members of the West Point class of 1985 Company F-4 Frog Book Club. Accomplished professionals with a keen appreciation of history all, these fine gentlemen carefully read my manuscript. In the best military fashion, they provided me with a detailed and thorough after-action report that contained countless superb suggestions for enhancing the manuscript. Thanks again, guys!

Fine artwork enriches the written word. In *A Brutal Reckoning,* I'm thrilled to introduce readers to five evocative paintings that my dear friend Keith Rocco rendered for the Horseshoe Bend National Military Park. They dramatically convey the critical moments of that horrific battle, so fraught with baleful consequences for the Native inhabitants of the American South. I'm similarly grateful to Herb Roe for permission to use his haunting painting of Hernando de Soto burning the Native town of Mabila and to Dori DeCamillis, artist and owner of Red Dot Gallery in Birmingham, Alabama, for permission to use her beautiful painting *"Italwas."*

COVID presented unique research challenges. I thank William A. Vaughan, PhD, of Ridgeland, Mississippi, for conducting essential research on my behalf at the Mississippi Department of Archives and History when the pandemic prevented my travel there.

In this, our third book together, I am deeply grateful to my literary agent Deborah Grosvenor for her enthusiastic support of my work, her wonderful suggestions and critiques, and her friendship. It continues also to be my great good fortune to work with Andrew Miller, my editor at Knopf, for whom I have the utmost admiration. I'd also like to thank the associate editor Todd Portnowitz for his many astute suggestions, the editorial assistant Tiara Sharma for skillfully easing *A Brutal Reckoning* through the editorial process, and the copy editor Ingrid Sterner for saving me from numerous embarrassing errors.

My deepest debt will always be to my wife, Antonia. Her emotional support and encouragement are of inestimable value.

NOTES

ABBREVIATIONS

ADAH: Alabama Department of Archives and History, Montgomery
AGI: Archivo General de las Indias, Newberry Library, Chicago
ASP-FR: American State Papers: Foreign Relations
ASP-IA: American State Papers: Indian Affairs
ASP-MA: American State Papers: Military Affairs
BIA: Bureau of Indian Affairs
CIART: Records of the Cherokee Indian Agency in Tennessee, 1801–1835
CLF: J. F. H. Claiborne Collection: Book F, Letters and Papers Relating to the Indian
    Wars
DC: Lyman C. Draper Collection
FSA: Florida State Archives, Tallahassee
GA: Georgia Archives, Morrow
HBNMP: Horseshoe Bend National Military Park, Daviston, Ala.
HNOC: Historic New Orleans Collection
LC: Library of Congress, Washington, D.C.
MDAH: Mississippi Department of Archives and History, Jackson
NA: National Archives and Records Administration, Washington, D.C.
NRS: National Records of Scotland, Edinburgh
PFP: Pickett Family Papers, Alabama Department of Archives and History,
    Montgomery
PPC: Papeles Procedentes de Cuba
TSLA: Tennessee State Library and Archives, Nashville
UGA: University of Georgia, Athens
WHS: Wisconsin Historical Society, Madison

EPIGRAPHS

1. [Gentleman of Elvas], *Narratives*, 81.
2. "History of the Church in Russia," 264.
3. Crockett, *Narrative*, 88–89.

A NOTE TO READERS

1. Paredes, "Back from Disappearance," 123–39.
2. National Museum of the American Indian website, americanindian.si.edu.

PROLOGUE

1. Parton, *Life of Jackson,* 1:384–97; Thruston, "Nashville Inn," 174–75.

1 FROM THE ASHES OF THE ENTRADA

1. Pickett, *History of Alabama,* 19–20; Hudson, *Southeastern Indians,* 74; Hudson and Tesser, introduction to *Forgotten Centuries,* 6.
2. "Conquistador Clothing," www.nps.gov; Pickett, *History of Alabama,* 20.
3. Green, *Politics of Removal,* 11; Hudson, *Southeastern Indians,* 108–12; Pickett, *History of Alabama,* 22.
4. Muscogee was the predominant language family in the Southeast. Once spoken in Louisiana, Mississippi, Alabama, and Georgia, it included five closely related groups of languages: Choctaw-Chickasaw, Apalachee, Alabama-Koasati (Coushatta), Mikasuki-Hitchiti, and Muscogee-Seminole. Many place-names in modern Alabama are derived from Muscogean words, including the word "Alabama" itself. In addition to their mother tongues, some southeastern Indians, as well as Europeans, used a lingua franca called the Mobilian trade jargon comprising words from Choctaw, Alabama, and Koasati. Hudson, *Southeastern Indians,* 23–24.
5. Ibid., 3, 77–79; Knight, "Formation of the Creeks," 373–75, 378–79; Pickett, *History of Alabama,* 56.
6. Pickett, *History of Alabama,* 51–55.
7. Bourne, *Narratives of de Soto,* 53.
8. Hudson, *Southeastern Indians,* 112; Pickett, *History of Alabama,* 27–29; Snyder, "Conquered Enemies," 276; Hally, "Chiefdom of Coosa," 16; Knight, "Formation of the Creeks," 381–82; Widmer, "Structure of Southeastern Chiefdoms," 127.
9. [Gentleman of Elvas], *Narratives,* 81; Hudson, *Southeastern Indians,* 113.
10. Hudson, *Southeastern Indians,* 114–15; Duncan, *Hernando de Soto,* 372–75.
11. Duncan, *Hernando de Soto,* 376–82.
12. Ibid., 382–87.
13. Pickett, *History of Alabama,* 40; Hudson, *Southeastern Indians,* 118; Duncan, *Hernando de Soto,* 387–90.
14. Hudson, *Southeastern Indians,* 5, 105; Hudson and Tesser, introduction to *Forgotten Centuries,* 9; Hally, "Chiefdoms of Coosa," 17–18.
15. Duncan, *Hernando de Soto,* 388; Hudson and Tesser, introduction to *Forgotten Centuries,* 10; Worth, "Later Spanish Military Expeditions," 104–5; Knight, "Formation of the Creeks," 379.
16. Hudson and Tesser, introduction to *Forgotten Centuries,* 12; Knight, "Formation of the Creeks," 379. The Catawbas of North Carolina are sometimes factored into the mix, but because their conflicts were with other Indian tribes or white settlers from the north, and their collapse relatively rapid, they played no appreciable role in the larger fortunes of the Creek Indians or the British colonists who confronted them.

17. Green, *Politics of Indian Removal*, 14; Crane, "Origin," 342; Braund, *Deerskins and Duffels*, 3–6, 13–14; Walker, "Creek Confederacy," 374–75; Wright, *Creeks and Seminoles*, 5; Halbert and Ball, *Creek War*, 23–24; Debo, *Road to Disappearance*, 3; Wesley, *Journal*, 1:65; Knight, "Formation of the Creek Confederacy," 394–96; Roosevelt, *Winning of the West*, 1:56–65; Section 15—Mordecai notes, in Pickett, "Some Interesting Notes."

2 A ROPE OF SAND

1. Walker, "Creek Confederacy," 381–82; Braund, "Slavery," 604; Hassig, "Internal Conflict," 252; Stiggins, *Creek Indian History*, 66; Saunt, *New Order*, 21; Ethridge, *Creek Country*, 109.
2. Walker, "Creek Confederacy," 383; Nairne, *Muskhogean Journals*, 32; Green, *Politics of Removal*, 6; Roosevelt, *Winning of the West*, 1:59, 64–65; Swan, "Manners and Arts," 279.
3. Green, *Politics of Removal*, 10; Debo, *Road to Disappearance*, 6–7; Walker, "Creek Confederacy," 383; Gatschet, *Migration Legend*, 122. Clans were associated with either white (*Hathagalgi*) or red (*Tcilokogalgi*) talwas. The Wind Clan was preeminent in white talwas. In red talwas, no single clan wielded comparable influence.
4. Green, *Politics of Removal*, 10–11; Swanton, "Social Organization," 461–63; Hassig, "Creek Intertown Relations," 479–83; Pope, *Tour*, 49–51; Bartram, *Travels*, 404, 565; Spoehr, "Creek Inter-town Relations," 152–53.
5. Hassig, "Internal Conflict," 253; Hudson, *Southeastern Indians*, 224; Nairne, *Muskhogean Journals*, 35–36; Braund, *Deerskins and Duffels*, 21, 23; Green, "McGillivray," 50; Swan, "Manners and Arts," 279; Walker, "Creek Confederacy," 252–53.
6. Debo, *Road to Disappearance*, 9–12; Swan, "Manners and Arts," 262–66; Bartram, *Travels*, 562–65; Hawkins, *Creek Confederacy*, 71–72; Taitt, "Journal," 503; Ethridge, *Creek Country*, 75.
7. Ethridge, *Creek Country*, 75; Bartram, *Travels*, 564–65; Walker, "Creek Confederacy," 378.
8. Stiggins, *Creek Indian History*, 65; Braund, *Deerskins and Duffels*, 268; Braund, "Guardians," 241–42; Braund, "Reflections," 262; Martin, *Sacred Revolt*, 20–21; Hudson, *Southeastern Indians*, 320; Bartram, *Travels*, 544; Bell, "Separate People," 334.
9. Gatschet, *Migration Legend*, 158–59; Griffith, *McIntosh and Weatherford*, 23; Snyder, "Adopted Kin," 266–68; Swan, "Manners and Arts," 280; Debo, *Road to Disappearance*, 24–25; Corkran, *Creek Frontier*, 29–30.
10. Green, *Politics of Removal*, 8; Braund, "Slavery," 602; Snyder, "Adopted Kin," 264–65; Campbell, "Account," 161; Walker, "Creek Confederacy," 386.
11. Braund, "Red Sticks," 87–88; Hudson, *Southeastern Indians*, 239–40, 245; Willett, *Narrative*, 103–4; Walker, "Creek Confederacy," 385; Hawkins, *Creek Confederacy*, 72; Stiggins, *Creek Indian History*, 75; Feiler, *Bossu's Travels*, 135.
12. Milford, *Memoirs*, 109; Hudson, *Southeastern Indians*, 240; Corkran, *Creek Frontier*, 30.
13. Hudson, *Southeastern Indians*, 117–18; Feiler, *Bossu's Travels*, 142; Stiggins, *Creek Indian History*, 54–55; Taitt, "Journal," 503, 507; Swan, "Manners and Arts," 266–67; Willett, *Narrative*, 102.
14. Hawkins, *Creek Confederacy*, 75, 80; Walker, "Creek Confederacy," 386–87; Swan, "Manners and Arts," 267–68; Payne, "Green-Corn Ceremony," 19–28; "Talk of Creek Leaders, June 11, 1735," in Coleman, *Colonial Records*, 20:382; Stiggins, *Creek Indian History*, 60–62.

15. "Talk of Creek Leaders, June 11, 1735," in Coleman, *Colonial Records*, 20:381; Braund, "Red Sticks," 87.

16. Hudson, *Southeastern Indians*, 120–24; Hawkins, *Creek Confederacy*, 80; Swan, "Manners and Arts," 270–71; Bartram, *Travels*, 397; Feiler, *Bossu's Travels*, 145.

17. Hudson, *Southeastern Indians*, 180–82; Adair, *American Indians*, 36; Taitt, "Journal," 539, 540–51.

18. Stiggins, *Creek Indian History*, 51–52; Corkran, *Creek Frontier*, 23; Ethridge, *Creek Country*, 109; Bartram, *Travels*, 391; Walker, "Creek Confederacy," 381; Burckhard and Petersen, *Partners in the Lord's Work*, 61–62; Feiler, *Bossu's Travels*, 131–32; Wesley, *Journal*, 1:66.

19. Milfort, *Memoirs*, 131–32.

20. I have been unable to determine whether Creek condemnation of extramarital affairs stemmed from a desire to avoid social strife or moral repugnance. Walker, "Creek Confederacy," 381; Swan, "Manners and Arts," 268–69; Hawkins, *Creek Confederacy*, 69; Broberg, "Sexual Mores," 33–39.

21. Bartram, *Travels*, 544; Feiler, *Bossu's Travels*, 131, 133; Campbell, "Account," 162; "Ranger's Report," 221.

22. Walker, "Creek Confederacy," 380; Hudson, *Southeastern Indians*, 264.

23. Bartram, *Travels*, 386, 399–400; Hudson, *Southeastern Indians*, 29–30, 261.

24. Swan, "Manners and Arts," 274; Taitt, "Journal," 513; Campbell, "Account of the Creek Nation," 161; Feiler, *Bossu's Travels*, 131, 147; Ethridge, *Creek Country*, 57; Taylor, "Alibamu Field Notes"; Bartram, *Travels*, 559; Walker, "Creek Confederacy," 374–77; Braund, *Deerskins and Duffels*, 19.

25. Swan, "Manners and Arts," 255–57; Ethridge, *Creek Country*, 11, 18–22, 31, 54–56; Hall, "Landscape Considerations," 222–28; Campbell, "Account of the Creek Nation," 158.

26. Swan, "Manners and Arts," 258.

3 BETWEEN THREE FIRES

1. Section 15—Mordecai notes, in Pickett, "Some Interesting Notes"; Browne, "Rise and Fall," 44; Green, *Politics of Removal*, 28; Mason, "Culture Change," 1.

2. Green, *Politics of Removal*, 19; Braund, *Deerskins and Duffels*, 32; Snyder, "Conquered Enemies," 277; Ramsey, "Something Cloudy," 58; Nairne, *Muskhogean Journals*, 75–76.

3. Debo, *Road to Disappearance*, 6.

4. Green, *Politics of Removal*, 11–12; Braund, *Deerskins and Duffels*, 5–6; Knight, "Formation of the Creeks," 387–88.

5. Hudson, *Southeastern Indians*, 439; Ramsey, "Something Cloudy," 44–46, 55–58, 70–72.

6. As a prominent Lower Creek micco declaimed, "The Almighty at first ordained that the Indians and white men should wash together and be alike, but the white men took advantage and bathed first, the Indians afterwards, by which means the Indians got stained by the sediment left in the water by the white men. The Negroes washed in muddy water, on which it was ordained that they should become slaves." Braund, "Slavery," 605–6, 611–12; Hopoithle Micco to the King of England, Sept. 3, 1811, Thomas Cochrane Papers, NRS.

7. Braund, *Deerskins and Duffels*, 58; Pressley, "Scottish Merchants," 150.

8. Pickett, *History of Alabama*, 156, 207, 250; Feiler, *Bossu's Travels*, 142–44; Debo, *Road to Disappearance*, 32.

9. Adair, *American Indians*, 260.

10. Debo, *Road to Disappearance*, 31–34; "Ranger's Report," 221; Pickett, *History of Alabama*, 207–9; Saunt, *Unworthy Republic*, xiii; Pressly, "Scottish Merchants," 139–40; Green, *Politics of Removal*, 23.

11. Pickett, *History of Alabama*, 263; Saunt, *New Order*, 12; Green, *Politics of Removal*, 28–30; Pressly, "Scottish Merchants," 141–52; "Observations of Superintendent John Stuart," 825.

12. Braund, *Deerskins and Duffels*, 78, 83–84; Doan, "Irish and Scots," 12.

13. The captains of the Indian trade, both legitimate and dubious, were the Irishman George Galphin and his partner the Scotsman Lachlan McGillivray, both of whom would come to loom large in Creek affairs. Originally based in Charleston and Augusta, they soon opened up branches in British East and West Florida. Braund, "Guardians," 247; Doan, "Irish and Scots," 10.

14. Bartram, *Travels*, 392–93; Wesley, *Journal*, 1:67–68; Hudson, *Southeastern Indians*, 441; Swanton, "Social Organization," 453; Thrower, "Casualties and Consequences," 14–15; Corbitt, "Papers IV," 276–77.

15. Pressly, "Scottish Merchants," 152, 161–62; Braund, *Deerskins and Duffels*, 69–72.

16. Thrower, "Casualties and Consequences," 14–15; Braund, *Deerskins and Duffels*, 76–77; Saunt, *New Order*, 47, 50; Taitt, "Journal," 515, 539.

17. Bast, "Creek Indian Affairs," 2, 3–17; Braund, "Slavery," 618; Snyder, "Conquered Enemies," 259; Foster, *Hawkins*, 429; Saunt, *New Order*, 54, 57, 61; Kokomoor, "Burning and Destroying," 300–304.

18. Hamilton, *Colonial Mobile*, 252–55; Stiggins, *Creek Indian History*, 79–80.

19. Braund, *Deerskins and Duffels*, 170, 180, 182.

20. Saunt, *New Order*, 67–69, 75; Caughey, *McGillivray*, xv–xvi; Green, *Politics of Removal*, 33; Green, "McGillivray," 41–43; Pope, *Tour*, 48; Braund, "Slavery," 619; Langley, "Tribal Identity," 234–37; Corbitt, "Papers IV," 279.

21. Saunt, *New Order*, 62–63, 80; Green, "McGillivray," 49–50; Green, *Politics of Removal*, 32–33.

22. Kokomoor, "Burning and Destroying," 302; Caughey, *McGillivray*, 92–93; Dowd, *Spirited Resistance*, 93.

23. Kinnaird, "International Rivalry," 60; Watson, "Continuity in Commerce," 548–53; Green, "McGillivray," 46–48; Swan, "Manners and Arts," 252; Dowd, *Spirited Resistance*, 94; Doan, "Irish and Scots," 13; Saunt, *New Order*, 78–79.

24. Feiler, *Bossu's Travels*, 138; Milfort, *Memoirs*, 65–66; Saunt, *New Order*, 83–84; Dowd, *Spirited Resistance*, 96, 98; Snyder, "Conquered Enemies," 262; Haynes, "Creek Border Patrols," 177; Swan, "Manners and Arts," 281; Green, *Politics of Removal*, 34–35.

25. *Niles' Weekly Register*, Dec. 28, 1811; Caughey, *McGillivray*, 153–57; Snyder, "Conquered Enemies," 268; Haynes, "Creek Border Patrols," 8, 9, 191, 193–94, 206–7; Braund, "Reflections," 272; Downes, "Creek-American Relations," 170.

26. Snyder, "Conquered Enemies," 278.

27. Ibid., 282–83; Braund, "Reflections," 262.

28. Green, "McGillivray," 54; Downes, "Creek-American Relations," 164, 172.

29. Downes, "Creek-American Relations," 174–84; Green, "McGillivray," 54; Green, *Politics of Removal*, 35–36; Willett, *Narrative*, 101; Debo, *Road to Disappearance*, 49–52.

30. Green, "McGillivray," 58–60; Green, *Politics of Removal*, 36.

31. Saunt, *New Order*, 99–100; Haynes, "Creek Border Patrols," 251; "Alabama Indian Chiefs," 19; Stiggins, *Creek Indian History*, 77–78.

4 THE SWEETS OF CIVILIZATION

1. Braund, *Deerskins and Duffels,* 9; Stiggins, *Creek Indian History,* 75–76; Feiler, *Bossu's Travels,* 172; Nairne, *Muskhogean Journals,* 48.

2. Haynes, "Creek Border Patrols," 276–77; Woodward, *Reminiscences,* 83, 87; J. F. H. Claiborne, *Sam Dale,* 38–40, 43.

3. Haynes, "Creek Border Patrols," 277–83; Debo, *Road to Disappearance,* 62.

4. Henri, *Southern Indians and Benjamin Hawkins,* 32–54.

5. Debo, *Road to Disappearance,* 61–65; Henri, *Southern Indians and Benjamin Hawkins,* 55–58; "Treaty of Colerain," Transcribed Treaties, RG 46, M200, NA.

6. Hawkins, *Creek Country,* 8–11; Henri, *Southern Indians and Benjamin Hawkins,* 59–80; Frank, *Creeks and Southerners,* 89; Saunt, *New Order,* 139, 153; Thrower, "Casualties and Consequences," 13. Hawkins's official title was "Principal Temporary Agent for Indian Affairs South of the Ohio River."

7. Green, *Politics of Indian Removal,* 29; Ethridge, *Creek Country,* 105–7; Debo, *Road to Disappearance,* 65–67; Saunt, *New Order,* 179; Foster, *Hawkins,* 314–15; Hawkins, *Creek Confederacy,* 67–68; Dowd, *Spirited Resistance,* 149.

8. Henri, *Southern Indians and Benjamin Hawkins,* 57; Saunt, *New Order,* 180; "Alabama Indian Chiefs," 15, 30; Woodward, *Reminiscences,* 116.

9. Mason, "Culture Change," 72–73; Green, *Politics of Removal,* 38; Hawkins, *Creek Country,* 24.

10. Saunt, *New Order,* 154–64; Braund, "Reflections," 259; Dowd, *Spirited Resistance,* 150–51; Ethridge, *Creek Country,* 164–66; Thrower, "Casualties and Consequences," 12–13.

11. Wallace, *Jefferson's Indian Policy,* 206–7, 221; *Niles' Weekly Register,* Dec. 28, 1811; Schwartzman and Barnard, "Trail of Broken Promises," 700; McKenney and Hall, *Indian Tribes,* 1:306.

12. Debo, *Road to Disappearance,* 72–73; Schwartzman and Barnard, "Trail of Broken Promises," 700.

13. Cozzens, *Tecumseh and the Prophet,* 144; Jefferson to Harrison, 1803, www.digitalhistory.uh.edu.

14. Jefferson to Jackson, Sept. 19, 1803, Jackson Papers, LC.

15. Jefferson to Hawkins, Feb. 18, 1803, in Bergh, *Jefferson's Writings,* 362–63.

16. Dreisback, "Death of McIntosh"; Frank, *Creeks and Southerners,* 100–101; McKenney and Hall, *Indian Tribes,* 1:305.

17. Janson, *Stranger in America,* 222; Griffith, *McIntosh and Weatherford,* 59–60.

18. Jefferson to Friend McIntosh and Chiefs of the Creek Nation, Nov. 1, 1805, Jefferson Papers, LC; Hawkins to John Milledge, June 9, 1806, in Grant, *Hawkins,* 2:510; Griffith, *McIntosh and Weatherford,* 59–60; Frank, "McIntosh," 39; Southerland and Brown, *Federal Road,* 20; Green, *Politics of Indian Removal,* 39–40.

5 THE HUNGRY YEARS

1. Mauelshagen and Davis, "Moravians' Plan," 361–62.

2. "Journal of Benjamin Hawkins," July 15, 1804, Hawkins to Henry Dearborn, July 9, Sept. 16, and Oct. 8, 1807, all in Grant, *Hawkins,* 2:476–77; Saunt, *New Order,* 154–55, 204–29; Ethridge, *Creek Country,* 182, 186, 219; Burckhard and Petersen, *Partners in the Lord's Work,* 48, 62–63.

3. Swanton, *Social Organization,* 478–79; Cozzens, *Tecumseh and the Prophet,* 21, 263–69.

4. Cozzens, *Tecumseh and the Prophet,* 70.

5. Ibid., 269–70; Halbert and Ball, *Creek War,* 40; Halbert, "Seekaboo and Tecumseh," 10YY1, Tecumseh Papers, DC, WHS.

6. Cozzens, *Tecumseh and the Prophet,* 270; Taitt, "Journal," 502, 511; Hawkins, *Creek Confederacy,* 27–28.

7. Gaines, "Letters," 186–87; Hall, "Landscape," 226–28; Hudson, *Creek Paths,* 26; Sunderland and Brown, *Federal Road,* 35–36; Thrower, "Casualties and Consequences," 11–12.

8. Hudson, *Creek Paths,* 79–83.

9. Hopoithle Micco to the King's Most Excellent Majesty, Sept. 1, 1811, Cochrane Papers.

10. Hawkins, *Creek Paths,* 83; Eades, "Life," 92.

11. Hawkins, *Creek Paths,* 84–85; *Cincinnati Liberty Hall,* Dec. 12, 1811.

12. Hawkins, *Creek Paths,* 85.

13. *Georgia Argus,* Sept. 11, 1811.

14. *Savannah Republican,* Oct. 17, 1811.

15. Griffith, *McIntosh and Weatherford,* 5–6, 18, 77–78, 98; Thompson, *Weatherford,* 835–37; Samuel Manac [*sic*] Deposition, Aug. 12, 1813, and Section 12—Robert James notes, both in Pickett, "Some Interesting Notes"; Halbert, "William Weatherford," 10YY37, Tecumseh Papers; J. D. Dreisbach to Lyman C. Draper, July 1874, VV62, Georgia, South Carolina, and Alabama Papers, DC, WHS; Hawkins to Eustis, Jan. 7, 1812, Hawkins Papers, GA; Griffith, *McIntosh and Weatherford,* 253; Stiggins, *Creek Indian History,* 86–87; Woodward, *Reminiscences,* 37, 94–95; Cozzens, *Tecumseh and the Prophet,* 271–72.

6 RISE OF THE RED STICKS

1. Gaines, *Reminiscences,* 151–52.

2. Waselkov and Wood, "Creek War," 4; Mauelshagen and Davis, "Moravians' Plan," 362; Dowd, *Spirited Resistance,* 167.

3. Cozzens, *Tecumseh and the Prophet,* 158–62; Waselkov and Wood, "Creek War," 4–5; Stiggins, *Creek Indian History,* 89.

4. Waselkov and Wood, "Creek War," 5; Martin, *Sacred Revolt,* 35; Stiggins, *Creek Indian History,* 158; Feiler, *Bossu's Travels,* 149.

5. Wright, *Creeks and Seminoles,* 168–69; Stiggins, *Creek Indian History,* 90, 121; "Alabama Indian Chiefs," 20; Griffith, *McIntosh and Weatherford,* 80.

6. Halbert, "Creek Red Stick."

7. Samuel Manac [*sic*] Deposition, Aug. 3, 1813, ADAH; Owsley, "Prophet of War," 274.

8. Cozzens, *Tecumseh and the Prophet,* 290–91; Eades, "Life," 92.

9. Southerland and Brown, *Federal Road,* 36; Benjamin Hawkins to William Hawkins, n.d., in *Georgia Journal,* June 17, 1812; Benjamin Hawkins to David Mitchell, April 6, 1812, Hawkins Papers; Benjamin Hawkins to Eustis, May 11, 1812, in *ASP-IA,* 809.

10. Hawkins to Eustis, July 13, 1812, Hawkins Papers.

11. Kanon, "Kidnapping," 15.

12. 23rd Cong., *Jesse Manley,* 1; Kanon, "Kidnapping," 3–4; George Colbert to Isaac Roberts, May 22, 1812, in *Philadelphia Aurora General Advertiser,* July 2, 1812; "Extract of Letter from William Henry to John J. Henry, June 26, 1812," contained in Willie Blount to John Armstrong, n.d., in *ASP-IA,* 812.

13. 23rd Cong., *Jesse Manley,* 1; "Extract of Letter from William Henry to John J. Henry, June 26, 1812," contained in Willie Blount to John Armstrong, n.d., in *ASP-IA,* 812; Martha Crawley deposition, Aug. 11, 1812, in Bassett, *Papers,* 1:225; Thomas Johnson to Andrew Jackson, May 27, 1812, in Moser, *Papers,* 2:299.

14. George Colbert to Isaac Roberts, May 22 and 24, 1812, in *Philadelphia Aurora General Advertiser,* July 2, 1812; Martha Crawley deposition, Aug. 11, 1812, in Bassett, *Papers,* 1:225; "Extracts from Memoranda."

15. Martha Crawley deposition, Aug. 11, 1812, in Bassett, *Papers,* 1:225; "Extracts from Memoranda"; Gaines, "Reminiscences," 153–54.

16. Cozzens, *Tecumseh and the Prophet,* 312; Kanon, "Kidnapping," 3.

17. Jackson to Blount, June 4, 1812, Jackson Papers.

18. Hawkins, *Creek Country,* 9; Kanon, "Kidnapping," 5; Thomas Johnson to Jackson, May 27, 1812, in Moser, *Papers,* 2:298; Call, "Journal," 8, Call Papers, FSA; *Wilson's Knoxville Gazette,* May 25 and June 15, 1812; Section 3—Patrick May notes, in Pickett, "Some Interesting Notes"; Gaines, "Reminiscences," 153; John Sevier to George Washington Sevier, May 31, 1812, in Sevier and Madden, *Sevier Family History,* 189.

19. Blount to Eustis, June 25 and July 26, 1812, in *ASP-IA,* 813–14.

20. Hawkins to Eustis, May 25, 1812, in *ASP-IA,* 811; Big Warrior to Hawkins, June 17, 1812, Hawkins Papers.

21. Hawkins to Eustis, Oct. 13, 1812, in *Virginia Patriot,* Nov. 20, 1812; James Robertson to John Armstrong, March 4, 1813, Matthews Collection, TSLA; Big Warrior to Hawkins, April 26, 1813, Hawkins to Eustis, Oct. 12, Nov. 2 and 9, 1812, Jan. 11 and March 25, 1813, and Hampton to Hawkins, Nov. 24, 1812, in *ASP-IA,* 811–13, 843.

22. *Virginia Patriot,* Nov. 20, 1812; Pound, "Hawkins," 396.

23. Cozzens, *Tecumseh and the Prophet,* 355–56; Hawkins to John Armstrong, May 3, 1813, in *ASP-IA,* 842; *Liberty Hall,* Feb. 27, 1813; J. C. Warren to David Mitchell, Hawkins Papers.

24. Hawkins to John Armstrong, March 25 and 29, April 6 and 22, and May 3, 1813, and Big Warrior and Alexander Cornells to Hawkins, April 25, 1813, in *ASP-IA,* 840, 843.

25. *Liberty Hall,* March 30, 1813; Nimrod Doyell to Hawkins, May 3, 1813, in *ASP-IA,* 844.

7 CIVIL WAR

1. Hawkins to Armstrong, Jan. 11, March 1, and April 24, 1813, in *ASP-IA,* 838–40.

2. Hawkins to Cornells, March 25, 1813, in *ASP-IA,* 839.

3. Linklater, *Artist in Treason,* 299–301; Hawkins to Armstrong, March 25, 1812, and to Tustunnugee Thlucco, Cornells, and McIntosh, April 24, 1813, in *ASP-IA,* 842; J. F. H. Claiborne, *Mississippi,* 318–19.

4. Big Warrior and Cornells to Hawkins, April 26, 1813, in *ASP-IA,* 843.

5. Hawkins to Armstrong, April 26, 1813, in *ASP-IA,* 844.

6. Henri, *Southern Indians and Hawkins,* 271, 273; Hawkins to David Mitchell, Feb. 15, 1813, Hawkins Papers; Hawkins to Armstrong, March 1, 1813, in *ASP-IA,* 838.

7. Hawkins to Tustunnugee Thlucco, Oche Hadjo, and every chief of the Upper Creeks, March 29, 1813, in *ASP-IA,* 839.

8. Hawkins to Armstrong, April 6, 1813, in *ASP-IA,* 840.

9. Dreisback, "Weatherford"; Saunt, "Taking Account of Property," 739.

10. Stiggins, *Creek Indian History,* 89–90.

11. Nimrod Doyell to Hawkins, May 3, 1813, and Big Warrior and Cornells to Hawkins,

April 21 and 26, 1813, in *ASP-IA,* 843–44; Hawkins to David Mitchell, April 26, 1813, Hawkins Papers; Big Warrior and Cornells to James Caller, April 18, 1813, Caller Papers, ADAH; I. G. Gore to Lyman C. Draper, Dec. 15, 1881, 4YY20, Tecumseh Papers.

12. Nimrod Doyell to Hawkins, May 3, 1813, in *ASP-IA,* 844.

13. Hawkins to Mitchell, May 31, 1813, Hawkins Papers; Hawkins to Armstrong, June 7, 1813, in *ASP-IA,* 844.

14. Hawkins was not alone in his opinion. Governor Mitchell heard from a state official in the Creek country who similarly discounted rumors of impending trouble. "If there was among a few in the Upper towns a disposition to hostility," the man reported, "it is completely suppressed, and the chiefs have such an overwhelming majority of the nation in their favor, that if there are a few who meditate mischief they will not dare to perpetrate it." J. G. Warren to Mitchell, May 13, 1813, Hawkins Papers.

15. *Georgia Journal,* April 14, 1813.

16. Dowd, *Spirited Resistance,* 158; Saunt, *New Order,* 257–58; Martin, *Sacred Revolt,* 144; Stiggins, *Creek Indian History,* 135–36; Waselkov and Wood, "Creek War," 7–8, 16; Collins, "Packet from Canada," 69; Davis, "Remember Fort Mims," 628; "Report of Alexander Cornells," June 22, 1813, in *ASP-IA,* 845; Samuel Manac [*sic*] Deposition, Aug. 3, 1813, and Section 15—Mordecai [*sic*] notes, in Pickett, "Some Interesting Notes"; Doan, "Irish and Scots," 15–16; J. F. H. Claiborne, *Sam Dale,* 67; Braund, *Deerskins and Duffels,* 183–84; Braund, "Reflections," 266; *Niles' Register,* Aug. 21, 1813.

17. Halbert and Ball, *Creek War,* 246–47; Waselkov and Wood, "Creek War," 9; Hawkins, *Creek Confederacy,* 83–84; Waselkov, "Return to the Holy Ground," 29, 32.

18. Waselkov and Wood, "Creek War," 9; Hawkins to Armstrong, June 28, 1813, in *ASP-IA,* 847; Kanon, "Slow, Laborious Slaughter," 4.

19. Quoted in Halbert and Ball, *Creek War,* 89–90.

20. Stiggins, *Creek Indian History,* 92–94; "Report of Alexander Cornells," June 22, 1813, 846; Owsley, "Prophet of War," 277–78.

21. "Report of Alexander Cornells," June 22, 1813, 846.

22. Hawkins to Mitchell, July 11, 1813, Hawkins Papers; "Report of Alexander Cornells," June 22, 1813, 846; Burckhard and Petersen, *Partners in the Lord's Work,* 75–76; Saunt, "Taking Account of Property," 750.

23. Mitchell to Hawkins, June 26, 1813, in *Augusta Chronicle,* July 30, 1813; "Report of Alexander Cornells," June 22, 1813, 846.

24. Hawkins's undated message [June 23, 1813?], in *Milledgeville Journal,* July 14, 1813; Hawkins to Mitchell, June 24, 1813, Hawkins Papers.

25. Hawkins's addendum to "Report of Alexander Cornells," June 22, 1813, and Talosee Fixico to Hawkins, July 5, 1813, in *ASP-IA,* 847, 848.

26. Cozzens, *Tecumseh and the Prophet,* 368–74.

27. Hawkins's addendum to "Report of Alexander Cornells," June 22, 1813, 848; James Duroceau to Hawkins, July 7, 1813, Hawkins to Mitchell, July 11 and 22, 1813, Big Warrior to Hawkins, July 26, 1813, and Big Warrior and Little Prince to Robert Walton, July 24, 1813, Hawkins Papers; Cusseta King to Hawkins, July 10, 1813, in *ASP-IA,* 849; Stiggins, *Creek Indian History,* 95–97.

28. Braund, "Reflections," 265; Halbert and Ball, *Creek War,* 94; John Ross to Return Meigs, July 30, 1813, Cook Collection, HNOC; Creek chiefs to Return Meigs, July 23, 1813, Allen Collection, University of Tennessee; Hawkins to Mitchell, July 27, 1813, Big Warrior and Little Prince to Robert Walton, July 24, 1813, Big Warrior and Tustunnugee Hopoie to Hawkins, Aug. 4, 1813, and "Extracts of Occurrences in the Agency

for Indian Affairs," Aug. 13, 1813, Hawkins Papers; Hawkins to Armstrong, July 28, 1813, in *ASP-IA*, 850; Hawkins, *Creek Confederacy*, 83–84.

29. Hawkins, letter to the editors, Oct. 31, 1813, in *University Gazette*, Nov. 19, 1813.

30. Hawkins to Thomas Pinckney, July 9, 1813, and to Armstrong, Aug. 22 and Sept. 4, 1813, in *ASP-IA;* Mitchell to David Blackshear, Aug. 4, 1813, Reid Collection, UGA; Hawkins to Mitchell, Aug. 28, 1813, and "Extracts of Occurrences in the Agency for Indian Affairs," Aug. 13–23, 1813, Hawkins Papers; Weir, *Paradise of Blood*, 176. In two letters, Hawkins refers to the talwa that McIntosh attacked as Tallassee; in a third he suggests it was the nearby Chattucchufaulee.

31. Hawkins to Armstrong, Aug. 22 and 23 and Sept. 6 and 13, 1813, in *ASP-IA*, 851–53; Timothy Bernard to Mitchell, Aug. 28, 1813, and David Adams to Mitchell, July 13, 1813, Cuyler Collection, UGA; Hawkins to Armstrong, Sept. 14, 1813, Hawkins Papers.

8 STARK MAD

1. The total number of Red Stick fighting men is uncertain. At the outset of the conflict, Peter McQueen boasted to the Spanish governor Mateo González Manrique of West Florida that forty-eight hundred warriors had answered the call. In 1791, Alexander McGillivray estimated the number of "gun-men" in the entire Creek confederacy to be between five thousand and six thousand; the "useless old men, the women, may be reckoned as three times the number of gun-men, making in the whole about 25,000 or 26,000 souls." In view of the slight increase in the Creek population between then and 1813 and calculating friendly Creek warriors at no more than two thousand, a figure of forty-eight hundred Red Stick combatants seems reasonable. Hawkins to John Floyd, Sept. 30, 1813, in *ASP-IA*, 854; Swan, "Manners and Arts," 263; *Columbian Museum and Savannah Advertiser*, April 21, 1814.

2. Waselkov, *Conquering Spirit*, 16–17; Halbert and Ball, *Creek War*, 31–32.

3. McGillivray to William Panton, May 20, 1789, in Corbitt, "Papers IV," 285; Halbert and Ball, *Creek War*, 32–34.

4. Ephraim Kirby to Jefferson, May 1, 1804, in Carter, *Territorial Papers*, 6:322–25; Halbert and Ball, *Creek War*, 32, 34.

5. Waselkov, *Conquering Spirit*, 18–30; Davis, "Remember Fort Mims," 612–28; Halbert, "Incidents at Fort Mims," 10YY86, Tecumseh Papers; J. D. Dreisbach to Lyman C. Draper, VV62, Georgia, Alabama, and South Carolina Papers, DC, WHS; Section 2— May notes, in Pickett, "Some Interesting Notes"; Collins, "Packet from Canada," 73; Hawkins to Wilkinson, Oct. 21, 1813, in *Hampshire Gazette*, Oct. 20, 1813; Thrower, "Casualties and Consequences," 18.

6. Stiggins, *Creek Indian History*, 92–93; Owsley, *Struggle for the Gulf Borderlands*, 27.

7. Pickett, *History of Alabama*, 453; González Manrique to Juan Ruiz de Apodaca, July 13, 1813, No. 94, Legajo 1794, PPC, AGI; Sparks, *Memories*, 478; Wright, *Creeks and Seminoles*, 167.

8. Owsley, *Struggle for the Gulf Borderlands*, 28; Collins, "Packet from Canada," 56–58; Harry Toulmin to Ferdinand Claiborne, July 13, 1813, James Cornells Deposition, Aug. 1, 1813, David Tate Deposition, Aug. 1, 1813, Claiborne to Armstrong, Aug. 12, 1813, and Claiborne to Mitchell, Aug. 14, 1813, CLF, MDAH.

9. Samuel Manac [*sic*] Deposition, Aug. 3, 1813, ADAH; Woodward, *Reminiscences*, 94; Halbert and Ball, *Creek War*, 93–94; Collins, "Packet from Canada," 72–75.

10. Stiggins, *Creek Indian History*, 98–99; Harry Toulmin to Ferdinand Claiborne, July 31,

1813, and James Cornells Deposition, Aug. 1, 1813, CLF; Holmes to Armstrong, Aug. 3, 1813, in Carter, *Territorial Papers,* 6:390; Hall, "Landscape," 228–29; Big Warrior to Hawkins, Aug. 4, 1813, in *ASP-IA,* 851; Toulmin to Claiborne, July 23, 1813, Toulmin Letters, ADAH; Woodward, *Reminiscences,* 97; *Niles' Weekly Register,* Sept. 4, 1813; "A Respectable Gentleman" to Hawkins, Aug. 12, 1813, in *Mirror of the Times,* Sept. 11, 1813.

11. Owsley, *Struggle for the Gulf Borderlands,* 20–24; John Jones to Thomas Hart Benton, July 4, 1814, Jackson Papers; González Manrique to Ruiz de Apodaca, Jan. 2, 1813, No. 1432, Legajo 1794, and July 13, 1813, No. 94, Legajo 1794, PPC.

12. Weir, *Paradise of Blood,* 121, 123; Innerarity, "Prelude," 251–53; Harry Toulmin to Ferdinand Claiborne, July 23, 1813, Toulmin Letters.

13. González Manrique to Ruiz de Apodaca, July 13, 1813, No. 94, Legajo 1794, PPC; David Tate Deposition, Aug. 1, 1813, CLF; Innerarity, "Prelude," 249–50.

14. González Manrique to Ruiz de Apodaca, July 13, 1813, No. 94, Legajo 1794, PPC; Innerarity, "Prelude," 254–55; David Tate Deposition, Aug. 1, 1813, CLF.

15. Halbert and Ball, *Creek War,* 128–29; González Manrique to Ruiz de Apodaca, Aug. 16, 1813, No. 96, and Sept. 3, 1813, Legajo 1794, PPC; Innerarity, "Prelude," 256–57.

16. John Hanes et al. to Wilkinson, April 17, 1813, Creek War Military Records Collection, ADAH; Lengel, "Road to Fort Mims," 19–23; Caller to Jefferson, Dec. 17, 1804, in Carter, *Territorial Papers,* 5:367; Holmes to Caller et al., Sept. 8, 1810, Toulmin to John Graham, March 10 and Aug. 5, 1812, and Toulmin to Edward Tiffin, June 7, 1814, in Carter, *Territorial Papers,* 6:113–14, 283–84, 306–7, 443; Toulmin to Holmes, July 3, 1813, series A, vol. 14, Governors' Papers, MDAH.

17. Toulmin to Ferdinand Claiborne, July 23, 1813, Toulmin Letters; Toulmin to Claiborne, July 31, 1813, CLF; Gaines, "Reminiscences," 157; Stiggins, *Creek Indian History,* 99–100; Halbert and Ball, *Creek War,* 99–100.

18. J. F. H. Claiborne, *Mississippi,* 332; Claiborne to Caller, June 27, 1812, to Armstrong, Aug. 12, 1813, and to Mitchell, Aug. 14, 1813, CLF, MDAH.

19. Claiborne to George Poindexter, Nov. 26, 1812, John C. Cox et al. to Claiborne, March 22, 1813, Claiborne to Wilkinson, March 18, 1813, "Morning Report of 1st Regiment Mississippi Territory Volunteers, July 1813," Claiborne to Flournoy, July 8, 1813, and Toulmin to Claiborne, July 2, 1813, CLF; Holmes to Armstrong, July 27, 1813, in Carter, *Territorial Papers,* 6:388–89; J. F. H. Claiborne, *Mississippi,* 87–88.

20. Claiborne to Mitchell, Aug. 14, 1813, CLF.

21. Toulmin to Claiborne, July 31, 1813, CLF; Halbert and Ball, *Creek War,* 120–24; Halbert, "Correction of a Statement in Regard to Choctaw Renegades of the Creek War of 1813–14," 10YY50, Tecumseh Papers.

22. Toulmin to Claiborne, July 23, 1813, Toulmin Letters.

23. Halbert and Ball, *Creek War,* 105–6; Halbert, "Incidents of the Creek War," 10YY91, Tecumseh Papers; Halbert, "Creek War Incidents," 96.

24. Halbert, "Creek War Incidents," 97.

25. Halbert, "Visit of Pushmataha to Fort Madison," 10YY47, and "Events in the Life of Pushmataha," 10YY54, Tecumseh Papers; Lincecum, *Pushmataha,* xv–xvi, 26, 28–29, 93.

9 TERROR IN THE TENSAW

1. Joseph Kennedy to Claiborne, July 24, 1813, and Claiborne to Mitchell, Aug. 14, 1813, CLF; Toulmin to Claiborne, July 23, 1813, Toulmin Letters; Holmes to Armstrong, Aug. 30, 1813, in Carter, *Territorial Papers,* 6:396–97.

2. Stiggins, *Creek Indian History,* 99–100; Woodward, *Reminiscences,* 86–87.

3. Caller to Claiborne, July 20, 1813, Caller Papers; Halbert and Ball, *Creek War,* 129–30; Section 2—Creagh notes, and Section 3—May notes, in Pickett, "Some Interesting Notes"; "Late George W. Creagh," *Flag and Advertiser,* Dec. 7, 1848.

4. Section 3—May notes, in Pickett, "Some Interesting Notes"; J. F. H. Claiborne, *Sam Dale,* 73.

5. Halbert and Ball, *Creek War,* 135–36; Halbert "Battle of Burnt Corn Creek," 10YY82, Tecumseh Papers; J. F. H. Claiborne, *Sam Dale,* 74; Section 2—Creagh notes, Section 3—May notes, and Section 4—Thomas G. Holmes notes, in Pickett, "Some Interesting Notes"; "Late George W. Creagh," *Flag and Advertiser,* Dec. 7, 1848.

6. Stiggins, *Creek Indian History,* 100–101; Section 2—Creagh notes, and Section 4—Thomas G. Holmes notes, in Pickett, "Some Interesting Notes"; W. W. Osborne to Carson, July 28, 1813, and Claiborne to Bailey et al., CLF.

7. Stiggins, *Creek Indian History,* 101.

8. David, "Remember Fort Mims," 629–30.

9. Halbert and Ball, *Creek War,* 141–42; Carson to Claiborne, July 30, 1813, Carson Letters, ADAH; Toulmin to Holmes, Aug. 2, 1813, Governors' Papers.

10. Stiggins, *Creek Indian History,* 102–5; Griffith, *McIntosh and Weatherford,* 88–92, 99; Woodward, *Reminiscences,* 96–97; J. D. Dreisbach to Lyman C. Draper, July 1874, VV62, Georgia, Alabama, and South Carolina Papers.

11. Thrower, "Casualties and Consequences," 19–21; Stiggins, *Creek Indian History,* 106–7; Woodward, *Reminiscences,* 97; Owsley, "Prophet of War," 281; Hawkins to Toulmin, Oct. 23, 1813, Jackson Papers; Hawkins to John Floyd, Sept. 30, 1813, in *APS-IA,* 854; Andrew Montgomery to Samuel Montgomery, Sept. 4, 1813, in unidentified newspaper clipping, CLF.

12. Waselkov, *Conquering Spirit,* 117–18, 277; Halbert, "An Incident at Fort Mims," 10YY83, and "Escape of Nehemiah Page," 10YY84, Tecumseh Papers; Halbert and Ball, *Creek War,* 147; Lackey, *Frontier Claims,* 34; Pickett, *History of Alabama,* 535.

13. Daniel Beasley to Claiborne, Aug. 6, 1813, CLF; Waselkov, *Conquering Spirit,* 120–21, 225; Halbert and Ball, *Creek War,* 148; Section 4—Thomas G. Holmes notes, in Pickett, "Some Interesting Notes."

14. *Washington Republican,* Dec. 1, 1813; Flournoy to Claiborne, Aug. 10, 1813, Toulmin to Claiborne, Aug. 12, 1813, CLF.

15. Claiborne to Holmes, Aug. 12, 1813, CLF.

16. Halbert, "Incidents of Fort Mims," 10YY85, Tecumseh Papers; Section 4—Thomas G. Holmes notes, in Pickett, "Some Interesting Notes"; Waselkov, *Conquering Spirit,* 126; Claiborne to Beasley, Feb. 15, 1813, CLF.

17. Beasley to Claiborne, Aug. 6, 1813, CLF; Halbert, "Incidents of Fort Mims."

18. Claiborne to Beasley, Aug. 7, 1813, CLF; J. F. H. Claiborne, *Sam Dale,* 101.

19. Section 4—Thomas G. Holmes notes, and Osborne to Claiborne, Aug. 24, 1813, in Section 7—"Interesting papers," in Pickett, "Some Interesting Notes"; Beasley to Claiborne, Aug. 12 and 14, 1813, CLF; "Extract of a Letter from Judge Toulmin to the Governor, September 11, 1813," in *Augusta Chronicle,* Oct. 13, 1813; Toulmin, letter to the editor, *Raleigh Register,* Sept. 7, 1813; Halbert, "Incidents of Fort Mims"; Waselkov, *Conquering Spirit,* 225–27; Brannon, "Osborne."

20. Stiggins, *Creek Indian History,* 108.

21. Griffith, *McIntosh and Weatherford,* 101; Woodward, *Reminiscences,* 98; Halbert, "William Weatherford and Dixon Moniac," 10YY34, Tecumseh Papers.

22. "Statement of Hugh Cassity, a Choctaw Indian, Signed by Joseph Carson, August 23, 1813," Claiborne to Flournoy, Sept. 3, 1813, and Claiborne to Joseph Kennedy, Aug. 25, 1813, CLF; Toulmin to Holmes, Aug. 27, 1813, in Doster, "Letters," 278–80.

23. Beasley to Claiborne, Aug. 14 and 30, 1813, CFP; Section 4—Thomas G. Holmes notes, in Pickett, "Some Interesting Notes"; Waselkov, *Conquering Spirit*, 126.

24. Stiggins, *Creek Indian History*, 109–10; J. D. Dreisbach to Lyman C. Draper, July 1874, VV62, Georgia, Alabama, and South Carolina Papers; H. S. Halbert to Lyman C. Draper, Oct. 31, 1887, 10YY35, Tecumseh Papers; Sections 4 and 25—Thomas G. Holmes notes, in Pickett, "Some Interesting Notes"; Woodward, *Reminiscences*, 98; Hawkins to Armstrong, Oct. 11, 1813, in *ASP-IA*, 852.

25. Toulmin to the editor, *Raleigh Register*, Sept. 7, 1813; Halbert, "A Fort Mims Incident," 10YY84, Tecumseh Papers; Halbert, "Incidents of Fort Mims"; Hawkins to John Floyd, Sept. 25, 1813, in *Georgia Journal*, Sept. 29, 1813; Beasley to Claiborne, Aug. 30, 1813, CFP; Section 12—James notes, in Pickett, "Some Interesting Notes"; Toulmin to Flournoy, Aug. 30, 1813, in Doster, "Letters," 283; Woodward, *Reminiscences*, 98; Stiggins, *Creek Indian History*, 111; Waselkov, *Conquering Spirit*, 56–57, 243.

26. Halbert, "Incidents of Fort Mims"; Sections 4 and 25—Thomas G. Holmes notes, in Pickett, "Some Interesting Notes"; Claiborne to Flournoy, Sept. 3, 1813, CLF; Woodward, *Reminiscences*, 99; Stiggins, *Creek Indian History*, 114; Hawkins to Armstrong, Oct. 11, 1813, in *ASP-IA*, 852.

27. J. D. Dreisbach to Lyman C. Draper, July 1874, VV62, Georgia, Alabama, and South Carolina Papers; Halbert, "Incidents of Fort Mims"; Section 4—Thomas G. Holmes notes, in Pickett, "Some Interesting Notes"; Halbert and Ball, *Creek War*, 173; Toulmin to the editor, *Raleigh Register*, Sept. 7, 1813.

28. Halbert and Ball, *Creek War*, 173–74; Meeks, *Romantic Passages*, 254–55; Griffith, *McIntosh and Weatherford*, 107–8.

29. Sections 4 and 25—Thomas G. Holmes notes, in Pickett, "Some Interesting Notes"; Toulmin to the editor, *Raleigh Register*, Sept. 7, 1813.

30. Section 12—James notes, and Section 25—Thomas G. Holmes notes, in Pickett, "Some Interesting Notes"; Stiggins, *Creek Indian History*, 112; Toulmin to the editor, *Raleigh Register*, Sept. 7, 1813; Halbert and Ball, *Creek War*, 158–59, 174–75; Halbert, "Incidents of Fort Mims"; Waselkov, *Conquering Spirit*, 236, 243, 249; Hawkins to Armstrong, Sept. 17, 1813, in *ASP-IA*, 853.

31. Section 4—Thomas G. Holmes notes, in Pickett, "Some Interesting Notes"; Waselkov, *Conquering Spirit*, 191–93; González Manrique to Ruiz de Apodaca, Oct. 2, 1813, No. 168, Legajo 1794, PPC; Hawkins to Armstrong, Sept. 21, 1813, in *ASP-IA*, 853; Stiggins, *Creek Indian History*, 113–14; Lackey, *Frontier Claims*, 45–48; Andrew Montgomery to Samuel Montgomery, Sept. 4, 1813, in unidentified newspaper clipping, CLF. The commanding officer of a detachment dispatched to inter the decomposed remains of the Fort Mims dead on September 26 swore he had counted at least a hundred dead warriors. "We cannot be mistaken as to their being Indians," he explained, "as they were interred with their war clubs and implements." The presence of war clubs by a cadaver was not positive proof, however, because Creek warriors sometimes left their war clubs beside the bodies of victims. Joseph Kennedy to Claiborne, Sept. 29, 1813, CFP.

32. Section 12—James notes, and Section 25—Thomas G. Holmes notes, in Pickett, "Some Interesting Notes."

33. Toulmin to Claiborne, Sept. 6, 1813, CLF.

34. Pickett, *History of Alabama,* 475; Halbert, "Incidents of the Creek War of 1813," 10YY21, Tecumseh Papers; Halbert and Ball, *Creek War,* III, 177–81.

35. Halbert and Ball, *Creek War,* 177–92; Halbert, "Incidents of the Creek War of 1813," 10YY91, Tecumseh Papers; Section 2—Creagh notes, in Pickett, "Some Interesting Notes."

36. Halbert and Ball, *Creek War,* 225–27; Owsley, *Struggle for the Gulf Borderlands,* 39; Halbert, "Creek War Incidents," 102–7; Halbert, "Incidents of the Creek War of 1813," 10YY91, Tecumseh Papers; González Manrique to Ruiz de Apodaca, Oct. 2, 1813, No. 168, Legajo 1794, PPC; González Manrique to "Gentlemen," Sept. 29, 1813, in *Mirror of the Times,* Feb. 19, 1814.

37. Durant to Charles Cameron, Sept. 11, 1813, Durant et al. to Cameron, Sept. 11, 1813, and Edward Handfield to Cameron, Oct. 28, 1813, Cochrane Papers; Toulmin to Claiborne, Sept. 18, 1813, in *Mississippi Republican,* Oct. 20, 1813.

38. Claiborne to Flournoy, Sept. 3, 1813, and William Malone et al. to Claiborne, CLF; Section 1—Jeremiah Austill notes, in Pickett, "Some Interesting Notes"; J. F. H. Claiborne, *Mississippi,* 486–88; Eades, "Life," 97; Halbert and Ball, *Creek War,* 116.

39. Claiborne to Holmes, Sept. 4, 1813, CLF; Toulmin to Holmes, Sept. 11, 1813, in *Augusta Chronicle,* Oct. 13, 1813.

40. J. F. H. Claiborne, *Mississippi,* 321; Claiborne to Flournoy, Sept. 3, 1813, Toulmin to Claiborne, Sept. 6, 1813, and Claiborne to Toulmin, Sept. 12, 1813, CLF; Toulmin to Madison, Sept. 11, 1813, Madison Papers, LC.

41. Section 4—Thomas G. Holmes notes, Kennedy to Claiborne, Sept. 9, 1813, in Section 7—Interesting Papers, and Section 12—James notes, in Pickett, "Some Interesting Notes"; Claiborne to Wilkinson, March 18, 1813, Kennedy to Claiborne, Sept. 9 and 26, 1813, and Claiborne to Kennedy, Sept. 22, 1813, CLF; Halbert, "Burial of the Dead at Fort Mims," 10YY9, "Incidents of the Creek War of 1813," 10YY91, and Henry S. Halbert to Lyman C. Draper, Oct. 3, 1887, 10YY35, Tecumseh Papers.

10 THE EMERGENCE OF OLD HICKORY

1. Toulmin to the editor, *Raleigh Register,* Sept. 7, 1813, in *American Commercial and Daily Advertiser,* Oct. 20, 1813; Braund, "Reflections," 263; Thrower, "Casualties and Consequences," 17, 21; Saunt, *New Order,* 269–71; Parton, *Jackson,* 1:449.

2. *Augusta Chronicle,* Sept. 3, 1813; *Nashville Whig,* Sept. 7, 1813; Blount to Mitchell, Aug. 8, 1813, and Mitchell to Blount, Aug. 26, 1813, in *National Intelligencer,* Nov. 20, 1813.

3. Remini, *Jackson and American Empire,* 1–25; Brand, *Jackson,* 9–30; Faust, *Another Look,* 203.

4. Remini, *Jackson and American Empire,* 13–14, 32–33, 44–45.

5. Buell, *Jackson,* 1:68–69.

6. Benton, *Thirty Years' View,* 1:739; Parton, *Jackson,* 1:337–38.

7. Parton, *Jackson,* 1:219.

8. Jackson to Colonel McKinney, May 10, 1802, and Jackson to Willie Blount, in Bassett, *Correspondence,* 1:62, 201–2.

9. Brand, *Jackson,* 120–70.

10. Bassett, *Correspondence,* 1:222–23.

11. Jackson to Blount, June 5 and July 8, 1812, in Moser, *Papers,* 2:301, 311–12; Jackson to Blount, June 4 and 17 and July 3, 1812, in Bassett, *Correspondence,* 1:225–29; *Democratic Clarion,* July 8, 1812.

12. Blount to Jackson, July 21, 1812, and Jackson to the Tennessee Volunteers, July 31, 1812, in Moser, *Papers*, 2:316–18.
13. *Niles' Weekly Register*, Sept. 26, 1812.
14. Jackson to Blount, Sept. 8, 1812, in Moser, *Papers*, 2:319.
15. Parton, *Jackson*, 1:365–68; General Orders, Nov. 23, 1812, in Bassett, *Correspondence*, 1:243.
16. Parton, *Jackson*, 1:368–69.
17. Ibid., 377–80; Jackson to Armstrong, March 15, 1813, and to Madison, March 15, 1813, in Bassett, *Correspondence*, 1:289–94.
18. Parton, *Jackson*, 383–84; Jackson to William B. Lewis, April 9, 1813, in Bassett, *Correspondence*, 1:295; Kanon, "Glories in the Field," 48–49.
19. Martin, *Self Vindication*, 18–19.
20. Remini, *Jackson and American Empire*, 180.
21. Parton, *Jackson*, 1:339; Remini, *Jackson and American Empire*, 161; Benton, *Thirty Years' View*, 1:738.
22. Remini, *Jackson and American Empire*, 132–34, 144; "Andrew Jackson's Log Cabin," stereoscopic view by C. C. Giers, ca. 1875, Andrew Jackson Collection, TSLA.
23. Parton, *Jackson*, 392–97; "Thomas H. Benton's Account of His Duel with Jackson, Sept. 10, 1813," in Bassett, *Correspondence*, 1:317–18.
24. Gaines, "Reminiscences," 158–61; John McKee to John Pitchlynn, Sept. 14, 1813, Jackson Papers, LC; Parton, *Jackson*, 1:422–23; Kanon, *Tennesseans at War*, 68.
25. Parton, *Jackson*, 1:369, 435; DeWitt, "Coffee Letters," 265–66; Royall, *Letters from Alabama*, 44–45.
26. Reid to "Dear Sir," Nov. 6, 1812, and to his mother, Sept. 19, 1813, Reid Papers, LC; Parton, *Jackson*, 1:422, 449–50; Martin, *Self Vindication*, 13, 16–17.
27. *Nashville Whig*, Sept. 28, 1813; Kanon, "Before Horseshoe Bend," 108; Pickett, *History of Alabama*, 434; Ephraim Foster to William Graham, Feb. 28, 1814, Gilder Lehrman Institute; Royall, *Letters from Alabama*, 43; Jackson to Holmes, Sept. 26, 1813, in Bassett, *Correspondence*, 1:322–23; Parton, *Jackson*, 1:424.
28. Blount to Flournoy, Oct. 15, 1813, in *ASP-IA*, 855–56.
29. Wallis, *Crockett*, xviii, 6, 8, 13, 65, 67; Folmsbee, "Early Career," 64–66; Crockett, *Narrative*, 71–73.
30. Call, "Journal," 10–13, Call Papers.
31. Parton, *Jackson*, 1:424–25; Gaines, "Reminiscences," 161; Sept. 28, 1813, entry in undated report of John McKee, Jackson Papers; Jackson to Holmes, Sept. 26, 1813, and Jackson to Coffee, Sept. 27, 1813, in Bassett, *Correspondence*, 1:322–24; Jackson to Coffee, Sept. 29, 1813, in Moser, *Papers*, 2:431.

1 1 INVASION OF THE TENNESSEANS

1. Abram, "'To Keep Bright the Bonds of Friendship,'" 228–43; Abram, *Forging a Cherokee-American Alliance*, 37–60; Meigs to the Cherokee Volunteers, Oct. 1813, Gideon Morgan Papers, TSLA; *Montgomery Advertiser*, March 6, 1911; Jackson to Coffee, Oct. 7, 1813, in Bassett, *Correspondence*, 1:329; John Strother to Jackson, Oct. 9, 1813, Jackson Papers.
2. Crockett, *Narrative*, 75–82; Folmsbee, "Early Career," 65–66; Coffee to Jackson, Oct. 6, 1813, Jackson Papers; Reid to his father, Oct. 17, 1813, Reid Papers.
3. Robert Grierson to Hawkins, Sept. 23, 1813, Hawkins Papers; John Strother to Jackson,

Oct. 5, 1813, McKee to Coffee, Oct. 21, 1813, and Path Killer to Jackson, Oct. 22, 1813, in Moser, *Papers*, 2:433–34, 439–40; Cozzens, *Tecumseh and the Prophet*, 413.

4. Parton, *Jackson*, 547–49; Kanon, "Before Horseshoe Bend," 106.

5. Reid to his father, Oct. 17, 1783, Reid Papers.

6. Ibid.; Jackson to Peter Perkins, Oct. 20, 1813, and Jackson to Blount, Oct. 20, 1813, Jackson Papers; Read, Mitchell, and Company to Jackson, Oct. 18, 1813, and Jackson to Flournoy et al., Oct. 23, 1813, in Bassett, *Correspondence*, 1:333, 335.

7. Coffee to Jackson, Oct. 22, 1813, in Moser, *Papers*, 2:438; Crockett, *Narrative*, 83–84; John Coffee to Mary Coffee, Oct. 24, 1813, Coffee Letters, Dyas Collection, TSLA.

8. Path Killer to Jackson, Oct. 22, 1813, in Moser, *Papers*, 2:439–40; John Reid to Elizabeth Reid, Oct. 24, 1813, Reid Papers; Owsley, *Struggle for the Gulf Borderlands*, 64.

9. Jackson to Chief Chinnabee, Oct. 19, 1813, Jackson to William Lewis, Oct. 24, 1813, Jackson to Blount, Oct. 24, 1813, and Jackson "to the Troops," Oct. 24, 1813, in Bassett, *Correspondence*, 1:334–38; Jackson to Path Killer, Oct. 24, 1813, in Moser, *Papers*, 2:441; John Reid to Elizabeth Reid, Oct. 24, 1813, Reid Papers; Kanon, *Tennesseans at War*, 74.

10. Gilbert, *Frontier Militiaman*, 27.

11. Henderson, "Littafuchee," 235–50; Braund, "Reflections," 276; John Reid to Elizabeth Reid, Oct. 29, 1813, Reid Papers; Jackson to Leroy Pope, Oct. 31, 1813, in Moser, *Papers*, 2:442–43; *Nashville Clarion and Tennessee Gazette*, Nov. 16, 1813; Edward D. Hobbs Claim, n.d., Cook Collection.

12. Call, "Journal," 19, Call Papers; John Reid to Nathan Reid, Nov. 6, 1813, Reid Papers.

13. Order to John Coffee dated Nov. 2, 1813, Coffee to Jackson, Nov. 2, 1813, and Jackson to Blount, Nov. 4, 1813, in Bassett, *Correspondence*, 1:340–41; Path Killer to Jackson, Oct. 25, 1813, Jackson Papers; John Reid to Nathan Reid, Nov. 6, 1813, Reid Papers; Coffee to Jackson, Nov. 4, 1813, in *Nashville Whig*, Nov. 9, 1813; Abram, " 'To Keep Bright the Bonds of Friendship,' " 243; Milford, *Memoirs*, 110; Crockett, *Narrative*, 87.

14. Crockett, *Narrative*, 89–90; Coffee to Jackson, Nov. 3, 1813, Cook Collection; Coffee to Jackson, Nov. 4, 1813, in *Nashville Whig*, Nov. 9, 1813; Call, "Journal," 20, Call Papers; Thrower, "Casualties and Consequences," 22 23.

15. Coffee to Jackson, Nov. 3, 1813, Cook Collection; John Reid to his father, Nov. 6, 1813, Reid Papers; Jackson to Leroy Pope, Nov. 4, 1813, in Bassett, *Correspondence*, 1:34.

16. Jackson to Blount, Nov. 4, 1813; John Coffee to Mary Coffee, Nov. 4, 1813, Coffee Letters; J. Norvell letter, Nov. 4, 1813, in *Nashville Whig*, Nov. 9, 1813.

17. John Reid to Elizabeth Reid, Nov. 4, 1813, Reid Papers.

18. Call, "Journal," 19–20, Call Papers.

19. John Lowry to Jackson and John Strother, Nov. 7, 1813, in Moser, *Papers*, 2:445–46.

20. J. Norvell letter, in *Nashville Whig*, Nov. 9, 1813; Crockett, *Narrative*, 89–90.

21. Parton, *Jackson*, 439; Jackson to William Moore, Nov. 15, 1833, Jackson Collections, TSLA; Andrew Jackson to Rachel Jackson, Dec. 19, 1813, in Bassett, *Correspondence*, 1:400–401; Andrew Jackson to Rachel Jackson, in Moser, *Papers*, 2:520.

22. Reid to his father, Nov. 6, 1813, and to Elizabeth Reid, Nov. 7, 1813, Reid Papers; Path Killer to Jackson, Oct. 25, 1813, Jackson Papers; Parton, *Jackson*, 1:452; *Washington Monitor*, Dec. 4, 1813; Jackson to Blount, Nov. 15, 1813, and Jackson to Armstrong, Nov. 20, 1813, in Bassett, *Correspondence*, 1:348, 355–56.

23. Jackson to Blount, Nov. 11, 1813, in Brannan, *Official Letters*, 265; Andrew Jackson to Rachel Jackson, Nov. 12, 1813, in Moser, *Papers*, 2:448; Jackson to Cocke, Nov. 16, 1813, in Bassett, *Correspondence*, 1:353.

24. Reid to his father, Nov. 21, 1813, Reid Papers; Call, "Journal," 21–22, Call Papers;

McCown, "Hartsell Memoranda," 125; Weir, *Paradise of Blood*, 221–22; White to Jackson, Nov. 7, 1813, and Jackson to Blount, Nov. 15, 1813, in Bassett, *Correspondence*, 1:350–51, 357; White, *Memoir*, 25; *Washington Monitor*, Dec. 4, 1813; Parton, *Jackson*, 1:450–51; Andrew Jackson to Rachel Jackson, Nov. 12, 1813, in Moser, *Papers*, 2:448.

25. Weir, *Paradise of Blood*, 222–23; Call, "Journal," 22, Call Papers; Jackson to Blount, Nov. 11, 1813, in Brannan, *Official Letters*, 265; Crockett, *Narrative*, 90–93; Kanon, *Tennesseans at War*, 78–79; Coffee to John Donelson, Nov. 12, 1813, in Coffee, "Letters," 444–45; Reid to his father, Dec. 24, 1813, Reid Papers.

26. Jackson to Blount, Nov. 11, 1813, in Brannan, *Official Letters*, 265; John Reid to Elizabeth Reid, Nov. 11, 1813, and John Reid to his father, Nov. 12, 1813, Reid Papers; Ephraim Foster to William Graham, Feb. 28, 1814, Jackson Papers; Jackson to Holmes, Nov. 4, 1813, Jackson Letters, Gilder Lehrman Institute.

27. Call, "Journal," 25–26, Call Papers; Samuel Bains letter, Nov. 25, 1813, ADAH; Petition of Mounted Riflemen, Platoon Officers, Nov. 12, 1813, and Petition of Company-Grade Officers of the Second Tennessee Volunteers, Nov. 13, 1813, Jackson Papers; Jackson to Blount, Nov. 14, 1813, Jackson to Cocke, Nov. 16, 1813, and William Lewis to Jackson, Nov. 20, 1813, in Barrett, *Correspondence*, 1:345, 353–54, 358.

28. Robert Grierson to Jackson, Nov. 13, 1813, and Jackson to Grierson, Nov. 17, 1813, in Moser, *Papers*, 2:452, 455–56; Jackson to Cocke, Nov. 18, 1813, in Bassett, *Correspondence*, 1:354; Kanon, *Tennesseans at War*, 80; Ephraim Foster to William Graham, Feb. 28, 1814, Jackson Papers.

29. Parton, *Jackson*, 1:451, 455; Cocke to Jackson, Nov. 14, 1813, in Bassett, *Correspondence*, 1:346; Hickey, *War of 1812*, 78.

30. Hemperley, "Hawkins' Trip," 131–32; Parton, *Jackson*, 452; Kanon, *Tennesseans at War*, 80–82; White to Cocke, Nov. 24, 1813, in *Nashville Whig*, Nov. 24, 1813; Cocke to Jackson, Nov. 27, 1813, and Jackson to Cocke, Dec. 2, 1813, in Bassett, *Correspondence*, 1:361, 364; Thrower, "Casualties and Consequences."

31. Stiggins, *Creek Indian History*, 122–24; Braund, "Reflections," 272–74; *Washington Mirror*, Dec. 4, 1813; Robert Grierson to Jackson, Nov. 13, 1813, in Moser, *Papers*, 2:452–53; Big Warrior and Little Prince to Hawkins, Oct. 7, 1813, Hawkins Papers.

12 THE RED STICKS RESILIENT

1. Thomas Bourke to Mitchell, Aug. 12, 1813, Mitchell to Bourke, Aug. 24, 1813, Monroe to Mitchell, Sept. 4, 1813, Daniel Parker to Mitchell, Sept. 15, 1813, Pinckney to Mitchell, Aug. 22, 1813, and Mitchell to Armstrong, Oct. 5, 1813, in *National Intelligencer*, Nov. 5, 1813; Tait, "Journal," 432.

2. Floyd, "Letters," 228, 229; Northern, *Men of Mark*, 91–92; *Washington Monitor*, Sept. 4, 1813; *Mirror of the Times*, Sept. 11, 1813; Tait, "Journal," 433; Hawkins to Armstrong, Sept. 21, 1813, in *ASP-IA*, 853.

3. Pinckney, *Thomas Pinckney*, 21–24, 79–81, 152–54, 189–94.

4. Pinckney to Jackson, Nov. 16 and 29, 1813, Jackson to Pinckney, Dec. 3, 1813, in Bassett, *Correspondence*, 1:352–55, 363–64; Owsley, *Struggle for the Gulf Borderlands*, 44–45.

5. Jackson to Pinckney, Dec. 11, 1813, in Bassett, *Correspondence*, 1:384–85.

6. Big Warrior and Little Prince to Hawkins, Oct. 7, 1813, Hawkins Papers; Big Warrior et al. to Floyd, Nov. 18, 1813, in Southerland and Brown, *Federal Road*, 42–43; Floyd to Jackson, Dec. 18, 1813, Jackson Papers.

7. Floyd, "Letters," 231, 233; Tait, "Journal," 434–35; Owsley, *Struggle for the Gulf Border-lands,* 51; *Columbian Museum and Savannah Advertiser,* March 3, 1814; Floyd to Jackson, Dec. 18, 1813, Jackson Papers.

8. Southerland and Brown, *Federal Road,* 43; Floyd to Jackson, Dec. 18, 1813, Jackson Papers; Weir, *Paradise of Blood,* 244; Bartram, *Travels,* 448–56; Stiggins, *Creek Indian History,* 124–25.

9. Floyd to Pinckney, Dec. 4, 1813, in Brannan, *Official Letters,* 283; John Floyd to Mary Floyd, Dec. 5, 1813, in Floyd, "Letters," 235; Tait, "Journal," 436.

10. Stiggins, *Creek Indian History,* 125–26.

11. Floyd to Pinckney, Dec. 4, 1813, in Brannan, *Official Letters,* 283–84; John Floyd to Mary Floyd, Dec. 5, 1813, in Floyd, "Letters," 235; Stiggins, *Creek Indian History,* 126.

12. John Floyd to Mary Floyd, Dec. 5, 1813, in Floyd, "Letters," 235; Stiggins, *Creek Indian History,* 126; Tait, "Journal," 436; Pickett, *History of Alabama,* 489n31.

13. Stiggins, *Creek Indian History,* 126; John Floyd to Mary Floyd, Dec. 5, 1813, in Floyd, "Letters," 235.

14. "Heroism!," *Georgia Journal,* Dec. 15, 1813.

15. John Floyd to Mary Floyd, Dec. 5, 1813, in Floyd, "Letters," 235–36; Floyd to Pinckney, Dec. 4, 1813, in Brannan, *Official Letters,* 284; Stiggins, *Creek Indian History,* 126–27.

16. Floyd to Pinckney, Dec. 4, 1813, in Brannan, *Official Letters,* 285; Tait, "Journal," 436; Stiggins, *Creek Indian History,* 127; *Georgia Journal,* Dec. 15, 1813.

17. Pinckney to Jackson, Dec. 12, 1813, in Moser, *Jackson Papers,* 2:487; Floyd to Jackson, Dec. 18, 1813, Jackson Papers; Owsley, *Struggle for the Gulf Borderlands,* 55.

18. Weir, *Paradise of Blood,* 255.

19. Adams to Early, Dec. 24, 1813, in Hays, "Georgia Military Affairs, 1801–1813," 3:316, unpublished compilation, GA.

20. Hemperley, "Hawkins' Trip," 130; Hawkins, *Creek Confederacy,* 45.

21. Adams to Early, Dec. 24, 1813, in Hays, "Georgia Military Affairs, 1801–1813," 3:316–20.

22. Gaines, "Reminiscences," 158–60; Section 14—Gaines notes, in Pickett, "Some Interesting Notes"; Claiborne to Flournoy, Sept. 21, 1813, CFP.

23. Claiborne to Flournoy, Oct. 22 and Nov. 6, 1813, Claiborne to Peter Isler, Oct. 29 and Nov. 25, 1813, Claiborne to Jackson, Nov. 12, 1813, and Flournoy to Claiborne, Oct. 28, 1813, CLF; Halbert and Ball, *Creek War,* 219–22; J. F. H. Claiborne, *Sam Dale,* 118–19.

24. Jones to Claiborne, Nov. 26, 1813, CLF; Section 1—Austill notes, and Section 2—Creagh notes, in Pickett, "Some Interesting Notes."

25. Halbert and Ball, *Creek War,* 231–35; Halbert, "Creek War Incidents," 98; Section 1—Austill notes, and Section 2—Creagh notes, in Pickett, "Some Interesting Notes"; Austill, "Canoe Battle," ADAH; J. F. H. Claiborne, *Sam Dale,* 119–27.

26. Flournoy to Claiborne, Nov. 7, 1813, Holmes to Claiborne, Nov. 10, 1813, Claiborne to Holmes, Nov. 12, 1813, CLF; Owsley, *Struggle for the Gulf Borderlands,* 46.

27. Claiborne to Flournoy, Nov. 12, 1813, Claiborne to Holmes, Nov. 21, 1813, and Claiborne to Peter Isler, Nov. 25, 1813, CLF; Halbert and Ball, *Creek War,* 241.

28. Claiborne to Jackson, Nov. 12 and 29, 1813, CLF; Halbert and Ball, *Creek War,* 242–43.

29. Claiborne to Jackson, Nov. 29, 1813, CLF.

30. Stiggins, *Creek Indian History,* 116; Meeks, *Romantic Passages,* 278–79; Cocks, "Catalogue of Trees," 189–94; J. F. H. Claiborne, *Sam Dale,* 140; Halbert, "Battle of the Holy Ground," 10YY96, and Henry Halbert to Lyman Draper, June 24, 1887, 10YY2, Tecumseh Papers; Halbert and Ball, *Creek War,* 246–48; Neal Smith to James Smiley, Jan. 8, 1814, ADAH; Russell to James Robertson, Jan. 9, 1814, in *Clarion and*

Tennessee State Gazette, March 1, 1814; Waselkov, "Return to the Holy Ground," 32, 36–37.

31. Officers of Carson's Regiment to Claiborne, Dec. 8, 1813, CLF; Halbert and Ball, *Creek War,* 244.

32. J. F. H. Claiborne, *Sam Dale,* 139; Halbert and Ball, *Creek War,* 343–44.

33. Section 2—Creagh notes, in Pickett, "Some Interesting Notes"; Halbert and Ball, *Creek War,* 346; Claiborne to Armstrong, Jan. 24, 1814, CLF; Russell to James Robertson, Jan. 9, 1814, in *Clarion and Tennessee State Gazette,* March 1, 1814.

34. Stiggins, *Creek Indian History,* 117–19; Testimony of Caesar, Jan. 18, 1814, Jackson Papers.

35. Halbert and Ball, *Creek War,* 346; Claiborne to Armstrong, Jan. 1, 1814, CLF; Russell to James Robertson, Jan. 9, 1814, in *Clarion and Tennessee State Gazette,* March 1, 1814.

36. Claiborne to Armstrong, Jan. 1, 1814, CLF; Joseph M. Wilcox to his father, Jan. 1, 1814, in *Narrative,* 5; Griffith, *McIntosh and Weatherford,* 129; Weir, *Paradise of Blood,* 287.

37. Claiborne to Armstrong, Jan. 1, 1814, CLF; Stiggins, *Creek Indian History,* 118; Austill, "Autobiography," 86; Russell to James Robertson, Jan. 9, 1814, in *Clarion and Tennessee State Gazette,* March 1, 1814; Halbert, "Battle of the Holy Ground"; Henry Halbert to Lyman Draper, Feb. 24, 1896, 10YY12, Tecumseh Papers; Neal Smith to James Smylie, Jan. 18, 1814, Smith Letter, ADAH; Joseph M. Wilcox to his father, Jan. 1, 1814, in *Narrative,* 5; Halbert and Ball, *Creek War,* 250–52.

38. Halbert, "Battle of the Holy Ground," "Pushmataha Continued," 10YY48, and Henry Halbert to Lyman Draper, Feb. 24, 1886, and June 24, 1887, 10YY2, Tecumseh Papers; Halbert, "Creek War Incidents," 105; Neal Smith to James Smiley, Jan. 8, 1814, Smith Letter, ADAH; Section 2—Creagh notes, Pickett, "Some Interesting Notes"; Testimony of Caesar, Jan. 18, 1814, Jackson Papers; Joseph M. Wilcox to his father, Jan. 1, 1814, in *Narrative,* 6; Nathaniel Claiborne, *Notes,* 25; Halbert and Ball, *Creek War,* 256–58.

39. Halbert and Ball, *Creek War,* 255–56; Griffith, *McIntosh and Weatherford,* 129–30; J. D. Dreisbach to Lyman Draper, July 1874, VV62, Tecumseh Papers; J. F. H. Claiborne, *Sam Dale,* 140–41; Woodward, *Reminiscences,* 100–101; Eggleston, *Red Eagle,* 222–25; Waselkov, "Return to the Holy Ground," 37.

40. Austill, "Autobiography," 86–87; Halbert, "Battle of the Holy Ground"; Halbert and Ball, *Creek War,* 259–60.

41. Claiborne to Armstrong, Jan. 1, 1814, CLF; Joseph M. Wilcox to his father, Jan. 1, 1814, in *Narrative,* 6; Halbert, "Battle of the Holy Ground"; Halbert and Ball, *Creek War,* 259–61.

42. Claiborne to Armstrong, Jan. 1 and 24, 1814, and R. B. Moore to Claiborne, Jan. 1, 1814, CLF; Joseph M. Wilcox to his father, Jan. 1, 1814, in *Narrative,* 6; Section 2—Creagh notes, in Pickett, "Some Interesting Notes"; Weir, *Paradise of Blood,* 297.

43. Halbert and Ball, *Creek War,* 262; Halbert, "Creek War Incidents," 100–101.

44. J. F. H. Claiborne, *Mississippi,* 340; Russell to Pinckney, Jan. 15, 1814, RG107, M221, NA.

13 ALL WE LACK IS POWDER AND LEAD

1. Halbert, "Creek War Incidents," 99–100; Stiggins, *Creek Indian History,* 121–22.

2. Woodward, *Reminiscences,* 101; Stiggins, *Creek Indian History,* 128; Floyd to Pinckney, Jan. 27, 1814, in *Mirror of the Times,* Feb. 5, 1814; John Durant to Alexander Durant, n.d., Claiborne Family Collection, ADAH; Russell to Claiborne, Jan. 15, 1814, CLF.

3. González Manrique to Ruiz de Apodaca, Dec. 31, 1813, No. 226, Legajo 1794, PPC.

4. Russell to Claiborne, Jan. 15, 1814, CLF; Pinckney to Armstrong, Feb. 3, 1814, RG107, M221, NA; Owsley, *Struggle for the Gulf Borderlands*, 48.

5. Some accounts credit Captain Dinkins with only one barge; the most reliable, however, accord him two boats and an escort of sixty infantrymen. Walter Bourke to Joseph Wilcox, Jan. 19, 1814, in *Narrative*, 8; J. F. H. Claiborne, *Sam Dale*, 143; Section 2—Creagh notes, in Pickett, "Some Interesting Notes"; Pickett, *History of Alabama*, 577.

6. J. F. H. Claiborne, *Sam Dale*, 144–46; Section 2—Creagh notes, in Pickett, "Some Interesting Notes"; Austill, "Autobiography," 87; Walter Bourke to Wilcox, Jan. 19, 1814, in *Narrative*, 9–11; Pinckney to Jackson, March 8, 1814, Jackson Papers; Stiggins, *Creek Indian History*, 155.

7. Gaines, "Reminiscences," 161; Adam James to the Head Chief of the Creek Nation, Nov. 29, 1813, ADAH; McKee to Coffee, Oct. 21, 1813, James Allen to Jackson, Jan. 9, 1814, George and James Colbert to Jackson, Jan. 10, 1814, and McKee's undated report, Jackson Papers; Moshulitubbee to Armstrong, Dec. 31, 1813, in Carter, *Territorial Papers*, 6:442.

8. Floyd to Jackson, Jan. 2 and 24, 1814, Jackson Papers; Owsley, *Struggle for the Gulf Borderlands*, 56; Tait, "Journal," 438.

9. Floyd to Pinckney, Jan. 27, 1814, in *Mirror of the Times*, Feb. 5, 1814; Tait, "Journal," 438; Stiggins, *Creek Indian History*, 164n.

10. Stiggins, *Creek Indian History*, 129–32; Griffith, *McIntosh and Weatherford*, 134–35; Floyd to Pinckney, Jan. 27, 1814, in *Mirror of the Times*, Feb. 5, 1814; Owsley, *Struggle for the Gulf Borderlands*, 57; Woodward, *Reminiscences*, 102. According to Woodward and Stiggins, Weatherford went home. Other versions of the episode contend that Weatherford relented and joined the attack. Henry Halbert to Lyman Draper, April 2, 1886, 10YY16, Halbert, "William Weatherford," 10YY37, "Floyd and Weatherford and the Battle of Calabee Swamp," 10YY46, and "The Battle of Calabee Swamp," 10YY97, Tecumseh Papers; Rowland, *Jackson's Campaign*, 117.

11. Halbert, "The Battle of Calabee Swamp," 10YY45, and "The Battle of Calabee Swamp, January 26 [*sic*], 1814," 10YY97, Tecumseh Papers; *Georgia Journal*, March 16, 1814; Floyd to Pinckney, Jan. 27, 1814, in *Augusta Chronicle*, Feb. 4, 1814; Northern, *Men of Mark*, 93.

12. Floyd to Pinckney, Jan. 27, 1814, in *Augusta Chronicle*, Feb. 4, 1814; Floyd to Pinckney, Jan. 31, 1814, in *Columbus Museum and Savannah Advertiser*, Feb. 17, 1814; Halbert, "William Weatherford," "Floyd and Weatherford and the Battle of Calabee Swamp," and "Battle of Calabee Swamp," 10YY103, Tecumseh Papers.

13. Floyd to Pinckney, Jan. 27, 1814, in *Augusta Chronicle*, Feb. 4, 1814; Woodward, "Reminiscences," 102; Halbert, "Battle of Calabee Swamp," 10YY45, Tecumseh Papers.

14. Floyd to Pinckney, Jan. 27, 1814, in *Augusta Chronicle*, Feb. 4, 1814; Tait, "Journal," 438–39.

15. Stiggins, *Creek Indian History*, 132, 135.

16. Floyd to Jackson, Feb. 4, 1814, Jackson Papers; Stiggins, *Creek Indian History*, 132.

17. Halbert, "Tecumseh's Chickasaw Visit," 4YY75, Tecumseh Papers.

18. Halbert, "Battle of Calabee Swamp"; Floyd to Pinckney, Jan. 31, and Feb. 2, 1814, in *Columbus Museum and Savannah Advertiser*, Feb. 17, 1814; Charles Williamson et al. to Floyd, March 3, 1814, in *Georgia Journal*, March 9, 1814; *Mirror of the Times*, March 4, 1814; *Georgia Journal*, Feb. 9, 1814; Owsley, *Struggle for the Gulf Borderlands*, 59–60.

19. Floyd to Jackson, Feb. 4, 1814, Jackson Papers.

14 TENNESSEANS TO THE REAR

1. Las Cases, *Journal*, 4:197.
2. Parton, *Jackson*, 1:460–64; Reid and Eaton, *Jackson*, 70–72; Samuel Bains to Christiana Bains, Nov. 25, 1813, Samuel Bains Letter, and "Autobiography of Rev. Ebenezer Hearn," ADAH; Reid to "Dear Sir," Nov. 21, 1813, and to Betsy Reid, Nov. 23, 1813, Reid Papers; Martin, *Self Vindication*, 4, 28; Jackson to Robert Hays, Jan. 14, 1814, Jackson Papers; Call, "Journal," 28–33, Call Papers.
3. John Reid to Betsy Reid, Dec. 3, 1813, Reid Papers; Jackson to Cocke, Dec. 2, 1813, Cocke to Jackson, Dec. 3, 1813, and Jackson to Coffee, Dec. 5, 1813, in Bassett, *Correspondence*, 1:364, 368; Jackson to Pinckney, Dec. 13, 1813, in Moser, *Papers*, 2:484.
4. Jackson to Blackburn, Dec. 3, 1813, in Bassett, *Correspondence*, 1:365; Reid and Eaton, *Jackson*, 74–75.
5. John Reid to Betsy Reid, Dec. 3, 1813, Reid Papers; Martin to Jackson, Dec. 4, 1813, and Jackson to Martin, Dec. 6, 1813, in Martin, *Self Vindication*, 4–9.
6. Martin, *Self Vindication*, 10–18, 20, 24–26, 30–34; Parton, *Jackson*, 468–71; Kanon, *Tennesseans at War*, 84; Jackson to Coffee, Dec. 11, 1813, in Bassett, *Correspondence*, 1:382–83.
7. Call, "Journal," 40–43, Call Papers; John Farr and Moses Glasscock statements, in Martin, *Self Vindication*, 35–36; Parton, *Jackson*, 471–75; Andrew Jackson to Rachel Jackson, Dec. 29, 1813, Jackson Papers.
8. Call, "Journal," 44–45, Call Papers.
9. Ibid., 45; Parton, *Jackson*, 84–89; Jackson to Blount, Dec. 12, 1813, in Moser, *Papers*, 2:479–80; Jackson to Blount, Dec. 13, 1813, in Bassett, *Correspondence*, 1:390–91.
10. Jackson to Coffee, Dec. 12, 1813, Jackson to Cocke, Dec. 15, 1813, and Jackson to Armstrong, Dec. 30, 1813, in Bassett, *Correspondence*, 1:386, 389, 423–24; Parton, *Jackson*, 89; McCown, "Hartsell Memoranda," 127–29, 131; Kanon, *Tennesseans at War*, 87.
11. Reid and Eaton, *Jackson*, 99; Jackson to Coffee, Dec. 18, 1813, in Bassett, *Correspondence*, 1:397.
12. Coffee to Jackson, Dec. 18, 20, and 28, 1813, in Bassett, *Correspondence*, 398, 401, 413; Call, "Journal," 53, 58, Call Papers.
13. Wallis, "Crockett," 117–18; Folmsbee, "Early Career," 69.
14. John Coffee to Mary Coffee, Dec. 19 and 27, 1813, John Coffee to John Donelson, Dec. 22, 1813, in Coffee, "Letters," 177–78; Reid and Eaton, *Jackson*, 99–108; Andrew Jackson to Rachel Jackson, Dec. 19, 1813, and Jackson to Hugh White, Jan. 6, 1814, in Bassett, *Correspondence*, 401, 435.
15. Blount to Jackson, Dec. 22, 1813, and Jackson to Blount, Dec. 28, 1813, in Parton, *Jackson*, 1:478–79, 482–83.
16. Jackson to Blount, Dec. 29, 1813, in Bassett, *Correspondence*, 1:416–19.
17. Andrew Jackson to Rachel Jackson, Dec. 19, 1813, in Bassett, *Correspondence*, 401; Call, "Journal," 64, Call Papers, FSA.
18. Hickey, *War of 1812*, 77–78, 111–12, 125, 164–65.
19. McCown, "Hartsell Memoranda," 136–38; Jackson to Pinckney, Dec. 31, 1813, in Moser, *Jackson Letters*, 2:519–20.
20. Jackson to Coffee, Dec. 31, 1813, in Bassett, *Correspondence*, 1:429; Parton, *Jackson*, 506–7.
21. Call, "Journal," 65–68, Call Papers; Reid and Eaton, *Jackson*, 112–16.
22. McCown, "Hartsell Memoranda," 141; Gideon Morgan to Armstrong, May 5, 1814, Morgan Papers; Jackson to Cocke, Dec. 28, 1813, in Bassett, *Correspondence*, 1:414–15.
23. Carroll to the Citizens of West Tennessee, n.d., in *Nashville Whig*, Dec. 15, 1813; Jackson

to Carroll, Dec. 23, 1813, Jackson to Blount, Dec. 26, 1813, Jackson to Armstrong, Dec. 30, 1813, Jackson to Blount, Jan. 7, 1814, and Jackson to Pinckney, Jan. 29, 1814, in Bassett, *Correspondence*, 1:407–8, 409–10, 424, 436, 447; Carroll to Jackson, Dec. 23, 1813, and Jackson to Pinckney, Dec. 24, 1813, in Moser, *Jackson Letters*, 2:500–501, 502–3.

15 JACKSON COURTS DISASTER

1. Blount to Cocke, Jan. 3, 1814, OSW, LR, RG107, M221, NA; Pinckney to Jackson, Jan. 9, 1814, in Bassett, *Correspondence*, 1:438–39.
2. Pinckney to Jackson, Jan. 9, 1814, and Jackson to Pinckney, Jan. 29, 1814, in Bassett, *Correspondence*, 447–48; John Reid to Nathan Reid, Feb. 14, 1814, Reid Papers.
3. John Reid to Nathan Reid, Feb. 14, 1814, Reid Papers; Lemuel Snow to his wife, Jan. 2, 1814, Snow Letter, ADAH.
4. McKenney and Hall, *Indian Tribes*, 101–2, 104–10.
5. Jackson to Hugh White, Jan. 6, 1814, Jackson to John Williams, Jan. 7, 1814, and Jackson to Pinckney, Jan. 29, 1814, in Bassett, *Correspondence*, 1:436, 438, 447–48; Return J. Meigs to Jackson, Feb. 1, 1814, Jackson Papers; Weir, *Paradise of Blood*, 358–59.
6. Call, "Journal," 79–81, Call Papers; Coffee to John Donelson, Jan. 28, 1814, Coffee Letters; Jackson to Pinckney, Jan. 29, 1814, in Bassett, *Correspondence*, 1:449.
7. Andrew Jackson to Rachel Jackson, Jan. 28, 1814, and Jackson to Pinckney, Jan. 29, 1814, in Bassett, *Correspondence*, 1:444–45, 449–50; Call, "Journal," 82–85, Call Papers; Ephraim Foster to Robert Foster, Jan. 29, 1814, Braund Papers, HBNMP; John Coffee to Mary Coffee, Jan. 30, 1814, Coffee Letters.
8. Call, "Journal," 86–88, Call Papers.
9. Andrew Jackson to Rachel Jackson, Jan. 28, 1814, and Jackson to Pinckney, Feb. 17, 1814, in Bassett, *Correspondence*, 1:445, 465; Reid and Eaton, *Jackson*, 129–30.
10. Call, "Journal," 88, Call Papers.
11. Andrew Jackson to Rachel Jackson, Jan. 28, 1814, and Jackson to Pinckney, Jan. 29, 1814, in Bassett, *Correspondence*, 1:445–46, 451; Reid and Eaton, *Jackson*, 131–32.
12. Reid and Eaton, *Jackson*, 132–33; Jackson to Pinckney, Jan. 29, 1814, in Bassett, *Correspondence*, 1:451; Call, "Journal," 88–89, Call Papers; Ephraim Foster to Robert Foster, Jan. 29, 1814, Braund Papers; Court Martial of Colonel Nicholas Perkins, Jan. 27, 1814, and Stump to Jackson, Jan. 31, 1814, Jackson Papers; John Reid to Nathan Reid, Feb. 14, 1814, Reid Papers; Abram, "'To Keep Bright the Bonds of Friendship,'" 145; Mooney, "Myths of the Cherokees," 92; Cocke to Early, Jan. 28, 1814, Cuyler Collection, UGA.
13. Andrew Jackson to Rachel Jackson, Jan. 28, 1814, Jackson Papers.
14. Call, "Journal," 90, Call Papers; Ephraim Foster to Robert Foster, Jan. 29, 1814, Braund Papers; Jackson to Pinckney, Jan. 29, 1814, in Bassett, *Correspondence*, 1:452; "Interesting Old Gun."
15. Reid and Eaton, *Jackson*, 137; Coffee to John Donelson, Jan. 28, 1814, in Coffee, "Letters," 180.
16. Reid and Eaton, *Jackson*, 136–37; Call, "Journal," 92, Call Papers.
17. Jackson to Pinckney, Jan. 29, 1814, in Bassett, *Correspondence*, 1:453.
18. Quoted in Parton, *Jackson*, 1:498; Kanon, "Before Horseshoe Bend," 118.
19. Overton to Jackson, Feb. 2, 1814, in Moser, *Jackson Letters*, 3:29–30; William B. Lewis to Jackson, Jan. 26, 1814, and Andrew Jackson to Rachel Jackson, Jan. 28, 1814, in Bassett, *Correspondence*, 1:447.

20. Jackson to Coffee, Feb. 17, 1814, in Moser, *Jackson Letters,* 3:33; Andrew Jackson to Rachel Jackson, Jan. 28 and Feb. 17, 1814, in Bassett, *Correspondence,* 1:447, 464.

21. Rachel Jackson to Andrew Jackson, Feb. 10, 1814, in Bassett, *Correspondence,* 1:459–60.

22. Andrew Jackson to Rachel Jackson, Feb. 21, 1814, in Moser, *Jackson Letters,* 3:34.

23. Quoted in Kanon, *Tennesseans at War,* 93.

24. Call, "Journal," 92–94, Call Papers; Jackson to Call, Jan. 30, 1814, in Bassett, *Correspondence,* 1:450.

25. William Lewis to Jackson, Jan. 26, 1814, Andrew Jackson to Rachel Jackson, Jan. 28, 1814, Rachel Jackson to Andrew Jackson, March 11, 1814, Jackson to Blount, March 10, 1814, Pinckney to Jackson, March 11, 1814, Andrew Jackson to Rachel Jackson, March 12, 1814, and Doherty to Jackson, March 2 and 6, 1814, in Bassett, *Correspondence,* 1:447, 473–78; Jackson to Blount, Feb. 8 and March 20, 1814, Blount to Jackson, March 13 and 20, 1814, and Pinckney to Jackson, March 13, 1814, Jackson Papers; Armstrong, "George Doherty," *Some Tennessee Heroes,* vol. 4 (no pagination); Jackson to Pinckney, March 2 and 6, 1814, in Moser, *Jackson Letters,* 3:36; John Coffee to Mary Coffee, Coffee Letters; Parton, *Jackson,* 1:500–501.

26. Parton, *Jackson,* 1:501; Jackson to Anthony, March 5, 1814, Jackson Papers; John Reid to Betsy Reid, March 11, 1814, Reid Papers.

27. Scott, *Memoir,* 33–36; Parton, *Jackson,* 1:499–500; Pinckney to Jackson, Feb. 10, 1814, Jackson Papers; Jackson to Pinckney, Feb. 12, 1814, in Bassett, *Correspondence,* 1:461.

16 A SLOW, LABORIOUS SLAUGHTER

1. Jackson to Pinckney, March 4, 1814, in Bassett, *Correspondence,* 1:474; Jackson to Pinckney, March 7, 1814, in Moser, *Jackson Letters,* 3:43.

2. Parton, *Jackson,* 1:507–8.

3. "Proceedings of Courts-Martial," 251, 256–58.

4. Parton, *Jackson,* 1:508–11; *Review of the Battle of the Horseshoe,* 6–7; General Orders, Case of John Woods, March 14, 1814, Jackson to Woods, March 14, 1814, and Jackson to Pinckney, March 14, 1814, in Bassett, *Correspondence,* 1:479–81; Royall, *Letters from Alabama,* 117.

5. Jackson to Pinckney, March 14, 1814, in Bassett, *Correspondence,* 1:481; Record of the Strength of General Jackson's Division of Militia from the State of Tennessee in the Service of the United States, April 2, 1814, Jackson Collection; Hale and Merritt, *History of Tennessee,* 2:259–60; Morgan to Jackson, Feb. 5 and 9, 1814, Jackson Papers; Abram, *Forging a Cherokee-American Alliance,* 75; Coffee to Jackson, April 1, 1814, in *Niles' Weekly Register,* April 30, 1814; "Our Correspondence," *Richmond Dispatch,* Sept. 16, 1861.

6. Jackson to Pinckney, Feb. 16, 1814, and Pinckney to Jackson, Feb. 17 and 26, 1814, in Bassett, *Correspondence,* 1:462–63, 466–67, 470–71; John Reid to Nathan Reid, March 15, 1814, Reid Papers.

7. Rachel Jackson to Andrew Jackson, March 21, 1814, in Bassett, *Correspondence,* 482–83; Reid and Eaton, *Jackson,* 148.

8. Jackson to Pinckney, March 22, 1814, in Bassett, *Correspondence,* 1:484; John Reid to Nathan Reid, March 15, 1814, Reid Papers; Jackson to John Hutchings, March 22, 1814, Jackson Papers.

9. Jackson to John Hutchings, March 22, 1814, and Jackson to Robert Steele, March 22, 1814, Jackson Papers.

10. Jackson to Pinckney, March 23, 1814, Jackson Papers.

11. John Reid to Betsy Reid, March 21, 1814, Reid Papers; Jackson to Pinckney, March 23, 1814, Jackson Papers; John Coffee to Mary Coffee, March 22, 1814, Coffee Letters.

12. General Orders, Fort Williams, March 24, 1814, in Bassett, *Correspondence*, 1:486–88.

13. Kanon, *Tennesseans at War*, 99; Reid and Eaton, *Jackson*, 149; John Coffee to Mary Coffee, April 1, 1814, Coffee Letters.

14. Isham, "Western Muscogee Perspective," 247–48.

15. Sheldon, "Archeology," 98–99, 101, 102; Parton, *Jackson*, 514; Reid to a friend, March 29, 1814, in *Clarion and Tennessee State Gazette*, April 12, 1814; Jackson to Blount, March 31, 1814, in Bassett, *Correspondence*, 1:490.

16. Kanon, "Slow, Laborious Slaughter," 6; Jensen, "Horseshoe Bend," 146, 148–51, 153.

17. Jackson to Blount, March 31, 1814, in Bassett, *Correspondence*, 1:489; Coffee to Jackson, April 1, 1814, in Morse, *Jackson Letters*, 3:55.

18. Jackson to Pinckney, March 28, 1814, in Bassett, *Correspondence*, 1:488–89; John Reid to Nathan Reid, April 5, 1814, Reid Papers.

19. Kanon, "Slow, Laborious Slaughter," 7; Jackson to Blount, March 31, 1814, in Bassett, *Correspondence*, 1:490; John Reid to Betsy Reid, April 1, 1814, and to Nathan Reid, April 5, 1814, Reid Papers; Halbert, "Incidents of the Battle of the Horse Shoe-II," 10YY57, Tecumseh Papers; Carroll to a friend, April 1, 1814, in *Clarion and Tennessee State Gazette*, April 12, 1814; Parton, *Jackson*, 1:517; John Coffee to Mary Coffee, April 2, 1814, Jackson Collection.

20. *Life of Sam Houston*, 1; Heiskell, *Andrew Jackson and Early Tennessee*, 2:154–55; Haley, *Houston*, 8–9, 11–12.

21. President James Monroe later presented Tucfo, Reese, and their companion with ornately decorated rifles in honor of their exploits. "Charles Reese Sr.," *Montgomery Advertiser*, March 26, 1911; Abram, "Cherokees in the Creek War," 133; Abram, *Forging a Cherokee-American Alliance*, 79; Agnew, "Whale's Rifle," 472; Coffee to Jackson, April 1, 1814, in Morse, *Correspondence*, 3:55.

22. Coffee to Jackson, April 1, 1814, in Morse, *Correspondence*, 3:55; Kanon, "Slow, Laborious Slaughter," 6; "Our Correspondence," *Richmond Dispatch*, Sept. 16, 1861; Morgan to Jackson, April 1, 1814, in *Clarion and Tennessee State Gazette*, April 1, 1814.

23. Kanon, "Slow, Laborious Slaughter," 6; Nathaniel Claiborne, *Notes*, 40–41.

24. Kanon, *Tennesseans at War*, 101; Kanon, "Slow, Laborious Slaughter," 7; Parton, *Jackson*, 1:517; Jackson to Blount, March 31, 1814, in Bassett, *Correspondence*, 1:491, 492; Halbert, "Incidents of the Battle of the Horse Shoe-II"; Carroll to a friend, April 1, 1814, in *Clarion and Tennessee State Gazette*, April 12, 1814; John Reid to Betsy Reid, April 1, 1814, and to Nathan Reid, April 5, 1814, Reid Papers.

25. Kanon, *Tennesseans at War*, 101; Alexander McCulloch to Francis McCulloch, April 1, 1814, in Cutrer, "Tallapoosa," 98; John Reid to Betsy Reid, April 1, 1814, Reid Papers.

26. Halbert, "Horse Shoe Incidents," 10YY101, Tecumseh Papers; Braund, "Red Sticks," 97.

27. Haley, *Houston*, 15; *Life of Sam Houston*, 2; Heiskell, *Andrew Jackson and Early Tennessee*, 2:155.

28. McKenney and Hall, *Indian Tribes*, 1:106–7; Martin, *Sacred Revolt*, 1; John Reid to Betsy Reid, April 1, 1814, Reid Papers.

29. Jackson to Blount, March 31, 1814, in Bassett, *Correspondence*, 1:492; Halbert, "Incidents of the Battle of the Horse-Shoe," 10YY57, Tecumseh Papers; *Montgomery Advertiser*, March 26, 1811.

30. Coffee to Jackson, April 1, 1814, in Morse, *Papers*, 3:55; Alexander McCulloch to Francis

McCulloch, April 1, 1814, McCulloch Family Papers, University of Texas; "Our Correspondence," *Richmond Dispatch,* Sept. 16, 1861.

31. Kanon, *Tennesseans at War,* 102; Coffee to Houston, April 25, 1828, Jackson Collections; Hanley, *Houston,* 15; *Life of Sam Houston,* 2.

32. Halbert, "Incidents of the Battle of the Horse-Shoe," 10YY56, and "An Incident of the Battle of the Horse Shoe," 10YY57, Tecumseh Papers.

33. Haley, *Houston,* 16; *Life of Sam Houston,* 3; Parton, *Jackson,* 1:521.

34. McKenney and Hall, *Indian Tribes,* 1:107.

35. Halbert, "Incidents of the Battle of the Horse Shoe-II" and "Horse Shoe Incidents," 10YY94, Tecumseh Papers; Kanon, *Tennesseans at War,* 104; Braund, "Reflections," 281–82; "A Veteran Hero," *Montgomery Weekly Public Ledger,* Sept. 11, 1883.

36. Coffee to Houston, April 25, 1828, Jackson Collections; *Review of Horseshoe,* 4–5; Jackson to Blount, March 3, 1814, in Bassett, *Correspondence,* 1:492.

37. "Extract of a Letter from a Distinguished Officer Dated March 29, 1814," in *Clarion and Tennessee State Gazette,* April 12, 1814; John Coffee to Mary Coffee, April 1, 1814, Coffee Letters; Levi Lee Diary, March 27, 1814, TSLA; Coffee to John Donelson, April 1, 1814, in Coffee, "Letters," 182; Meigs to John Armstrong, June 4, 1814, RG 75, BIA, CIART, NA; "Cherokee Warriors," *Niles' Weekly Register,* April 19, 1817; Mooney, "Myths of the Cherokees," 96.

38. McKenney and Hall, *Indian Tribes,* 1:107–8; James Moore and James Taylor to David Adams, May 20, 1814, Cuyler Collection, UGA.

39. Andrew Jackson to Rachel Jackson, April 1, 1814, in Bassett, *Correspondence,* 1:493; Coffee to John Donelson, April 1, 1814, in Coffee, "Letters," 182.

I 7 AN ELUSIVE PEACE

1. Section 12—James notes, in Pickett, "Some Interesting Notes."

2. Dowd, *Spirited Resistance,* 187; Akers, "Unexpected Challenge," 241; Green, *Politics of Indian Removal,* 42; Woodward, *Reminiscences,* 42–43; J. A. Gordon to Charles Cameron, April 13, 1814, Cochrane Papers.

3. Jackson to James Baxter, April 1, 1814, Jackson Papers; "Proclamation to the Officers and Soldiers Who Have Lately Returned from the Expedition to the Tallapoosa," April 2, 1814, in Bassett, *Correspondence,* 1:494–95.

4. Jackson to John Armstrong, April 25, 1814, in *ASP-MA,* 3:790; Coffee to John Donelson, April 26, 1814, Coffee Letters; Undated memorandum of John Reid, in Bassett, *Correspondence,* 1:500.

5. Jackson to John Armstrong, April 25, 1814, in *ASP-MA,* 3:790; John Coffee to Mary Coffee, April 6, 1814, Coffee Letters; Joseph Graham to Pinckney, April 6, 1814, in Graham, *General Joseph Graham,* 154; Pinckney to Jackson, April 7, 14, and 16, 1814, Jackson to Pinckney, April 5, 1814, in Bassett, *Correspondence,* 1:495, 496, 501–2, 506; Jackson to Pinckney, April 14, 1814, in Moser, *Papers,* 3:62; Owsley, *Struggle for the Gulf Borderlands,* 83.

6. Hawkins, *Creek Confederacy,* 38; Willett, *Narrative,* 104.

7. John Coffee to Mary Coffee, April 18, 1814, Coffee Letters.

8. There are multiple versions of Weatherford's surrender to Jackson and the words that passed between them. Some are clearly fanciful, others likely embellished. I have attempted to reconstruct the scene—beyond doubt one of the most symbolically

dramatic of the Creek War—incorporating the most plausible elements from what I judge to be reliable sources. Woodward, "Reminiscences," 91–94; Orr, "Surrender of Weatherford," 57–58; J. D. Driesbach to Lyman Draper, July 1814, VV62, Tecumseh Papers; Reid and Eaton, *Jackson*, 164–65.

9. Griffith, *McIntosh and Weatherford*, 154–55; Reid and Eaton, *Jackson*, 165–66.

10. Kanon, *Tennesseans at War*, 106; Jackson to Blount, April 18, 1814, in Bassett, *Correspondence*, 1:503.

11. Waselkov, "Fort Jackson," 162; Joseph Graham to Pinckney, June 14, 1814, Graham Papers, Southern Historical Collection, University of North Carolina, Chapel Hill; Thompson, *Weatherford*, 568.

12. Stiggins, *Creek Indian History*, 135–36; J. A. Pearson to Joseph Graham, June 14, 1814, in Graham, *General Joseph Graham*, 157; Edmund Gaines to James Monroe, June 2, 1815, Jackson Papers.

13. Jackson to Blount, April 18, 1814, in Bassett, *Correspondence*, 1:503; John Jones to Thomas Hart Benton, July 4, 1814, and Benton to Flournoy, July 5, 1814, Jackson Collections; Halbert, "Creek War Incidents," 102.

14. Halbert, "Pushmataha Continued," "Charley Hoentubbee's Version of the Incident of Pushmataha and the Young Choctaw Renegades," 10YY58, "Incident of Pushmataha and the Choctaw Renegades: Captain Doss's Version," 10YY59, and "The Campbell Stonie Hadjo Version of the Incident of Pushmataha and the Choctaw Renegades," 10YY60, Tecumseh Papers.

15. Graham to William Hawkins, April 25, 1814, in *Liberty Hall*, June 14, 1814; Williams, "Joseph Graham"; Mahon, "Carolina Brigade," 422.

16. Parton, *Jackson*, 1:579–80; Graham to William Hawkins, April 25, 1814, in *Liberty Hall*, June 14, 1814; Benjamin Hawkins to William Hawkins, April 26, 1814, in *Charleston Courier*, May 24, 1814.

17. Armstrong to Pinckney, March 17 and 28, 1814, in *ASP-IA*, 1:836–37; Pinckney to Jackson, April 18, 1814, Jackson Papers.

18. Jackson to Armstrong, April 25, 1814, in Bassett, *Correspondence*, 1:508.

19. George Doherty et al. to George Campbell, April 6, 1814, and Coffee to William Lewis, April 18, 1814, in Bassett, *Correspondence*, 1:497, 2:4; Owsley, *Struggle for the Gulf Borderlands*, 86–87; Pinckney to Hawkins, April 22, 1814, in *ASP-IA*, 1:858.

20. Rachel Jackson to Andrew Jackson, April 12, 1814, and Overton to Jackson, May 8, 1814, in Bassett, *Correspondence*, 1:499, 2:1.

21. *Nashville Whig*, May 16, 1814; Parton, *Jackson*, 1:542; Andrew Jackson to Rachel Jackson, May 2, 1814, in Moser, *Papers*, 3:71; Holmes to Blount, April 20, 1814, Jackson Papers.

22. Quoted in *Nashville Whig*, May 16, 1814.

18 BETRAYAL AT FORT JACKSON

1. Waselkov, "Fort Jackson and the Aftermath," 162–63; Mahon, "Carolina Brigade," 423; Pearson to Graham, June 13, 1814, in Graham, *General Joseph Graham*, 156–57; Graham to Pinckney, May 21 and June 7, 1814, Joseph Graham Mississippi Territory Military Records, ADAH.

2. Halbert, "Creek War Incidents," 101–2.

3. Hawkins to Pinckney, April 25, 1814, in *ASP-IA*, 1:858; Statement of Jake Turner, July 12, 1814, Jackson Papers; Waselkov, "Fort Jackson and the Aftermath," 163.

4. Horsman, *War of 1812*, 226; Graham to Pinckney, July 16, 1814, Graham Mississippi Ter-

ritory Military Records; Charles Cameron to Earl Bathurst, April 17 and July 4, 1814, Cochrane Papers; Heidler, "Where All Behaved Well," 184.

5. Horsman, *War of 1812*, 225–26; Alexander Durant et al. to Cochrane, n.d., contained in Cochrane to Charles Cameron, June 23, 1814, Cochrane Papers; Heidler, "Where All Behaved Well," 184; Mahon, "British Strategy," 287–88.

6. Cochrane to Charles Cameron, July 4, 1814, and Cameron to Earl Bathurst, July 4, 1814, Cochrane Papers; Mahon, "British Strategy," 288–90; Owsley, *Struggle for the Gulf Borderlands*, 98.

7. Big Warrior et al. to Hawkins, June 13, 1814, in *American and Commercial Daily Advertiser*, July 2, 1814; George Gaines to James Gaines, June 11, 1814, in Gaines, "Letters," 190.

8. Reid and Eaton, *Jackson*, 182.

9. Jackson to Williams, May 18, 1814, in Bassett, *Correspondence*, 2:3–4.

10. Reid and Eaton, *Jackson*, 182; Parton, *Jackson*, 1:549; Armstrong to Jackson, May 22, 24, and 28, 1814, and Jackson to Armstrong, June 13, 1814, in Bassett, *Correspondence*, 2:3–5, 7–8.

11. Jackson to Armstrong, July 16, 1814, and to Rachel Jackson, July 16, 1814, in Morse, *Papers*, 3:86, 89; Faust, "Another Look," 213–14; Waselkov, "Fort Jackson and the Aftermath," 165.

12. Jackson to Hawkins, July 11, 1814, Jackson to Coffee, July 17, 1814, and Jackson to Armstrong, July 31, 1814, in Bassett, *Correspondence*, 2:15–17, 23.

13. Owsley, *Struggle for the Gulf Borderlands*, 89; Parton, *Jackson*, 1:116–17.

14. Andrew Jackson to Rachel Jackson, Aug. 5, 1814, and to the Cherokee and Creek Indians, Aug. 5, 1814, in Moser, *Papers*, 3:103–4; Meigs to Jackson, Aug. 4, 1814, Jackson Papers; Remini, *Jackson and American Empire*, 226–27; "Extracts from the Minutes of Occurrences at Fort Jackson," BIA, Documents Regarding Negotiations of Ratified Indian Treaties, RG 75, NA; Jackson to Blount, Aug. 9, 1814, in Bassett, *Correspondence*, 2:24.

15. Big Warrior to Hawkins, April 6, 1814, in Moser, *Papers*, 3:106–8.

16. "Extracts from the Minutes of Occurrences at Fort Jackson"; Saunt, "Taking Account of Property," 739; Jackson to Big Warrior, Aug. 7, 1814, in Moser, *Papers*, 3:109–11; Jackson to Gaines, Nov. 26, 1815, Jackson Papers.

17. Hawkins to Pinckney, Aug. 8, 1814, and "Articles of Agreement and Capitulation, Made and Concluded This Ninth Day of August, 1814, Between Major General Andrew Jackson, on Behalf of the President of the United States of America, and the Chiefs, Deputies, and Warriors of the Creek Nation," in *ASP-IA*, 826–27, 837–38; "Extracts from the Minutes of Occurrences at Fort Jackson"; Jackson to Blount, Aug. 9, 1814, in Bassett, *Correspondence*, 2:24; Saunt, "Taking Account of Property," 739–40; Thrower, "Casualties and Consequences," 25–26; Owsley, *Struggle for the Gulf Borderlands*, 91, 96–97; Big Warrior to Jackson, Oct. 3, 1815, Mitchell Papers, Ayers Collection, Newberry Library, Chicago; "Creek Treaty," *Clarion and Tennessee State Gazette*, Aug. 23, 1814.

18. Waselkov, "Fort Jackson and the Aftermath," 165; Andrew Jackson to Rachel Jackson, Aug. 10, 1814, in Moser, *Papers*, 3:115; Jackson to Overton, Aug. 20, 1814, and Big Warrior to Jackson, April 16, 1816, Jackson Papers; Jackson to Armstrong, Aug. 10, 1814, in Bassett, *Correspondence*, 2:24; Remini, *Jackson and American Empire*, 228–31.

19 A SCALP FOR A SCALP

1. Pigot to Cochrane, June 8, 1814, Cochrane Papers; Hawkins to Early, Aug. 23, 1814, Cuyler Collection, UGA.

2. Mahon, "British Strategy," 287–88.

3. Ibid., 289–91; Owsley, "Prophet of War," 283; Owsley, "British and Indian Activities," 115; Doyle, "Panton, Leslie Letters," 63.

4. Mahon, "British Strategy," 293, 295; Jackson to Armstrong, Aug. 10, 1814, William Robinson and Charles Muir to Jackson, July 28, 1814, and Jackson to González Manrique, Aug. 24, 1814, in Bassett, *Correspondence*, 2:21–22, 25–26, 28–29.

5. Horsman, *War of 1812*, 231–32; Waselkov, "Fort Jackson and the Aftermath," 163; Remini, *Jackson and American Empire*, 236–38; Owsley, "Prophet of War," 284; Owsley, *Struggle for the Gulf Borderlands*, 188–89.

6. Remini, *Jackson and American Empire*, 240–44; Horsman, *War of 1812*, 234–45; Andrew Jackson to Rachel Jackson, Oct. 20, 1814, Monroe to Jackson, Oct. 21, 1814, and Jackson to Monroe, Oct. 26, 1814, in Bassett, *Correspondence*, 2:79–83.

7. Owsley, *Struggle for the Gulf Borderlands*, 175.

8. Mahon, "British Strategy," 297; Bourchier, *Memoir*, 1:329–30.

9. Waselkov, "Fort Jackson and the Aftermath," 166; Owsley, "Prophet of War," 284.

10. Owsley, *Struggle for the Gulf Borderlands*, 176–77; Mahon, "British Strategy," 299; Wright, "Note on the First Seminole War," 567.

11. Mahon, "British Strategy," 299; Remini, *Jackson and American Empire*, 302–3.

12. Mahon, "British Strategy," 299–301; Hawkins to Nicolls, May 28, 1815, in *Niles' Weekly Register*, June 24, 1815; Owsley, *Struggle for the Gulf Borderlands*, 180–81; Owsley, "Prophet of War," 285.

13. Owsley, *Struggle for the Gulf Borderlands*, 180–81; Owsley, "Prophet of War," 285–87; *Niles' Weekly Register*, June 13, 1818; Mahon, "British Strategy," 301; *Niles' Weekly Register*, March 15, 1817.

14. Edmund Doyle to John Innerarity, June 17, 1817, in Doyle, "Panton, Leslie Papers," 62; Owsley, "Prophet of War," 287; Alexander Arbuthnot to Nicolls, Aug. 26, 1817, and Arbuthnot to Charles Bagot, Jan. 27, 1818, in *ASP-FR*, 3:378–79, 585; Thomas Barnard to David Mitchell, April 30, 1818, in *Niles' Weekly Register*, June 13, 1818.

15. Mahon, "First Seminole War," 62–64; Calhoun to Jackson, Dec. 26, 1817, Jackson Papers; T. Frederick Davis, "Milly Francis," 264–65.

16. Mahon, "First Seminole War," 64–65.

17. Ibid., 65–66; Jackson to Monroe, June 2, 1818, Monroe to Jackson, July 19, 1818, in Bassett, *Correspondence*, 2:377–78, 382–83.

18. *Niles' Weekly Register*, June 13, 1818; Jackson to Calhoun, April 8, 1818, William Hambly to Jackson, May 2, 1818, Alexander Arbuthnot to John Arbuthnot, April 2, 1818, in *ASP-FR*, 3:574–75, 577–78, 584; Owsley, "Prophet of War," 288; T. Frederick Davis, "Milly Francis," 256–57.

19. Cinnamon Bair, "McQueen Lost All, but Never Gave Up," *Ledger*, Aug. 21, 2012; "Peter McQueen," *Macon History*, maconhistory.weebly.com; "Great Leader: Peter McQueen of the Creek," *Great Warriors Path*, greatwarriorspath.blogspot.com; Michael Klosterboer, "Osceola," in *Encyclopedia of Alabama History*, encyclopediaofalabama.org; "Peter McQueen," *Digital Alabama*, digitalalabama.com; "Alabama Indian Chiefs," 37.

20 SHADES OF GENOCIDE

1. Pickett, *History of Alabama*, 614–22; Debo, *Road to Disappearance*, 86.

2. Jackson to Monroe, March 4, 1817, in Bassett, *Correspondence*, 3:279–82; Green, *Politics of Indian Removal*, 48–49.

3. Quoted in Green, *Politics of Indian Removal*, 46.

4. James Monroe, First Annual Message to Congress, Dec. 12, 1817, in Richardson, *Messages and Papers of the Presidents*, 2:585.

5. Stiggins, *Creek Indian History*, 82.

6. Debo, *Road to Disappearance*, 85–86; Saunt, *Unworthy Republic*, 33; Green, *Politics of Indian Removal*, 59; McKenney and Hall, *Indian Tribes*, 1:282.

7. *Niles' Weekly Register*, Nov. 7, 1818; McKenney and Hall, *Indian Tribes*, 1:308.

8. William Baldwin to William Darlington, April 19, 1817, in Darlington, *Reliquiae Baldwinianae*, 215–17; Green, *Politics of Indian Removal*, 57.

9. Saunt, *Unworthy Republic*, 33–34, 56–57.

10. Debo, *Road to Disappearance*, 86; Green, *Politics of Indian Removal*, 75; Schwartzman and Barnard, "Trail of Broken Promises," 707–8.

11. *Niles' Weekly Register*, Dec. 4, 1824; Debo, *Road to Disappearance*, 88.

12. McKenney and Hall, *Indian Tribes*, 1:282, 307–8; Green, *Politics of Indian Removal*, 87–88; Declaration of Chiefs of the Cowetas, Talladegas, et al., Jan. 25, 1815, in *ASP-IA*, 2:579; John Smylie to James Smylie, May 7, 1825, John Smylie Letter, ADAH; Frank, "McIntosh," 21; Benjamin Hawkins Jr. to Troup, April 10, 1825, Cuyler Collection, GA.

13. Griffith, *McIntosh and Weatherford*, 238–47; Troup to McIntosh, April 9, 1825, in Harden, *Life of Troup*, 273–74.

14. Griffith, *McIntosh and Weatherford*, 249–50; McKenney and Hall, *Indian Tribes*, 109–10, 309–10; Schwartzman and Barnard, "Trail of Broken Promises," 716–17; Alexander Ware to Troup, May 1, 1825, in Harden, *Life of Troup*, 275–76; "Death of McIntosh," 31–32.

15. Griffith, *McIntosh and Weatherford*, 250–54; Dreisback, "Weatherford."

16. *Niles' Weekly Register*, May 28, 1825; Saunt, *Unworthy Republic*, 35–37; McKenney and Hall, *Indian Tribes*, 1:282–83; Green, *Politics of Indian Removal*, 108, 111.

17. Charles Francis Adams, *Memoirs of John Quincy Adams*, 7:87, 106; Hryniewicki, "Creek Treaty of Washington, 1826," 425–41; 19th Cong., *Creek Lands in Georgia*, 3–9; Green, *Politics of Indian Removal*, 125.

18. Griffith, *McIntosh and Weatherford*, 268; Debo, *Road to Disappearance*, 95; *Tuscumbia Patriot*, Nov. 30, 1827; *New-York American for the Country*, Aug. 31, 1827; *Savannah Georgian*, April 4, 1828; Green, *Politics of Indian Removal*, 155.

19. Saunt, *Unworthy Republic*, 48; Green, *Politics of Indian Removal*, 155.

20. President Andrew Jackson's First Annual Message, Dec. 28, 1829, in Richardson, *Messages and Papers*, 3:1019–22.

21. Quoted in Saunt, *Unworthy Republic*, 49.

22. Jackson to Pitchlynn, Aug. 5, 1830, Jackson Papers.

23. Green, *Politics of Indian Removal*, 156.

24. Saunt, *Unworthy Republic*, 108; Green, *Politics of Indian Removal*, 168–69; Nehah Micco to Eaton, April 8, 1831, and Eaton to the Red Men of the Muscogee Nation of Indians, May 16, 1831, in *Correspondence on the Subject of the Emigration of Indians*, 2:424–25, 290.

25. Moor to Nehah Micco, Dec. 4, 1831, in *Correspondence on the Subject of the Emigration of Indians*, 2:709.

26. Green, *Politics of Indian Removal*, 177–78; Debo, *Road to Disappearance*, 99; Ellisor, "Like So Many Wolves," 1–3.

27. Payne, "Green-Corn Dance," 16–18.

28. Debo, *Road to Disappearance*, 100–101; Green, *Politics of Indian Removal*, 179–81; *Montgomery Mercantile Advertiser*, Oct. 7, 1833; *Huntsville Democrat*, Oct. 3, 1833.

29. Foreman, *Indian Removal*, 147–50.

30. Quoted in ibid., 153–54.
31. Quoted in ibid., 166–67, 175; Ellisor, "Like So Many Wolves," 10; Debo, *Road to Disappearance,* 102.
32. Gerstaecker, *Wild Sports,* iii, 276–77.
33. Debo, *Road to Disappearance,* 104–7. For a comprehensive study of the Creek removal, see Haveman, *Rivers of Sand.*
34. Charles Francis Adams, *Memoirs of John Quincy Adams,* 10:491–92; Owsley, "Pattern of Migration," 147–76.

BIBLIOGRAPHY

BOOKS

Abernathy, Thomas P. *The Formative Period in Alabama, 1815–1828.* Tuscaloosa: University of Alabama Press, 1965. Reprint, 1990.

Abram, Susan M. *Forging a Cherokee-American Alliance in the Creek War.* Tuscaloosa: University of Alabama Press, 2015.

Adair, James. *The History of the American Indians; Particularly Those Nations Adjoining to the Mississippi, East and West Florida, Georgia, South and North Carolina, and Virginia.* London: Edward and Charles Dilly, 1775.

Adams, Charles Francis, ed. *Memoirs of John Quincy Adams, Containing Portions of His Diary from 1795 to 1848.* 12 vols. Philadelphia: J. B. Lippincott, 1875.

Adams, Henry. *The War of 1812.* Washington, D.C.: Infantry Journal, 1944.

American State Papers: Documents, Legislative and Executive, of the Congress of the United States. 38 vols. Washington, D.C.: Gales & Seaton, 1832–1861.

Armstrong, Zella. *Some Tennessee Heroes of the Revolution, Compiled from Pension Statements.* 4 vols. Chattanooga: Lookout, 1933–1944.

Atkins, Edmond. *Indians of the Southern Colonial Frontier: The Edmond Atkins Report and Plan of 1755.* Columbia: University of South Carolina Press, 1954.

Bartram, William. *Travels and Other Writings.* New York: Library of America, 1996.

Bassett, John S., ed. *Correspondence of Andrew Jackson.* 7 vols. Washington, D.C.: Carnegie Institution of Washington, 1926–1935.

Benton, Thomas Hart. *Thirty Years' View; or, A History of the Workings of the American Government for Thirty Years, from 1820 to 1850.* 2 vols. New York: D. Appleton, 1854.

Bergh, Albert E., ed. *The Writings of Thomas Jefferson.* 20 vols. Washington, D.C.: Thomas Jefferson Memorial Association, 1903.

Bourchier, Lady [Jane Barbara]. *Memoir of the Life of Admiral Sir Edward Codrington, with Selections from His Public and Private Correspondence.* 2 vols. London: Longmans, Green, 1873.

Bourne, Edward G. *Narratives of the Career of Hernando de Soto.* 2 vols. New York: A. S. Barnes, 1904.

Brands, H. W. *Andrew Jackson, His Life and Times.* New York: Doubleday, 2005.

Brannan, John, ed. *Official Letters of the Military and Naval Officers of the United States, During the War with Great Britain.* Washington, D.C.: Way and Gideon, 1823.

Braund, Kathryn E. Holland. *Deerskins and Duffels: Creek Indian Trade with Anglo-America, 1685–1815.* Lincoln: University of Nebraska Press, 1993.

———, ed. *Tohopeka: Rethinking the Creek War and the War of 1812.* Tuscaloosa: University of Alabama Press, 2012.

Brewer, W. *Alabama: Her History, Resources, War Record, and Public Men.* Montgomery, Ala.: Barrett & Brown, 1872.

Brown, Lynda W., et al. *Alabama History: An Annotated Bibliography.* Westport, Conn.: Greenwood Press, 1998.

Buell, Augustus C. *History of Andrew Jackson: Pioneer, Patriot, Soldier, Politician.* 2 vols. New York: Charles Scribner's Sons, 1904.

Burckhard, Johann C., and Karsten Petersen. *Partners in the Lord's Work: The Diary of Two Moravian Missionaries in the Creek Indian Country, 1807–1813.* Atlanta: Georgia State College, 1969.

Carter, Clarence E., ed. *The Territorial Papers of the United States.* 28 vols. Washington, D.C.: Government Printing Office, 1934–1975.

Caughey, John W. *McGillivray of the Creeks.* Norman: University of Oklahoma Press, 1938. Reprint, 2007.

Claiborne, J. F. H. *Life and Times of Gen. Sam Dale, the Mississippi Partisan.* New York: Harper & Brothers, 1860.

———. *Mississippi, as a Province, Territory, and State, with Biographical Notices of Eminent Citizens.* 2 vols. Jackson, Miss.: Power & Barksdale, 1880.

Claiborne, Nathaniel H. *Notes on the War in the South.* Richmond: William Ramsay, 1819.

Coleman, Kenneth, and Milton Ready, eds. *The Colonial Records of the State of Georgia.* 32 vols. Athens: University of Georgia Press, 1982.

Corkran, David H. *The Creek Frontier, 1540–1873.* Norman: University of Oklahoma Press, 1967.

Covington, James W. *The Seminoles of Florida.* Gainesville: University of Florida Press, 1998.

Cozzens, Peter. *Tecumseh and the Prophet: The Shawnee Brothers Who Defied a Nation.* New York: Alfred A. Knopf, 2020.

Crockett, David. *Narrative of the Life of David Crockett of the State of Tennessee, Written by Himself.* Philadelphia: E. L. Carey and A. Hart, 1834.

Darlington, William, ed. *Reliquiae Baldwinianae: Selections from the Correspondence of the Late William Baldwin, M.D., Surgeon in the U.S. Navy.* Philadelphia: Kimber and Sharpless, 1843.

Debo, Angie. *The Road to Disappearance: A History of the Creek Indians.* Norman: University of Oklahoma Press, 1941. Reprint, 1979.

Denny, Ebenezer. *Military Journal of Major Ebenezer Denny.* Philadelphia: J. P. Lippincott, 1859.

Dowd, Gregory Evans. *A Spirited Resistance: The North American Indian Struggle for Unity, 1745–1815.* Baltimore: Johns Hopkins University Press, 1992.

Duncan, David E. *Hernando de Soto: A Savage Quest in the Americas.* New York: Crown, 1995.

Eggleston, George C. *Red Eagle and the Wars with the Creek Indians of Alabama.* New York: Dodd, Mead, 1878.

Ellisor, John T. *The Second Creek War: Interethnic Conflict and Collusion on a Collapsing Frontier.* Lincoln: University of Nebraska Press, 2010.

Ethridge, Robbie. *Creek Country: The Creek Indians and Their World.* Chapel Hill: University of North Carolina Press, 2003.

Feiler, Seymour, ed. *Jean-Bernard Bossu's Travels in the Interior of North America, 1751–1762.* Norman: University of Oklahoma Press, 1962.

Foreman, Grant. *Indian Removal: The Emigration of the Five Civilized Tribes of Indians.* Norman: University of Oklahoma Press, 1932.

Foster, H. Thomas, ed. *The Collected Works of Benjamin Hawkins, 1796–1810.* Tuscaloosa: University of Alabama Press, 2003.

Frank, Andrew K. *Creeks and Southerners: Biculturalism on the Early American Frontier.* Lincoln: University of Nebraska Press, 2005.

Gatschet, Albert S. *A Migration Legend of the Creek Indians.* Philadelphia: D. G. Brinton, 1884.

[Gentleman of Elvas]. *Narratives of the Career of Hernando de Soto in the Conquest of Florida.* New York: [Bradford Club], 1866.

Gerstaecker, Frederick. *Wild Sports of the Far West.* Boston: Crosby and Nichols, 1864.

Gilbert, Ed. *Frontier Militiaman in the War of 1812: Southwestern Frontier.* Oxford, U.K.: Osprey, 2008.

Graham, William A. *General Joseph Graham and His Papers on North Carolina Revolutionary War History.* Raleigh, N.C.: Edwards and Broughton, 1904.

Grant, C. L., ed. *Letters, Journals, and Writings of Benjamin Hawkins.* 2 vols. Savannah: Beehive Press, 1980.

Green, Michael D. *The Politics of Indian Removal: Creek Government and Society in Crisis.* Lincoln: University of Nebraska Press, 1982.

Griffith, Benjamin W., Jr. *McIntosh and Weatherford, Creek Indian Leaders.* Tuscaloosa: University of Alabama Press, 1988.

Hahn, Steven C. *The Invention of the Creek Nation, 1670–1763.* Lincoln: University of Nebraska Press, 2004.

Halbert, Henry S., and Timothy H. Ball. *The Creek War of 1813 and 1814.* Chicago: Donohue & Henneberry, 1895.

Hale, Will T., and Dixon L. Merritt. *A History of Tennessee and Tennesseans.* 8 vols. Chicago: Lewis, 1913.

Haley, James L. *Sam Houston.* Norman: University of Oklahoma Press, 2002.

Hamilton, Peter J. *Colonial Mobile.* Boston: Houghton Mifflin, 1897.

Harden, Edward J. *The Life of George M. Troup.* Savannah: E. J. Purse, 1854.

Haveman, Christopher D. *Rivers of Sand: Creek Indian Emigration, Relocation, and Ethnic Cleansing in the American South.* Lincoln: University of Nebraska Press, 2016.

Hawkins, Benjamin. *Creek Confederacy and a Sketch of the Creek Country.* Savannah: Georgia Historical Society, 1848.

Hawkins, John D. *A Biographical Sketch and Incidents of the Life and Services of the Late Col. Benjamin Hawkins, Superintendent of All the Indians South of the Ohio.* N.p., 1848.

Heidler, David S., and Jeanne T. Heidler. *Old Hickory's War: Andrew Jackson and the Quest for Empire.* Baton Rouge: Louisiana State University Press, 2003.

Heiskell, S. G. *Andrew Jackson and Early Tennessee History Illustrated.* 2 vols. Nashville: Ambrose Printing Company, 1920.

Henri, Florette. *The Southern Indians and Benjamin Hawkins, 1796–1816.* Norman: University of Oklahoma Press, 1986.

Hickey, Donald R. *The War of 1812.* Urbana: University of Illinois Press, 1989.

Holland, James W. *Andrew Jackson and the Creek War: Victory at the Horseshoe.* Tuscaloosa: University of Alabama Press, 1968.

Horsman, Reginald. *Expansion and American Indian Policy, 1783–1812.* Norman: University of Oklahoma Press, 1967. Reprint, 1992.

———. *The War of 1812.* New York: Alfred A. Knopf, 1969.

Hudson, Angela P. *Creek Paths and Federal Roads: Indians, Settlers, and Slaves and the Making of the American South*. Chapel Hill: University of North Carolina Press, 2010.

Hudson, Charles. *The Southeastern Indians*. Knoxville: University of Tennessee Press, 1976. Reprint, 1979.

Hudson, Charles, and Carmen C. Tesser, eds. *The Forgotten Centuries: Indians and Europeans in the American South, 1521–1704*. Athens: University of Georgia Press, 2004.

James, Marquis. *Andrew Jackson, the Border Captain*. New York: Grosset & Dunlap, 1933.

Janson, Charles W. *The Stranger in America, 1793–1806*. London: Albion Press, 1807.

Kanon, Tom. *Tennesseans at War, 1812–1815*. Tuscaloosa: University of Alabama Press, 2014.

Lackey, Richard S., ed. *Frontier Claims in the Lower South: Records of Claims Filed by Citizens of the Alabama and Tombigbee Settlements in the Mississippi Territory for Depredations by the Creek Indians During the War of 1812*. New Orleans: Polyanthos, 1977.

Las Cases, Emanuel-Augustus-Dieudonné. *Journal of the Private Life and Conversations of the Emperor Napoleon at Saint Helena*. 4 vols. London: Henry Colburn, 1824.

Life of General Sam Houston. Washington, D.C.: J. T. Towers, 1856.

Lincecum, Gideon. *Pushmataha: A Choctaw Leader and His People*. Tuscaloosa: University of Alabama Press, 2004.

Linklater, Andro. *An Artist in Treason: The Extraordinary Double Life of General James Wilkinson*. New York: Walker, 2009.

Martin, Joel W. *Sacred Revolt: The Muskogees' Struggle for a New World*. Boston: Beacon Press, 1991.

[Martin, William]. *The Self Vindication of Colonel William Martin, Against Certain Charges and Aspersions Made Against Him by Gen. Andrew Jackson and Others*. Nashville: John S. Simpson, 1829.

McKenney, Thomas L., and William Hall. *History of the Indian Tribes of North America*. 3 vols. Philadelphia: Greenough, Rice & Clark, 1838–1844.

Meek, A. B. *Romantic Passages in Southwestern History*. Mobile: S. H. Goetzel, 1857.

Milfort, Louis L. *Memoirs; or, A Quick Glance at My Various Travels and My Sojourn in the Creek Nation*. Savannah: Beehive Press, 1972.

Moser, Harold D., et al. *The Papers of Andrew Jackson*. 10 vols. Knoxville: University of Tennessee Press, 1980–.

Nairne, Thomas. *Nairne's Muskhogean Journals*. Jackson: University of Mississippi Press, 1988.

A Narrative of the Life and Death of Lieut. Joseph Morgan Willcox, Who Was Massacred by the Creek Indians, on the Alabama River (Miss. Ter.) on the 15th of January 1814. Marietta, Ohio: R. Prentiss, 1816.

Northern, William J., ed. *Men of Mark in Georgia*. Atlanta: A. B. Caldwell, 1907.

O'Brien, Sean Michael. *In Bitterness and in Tears: Andrew Jackson's Destruction of the Creeks and Seminoles*. Westport, Conn.: Praeger, 2003.

Owsley, Frank L., Jr. *Struggle for the Gulf Borderlands: The Creek War and the Battle of New Orleans, 1812–1815*. Tuscaloosa: University of Alabama Press, 1981. Reprint, 2000.

Parton, James. *Life of Andrew Jackson*. 3 vols. Boston: Fields, Osgood, 1870.

Pate, James P. *Reminiscences of George Strother Gaines, Pioneer Statesman of Early Alabama and Mississippi, 1805–1843*. Tuscaloosa: University of Alabama Press, 1998.

Pickett, Albert J. *History of Alabama and Incidentally of Georgia and Mississippi, from the Earliest Period*. Charleston, S.C.: Walker and James, 1851. Reprint, 2018.

Piker, Joshua. *Okfuskee: A Creek Indian Town in Colonial America*. Cambridge, Mass.: Harvard University Press, 2004.

Pinckney, Charles C. *Life of General Thomas Pinckney*. Boston: Houghton, Mifflin, 1895.

Pope, John. *A Tour Through the Southern and Western Territories of the United States of North-America*. Richmond: for the author, 1792.

Reid, John, and John H. Eaton. *The New Life of Andrew Jackson, Major General in the Service of the United States*. Philadelphia: M. Carey and Son, 1817.

Remini, Robert V. *Andrew Jackson and His Indian Wars*. New York: Viking, 2001.

———. *Andrew Jackson and the Course of American Empire, 1767–1821*. New York: Harper & Row, 1977.

Richardson, James D., comp. *A Compilation of the Messages and Papers of the Presidents*. 20 vols. New York: Bureau of National Literature, 1897.

Roosevelt, Theodore. *The Winning of the West*. 4 vols. New York: G. P. Putnam's Sons, 1889.

Rowland, Eron. *Andrew Jackson's Campaign Against the British; or, The Mississippi Territory in the War of 1812*. New York: Macmillan, 1926.

Royall, Anne. *Letters from Alabama on Various Subjects*. Washington, D.C., 1830.

Satz, Ronald N. *American Indian Policy in the Jacksonian Era*. Lincoln: University of Nebraska Press, 1975.

Saunt, Claudio. *A New Order of Things: Property, Power, and the Transformation of the Creek Indians, 1733–1816*. Cambridge, U.K.: Cambridge University Press, 1999.

———. *Unworthy Republic: The Dispossession of Native Americans and the Road to Indian Territory*. New York: W. W. Norton, 2020.

Scott, Nancy N., ed. *A Memoir of Hugh Lawson White*. Philadelphia: J. B. Lippincott, 1856.

Sevier, Cora B., and Nancy S. Madden. *Sevier Family History, with the Collected Letters of Gen. John Sevier, First Governor of Tennessee*. Washington, D.C.: Nancy S. Madden, 1961.

Southerland, Henry D., Jr., and Jerry E. Brown. *The Federal Road Through Georgia, the Creek Nation, and Alabama, 1806–1863*. Tuscaloosa: University of Alabama Press, 1989.

Sparks, William H. *The Memories of Fifty Years*. Philadelphia: J. W. Burke, 1870.

Stagg, J. C. A., ed. *The Papers of James Madison: Digital Edition*. Charlottesville: University of Virginia Press, 2010.

Stiggins, George. *Creek Indian History: A Historical Narrative of the Genealogy, Traditions, and Downfall of the Ispocoga or Creek Indian Tribe of Indians*. Birmingham, Ala.: Birmingham Public Library Press, 1989.

Swanton, John R. *Early History of the Creek Indians and Their Neighbors*. Washington, D.C.: Government Printing Office, 1922.

Thompson, Lynn H. *William Weatherford: His Country and His People*. Bay Minette, Ala.: Lavender, 1991.

Wallace, Anthony F. C. *Jefferson and the Indians: The Tragic Fate of the First Americans*. Cambridge, Mass.: Belknap Press of Harvard University Press, 1999.

Wallis, Michael. *David Crockett, the Lion of the West*. New York: W. W. Norton, 2011.

Waselkov, Gregory A. *A Conquering Spirit: Fort Mims and the Redstick War of 1813–1814*. Tuscaloosa: University of Alabama Press, 2006.

Waselkov, Gregory A., and Raven M. Christopher. *Archeological Identification of Creek War Sites, Part 2*. Mobile: University of South Alabama, 2012.

Weir, Howard T. *A Paradise of Blood: The Creek War of 1813–1814*. Yardley, Pa.: Westholme, 2016.

Wesley, John. *Journal of Rev. John Wesley, A.M.* 8 vols. London: Epworth Press, 1938.

Willett, William M. *A Narrative of the Military Actions of Colonel Marinus Willett, Taken Chiefly from His Own Manuscript*. New York: G. & C. & H. Carvill, 1831.

Woodward, Thomas S. *Woodward's Reminiscences of the Creek, or Muscogee Indians, Contained in Letters to Friends in Georgia and Alabama*. Montgomery, Ala.: Barrett & Wimbish, 1859.

Wright, J. Leitch. *Creeks and Seminoles: The Destruction and Regeneration of the Muscogulge People*. Lincoln: University of Nebraska Press, 1990.

406 *Bibliography*

ARTICLES, ADDRESSES, AND ESSAYS

Abram, Susan M. "Cherokees in the Creek War: A Band of Brothers." In Braund, *Tohopeka*.
———. "'To Keep Bright the Bonds of Friendship': The Making of a Cherokee-American Alliance During the Creek War." *Tennessee Historical Quarterly* 71, no. 3 (Fall 2012).
"Account of Col. Caller's Powder Expedition, July 1813." *Alabama Historical Reporter* 1, no. 4 (Jan. 1880).
Agnew, Brad. "The Whale's Rifle." *Chronicles of Oklahoma* 56, no. 4 (Winter 1978–1979).
"Alabama Indian Chiefs." *Alabama Historical Quarterly* 13, nos. 1–4 (1951).
Austill, Jeremy. "Autobiography." *Alabama Historical Quarterly* 6, no. 1 (Spring 1994).
———. "The Canoe Battle." *Alabama Historical Reporter* 2, no. 9 (Aug. 1884).
Barnard, Susan K., and Grace M. Schwartzman. "Tecumseh and the Creek Indian War of 1813–1814 in Northern Georgia." *Georgia Historical Quarterly* 82, no. 3 (Fall 1998).
Bast, Homer. "Creek Indian Affairs, 1775–1778." *Georgia Historical Quarterly* 33, no. 1 (March 1949).
"Battle of the Holy Ground." *Alabama Historical Reporter* 1, no. 10 (July 1880).
Bell, Amelia R. "Separate People: Speaking of Creek Men and Women." *American Anthropologist,* n.s., 92, no. 2 (June 1990).
Bonner, James C. "William McIntosh." In *Georgians in Profile: Historical Essays in Honor of Ellis Merton Coulter,* edited by Horace Montgomery. Athens: University of Georgia Press, 1958.
Boyd, Mark F. "Events at Prospect Bluff on the Apalachicola River, 1808–1818." *Florida Historical Quarterly* 16, no. 2 (Oct. 1937).
Brannon, Peter A. "More About Mordacai." *Alabama Historical Quarterly* 20, no. 1 (1958).
———. "Spruce McCall Osborne." *Alabama Historical Quarterly* 5, no. 1 (Spring 1943).
Braund, Kathryn E. Holland. "The Creek Indians, Blacks, and Slavery." *Journal of Southern History* 57, no. 4 (Nov. 1991).
———. "Guardians of Tradition and Handmaidens to Change: Women's Roles in Creek Economic and Social Life During the Eighteenth Century." *American Indian Quarterly* 14, no. 3 (Summer 1990).
———. "Red Sticks." In Braund, *Tohopeka*.
———. "Reflections on 'Shee Coocys' and the Motherless Child: Creek Women in a Time of War." *Alabama Review* 64, no. 4 (Oct. 2011).
———. "'Resolved Not to Yield': Tohopeka Two Hundred Years On." *Alabama Review* 67, no. 3 (July 2014).
Briceland, Alan V. "Ephraim Kirby: Mr. Jefferson's Emissary on the Tombigbee-Mobile Frontier in 1804." *Alabama Review* 24, no. 2 (April 1971).
Browne, Eric E. "The Rise and Fall of the Westo Indians." *Early Georgia* 28, no. 1 (2000).
Campbell, Thomas. "Thomas Campbell to Lord Deane Gordon: An Account of the Creek Indian Nation, 1764." *Florida Historical Society Quarterly* 8, no. 3 (Jan. 1930).
Cave, Alfred A. "Andrew Jackson and the Indian Removal Act of 1830." *Historian* 65, no. 6 (Winter 2003).
Cocks, R. S. "Catalogue of Trees Growing Naturally in the Vicinity of Sardis, Dallas County, Alabama." *Journal of the Arnold Arboretum* 6, no. 4 (Oct. 1925).
Coffee, John. "Letters from Gen. Coffee." *American Historical Magazine* 6, no. 2 (April 1901).
Collins, Robert P. "'A Packet from Canada': Telling Conspiracy Stories on the 1813 Creek Frontier." In Braund, *Tohopeka*.

Corbitt, D. C. "Papers Relating to the Georgia-Florida Frontier, 1784–1800, II." *Georgia Historical Quarterly* 21, no. 1 (March 1937).

———. "Papers Relating to the Georgia-Florida Frontier, 1784–1800, IV." *Georgia Historical Quarterly* 21, no. 3 (Sept. 1937).

———. "Papers Relating to the Georgia-Florida Frontier, 1784–1800, VII." *Georgia Historical Quarterly* 22, no. 2 (June 1938).

———. "Papers Relating to the Georgia-Florida Frontier, 1784–1800, X." *Georgia Historical Quarterly* 23, no. 1 (March 1939).

Coulter, E. M. "The Creek Troubles of 1793." *Georgia Historical Quarterly* 11, no. 3 (Sept. 1927).

Crane, Verner W. "The Origin of the Name of the Creek Indians." *Mississippi Valley Historical Review* 5, no. 3 (Dec. 1918).

Cutrer, Thomas W. "'The Tallapoosa Might Truly Be Called the River of Blood': Major Alexander McCulloch and the Battle of Horseshoe Bend." *Alabama Review* 43, no. 1 (1990).

Davis, Karl. "'Remember Fort Mims': Reinterpreting the Origins of the Creek War." *Journal of the Early Republic* 22, no. 4 (Winter 2002).

Davis, T. Frederick. "Milly Francis and Duncan McKrimmon: An Authentic Florida Pocahontas." *Florida Historical Quarterly* 21, no. 3 (Feb. 1943).

"The Death of McIntosh." *Arrow Points* 10, no. 2 (Feb. 1925).

"Deposition of Samuel Manac [*sic*], of Lawful Age, a Warrior of the Creek Nation." *Alabama Historical Reporter* 1, no. 9 (June 1880).

DeWitt, John H. "Letters of General John Coffee to His Wife, 1813–1815." *Tennessee Historical Magazine* 2, no. 4 (Dec. 1916).

Din, Gilbert C. "William Augustus Bowles on the Gulf Coast, 1787–1803." *Florida Historical Quarterly* 89, no. 1 (2010).

Doan, James E. "How the Irish and Scots Became Indians: Colonial Traders and Agents and the Southeastern Tribes." *New Hibernia Review* 3, no. 3 (Autumn 1999).

Doster, James F. "Early Settlements on the Tombigbee and Tensaw Rivers." *Alabama Review* 12 (1959).

———. "Letters Relating to the Tragedy of Fort Mims: August–September 1813." *Alabama Review* 14, no. 4 (Oct. 1961).

Dowd, Gregory E. "Thinking Outside the Circle: Tecumseh's 1811 Mission." In Braund, *Tohopeka.*

Downes, Randolph C. "Creek-American Relations, 1782–1790." *Georgia Historical Quarterly* 21, no. 2 (June 1937).

Doyle, Edmund. "The Panton, Leslie Papers." *Florida Historical Quarterly* 18, no. 1 (July 1939).

Dreisback, J. D. "The Tragic Death of Gen. Wm. McIntosh, a Leading Chief of the Muscogee or Creek Indians." *Alabama Historical Reporter* 3, no. 7 (July 1885).

———. "Weatherford—'The Red Eagle.'" *Alabama Historical Reporter* 2, no. 2 (Jan. 1884).

Eades, Margaret. "Life of Margaret Ervin Austill." *Alabama Historical Quarterly* 6, no. 1 (Spring 1944).

Ellisor, John T. "'Like So Many Wolves': Creek Removal in the Cherokee Country, 1835–1838." *Journal of East Tennessee History* 71 (1999).

———. "'Wild People in the Woods': General Jackson, Savannah Jack, and the First Seminole War in the Alabama Territory." *Alabama Review* 70, no. 3 (July 2017).

"Extracts from Memoranda of George S. Gaines." *Alabama Historical Reporter* 2, no. 6 (May 1884).

Fabel, Robin F. A., and Robert R. Rea, eds. "Lieutenant Thomas Campbell's Sojourn Among the Creeks." *Alabama Historical Quarterly* 36, no. 2 (Summer 1974).

Faust, Richard H. "Another Look at General Jackson and the Indians of the Mississippi Territory." *Alabama Review* 28, no. 2 (April 1975).

Floyd, John. "Letters of John Floyd, 1813–1838." *Georgia Historical Quarterly* 33, no. 3 (Sept. 1949).

Folmsbee, Stanley J., and Anna Grace Catron. "The Early Career of David Crockett." *East Tennessee Historical Society's Publications* 28 (1956).

Frank, Andrew K. "The Rise and Fall of William McIntosh: Authority and Identity on the Early American Frontier." *Georgia Historical Quarterly* 86, no. 1 (Spring 2002).

Gaines, George S. "Gaines' Reminiscences." *Alabama Historical Quarterly* 26, nos. 3 and 4 (Fall and Winter 1964).

———. "Letters from George Strother Gaines Relating to Events in South Alabama, 1805–1814." *Transactions of the Alabama Historical Society* 3 (1899).

Gatschet, Albert S. "Towns and Villages of the Creek Confederacy in the XVIII and XIX Centuries." *Publications of the Alabama Historical Society* 1 (1901).

Green, Michael D. "Alexander McGillivray." In *American Indian Leaders: Studies in Diversity,* edited by R. David Edmunds. Lincoln: University of Nebraska Press, 1980.

Haas, Mary R. "Creek Inter-town Relations." *American Anthropologist* 42, no. 3 (July–Sept. 1940).

Halbert, Henry S. "The Creek Red Stick." *Alabama Historical Reporter* 2, no. 6 (May 1884).

———. "Creek War Incidents." *Transactions of the Alabama Historical Society* 2 (1897–1898).

———. "Ensign Isaac W. Davis and Hanson's Mill." *Gulf States Historical Magazine* 1 (July 1902–May 1903).

———. "An Incident of Fort Mimms [*sic*]." *Alabama Historical Reporter* 2, no. 6 (May 1884).

———. "The Vengeance of Olohtie." *Alabama Historical Reporter* 2, no. 8 (July 1884).

Hall, Arthur H. "The Red Stick War." *Chronicles of Oklahoma* 12, no. 3 (Sept. 1934).

Hall, John C. "Landscape Considerations for the Creek War in Alabama, 1811–1814." *Alabama Review* 67, no. 3 (July 2014).

Hally, David J. "The Chiefdom of Coosa." In Hudson and Tesser, *Forgotten Centuries.*

Hassig, Ron. "Internal Conflict in the Creek War of 1813–1814." *Ethnohistory* 21, no. 3 (Summer 1974).

Haveman, Christopher D. "Final Resistance: Creek Removal from the Alabama Homeland." *Alabama Heritage* 89 (Summer 2008): 9–19.

Heidler, David S., and Jeanne T. Heidler. "'Where All Behave Well': Fort Bowyer and the War on the Gulf, 1814–1815." In Braund, *Tohopeka.*

Hemperley, Marion R. "Benjamin Hawkins' Trip Across Georgia in 1796." *Georgia Historical Quarterly* 55, no. 1 (Spring 1971).

Henderson, T. R. "The Destruction of Littafuchee, and a Brief History of American Settlement." *Alabama Review* 67, no. 3 (July 2014).

Hilton, Sylvia L. "Spanish Archives." *American Indian Quarterly* 17, no. 2 (Spring 1993).

"A History of the Church in Russia." *Christian Remembrancer* 10 (Oct. 1845).

Holmes, Jack D. L. "Benjamin Hawkins and United States Attempts to Teach Farming to Southeastern Indians." *Agricultural History* 60, no. 2 (Spring 1986).

Howe, Daniel W. "Why the Scottish Enlightenment Was Useful to the Framers of the American Constitution." *Comparative Studies in Society and History* 31, no. 3 (July 1989).

Hryniewicki, Richard J. "The Creek Treaty of November 15, 1827." *Georgia Historical Quarterly* 52, no. 1 (March 1968).

———. "The Creek Treaty of Washington, 1826." *Georgia Historical Quarterly* 48, no. 4 (Dec. 1964).

Hudson, Charles. "The Hernando de Soto Expedition, 1539–1543." In Hudson and Tesser, eds., *Forgotten Centuries.*

Hudson, Charles, and Carmen C. Tesser. Introduction to *Forgotten Centuries,* edited by Hudson and Tesser.

Innerarity, John. "A Prelude to the Creek War of 1813–1814: In a Letter of John Innerarity to James Innerarity." *Florida Historical Quarterly* 18, no. 4 (April 1940).

"An Interesting Old Gun." *Alabama Historical Reporter* 3, no. 6 (June 1885).

Isham, Ted. "Afterword: The Western Muscogee (Creek) Perspective." In Braund, *Tohopeka.*

Jensen, Ove. "Horseshoe Bend: A Living Memorial." In Braund, *Tohopeka.*

Kanon, Tom. "Before Horseshoe Bend: Andrew Jackson's Campaigns in the Creek War Prior to Horseshoe Bend." In Braund, *Tohopeka.*

———. " 'Glories in the Field': John Cocke vs. Andrew Jackson During the War of 1812." *Journal of East Tennessee History* 71 (1999).

———. "The Kidnapping of Martha Crawley and Settler-Indian Relations Prior to the War of 1812." *Tennessee Historical Quarterly* 64, no. 1 (Spring 2005).

———. "A Slow, Laborious Slaughter: The Battle of Horseshoe Bend." *Tennessee Historical Quarterly* 58, no. 1 (Spring 1989).

Kinnaird, Lawrence. "International Rivalry in the Creek Country: Part I: The Ascendency of Alexander McGillivray, 1783–1789." *Florida Historical Quarterly* 10, no. 2 (Oct. 1931).

Knight, Vernon J., Jr. "The Formation of the Creeks." In Hudson and Tesser, *Forgotten Centuries.*

Kokomoor, Kevin. " 'Burning and Destroying All Before Them': Creeks and Seminoles on Georgia's Revolutionary Frontier." *Georgia Historical Quarterly* 98, no. 4 (Winter 2014).

Langley, Linda. "The Tribal Identity of Alexander McGillivray: A Review of the Historical and Ethnographic Data." *Louisiana History: The Journal of the Louisiana Historical Association* 46, no. 2 (Spring 2005).

Lengel, Leland. "The Road to Fort Mims: Judge Harry Toulmin's Observations on the Creek War, 1811–1813." *Alabama Review* 29, no. 1 (Jan. 1976).

Mahon, John K. "British Strategy and Southern Indians: War of 1812." *Florida Historical Quarterly* 44, no. 4 (April 1966).

———. "The Carolina Brigade Sent Against the Creek Indians in 1814." *North Carolina Historical Review* 28, no. 4 (Oct. 1951).

———. "The First Seminole War, November 21, 1817–May 24, 1818." *Florida Historical Quarterly* 77, no. 1 (Summer 1998).

Mason, Carol I. "Eighteenth Century Culture Change Among the Lower Creeks." *Florida Anthropologist* 26, no. 3 (Sept. 1963).

Mauelshagen, Carl, and Gerald H. Davis. "The Moravians' Plan for a Mission Among the Creek Indians, 1803–1804." *Georgia Historical Quarterly* 51, no. 3 (Sept. 1967).

McAlister, Lyle N. "William Augustus Bowles and the State of Muskogee." *Florida Historical Quarterly* 40, no. 4 (April 1962).

McCown, Mary H., ed. "The 'J. Hartsell Memora': The Journal of a Tennessee Captain in the War of 1812." *East Tennessee Historical Society's Publications* 11 (1939).

———. "The 'J. Hartsell Memora': The Journal of a Tennessee Captain in the War of 1812 [Part II]." *East Tennessee Historical Society's Publications* 11 (1939).

Mooney, James. "Myths of the Cherokee." In *Nineteenth Annual Report of the Bureau of American Ethnology*. Washington, D.C.: Government Printing Office, 1902.

Nuñez, Theron A., Jr. "Creek Nativism and the Creek War of 1813–1814." *Ethnohistory* 5, no. 1 (Winter 1958).

"Observations of Superintendent John Stuart and Governor James Grant of East Florida on the Proposed Plan of 1764 for the Future Management of Indian Affairs." *American Historical Review* 20, no. 4 (July 1915).

Orr, William G. "Surrender of Weatherford." *Transactions of the Alabama Historical Society* 2 (1898).

[Owen, Thomas M.]. "Alabama Indian Chiefs." *Alabama Historical Quarterly* 13, nos. 1–4 (1951).

———. "Indian Trading Houses." *Alabama Historical Quarterly* 13, nos. 1–4 (1951).

———. "Indian Wars in Alabama." *Alabama Historical Quarterly* 13, nos. 1–4 (1951).

———. "Name Places Affected by the Indian War of 1813–14." *Alabama Historical Quarterly* 13, nos. 1–4 (1951).

———. "White Men Associated with Indian Life." *Alabama Historical Quarterly* 13, nos. 1–4 (1951).

Owsley, Frank L., Jr. "British and Indian Activities in Spanish West Florida During the War of 1812." *Florida Historical Quarterly* 46, no. 2 (Oct. 1967).

———. "The Pattern of Migration and Settlement on the Southern Frontier." *Journal of Southern History* 11, no. 2 (May 1945).

———. "Prophet of War: Josiah Francis and the Creek War." *American Indian Quarterly* 9, no. 3 (Summer 1985).

Paredes, J. Anthony. "Back from Disappearance: The Alabama Creek Indian Community." In *Southeastern Indians Since the Removal Era*, edited by Walter L. Williams. Athens: University of Georgia Press, 1979.

———. "A Reexamination of Creek Indian Population Trends: 1738–1832." *American Indian Culture and Research Journal* 6, no. 4 (1983).

Parker, James W. "Digging Twice: Camps and Historical Sites Associated with the War of 1812 and the Creek War of 1813–1814." In Braund, *Tohopeka*.

Payne, John H. "The Green-Corn Dance." *Continental Monthly* 1 (Jan. 1862).

Peeler, Elizabeth H. "The Policies of Willie Blount as Governor of Tennessee, 1809–1815." *Tennessee Historical Quarterly* 1, no. 4 (Dec. 1942).

Porter, Charlotte M. "William Bartram's Travels in the Indian Nations." *Florida Historical Quarterly* 70, no. 4 (April 1992).

Pound, Merritt B. "Benjamin Hawkins, Indian Agent." *Georgia Historical Quarterly* 13, no. 4 (Dec. 1929).

Pressly, Paul M. "Scottish Merchants and the Shaping of Colonial Georgia." *Georgia Historical Quarterly* 91, no. 2 (Summer 2007).

"Proceedings of Courts-Martial in the Creek War." *American Historical Magazine* 6, no. 3 (July 1901).

Prucha, Francis P. "Andrew Jackson's Indian Policy: A Reassessment." *Journal of American History* 56, no. 3 (Dec. 1969).

Ramsey, William L. "'Something Cloudy in Their Looks': The Origins of the Yamasee War Reconsidered." *Journal of American History* 90, no. 1 (June 2003).

"A Ranger's Report of Travels with General Oglethorpe, 1739–1742." In *Travels in the American Colonies*, edited by Newton D. Mereness. New York: Macmillan, 1916.

A Review of the Battle of the Horseshoe, and of the Facts Relating to the Killing of Sixteen Indians on the Morning After the Battle by the Orders of Gen. Andrew Jackson. N.p., n.d.

Rucker, Brian R. "In the Shadow of Jackson: Uriah Blue's Expedition into West Florida." *Florida Historical Quarterly* 73, no. 3 (Jan. 1995).

"Samuel Bains Letter." *Alabama Historical Quarterly* 19, nos. 3 and 4 (Fall and Winter 1957).

Saunt, Claudio. "Taking Account of Property: Stratification Among the Creek Indians in the Early Nineteenth Century." *William and Mary Quarterly* 57, no. 4 (Oct. 2000).

Schwartzman, Grace M., and Susan K. Barnard. "A Trail of Broken Promises: Georgians and Muscogee/Creek Treaties, 1796–1826." *Georgia Historical Quarterly* 75, no. 4 (Winter 1991).

Sheldon, Craig T., Jr. "Archaeology, Geography, and the Creek War in Alabama." In Braund, *Tohopeka*.

Smith, Maurice G. "Notes on the Depopulation of Aboriginal America." *American Anthropologist*, n.s., 30, no. 4 (Oct.–Dec. 1928).

Snyder, Christina. "Adopted Kin and Owned People: The Creek Indians and Their Captives." *Journal of Southern History* 73, no. 2 (May 2007).

Spoehr, Alexander. "Creek Inter-town Relations." *American Anthropologist*, n.s., 43, no. 1 (Jan.–March 1941).

Swan, Caleb. "Position and State of Manners and Arts in the Creek, or Muscogee Nation in 1791." In *Information Respecting the History, Condition, and Prospects of the Indian Tribes of the United States* 5, edited by Henry R. Schoolcraft. Philadelphia: J. B. Lippincott, 1856.

Swanton, John R. "Religious Beliefs and Medical Practices of the Creek Indians." In *Forty-Second Annual Report of the Bureau of American Ethnology to the Secretary of the Smithsonian Institution, 1924–1925*. Washington, D.C.: Government Printing Office, 1928.

———. "Social Organization and Social Usages of the Indians of the Creek Confederacy." In *Forty-Second Annual Report of the Bureau of American Ethnology to the Secretary of the Smithsonian Institution, 1924–1925*. Washington, D.C.: Government Printing Office, 1928.

Symonds, Craig. "The Failure of America's Indian Policy on the Southwestern Frontier, 1785–1793." *Tennessee Historical Quarterly* 35, no. 1 (Spring 1976).

Tait, James A. "Journal of James A. Tait for the Year 1813." Edited by Peter A. Brannon. *Alabama Historical Quarterly* 2, no. 4 (Winter 1940).

Taitt, David. "David Taitt's Journal of a Journey Through the Creek Country, 1772." In *Travels in the American Colonies*, edited by Newton D. Mereness. New York: Macmillan, 1916.

Tarvin, Marion E. "The Muscogees or Creek Indians, 1519 to 1893." *Alabama Historical Quarterly* 17, no. 4 (Fall 1955).

Thrower, Robert G. "Casualties and Consequences of the Creek War: A Modern Creek Perspective." In Braund, *Tohopeka*.

Thruston, Gates P. "The Nashville Inn." *American Historical Magazine and Tennessee Historical Society Quarterly* 7, no. 2 (April 1902).

Walker, Willard. "The Creek Confederacy Before Removal." In *Handbook of North American Indians*. Vol. 14, *Southeast*, edited by Raymond D. Fogelson. Washington, D.C.: Smithsonian Institution, 2004.

Walker, William A., Jr. "Martial Sons: Tennessee Enthusiasm for the War of 1812." *Tennessee Historical Quarterly* 20, no. 1 (March 1961).

Waselkov, Gregory A. "Fort Jackson and the Aftermath." In Braund, *Tohopeka*.

———. "A Reinterpretation of the Creek Indian Barricade at Horseshoe Bend." *Journal of Alabama Archaeology* 32, no. 2 (Dec. 1986).

————. "Return to the Holy Ground: The Legendary Battle Site Discovered." *Alabama Heritage* 101 (Aug. 2011).

Waselkov, Gregory A., and Brian M. Wood. "The Creek War of 1813–1814: Effects on Creek Society and Settlement Pattern." *Journal of Alabama Archaeology* 32, no. 1 (June 1986).

Watkins, John A. "The Mississippi Panic of 1813." *Publications of the Mississippi Historical Society* 4 (1901).

Watson, Thomas D. "Continuity in Commerce: Development of the Panton, Leslie and Company Trade Monopoly in West Florida." *Florida Historical Quarterly* 54, no. 4 (April 1976).

————. "Striving for Sovereignty: McGillivray, Creek Warfare, and Diplomacy, 1783–1790." *Florida Historical Quarterly* 58, no. 4 (April 1980).

Whitaker, Arthur P. "Alexander McGillivray, 1789–1793—Part I." *North Carolina Historical Review* 5, no. 2 (April 1928).

————. "Alexander McGillivray, 1789–1793—Part II." *North Carolina Historical Review* 5, no. 3 (May 1928).

Widmer, Randolph J. "The Structure of Southeastern Chiefdoms." In Hudson and Tesser, *Forgotten Centuries.*

Williams, Samuel C. "A Forgotten Campaign." *Tennessee Historical Magazine* 8, no. 4 (Jan. 1925).

Worth, John E. "Late Spanish Military Expeditions in the Interior Southeast, 1597–1628." In Hudson and Tesser, *Forgotten Centuries.*

Wright, J. Leitch. "Creek-American Treaty of 1790: Alexander McGillivray and the Diplomacy of the Old Southwest." *Georgia Historical Quarterly* 51, no. 4 (Dec. 1967).

————. "A Note on the First Seminole War as Seen by the Indians, Negroes, and Their British Advisers." *Journal of Southern History* 34, no. 4 (Nov. 1968).

Wright, Marcus J. "The Battle of Tohopeka, or Horse-Shoe: General Andrew Jackson's Original Report." *Magazine of American History with Notes and Queries* 19 (Jan.–June 1888).

GOVERNMENT DOCUMENTS

Correspondence on the Subject of the Emigration of Indians: Between the 30th November 1831, and 27th December 1833, with Abstracts of Expenditures by Disbursing Agents, in the Removal and Subsistence of Indians, &c. &c. Furnished in Answer to a Resolution of the Senate, of 27th December 1833, by the Commissary General of Subsistence. 5 vols. Washington, D.C.: D. Green, 1834–1835.

19th Cong., 2nd sess. House Document 76. *Creek Lands in Georgia.*

19th Cong., 2nd sess. House Document 79. *Friendly Creek Indians.*

22nd Cong., 2nd sess. House Report No. 127. *Friendly Creek Indians.*

23rd Cong., 1st sess. House Report No. 402. *Jesse Manley.*

MANUSCRIPTS

Alabama Department of Archives and History, Montgomery
    Alabama Governor Administrative Files

Jeremiah Austill, "The Canoe Battle"
Samuel Bains Letter
James Caller Papers
Joseph Carson Letter
Claiborne Family Collection
John Coffee Papers
Creek War Military Records Collection
Joseph Graham Mississippi Territory Military Records
Ebenezer Hearn Autobiography
Adam James Letter
Kendall Lewis Correspondence
Samuel Manac [Moniac] Deposition
Pickett Family Papers
    Albert J. Pickett, "Some Interesting Notes upon the History of Alabama"
        Section 1, "Notes Furnished by Col. Jeremiah Austill in Relation to the 'Canoe Fight': and Other Engagements in Which He Was Concerned in the Memorable Years 1813–1814"
        Section 2, "Notes Furnished by Col. G. W. Creagh of Clarke County, Alabama, in Relation to the Battle of 'Burnt Corn,' the 'Canoe Fight,' and Other Engagements in Which He Was Concerned in 1813–1814"
        Section 3, "Notes Furnished by Gen. Patrick May of Greene County, Ala., in Relation to the 'Burnt Corn Fight' and Many Other Things Which Happened in the Years 1813, 1814"
        Section 4, "Notes of Doctor Thomas G. Holmes of Baldwin County, Ala., in Relation to the 'Burnt Canoe Expedition,' the Massacre of 553 Men, Women, and Children at Fort Mims, and Other Things Which Happened in the Trying Times of 1813–1814"
        Section 5, "Notes Furnished by the Honorable John F. H. Claiborne of Natchez, Ms., in Relation to Gen. Sam Dale, Etc."
        Section 7, "Interesting Papers in Relation to the Indian Hostilities in 1813–814"
        Section 12, "Notes Taken from the Lips of Col. Robert James of Clarke County Relative to Zachariah McGirth and Weatherford"
        Section 14, "Notes Taken from the Lips of Mr. George S. Gaines in Relation to His Early Settlement in Alabama, Etc."
        Section 15, "Notes Taken from the Lips of Abram Mordecai an Old Jew 92 Years of Age Who Had Lived 60 Years Among the Creek Indians, Also, the Conversations of James Mare Who Had Lived Nearly All His Life Among the Creeks"
        Section 21, "Notes on the Life and Character of the Honorable Harry Toulmin"
        Section 25, "Notes Taken from the Lips of Dr. Thos. G. Holmes in Relation to the Various Expeditions of Capt. Blue, Colonel Benton, and Others"
Neal Smith Letter
John Smylie Letter
Lemuel E. Snow Letter
Harry Toulmin Letters
Thomas Vaughan Letter

WPA Alabama Writers Project
  Benjamin D. Baker, "Mobile County Miscellaneous Manuscript"
  Indian and Colonials Folklore
  Mobile County Folklore

Georgia Archives, Morrow
  Benjamin Hawkins Papers

Gilder Lehrman Institute of American History, New York
  "A Correct View of the Battle of the Horseshoe, March 27, 1814"
  Ephraim H. Foster Letter
  Andrew Jackson Letters

Historic New Orleans Collection, New Orleans
  William C. Cook War of 1812 in the South Collection

Horseshoe Bend National Military Park, Daviston, Alabama
  Kathryn Braund Papers

Library of Congress, Washington, D.C.
  Andrew Jackson Papers
  Thomas Jefferson Papers
  James Madison Papers
  John Reid Papers

Mississippi Department of Archives and History, Jackson
  J. F. H. Claiborne Collection: Book F, Letters and Papers Relating to the Indian
    Wars, 1812–1816
  Governors' Papers

National Anthropological Archives, Smithsonian Institution, Washington, D.C.
  Taylor, Lydia A., "Alibamu Field Notes, Miscellaneous Subjects (Series 1)"

National Archives and Records Administration, Washington, D.C.
  Record Group 46: Records of the U.S. Senate
    Transcribed Treaties (M200)
  Record Group 75: Records of the Bureau of Indian Affairs
    Records of the Cherokee Indian Agency in Tennessee, 1801–1835 (M208)
    Documents Regarding Negotiations of Ratified Indian Treaties, 1801–1869 (T494)
  Record Group 107: Records of the Office of the Secretary of War
    Letters Received, 1800–1889 (M221)

National Records of Scotland, Edinburgh
  Thomas Cochrane Papers

Newberry Library, Chicago
  Edward E. Ayers Collection
    Benjamin Hawkins Letters
    David B. Mitchell Papers

Papeles Procedentes de Cuba, del Archivo General de las Indias, Sevilla, España, Legajos 1794 and 1795, in "Spanish-Language Transcripts of Selected Documents from Various Archives in Mexico"
John Ross Letter and Report

New-York Historical Society, New York
Albert Gallatin Papers

State Library and Archives of Florida, Tallahassee
Richard Keith Call Papers
"The Journal of Governor Richard K. Call"

Tennessee State Library and Archives, Nashville
Claiborne Family Papers
Dyas Collection
John Coffee Letters
Andrew Jackson Collections
Levi Lee Diary
Gideon Morgan Papers

University of Georgia, Hargrett Rare Book and Manuscript Library, Athens
Telamon Cuyler Collection
Keith M. Read Collection

University of North Carolina, Wilson Special Collections Library, Chapel Hill
Southern Historical Collection
Joseph Graham Papers

University of Tennessee, Betsey B. Creekmore Special Collections and University Archives, Knoxville
Penelope Johnson Allen Collection

University of Texas, Briscoe Center for American History, Austin
Ben and Henry Eustace McCulloch Papers

Wisconsin Historical Society, Madison
Lyman C. Draper Collection
Georgia, South Carolina, and Alabama Papers (Series VV)
Tecumseh Papers (Series 10YY)

NEWSPAPERS

American and Commercial Daily Advertiser (Baltimore)
Augusta Chronicle (Ga.)
Carthage Gazette (Tenn.)
Charleston Courier (S.C.)
Clarion and Tennessee State Gazette (Nashville)

Columbian Museum and Savannah Advertiser
Democratic Clarion (Nashville)
Federal Republican (Georgetown, Washington, D.C.)
Georgia Argus (Milledgeville)
Georgia Journal (Milledgeville)
Hampshire Gazette (Northampton, Mass.)
Huntsville Democrat
Ledger (Lakeland, Fla.)
Liberty Hall (Cincinnati)
Memphis Weekly Public Ledger
Mirror of the Times (Augusta, Ga.)
Mississippi Republican (Natchez)
Mobile Mercantile Advertiser
Montgomery Advertiser
Montgomery Flag & Advertiser
Nashville Whig
National Intelligencer (Washington, D.C.)
New-York American for the Country (Ithaca)
New York Columbian
New York Spectator
Niles' Weekly Register
Pennsylvania Correspondent and Farmers' Advertiser (Doylestown)
Raleigh Register (N.C.)
Republican and Savannah Evening Ledger
Richmond Dispatch
Savannah Republican
Tuscumbia Patriot (Ala.)
Universal Gazette (Washington, D.C.)
Virginia Patriot (Richmond)
Washington Monitor (Ga.)
Washington Republican (Mississippi Territory)
Weekly Aurora (Philadelphia)
Wilson's Knoxville Gazette (Tenn.)

DISSERTATIONS AND THESES

Broberg, Lisa L. "Sexual Mores Among the Eastern Woodland Indians." Master's thesis, College of William and Mary, 1984.

Haynes, Joshua. "Patrolling the Border: Theft and Violence on the Creek-Georgia Frontier, 1770–1796." PhD diss., University of Georgia, 2013.

INTERNET SOURCES

Feller, Daniel, ed. *Papers of Andrew Jackson, Digital Edition.* Charlottesville: University of Virginia, Rotunda, 2015–. rotunda.upress.virginia.edu.

"Great Leader: Peter McQueen of the Creek." *Great Warriors Path.* greatwarriorspath .blogspot.com.

Lowery, Charles. "The Great Migration to the Mississippi Territory, 1798–1819." *Mississippi History Now, an Online Publication of the Mississippi Historical Society.* www.ms historynow.mdah.ms.gov.

"Peter McQueen," *Digital Alabama.* digitalalabama.com.

"Peter McQueen." *Macon History.* maconhistory.weebly.com.

Williams, Max R. "Joseph Graham." In *Dictionary of North Carolina Biography,* edited by William S. Powell. 6 vols. Chapel Hill: University of North Carolina Press, 1979–1986. www.ncpedia.org.

INDEX

ILLUSTRATION CREDITS

Andrew Jackson: Smithsonian American Art Museum, transfer from the National Institute

Hernando de Soto: Digital Public Library of America, from *Retratos de los Españoles Ilustres*, Madrid, 1791

Hernando de Soto Burns Mabila: Courtesy of Herb Roe

Italwas: Courtesy of Dori DeCamillas, owner of Red Dot Gallery, Birmingham, Alabama

John Oglethorpe: The Miriam and Ira D. Wallach Division of Art, Prints and Photographs: Picture Collections, The New York Public Library Digital Collections

Family group on the Georgia frontier: Irma and Paul Milstein Division of United States History, Local History and Genealogy, The New York Public Library Digital Collections

Benjamin Hawkins: The Miriam and Ira D. Wallach Division of Art, Prints and Photographs: Picture Collections, The New York Public Library Digital Collections

Josiah Francis: The British Museum

Jim Boy: National Portrait Gallery, Smithsonian Institution; gift of Betty A. and Lloyd G. Schemer

Big Warrior: John Frost, *Pictorial Life of Andrew Jackson*

Hopoithle Micco: The Miriam and Ira D. Wallach Division of Art, Prints and Photographs: Picture Collections, The New York Public Library Digital Collections

William McIntosh: National Portrait Gallery, Smithsonian Institution

Pushmataha: National Portrait Gallery, Smithsonian Institution

Burnt Corn Creek: Alabama Department of Archives and History

Fort Mims massacre: Author's collection

John Floyd: Hargrett Rare Book and Manuscript Library, University of Georgia Libraries

Andrew Jackson as a major general: Smithsonian American Art Museum; gift of International Business Machines Corporation

Rachel Jackson: Courtesy Tennessee State Library and Archives

John Coffee: undefined, Calvert Brothers, Library Photography Collection, Tennessee State Library and Archives, Drawer 5, Folder 80, Tennessee Virtual Archives

John H. Cocke: White House Historical Association (White House Collection)

Thomas Pinckney: National Portrait Gallery, Smithsonian Institution; gift of Elise Pinckney

David Crockett: Dallas Museum of Art. The Karl and Esther Hoblitzelle Collection; gift of the Hoblitzelle Foundation

John Call: Courtesy of Florida Memory, State Archives of Florida

Tennessee Volunteers: National Park Service, Harpers Ferry Center, Commissioned Art Collection. Artist Keith Rocco

Battle of Tallushatchee: 1848, Tennessee Virtual Archive, Drawer 10, Folder 247, Tennessee State Library & Archives, Library Photograph Collection

Battle of Talladega: Courtesy of Tennessee State Library & Archives

Jackson faces down a brigade of hungry and discontented volunteers: Courtesy of Tennessee State Library & Archives

The Holy Ground Battlefield: Creative Commons, Rivers Langley

Menawa: National Portrait Gallery, Smithsonian Institution

The Battle of Enitachopco: John Frost, *Pictorial Life of Andrew Jackson*

Cherokee warriors cross the Tallapoosa River: National Park Service, Harpers Ferry Center, Commissioned Art Collection. Artist Keith Rocco

Cherokee warriors infiltrate Tohopeka: National Park Service, Harpers Ferry Center, Commissioned Art Collection. Artist Keith Rocco

The Thirty-Ninth United States Infantry charge the Red Stick breastworks: National Park Service, Harpers Ferry Center, Commissioned Art Collection. Artist Keith Rocco

The Red Sticks defend their barricade: National Park Service, Harpers Ferry Center, Commissioned Art Collection. Artist Keith Rocco

Sam Houston in later life: William Emerson Strong Photograph Album, David M. Rubenstein Rare Book and Manuscript Library, Duke University

Andrew Jackson rides over the Horseshoe Bend battlefield: National Park Service, Harpers Ferry Center, Commissioned Art Collection. Artist Keith Rocco

The surrender of William Weatherford: Author's collection

Opothle Yoholo: Digital Public Library of America

Chiefs of the Creek nation in 1829: Irma and Paul Milstein Division of United States History, Local History and Genealogy, The New York Public Library Digital Collections

A NOTE ABOUT THE AUTHOR

Peter Cozzens is the author or editor of seventeen acclaimed books on the American Civil War and the Indian Wars of the American West, and a member of the Advisory Council of the Lincoln Prize. In 2002 he was awarded the American Foreign Service Association's highest honor, the William R. Rivkin Award, given annually to one Foreign Service Officer for exemplary moral courage, integrity, and constructive dissent. He lives in Kensington, Maryland.

A NOTE ON THE TYPE

This book was set in Janson, a typeface long thought to have been made by the Dutchman Anton Janson, who was a practicing typefounder in Leipzig during the years 1668–1687. However, it has been conclusively demonstrated that these types are actually the work of Nicholas Kis (1650–1702), a Hungarian, who most probably learned his trade from the master Dutch typefounder Dirk Voskens.

Composed by North Market Street Graphics, Lancaster, Pennsylvania

Printed and bound by Berryville Graphics, Berryville, Virginia

Designed by Maggie Hinders

Maps by Mapping Specialists, Fitchburg, Wisconsin